CENTRAL EUROPE

LUKA IVAN JUKIC

Central Europe

*The Death of a Civilization
and the Life of an Idea*

HURST & COMPANY, LONDON

First published in the United Kingdom in 2025 by
C. Hurst & Co. (Publishers) Ltd.,
New Wing, Somerset House, Strand, London WC2R 1LA
Copyright © Luka Ivan Jukic, 2025
All rights reserved.

The right of Luka Ivan Jukic to be identified as the author of this publication is asserted by him in accordance with the Copyright, Designs and Patents Act, 1988.

Distributed in the United States, Canada and Latin America by Oxford University Press, 198 Madison Avenue, New York, NY 10016, United States of America.

A Cataloguing-in-Publication data record for this book is available from the British Library.

ISBN: 9781911723981

This book is printed using paper from registered sustainable and managed sources.

www.hurstpublishers.com

Printed and Bound in Great Britain by Bell and Bain Ltd, Glasgow

Baki Mari

CONTENTS

Acknowledgements	ix
Introduction	1

PART I
THE RISE
1740–1848

1. Before Central Europe	15
2. The Enlightenment Challenge	33
3. *Finis Romae*	55
4. The Age of Cosmopolitanism	67
5. Reform and Revolt	83

PART II
THE PRIDE
1848–1918

6. The Lost Partition	105
7. Into the Furnace of Modernity	125
8. Central Europe Remade	141
9. The Age of Nationalism	157
10. The Spirit of Secession	177
11. The New Old Regime	193
12. Between Western Civilization and Eastern Barbarism	211
13. Plunge into the Abyss	221

PART III
THE FALL
1918–1948

14. Geese into the Fog	235
15. The Central European Crisis	255
16. The Death of a Civilization	275

PART IV
THE LIFE
1948–

17. Liberated from History	291
18. The Birth of an Idea	307
19. The Life of an Idea	319
20. The Return of Central Europe?	327
Notes	337
Bibliography	371
Index	405

ACKNOWLEDGEMENTS

This book would have been impossible to write without the hard work and support of countless people. There are several I would like to thank in particular. First of all, I would like to thank Michael Dwyer of Hurst Publishers for initiating the long process that led to this book's creation. Alice Clarke has been a wonderful editor, guiding me along the long and winding process to publication. Alasdair Craig was similarly invaluable, helping transform the manuscript into the best book it could be. Also at Hurst I would like to thank Kathleen May, Daisy Leitch, Raminta Uselytė, Rubi Kumari, and Jess Winstanley for all their work on the production and marketing side. For their kind words of endorsement, I am grateful to Peter Pomerantsev, Martyn Rady, Brendan Simms, Pauline Terreehorst, and Peter Frankopan.

The staff of the SSEES Library and German Historical Institute in London deserve great credit for running the two institutions that did most to facilitate the extensive research that this book required and whose rich shelves were a source of endless curiosity and inspiration. A special thanks also goes to Paul Lay and Alastair Benn at *Engelsberg Ideas*, who generously hosted a great deal of my writing in the run up to the book's publication. I am grateful to all those who taught me over the years at the University of Glasgow, the School of Slavonic and East European Studies at UCL, and Jagiellonian University in Krakow, who formed my understanding of and approach to history (and much else) in more ways than I can imagine. In particular Thomas Lorman, who advised me at UCL and did much to shape my views on Central European history. I want to thank Áron Kecskés, Sebastian Schnorrenberg, Wessie du Toit, and Tim Willems for their feedback on early drafts. Similarly, I am eternally grateful to my father Paul, who offered invaluable criticism and encouragement every step of the way, to my mother Ivanka, who made me the man I am today, and to Zoe and our loyal hound Maui, who kept me sane throughout.

INTRODUCTION

I assume there is such a thing as Central Europe, even though many people deny its existence.

Czesław Miłosz

The year was 1988. More than four decades had passed since the end of the Second World War: four decades in which Europeans had grown accustomed to their continent's division in two. Adorned with barbed wire, supported by minefields, and patrolled by watchful guards in concrete towers, a narrow strip of land running across the heart of the continent had been transformed into an insurmountable barrier that separated communist East from liberal-democratic West. Contact across this 'iron curtain' was minimal. The Soviet Union controlled the movement of its citizens obsessively. It kept a watchful eye on its Eastern European satellites to ensure they would do the same, even going as far as to invade Hungary in 1956 and Czechoslovakia in 1968 to prevent their liberalization. For the vast majority of those in Eastern Europe, a trip to 'the West' was unthinkable. There could only be an escape.

In 1985 something changed. After three elderly general secretaries dropped dead in their posts in the span of just four years, the Soviet leadership opted for the 'youthful' fifty-four-year-old reformer Mikhail Gorbachev to lead party and country. His signature policies amounted to a complete overhaul of the insular Soviet system. No longer, Gorbachev thought, should the East fear the West, nor the West the East. In this newfound spirit of openness, four Soviet writers were allowed to leave their country for the first time in their lives in May 1988. They soared across a vast and unfamiliar continent and touched down in distant Lisbon. On the city's outskirts, the resplendent Rococo Palace of Queluz would play host to a spectacular gathering of literary men and women from both sides of the iron curtain in a grand act of cross-cultural reconciliation. Or so it was hoped.

CENTRAL EUROPE

Very quickly, fault lines emerged. One Russian writer, expressing her incredulity at the 'stubbornness with which everybody talks about Central Europe', dismissed the presence of the Red Army there as a mere 'climatic factor'. This drew the ire of the Hungarian writer György Konrád, whose homeland had been invaded by Soviet troops just a few decades before. Sooner or later, 'you will have to confront the role of your country in the world' he told her. Heated debates followed, drawing in ever more writers from ever more countries. Salman Rushdie eventually chimed in, calling the Russian writers' denial of the existence of Central Europe a 'colonial act'.

The Nobel Prize-winning Russian author Joseph Brodsky took offence, declaring emphatically that in 'the name of literature, there is no such a thing as a "Central Europe" ... There is Polish literature, Czech literature, Slovak literature, Serbo-Croatian literature, Hungarian and so forth'. His fellow Nobel Prize winner, the Pole Czesław Miłosz, interjected: 'Divide et impera. This is a colonial principle and you are for that'. 'Divide et impera. In what way, Czeslaw? I don't understand you. Could you specify?' asked Brodsky. 'Central Europe, as Susan Sontag said, is an anti-Soviet concept provoked by the occupation of those countries ... I am afraid that there is a certain taboo in Russian literature and this taboo is empire'. What had been intended as a conference that would foster mutual understanding had been poisoned by a bitter cloud of misunderstanding.[1]

The Lisbon Conference was derailed by a seemingly simple question: Does Central Europe exist? To this day, few seem to know for certain. A political map of Europe gives few clues as to where it may lie. A geographic map only adds to the confusion. Ukraine's foreign minister Dmytro Kuleba declared in 2021 that his country 'is and always has been a Central European state', a claim few geographers would endorse.[2] People in Croatia and Romania often think of themselves as the same, but this is no less a point of contention. As far as the United Nations is concerned there is no Central Europe. Instead, its statistical agency lumps together most of the countries mentioned above as parts of 'Eastern Europe'.

In a farcical diplomatic replay of the literary debates that had taken place two decades before, the Russian and Czech foreign ministers sparred over the question of Central Europe in 2009. The concrete issue was the placement of U.S. missile defence systems in Poland and Czechia—now sovereign democratic states—which Russia's Foreign Minister Sergey Lavrov objected to on the grounds that their placement in 'Eastern Europe' clearly threatened Russia's security. His Czech counterpart Karel Schwarzenberg quickly replied: 'the radar base definitely isn't [going to be] placed in Eastern Europe, it's in Central Europe ... just look at the geography'.[3] Lavrov, evincing a wilful ignorance, simply pointed to the UN's definition.

For those who believe their country to be a part of Central Europe today—Czechs, Slovaks, Poles, Hungarians, and others—Eastern Europe is by and large considered a frustrating and outdated designation. This is not only because it conjures up images of a greyer, poorer, and less European Europe, but also thanks to precisely the dynamic on display above. For a neutral observer the term Eastern Europe can easily serve as an innocuous descriptor. But it can also be deployed as a rhetorical sleight of hand that relegates a country to Russia's sphere of influence.[4]

Lavrov invoked Eastern Europe to make a point about the closeness of the missiles to Russia. Schwarzenberg countered with 'Central Europe' to emphasize their distance and, by extension, the distance of the countries they were in. Of course, many Russians would undoubtedly see this as a different kind of rhetorical sleight of hand that belittles their own great power status and natural dominion over vast swathes of Europe's east. Kuleba's insistence on Central European status for Ukraine was deployed with similar political reasoning in mind. It was accompanied by a condemnation of the centuries Ukrainians spent in a common state with their Russian neighbours, first in the Russian Empire and then the Soviet Union, as a period when Ukraine was 'integrated into what is now artificially called "Eastern Europe"'.

For Schwarzenberg, Kuleba, and countless others, this is an issue of fundamental importance to their sense of national identity and their country's place in the world. Perhaps they might once have been part of some Eastern Europe tied to Moscow, but no longer. Cognisant of this verbal minefield, journalists and academics often use the phrase 'Central and Eastern Europe', leaving it to the reader to decide where they place the border between the two. So Central Europe does exist, perhaps, but it is beyond their authority to pronounce on its exact borders. On this question the more zealous proponents of Central Europe are usually no better, convinced as they are that their country sits on the right side of the border between Central and Eastern Europe.

This debate largely owes its prominence to an essay written by the Czech writer Milan Kundera, published internationally in 1983/4 and best known in English as 'The Tragedy of Central Europe'. At a time when the division of Europe into an advanced capitalist West and a backwards communist East seemed natural and permanent, he argued that countries like Hungary, Poland, and Czechoslovakia sitting behind the iron curtain were integral parts of 'the West' as members of an amorphous cultural entity called Central Europe. The moment such a country was 'no longer European', it was 'driven from its own destiny, beyond its own history: it loses its sense of identity'. The phrase 'to die for one's country and for Europe' supposedly could not even be 'thought' in Moscow or Leningrad, but only in 'Budapest or Warsaw'. These countries were not only European, but the most European. That Western Europe could not see or acknowledge this and did not even lift a finger to aid Central Europe as it was subjugated by a quasi-Oriental Russia after the Second World War was the 'Tragedy of Central Europe'.[5]

Kundera's essay sparked considerable controversy on both sides of the iron curtain.[6] It ignited a protracted debate around the question of Central Europe's existence, initially driven by dissident intellectuals who longed for an end to communist rule and all that came with it. The force of attraction was immense. Eastern Europe represented everything terrible about the communist present: backwardness, repression, conformity. Central Europe—at least to its enlightened proponents—represented everything wonderful about the supposedly more European past and a promised European future: progress, freedom, cosmopolitanism, openness. As Czesław Miłosz put it: 'Central Europe is an act of faith, a project, let us say, even a utopia'.[7]

Galvanized by Kundera's hit essay, the 1980s saw a flood of newspapers, magazines, journals, speeches, conferences, and books devoted to the issue of Central Europe.[8] Did it exist? Where did its borders lie? Is it a fate or a culture? A concept or category? Utopia or reality? Every word printed, every invocation, every person converted to its possibilities brought it one step closer to existence but seemingly took everyone two steps away from understanding what exactly it was. It is no wonder that, confronted with the concept of Central Europe for the first time in 1988, some Russian writers were utterly perplexed by it. After all, those who discussed it intensely for years were equally perplexed, even if they were certain of its existence. 'We live in a region that no longer exists, and we speak about and discuss no other [region] so much as this Central Europe that perhaps never existed' opined the historian Péter Hanák in 1988.[9]

These debates might have come to naught had the iron curtain and the communist regimes behind it not fallen like dominos from 1989 to 1991.

INTRODUCTION

Pro-Western dissidents that had been forced into the shadows suddenly found themselves leading revolutions. As if embodying the ephemeral cosmopolitan spirit of Central Europe, the dissident playwright Václav Havel was elected the first president of a revived democratic Czechoslovakia. His and other newly freed countries clamoured to join the transatlantic liberal democratic order as a fulfilment of the promise of the revolutions of 1989.

Multi-party democracies were established, capitalism unleashed, liberal freedoms enshrined. The American political scientist Francis Fukuyama speculated in his 1989 essay 'The End of History?' that Western victory in the Cold War would be 'the end point of mankind's ideological evolution' and represented the 'universalization of Western liberal democracy as the final form of human government'.[10] It was a thesis for which Central Europe would act as the first proof. When his essay was expanded into a book three years later the question mark had been dropped, fuelling a common reading of the book that does not stray far from its seemingly triumphant title. History was over, and Central Europe's Westward march had ended it.

New political elites—in many cases the 'reformed' old elites—were keen to stress not only that communism was a failed project, but that its existence in their countries was an illegitimate historical anomaly imposed by a foreign entity: Russia, or Serbia in post-Yugoslav contexts. This could only be corrected by their 'return' to the West. By the 'reunification' of Europe. As Larry Wolff put it, Central Europe would act as the 'ideological antidote to the iron curtain'.[11] Poland, Hungary, and Czechoslovakia (from 1993 split into the Czech and Slovak Republics) made ample use of it to argue for their rapid admission into the European Union and NATO. Their 1991 declaration proclaiming the formation of the Visegrád Group to aid their joint accession to these institutions made it explicit that they all belonged to Central Europe, a fact so obvious that did not even need explanation. It appears it does exist then. After all, has history not given its verdict?

All four Visegrád countries, plus Slovenia and Lithuania, were welcomed into the EU in 2004. Romania and Croatia achieved prized EU membership in 2007 and 2013, respectively. Ukraine, meanwhile, took on the role of an archetypal Kunderian state in the wake of Russia's full-scale invasion in 2022. Its flag went up across Europe on homes, government buildings, and businesses. The European flag did the same across Ukraine as the whole continent seemingly came together to recognize

Ukraine's suffering for the very idea of Europe. As if to drive the point home, Kundera allowed his essay to be published in book format shortly before his death in 2023.[12] In a speech made in Bratislava that same year French President Emmanuel Macron quoted 'The Tragedy of Central Europe' at length. He declared that he did not believe there is such a thing as 'Eastern Europe' and 'Western Europe', only a single Europe artificially divided by the Soviet Union. 'My message is simple' he went on, 'in the times we are living in, we must not let the West be kidnapped a second time. We will not let Europe be kidnapped a second time'.[13]

Though absent, Kundera's name haunted the Lisbon Conference. His essay was the cornerstone of the whole transatlantic debate on Central Europe, one that seemed to presage the eventual collapse of communism and 'reunification of Europe'. It was so central, many lamented, that it made Central Europe seem like Kundera's invention. But the term was not his invention, nor was it a Cold War neologism invented to divide the Soviet-led Eastern Bloc. It was a product of the nineteenth century, one that by 1984 had long disappeared from popular use. According to the narrative presented in Kundera's essay, this disappearance was a result of the West's ignorance and disregard for its other half, but this is not quite the case.

'Central Europe' fell out of use because the place the term was coined to describe was so thoroughly obliterated by two world wars and as many totalitarian systems that it ceased to exist as a distinct political, cultural, or social entity. While nations described as Central European today certainly have their roots in the Central Europe of old, much of the continuity between the two has long since been broken. From the late eighteenth century to the end of the First World War, Central Europe was identifiable as a constellation of linguistically and religiously diverse polities and societies that eventually developed into the great powers of the German Reich and Austria-Hungary. Both were eclectic unions of various kingdoms, duchies, archduchies, free cities, and other crownlands whose precise relationship to their rulers and each other had been a subject of near constant debate for centuries. What united this assemblage of territories was a political link to the House of Habsburg inherited from the long eighteenth century, their cultural position in Europe between an Anglo-French 'West' and a Russian-Slavic 'East', and the position of standard High German as the regional language of high culture, social advancement, and intraregional communication.

In the nineteenth and twentieth centuries many Germans argued the emergence of such a space, the primacy of German within it, and the

INTRODUCTION

power of the German Reich itself was the result of some innate Germanic superiority. Conversely, many from nations ostensibly oppressed by this state of affairs interpreted it as evidence of nefarious German imperialism. Neither of these polemical views has stood the test of time. Central Europe was not a predestined fate, but the result of a number of historically contingent events and decisions in the eighteenth and early nineteenth centuries; a novel historical situation whose existence was tied to specific circumstances whose disappearance it did not survive.

In the aftermath of the First World War, Central Europe was shattered politically by the collapse of the multinational, multireligious, and composite German and Austro-Hungarian states, who had entered and lost the war together. Out of their collapse emerged Germany, Austria, Poland, Czechoslovakia, Hungary, Yugoslavia, Lithuania, and Romania, states whose legitimacy rested on the notion that their existence reflected the will of their titular nations. But many of these states were almost as diverse as the empires that came before them and they struggled to build legitimacy with 'national majorities' as much as their 'national minorities'. Germany, for all its weaknesses, was still the largest and most powerful country in the region, from 1933 under the rule of antisemitic Pan-German ultranationalists that held nothing but deep contempt for the Central Europe of old, particularly as embodied by the multinational realm of the Habsburgs. From 1938 to 1941 they reshaped the region with impunity, introducing a new, chaotic hierarchy of 'races' in which Germans stood on top and Jews, Roma, and certain Slavs stood at the bottom.

The war Germany unleashed in 'the East' was waged on a near-apocalyptic scale as a radical racial war that would reshape the global balance of power for centuries to come. Tens of millions would perish. Jews would be targeted for complete elimination. Great multinational metropolises would be reduced to rubble, some all but wiped off the face of the earth. Millions upon millions of Europeans would be displaced, including over ten million Germans from the eastern half of the continent. People, nations, and ideas would survive this catastrophe battered, scarred, and displaced, but Central Europe would not. Its map was redrawn yet again, this time with the outcome—if not always the aim—of creating homogenized nation-states dotted with equally homogeneous cities. Backed by Soviet arms, communist parties took power in most of them. Germany was reinvented as a liberal and democratic nation-state in its west. In its east, a Stalinist one. In between them descended an iron curtain.

CENTRAL EUROPE

Central European civilization died a gruesome death in 1918–48. The scale of the catastrophe is difficult to comprehend, especially for those from Western European countries that have had relatively stable borders for centuries. Most urban centres were left bearing almost no resemblance to their prewar selves. If not physically destroyed, their character was irreparably changed by the loss of prewar populations and the relocation of new national majorities from the countryside into the cities. For all the social inequalities, national conflicts, and political sclerosis, the contrast between that secure 'world of yesterday' and the horrors that followed its demise made Central Europe seem to generations of nostalgics like a lost paradise. By mid-century it was an unrecognizable, traumatized ruin, turned into the frontline of a global Cold War. This book seeks to answer why it came to be so; how and why a distinct place called Central Europe emerged in the first place; how and why it was so absolutely destroyed in the twentieth century; and how and why it lives on as an idea that emerged from a place called Eastern Europe in the waning days of the Cold War.

* * *

It is rare to find a definition of Central Europe without a list of countries. Poland, Czechia, Slovakia, Hungary, Germany, and Austria are more or less universally included. Slovenia, Croatia, Romania, and Lithuania less so. Ukraine, Belarus, Latvia, Serbia rarely. The inclusion of Switzerland, Luxembourg, and Liechtenstein varies but is of little practical consequence considering their passive role in modern European history. Whatever the set given by one historian or another, all convey a similar message. Some collection of nation-states together add up to Central Europe. Its history, then, is simply the collection of national histories of its constituent members.[14] In such an approach there is little to differentiate Central and Eastern European history beyond the set of countries chosen for analysis. This book will not take such an approach. In fact, it will attempt the opposite: to disentangle the history of Central Europe from the histories of the many nations that have emerged from it, and to show that Central European history is much more than the sum of its parts.

This is no easy task. Every country now considered Central European is a 'nation-state'. The primary concern of historians in each has traditionally been strictly national. History-writing in most began as an explicit nation-building exercise and nationalist schools of history have usually

INTRODUCTION

been dominant, to say nothing of the narratives they developed.[15] Even Germany, in the early twenty-first century considered an archetypally open, cosmopolitan, and 'post-nationalist' country, struggles to overcome the national paradigm in its history. This is not so much the fault of historians as it is reflective of a wider Central European problem. The territories of all these countries were bewilderingly diverse in terms of state forms, languages, religions, and nationalities right up until the Second World War.[16] But to open up the bounds of history beyond the national raises countless questions, particularly for Germany.

Until 1806 there was no 'Germany' but only a Holy Roman Empire in which the majority of German-speakers lived, and which consisted of nearly 2,000 sovereign territories. These included tiny estates ruled by imperial knights, ecclesiastical states ruled by elected bishops, and fully-fledged kingdoms, duchies, and principalities. Setting aside its decentralization and institutionalized Catholic-Protestant divide, even its 'Germanness' was questionable. The imperial title was of pan-European importance and gave its holder the highest status of any secular ruler on the continent. As its name suggests, its legitimacy was rooted in claims to the inheritance of Rome, not an ethnically-conceived German nation. Historically, the Empire included large parts of Italy, the Netherlands, and French-speaking territories to the west. The only kingdom in the Empire, that of Bohemia, which largely corresponds to today's Czechia, was a predominantly Slavic state. Slavic-speaking peasants also formed majorities in large swathes of Austria, Saxony, and Prussia. To top it all off, the opulent residences in which the rulers of all these states lived were highly cosmopolitan and by the eighteenth century more likely to be French than German-speaking. Not only did the boundaries of the Empire not correspond to those of modern Germany, but the two countries most important to the history of the Empire and Germany up until 1918—Austria and Prussia—are not part of modern Germany at all.

This brings us to the second issue. The Austrian House of Habsburg nominally ruled all of what is today Germany for centuries as heads of the Empire. But over the dynasty's long history they also ruled Spain, parts of Italy, France, and the Low Countries, as well as the Kingdom of Hungary (which had a personal union with Croatia), and a Kingdom of Galicia whose territory is today part of Poland, Romania, and Ukraine. Strangely for what was once the centre of the Empire, Austria was usually excluded from 'German' history altogether well into the twentieth century, in large part because history writing in Germany was dominated by a Prussian-oriented school keen to legitimize Bismarck's 'lesser German' Reich. But also, perhaps, because the inclusion of Austria raises many further questions about the bounds of German history.[17]

If 'Austria'—which was really a number of imperial territories under the hereditary rule of the Austrian Habsburgs—is included within the bounds of 'German history' then Slovenia is suddenly drawn in as well. Slovenes were spread across three Austrian imperial duchies of Carinthia, Styria, and Carniola. Then there is also no reason not to include Bohemia considering it was a hereditary Habsburg land associated with the Empire. The inclusion of Austria in German history has therefore already entangled the Slavic Czechs and Slovenes. But can developments in these territories really be understood by ignoring the territories outside the Empire that the Habsburgs ruled? Hungary and Galicia then become a part of 'German history', drawing Hungarians, Slovaks, Croats, Serbs, Romanians, Poles, and Ukrainians into a story that no longer sounds very German.

One could counter that Hungary or Galicia should not in any case be included in the grand sweep of German history because they were not a part of 'Germany' as defined by the borders of the Holy Roman Empire. But then was Prussia 'Germany' if it too was outside of the Empire? And what of the fact that Prussia's own history is intimately entangled with that of Poland? What justifies the inclusion of those extraimperial territories ruled by the Hohenzollerns while those ruled by the Habsburgs are excluded? It could not possibly be the simple presence of Germans or the German language because both were present in the Kingdom of Hungary. The wider the bounds of German history push, the less German they become. 'National history' dissolves into a wider Central European goulash.

This is something those from smaller, 'East-Central' European countries are exceedingly familiar with.[18] Hungarian, Polish, Czech, Slovak, Romanian, Slovenian, Serbian, and Croatian historians are faced with their own reverse Austrian issue. All their countries were wholly or partially under the rule of the Habsburgs until 1918, which means they spent much of their history sharing a capital of sorts with the largely German Holy Roman Empire even if most were outside of it. At the same time, large parts of modern Croatia, Romania, Poland, and Serbia were under Italian, Russian, or Turkish rule or influence, meaning their history is not exclusively Central European. This made it easier to deemphasize, condemn, or ignore the German link altogether as these countries sought to establish themselves as nation-states in the twentieth century, joining a similar ignorance from the German side concurrently looking to deem-

INTRODUCTION

phasize, condemn, or ignore anything that smacked of German imperialism or chauvinism in the wake of the Second World War.[19]

For much of their modern histories this was not really a concern. Nationalism as a mass political phenomenon only emerged in the late nineteenth century. To treat it as the single defining feature of either Central or Eastern European history is misleading. Religious, linguistic, national, state, dynastic, or even class-based identities had vastly different political implications depending on the eye of the beholder. In some eras they coexisted with ease, in others they did not. But nationalism was never the sole driving force in Central European history. Indeed, its course from the late eighteenth to early twentieth century tended towards the inclusion of more and more people in public life rather than their exclusion. It broke down rather than erected social barriers, whether based on religion, social class, language or sex. Though there were many Central European states, nations, and monarchs, they were ultimately all forced to build their futures upon a common fate.

Could this fate ultimately be called a 'civilization'? This notoriously slippery term means many things in different contexts. One can refer to human, modern, or global civilization just as easily as Chinese, Christian, or classical civilization. In the nineteenth century, European states pursued 'civilizing' missions across the world. Different nineteenth-century societies with their own languages, customs, ideas, and outlooks like Russia, Britain, or France are often described as their own civilizations. But they are just as easily termed empires, states, or even nations, making the lines between these terms ambiguous during this all-important period. None of these additional terms apply to Central Europe, however.

As many things as Central Europeans shared, a single state was never one of them, even if the role of Habsburgs as leaders of both the Holy Roman Empire and the German Confederation and a vast Danubian realm did provide a vague institutional umbrella until 1866. Nation can be discarded outright as there was never any semblance of common nationhood beyond perhaps the imperially-loyal Homo Austriacus. Though multiple 'empires' are central to its history, one single empire never covered the whole of Central Europe. 'Space' and 'region' are apt, and I use them occasionally out of convenience, but they are also insufficient. They are too geographical, perhaps, to capture the multifarious social, economic, cultural, linguistic, and political links that bound people along with the lands they lived on together. 'Civilization' is ultimately an invitation to think bigger, to overcome narrow constraints set by national historiographies, and to remind us that no historical society can be understood as a fixed state, but only as a process of continuous and common development. Much must be left out of this book. To do justice to every development, every experience, every facet of state and society in this period in every country discussed would take thousands, perhaps tens of thousands of pages. This book is only one attempt to tell a history of Central Europe as a whole rather than a collection of parts.

PART I

THE RISE
1740–1848

1

BEFORE CENTRAL EUROPE

On 30 September 1790, Frankfurt awoke to the sound of storm bells ringing. Under the warm glow of the morning twilight, the city rapidly came alive. The tolling echoing through the narrow medieval streets was joined by the marching music of the citizens' militia. Colourful figures rushed to find their pre-determined places, wading through amorphous crowds gathering where they could. Spectators perched themselves on windowsills and roofs. The previous night, the gates offering passage through the thick and imposing fortifications surrounding the city had been sealed. All but a few choice foreigners had first been asked to leave. Nothing could be left to chance as the Free Imperial City of Frankfurt staged one of the oldest and most extravagant political rituals on the European continent. The sense of 'joy and merry anticipation' was undoubtably palpable.[1]

As the Frankfurt native Johann Wolfgang von Goethe later recalled, there 'was no [Frankfurter] of a certain age who would not have regarded [these events], and their attendant circumstances, as the crowning glory of his whole life'.[2] This was no less true for many of the visitors. Klemens von Metternich, a native of the Rhineland, described it as 'one of the most sublime and simultaneously magnificent spectacles that the world has ever seen'.[3] It would mark the young aristocrat's debut on the European political stage at the age of seventeen. Wolfgang Amadeus Mozart, who hailed from picturesque Salzburg just north of the Alps, was certainly no debutant. He travelled in style from Vienna in his own luxurious carriage hoping to revive his flagging career, even pawning family furniture and taking on a large loan to finance the journey. His unplanned concert ended up a flop.[4] Mozart and the other great composers in attendance were nothing but a sideshow. They could never hope to compete with the innumerable imperial knights and counts, dukes, prince-bishops, kings, queens, and foreign ambassadors that had come to witness and participate in the election, anointment, and coronation of the 'Most Serene, Most Powerful, and Most Invincible Roman Emperor'.

From the late sixteenth century, it had been Frankfurt's privilege to host the series of magnificent ceremonies that conferred Europe's most prestigious title to its new bearer, beginning with their election as King of the Romans. This was what brought throngs of spectators onto the streets on 30 September as a procession of elaborately dressed figures, graciously decorated horses, and opulent carriages made their way from the Römer, Frankfurt's city hall, to the Cathedral of Saint Bartholomew. Leading it was a unique triumvirate of ecclesiastical electors, their clerical and political roles fused into one: the Prince-Archbishops of Cologne, Mainz, and Trier. The remaining secular five of Saxony, Brandenburg, Bohemia, Bavaria, and Hanover were represented by envoys, closely following behind.

Trumpets and drums marked the triumphant arrival of the eight electors in the church before the first of many musical pieces began. An elaborate ritual followed during which each of the electors and their representatives swore an oath on the Bible 'that with all my reason and understanding, with God's help, I want to choose a secular head for the Christian people, that is, to elevate a Roman King to future Emperor'.[5] The electors conferred in secret to make their choice while the crowd in the church waited with 'nervous anticipation'. When they finally emerged, there was 'an outburst of joy and curiosity' quickly followed by a 'silence even deeper than the first' as a representative of the Archbishop of Mainz announced the result:[6]

> I Friedrich Carl Joseph by the Grace of God of the Holy See Archbishop of Mainz, of the Holy Roman Empire through Germania Archchancellor and Elector ... name, elect, and choose to elevate the most serene, mighty prince and lord Leopold the second, King of Hungary and Bohemia ... Archduke of Austria, Duke of Burgundy and Lothringia, Grand Duke of Tuscany ... free and thoughtful and self-willed, to Roman King and future Roman Emperor, and to be the leader of the Holy Roman Empire of the German nation.

When he concluded with the words *Vivat Rex*—long live the king—the crowd erupted into cries of *Vivat!* A *Te Deum*—hymn of thanksgiving— began as the doors of the church were flung open, joined by the cheers of the people outside, the ringing of the city's bells, and the thunderous roars of a hundred cannons that announced to the world a new King of the Romans—Leopold II of the House of Habsburg.[7] As the electors paraded out of the church, the crowd singled out Leopold's brother, the Archbishop-Elector of Cologne Maximilian Francis, for particularly 'rousing and fiery' adoration. '*Vivat* Leopold, *Vivat* Maximilian, *Vivat* Austria!' they cheered as he passed by.[8]

The scenes of jubilation offered a welcome respite from the nervous excitement of the previous several months. Like countless others attached to the electoral delegations, the Saxon elector's secretary Rudolph Hommel had arrived in Frankfurt weeks before. He found the setting ill-fitting for the grand occasion. The labyrinthine medieval Römer was 'old-fashioned', the square it stood on 'small' and 'uneven'. The path the procession would follow to the cathedral led through 'narrow dirty alleys,' truly 'abhorrent' for such an event.[9] Of much more interest were the homes of the various delegations quartered around the city. Their coats of arms were painted above the door of every building that hosted someone from a delegation, the largest of all placed above the headquarters of Leopold's own Bohemian delegation. The delegations evidently arrived in style, with handsome horses pulling modern coaches containing many of the continent's leading aristocrats and their coteries.[10] In the weeks and months leading up to the election they passed the time as eighteenth-century aristocrats usually did: with concerts conducted by famous composers; with plays, ballets, and operas put on in French and German by three different theatre companies; and with trips to the nearby spa town of Wilhelmsbad, where they could even indulge in gambling, banned in Frankfurt in the run up to the coronation in the interests of public order.[11]

On 2 October the spectacle continued. The imperial regalia arrived with great pomp from the Free Imperial Cities of Aachen and Nuremberg, announced as usual with the ringing of bells and the firing of cannons. One can only imagine how a humble, pious Christian would have felt seeing a tooth of John the Baptist or a piece of the tablecloth used in the Last Supper passing before them. There were also relics of political significance, such as Charlemagne's supposed sword, the imperial orb and sceptre, and the glittering, bejewelled majesty of the golden imperial crown itself. Two days later Leopold ceremonially paraded into the city to sign his electoral capitulation, joined by 'incalculable guests' including Papal, Russian, and Sardinian legations and the King and Queen of Naples and Sicily.¹² The procession took hours to pass, accompanied by so much noise that days later Hommel joked he could 'still hear the Te Deum, the roar of the cannons, and the even greater roar of the people'.¹³

On 7 October two trumpeters informed the city that the coronation would take place that Saturday. After a solemn procession to the cathedral, a labyrinthine three-hour coronation mass followed in five stages, interspersed with hymns, reading of texts from the Bible, and instrumental music, all likely conducted by the imperial Kapellmeister Antonio Salieri.¹⁴ It culminated in Leopold's anointment, after which he was symbolically transformed from a mere prince into the Roman Emperor. He was then adorned with the various relics—ring, sword, sceptre, orb—and the three ecclesiastical electors placed the crown upon his head. 'Everything, down to the most trifling details, spoke to the spirit and the heart, through the power of tradition as well as through the aggregation of so much splendour', noted Metternich.¹⁵ The new Emperor Leopold II then paraded back to the Römer, once again amidst the deafening sound of *Vivat* and cannon fire. There he addressed the people before turning his attention to the ceremonial banquet with the highest dignitaries of the Empire. Here the princes had the chance to perform their ceremonial 'imperial dish-carrying duties' in which they served the food in a strictly prescribed sequence with their hats under their arms. The young Metternich, there representing the Catholic Rhenish and Westphalian imperial counts, was twenty-fifth.¹⁶ It clearly did not fail to make an impression.

* * *

In February 1790, Leopold was known to Europe as Pietro Leopoldo, Grand Duke of Tuscany. He had been born in the magnificent Viennese palace of Schönbrunn in 1737. As the ninth child and third son of Emperor Francis I and the Empress Maria Theresa, his destiny seemed to be that of a minor aristocrat. It was only thanks to one brother's death in 1761 that the Grand Duchy of Tuscany fell to him, transforming him into a sovereign prince. He ruled Tuscany as a model enlightened reformer, liberalizing trade, draining swamps, founding schools, promoting religious tolerance, and building canals, roads, and hospitals. The 1786 penal code he promulgated made Tuscany the first modern state to abolish the death penalty. A reflection, perhaps, of the 'good, generous and compassionate heart' his mother had always seen in him.¹⁷

BEFORE CENTRAL EUROPE

As the French estates revolted against their monarch in 1789, he welcomed it as an opportunity for France to take the lead and serve as a model for the rest of the continent.[18] Behind his moderate, enlightened constitutionalism stood a biting critique of his elder brother Joseph II, who had frustrated his own constitutional designs only a few years earlier. An enlightened monarch of a different, 'absolutist' sort, Joseph inherited the imperial title in 1765 and the bulk of the family lands upon Maria Theresa's death in 1780, seeing his younger brother's realm as little more than a minor family protectorate. But Joseph's failure to produce any lasting offspring set Leopold on the path to much greater things. By October 1790, he had taken on the most impressive, but also most complicated inheritance in Europe.

The House of Habsburg had humble medieval origins, but a series of fortunate inheritances around the year 1500 transformed it into a global power, with kingdoms, duchies, and estates across Europe and the world. The list of modern European countries whose territories were wholly or partly ruled by this family at some point in history is staggering: Spain, Portugal, Belgium, the Netherlands, Luxembourg, Austria, Czechia, Slovakia, Hungary, Croatia, Bosnia, Slovenia, Germany, Italy, Poland, Romania, Serbia, France, Ukraine, and Switzerland. From the mid-sixteenth century the family was divided into two lines. One ruled Spain and its vast overseas colonies, the other ruled disparate lands at the heart of Europe and held the imperial title. It was this latter, Austrian line whose strange inheritance would shape the Central Europe to come, binding together the fate of the Holy Roman Empire and its successors with that of the Austrian Habsburgs' extensive territorial realm.

The territorial core of this Austrian Habsburg inheritance was a group of contiguous crownlands—territories ruled directly as family 'properties'—on and beyond the eastern edge of the Holy Roman Empire. Some—like the kingdoms of Hungary and Croatia or the Archduchy of Austria—bore names familiar to modern readers but with very different boundaries and political identities to the modern nation-states. Others—like Moravia, Transylvania, or Galicia—have been lost to time. They were all distinct legal and political entities, with their own histories, proud nobilities, and local conditions that begged the question of whether or not they could ever be integrated into a single 'Habsburg Monarchy' (colloquially referred to simply as Austria). To add to the complexity, while Bohemia, Moravia, Silesia, and the Austrian duchies were part of the Holy Roman Empire, the kingdoms of Hungary and Croatia as well as the Principality of Transylvania were not and never had been, implying a 'sovereign' status seemingly incongruous with being amalgamated into a centralized state.

Leopold's mother Maria Theresa—who ruled them from 1740 to 1780—was the first in the family who attempted to form the trappings of a unified state. And his brother Joseph II, ruling from 1780 to 1790, then pursued a far more aggressive centralizing mission that brought that nascent state to the brink of collapse. He was a classic enlightened absolutist, running roughshod over the privileges and sensibilities of the established orders—principally the landed nobility and the clergy—hoping to build up a unified, centralized bureaucratic monarchy that left them with no voice in matters of taxation, conscription, law-making, and so on.

Leopold II thus inherited a realm in crisis. In 1789, encouraged by the revolution in France, the estates of the Austrian Netherlands had risen up against their Habsburg rulers while the armies of the latter were bogged down in the Balkans in an ultimately fruitless war against the Ottomans. On his deathbed, Joseph had called the estates of Bohemia and Hungary to meet for the first time in decades, the latter on the verge of a full-scale revolt. Sabre-rattling from Leopold's powerful Prussian neighbour to the north threatened to turn an internal crisis into an all-out European war. But there was a way out. Leopold believed in a more consensual form of enlightened government that was based on cooperation between the monarch and the privileged classes—or 'estates'—of nobles, clergy, and cities. These estates were represented in assemblies—'diets'—that met in each individual crownland; or, in the case of the Holy Roman Empire, in the Imperial Diet.

The contrast between the governing styles of the two brothers was quickly apparent as Leopold made his way north from Tuscany in early 1790.[19] In March, safely installed in Vienna, he devoted himself with a manic energy to realizing his grand plan to save the family inheritance.[20] His ritualized public debut came on 6 April, when a carefully planned 'inauguration' took place to reassure the Lower Austrian estates and, by extension, those of the whole Austrian 'heartlands'. Alongside some territories scattered across the Holy Roman Empire further west, this core of seven crownlands on the eastern edge of the Empire were known as the 'hereditary lands' or Austrian duchies, largely corresponding to modern Austria and Slovenia. The most important of these was Lower Austria, which contained Vienna.

The ceremonial act of reconciliation between the House of Habsburg and the Lower Austrian elites began with a procession of the estates from their home—the Landhaus—to the Hofburg (the imperial palace), a short walk through the narrow Viennese streets. Leopold and his court then joined the procession as it continued to St. Stephen's Cathedral at the heart of the inner city. After a solemn mass, they returned to the Hofburg, where in the great hall both sides made eloquent pronouncements of the trust they placed in each other before Leopold swore to uphold the 'privileges, freedoms, usages, rights, and immunities' of the Lower Austrian estates. In turn, the estates swore their own oath of fealty to their new monarch. A ceremonial banquet closed out the day.[21]

The significance of the ceremony reached far beyond the bounds of Lower Austria. Parading through the streets of the imperial capital, Leopold's commitment to consensual rule with the estates was on display for all to see. Not since his own mother's reign in the 1740s had the monarchy seen anything like it, his brother Joseph having spurned such customary ceremonies. Even worse, Joseph had hoarded the crowns of Hungary and Bohemia as well as the bejewelled 'archducal hat' of Lower Austria in Vienna in an act of symbolic centralization. The day after his inauguration, Leopold made up for this by returning the archducal hat to its traditional home near Vienna.[22] It was just one of many steps that had to be taken to clean up the mess Joseph had left behind and stave off the spectre of dynastic collapse that had menaced the family since the beginning of the century.

No house, no matter how illustrious, was immune from the consequences of impotence. On 1 November 1700, the last Spanish Habsburg king died without an heir, engulfing Europe in a long war of succession in which the Austrian Habsburgs were forced to relinquish claims to Spain and its globe-spanning colonies for good. By 1790 the family motto *Austrae est imperare orbi universe* (all the world is subject to Austria) appeared a distant fantasy—one immortalized in stone by the magnificent Baroque Karlskirche in Vienna and its two imposing columns built to represent the pillars of Hercules that separate the Mediterranean from the Atlantic. They reflected Leopold's grandfather's life-long obsession with the lost Spanish title and the closed path to global monarchy it represented. At his Viennese court, Spanish language, customs, art and fashion were nurtured with a longing pride by the man who still styled himself 'king of Spain'. He was only stopped from building a Viennese replica of the Escorial Palace in Madrid because he ran out of money.[23]

His death in 1740 brought a further blow to the family. He too had failed to produce a male heir. Before his death, he worked tirelessly to ensure that the estates of the various Habsburg crownlands would allow his daughter Maria Theresa—Leopold's mother—to inherit them. He created in the process what was later considered the founding constitutional charter of the Habsburg Monarchy: the various 'Pragmatic Sanctions', which established that the crownlands would pass indivisibly to any heir, male or female, implying they were parts of a single whole. Rapacious neighbours thought the young heiress—who could not be emperor on account of her sex—would put up little resistance to an assault on the family's imperial territories. Supported by France, Saxony and Bavaria launched what one French general predicted would 'resemble an occupation rather than a war'.[24] But Maria Theresa proved a far more formidable opponent than her adversaries expected. She defeated them and eventually secured the imperial throne for her husband, Francis Stephen of Lorraine. Yet Maria Theresa's reign was marked by one consequential failure.

In 1740, a young Frederick II, later known as 'the Great', inherited the Prussian crown from his pious and parsimonious father, Frederick William I.[25] His House of Hohenzollern had ruled a set of relatively poor and indefensible territories scattered across Northern Europe for centuries, the most important of which was the Electorate of Brandenburg centred on Berlin and the nearby court city of Potsdam. On the basis of the family's only extraimperial territory—sandy Prussia on the Baltic—Frederick II's grandfather had invented a royal title out of thin air in 1701, crowning himself king in Königsberg. It was an ostentatious display of dynastic ambition. It did not change that most of the family lands remained in the Holy Roman Empire nor that Prussia proper was outside of it. All it did was provide the head of the Hohenzollern dynasty with a dignified title that implied that—at least somewhere—he was sovereign, even if he remained a vassal within the Empire.

Even though 'Prussia' now referred to the Hohenzollern lands in their entirety, the 'kingdom' left to Frederick II was still modest in size. The overflowing coffers and enormous standing army built up by his father gave him the opportunity to change that. Just months after his accession, he staged an audacious and outrageous invasion of the wealthy Habsburg province of Silesia. Almost overnight, Frederick increased Prussia's population by 50 per cent and its territory by a third, at the manageable cost of Maria Theresa's lifelong enmity and two more wars to defend it.[26] Prussian victory in the second of those—the Seven Years' War—made clear that the era of Austrian unipolarity in the Holy Roman Empire had ended. Austro-Prussian dualism had become a permanent feature of imperial and, later, Central European politics.

Prussian power was given an added boon later in the century thanks to the decline of the Polish-Lithuanian Commonwealth. An elective monarchy dominated by an enormous and proud nobility that stretched from the eastern boundaries of the Empire to what was then a distant Russia, Poland-Lithuania had been one of the largest countries on the continent since its creation in 1569. But by the late eighteenth century, it had been reduced to a de facto Russian vassal. A further round of political chaos precipitated its rapacious partition by Prussia, Austria, and Russia in 1772. Two further partitions followed in 1793 and 1795, wiping it off the map of Europe for good and leaving the three partitioning powers with the challenge of integrating huge numbers of patriotic Polish nobles, poor Slavic peasants, and hundreds of thousands of Jews into their developing states.

The traditionally-minded Empress Maria Theresa saw the first partition as dishonourable 'policy *à la prussienne*', but the Habsburgs could not sit idly by as two regional adversaries aggrandized themselves at Vienna's expense.[27] Her Chief Librarian Adam František Kollár helped assuage her conscience by digging up medieval Hungarian claims to parts of 'Little- or Red-Russia'. The Habsburgs thus claimed they were simply restoring the 'Kingdom of Galicia and Lodomeria' that was rightfully theirs. The Hohenzollerns, for their part, pretended they were reunifying the ancient Kingdom of Prussia. The Russians claimed to be 'reuniting' the east Slavic lands that belonged to the medieval polity of Kyivan Rus'.[28] But these claims were novelties and so were the polities created by them. The ancestors of the Hohenzollerns were minor nobles who had helped annihilate the original pagan Prussians. The vague Hungarian claim used to justify Galicia's creation had never corresponded to a lasting political reality. 'Russia' was a rebranded Grand Duchy of Muscovy seeking justification for expanding an empire that its elite were far more fixated on than some recreated medieval Rus'. The ideological pretexts given by the partitioning powers and the propaganda that accompanied them only served to obscure the naked opportunism of the partition.

Prussia was, after all, a state built on opportunism. King Frederick William II perhaps had this in mind in 1790, when the consequences of Josephine absolutism had left his great Habsburg rival teetering on the brink. He massed nearly 200,000 troops in Silesia as he lent support to the revolting Belgians and the defiant Hungarians, and signed an alliance with a Polish-Lithuanian state in the midst of a 'revolution' that its nobles and king hoped would turn it into a stable constitutional monarchy.[29] Frederick William was suspicious of Leopold's pacifist overtures but was forced by his Dutch and English allies to negotiate and avoid a general war. And so, in the small Silesian town of Reichenbach, representatives of the Prussian and Austrian monarchs met in late June 1790 in an attempt to reconcile the Empire's two great powers, the leading of which undoubtedly remained the latter. After weeks of negotiations, they signed a treaty on 27 July that restored the status quo ante bellum. Prussia promised to withdraw support for the rebellious estates in Belgium and Hungary while Austria promised to end its war with the Ottomans without annexations, thus leaving the balance of power unchanged. As an added bonus, Frederick William promised to support Leopold's accession to the imperial throne.

On 30 September 1790, after a seven-day trip from Vienna, Leopold arrived in the small town of Aschaffenberg on the Main with most of his family. Just an hour later, news arrived from nearby Frankfurt. Leopold had been unanimously elected King of the Romans. Nine days later, he would be crowned Roman Emperor. 'Applaud happy Germania', read one of Frankfurt's many celebratory illuminations, 'you possess an Emperor with the kindness of Trajan, the clemency of Titus, the wisdom of Aurelius ... Ceaser Augustus *LEOPOLD II*'.[30]

* * *

For those familiar with a narrative of Roman decline and fall in 476 CE, the fact that Europe's great aristocrats gathered for an extravagant election and coronation of a Roman Emperor—in Frankfurt of all places—a millennium later may seem hopelessly anachronistic. Adjectives like this are often used to describe the 'Holy Roman Empire' more generally, not least thanks to some dismissive contemporaries. Chief amongst them was Voltaire, who famously quipped that it was neither holy, nor Roman, nor an empire—more a reflection of his own biases and distaste for Maria Theresa than a description of reality.[31]

It owed its existence not to a territory, but to a title. In 800 CE, Pope Leo III crowned Charlemagne Emperor of the Romans on the pretext that the position was vacant since the actual Roman emperor in Constantinople had been deposed and replaced by his mother, who supposedly could not hold the title. Centuries later, this Roman Empire in the east was anachronistically dubbed a separate 'Byzantine' phenomenon, marginalized ever since in Western European conceptions of history, reflecting the longstanding Catholic claim that the Holy Roman Empire represented true continuity with the world of antiquity.[32] While the original title had been a recognition of Charlemagne's power through his vast Frankish kingdom, it did not in and of itself correspond to any territory. Nor did it really have the significance it would later take on. Only gradually did a vague territorially defined 'Holy Roman Empire' emerge, roughly corresponding to today's Germany, Austria, Switzerland, the Low Countries, Czechia, and parts of many other countries.

By the eighteenth century, the Holy Roman Empire had evolved into perhaps the most unique political entity in European history. As the contemporary jurist Johann Jakob Moser put it: 'no school word, or a few words, or way of government of other states is suited to make our way of government understandable'.[33] It included within its legal-institutional order states like Mainz, Cologne and Trier ruled by elected noble bishops, free imperial cities like Hamburg and Frankfurt governed by urban oligarchies, miniscule sovereign estates of imperial counts and knights like the Metternichs, and countless princely states both large and small. Any ruler who was an 'immediate' vassal of the emperor was known as a 'prince', enjoying a distinct form of sovereignty called *Landeshoheit*— roughly translated as territorial sovereignty—which meant that subordinate nobles (if there were any) could not have their own military forces. Such princes could enter freely into treaties with foreign powers, with the caveat that these could not be aimed against the emperor or Empire.[34]

They were all part of a porous and diffuse feudal landscape in which symbolic acts of participation mattered more than direct authority; an empire of titles, rights, privileges, and obligations as much as territories.[35] It did not so much consist of states as of areas distinguished by unique institutions, laws and customs with different authorities for different social groups. The delineation of precise political boundaries is nearly impossible.[36] A knight or prince could have some territory that was sovereign while also holding estates subordinate to other princes. Meanwhile a neighbouring prince-bishop's ecclesiastical authority could reach into their own lands even if their princely authority did not. In the Rhineland in the west of the Empire, where most of the imperial knights and ecclesiastical states were located, the tangle of sovereignties was particularly acute. There was not even a clear border with France, where countless imperial nobles also had estates and saw the country as a natural part of their 'geo-cultural landscape'.[37]

The entire institutional order of the Holy Roman Empire was designed to maintain this web of princely, aristocratic, ecclesiastical, and imperial authority. It was simultaneously an arena of international relations, where leading princes vied for power and influence, and a self-contained political world of estates. The coronation of an emperor was important not just because of the political power it gave its holder, but because it was an opportunity to enact a feudal hierarchy of status for all to see. Amongst imperial nobles this was considered an issue of paramount importance. Questions of precedence were haggled over and defended with unbelievable persistence, baffling and amusing outsiders in equal measure.

By 1790 it was certainly a far cry from Charlemagne's early medieval kingdom, to say nothing of the Roman Empire of antiquity. But certain elements of this long political tradition remained integral to the Empire's place in Europe as well as the importance of it to the House of Habsburg, the most important undoubtedly being its universalism. The world has grown accustomed to thinking in terms of plural empires, but for the vast majority of European history there was only one empire: the Roman Empire. According to the Bible, it was the last of four world empires whose own fall would herald the end of the world. The singularity of this Roman imperial title was such that even eighteenth-century French or English authors wrote simply of 'the Empire', the capital 'E' differentiating it from the 'empires' European powers forged on distant shores.[38] It was a political idea upheld by the universalist Roman Catholic Church, with the pious Habsburgs representing its most stalwart defenders. In the church and parts of the Habsburg Monarchy the Latin tongue of the Romans remained in use far longer than anywhere else in Europe.[39]

That Roman legacies mediated through the Middle Ages remained so central to the eighteenth-century Habsburg patrimony provided easy fodder for enlightened ridicule. Yet the language, church, and empire of the Romans were a shared European legacy, ones that were inherently universalist. Latin had for centuries been the universal tongue of Europe's educated elite. 'Catholic' was simply the Greek word for universal, with the church bearing this name serving for centuries as the only established church of Western Christians in Europe. And the title of emperor stood above every other secular title on the European continent. It signified a sovereign above sovereigns, a 'secular head for the Christian people'.[40]

The singularity of the imperial title was recognized universally by Western Christians. Recognized, and also constantly reinforced by their participation in its reproduction. The assembled nobles, royals, and dignitaries at Leopold's coronation represented just about every corner of the continent. The duke and prince-elector of Hanover was the British King George III. The prince-elector of Brandenburg was the Prussian King Frederick William II. The kings of France and Sweden both acted as guarantors of the imperial order pursuant to the Peace of Westphalia signed in 1648. The former was Leopold II's brother-in-law through his sister Marie Antoinette. Leopold's other sister was Queen of Naples and Sicily and his in-laws were the king and queen of Spain. They existed in a world of status unbounded by geography. In Montesquieu's words, for them Europe was just 'a state made up of several provinces'.[41] They intermarried across the continent with little care for origins or language. They could begin life on one end of the continent and finish it on the other with no change in their station in life. Indeed, usually such movement was an attempt to rise up the ladder of status. They differentiated themselves from the masses through the use of prestigious vernaculars like Spanish, Italian, and especially French.

The oddest thing about this Habsburg universalism was how limited it was. By 1790 England, Spain, France, Italian states, the Netherlands, Scandinavian countries, and Scotland had long since made political, cultural, or confessional declarations of independence from the Empire, the Roman Catholic Church, or Latin and the culture of classical Rome. They asserted royal sovereignty, promoted vernacular languages, and rejected the Roman church's claim to the spiritual leadership of Western Christendom. But the pillars of Habsburg legitimacy in the Empire and in their own territorial lands required an entirely different approach—one that respected the authority of the Catholic Church, maintained the symbolic order of the Empire, and kept Latin alive as a neutral language of administration.

* * *

As the festivities in Frankfurt wrapped up, Leopold received some welcome news. The rebellious Hungarian diet—deprived of Prussian support—had finally agreed to the restoration of the pre-Josephine status quo. The Kingdom of Hungary—or lands under the Crown of St. Stephen—was a realm unlike any other ruled by the Habsburgs. For one, it was enormous. In its broadest possible definition, it was about the size of all the other crownlands combined, larger than the modern United Kingdom. It stretched across the Pannonian Plain, buttressed by dramatic

Carpathian peaks to the north and east and the Dinaric Alps to the south, with the long Danube running through its heart. It stood completely outside the Empire and had a large and powerful noble elite that jealously guarded their rights and privileges, which they expected every new king to re-affirm in person, as Leopold would at his coronation in Pressburg (modern-day Bratislava) in early November 1790.

In true premodern form, this noble elite prided themselves as the *Natio Hungarica*—Hungarian nation—a privileged martial class with the right to administer their own affairs.[42] Nearly five per cent of the population belonged to this 'nation' in the late eighteenth century, while the bourgeoisie was perhaps half that size and spread across dozens of distant cities.[43] Many poorer, 'sandaled' nobles lived a meagre existence scarcely distinguishable from the vast majority of the population that lived off the land as serfs or peasants. Atop it all stood a small class of wealthy aristocrats—or magnates—who alone enjoyed the right to sit directly in the upper house of the diet. The lower house, by contrast, filled with representatives of the lower nobility, was a hotbed of patriotic agitation. To add to the complexity, Hungary contained two autonomous crownlands within it. One was the Kingdom of Croatia-Slavonia in the southwest, the other the Principality of Transylvania in the east. The latter was uniquely ruled by a union of three different 'nations' representing estates of Hungarian nobles, Saxon burghers, and the militarized Szeklers (often considered a sub-group of Magyars), even though Romanians formed an unrepresented majority. Croatia-Slavonia meanwhile had its own native nobility that through the centuries had become deeply intertwined with the wider Hungarian nobility.

Hungary was one of the most linguistically diverse countries in Europe.[44] Thirty to forty per cent spoke Magyar, a unique language brought into Europe from the Eurasian steppe by the nomadic tribes that invaded the Pannonian Plain and established the Kingdom of Hungary in the Middle Ages. But most Hungarians spoke Slavic, German, and Romance vernaculars, while the official language was Latin. This linguistic diversity was one of the country's most widely remarked-upon features. The exiled Bohemian scholar Jan Amos Comenius remarked in 1659 that 'such a confusion of nations, languages and customs either leads to barbarism or smells of it'.[45] Supporters of Latin would have countered that the official use of Latin made this irrelevant as 'in some respects [it was] not foreign to anyone'.[46] This is in large part why Latin survived as a living language longer in Hungary than anywhere else in Europe save the

Vatican, providing a never-ending source of bemusement for foreign travellers shocked to find innkeepers, coachmen, and shepherds speaking the supposedly dead Roman tongue well into the nineteenth century.

Hungary had historically been the primary battleground in the great struggle between the Habsburgs and the Ottoman Empire that had raged since the sixteenth century. Indeed, both Hungary and Bohemia had only come into Habsburg hands because their king fell in battle against the Ottomans in 1526. It took the Great Turkish War, which came to an end in 1699, for the Habsburgs to finally reconquer most of a kingdom that had been in the family for a century and a half. The long Habsburg border nonetheless remained a specially administered Military Frontier ruled directly from Vienna and populated by free peasants expected to defend their border homes and serve in the army more broadly. Over the course of the eighteenth century, Hungary was once again recast in a Christian image. The city skylines once dominated by minarets saw churches emerge in their place. The Muslim merchants and administrators were expelled and colonists from across Habsburg Europe poured in to settle the devastated countryside.

Buda (Ofen in German), the old Hungarian capital, only hosted its first diet since the reconquest in 1790, but Leopold requested the coronation take place in Pressburg, which had served as the capital through the long Ottoman wars. Just a few dozen kilometres downstream from Vienna along the Danube, Pressburg enjoyed a symbiotic relationship with the imperial capital. While other Hungarian towns stagnated or declined, Pressburg flourished thanks to its proximity to Vienna and its role as Hungary's administrative centre, which in turn made it an attractive place of residence for wealthy nobles.[47] By 1790 many of the fortifications that once constricted the inner city had been torn down and the square Baroque castle that loomed over the city had been transformed into a royal palace. It was a cultured European city, with one visitor reporting that it had 'comfortable inns, beautiful coffee houses, four printing houses, four bookshops, and an art shop'.[48]

As had been the case in Frankfurt, the royal coronation was cause for weeks of ceremony that transformed Pressburg into a magnificent political stage. It began on 30 October with the ceremonial arrival of the regalia, accompanied by the usual bells, trumpets, and drums. In this case the celebrated crown, sceptre, orb, sword, coat, and gloves were those of Saint Stephen, the Hungarian king who had converted to Christianity and founded the kingdom around 1000 CE.[49] On 10 November the estates lined the streets of Pressburg to greet the man that promised to restore all that Joseph had ostentatiously deprived them of. As peeling bells echoed, Leopold made his triumphal entry in full, colourful, embroidered Hungarian dress. A speech of welcome was given in Latin, which Leopold responded to in the same language. A huge parade followed, involving multi-coloured citizens' militias raised for the occasion by the city, and the day closed out with a banquet and Pressburg illuminated.[50]

The following day Leopold opened the diet, addressing the nobles in their 'native' Latin. The next three days saw the elevation of his son to palatine (viceroy), a position left vacant by Joseph, accompanied by much celebration. Finally, on 15 November, the coronation took place, followed by Leopold's swearing of the Latin oath to uphold the nation's rights and privileges. One notable Hungarian peculiarity was the constant presence throughout of ten colourful banners representing the ten lands once ruled under St. Stephen's crown, including Galicia and Lodmoeria as well as Croatia, Slavonia, and Dalmatia.[51] The ceremony culminated in a unique spectacle up on the hill in front of the palace. Leopold rode his horse onto an artificial mound and pointed St. Stephen's sword in each of the cardinal directions to signify he would protect the kingdom against any and all external threats.[52]

By 1791, Leopold had comfortably seen off the threats that faced him upon his accession, but one final symbolic gesture remained. North of the Austrian duchies stood the richest of all the Habsburg crownlands. The Lands of the Crown of Saint Wenceslaus—usually colloquially referred to simply as Bohemia—included the Kingdom of Bohemia, Margravate of Moravia, and Silesian Duchies of which only a small sliver was left over after Frederick's conquest earlier in the century. As the crown of St. Wenceslas made its way to Prague ahead of Leopold's coronation, it was cheered on in countless Bohemian towns along the way. It arrived in the city on 9 August 1791, celebrated not just as the return of an old relic, but as the rejuvenation of the kingdom itself.[53]

Prague was—and still is—a city dominated by the castle complex across the river from the medieval old town. A looming reminder of Bohemia's storied history. Prague hosted sovereign native kings in the Middle Ages and even served as the primary residence of the long-reigning Habsburg Emperor Rudolph II. This apotheosis of Prague's centrality was followed just a few years after Rudolph's death in 1612 by the most troubled period in Bohemian history, when the Third Defenestration of Prague kickstarted the gruelling Thirty Years' War that left it devastated and much of its native nobility dead or dispossessed.

BEFORE CENTRAL EUROPE

Bohemia's rebellious past was a distant memory by 1790, but few wanted to see their country's individuality dissolved entirely. It was much more tightly integrated into the Habsburg state than Hungary, with a smaller aristocratic class that formed the backbone of the wider imperial and Habsburg elite. The diet called in 1790 ended up being the largest since the 1620s, with an opposition party hoping to press Leopold on his commitment to estates-based governance and secure a more favourable settlement for the country akin to that of Hungary.[54] In the end, they had to settle for a mere coronation, recognizing the political personality of Bohemia without any actual political power being ceded to Prague. It was a recognition nonetheless that they lived in a real kingdom and not simply under an empty title.

Leopold was greeted in the royal castle on 31 August 1791 after a triumphal entry. The Highest Burggrave Count Heinrich Rottenhan addressed him in the—to Leopold incomprehensible—'Bohemian' language. It was not Rottenhan's mother tongue, but this incantation served as a symbol of the kingdom's distinctiveness. The ritualized use of the 'Bohemian' language was even more pronounced at the oath-taking ceremony of the estates, when the majority of those assembled chose to use the kingdom's native Slavic tongue instead of the German that followed. This carefully crafted political instrument was only deployed thanks to the help of the scholar Joseph Dobrovský, who translated the various addresses from their original German into an archaic 'Bohemian' for the occasion, harkening back to the glory days of Bohemia's sovereign existence.[55]

The coronation itself took place on 6 September, its details not dissimilar to those in Frankfurt and Pressburg. Colourful citizens' militias lined the streets, cannons roared, bells rang, nobles swore oaths, and a city rejoiced under the glow of illuminations and fireworks. In the evening, Leopold and the many Bohemian and imperial notables gathered in the Estates Theatre built by the enlightened Count Anton von Nostitz. The estates had commissioned a brand-new opera to mark the occasion, *La clemenza di Tito*—The Clemency of Titus—authored and conducted by Mozart.

2

THE ENLIGHTENMENT CHALLENGE

True to enlightened form, Leopold II closed out his stay in Prague with a visit to the Royal Bohemian Society of Sciences. On 25 September 1791 it held an open session in its headquarters in the sprawling Clementinum in Prague's old town, attended by Leopold, his son Francis, and several other dignitaries. Speakers showcased the achievements of the Bohemian Enlightenment, lecturing on local politics and culture, natural sciences, minerology, anatomy, and more. Towards the end, Joseph Dobrovský delivered what became the most famous of all the lectures 'On the Loyalty and Devotion of the Slavic Peoples to the Arch-House of Austria'.[1]

A native Bohemian—though born in Hungary as his officer father was stationed there in 1753—Dobrovský's first years had been spent in the western Bohemian town of Bischofsteinitz. It was part of a whole ring of territories on the edge of Bohemia—bordering surrounding German states—that were overwhelmingly German-speaking, dubbed in a later epoch the 'Sudetenland'. It was a change then when he was sent deep into the Slavic-speaking interior for secondary school. The Czech boys mocked and played pranks on 'Germans' like Dobrovský, but this did not stop him from picking up a deep admiration for the 'Bohemian' language.[2] In time he proved to be an incredibly talented linguist, studying Arabic, Chaldean, and Syriac and slated for a professorship in Oriental languages.

In the late eighteenth century, however, academia was just one venue amongst many for the pursuit of enlightenment. Of much more long-term significance for Dobrovský than his degrees was his position as a tutor in the house of Count Anton von Nostitz, the intellectual centre of the whole Bohemian Enlightenment. Under the patronage of this patriotic noble, Dobrovský would in time become one of its leading lights for his pioneering work on the 'Bohemian' language. Known to its own speakers and today's world as 'Czech', it was the language of the majority of the kingdom's inhabitants but had been relegated by decades of elite neglect to the position of a largely peasant tongue. Dobrovský's original intent with his lecture in Leopold's presence was to make an appeal for Joseph's Germanizing measures to be relaxed and Czech given official support, but the high official that had to approve all the speeches insisted he leave it out.

Dobrovský was thus forced to stick to his main topic. Bohemians, he said, 'as a tribe of the large, widely-spread Slavic nation [*Völkerschaft*], consider it our greatest glory, along with other Slavic peoples, to have preserved the German imperial house in its greatness and prestige, and to be able to further secure the Austrian Monarchy through the combined forces of all other Slavic peoples against all enemy attacks'. Leopold, he pointed out, bore the title of four whole Slavic kingdoms in Croatia and Dalmatia, Slavonia, Bohemia, and Galicia. Northern Hungary, meanwhile, was full of Slovaks while the inner Austrian duchies of Styria, Carinthia, and Carniola were full of 'Winds' (Slovenes). It was clear, he concluded, that the number of Slavs was equal to every other people in the Habsburg Monarchy combined.[3]

Underneath the aristocratic edifice of the Holy Roman Empire, and of the extraimperial Habsburg and Hohenzollern crownlands, stood a melange of peoples with astounding variety in languages, faiths, and identities. The vast majority were peasants who lived off the land, many in conditions of serfdom that often resembled slavery, especially in Prussia proper, Galicia, and Hungary, where the large classes of 'Junker', Polish and Hungarian gentry lords dominated their respective countrysides. 'A noble Hungarian man', wrote one such lord from Transylvania, differs from 'his peasant, as much as an owner differs from his property'.[4]

The speech of the overwhelmingly illiterate peasantry was highly localized, as were their identities. Their awareness of the wider world was largely mediated through their local church, far and away the most important social institution for the rural masses. Religion was usually the only thing they shared with their distant rulers, who appeared in sermons and proclamations as almost semi-mythic figures few were likely to ever encounter in the flesh. Little attention was afforded to them by their rulers, who lived aloof lives at court cities surrounded by men and women of their stature—at least, that is, until the Age of Enlightenment.

Dobrovský, Leopold II, the Bohemian Society of Sciences, and all the subjects discussed were products of the Enlightenment's intellectual revolution that so transformed the way Europeans thought about the world.

THE ENLIGHTENMENT CHALLENGE

By 1791, this process was at its zenith; it had upended all the assumptions that underpinned the strangely limited universalism of a Roman-medieval provenance that defined the peculiar Habsburg-ruled world in the heart of Europe, provoking debates on a huge array of political, social, and cultural questions that touched on every bit of the Habsburg inheritance. To the enlightened mind, everything about that inheritance appeared irrational, outdated, and peculiar.

The Holy Roman Empire, with its maze of overlapping authority, seemingly infinite political units, and total lack of centralized power, confounded any precise definition or theory of statehood. To whom did a forward-thinking subject owe his loyalty? To the emperor? To a 'state'? To some abstract imperial or national ideal? Though composite monarchies that amalgamated several states into one—such as Great Britain—were not unusual, the sheer number and ambiguity of relations in the Habsburg case was singular. Some states were in the Holy Roman Empire, others were not. Some were dominated by small cosmopolitan aristocracies, others by large native gentries. To whom, once again, did they owe their loyalty? Unconditionally to their Habsburg ruler? To their crownland? To some abstract imperial or national ideal? These questions, which emerged in the ferment of the eighteenth-century Age of Enlightenment, would end up shaping political debate in Central Europe up into the twentieth century.

* * *

What is 'enlightenment'? The eighteenth-century Reverend Johann Friedrich Zöllner thought the question to be 'almost as important as what is truth?'[5] In an essay published in 1784 in response to Zöllner, the Königsberg philosopher Immanuel Kant argued: 'Enlightenment is man's emergence from his self-inflicted immaturity'. And its motto was *Sapere Aude!* (Dare to think). In this Age of Enlightenment, every old certainty had come under question, every superstition had been challenged, and every old value cast aside. Characteristic of the 'enlightened' was a commitment to rationalism, scorn for the darkness of 'superstition', belief in the power of one's own intellect, but beyond that the exact bounds of the Enlightenment have always been a subject of debate. Christian Gotthilf Salzmann joked that he knew 'one young fop who thought he was enlightened simply because he could speak French'.[6] It was an easy mistake to make.

The Enlightenment's spread across Europe in the eighteenth century was closely related to the hegemony of French language and culture amongst Europe's well-born elites. French was Europe's first entirely secular lingua franca; by the end of the eighteenth century the ability to speak it was a marker of a cultured individual from Paris to St. Petersburg, particularly when accompanied—as it often was—by the adoption of French dress, manners, and attitudes. But there was never quite a wholesale and uncritical adoption of ideas emanating from France. The Enlightenment was 'more like a language than a single idea, imposing by its very nature certain modes of thought on those who use it, while remaining always at the same time the expression, in any actual usage, of particular desires and meanings and a response to particular conditions', as aptly put by Lionel Gossman.[7] In the Holy Roman Empire and the most tightly integrated Hohenzollern and Habsburg lands— extending to Prussia proper in the former case and Galicia, Hungary, Croatia, and Transylvania in the latter—two very distinct streams of enlightened thought shaped political, cultural and social development in this Age of Enlightenment: one coming from France, the other emanating from the mostly Protestant north of the Empire while taking considerable inspiration from Great Britain. There was not so much a geographic divide in which one or the other predominated as there was a complicated web of influence.

What made this northern Enlightenment uniquely important for the formation of Central Europe was what it did with the German language. At the turn of the eighteenth century, German was thought of as little better than Magyar, Czech, or other Slavic vernaculars, none worthy of the same status as Latin, Italian, or French, languages in which philosophy, literature, and poetry could all be written and whose very use displayed culture and refinement. An 'anxiety of deficit' reigned—typical when transitioning from Latin to vernacular high culture—where it was feared the 'poverty' of the vernacular could not compete with the 'riches' of Latin.[8] Several competing standards and countless dialects made it difficult to define what good or proper German was. It lacked accepted vocabulary to express scientific or philosophical thoughts, and it was not believed to have the refinement for artistic prose or poetry. Some attempts had been made to elevate German in the seventeenth century, but they withered away against the rising tide of French.[9]

In 1682 one French writer triumphantly declared: 'It is the glory of France to have succeeded in establishing the rules for all the fine arts.

THE ENLIGHTENMENT CHALLENGE

During the past twenty years, scholarly dissertations have regulated drama, epic poetry, epigrams, eclogues, painting, music, history and rhetoric. All branches of knowledge are now conducted in our language'.[10] A literary debate erupted soon after around the question of whether or not contemporary France had actually achieved a level of culture equal to that of the ancient Greeks and Romans. The Académie Française gave its verdict in 1694, declaring that French was in the same state as Latin was in Cicero's time.[11] The difference was that classical Rome and Greece were imitated as universal models, whereas France was a clearly existing entity ruled by a monarch traditionally hostile to both the Habsburgs and the Empire at large.

Latin, French and Italian were also foreign languages, spoken only by those educated few who could afford to adopt them. Not every 'young fop' could be counted on to become a Frenchman as easily as could a Habsburg, Hohenzollern or Metternich with their coteries of paid tutors. While the French celebrated the apotheosis of their cultural hegemony, the most eminent German philosopher of the day was lamenting the sorry state of German pride in the wake of the Thirty Years' War, which had raged from 1618–48 and devastated much of the Empire. Gottfried Wilhelm Leibniz proposed it would be saved by increasing the number of people who 'lead a freer life, who take pleasure in histories and journeys, who sometimes enliven themselves with a pleasant book and, when in society they encounter a learned and eloquent man, listen to him with particular eagerness'.[12] That is, it would be saved by spreading enlightenment, which the German vernacular would have to be able to convey if it were to influence the wider population.

Taking up Leibniz's call, the young Saxon philosopher Christian Thomasius became the first person to hold a course of lectures in German in 1687, but peppered his speech with so many Latin words, phrases and constructions that it was incomprehensible to anyone who did not know the ancient tongue.[13] The native Silesian Christian Wolff carried the regeneration of German a step further, developing a distinctly German philosophical language free from Latin or French constraints.[14] Besides contributing to the cultivation of German, Wolff and Thomasius helped transform the way Germans thought about political power. They espoused a vision of harmony between the princely states of the Empire and their societies, seeing the former's task as increasing the productivity and well-being of the latter through proactive intervention. Progress, they argued, would come from the legitimate rulers.

Indeed, it was largely thanks to the patronage of those princes that the Enlightenment was able to flourish in the Holy Roman Empire. By 1800 France had twenty-two universities and England just two, but in the Empire there were nearly fifty, many of which had been founded in the previous century by enlightened monarchs.[15] The University of Göttingen, for example, was founded by the Elector of Hanover and King of Great Britain George II in 1734 with the express purpose of spreading enlightenment, quickly becoming a renowned centre of scholarship and drawing students from across Europe. The multitude of universities helped Wolff's influence in particular spread far and wide, with 112 chairs at German universities occupied by supporters of his philosophy by the mid-1730s.[16] Johann Christoph Gottsched later told an anecdote of a simple peasant who had obtained a complete understanding of mathematics from one of Wolff's books.[17] True or not, it illustrates the thrust of the enlightened drive to use the vernacular. If common people could be taught in a language they understood, they too could be educated, cultivated and refined.

Who exactly were these German-speakers they wanted to help reach enlightenment? Most lived in one of the countless states of the Holy Roman Empire. Indeed, in the eighteenth century, the Empire was often simply equated with 'Germany', reflected in the unofficial suffix 'of the German nation' or the shorthand 'Roman-German Empire'. The ancient Romans had referred to the 'barbarians' north of the Alps collectively as 'Germans'. Over the centuries and especially after the discovery of the Roman historian Tacitus's *Germania* during the Renaissance, this identification with a Germany stretching back to antiquity became increasingly important to many of those living within the Empire.[18]

But speakers of German dialects were by no means limited to 'Germany'. The region of Prussia from which the Hohenzollern state took its name was historically associated with Poland, even though it contained many German-speakers alongside speakers of Baltic and Slavic languages. Further east along the Baltic coast an even smaller class of German landowners and burghers dominated what are today Estonia and Latvia, under Russian rule from the early eighteenth century. There were German settler-farmers in Croatia, Slavonia, Galicia, and—most notably—Hungary. The Germans of Habsburg-ruled Hungary amounted to about ten per cent of the population, mostly divided into three main groups: a small community of Lutheran burghers in the north known as the Zipsers, the far more numerous, largely Catholic 'Swabians' settled

THE ENLIGHTENMENT CHALLENGE

across the Pannonian Plain, and the Saxons of Transylvania, a whole corporate nation in their own right.[19]

The situation in Hungary was a microcosm of the general differences that marked out 'Germans' across Europe. For one, they were confessionally divided into Catholic, Lutheran and Calvinist churches. The south and west of Germany was largely Catholic, the north largely Protestant. Then there was the question of 'tribes' identified with traditional regions, like Swabians, Bavarians or Franconians. Often people recognized they were German in some general sense but felt much more strongly attached to these 'tribal' regions. In large part this was because the tribes were associated with certain dialects, which were not always mutually intelligible. Low German dialects in the north were in many ways linguistically closer to Dutch or Frisian than to High German, although by the eighteenth century Low German's written functions had narrowed considerably from its previous heyday.[20]

Insofar as people took pride in Germany, celebrated 'German liberties', or contrasted the 'German nation' with the French or Italian, they were usually contrasting the political entity of the Empire and its peculiar institutional order, not invoking a more abstract national state that did not yet exist. The emperors—customarily Austrian Habsburgs since the fifteenth century—were the pinnacle of this order. They were thus the main target of devotion, with prayers said for them in churches and synagogues across the Empire. They were the ultimate source of legal authority and legitimacy, with the ability to grant special distinctions and privileges as well as act as ultimate arbiter in legal disputes. And, fundamentally, they were meant to act as protectors of the whole realm. Though there was no standing imperial army, the emperor raised one in times of crisis and war to defend the Empire and its internal order.

Local elites in the west of the Holy Roman Empire were especially interested in the maintenance of this imperial order in all its contradictions. They were close to France, vulnerable to exacting invasions, occupations and even outright annexation. The Rhineland was full of small and complicated entities without much power of their own: small free cities, archbishoprics, and sovereign estates of knights and counts who were considered 'immediate' to the emperor since they had no other local lord. Their unique liberties thus depended on the protection afforded by their place in the Empire.

In the east, it was a different matter altogether. There, due to the unique way the Empire had expanded eastwards in the Middle Ages, large territorial states like Prussia, Saxony, Bavaria, and the Habsburg Monarchy dominated without the extreme complexity that defined the west. The monarchs of these states had their own self-contained world of estates under their watch, with nobles, cities and armies that were loyal only to them. They were meant to be loyal to the Empire and its elected leader, but sometimes they were not, entering alliances with foreign powers such as France to fight against the Habsburgs. But the results of such escapades were often disastrous. The Prussian King Frederick William I warned his son Frederick II never to wage an aggressive war nor ally against the emperor, lest he be 'punished by the hand of God' like the proud Saxon King Augustus II. But Frederick II had none of his father's sense of loyalty and deference.[21]

Shortly after coming to power in 1740, he invaded and annexed the bulk of Habsburg Silesia. For the enlightened, rational, Francophone Prussian king, the Empire was little more than an obstacle to be overcome in his pursuit of glory. He dismissed it as 'bizarre', 'a chaos of little states' dominated by his arch-enemy Maria Theresa.[22] Frederick 'the Great' advanced a distinctly more modern theory of politics than his father, following Wolff and others in seeing the monarch not as first among aristocratic equals restricted in action within a wider imperial order, but the very embodiment of the sovereign state in whose interests it was his duty to act. Though Frederick's Prussia was certainly no enlightened utopia, it was ruled by a secular monarch who seemed to have succeeded in subordinating the interests of the provincial landed nobility—the infamous 'Junkers' as they were dubbed in the nineteenth century—to that of the wider 'state', channelling their sons into administrative and military service while preserving their privileged position in the countryside. And he put the interests of his 'state' above traditional notions of fealty, as was clearly demonstrated in 1750 when he became the only prince in the Empire to ban the traditional prayers to the emperor in the (largely Protestant) churches under his rule.[23]

The Habsburg realm, in contrast to Frederick's Prussia, was a composite monarchy of composite monarchies. To recap, the crownlands Maria Theresa inherited within the Empire included the far-off Austrian Netherlands, an archipelago of small territories scattered across southern Germany, the core Austrian duchies on the southeast of the Empire, and the Bohemian lands above them. Beyond that there was the large Kingdom of Hungary with Croatia and Transylvania to the east as well as a group of duchies in northern Italy. With the partitions of Poland later in her reign the large territory of Galicia was added to the mix. There was no concept that brought unity to all these territories beyond the family that ruled them and the Pragmatic Sanctions, which meant the most important of them—roughly the territories of what would come to be known as the Habsburg Monarchy or simply Austria—would be inherited by a single heir, male or female.

In 1740 a spirit of old-fashioned Catholic piety reigned in Vienna alongside fiscal and administrative chaos, which contributed to Maria Theresa's inability to defeat Prussia in the Silesian wars. This frustration left her convinced of the necessity of reform, which proceeded slowly and carefully from the late 1740s.[24] In practice, this entailed centralization at the expense of local aristocracies, but it also meant developing a raison d'être. Her focus was thus integrating the imperial heartlands of the Austrian duchies and Bohemia. Modelled on Prussia, over the years she created an administrative, judicial and military unity of these core lands where none had before existed.[25] Even where—as in Hungary—Maria Theresa avoided outright centralization, she founded several new institutions whose purpose was to draw noble sons into state service. The Theresianum was meant to prepare young men for the civil service, a military academy in Wiener Neustadt to produce loyal officers, and the Oriental Academy to train young diplomats. The Military Order of Maria Theresa and Order of Saint Stephen rewarded exceptional military and civil service, respectively.[26] A special Hungarian Noble Guard was also created to help build loyalty amongst the provincial Hungarian nobility, with its members performing ceremonial duties while also learning sciences and languages and being given a path to join the army or civil service.[27] In a world where nation and nobility were often synonymous, this drawing together of nobles from across Habsburg lands was a crucial method of integrating disparate territories into a common state. As the example of the Polish-Lithuanian Commonwealth—or even that of Great Britain—showed, a diverse early-modern composite state could indeed be integrated if its elite shared a common purpose and identity.

The construction of a Habsburg Monarchy partly within and partly outside of the Holy Roman Empire raised the question of where exactly the Habsburgs' priorities lay. This became an issue of heated public debate in the Empire during the three wars fought against Frederick's Prussia and was tied up with wider questions around patriotism and 'love of the fatherland'.[28] Many in the 'third Germany'—those parts of the Empire neither Austrian nor Prussian—lamented what seemed like the breakdown of the order that protected their liberties, accentuated by the fact that during the Silesian Wars propagandists on both the Habsburg and Hohenzollern sides claimed they were simply protecting 'imperial unity'.

For Friedrich Karl Moser, it was difficult to decide where his loyalties lie during the Seven Years' War that lasted from 1756–63. He was a Protestant from Württemberg in southern Germany but lived in Frankfurt, where he worked a jurist and writer. Initially he was a supporter of Frederick, portraying the war as a struggle to preserve the imperial order against an intolerant Catholic emperor overstepping his authority. But he later became disillusioned with Prussia when he realized Frederick cared more for his own state than the Empire. While attending Joseph II's 1764 coronation in Frankfurt, he accepted a position as a writer in imperial service. The following year he published the widely-read tract *Concerning the German National Spirit*, in which he condemned the disloyalty of princes and their subordinates to the imperial fatherland, now portraying the Habsburgs as its true defenders. While some approved of his work, he was met with a torrent of criticism, showing how controversial the question of imperial patriotism was at a time when modern states being formed within the Empire were building their own sense of patriotism.[29]

Thomas Abbt, one of Moser's early critics, advanced a patriotism tied purely to the monarchical state, not to an abstract 'Germany' represented by the Empire. Though not from there originally, he claimed Prussia was his true 'fatherland'.[30] While this idea of Prussian patriotism was certainly harmful for imperial unity, the notion of 'Austrian' patriotism was even more explosive. Moser lost his imperial patron when he distinguished between 'good Austrian' and 'good imperial' policies in an essay, implying that the Habsburgs did not always have the Empire's best interests at heart.

Moser was simply acknowledging reality, however. The Habsburg matriarch Maria Theresa thought little of the imperial title—which she herself did not hold—firmly placing the Habsburg dynastic interest above all else, something naturally tied to the emerging bureaucratic state.[31] Her son Joseph II, who became emperor in 1765 upon his father's death, was even more disparaging. Like Frederick, he saw the Holy Roman Empire as strange and outdated. He was obsessed with the idea of exchanging the distant Austrian Netherlands for neighbouring Bavaria, which alienated many imperial elites who saw it as an attempt at naked self-aggrandizement at the expense of lesser princes. Some even threw their lot in with Frederick in response, with Prussia, Hanover and Saxony forming a League of Princes in 1785 to retain the status quo.

THE ENLIGHTENMENT CHALLENGE

By 1790 the Holy Roman Empire had thus reached an impasse. Enlightenment ideas had encouraged princes and their subordinates to consolidate the territories under their direct rule into centralizing states in which the monarch was seen as the embodiment of all sovereignty and authority. Frustrated with their inability to crush the Prussian challenge, the Habsburgs focused on their own affairs while neglecting the Empire, leaving many enlightened writers and lesser princes questioning how committed the ostensible leaders of the whole imperial order were to its maintenance. Few outside Prussia or Austria could imagine life beyond the Empire, yet fewer still could imagine how reforming the Empire into something more akin to a 'normal' state would be possible as long as its two great powers remained hostile to each other and indifferent at best to its institutions.

* * *

On 28 September 1749, Maria Theresa received a portly Prussian and his wife in the magnificent palace of Schönbrunn on the western outskirts of Vienna. The couple—Johann Christoph Gottsched and his wife Luise—had come from Saxony, where Gottsched was a professor of philosophy at the University of Leipzig. But more important than his post was the reputation he had earned himself as Europe's foremost authority on the German language.

When Gottsched had arrived in Leipzig in the early 1720s, the movement to embrace German as a literary language was still in its infancy. French was the dominant court language while Latin remained the preferred scholarly language of imperial universities, reinforced by the fact that in Catholic states such as the Habsburg Monarchy the Jesuit Order controlled education from top to bottom with a Latin-medium curriculum focused on the classics. Gottsched, meanwhile, was one of a growing number of educated Germans who wanted to see their mother tongue take over all the functions fulfilled by these foreign tongues. After briefly publishing two German-language 'moral weeklies', his efforts turned to the reorganization of the Leipzig-based German Society dedicated to the cultivation of the language.

Through the German Society and a whole series of publications on to the German language, Gottsched promoted the Saxon dialect used by the educated elite of Leipzig as the standard all Germans should aspire to. This was supported by the fact that Luther had deployed a similar High

German in his translation of the Bible, already familiar to Protestants through their liturgy for centuries. The wider the dialect spread the more difficult it was to deny. Gottsched was a pedantic linguistic reformer and energetic organizer, quickly turning the German Society into a model for other patriot-cultivators to follow. Sister societies sprouted up across German-speaking Europe, gradually harmonizing the way educated Germans wrote.

In the wake of her meeting with the Gottscheds, Maria Theresa apologized to Luise—who was herself one of the most accomplished women of letters in eighteenth-century Germany as a translator and dramatist—for the 'very poor language' of the Austrians. Aristocrats in Vienna customarily spoke French, Italian, Latin, even Spanish, but thought little of their German. They often spoke it with thick lower-class dialects learned from their maids, as was the case with Maria Theresa herself. But as her meeting with the man she called 'the master of the German language' revealed, by the mid-eighteenth century those in the imperial capital were also beginning to take an interest in the German language.[32]

Maria Theresa was building a growing administrative state, but the Jesuit institutions that dominated education were increasingly seen as useless for training the educated civil servants needed to run it. As the enlightened Croatian priest Baltazar Adam Krčelić complained, '[we] ate and were fed metaphysical fruits, but we were not allowed to think about the state, political, military and economic sciences or public law'.[33] Indeed, the modern political, economic and legal theories that were underpinning the pursuit of 'enlightened absolutism' in the Holy Roman Empire were being written in German, not Latin. Many leading aristocrats had long since realized this. Three of six members of Maria Theresa's Council of State set up in 1761 studied in northern Germany, including her powerful State Chancellor Wenzel Anton von Kaunitz, a Francophile Bohemian who had been instilled with the philosophy of Wolff and Thomasius at Leipzig.[34]

From the early 1750s, the Jesuits were gradually pushed out of all spheres of public life. Their control over censorship was abolished in 1751, enabling a flood of enlightened German publications. The universities of Vienna and Prague were brought under state control with a new emphasis on Wolffian natural law instead of Jesuit Aristotelianism. Chairs of German language and literature were created to increase the language's prestige. More broadly, the impact of Enlightenment rationalism made itself felt by the de-confessionalization of public life through the reduction

THE ENLIGHTENMENT CHALLENGE

of public holidays on church festivals, taxing of the Catholic Church, restriction of monasteries, and the regulation of priestly education.[35]

The career of Joseph von Sonnenfels—the face of the new bureaucracy—was emblematic of how important German was to the transformation of the Habsburg Monarchy from a ramshackle collection of crownlands under a Baroque Catholic monarch into a modern enlightened state. He envisioned the Habsburg Monarchy as a single fatherland to which all its inhabitants should owe their allegiance as equal citizens rather than subjects.[36] Sonnenfels co-founded the Vienna branch of Gottsched's German Society in 1761, enthusiastically promoting the High German standard in Vienna. He deployed it in his popular course on 'cameral and administrative sciences', which students from across the Habsburg Monarchy flocked to because it enjoyed Maria Theresa's stamp of approval.

Over the course of her reign, Maria Theresa displayed an increasing predilection for the use of German by her subordinates, especially those who had attended Sonnenfels's fashionable course.[37] The promise of a prestigious career in state service drew not just those from the imperial heartlands onto the course, but also Orthodox Serbs and Ruthenians alongside Transylvanians, Croatians and Hungarians, many returning to various parts of Hungary to 'domesticate' it. By the time Joseph II came to power in 1780 German had come to seem like the natural language of state administration. Four years later he declared it the official language of the whole Habsburg Monarchy.[38]

This Viennese triumph was the final proof that High German had been elevated to the status of a respected and prestigious language of high culture. Within both the Holy Roman Empire and the wider Habsburg and Hohenzollern lands, it had become the written language of choice in nearly every urban centre, no matter the languages of the rural masses surrounding them. By Leopold II's time, today's Bratislava, Prague, Budapest, Zagreb, and Ljubljana—cities that act as national capitals for Slovakia, Czechia, Hungary, Croatia, and Slovenia—were better known to their well-to-do residents and the authorities in Vienna as Pressburg, Prag, Ofen & Pest, Agram, and Laibach.

These cities, along with smaller regional centres, were not so much linguistic islands as nodes in a network of interconnected urban centres in which a culture of German literacy had taken hold. Multiple factors contributed to this dominance: existing German populations, migrations of German-speaking officials, soldiers, officers, craftsmen, and merchants, the social and cultural draw of the prestigious language, and the unstandardized and uncultivated nature of the native vernaculars that should have offered it competition. All this was naturally supported by institutional links to Vienna as well as countless individual ties through the military, state administration, education, and personal networks.

It was a language that united the tens of thousands of state employees, writers, academics, intellectually minded aristocrats and princes involved in the administration and education of these enlightened absolutist states who, despite their official posts or station in life, were all participants in an emerging public sphere independent from either the state or the church. Literate people could now interact in an atmosphere of equality, whether through correspondence or in person at new social institutions like coffee houses, masonic lodges, private learned societies, and salons. The activities of all these institutions revolved around the publication and discussion of printed works. While Latin, French, and other vernaculars were used in the eighteenth-century public sphere both in the Empire and Habsburg Monarchy, the increasing use of German was visible everywhere.

This German-language public sphere showed little concern for political boundaries or national origins. As Hagen Schulze put it, many of those writing in German were proclaiming their 'allegiance to the unity of an enlightened middle-class spirit which stood above territorial boundaries and consciously distanced itself from the French language and culture prevalent in court life'.[39] The first private learned society in the Habsburg Monarchy was the Societas eruditorum incognitorum in terris Austriacis, established in Moravian Olmütz in 1746 by a Slavonian nobleman.[40] The founder, Joseph von Petrasch, was a member of Sonnenfels' Vienna-based German Society and it counted amongst its members local scholars and nobles as well as prominent 'corresponding members' like Gottsched and the Slavic Hungarian polymath Matthias Bel.[41]

Bel was a particularly striking example of the eighteenth-century exchanges that affected intellectual life in Habsburg-ruled lands through the newly-cultivated German standard. He described himself as 'by language a Slav, by nation a Hungarian, by erudition a German'. Neither in the Baroque Catholic realm he was born into nor in the enlightened one in which he died was there any contradiction in such an identity. If anything, it was precisely what would be expected of someone of his background and life experiences. Born into a Slavic peasant family in northern Hungary, he attended Protestant schools in Neusohl and Pressburg. There he perfected his German and came under the strong influence of Pietism, an influential Lutheran reform movement that spread into the staunchly Catholic

Habsburg Monarchy through such schools and students attending northern German universities. It was thanks to this connection that a teacher encouraged him to study at the Pietist stronghold of Halle in Prussia. A few years later he returned to Hungary where he eventually became the rector of the Lutheran Lyceum in Pressburg and pastor to the German Lutheran congregation there, promoting the ideas he learned at Halle.[42]

Though the Societas eruditorum incognitorum was dissolved in 1751, its use of German was a portend for things to come. The following year the first lasting learned society in Hungary was founded in Pressburg with the purely German name Pressburgischen Gesselschaft der Freunde der Wissenschaften. Its main organizer was Karl Gottlieb Windisch, who was born in the city and attended the Lutheran Lyceum where Bel had served as rector. He took inspiration from Gottsched, hoping to aid the cultivation of the German language.[43] The year after the society shut down in 1763, Windisch founded the first lasting Hungarian newspaper, the German-language *Pressburger Zeitung*, providing a native accompaniment to the mostly German-language newspapers that were already being read by the Hungarian public.[44]

Many more followed in the late eighteenth and early nineteenth century, including the first literary journal, the *Merkur von Ungarn*.[45] Such publications sought not only to transmit enlightened ideas and leading literature of the day to Hungarian audiences, but also to keep the broader German-speaking public informed about Hungary. The situation was not too different in Croatia, which received its own German-language paper in 1784 and another in 1787.[46] When in 1779 a pamphlet appeared in Pressburg calling for a 'Hungarian national theatre', there was no question what language it would employ. Falling short of a true 'national' theatre, in 1786 Joseph II sponsored the building of a new theatre building in Ofen to house a permanent German theatre that had until then been in Pressburg. From 1806–12 an ever more ambitious project saw the building of a city theatre in Pest that would be the largest theatre in German-speaking Europe.[47]

* * *

György Bessenyei looked upon his homeland with dismay. In the 1760s, the Hungarian nobleman had joined Maria Theresa's Hungarian Guard, coming face to face with the flourishing of German culture in Vienna. The contrast with Hungary was stark. Latin remained the official language of the linguistically diverse country and enlightened arguments for vernacularization had made little to no impact. The scattered urban centres were dominated by German, the small class of wealthy magnates followed Viennese and European fashions in speaking French or German, while the substantial, largely Magyar-speaking landed nobility was taking more pride than ever in Latin as a symbol of their unique privileges as they faced the threat of centralization from Vienna.[48]

Whatever differences they might have had amongst themselves, Hungary's noble 'nation' saw the use of Latin as one of the defining features of the kingdom and their own identity. When in 1784 Joseph II imposed German as the administrative language of the Kingdom of Hungary, its impact on vernaculars was a minor concern. Zagreb County sent a petition of protest, contrasting German—which was 'virtually unknown to most inhabitants of the kingdom', though the same could have been said about Latin—with the 'uniform purity of the Latin idiom'.[49] Other lines of protest were also included, stressing the loyalty of the nobility, the impracticality of the decree, and the injustice of dismissing loyal servants just because they could not learn German.[50] Joseph saw the measure as purely practical, but he dramatically underestimated the attachment of the Hungarian nobility to a language that he considered as good as dead.

Bessenyei and like-minded Hungarian patriots agreed that Latin's time was up, but for their own reasons. 'Take note of this great truth', he wrote in 1778, 'that never on this earth could a nation claim wisdom or depth for itself until it introduced knowledge and scholarship in its own language'.[51] Following the same argument once set forth by Leibniz, he concluded that 'the first concern of a nation that wishes to spread knowledge among its own inhabitants and by such means work for their knowledge and happiness be the cultivation of that language to perfection'.[52]

In the 1770s, Bessenyei gathered around himself a literary circle of Magyar patriot-cultivators in Vienna whose goal was to elevate their language and thereby spread enlightenment into their native realm. Their mission soon found a wider resonance. With remarkable speed over the following two decades, Magyar authors developed the literary, philosophical, geographic, and scientific terminology needed for a commonly accepted standard.[53] In 1780, a decade after the *Pressburger Zeitung* had first been published, the first Magyar newspaper emerged in the form of *Magyar Hírmondó*, joined in the following decade by the *Magyar Kurír* and hundreds of pamphlets taking advantage of lax Josephine censorship.[54]

THE ENLIGHTENMENT CHALLENGE

Neither of these newspapers was founded in distant Ofen-Pest, but in Pressburg and Vienna. In these two cities—separated by less than 100 kilometres along the Danube—the Magyar-language press was born alongside its thriving German equivalent.[55]

In the first half of the eighteenth century the vast majority of books published in Hungary were still Latin, but this changed rapidly from the 1770s in favour of Magyar, alongside a similar boom in German publishing.[56] Patriotic nobles were once again essential, both as a reading public and as patrons of private libraries, reading societies, and periodicals. They were not necessarily motivated by linguistic nationalism, however. German-language institutions and publications like the Pressburgischen Gesselschaft der Freunde der Wissenschaften and the *Merkur von Ungarn* had the same patriotic-enlightening goals and noble patrons as Hungarian ones. There was nothing unusual about the fact that Dániel Tállyay could participate in the publishing of three Pressburg-based papers in three different languages: German, Magyar, and Slovak.[57] Hungary's elites—nobles, clergy, administrators, and educated commoners alike—were extremely multilingual. A survey of officials in an office of the Royal Chamber from 1788 provides some insight. The majority of the 223 respondents spoke four languages, usually Latin, German, Magyar, and another.[58]

The movement to enrich Magyar was given added impetus by the fact that in the late eighteenth century it had become commonplace in German publishing to predict its imminent extinction. Maria Theresa's court librarian—himself a northern Hungarian Slav—Adam František Kollár (incorrectly) wrote in an anonymously published pamphlet in 1763 that the Kingdom of Hungary was mostly Slavic while 'the people who just use the Hungarian idiom, have the smallest part of Hungary; indeed, it is to be feared that their tongue will pass away'.[59] This was then picked up by August Ludwig Schlözer in his popular *General Northern History* and subsequently by Johann Gottfried Herder in his widely read *Ideen zur Philosophie der Geschichte der Menschheit*—named the most popular work in Hungary by the *Pressburger Zeitung* in 1795—where he predicted that Magyar would disappear completely amidst an 'ocean of surrounding' German, Slav, and Romanian speakers.[60]

The 1790 Hungarian diet—which was the first to meet in the ancient capital of Buda since the Ottomans had conquered it in the late fifteenth century—had an almost revolutionary atmosphere. Diets were accompanied by a flurry of pamphlets, books and manifestos as various factions or individuals sought to promote their agenda. Years of Josephine absolutism, Germanization, and predictions of national extinction seemed to demand a radical approach if the noble 'Hungarian nation' and its liberties were to be preserved. The patriotic opposition developed a whole political program arguing that Joseph was an illegitimate king—the 'hatted king' as they sardonically referred to him—and that the right to elect a new one had therefore reverted to the nobility. Their base of support was the lower house, where the mass of lesser provincial nobles was represented through county delegates, as opposed to the upper house where the wealthy cosmopolitan aristocrats and clergy sat in person. The latter group was tied to the Habsburg crown through their professional careers and personal networks, while the former was by and large not. Each had their own vision of Hungary and its position in the wider monarchy.[61]

When the diet began, both chambers first met independently. Aristocrats in the upper house took turns repenting for their service of Josephine absolutism while those in the lower house began to develop a clear political program driven by reformist delegates. Though Latin had been restored as the country's official language when Joseph repealed his Germanization decree, these sessions of the lower house took place exclusively in Magyar. Even more significantly, the bulk of this lower house pushed for the abandonment of Latin altogether and its replacement by Magyar. If Latin was to be abandoned as a dead language, they reasoned, then why not replace it with the country's own living language. In the run up to the diet, proponents of Magyarization had waged a relentless press campaign arguing for the necessity of abandoning Latin. They were optimistic about how easy it would be to switch and painted apocalyptic pictures of a Hungarian nation that itself could cease to exist if Magyar was not introduced as the country's official language.[62]

* * *

Fears of language-death were by no means limited to Hungary. With the exception of Galicia with its large and proud Polish nobility, Slavic lands ruled by the Habsburgs were entirely dominated by German-speaking urban centres in which local Slavic vernaculars were looked down upon as the language of the lower classes. In heavily urbanized Bohemia—where the nobility had almost entirely abandoned Czech—the situation was seen as particularly dire by enlightened promoters of the vernacular.[63] The distinguished Bohemian historian and passionate defender of the Czech language Franz Martin Pelzl—who worked with Dobrovský in the

THE ENLIGHTENMENT CHALLENGE

Nostitz household—lamented in 1791 that 'in fifty years ... it will be difficult to even flush out a Czech [in Bohemian cities]'.[64]

As in the Magyar case and the German one before it, a lack of standardization and refinement made it difficult to convince educated Bohemians that Czech was worth learning, let alone using for scholarly pursuits. But this was also bound up with a wider problem that afflicted Slavic scholars. Who exactly were these Slavs?

The notion that the tens of millions of Slavs scattered across Europe formed a single people or nation—the largest in Europe—with one language consisting of many dialects was by this time an accepted fact in German-speaking Europe and was central to early Slavic scholarship. From the Dalmatian coast to distant Russia and everywhere in between, Slavic speech was similar enough for a close kinship to be widely recognized. The Sorb Michał Frencel, for example, wrote a note of welcome to Peter the Great in 1697 when he was expected to visit Dresden, praising him as a 'great tsar and grand duke' who 'with many thousands of millions of subjects speaks in our Wendish or Sarmatian language'.[65] Just a year later, the Russian nobleman Pyotr Tolstoy noted matter-of-factly that the inhabitants of the small Republic of Ragusa (Dubrovnik) 'all speak the Slavic language'. When he met its leader, they spoke this 'Slavic language' together.[66] Slavs from the Dalmatian coast—most of which was ruled by Venice—had for centuries called their own language simply 'Slavic' or 'Illyrian' in a similar way that Frencel spoke of his 'Wendish'.

When Dobrovský therefore described Czechs as just a 'tribe' of a great Slavic unity it was nothing new. Nor was it thought of as anything that marginalized or belittled the identities of these individual 'tribes'. But while notions of Slavic commonality had been around for centuries, the Göttingen-based historian August Ludwig von Schlözer was the first to give it real academic legitimacy when in his 1773 *General Northern History* he explored Slavic history as a single whole and divided Slavs not into languages but dialects.[67] It was a foundational work of German-language Slavistics, praised in the opening of his own masterwork by the prominent Slovene scholar Bartholomeus Kopitar as the work that 'began to shed light' on the history of 'this so divided nation'.[68]

The greatest divide that kept Slavs apart was not so much geography as class. Slavic commoners across the Habsburg Monarchy who moved up in the world through education or state service inevitably picked up German or Latin or both and therefore entered a social world completely detached from the Slavic—likely peasant—world of their youth. Even when they took an interest in that Slavic world, in its language, culture, and history, they used the Latin and German languages of erudition to explore them and, thus, were part of a diffuse regional public sphere not troubled by boundaries. Dobrovský wrote his works almost entirely in German, but his works on the history of the Czech language—conceived of as a 'dialect' of Slavic—and later German-Czech dictionaries would be vital to the language's codification.

After his long stay in the household of the enlightened Count Nostitz, he worked under the patronage of Count Franz Joseph Kinsky, one of many enlightened aristocrats crucial for the replication of Enlightenment initiatives across the Habsburg Monarchy, particularly in provincial surroundings with fewer opportunities. Like in the Holy Roman Empire more broadly, it was impossible for anyone to make a living off freelance intellectual production.[69]

The Carniolan nobleman Sigmund Zois von Edelstein would play a similarly central role in the early study and national development of the Slavs living primarily in the Austrian duchies of Carniola, Carinthia, and Styria. In the 1780s Zois formed a circle of enlightened intellectuals that met at his mansion in Laibach, some of whom would go on to become prominent scholars of Slavic languages and culture and, in the process, begin the codification of a specifically Slovene language. Anton Tomaž Linhart, for example, who would later be considered the father of Slovene historiography, had a background typical for Habsburg intellectuals of the time. Born into a Moravian family that had immigrated to Carniola, he later moved to Vienna where he worked and studied under Sonnenfels and wrote his first poetry in German.[70] Upon his return to Laibach in 1780, he became involved with Zois' circle and switched to writing exclusively in Slovene.[71] He supported himself through a variety of local administrative posts, but became famous for his (German) two-volume *Attempt at a History of Carniola and the Other Lands of the Southern Slavs of Austria*, published in 1788 and 1791. In it, he asserted that Austria should rightly be called a Slavic state like Russia and that 'no nation deserves as much attention of historians, philosophers, and statesmen as the Slavs'.[72]

He had perhaps been inspired by Karl Gottlob von Anton, whose 1783 *First Lines of an Attempt on the Ancient Slavs' Origins, Manners, Customs, Opinions and Knowledge* recognized diffidently how much Slavic scholarship still had to explore. Though Anton wrote about Slavs more broadly, he was inspired by the Lusatian Slavs, also known as Wends or Sorbs. Though a native Silesian, Anton had moved to Görlitz in Saxony where

THE ENLIGHTENMENT CHALLENGE

he took an interest in these local Saxon Slavs. They made up perhaps a tenth of the population and their speech enjoyed a similar low status to Slovene.[73] To add to the similarities, Sorbs were often known in German as Wends and Slovenes as Winds, both effectively just an old term for Slavs.[74] Anton and Linhart were naturally connected by Dobrovský, who was central to a whole correspondence network of scholars interested in the language and history of the Slavs.[75]

The philosopher Johann Gottfried Herder, to whom almost mythical sway over the national development of Slavic nations is often attributed, based the famous 'Slav Chapter' of his *Ideen* on the writings of Schlözer, Anton, Dobrovský, and other such Germanophone scholars. Anton knew Herder personally, connected through a mutual acquaintance who was in the same circle as Herder, Goethe, and the celebrated playwright Friedrich Schiller.[76] As Slavs were just beginning the cultivation and study of their own languages, these three Germans were bringing the refinement of German to its apotheosis.

What made them so special for German culture was their pursuit of truly original, German style, rather than the imitation of inherited classical or French forms. At the age of twenty-one, the native Frankfurter Goethe travelled to French-ruled Strasbourg, where he was deeply moved by the looming gothic cathedral. It inspired an essay in which he wrote that 'the only true art is characteristic art. If its influence arises from deep, harmonious, independent feeling, from feeling peculiar to itself, oblivious, yes, ignorant of everything foreign, then it is whole and living, whether it be born from crude savagery or cultured sentiment'.[77] In a sense this was Herder speaking through Goethe. The pair had met in Strasbourg, which Goethe later recognized as the turning-point of his life.[78] Unlike the aristocrats who saw France as synonymous with culture and civilization or Humanists who saw the same in antiquity, Herder stressed that 'truth, value, and beauty are not one, but many'.[79] He condemned the classicism Goethe had been raised to admire and encouraged him instead to find inspiration in authentic folk poetry and medieval history, instances where art had flourished under supposedly natural circumstances uncorrupted by imposed universalist models.[80]

In Herder's eyes all values and thoughts were rooted in their own national contexts. Nations were not political entities tied to a certain state and its legal tradition, but cultural entities tied to language, customs, and history. He was particularly fond of folk culture, which he saw as the most authentic expression of cultural individuality. At the time this was a message of radical cultural liberation, aimed not just at Germans but at the Slavic and Baltic peasant *Volk* of Europe's east. Herder studied at Königsberg and spent several years in Riga, a Russian town on the Baltic ruled by a German patrician elite but surrounded by Latvian-speaking peasants. Though he did not have more than cursory interactions with them, his experience there gave him his sympathies for the culture of the scorned common people that he developed over the course of his life into a grand but unsystematic philosophy which Tim Blanning likened to 'nothing less than a revolution in the way in which Germans viewed their culture'.[81] This was a romantic cosmopolitan cultural nationalism, which stood in explicit opposition to French universalism, and which became incredibly influential throughout Central Europe well into the nineteenth century.

* * *

Leopold II's visit to the Royal Bohemian Society of Sciences had offered a picture of the proto-Central European Enlightenment in miniature, in all its triumphs and contradictions. On 25 September 1791, the emperor, provincial aristocrats and commoners discussed topics of secular scholarly interest on the former site of a religious order that just twenty years earlier maintained a stranglehold on intellectual life in the Habsburg Monarchy. The German that they used to discuss a whole range of topics had a century earlier been a maligned, unstandardized language, hardly fit for such an intellectual exchange. And a speaker celebrated the fact that the Habsburgs did not just rule kingdoms and duchies represented by noble 'nations', but also peoples with different languages, customs, religions, and identities not necessarily congruent with the political entities that may or may not have borne their names. Behind the imperial, Latinate, Catholic façade stood nobles, educated commoners, courts, institutions, princes—if not quite whole societies—transformed by the intellectual revolution of the Enlightenment.

3

FINIS ROMAE

While attending Leopold II's imperial coronation in Frankfurt in late 1790, the Bohemian Count Kaspar von Sternberg made a worrying observation. In the great hall of the Römer adorned with portraits of the emperors, there was only space for one more. 'Is this supposed to be a bad omen?' he asked in his diary. On 28 February 1792 Leopold felt a sudden pain in his chest. Two days later he was dead.[1] His short reign as Roman Emperor would fade into a historical footnote, overshadowed by events out of his control, his personality outshone by bombastic personalities that would reshape the face of Europe. His coronation was, as Sternberg put it, 'the last time Germany showed itself here in splendour and dignity'.[2]

Leopold told the Badenese minister Wilhelm von Edelsheim two days before his imperial coronation that the French Revolution that had broken out in 1789 posed no threat to Germany, 'for our nation is neither so corrupt, nor so dejected, nor so enthusiastic'.[3] Few enlightened Germans would have disagreed. News of the French Revolution had been received with almost universal acclaim.[4] Schlözer remarked that the revolution had 'taught in practice what we Germans have long known in theory, that the Sovereign is responsible to his people'.[5] Leopold's election and coronation against the backdrop of the events in France would be celebrated by many enlightened members of the middle class as a great national event that proved the superiority of German ways, with the peaceful and consensual elevation of an enlightened prince to the highest office in the land.[6] The contrast seemed to grow as the revolution progressed and radicalized, dissipating much of the initial enthusiasm in Germany.

Indeed, the struggle against the French and their revolution would define the reign of Francis II. Before he had even had a chance to don the imperial crown, he was embroiled in the first of many wars against revolutionary France that would continue almost unabated for over two decades. Though born and initially raised in Florence, Francis spent six years in Vienna preparing for his future role as emperor under Joseph. In a sign of the changing times, he was the first Habsburg in generations whose preferred language was German, speaking it with a light Viennese accent. Partly thanks to the influence of his tutors, he developed far more conservative views than his father or uncle.[7] Those views would only harden as the revolution culminated in the shocking execution of the French king and queen—Louis XVI and Leopold's sister Marie Antoinette. The established orders rallied behind their princes to hold back the tide of the godless secularism emanating from Paris. The free press gave way to strict censorship. Private societies like the freemasons were banned. Those who had once taken most pride in their enlightenment were now placed under the deepest suspicion.

French military victories shook the Holy Roman Empire to its core. The War of the First Coalition ended in defeat in 1797, forcing the Habsburgs to cede Belgium and pushing France's border onto the Rhine. The anti-French coalition was defeated again in 1801, forcing the Imperial Diet to compensate those who had lost their estates to the French Republic with 'mediatized' land from ecclesiastical estates and cities, completely upending the imperial order in the interests of preserving it. To add to the confusion, in 1804 Napoleon crowned himself 'Emperor of the French'. It was an unprecedented act that implied that the Roman imperial title's monopoly on imperial dignity had been broken—though he still recognized it as superior to his own. The Russian Tsar Alexander I expected a wave of outrage to sweep the Holy Roman Empire due to what seemed like a pure usurpation of the imperial title. Francis II instead matched Napoleon's act by proclaiming himself 'Emperor of Austria' and the Habsburg Monarchy an indivisible realm.[8] This was partly so as not to be outdone, but partly too because the Holy Roman Empire's centrality to the European political order was clearly waning.[9]

France and Austria once again went to war in 1805, with Napoleon's victory allowing him to dictate a radical reorganization of the Holy Roman Empire, merging most of the smaller territories into enlarged princely states under French direction. In 1806—under Napoleonic pressure—all the imperial territories that were not part of Austria, Prussia or France seceded from the Empire and announced the formation of the Confederated States of the Rhine under French protection. The pace of political change was almost incomprehensible. An Austrian envoy to Regensburg commented at the end of July that 'the consternation which is aroused in the Imperial Diet by this impending strange catastrophe is beyond description'.[10]

In 1806, some months after the formation of the Rhenish Confederation, rumours began to spread that there was no longer an emperor. The historian Heinrich Leo would later recall that when the rumour reached farmers in his home region of Thuringia, they refused to believe it. They instead looked forward to the day that the emperor could punish those spreading such falsehoods.[11] That day would never come. Earlier in the year, the Habsburg court began the painstaking process of deciding how to legally dissolve the Holy Roman Empire. It was the culmination of a long process of Habsburg alienation from their most prestigious title as, from Maria Theresa's reign onwards, their focus had shifted from pan-European dynastic politics to state-building along the Danube. They had fought to defend the Holy Roman Empire repeatedly against the French revolutionary challenge, but their failure saw most of it conquered by Napoleon. After resolving the issues of what to do with its officials, archives, courts, the crown itself and more, Emperor Francis announced the 'cession'—not 'abdication'—of his title and the formal dissolution of the Holy Roman Empire.[12] There was no public announcement besides what was relayed through the press. No fanfare accompanied the final dissolution of the Roman Empire.[13]

Though the move was technically against imperial law, the only country that had the power to contest the emperor's announcement—France—had already ceased to recognize the Empire's existence. Sweden, a guarantor of the imperial constitution since the Peace of Westphalia, lodged an official protest, but its days as a great power were long gone. Prussia issued a formulaic expression of 'regret at the end of an honourable bond hallowed by time' without any intent of contesting it.[14] Its court historiographer Johannes von Müller had a far more intense reaction, suffering a nervous breakdown upon hearing the news.[15] An Austrian envoy to the Imperial Diet in Regensburg commented that the dissatisfaction 'is so great that a violent outbreak is to be feared. There has never been such an atmosphere in Germany'.[16] Quite the opposite turned out to be the case. Though private diaries and letters testify to the sense of shock and confusion felt by the Empire's former inhabitants, discussion of its demise was muted thanks to intense Napoleonic censorship, underscored by the execution of the Nuremberg bookseller Johann Philipp

Palm, accused of writing an anonymous patriotic, anti-French pamphlet condemning the Empire's dissolution.[17]

Goethe's mother wrote in her diary on 19 August 1806 that she felt 'as if an old friend were very ill. The doctors have given up hope of his recovery, and we are assured that he is going to die—and yet despite all this certainty, one is utterly shaken when the post arrives with the news of his death'. This was allegedly how the whole of Frankfurt felt. Never again would the city experience an imperial coronation. Never again would so many notables from across Europe grace it with their presence. For the first time, she reported, 'the emperor and the Empire were omitted from prayers in church ... It is as if we had one funeral after another—that is how our joys now look'.[18]

* * *

By 1806 Europe was a continent in disarray. 'It is as if a new world has emerged before our eyes', opined the geographer Georg Hassel in his *Statistical Outline of All the European States*. The French Revolution and its consequences had brought wars, revolutions, and occupations. Once venerable realms had now 'disappeared from the scene or become insignificant extras'. Hallowed ancient constitutions 'have been completely destroyed'.[19] The balance of power 'for whose preservation streams of European blood' had flown for centuries, was no more. Difficult as it may have been to come to grips with this changed continent, Hassel hoped that his book's meticulous statistical portrait could help. In service of this end, he deployed a hitherto unknown term: 'Central Europe'.[20]

Hassel was born in the northern German town of Wolfenbüttel in 1770, renowned for the presence of a large ducal lending library under the directorship of Gotthold Ephraim Lessing.[21] Raised and educated there and in the nearby university town of Helmstedt, he followed countless educated commoners into the civil service of his local principality. This in turn allowed him to pursue his true calling: geography.[22] After a book devoted to his native Principalities of Wolfenbüttel and Blankenburg, he turned his attention to much greater issues. 'The continent of Europe currently bows to the will of two ruling powers ... The whole West and South obeys the commanding orders of the Frankish Emperor just as the North and East obey the orders of the Autocrat of all Russians'. The only powers that stood in their way, that for Europe represented a 'guarantee of its political existence', were Habsburg Austria and Hohenzollern Prussia.[23]

Hassel thus divided Europe into four political zones. A Northern and Eastern Europe under Russian influence, French Southern and Western Europe, British 'Insular Europe', and a Central Europe consisting of Austria, Prussia, the princely German states, as well as the tiny Adriatic republics of Ragusa and Poljica that would not survive the Napoleonic era.[24] Not long after Hassel's book was published, this 'Central Europe' was given a visual expression by the Vienna-based cartographer Joseph Marx von Liechtenstern in his vast sixty-four-section 'Map of Central Europe or of the Hereditary Monarchies Austria and Prussia and all of the German States'.[25] Liechtenstern was one of the most widely cited cartographers of the early nineteenth century, combining a commitment to applying modern statistical methods to map-making with extensive personal knowledge of the Habsburg lands through his career as an administrator of aristocratic estates.[26] Whether thanks to the work of Hassel and Liechtenstern, or simply reflecting the value of the term, or some of both, 'Central Europe' entered into common German usage over the following decades. Often it would be used to mean something like 'core Europe', a usage attested already in 1808, but this was a definition always of secondary political importance.[27] When Prussia and Austria were written about as 'the ruling powers of Central Europe' or one spoke of 'the whole Austrian and Prussian state, so almost the entirety of Central Europe', there was little ambiguity in what the term meant.[28]

Hassel's work and Lichtenstern's map were widely reported on not just in Germany, but also in Britain, where in dailies and periodicals readers were introduced to his concept of *Mitteleuropa*.[29] It was translated everywhere literally as 'Middle Europe', a term that would in time be interchangeable with 'Central Europe'.[30] Prior to the First World War there was no autochthonous conception of Central Europe in the English language, with the concept from its very beginning borrowed purely from the German usage and translated—or not—according to the author's preference.[31] Though more expansive definitions would be offered and used over the following century as use of the term proliferated, this fundamental idea of a Middle or Central Europe whose core consisted of territories under the influence of Austria and Prussia, separate from Russia to the East and France to the West, would remain in use up until 1918, reflecting a unique historical situation that had been created in the eighteenth century.

Why nobody ever conceived of a place called 'Central Europe' before then is rather simple: there was no need for it. Given Europeans' understanding of geography, of their place in the world, of their identities and sense of belonging, it was unclear what the term could have meant before the turn of the nineteenth century. In large part this was thanks to the lasting influence of Greco-Roman antiquity on the European imagination. The first stirrings of German national feeling were prompted by the discovery of the Roman historian Tacitus' *Germania* in the fifteenth century. The Polish nobility imagined they were descendants of the ancient Sarmatians, who they knew only through Greek and Roman authors. Renaissance poets as far away as Lithuania would locate their country on the map in relation to Italy.[32] Naturally, they wrote in Latin, the common tongue of Europe's educated elite and its then-living link to antiquity. Artists depicted contemporary events or individuals in classical settings just as they depicted classical events or individuals in contemporary settings.

The English critic Samuel Johnson summed up this outlook succinctly in 1776: 'All our religion, all our arts, almost all that sets us above savages, has come from the shores of the Mediterranean'.[33] The urban Mediterranean culture of classical Greece and Rome was considered the peak of human civilization. Christian Europeans, wherever they lived and whatever language they spoke, sought to claim the heritage of antiquity if not emulate it. This also provided them with a simple geographic framework that would remain dominant into the nineteenth century. A cultured south stood in contrast to the barbarian north. In Johnson's time, British diplomacy was conducted by two separate departments, a Northern Department responsible for Russia, Sweden, Denmark, Poland-Lithuania, the Netherlands, and the Holy Roman Empire, and a Southern Department which dealt with France and other Mediterranean states. The German historian August Ludwig Schlözer's 1771 *General History of the North* distinguished a 'Nordic' Europe including Scandinavia, Russia, and Poland from a Southern Europe consisting of Greece, Italy, France, and Spain.[34] John Milton noted that he was interested in writing about Russia in his *Brief History of Moscovia* because it was 'the most northern Region of Europe reputed civil'.[35]

Not long before Milton's time, even that geographic certainty we know as Europe was a more ambiguous concept. Indeed, it was rarely used before the fifteenth century: the cultural community living on the western edge of Eurasia thought of themselves as part of Christendom, not Europe.[36] And yet even the word Christendom was not in common usage until the eleventh century, having been invented in the ninth.[37] Before that, Rome and its empire was essentially synonymous with the civilized world. Even for the ancient Greeks that came up with the word

'Europe', it meant little beyond the realm of myth.[38] The three continents they knew of and settled were culturally less important than the distinction between Greek and barbarian.

All of these semantic changes were reflective of major political, cultural, or religious developments that made past geographic paradigms less relevant. But there was rarely such a definite break that old paradigms had to be thrown out quickly and in their entirety. Though the Christian paradigm emerged in the ninth century, a Holy Roman Empire survived until 1806. Though the European paradigm replaced the Christian one in the fifteenth century, Christianity continues to be the dominant religion in Europe well into the twenty-first century. Though there was a reconceptualization of the north-south division of Europe in the late eighteenth century, such a dichotomy continued to be used well into the nineteenth. Still, essential to understanding their changing fortunes was the fact that Christendom, Rome, and Europe were and are words that reflect cultural, social, and political realities as much as geographic ones. In this regard, notions like Central, Eastern, and Western Europe are no different.

Towards the end of the eighteenth century, northwestern Europe—with its valuable global colonies and trade, its nascent capitalism and urbanization, and increasingly wealthy and empowered bourgeoisie—began to diverge from the rest of the continent, and indeed the world. Ideas of 'civilization' and progress—also new to the eighteenth century—provided the beneficiaries of this transformation the framework to interpret this divergence.[39] History was no longer understood as a cycle of repetition but a process of forward motion in which northwestern European states were furthest along and the further east one went the more backwards it was. Antiquity was still respected, but contemporary societies began to assert that they had in fact surpassed it and would continue to do so. Little by little, the notion of a barbarian north and cultured south was replaced with that of the civilized West and the backwards East, the latter often blending into a generalized 'Orient'.[40]

What truly demanded the emergence of the term Central Europe was not just a new East-West understanding of Europe's cultural geography, but the contemporaneous final collapse of the universalist Roman-Christian paradigm as an element of European politics and society around the turn of the nineteenth century. At the top of this order stood the House of Habsburg and, at its heart, the territories they ruled. Unmoored from the universalist institutions and ambitions of their past, this house and its territories would be forced to forge a new sense of purpose and identity between a new East and West.

The boundaries Hassel provided would have made little sense in the late seventeenth century. 'Austria' referred as much to the House of Habsburg as the duchies they ruled on the southeastern edge of the Holy Roman Empire, and its areas of influence extended to Italy, Iberia, and the Low Countries. The contiguous territories ruled beyond the Empire were hardly noteworthy, with the Ottoman Empire ruling most of the Danube basin, leaving the Habsburgs with only a rump Hungary and Croatia. Prussia was a duchy divided between the king of Poland and elector of Brandenburg without any area of influence at all. Russia was just one of three major powers in Northern Europe alongside Poland-Lithuania and Sweden. France was a powerful kingdom, but Habsburg lands made up the greater part of both Western and Southern Europe. It took a series of radical political transformations in the intervening years for 'Middle Europe' to emerge and an equally radical series of social, cultural, and intellectual transformations to make it relevant to its inhabitants.

* * *

The great irony of Central Europe was that the precise moment of its coinage came at a time when French power seemed to have made it redundant. As part of wider coalitions, both Austria and Prussia suffered crushing defeats to Napoleon in 1806 and 1807, followed in 1809 by another Austrian defeat. Both powers were brought to their knees, their armies humiliated in the field, their westernmost territories ceded to France and its satellites, and any influence they once had over the lands of what-was-once-the-Empire entirely lost. Napoleon instead recast Germany in his image.

The left bank of the Rhine became an integral part of France, while the model Kingdom of Westphalia in north-central Germany was given a written constitution that enshrined religious equality, abolished old privileges, and ended serfdom.[41] The newly elevated king of Württemberg abolished the old corporatist constitution in 1805 and declared his realm a single state. Three years later, Bavaria adopted a written constitution with a similar integrative aim. A slightly amended version of the Napoleonic code was then adopted in Baden in an effort to 'tighten the knot in the bonds between the ruler and his citizen'.[42] They adopted the royal-bureaucratic absolutism of Napoleon without troubling themselves with the liberal garb that came with it.

Napoleon's Germany was one in which princes and their bureaucrats were empowered over a cowed church and weakened—but not broken—territorial nobilities. True enthusiasts for the revolutionary ideas once espoused in Paris were few and far between, their growth in numbers discouraged by the fact that French rule was experienced as little more than an exacting foreign occupation. Indeed, Germans had soured on the very idea of 'enlightenment'. Robespierre dug the grave; Napoleon did the burying. It was not just that much of the infrastructure that had underpinned the German Enlightenment had been placed under suspicion or thrown into chaos, but the socio-political context seemed to demand entirely new ideas.

For Prussia, this was made patently clear in 1806. The army that had once been the state's pride was crushed by Napoleon at Jena before he proceeded to occupy the whole country and dictate a treaty that reduced it to a rump of its former self. The disaster was so great that King Frederick William III was convinced that root-and-branch reform was needed if the state was to survive. Often called the Stein-Hardenberg reforms after their two leading proponents, in just a few years Prussia adopted an organized cabinet system, liberalized trade and enterprise, purged and opened up the noble-dominated army, emancipated the peasantry, expanded citizenship in cities, provided Jews with equal civic rights, and more.[43] In part, the reforms continued an established pattern of top-down state reform that had been characteristic of the German Enlightenment. But they also signified the dawn of a new era in which educated Germans would come to expect much more from politics.

In the winter of 1807–8, while French troops were quartered around Berlin, the Saxon-born philosopher Johann Gottlieb Fichte gave a celebrated series *Addresses to the German Nation*. The watchword of his lectures was not enlightenment, but *Bildung*. This term had risen in prominence in the latter half of the eighteenth century, but it was in the ferment of the post-Enlightenment era that it became the lodestar of progressive thought. A term with no true English equivalent, *Bildung* combined the ideas of education, development, and cultivation into a single process that formed an individual into a self-actualized whole. It was largely thanks to Herder that *Bildung* was placed on a pedestal as of central importance for all those who desired the betterment of mankind. It meant for him not just an individual or nation's elevation to a higher state of being, but the fulfilment of the unique potential they contained within themselves. Fichte extended this idea to the whole 'German nation'. He saw it as an organic phenomenon rooted in its language, which through *Bildung* could be moulded into a power with the moral strength and courage to defeat the hated French, whose 'nation' he decried as an artificial phenomenon.[44]

This was, however, just one vision of what role *Bildung* could play in German society. For the geographer and naturalist Alexander von Humboldt, *Bildung* was not something that could be pursued with an expected outcome, but as an end in and of itself. In 1809 Humboldt was brought into the Prussian reform administration with the task of creating its first unified educational system. This he did, and the crowning glory of his work would be a university in Berlin founded in 1810, which rapidly became one of the most esteemed academic institutions in the world. Humboldt disliked the rigid hierarchical bureaucratic state that Frederick the Great had built, seeing it as stultifying the individual development of its citizens. His ideal state was instead one that allowed its citizens to develop freely, to achieve through *Bildung* their own full potential irrespective of their personal class or background. It was no longer sufficient for a state to simply produce good citizens—it had to produce good people. Students reached maturity only when they learned to think for themselves rather than repeat what they had been taught. Humboldt insisted in 1809 that this was entirely compatible with the interests of the state because fully-formed individuals would be inherently more useful to it, but time would show that the aspirations and expectations of the emerging educated middle class—the *Bildungsbürgertum*—were not entirely in line with those of the princes and aristocrats that continued to rule.[45]

In 1812 Napoleon marched on Russia with hundreds of thousands of soldiers drawn from his continental empire in a failed invasion that ultimately cost him everything. As the tide of war shifted, Austria and Prussia both switched from the French to the Russian side, convincing most of Napoleon's erstwhile German allies to do the same. Attempting to rouse their people for yet another war, they deployed vague appeals to German national feeling that mobilized students and middle-class publicists more than the masses. Some flocked to volunteer units known as the *Freikorps*, which made up for their small number with a prodigious poetic output. Others joined the new gymnastics movement, which the schoolteacher Friedrich Ludwig Jahn had founded in Berlin in 1811, hoping that through exercise the 'entire people will become manly and patriotic, and, feeling its power, will be reborn'.[46]

Amidst a torrent of anti-French publications, Ernst Moritz Arndt gained particularly notoriety for his nationalist belligerence. His war songs became nationalist anthems and his patriotic pamphlets achieved wide circulation, but his criticism reached beyond the Napoleonic foe. In an 1814 pamphlet he argued that the national struggle also meant returning to 'German customs' and fighting against 'aping of foreign manners' in a not-so-subtle critique of the 'Frenchified' nobility.[47] As France's defeat brought an end to the 'wars of liberation', Joseph Görres in his influential paper *Rheinischer Merkur* began to aim his criticism ever more towards German princes themselves and their supposedly 'un-German' behaviour. Criticism of the Prussian king proved to be the final straw, and the paper was banned in early 1816.[48]

Moderate German patriots or those simply uninterested in nationalism mocked the 'Germanomania' unleashed at the end of the Napoleonic Wars. Goethe declined to contribute to the propaganda effort when asked by Austria.[49] Napoleon responded to Austria's most dramatic call for Germans to rise up against the French with bewilderment, believing the Austrians were surely going to war to reassert their claim to Spain.[50] The call was in the end answered not by 'Germans', but Tyroleans rising up against Bavaria. Similarly, when a Saxon regiment was meant to be integrated into the Prussian army in 1815, the soldiers revolted against the hated Prussians.[51]

When the representatives of all of Europe's greater and lesser powers gathered in Vienna in 1814 to create a new European order, 'Germanomania' played no role whatsoever. The gathered men were not educated commoners like Arndt, Görres, or Jahn, but men like Klemens von Metternich, the haughty Rhenish imperial knight who had become Austria's powerful minister of foreign affairs after a meteoric rise through Habsburg service during the Napoleonic Wars. He had briefly even considered a de facto Austro-Prussian partition of Germany, recognizing that they inhabited a space he called *l'Europe intermediare* in which they had a common interest and should pursue common policies.[52] 'Placed between the great monarchies of the east and west of Europe', Austria and Prussia were 'called to hold the balance between these masses, which are drawn constantly toward the centre'.[53] The negotiations in Vienna soured him on the idea, but this still left the question of what exactly was to be restored.

Many princes—like the English king and former prince-elector of Hanover—wanted to see the old Holy Roman Empire return after a short interregnum. When Francis made a triumphal entry into Frankfurt,

Metternich reported scenes of such jubilation that 'all coronations were and remain nothing' by comparison.[54] But so much had changed in the last decade that a wholesale return to the Empire was all but impossible. For one thing, the cooperation of the consolidated princely German states had been predicated on them retaining their expanded borders, new royal distinctions, and true sovereignty. More important, perhaps, was the fact that Vienna's overriding concern was its own state security. The 'restoration' of the old order thus became a strange hybrid of old and new aimed at preserving the balance of power in Germany and Europe more broadly.

Hanover was restored with an added royal distinction. Saxony—which Prussia wanted to annex after is king had unwisely stuck by Napoleon too long—was much reduced but ultimately spared. Most of the Rhineland was given to Prussia as compensation, with a smaller chunk handed over to Bavaria. Austria's territorial expansion came along the Adriatic, with the territories of the former Venetian republic including Dalmatia and the Istrian peninsula as well as the former Republic of Ragusa. A new German Confederation was established as a union of sovereign princes, retaining the boundaries of the old Empire and consisting of thirty-nine equal members committed to mutual defence. It was seen as a successor of the Empire and as such the Habsburgs were given a role as hereditary leaders.[55] The 'Central Europe' that Georg Hassel described was back. For the first time in history, it had a firm boundaries in east and west. The diffuse, porous feudal landscape that had once defined the Rhineland and French territories to the west had been replaced by the hard borders of sovereign states committed to regulating everything under their control. For decades after the first partition of Poland-Lithuania, people moved freely across the partitioning powers as if nothing had happened. But by 1815 these too had become regulated boundaries, with nobles forced to choose where their new loyalties lay—with Prussia, Austria, or the Russian colossus that now stood on their border.[56]

4

THE AGE OF COSMOPOLITANISM

On a picturesque hill overlooking the town of Eisenach, hundreds of students and professors made their way up to the medieval castle of Wartburg. The date was 18 October 1817. Exactly 300 years before, Martin Luther's supposed nailing of his ninety-five theses on a Wittenberg church door had sparked the reformation. Now, on the site where Luther later produced his German translation of the New Testament, his act of religious protest was being celebrated as a great national holiday. The assembled students were members of *Burschenschaften* (fraternities) that had boomed in popularity since the end of the Napoleonic Wars. They carried the black-red-gold banner that had been used as a symbol of a prominent *Freikorps* unit as their flag, sang patriotic songs from the 'wars of liberation', and some even sported beards and long hair as symbols of their Germanness.

Lorenz Oken, a professor at Jena, gave one of the many speeches that day, announcing that students 'should give up all egoism, provincialism, and dialectism and raise themselves to the level of the whole nation'. It was a 'disgrace' for an educated student to be nothing but Saxon, Prussian, Austrian, and so on. 'May this national division disappear among us in the future and we be one body, one German nation'. The official program adopted called for Germany to become a unified constitutional monarchy, with guaranteed personal freedoms, equal rights, and ministers responsible to a freely-elected parliament.[1]

The Wartburg Festival was an inchoate manifestation of a growing nationalist subculture which flourished amongst students and educated men in northern German towns in the post-Napoleonic period. It was intimately tied up—though not entirely synonymous—with the growth of ideas that would come to be known as 'liberal'. Liberal nationalists hoped to fill the spiritual vacuum created by the Holy Roman Empire's demise with liberal constitutionalism on a national scale, as opposed to the aristocratic provincialism on a European scale represented by the German Confederation.

No single figure would become as synonymous with this post-Napoleonic aristocratic provincialism as Klemens von Metternich. He was the leading figure in the Congress of Vienna which shaped this order and the man most committed to its maintenance: indeed, it was dubbed by critics the 'Metternich system'. Metternich was a child of the Empire. Before its demise, his illustrious Rhenish family was part of the select circle of sovereign imperial knights and counts. This aristocratic lineage helped his father build a career as a diplomat, first in the service of the archbishop of Trier and then the Habsburg emperor himself. The family had estates both in the Rhineland and in Bohemia, the latter of which allowed his father to attend Leopold II's coronation as one of the Bohemian envoys, leaving it to Metternich to attend as head of the Catholic Rhenish and Westphalian imperial counts. As recounted earlier, he was amazed by the spectacle, one he would bear witness to two years later as Francis inherited the imperial title. By then Metternich was just nineteen. Over the following decades, the young man watched as French revolutionary and Napoleonic armies criss-crossed the continent bringing death, destruction, and revolutionary change wherever they went. Diplomatic postings in Francis's service in Dresden, Berlin, and Paris catapulted him to the pinnacle of European diplomacy. He was shrewd, hard-working, and loyal. In 1809 Francis made him his foreign minister.[2]

The Empire faded away, but Metternich's service to the Habsburg emperor continued. Austria, as he described it in 1819, had become his 'moral fatherland'. Like many men of his aristocratic background, he was Francophone but thoroughly Anglophile, admiring Britain as an orderly and free constitutional monarchy ruled by a responsible nobility. One sympathetic biographer likened him to 'a conservative British Whig' in political outlook.[3] While he did not envision transplanting British models onto Central Europe wholesale, his vision for the post-Napoleonic order was not one in which absolutist monarchs would dictate what they pleased to their subordinates, but one of harmony between legitimate princes and their estates. It was a very different kind of philosophy than that which had animated Maria Theresa and Joseph II, who sought—gradually in the former case, rapidly in the latter—to turn Bohemia, the Austrian duchies, Hungary, Galicia, and some other minor territories into a single indivisible state ruled from Vienna. Only in 1804 did this state really get an official name, when Francis announced the creation of an Austrian imperial title that would encompass all these lands. But this was a defensive response to Napoleon, not a sign of centralizing tendencies. In the patent announcing its creation, Francis described his realm under this title as consisting of 'independent kingdoms and states' that would henceforth 'retain unchanged their previous titles, constitutions, privileges, and relations'.[4] The project of a unified Habsburg state was indefinitely put on ice, with the existing Josephine bureaucracy left intact along with the privileged provincial elites and their estates.

The same was true in Prussia. Frederick William III gradually turned against his reformers, and his promise to provide the kingdom with a constitution never materialized. Instead, in 1823 he established a system of provincial diets which deliberated in private and had little real power. A national 'united diet' would only be called by the king if he needed new loans, which he would avoid throughout his long reign—lasting until 1840—by strict fiscal discipline.[5] While a certain administrative unity had been achieved during the age of reform, it applied only to the rump then under Prussian control. Not unlike Austria, after 1815 the Kingdom of Prussia remained a patchwork of distinct provinces with their own histories and identities.

Almost half of Prussia's citizens lived in a territory annexed to the Hohenzollern realm since 1793.[6] The majority shared a common German tongue, but many spoke other Germanic, Slavic, and Baltic vernaculars. The minority Calvinism of the Hohenzollerns was very different from the Lutheranism of the majority. Moreover, there were millions of Catholics in east and west along with Jews scattered across the country. Prussia proper in the far east had its origin in a medieval Baltic crusading state eventually secularized by the Hohenzollerns. The Grand Duchy of Posen was created out of the non-Prussian Polish territories annexed by Prussia. Neither had been part of the Holy Roman Empire, unlike the dynasty's sandy heartland of Brandenburg where Berlin and Potsdam were located. To the north of Brandenburg was Pomerania stretched along the Baltic, a source of some of the most loyal Junker lords. To the west was Prussian Saxony, an amalgamation of territories annexed during and after the Napoleonic wars. Then to the southeast there was Silesia, historically a land of the Bohemian crown whose Catholic nobility were deeply intertwined with the wider Habsburg elite, conquered by Frederick in 1740. And finally, there was the Rhineland, which stood apart from the rest of

Prussia in the far west of Germany, and was more densely populated, urbane, and Catholic than any other territory ruled by the Hohenzollerns. All that really united Prussians, Silesians, and Rhinelanders—Cologners, Berliners, and Königsbergers—was the Prussian king.

The princely successor states to the Holy Roman Empire sought to establish themselves as sovereign states with distinct identities. They had their own flags, anthems, currencies, uniforms for public officials and more.[7] They believed in the 'monarchical principle', the notion that sovereignty rested in the person of the monarch alone, rather than in the nation, whether conceived of as a collection of estates or a whole people.[8]

What frustrated liberals was less that Germans lacked a unified constitution, but that they lacked constitutions at all. Article 13 of the Federal Act of the German Confederation stipulated that each member state would provide 'an estate-based constitution', but it was an intentionally vague formulation that left the specifics to the princes. What made constitutions such an issue of importance was that they were expected to enshrine a political role for the growing 'educated middle class'—the *Bildungsbürgertum*. This was a vague and diverse strata of men and women who had imbibed the spirit of the Enlightenment and stood outside the bounds of the estates-based political order. They were largely bureaucrats, teachers, professors, and pastors, educated and literate people for whom *Bildung* or self-cultivation had become a marker of a status that made them no less worthy of political participation than those of noble birth.[9]

Indeed, it was precisely their *Bildung* that made them feel 'German'. The institutions of the princely state were limited, both by geography and status, but German language and culture was unlimited, universal, shared by the educated no matter their place of birth or even their religion. For educated middle-class Jews, *Bildung* was the ideal that promised them acceptance into mainstream society. By adopting the same secular ideal as their Christian counterparts, they were putting themselves on equal footing. This was indeed exactly what reformist bureaucrats hoped for when emancipating Jews, expecting them to transcend all the negative anti-Jewish stereotypes current at the time through self-cultivation. As Jews changed their names to Christian or German ones, fought in the army, and sent their sons into the same schools and universities as their Christian neighbours, all that once made them so distinct became less and less clear.[10]

At its core, this dawning liberalism was highly cosmopolitan. Liberal movements hoped to raise the spiritual, cultural and economic level of the

THE AGE OF COSMOPOLITANISM

'nation', understood as having a much wider definition than the narrowly noble nations of the past. Other nations doing the same were seen as complementary rather than as rivals. 'Fatherlands do not march against each other', Herder had written, 'they lie quietly side by side and help each other like families'.[11] Somewhat ironically, Metternich would insist into old age that he too was a cosmopolitan formed by the Enlightenment, his political philosophy grounded in mutual respect between existing states. But those who embraced 'liberal' ideas condemned this kind of cosmopolitanism for excluding those of common birth, and instead saw the 'reciprocal solidarity between various oppressed nationalities' as true cosmopolitanism.[12]

* * *

The Wartburg Festival concluded during the afternoon of 18 October 1817. The hundreds of students then marched two hours to another hill on the other side of Eisenach. Grand Duke Carl August of Saxe-Weimar, the local enlightened prince who had once patronized Goethe and Herder and the previous year had given his small state a constitution, had arranged a party for them there. They drank the evening away as eight bonfires burned on the hillside before the vast majority made their way down the hill for a night's rest. One young student called on the remaining few dozen to gather around the largest of the bonfires. Most had no idea what was going on as the student and a few accomplices threw bundles of paper made to look like books by 'anti-German' authors into the flames, later joined by a cane, wig, and corset.

This marginal event soon came to define the whole festival. Hysterical reports cast it as the culmination of a revolutionary occurrence. The burning of an Austrian corporal's cane, a Prussian cavalry uniform, and a pigtail from a Hessian officer's wig was the least of it.[13] As authorities in Postdam and Vienna investigated the festival, they convinced themselves there were 'highly pernicious and highly criminal' forces at work, that the 'mass of degenerate professors and students' identified by the Prussian deputy minister of police were just the tip of the iceberg.[14] A 'German revolution' loomed, Metternich ominously warned as the Prussians pointed to the eccentric founder of the gymnastics movement Friedrich Ludwig Jahn—who was indeed likely was behind the burnings—as the director of a vast revolutionary conspiracy.[15]

At about five o'clock on 23 March 1819, the playwright August von Kotzebue received a knock on the door. A young lad called Heinrich was there to see him. He was received cordially in the living room before drawing a dagger and stabbing Kotzebue to death while he cried: 'Here, you traitor to the fatherland!' The young man was not 'Heinrich' at all, but a messianic nationalist from Franconia named Carl Sand. He had been a student at Jena and had attended the Wartburg Festival, where he had thrown one of Kotzebue's works into the flames (before ever reading it, it appears).[16] Metternich convened a secret meeting in the Bohemian spa town of Carlsbad where the leaders of the German Confederation were finally convinced of the ominous threat facing them, agreeing to a unified regime of censorship and investigation of suspected revolutionaries. The *Burschenschaften* were banned, Jahn arrested, many gymnastics clubs shut down, and leading nationalist figures like Ernst Moritz Arndt suspended from their professorships. Even fashion items associated with German nationalism were banned.[17] The Carlsbad decrees were a confused reaction to the red herring of the 'Wartburg book-burnings'. There had been no revolutionary conspiracy.

Despite the new spirit of state repression, universities remained hotbeds of nationalist sentiment, many *Burschenschaften* soon recovered, countless supposedly non-political societies maintained a nationalist bent, and educated, propertied men held on to their hopes for political participation.[18] Those who felt themselves to be a part of the 'German nation' only grew. Though Germany lacked a cohesive 'national memory' or single national historical narrative, its most prominent early nineteenth century historians agreed that nations were the fundamental building blocks of history. Inspired by Romanticism, they saw history as something that should be written for and about the people, focusing not on the lives and deaths of monarchs but on the organic, historically-rooted, and unique whole that was the nation.[19]

These new conceptions of German history, along with a shared standard language and a fairly standardized literary corpus (that came to include more and more nationally minded writers from the 'Wars of Liberation'), made many schools a training ground for future nationalists. Otto von Bismarck, attending school in the 1820s, recalled with some irony that liberal and nationalist attitudes were a 'natural product of our [Prussian] state education'.[20] There was little to no central control over what materials were used in classrooms in any German state. The first school textbook written for 'German history', published in 1816 and widely used in the 1820s and 1830s, spoke of 'the history ... of our people' as an unbroken continuity with an 'ancient, pure, unmixed [German] tribe' inhabiting the territory of Germany for millennia.[21] It criticized the nobility for adopting French morality and 'immorality' in the seventeenth century and neglecting to care for the German language.[22] The author was a schoolteacher in the Rhineland for years before being appointed Director General of Schools for the Kingdom of Hanover in 1830. Germans of the 1820s and 1830s had already been socialized to think of themselves as part of a wider German nation before they even set foot in universities which were themselves breeding grounds of liberal nationalism.

Liberals did not have a monopoly on developing notions of 'Germanness', however. Though none of the princely states of the German Confederation and their still largely noble elites denied that they were 'German', they nurtured a more pluralistic idea of Germany, which celebrated rather than condemned regional or 'tribal' identities and sought to emphasize the leading role of nobles and princes in the national story. As the conservative Swiss jurist Carl Ludwig von Haller wrote in 1821: 'The nobility [is] not a privileged caste, not a separate people … but rather the most excellent, outstanding part of the people, its adornment, its glory'.[23] The purity of lineage imperial aristocrats had once prided themselves on was replaced by an emphasis on belonging to ancient German nobility. Genealogical handbooks stressed 'ancient German names' or 'Bavarian-Germanic origins'.[24]

Besides wishing to foster loyalty to their dynasties, princely establishments were keenly interested in 'historicizing' their states. Ostensibly bearers of tradition and stability, the princes ruling the German Confederation had in fact cannibalized the old Holy Roman Empire during the Napoleonic Wars, massively expanding their territories at its expense and coming to enjoy elevated royal distinctions. Dozens of historical societies sprang up across Germany after 1815, often with official support and always with a provincial or state-based focus to make these newly-expanded states and their borders appear more deeply rooted in German history than they really were.[25]

Initiatives promoting provincial identities—spearheaded by local aristocrats and notables in opposition to grander middle-class national visions—found fertile ground in the Habsburg Monarchy too. Such endeavours were permitted in Hungary, Galicia, Styria, Carniola, Tyrol, Carinthia, Upper Austria, and Salzburg alongside a series of specifically Slavic cultural institutes called *Maticas* starting with the Serbian one in Pest in 1826.[26] Bohemia too, where the estates were keen to assert their state's identity as a bilingual country with a long independent history, won royal approval for the founding of the Bohemian Museum in 1818. It had been the initiative of Kaspar von Sternberg, who had once been committed to a career in imperial institutions but turned his attention to his Bohemian homeland after the demise of the Holy Roman Empire. Part of the museum's scientific mission ended up being supporting the development of the kingdom's majority Slavic tongue.

This helped launch the career of the country's most important historian, František Palacký. A Moravian by birth, educated at the Lutheran Lyceum in Pressburg, he established himself in Prague with Joseph Dobrovský's help and in 1827 convinced Sternberg to begin publishing the museum's journal in Czech under his editorship.[27] That same year, Palacký was approached by the estates to become their official historiographer, tasked with writing a comprehensive history of Bohemia based on primary sources, something which would occupy him for the rest of his life. The first edition was published in German in 1836 to much acclaim. The king of Saxony, Bohemia's northern neighbour, sent Palacký a diamond ring as a sign of appreciation.[28]

The lack of interest in liberal nationalism on the part of German princes and their support for provincial identities presented an obvious conundrum for those who dreamed of a united German nation-state, particularly since Prussia and Austria were both ruled by conservative monarchs and Metternich had no appetite for radical change. Many liberals thus questioned whether these two leading German powers, with kingdoms that stretched far east beyond the bounds of 'Germany', should be part of it at all. One Rhenish liberal commented that when visiting Düsseldorf in 1836 the Prussian king appeared like 'a foreign curiosity from the steppes of Asia'. In the southwestern German states where liberals were most influential, they fancifully imagined a united Germany aligned with France that would exclude both Austria and Prussia.[29] Lacking any obvious path to the realization of their own aspirations, German liberal nationalists took up the causes of other nations fighting for freedom in a spirit of cosmopolitan cooperation. Above all else they supported Poland, which was seen as the great victim of the reactionary order; the restoration of its independence became a *cause célèbre*.

The victorious powers at the Congress of Vienna had opted to keep the Polish-Lithuanian Commonwealth partitioned while allowing Polish language and culture their place in public life. Krakow was given independence as a free city, with Polonophone students from all three partitioning powers (Prussia, Austria and Russia) guaranteed the right to study at

THE AGE OF COSMOPOLITANISM

its ancient university.[30] In Galicia, the Habsburgs encouraged a provincial patriotism that allowed pride in Poland as a cultural nation and loyalty to the emperor to exist side-by-side.[31] Prussian authorities permitted the use of Polish in education and cooperated with Polish nobles as well as the Catholic Church in the Grand Duchy of Posen, while Russia's Polonophile emperor Alexander I created a Kingdom of Poland in personal union with Russia out of territories that had mostly been part of the Napoleonic Duchy of Warsaw. In Warsaw another Polish-language university was founded in 1818, joining the much older Vilna University that also employed Polish although being outside of the Polish kingdom. The two universities together educated considerably more students than the three Russian-medium ones in the Russian Empire.[32]

Their situation was precarious, however. In 1830 a wave of revolutions swept over Europe. The overthrow of the French Bourbon king Charles X and the crowning of his cousin Louis-Philippe as the 'King of the French' in his place provided a catalyst for liberal uprisings elsewhere. It also emboldened German liberals, who managed to force the adoption of liberal constitutions in Saxony and Hanover in subsequent years. But this paled in comparison to the full-scale uprising that broke out in Russian Poland in November of 1830. Germany was swept by a wave of 'Poland enthusiasm'. Images of heroic Polish resistance graced paintings, banners, ceramic dishes, and pipes, and a whole genre of 'Polish songs' pervaded popular culture.[33] When the uprising was crushed thousands of Poles made their way through Germany into exile as part of the 'Great Emigration', providing Germans a chance to meet with their Polish heroes in person.[34]

'Poland enthusiasm' reached a crescendo at the 1832 Hambach festival, the first public demonstration of German liberal nationalism since the Carlsbad decrees and one that signified the transformation of German nationalism from a fringe student movement into one with broad middle-class support, as the presence of women testified.[35] Several Polish emigres attended alongside 20–30,000 participants. The white-red Polish flag symbolically flew alongside the German black-red-gold.[36] The organizers of the festival even raised the slogan: 'Without Poland's freedom, no German freedom ... let us fight for Poland's restoration, for the noble cause of all humanity!'[37]

This latest wave of revolutions offered a temporary reprieve for Metternich and his 'system'. Despite the near-omnipotent power critics often ascribed to him, Metternich was a mere servant of a single monarch.

His system was reliant on friendly rulers who shared his conservative worldview, particularly the Prussian and Russian monarchs allied to his own Austrian employer in a 'Holy Alliance' dedicated to quashing revolution wherever it may break out. The Carlsbad Decrees worked only insofar as they were enforced, which south German rulers had been reluctant to do in the 1820s as they tried to assert their sovereignty at the expense of the German Confederation.

Metternich used the renewed spectre of revolution to convince the states of the confederation in 1832 and 1834 to re-affirm the various repressive laws passed since 1819, but this success was bittersweet. That same year, the *Zollverein* (customs union) came into being, giving economic unity to Prussia, Bavaria, Saxony, Württemberg and most other south and central German states. Metternich felt it a blow to his system for two reasons. Firstly, he thought it alienated Austria from the rest of Germany. And secondly, it reduced the importance of the confederation since it had been negotiated outside of its purview. An added blow came the following year when Emperor Francis died and was replaced by his epileptic, feeble-minded son Ferdinand. With Ferdinand effectively unable to rule, the Habsburg Monarchy fell into the hands of a secret four-man State Conference consisting of two Habsburg archdukes, Metternich, and his arch-rival, the Bohemian Count Franz Anton Kolowrat.[38]

In the rudderless monarchy Metternich was able to exert more direct influence over internal affairs, but in truth the loss of his like-minded patron Francis left his system in a far more precarious position. Austrian administration remained chaotic, divided into three geographically-defined court offices—for the hereditary lands, Hungary and Transylvania—staffed by overworked and underpaid bureaucrats whose own generally more liberal ideas chafed against the conservatism of their superiors. The state's finances were in disarray, leading to calls from those like Kolowrat for the army's size to be reduced, anathema to Metternich who saw a strong army as essential to the maintenance of the international system. No one figure was powerful enough to change Austria's course, leaving contemporaries feeling like it had gone totally adrift.[39]

* * *

The Wartburg Festival had counted amongst its attendees several foreign students, including a Protestant Slav from northern Hungary named Ján Kollár. He had only recently arrived at the nearby University of Jena for his first term, finding a town teeming with students and dominated by academic life. Between duels and bouts of beer-induced revelry, they would often gather on the city's squares singing patriotic songs, especially Arndt's 'What is the German's Fatherland?' One of Kollár's first stops upon his arrival was to visit the most famous of all of Jena's residents: Goethe. He and a friend were welcomed with 'sublime courtesy', Kollár correcting Goethe's misapprehension that only Magyars live in Hungary. 'Sir, I am a Slovak or, if you will, a Slav, my colleague here is a half-Magyar, half-German'. The old poet laughed and asked if Kollár would be willing to collect and translate some Slovak folk songs for him. Goethe had heard much of their beauty.[40]

While Wartburg left a strong impression on Kollár, he found the picturesque surroundings of Jena even more striking. Wandering around the Thuringian countryside, he found 'Slavic names, but no Slavic inhabitants'.[41] Hundreds of years ago, in the wake of the great *Völkerwanderung* (migration period) around the collapse of the Western Roman Empire, Slavs had settled the entirety of what later became eastern Germany. Over the centuries German settlement shifted eastwards, swallowing up the Slavs; the memory of their presence was preserved only in the Germanized names of villages in places like Thuringia and Saxony and cities like Berlin, Leipzig, and Dresden. 'Every town, every village, every river and mountain that had a Slavic name seemed to me like a grave or a monument in this huge cemetery', Kollár wrote. It made him feel a deep sadness for 'the death of the Slavic nation ... oppressed and destroyed here'.[42]

Kollár was undoubtedly troubled by more than history. The early nineteenth century was the high point of German linguistic dominance in Central Europe. Leading Slavic intellectuals like Joseph Dobrovský wrote, published, and corresponded primarily in German, even though the standardization and cultivation of Czech was well underway. German-language educational and cultural institutions dominated intellectual life even where, as in Croatia, there was a native Slavic nobility. Magyar was displacing Latin in the Kingdom of Hungary, but it was a slow process whose impact was limited in most urban centres. The number of nationally conscious Slavs was growing, but they remained too small in number to sustain an independent public sphere. The fear that out of a combination of disinterest and neglect their languages would be lost and with them the nation itself remained ever-present.

The greatest challenge facing Slavic intellectuals was the lack of a common alternative means of communication to German. As Kollár lamented:

'When one wishes to make himself understood on any important matter to brother Slavs, he must use a foreign, non-Slavic tongue'.[43] By this point those who took a scholarly interest in Slavs in Central Europe took it as a given that they were a single people or nation consisting of various 'tribes' with their own 'dialects'. But there was no commonly accepted measure of which dialect was worthy of becoming a literary standard. Nor was it clear how to reconcile the many well-established Slavic vernacular literary and liturgical traditions. The question of which nations had the right to a literary standard was—and in many ways still is—tied up with which nations are seen as legitimate and which are not.

The German romantic Friedrich Schlegel had opined in a series of lectures held in Vienna in 1812 that the suppression of a native language was 'the worst barbarism', and yet his claim that every nation had a right to its own literature and linguistic development was caveated with the words 'every independent and significant nation'.[44] Liberal nationalists across Europe were cosmopolitan, supporting each other's endeavours, but agreed that some threshold that had to be reached for a nation to be considered legitimate enough for its peculiar development to be necessary. After all, as Schlegel noted, any nation 'whose language is allowed to become wild or kept in an unrefined state must itself become barbarous and unrefined'.[45] All nations had their place, but some were destined for greatness while others doomed to irrelevance.

As a solution to the question of Slavic literacy, Johann Popowitsch, a Styrian Slav professor of German language and rhetoric at the University of Vienna, wanted to develop a universal Slavic orthography.[46] He studied and lectured on a language whose standardization and cultivation was an active process during his lifetime, one that Slavic intellectuals watched with admiration and wanted to replicate in their own context. If Hanoverians, Bavarians, and Saxons saw the cultural nation they owed allegiance to as Germany, why would Slavic-speaking Bohemians, Croatians, or Moravians not search for the same?

Like Popowitsch, the Pest-based lawyer Ján Herkel' proposed all Slavs adopt universal orthography so that their work could easily be read by any other Slav even if the content of their writing was different.[47] To this end, he coined the term 'Pan-Slavism' in 1826 to denote 'unity in literature among all Slavs'.[48] But by then most Slavic literati recognized that the numerous dialects or tribes would need their own literary standards, many of which already existed. What they could not agree on, however, was precisely how many dialects there were. Nor could they agree on

THE AGE OF COSMOPOLITANISM

what to call them. For example, Dobrovský corresponded for years with Bartholomeus Kopitar—a native Carniolan and chief censor for Slavic and Greek books in Vienna—on the question of how to categorize the south Slavic dialects spoken in the southern Austrian duchies, Croatia, Slavonia, Dalmatia, Serbia, and the Ottoman-ruled Balkans. They floated names like Windish, Carinthian, Croatian, Bosnian, and Slavo-Serbian with various definitions and boundaries, but could never agree.[49]

For Kollár and his generation, however, such academic debates were far less inspiring than the modern spirit of romantic nationalism they came into contact with in places like Jena. Pavel Josef Šafařík, a fellow Protestant Slav from northern Hungary two years Kollár's junior, also studied there from 1815–17. He found it revelatory, both because of the spirit of liberal nationalism and the opportunity he had to establish the philosophical and historical foundations of his own thought. By the time he left Jena he had taken up the study of Slavs—of their history, languages and culture—as his calling. He got to know Dobrovský, Palacký and other Slavic luminaries and in 1826 published the first scholarly study of 'the Slavic language and literature' in all its 'dialects'. It was a huge inspiration to Slavs from all over Central Europe, especially since it effectively canonized Herder's description of the Slavic 'national character' as inherently peaceful and industrious.[50]

While Šafařík—who spent the 1820s teaching at the Serbian Gymnasium (secondary school) in Neusatz (Novi Sad) in southern Hungary—embraced scholarly pursuits, Kollár turned to literature. His allegorical, semi-autobiographical 1824 poem *The Daughter of Slava* extolled the virtues of the Slavic nation while describing a poet's journey through past and present Slavic lands. Through this and his work collecting and publishing Slovak folk songs with Šafařík, he became the leading proponent of Romantic literary Pan-Slavism.

Kollár's most influential idea was 'literary reciprocity'. He argued that for the Slavic nation to flourish, its tribes should coalesce around four literary standards: Russian, Polish, Czechoslovak, and 'Illyrian' (South Slavic).[51] The nationally minded should focus their attention on providing literary depth to each of these standards while also supporting the others and ultimately drawing them all closer together, even if they remained separate. His book-length treatment of the idea, published in German in 1837, provided a concrete program for how reciprocity might be achieved. Slavic bookshops and libraries selling books in all Slavic dialects were to be set up; chairs in Slavic studies would be created; teachers trained and sent out to teach Slavic dialects in schools; grammars, dictionaries, and other literary works published; and so on. He drew attention to the fact that the 'German nation' was divided into many more 'tribes' and states than the Slavic nation. He counted thirty-eight in Germany alone to say nothing of Norway, Sweden, or Holland, which he also counted as 'German'.[52] Slavs, by contrast, were divided only into 'four or five governments, namely, Russia, Austria, Prussia, Saxony and the Porte [Ottoman Empire]'.[53]

The comparison served to illustrate that his envisioned Slavic nation was not a political concept, but a purely philosophical and literary one.[54] In many ways it was a mirror image of the German 'cultural nation' that these Central European Slavs were hoping to emancipate themselves from.[55] This Slavic nation was somewhat vague, with many vernacular dialects, no coherent national historical narrative, and divided into many states, but nonetheless possessed a cultural, spiritual, and moral unity with a cosmopolitan higher purpose for all humanity. It is no wonder then that the works of German philosophers, poets, and writers were crucial for the formulation of a Pan-Slavist cultural agenda. The work of Herder provided philosophical underpinnings for language-based concepts of nationhood, the collection of folk poetry, and the world-historical meaning of Slavic unity. The works of Schiller, Goethe and Christoph Martin Wieland provided aesthetic and literary inspiration. And the extensive corpus of German-language scholarship on Slavic peoples and languages that had been built up during the Enlightenment proved an invaluable source for all future works.

In line with the peak of German cosmopolitan nationalism, the 1820s and 1830s would be the golden age of Slavic reciprocity as well as the peak of Slavic-German cooperation. The case of the Serbian philologist Vuk Karadžić is illustrative. In 1813 he left Serbia for Vienna, where he met Kopitar, who translated two collections of Serbian folk poetry Karadžić had collected in his native land and enthusiastically promoted them in the German press.[56] With Kopitar's encouragement, Karadžić began work on a Serbian grammar that would become the basis of the modern Serbian literary language. Thanks in large part to Kopitar, Karadžić's folk poetry was read by Goethe and Jacob Grimm, who became a lifelong friend and collaborator.

Karadžić and Kopitar were not quite Pan-Slavists, however. Neither wanted to subsume their own languages into a wider south Slavic literary standard. Both instead agreed that Slovene and Serbian were separate

THE AGE OF COSMOPOLITANISM

languages and that a Croatian language did not exist. While there was a rich literary tradition in the Croatian lands—encompassing Croatia, Dalmatia and Slavonia—writers generally stuck to their own dialects and without any consistent orthography. Broadly, there were three main Slavic dialect groups in the region, named after their differing words for 'what': Kajkavian, Čakavian, and Štokavian. Kajkavian was the dialect native to the northwest of Croatian, whose speakers Kopitar claimed were Slovenes. Čakavian was spoken along the Adriatic, and Štokavian was the most widespread dialect group that reached deep into the Ottoman-ruled Balkans. Karadžić and Kopitar both claimed Štokavians were Serbs, following the classification of other philologists.[57]

This diversity is in no small part why Kollár's four-standard reciprocity was so appealing to a young Slavic patriot from Croatia named Ljudevit Gaj. He had been born Ludwig Gay in northern Croatia to two German-speaking immigrants of Huguenot origin in 1809. After studying at Vienna and Graz, where he became acquainted with Šafařík's work as well as Kopitar's grammar, he moved to Pest in 1829.[58] A major centre of Pan-Slavism thanks to Kollár's presence, the two became close and Gaj wholeheartedly embraced the notion of Slavic reciprocity.[59] Influenced by Czech orthography, he published a Croatian grammar in Ofen in 1830. Characteristic of his generation, most of his writings from this period were in German, which he would continue to use throughout his life even when corresponding with other Pan-Slavists.[60] Nonetheless, his Croatian grammar was a milestone in the development of a Croatian literary standard he hoped would be accepted by all South Slavs—or Yugoslavs—including Slovenes.

Gaj was also building on a much older Croatian tradition of believing in and extolling Slavic unity, one he consciously stepped into when embracing the 'Illyrian' name.[61] The Illyrians were the inhabitants of the eastern Adriatic in classical times, their name surviving as a descriptor for the Slavs who took their place. 'Illyrianism' was seen as a way to overcome the 'tribal' boundaries between south Slavs and thus bring them one step closer to general Slavic unity within Kollár's four-standard framework. When Gaj founded the first Croatian-language newspaper in Habsburg Croatia, he thus called it *Danica Ilirska*, with his whole intellectual project of a Pan-Slavist-inspired standard for all south Slavs coming to be known as the Illyrian movement. This movement was crucial not just for the standardization of Croatian, but the adoption by the Croatian literary elite of the Štokavian dialect. Many Serbs were already

81

adopting a standard on the same dialect thanks to Karadžić, which put the two languages close together. The next major impediment to south Slavic unity was the Slovene standard. Some Slovenes like Stanko Vraz were won over to the Illyrian movement. He argued Slovenes had to abandon their language because a national literature supposedly needed five or six million users to be viable.[62] But Gaj ultimately failed to get Slovenes to abandon their language wholesale. In a sign of things to come, the Slovene France Prešeren wrote to Vraz that the whole Pan-Slavist project would likely 'remain a pious wish' and that the attempt to get Slovenes to abandon their 'dialect' in favour of Illyrian was 'impossible'.[63]

5

REFORM AND REVOLT

In the late 1830s, the Englishman John Paget found himself in Pest, one of many stops on his tour of Hungary and Transylvania, undertaken 'to extend the knowledge of that country in the west of Europe'.[1] As he walked along the Danube, he found one particularly 'handsome building with an exceedingly elegant portico' on the quay. It was the Lloyd Palace, whose first floor was occupied by the National Casino, a gentleman's club where well-to-do men could gather, converse, read and discuss periodicals, play cards and billiards, receive mail, or simply eat, drink, and relax. Despite the inescapable thick clouds of tobacco smoke, Paget was impressed enough to call it 'one of the best-managed clubs in Europe'.[2]

For its founder István Széchenyi, it was meant to be much more than a mere social club. He hoped it would become a catalyst for the forging of a modern, responsible, and enlightened Hungarian elite and turn a city of 'mud and dust' into a vibrant national capital. Széchenyi was an aristocrat of the highest pedigree. He had been born and raised in Vienna in an environment where French and German took precedence over Magyar and Latin, both of which he spoke poorly as a young man. He joined the imperial army as a lieutenant in 1809 at the age of seventeen, remaining an officer throughout the Napoleonic Wars and long after. He caroused with men and women of his stature across the continent, in Paris, London, Vienna, and beyond.[3]

France and England unceasingly impressed him with their economic, social, and cultural advancement. England in particular seemed to offer a vision of a brighter Hungarian future, with its air of gentle freedom and industrial advancement under the watchful gaze of a cultivated nobility and constitutional monarch. He thought of Hungary lovingly but disparagingly as a 'filthy little fatherland' that 'no one in [their] right mind' would want to live in. He was unfailingly loyal to the House of Habsburg but wanted to see Hungary transformed into the kind of country he had seen in Western Europe.[4]

Reform had been on the minds of many Hungarians since 1790, but as the passions stirred by Josephine absolutism dissipated it seemed like the country had returned to an apathetic slumber. The only lasting major change from that stormy year had been the beginning of a long but slow process of 'Magyarization'. In the first post-Napoleonic diet in 1825, as largely German-speaking Pressburg teemed with provincial Magyar nobles and wealthy cosmopolitan aristocrats, Széchenyi made his political debut. The buzz of the diet was what finally convinced him to devote his life fully to the betterment of his homeland. The National Casino had its beginnings there in the form of a room Széchenyi rented as a kind of open salon. But Széchenyi's most impressive achievement came as he made an abrupt and passionate announcement that he would donate a year's income for the foundation of a Hungarian Academy of Sciences. Others followed his lead. It would be the capstone of the Magyar language's cultivation and—Széchenyi hoped—help turn Pest into a truly Magyar city.[5]

Even though the vast provincial nobility embraced Magyarization, the small but growing urban 'middle class' largely did not. Ofen, Pest, and Pressburg were still outwardly 'German' cities in the early nineteenth century. Pest even sustained the largest theatre in the German-speaking world while a Magyar equivalent failed to take off. German periodicals flourished while Magyar ones struggled.[6] Much of this Germanness was simply reflective of a multinational population that shared German as their language of education and high culture. There were thousands of Slavs in Pest including the Pan-Slavist leader and clergyman Ján Kollár. Indeed, 'Pan-Slavism' had been coined by a local lawyer. The central Serbian cultural institution in the monarchy—the *Matica*—was also based in Pest, while the university press published important works in many of the kingdom's vernaculars.[7]

Széchenyi saw Germanization—or 'Austrianization'—as the greatest threat to Hungarian national development. He confided (in German) to his diary in 1829 that 'every day I see myself that Herder is right, the Hungarian nation will soon cease to exist'.[8] He was not disloyal to the Habsburgs, nor did he want independence from them, but like most of the Hungarian nobility he did not want to see the country become just another 'Austrian state' within a centralized monarchy in which all its specificities would have withered away. Széchenyi was prone to swerving bouts of extreme pessimism and wild optimism that continued even as his worries became increasingly anachronistic due to the slow but steady Magyarization of the kingdom. The model presented by his casino set off a veritable movement, with nearly thirty in Hungary and Transylvania by 1832.[9] His 1830 book *Credit*—written in Magyar—proved to be a runaway bestseller, quickly translated into German in which it was equally popular. He followed it up with two more books, forming a trilogy of liberal reformist works, the third of which was controversial enough that it had to be published in Leipzig before being smuggled back into Hungary, although it was sold in Vienna and Pressburg without issue like many such works which the authorities prevented from being published but found themselves powerless to stop from being distributed. It laid out concrete points to serve as a reform program at the 1832–6 diet.[10]

Austrian Chancellor and Foreign Minister Klemens von Metternich's suspicions (which were not difficult to rouse) had already been raised by the diet of 1825–7. He thought it overly political in addressing issues beyond the taxes and recruits it was meant to raise for the crown, and personally berated Széchenyi for joining the supposed 'opposition'. The diet of 1832–6 would be the first of many 'reform diets' in which there was a strong contingent of representatives inspired by liberal ideas. Thanks to Széchenyi, issues like a chain bridge linking Buda and Pest, a National Theatre, the regulation of the Danube as well as broader issues around the peasantry, cities and taxes were all on the agenda. Also largely thanks to Széchenyi, the diet passed a law that retained Latin-Magyar dualism, but made the Magyar version of laws authoritative, effectively making it the primary official tongue. It was just the latest in a long line of Magyarizing measures protested without effect by the most stalwart defenders of Latin, including the Croatian nobility (who generally spoke no Magyar), the Catholic clergy, and traditionalist aristocrats.[11]

Conservatives more broadly, however, remained the dominant force in the diet. They may have been fine with slow Magyarization, but thought of liberalism as a 'disease' that afflicted young people with 'religious indifference and futile cosmopolitanism'. Such views were particularly strong in the upper house, where conservative magnates close to the court and the Catholic high clergy sat. Széchenyi's reformist liberalism was in the minority but was becoming a powerful political force in its own right.[12] These reformers focused not on constitutional issues, but overcoming the 'barbarism' of Hungarian feudalism and building a civil society based on liberal principles like equality before the law, personal freedom, and the right to own property.[13]

The new liberalism was particularly inspiring to the thousands of law students who acted as scribes and secretaries, known as the 'Dietal youth'. Many were from Pest, scorning the 'cursed Germans' they lived amongst and agitating against 'reactionary' members of the diet. Lajos Kossuth was the most famous example, making his political debut as a representative of two absent magnates. Unlike the wealthy and well-connected Catholic aristocrat Széchenyi, Kossuth was a poor Calvinist noble from the northeast. Like many young liberals he admired Széchenyi, but the warm feeling would never be reciprocated. Kossuth became the editor of *Dietal Reports* during the diet as a mouthpiece of the more radical youth faction, something Széchenyi watched with trepidation as a 'dangerous means of oppositional propaganda'.[14]

When the diet came to an end in 1836, Kossuth—already under close watch by the authorities in Vienna—decided to continue his publishing endeavour by reporting on the county diets. He was explicitly banned from doing so because the deliberations of the county diets were not meant to be publicized, but he pressed ahead anyway, insisting it was entirely legal. From July 1836 to May 1837, Kossuth became the focal point for the liberal opposition in Hungary, building up a huge network of correspondents and subscribers as his *Dietal Reports* reported on liberal and reformist speeches made by politicians across the country. For the first time ever, a true liberal 'movement' appeared to be gaining traction in Hungary.[15]

To Metternich and many other conservatives at court, such a 'movement' appeared openly subversive, underlined by Kossuth's open flouting of censorship. With Metternich blaming pernicious Polish influence for the emergence of a new opposition, Kossuth was arrested in 1837 and imprisoned in Buda castle pending trial along with the Transylvanian opposition leader Miklós Wesselényi and dozens of others. Their arrests were illegal since nobles were meant to be given a fair trial before imprisonment, but Metternich felt the government's hand had been forced by what he imagined to be a much wider revolutionary conspiracy.[16] Though Széchenyi had not been involved, abhorring Kossuth's rebellious methods, Metternich lectured him on how everything in Hungary had supposedly been ruined over the past ten years thanks to Széchenyi's reformist agitation. Odd, Széchenyi remarked in his diary, because ten years ago Metternich had claimed that his house on the Rennweg at the edge of Vienna 'marks the frontier of civilisation'.[17]

* * *

Metternich's mixture of respect for the established estates and a paranoid fear that their work could veer off in the wrong direction was common amongst German princes and aristocrats. If even nobles—such as in Hungary—could not be fully trusted with political participation, the notion that the educated middle classes should be thrown into the mix remained an absurdity. As the liberal German magazine *Die Grenzboten* put it in 1844: 'Two completely opposed systems of government are fighting in Europe for physical and intellectual hegemony': in the west one based on participation in public life, and in the east one based on absolute governmental secrecy. 'In the middle of this European dualism stands Germany ... still wavering as to whether it should follow the western or the eastern system of government'. The 'thinking people' were unquestionably inclined towards the former, 'government officials' the latter, leading to 'coldness and discord between the governments and the educated classes' of Germany.[18]

By the 1840s, the states of the German Confederation found themselves locked in a standoff with their own people, many of whom resented the arbitrary, chaotic and autocratic nature of governance and how it stifled freedom of speech. The only real hope for a change of course was a change of government, which in the monarchical states of Central Europe could only mean a change of monarch. Prussian liberals and reformers—and many non-Prussian German ones—placed great hopes on Frederick William IV when he inherited the Prussian crown in June 1840. As the head of the second most populus and powerful state in Germany, one which had spearheaded the formation of the *Zollverein* that by then blanketed much of Germany, a change of course in Prussia would have been felt far beyond its borders. And there seemed to be little hope for the advancement of liberal ideas in Vienna. Moreover, Frederick William came to power amidst a wave of German patriotic fervour provoked by a crisis in Egypt that spiralled into an outrageous French demand that its border return to the Rhine. Though he was overweight, short-sighted and cared more for art and architecture than the military, the new Prussian king leapt at the opportunity to cast himself as the defender of Germany. As the ruler of most of the Rhineland he had a natural interest in its defence, but he also nurtured a Romantic nationalist devotion to the region, embracing and encouraging the manifestations of popular nationalism that accompanied the crisis.

Forced into retirement and solitude since the Carlsbad decrees, Ernst Moritz Arndt was suddenly not only allowed to return to his professorship by Frederick William, but even appointed rector of the University of Bonn in 1841. The Bavarian king Ludwig I sent him a complimentary letter.[19] In a grand expression of the Romantic nationalism that brothers-in-law Ludwig and Frederick William both shared, the latter wrote to the former in December 1840 of his passionate desire to 'see what is incontrovertibly the world's most important crown, the crown of Charlemagne' upon 'the head of the mightiest German prince'. 'I would like to hear it proclaimed that the Austrian monarch only as Roman Emperor [would] be President of the Confederation, the first Prince of Germany, the greatest leader of Christendom'.[20]

For the first time since the 'wars of liberation', German princes came to feel that nationalism was something they could manage to their advantage. Even Metternich, whose primary focus was European peace and the balance of power, thought the outpouring of patriotism was evidence of support for German unity rather than unification—for the legitimate rule of the German princes rather than a revolutionary desire to see them overthrown. After a visit to southern Germany in late 1841, he wrote effusively that he was 'struck by the momentum that has taken the national spirit in the best directions'.[21] This time there would be no reaction. On the contrary, the authority charged with investigating potential revolutionaries in the German Confederation was abolished in 1842. The ban on gymnastics societies was also lifted, allowing the movement to grow to 300 clubs by 1847.[22] Censorship in Prussia was loosened in 1841, flooding the public sphere with cheap new publications. The 1840s saw an unprecedented expansion in oppositional activity across Central Europe. Private clubs, societies and casinos offered spaces for free discussion and debate. Provincial diets provided forums for discontent to be voiced, even—as in Prussia—where their real responsibilities were limited. Newspapers, pamphlets, and books on controversial political topics proliferated to feed the curiosity of a growing literate public.

While Frederick William IV made some initial moves that suggested a more reformist course, he quickly provoked the ire of liberal opinion when he dispelled rumours that he was planning to call a constitutional assembly.[23] Their sense of bitter disappointment soon turned to exasperation when the king's peculiar political philosophy made itself apparent. Frederick William was a Romantic who dreamed of an ideal 'Christian state' in which everyone had their rightful place and would be represented according to their role in society. Few Hohenzollern kings were both so aware of their country's diversity and so convinced that it must be retained. As he himself told his people in 1842, it was impossible 'to come up with any kind of concept that could describe the political entity called Prussia'. It had 'no historical basis', rather consisting of 'an agglomeration of territories'. In his eyes it could only exist as a decentralized, Christian, estates-based monarchy.[24]

In the wake of the debates that had accompanied Frederick William IV's ascent to power in 1840, the provincial president of Prussia Theodor von Schön penned a pamphlet entitled *Where from and Where To?* Like Széchenyi, he was an admirer of English parliamentarism and economic liberalism, hoping to see Prussia mimic some of that liberal spirit that had made the country the envy of the world. It was distributed in private and sent to the king, who angrily responded that he would not allow a 'piece of paper' to come between him and his subjects. In May 1842, Schön's work was published without his approval with a long afterword attacking the king, eventually leading to his dismissal in June. When he returned to Königsberg, he was treated as a celebrity, unprecedented for a mere bureaucrat, with the provincial Prussian diet becoming just the latest of many to call for true freedom of speech in 1843.[25]

The Prussian liberal public's dissatisfaction with the status quo was starkly illustrated by the success of the *Rhenische Zeitung* based in Cologne. Initially born out of a desire of liberal Protestants in the Rhineland to counteract the influence of the dominant Catholic *Kölnische Zeitung*, it became more and more radical over the course of 1842 as the editorial line was taken over by Karl Marx. Originally from Trier, Marx had moved to Berlin in 1836 and joined a movement of intellectuals known as the 'Young Hegelians'. Their critiques of the established order were radical, as were their proposed solutions. Marx polemicized against the 'Christian state' Frederick William was building in Prussia, contrasting it instead with a 'rational state', which in practice meant a secular republic. No pillar of the establishment was spared criticism, not even Christianity itself. It did not take long for him to run afoul of the government even as his became one of the most popular papers in Germany, with the *Rheinische Zeitung* shut down in early 1843 and Marx going into exile in France.[26]

No such endeavour could have ever got off the ground in Austria in the first place, but there was an easy enough workaround. Ignaz Kuranda—a German-speaking Jewish Prague native who had bounced around Central Europe as a playwright, critic and liberal intellectual—decided to take advantage of the more favourable political climate to found *Die Grenzboten* in 1841. The following year he moved it to Saxon Leipzig, an industrializing centre of publishing—ideally placed between Prussia and Austria—that served as a port of call alongside distant Hamburg for authors of controversial texts from across Central Europe hoping to evade censors at home. From there they easily smuggled it across the border and got it into the hands of the liberal public they were aiming to reach. Kuranda rapidly turned the magazine into a leading voice of social and political reform, expressing a strong if sometimes vague desire to see both liberalism and nationalism triumphant in Germany.[27]

The success of liberal or radical endeavours like those pursued by Kuranda and Marx was evidence of not just the educated middle class demanding political power, but also frustration at the way in which princely states restricted freedom of speech and discussion in a radically changing world. Most Central Europeans still lived in villages or small towns, their lives regulated by the seasons and the religious calendar, and their life ambitions and prospects circumscribed by their station in life. But social and economic changes caused by the Industrial Revolution were increasingly straining these old ways to a breaking point, provoking intense interest in the 'social question'. The focus was largely on the 'pauperization' of groups whose traditional economic role seemed to be withering away as technological advancements reduced the value of their labour. But there were other issues, too: the problems of dire working conditions in emerging factories, atrocious living conditions in rapidly expanding cities, the impact of railroads, financialization of agriculture, and more. It all tied in to the question of whether or not the authoritarian methods of government represented by the princely states of Central Europe were fit to deal with such dynamic and modern issues.[28]

This came to a head in 1844, when the German public was gripped by news that in two small Silesian towns hundreds of weavers had marched on the homes and businesses of factory owners and destroyed their possessions. The weavers thought of themselves as a class of independent, self-employed workers, but had found themselves increasingly on the edge of grinding poverty and proletarianization. The creeping industrialization of the previous decades had transformed their social and economic position for the worse, while the arrogant manufacturers they blamed for their ills seemed to be living lavishly. The weavers displayed no true political consciousness. They told one aristocrat: 'We are not rebels, but loyal subjects of the King and all authority'. But the government panicked, sending the Prussian army to quell the revolt and killing twelve weavers in the process.[29] The Silesian weavers' revolt galvanized those who, like Marx, entertained vague visions of a society transformed by 'socialism' or 'communism'. The first workers' associations in Germany emerged in the summer of 1844, alongside a torrent of radical publications.[30] Marx thought it only proved that *'socialism cannot be realized without revolution'*.[31]

* * *

In his 1841 pamphlet *Austria and Its Future*, the disgruntled aristocratic civil servant Victor Franz von Andrian-Werburg warned that Austria now stood 'where France stood in 1788', on 'the eve of great events, of which the first quarter-century of the new era was only a prelude'.[32] Beyond mere failings of governance, Andrian-Werburg prophesized that it was the failure to develop an overarching 'Austrian' identity that spelled the monarchy's true doom. 'Austria is a purely imaginary name, which signifies no separate people, no country, no nation'. There were Hungarians, Slavs, Germans, and Italians (as well as Jews, Romanians and others he failed to mention) in the Habsburg Monarchy, but there was no 'Austrian nationality'.[33]

Andrian-Werburg was not entirely correct. There were indeed many civil servants, officers and aristocrats who thought of their identity primarily in terms of service to the Habsburg dynasty and its state. But he highlighted a central conundrum for all those who supported liberal ideas in the Habsburg Monarchy. If it was 'the nation', represented by the educated middle class, that would act as the force of progress against the conservative forces that ruled over Central Europe, which 'nation' was to fulfil this task in multinational Austria? There was no general 'Austrian' liberal movement, but rather many liberal nationalist movements, some of which—like the Hungarian one—only cared for part of the Habsburg Monarchy, others of which—like the German or Italian—looked to unite with co-nationals beyond its borders. Though they generally recognized their mission as a cosmopolitan European one, many of their ambitions were in tension with one another if not fundamentally irreconcilable.

In Hungary this had become clear in the 1830s as Magyar continued to displace Latin as the official language. Despite its internal divisions—between aristocrats and nobles, Catholics and Calvinists, traditionalist conservatives and liberal reformers—the noble 'Hungarian nation' represented in the diet overwhelmingly supported this transition. Its liberal members were the most enthusiastic, seeing 'Magyarization' as a prerequisite to the development of a modern nation-state on the Western model in which Hungarians would be free and equal citizens instead of serfs, burghers and nobles. The diet of 1839/40 saw this liberal faction organized like never before as the young Count Lajos Batthyány set up a 'Casino of the Opposition' to coordinate their activities. Their voice only grew louder once Lajos Kossuth was released from prison and allowed to set up the newspaper *Pesti Hírlap* in 1841. The authorities accepted that there was now an 'opposition' in Hungary and hoped they could keep Kossuth in check through censorship. But *Pesti Hírlap* rapidly became the voice of a new generation of Hungarian liberals who displayed a markedly more ambivalent attitude towards the House of Habsburg insofar as it was seen as a barrier to the advancement of liberal nationalist ideas. They demanded union with Transylvania and were strident in their assertion of Magyar linguistic supremacy.

Liberalism and Magyarization were intimately intertwined in their eyes, with Slav demands for cultural and linguistic autonomy not just rejected but taken as evidence of a nefarious 'Pan-Slavic' conspiracy (allegedly directed from Russia, which was doubly terrifying as a vast Slavic empire and the bastion of absolutism in Europe). Adding to this sense of unease was Herder's old prophecy that the Magyars would drown in a surrounding ocean of Slavs, Germans and Romanians, exacerbated by the Slavic predilection for exaggerating their numbers as well as their unity. Commonly cited was Bartholomeus Kopitar's claim that of twenty million souls under Habsburg rule thirteen million were Slavs, which proved that Austria was a Slavic state like Russia.[34] While to Slavic ears this was a point of optimism, for Magyars the suggestion that not only were they threatened by a Slavic flood from the East but that they were already living in it was positively apocalyptic.

A war of words had raged in Hungary over this very question of the state's fundamental identity since the publication of the 1833 pamphlet *Should we become Magyars?*, which rejected the imposition of the language of the Magyar minority on the diverse Hungarian whole. This Magyar-Hungarian distinction had been created in the early nineteenth century by literate burghers who defended their Latinate *Hungarus* identity against the encroachments of a Magyarizing nobility, but was soon picked up by representatives of non-Magyar nationalities seeking to combat Magyar claims to national 'ownership' of Hungary.[35]

Hungarian nationalists, by contrast, resolutely rejected the very notion of a distinction between the words Magyar and Hungarian, which did not exist in their own language, just as the distinction between Czech and

Bohemian did not exist in Czech. It was one of many topics debated by the Slav-friendly Bohemian Count Leo von Thun and the Magyar patriot Ferenc Pulszky in an exchange of German letters eventually published in 1843. Pulszky called the distinction a 'fashion' of 'Slavomaniacs' and argued that what Hungarians asked of the Slavs and Romanians was 'nothing more than what the English ask of the Celtic inhabitants of Wales and high Scotland, nothing more than the French ask of Brittany or Alsace'.[36]

Beyond the public sphere, the non-Magyars of the kingdom had little to no say in the matter. Transylvania's Romanian majority had no representation in either the Transylvanian or Hungarian diets. The vast majority lived off the land as farmers or shepherds, differentiating themselves from the peoples around them through their Romance tongue as well as their Orthodox and Greek Catholic faiths. It was priests of the latter confession in particular that were most active in developing a modern Romanian national consciousness from the late eighteenth century, basing it firmly in the supposedly pure Roman ancestry of the Romanians and the need to reawaken this Latinness after centuries of Slavic, German and Magyar influence. The most visible such influence was the fact that Romanians wrote their language in Cyrillic, an alphabet developed specifically for Slavs. For centuries Old Church Slavonic was the liturgical language of their Orthodox Church, persisting into the eighteenth century. From 1791 the clergy had hoped to have Romanians recognized as the fourth 'nation' in Transylvania to no great effect, with the established Magyars, Szeklers and Saxons having no intention of diluting their privileges.[37]

Rural Slovak, Serb and German commoners were similarly absent of a voice in Hungary's political institutions, although the Orthodox Serbs had ecclesiastical autonomy that their clergy saw as the basis of the community's existence.[38] Even Hungarian cities, most with a strongly non-Magyar character, had a weak voice in the diet. The only exceptions were the Saxon nation in Transylvania—whose elites were divided over the question of union with Hungary—and Croatia. As a once-independent kingdom tied to the Hungarian crown for centuries, the precise nature of the relationship between Croatia and Hungary was a subject of perpetual debate. Croatia had its own diet called the Sabor, but its nobility and political institutions were deeply intertwined with their Hungarian counterparts. While many nobles were happy to think of themselves as nothing but Hungarian, others resented the notion that Croatia was merely 'a part of Hungary, which needs to listen to its mother-country'.[39]

Ahead of the 1832–6 Hungarian diet, Croatia's chosen delegate to the upper house, Count Janko Drašković, penned an influential *Dissertation, or Treatise* which called for rapid national renewal, warning that 'we are in the centre of Europe, East and West threatens us, the first by the darkness … the second by the brightness, which still cannot be gazed by the feeble eyes of our people'.[40] Drašković was a leading patron of the Illyrian movement and gave political weight to Ljudevit Gaj's Pan-Slavic linguistic and cultural activities. What they and their many collaborators ultimately wanted to see was the creation of an 'Illyrian' (south Slavic) nation-state within the Habsburg Monarchy based on the 'state right' of Croatia (that is, the claim that its sovereignty was not a mere historical relic, but something embodied in its own unique national culture, history and political institutions). They wanted to see the 'Triune Kingdom' of Croatia, Slavonia and Dalmatia, the port city of Fiume (Rijeka), the Military Frontier, and Slovene-inhabited territories of Austria all integrated into this single 'Illyrian' entity.

In reality, this Illyrian movement was the product of a few largely German-speaking urban centres in northwest Croatia, principally Agram (Zagreb), Karlstadt (Karlovac), and Warasdin (Varaždin).[41] Just as Hungarian politics in the 1840s was increasingly defined by the rivalry between Széchenyi's spirit of moderate reform and Kossuth's Romantic radicalism, Croatian politics was being transformed by tensions between the patriotic Illyrianists and pro-Hungarian 'unionists' interested above all in the defence of feudal privileges. The latter founded their own Croatian-Hungarian party in 1841, matched by the official founding of the Illyrian Party that same year. Tense elections for the three Croatian county assemblies followed the next year. The triumph of the Illyrian Party in all three provoked a storm of outrage in Hungary, with panicked nationalists portraying it as part of the long-feared Pan-Slavic conspiracy. To diffuse tensions, Vienna banned the use of the Illyrian name. But Hungarian and Croatian delegates clashed like never before over linguistic questions at the 1843–4 Hungarian diet. Magyar made its final triumph in becoming Hungary's sole official language, and to rub salt into the wounds it was ordered that this be applied to Croatia too. Zagreb county elections in 1845 were marked by unprecedented clashes when a protest against alleged voter fraud turned violent and thirteen nationalist protesters were shot dead by the army.[42]

Most Germans—even within the Habsburg Monarchy—were entirely ignorant of events in Hungary. It was a foreign country to them and the

Slavs in general simply unimportant—a non-entity in world history, as Kant and Hegel had both dismissed them.[43] But those who did confront Central Europe's predicament of interweaving identities understood that national movements were not always complementary, and that their competing ambitions might even result in conflict. The first generation of German patriots had developed a philosophy that celebrated all that was peculiar, specific and vernacular. The next generation had implemented those ideals and helped the various nations of Central Europe elevate their vernacular cultures. Now the generation after was being forced to contend with the political implications of this whole cosmopolitan nationalist endeavour.

In his 1843 pamphlet *Is Austria German?*, the prolific Bohemian liberal writer Franz Schuselka addressed head on the question most likely to be on the minds of German nationalists when it came to the Habsburg Monarchy. While he acknowledged that Austria was a majority Slavic state, he did not accept sheer numbers as the most important criterion for determining the true national character of a land. Excepting the 'Frenchified nobility' that was in any case a 'dead branch on the tree of national life', the hereditary provinces of Austria—the Bohemian lands and Austrian duchies—represented 'a truly and entirely German country' thanks to the predominance of German *Bildung*. For him, the leading nation everywhere was represented by its educated bourgeoisie, something which Slavs lacked, hence their underdevelopment. Austria, which had lost its purpose with the end of the Holy Roman Empire, needed to find a new one, and for Schuselka that was to pursue 'genuinely German' politics, which in practice meant the integration of all of Central Europe under Austrian auspices through the spread of German culture.[44]

Schuselka's book was not the work of an isolated Slavophobe, but just one manifestation of liberal nationalist German attempts to deal with their 'Austrian question'. Paul Pfizer was even more explicit in his 1845 book *The Fatherland*, depicting a great confrontation between Germany and 'Russian Slavdom' as inevitable and thus calling for proactive German colonization of Hungary to serve as Germany's eastern bulwark. Following countless writers before him, he predicted the eventual dominance of Slavs in Hungary and argued the only way for Hungary to protect itself against this Slavicization was to strengthen its German element instead.[45] The *Völkerwanderung*, he noted, was not yet complete. The threat from Russia was nothing less than the 'subjugation and annihilation of the German world by the Slavic'.[46]

Such anti-Slavic paranoia inevitably had the greatest effect in Bohemia, where Slavs formed the majority but where the German language and culture of a considerable minority predominated. The dominant self-conception of Bohemian identity since the late Enlightenment was one that accommodated both Slavs and Germans within the framework of the shared kingdom. The promotion of this identity had driven the revival of the Czech language as well as interest in Bohemian history and patriotism. Outside of the kingdom, or amongst German liberals within it, this tended to be seen as a curiosity rather than something that implied Bohemia was not German. The Augsburg *Allgemeine Zeitung* placed news from Bohemia or Moravia in the 'Germany' section, while the native Bohemian Kuranda's *Grenzboten* showed little to no interest in the Czechs even as he wrote about their country as a natural part of Germany.[47] But the revival of Czech had given Slavic nationalists confidence that in turn terrified more chauvinistic German nationalists, with their conflicts playing out in the public sphere for all to see.

Josef Leonhard Knoll, a professor of history at Prague's university, had incessantly denounced nearly every Czech national endeavour over the course of the 1830s to the imperial authorities. He attacked the first volume of František Palacký's *History of Bohemia* and urged Vienna to suppress it before it created 'thirteen million Slavs burning with national fanaticism and hatred against the Germans'.[48] While Palacký portrayed Bohemian history as defined by the duality of its Slavic and German elements and had a tendency to embellish early Slavic history, it was hardly a work of Slavic fanaticism.[49] Vienna understood this, responding to complaints about Czech nationalism from the mayor of Prague himself by saying: 'Slavism is allowed unlimited freedom so long as it remains within the limits of the law, refrains from interfering in the jurisdiction of the governmental authorities and does not descend into political delusion'.[50]

German-speaking Bohemian liberals like Kuranda and Schuselka dreamed of a German nation-state of which Bohemia and Austria would simply be parts. They saw their movement as one common to all those in the German Confederation. Czech nationalists, by contrast, shared the view of patriotic aristocrats that Bohemia was more akin to a sovereign kingdom that should be given wide-ranging autonomy within the wider Habsburg Monarchy, with Bohemia, Moravia and Silesia ruled together as the lands of the Bohemian crown. Prague was their intellectual centre, hosting several cultural institutions that helped cultivate and spread Czech literacy, by the 1840s finding a growing public amongst literate priests, students and civil servants in major cities as well as smaller towns in eastern Bohemia.[51]

On top of this, Czech nationalists had a strong awareness of belonging to a greater Slavic whole, even if by the 1840s rising Slavic national consciousness was producing not Pan-Slavist convergence, but ever more literary standards and ever more conflicts. For example, Vuk Karadžić's vernacular standard was effectively rejected by the Serbian economic and cultural elites in Hungary. The community was dominated by a conservative Orthodox clergy that thought of their community primarily in religious terms, seeing Karadžić's linguistic innovation as a dangerous secular invention and clinging to the liturgical 'Slavo-Serb' language. Something similar occurred when a young generation of Ruthenians (Ukrainians) at the Greek Catholic seminary in Lemberg (Lviv) sought to develop a vernacular with phonetic orthography for the Ruthenians of eastern Galicia. Traditionalists associated with the Greek Catholic Church rejected such innovations, hoping to retain elements of the liturgy in any new standard.[52] Even the Slovenes could not agree on a single standard, with books published in four distinct Slovene alphabets with varying regional popularity.[53]

Perhaps the greatest blow to Kollár's life work came from his fellow Slovak Ľudovít Štúr. A generation younger, Štúr attended the Lutheran Lyceum in Pressburg and then went on to study at Halle where he became acquainted with the work of German philosophers and the works of Dobrovský, Kollár and Šafařík.[54] As the young Štúr matured, he came to see the Czech standard used by his fellow Slovaks—especially the Protestant minority to which Štúr, Kollár and Šafařík all belonged—as too detached from the common speech of the people it was meant to serve and instead advocated for the separate standardization of Slovak. His codification undertaken in the early 1840s took place within a Pan-Slavist framework, seeing Slovaks as a Slavic 'tribe' and their speech as a 'dialect', but was a rejection of Kollár's four-standard language. Kollár despised Štúr's standard as stinking 'of the stable and the tavern' but could do little to stop the growth of Slovak separatism from a common Czechoslovak literary language.[55]

The Czech journalist Karel Havlíček—who was six years younger than Štúr—was even more thoroughly disillusioned with the whole foundations of Kollár's project. Disabused of his youthful Pan-Slavism by a prolonged stay in Russia, he argued in a series of articles published in early 1846 that Slavic reciprocity was unworkable and that the four 'main tribes' of the Slavic nation were in fact four totally separate nations. 'Our country is not Slavdom, but Bohemia, Moravia, Silesia and Slovakia'. He held Pan-Slavism and cosmopolitanism in equal reproach, arguing that nobody 'could be a true cosmopolitan, since anyone who professed to love all loved nobody'.[56]

No Slavs under Habsburg rule differed so much from the others as the Poles, who generally would have agreed with Havlíček that they formed their own distinct nation, though they would have been unlikely to share his disdain for cosmopolitanism. Indeed, Poles were perhaps the most cosmopolitan of all European nationalists. Their repeated revolts against the three powers that partitioned the Polish-Lithuanian Commonwealth from 1772–95 provided fodder for Romantic nationalist idolatry and sent thousands of Poles into exile across Europe. Whether living in France, Germany, Russia, or Galicia, they seemed to share a common purpose in the restoration of the old Polish state—the 'Christ of nations' as the exiled poet Adam Mickiewicz put it—as part of the general struggle of European nations for freedom against autocracy.

Even decades after the partitions had wiped Poland-Lithuania off the map, Polish high culture continued to dominate the lands of the former commonwealth. These included the vast expanses of most of today's Ukraine, Belarus and Lithuania, where the peasantries were overwhelmingly non-Polish but most landowners identified as Poles even if they in fact had diverse origins. Moving up in the world as a commoner in most of the Habsburg Monarchy entailed adopting German language and culture, but in Galicia things were different. There even Austrian bureaucrats sent to administer the province on behalf of Vienna were often irresistibly drawn to Polishness, becoming overtly sympathetic to the Polish cause, marrying Polish women and watching their children become Polish nationalists.

The largely noble and aristocratic Polish nationalists in Galicia and Prussian-ruled territories thus saw their place in Central Europe as little more than a temporary inconvenience. 'Central Europe' indeed did not even factor into their thinking as a concept.[57] The failed anti-Russian revolution of 1830 shifted their attention to Austrian Galicia and Prussian-ruled Posen, where they plotted revolutions in conspiratorial societies. Finally, in February 1846, their long-planned uprising took place. It began near the city of Tarnów in western Galicia, where—unlike in the largely Ruthenian (Ukrainian) east—the peasantry was entirely Polish-speaking. But the attempts of nationalist nobles to rouse the peasantry even while promising an end to serfdom instead provoked an anti-noble revolt. Hundreds of nobles in the Tarnów-area alone were murdered and their manor houses burned to the ground, with the unrest spreading across western Galicia over subsequent weeks. The nationalist revolt was easily crushed—while the planned uprising in Posen was foiled by the Prussian authorities and its ringleaders arrested—and its supporters left reeling, blaming Austrian bureaucrats for allegedly turning their peasants against them. But their serfs, it seemed, felt they had little in common with those they saw as their oppressors, even if they may have shared the same Slavic tongue and Catholic faith.[58]

For Italian nationalists, just like their German counterparts, the Polish struggle for independence was celebrated as part of the cosmopolitan struggle of nations against Europe's reactionary monarchical regimes. Indeed, much like the Galician and Posen Poles, most Italians in the Habsburg Monarchy seemed like strangers to Central Europe. After 1815 the Habsburgs had tightened their grip on northern Italy. They directly annexed the territories of the old Venetian Republic, combining those on the Italian peninsula with Lombardy to create the new Kingdom of Lombardy-Venetia. Minor Habsburgs ruled the remaining duchies of Parma, Modena and Tuscany, while the Papal States were effectively under Habsburg protection.

Going back to Maria Theresa, Italian territories (that is, those part of geographic Italy) under Habsburg rule had always been treated as distinctly Italian even as Vienna had sought to integrate other crownlands into a single centralized state. German never became a language of importance in Lombardy-Venetia and the primacy of Italian language and culture was never under question.[59] To rule Italy, the cradle of so much of Europe's cultural and religious heritage, conferred a special kind of prestige that made it an end unto itself. Even in Dalmatia and Istria, places in the eastern Adriatic where urban centres were dominated by Italians and the hinterland by Slavs, this Italian cultural hegemony was permitted and institutionalized by the Habsburgs and not overturned in favour of German. All this meant for Italian nationalists was that the Habsburgs became the clearest enemy for the entire nation to rally against, immortalized in the 1847 'The Song of the Italians' which later became Italy's national anthem.

Poles, Italians, Germans, and Hungarians were all celebrated by European liberals as progressive 'historic' nations whose struggle for freedom was destined to shake the aristocratic establishment to its core.

The same was not true for 'unhistoric' nations like Czechs, Croats, Slovenes, Slovaks, Serbs, Ruthenians, and Romanians, who were instead scorned as mere 'remnants of peoples'—as Marx put it—whose national movements were cast as little more than tools of reaction.[60] Nor did this framework make clear what role the most disadvantaged of all Central European peoples—the Jews—were meant to play.

The Jews had ancient roots in Europe and an equally ancient history of persecution at the hands of their Christian neighbours. By the late eighteenth century, about half of the Jews in the world lived in the Polish-Lithuanian Commonwealth, which was remarkably tolerant by European standards.[61] The few Jews scattered across the Holy Roman Empire and Hungary by contrast lived mostly in small, extremely restricted communities, with the notable exception of wealthy 'court Jews' who served princes as bankers, moneylenders, or suppliers. Mayer Amschel Rothschild was one such figure, who in the late eighteenth century used his position serving the prince of Hesse-Kassel to rise out of the narrow confines of the Jewish ghetto of Frankfurt and found one of Europe's preeminent banking dynasties. Most Jews were nowhere near as lucky, forced to comply with often odious restrictions regulating their movement, place of residence, and relations with the Christians around them.

The partitions of Poland-Lithuania, the Jewish Enlightenment, Emperor Joseph II's 1782 Edict of Toleration, and the Napoleonic Wars and their consequences totally transformed this old state of affairs. By the early nineteenth century Jews in many urban centres of Central Europe were increasingly involved in secular forums of Christian society, though countless legal restrictions remained, which meant they were not legally considered equal to their Christian counterparts. Integration was strongly supported by the movement of Reform Judaism that emerged in Hamburg before spreading southwards to influence Jewish life in Berlin, Vienna and the other cities of the Habsburg Monarchy. Reform synagogues effectively mimicked Christian forms of worship, introducing German prayers and sermons, organs and choirs, and omitting prayers that marked Jews out as a separate people.[62]

Many established Jewish communities reacted strongly against this movement, holding fast to conservative forms of 'Orthodox' Judaism and rejecting Jewish integrationism or assimilationism. Beyond theological questions, the dispute between reform and Orthodox Judaism revolved around deep questions of Jewish identity. In Central Europe more broadly, the Jews were thought of primarily neither as a historic nor unhistoric nation, but in terms of a 'Question'. In the 1840s this 'Jewish Question' had become a hotly debated topic in the German public sphere, stimulated in part by a thriving Jewish press that included many German-language periodicals devoted to questions of Jewish interest.[63]

At root was the basic question of full Jewish emancipation and its potential consequences. If Jews were to be treated as equal to Christians, would they then become members of the same nation? Or would they always remain distinct? Proponents of Jewish distinctiveness often invoked old anti-Jewish stereotypes, while believers in the possibility of Jewish assimilation invoked liberal ideals of civic equality to argue that Jews could be equally patriotic Germans, Hungarians, Poles, and so on even while retaining their distinct faith. They wanted first and foremost to be recognized as equally worthy human beings, then as citizens, and only then as Jews.[64]

* * *

On a cold and rainy Berlin morning in April 1847, Prussia's great constitutional experiment got underway. Three years earlier, the Romantic King Frederick William IV had finally recognized his monarchy was in an 'unhealthy' state and had announced that a 'united diet' would meet within three years to approve new loans and taxes. The aim was to put the monarchy on a sounder financial footing to help fund a massive expansion of the already booming railways.

The weather was a good reflection of the mood of the country at large. A series of poor harvests caused by the same potato blight that brought famine to Ireland were a source of widespread hunger and rural despair. Rising grain prices then brought inflation, further immiserating the poorest of households. The Augsburg *Allgemeine Zeitung* published harrowing reports of bodies strewn across roads in Upper Silesia, where people were being forced to 'eat grass, the potato plants, bran, or the pea straw, stolen from the fields and spiced with herring gruel'. To add to the general sense of misery, an industrial recession would soon give rise to a fully-fledged financial crisis, temporarily stopping the country's industrialization in its tracks.[65] The representatives of Prussia's provincial estates, many of whom were liberals, wanted a government that responded to the severe challenges of the day. What they got instead was Frederick William reiterating his opposition to constitutions, announcing he would 'never allow a written piece of paper to come between Our Lord in Heaven and this country'.[66]

Already at the beginning of the 1840s, the frustration of Central European societies with the ineffectual, autocratic and chaotic nature of the governments that ruled over them was driving educated men and women to oppose their own princely states. Some were even driven to the radical republicanism espoused by the likes of Karl Marx, whose views were so extreme they could only be expressed far away from the German Confederation. In June 1847, many of these exiled republicans met in London for a secret congress that resulted in the establishment of a Communist League. Its statutes written later in the year by Marx called for nothing less than 'the abolition of the old bourgeois society based on class conflicts, and the establishment of a new society, without classes and without private property'. The idea would form the core of *The Communist Manifesto* that Marx was commissioned to write with his close collaborator Friedrich Engels, published in February 1848.[67]

In 1841 Andrian-Werburg had warned that Austria was standing on the precipice of a revolution. That was before the crop failures, the hunger, inflation, and 'pauperization' that affected everyone from peasants to factory workers to students, problems by no means limited to the Habsburg Monarchy.[68] The years since Andrian-Werburg's warning brought more crises, more criticism, more exasperation, but no change of course. Lajos Batthyány—the leader of a Hungarian opposition that had only grown bolder as the decade went on—echoed Andrian-Werburg when he warned in a speech to the upper house of the Hungarian diet in December 1847 that the only supporters the government had left were bureaucracy and bayonets.[69]

PART II

THE PRIDE
1848–1918

6

THE LOST PARTITION

In January 1848, a revolution broke out in Sicily against its autocratic Bourbon regime. It inspired an uprising in Paris a month later that started as a protest against repressive government measures but soon spiralled out of control. The French king Louise Philippe was forced to abdicate on 24 February. Unlike the first French Revolution, in which years passed before a republic was declared, this time it took place on the very same day as Louis Philippe's abdication.

News of the revolution in Paris reached Vienna on 29 February. That same day, a mysterious poster appeared on the city's Carinthian gate announcing that, 'In one month, Prince Metternich will be overthrown. Long live constitutional Austria!'[1] Excited citizens gathered into coffeehouses day after day as more news trickled in. Louis Philippe's abdication, the declaration of a French republic, demonstrations in Baden. There, a petition presented to the government penned by the radical republican Gustav von Struve had articulated what became known as the 'March demands': the replacement of standing armies with peoples' militias, freedom of speech, trial by jury, and the calling of a German national assembly.[2] Similar demands were presented to other German princes as they cowered at the sight of masses in the streets, many rapidly consenting to some of the March demands and appointing liberal 'March ministries'.

The authorities in Vienna appeared paralyzed as Austrian liberals followed in the footsteps of their foreign and German counterparts. A petition signed by 3,000 officials, lawyers and professors demanding, amongst other things, a parliament with legislative powers was drawn up. Liberal members of the Lower Austrian diet endorsed this call, warning that the very integrity of the monarchy was at stake. Amidst the growing tumult, a speech given to the Hungarian diet by Lajos Kossuth on 3 March began to circulate in Vienna in German translation. It condemned Habsburg absolutism as a 'pestilent air' which 'dulls our nerves and paralyses our spirit'. The only solution was far-reaching liberal reform in the entire monarchy—including enfranchising the urban middle classes—which in Hungary would be accompanied by de facto independence.[3]

The revolution in Austria came to a head on 13 March. Large crowds gathered outside the Landhaus where the Lower Austrian diet was in session. Random members of the crowd emerged to make impromptu speeches before one Tyrolean read out Kossuth's speech to rapturous cheers. Watching with nervous terror, the diet sent a small delegation to court asking for moderate reforms to diffuse the situation. But violence then broke out between the crowd and military that left dozens dead as the streets descended into chaos. Sensing the way the wind was blowing, Metternich handed in his resignation and slipped out of the city. As he fled, the feeble Emperor Ferdinand promised a constitution and the abolition of censorship.

On 15 March, a steamer set out from Pressburg with István Széchenyi, Lajos Kossuth, Lajos Batthyány, and other Hungarian political leaders on board to present a petition asking for a series of reforms. They wore ceremonial national dress and national cocardes. Even the Anglophile Széchenyi traded his usual umbrella for a ceremonial scimitar. They arrived in Vienna to delirious scenes. The revolution there had gone further than anyone had expected. Meanwhile, unbeknownst to the travelling Hungarian leaders, in Pest young radicals marched on the city hall and forced the municipal council to agree to a set of twelve liberal demands. On their second day in Vienna the Hungarians were received by Ferdinand, their king. For Széchenyi, it was a painful scene. The disabled monarch pleaded to the Palatine of Hungary, Archduke Stephen: 'I beg you, please don't take my throne away!' By the evening, he had given in to all the Hungarian demands, consenting to the formation of a liberal ministry under Batthyány and to unconditionally ratify any legislation passed by the diet.[4]

When Prussian King Frederick William IV received the news of the revolution in Paris, he was aghast. 'Satan is on the loose again', he remarked. He brought troops into the streets of Berlin even as the city stayed relatively quiet. Only when news of Metternich's fall reached Berlin did mass demonstrations follow, forcing the king to lift censorship, recall the united diet, and appoint a liberal ministry. Huge crowds gathered in front of the palace on 18 March to celebrate, but chaos ensued when shots were fired (for unclear reasons) and clashes between the army and demonstrators left hundreds dead, injured and imprisoned. The king ordered the army out of the city in response, and on 21 March attempted to further placate liberal opinion by announcing his support for a united Germany, riding through the streets of Berlin draped in the national black-red-gold colours that until recently were seen as a dangerous revolutionary symbol.[5]

By then the creation of a constitutional German nation-state was already in motion. The efforts of southwest German liberals to organize the first all-German elections were endorsed by the diet of the German Confederation, which officially recognized the black-red-gold tricolour as the confederative flag. On 2 April it repealed all the repressive measures passed since 1819.[6] The new Hungarian government meanwhile passed a raft of liberal and nationalist legislation in late March and early April (the 'April Laws'), approved in Vienna and capped off by the king's visit to Pressburg on 10 April, when he declared his wish 'from the depths of my heart [for] the happiness of my loyal Hungarian nation'.[7]

With bewildering speed, a wave of revolutions had transformed Central Europe. Amidst the widespread revolutionary joy there was little indication of the challenges faced by liberals in reconciling their cosmopolitanism with their nationalism in the years preceding 1848. Delegations from across the Habsburg Monarchy were joyfully greeted in Vienna, the theatricality of it all reinforced by the national costumes worn by the various nationalities to display their patriotism.[8] The semi-official *Wiener Zeitung* reported with pride in mid-March that thanks to the revolution 'the brotherhood of all the nations that are united under Austria's sceptre had been sealed'.[9]

On 17 March, the burial of five students killed in the revolutionary violence even brought together the Carniolian Catholic preacher Anton Füster and the liberal Rabbi Isaac Noah Mannheimer in what Füster later described triumphantly as 'the Old and the New Testament [marching] together under the banner of freedom'.[10] In Berlin, revolutionaries freed 254 Poles interned there since the abortive 1846 rising. They immediately formed a Polish legion of the National Guard. Its leader waved the German tricolour in front of cheering crowds.[11] The Polish National Committee formed in the Prussian city of Posen stressed the common revolutionary struggle of Poland and Germany just as Prague liberals demanded a common German-Slav front.[12] Even the Hamburg-based Franz Schuselka, author of the chauvinistic 1843 pamphlet *Is Austria*

German?, was touched: 'Germans, Hungarians, Slavs and Italians are joyfully joining hands for the great work of political and human redemption ... We all have the same goal—freedom—we all have the same external enemy—servitude'.[13]

The German Reich being planned in Frankfurt was supposed to encompass the whole of the German Confederation, which included much of the Habsburg Monarchy and its many predominantly Slavic lands. The Kingdom of Hungary represented much of the rest of it. German and Hungarian nationalists meanwhile endorsed the creation of Polish and Italian nation-states, both of which would have been built out of the remaining Habsburg lands. The creation of German, Hungarian, Polish, and Italian nation-states seemed to imply the Habsburg Monarchy would simply disappear off the face of the earth.[14] But it soon became apparent that the notion that the Habsburg Monarchy could be partitioned without resistance was far-fetched. For all their concessions, monarchs and their armies were not ready to unconditionally give in to the revolutions. Nor were nationalists as aligned as they might have initially seemed.

Already on 26 April the Austrian army crushed a minor uprising in Krakow after Polish nationalists attempted to turn it into a hub for revolutionary activity. In Posen, after Germans formed a National Committee of their own, cooperation with the Poles broke down and in early May Prussian troops crushed the small Polish army raised there. By then Polish leaders in Galicia were watching with horror as Ruthenians (Ukrainians)—who they largely considered a mere religious group—formed their own Supreme Ruthenian Council, which formulated its own national demands. The most important of these was the division of Galicia into Polish and Ruthenian halves (while clearly recognizing the millions of Ruthenians living in the Russian Empire as their own, too).[15]

Conflicts between national movements were particularly concerning for the new Hungarian government. Josip Jelačić had been appointed *ban* (viceroy) of Croatia in late March after a hastily assembled National Assembly in Zagreb demanded his appointment. His blend of Croatian patriotism and Habsburg loyalism would garner him the plaudits of Croatian nationalists but the scorn and suspicion of radicals across Europe. He refused to recognize the authority of the Batthyány government, instead demanding Croatia be given equal status to Hungary in the wider Habsburg Monarchy.[16]

Representatives of non-Magyar nations were not opposed to the April Laws but saw them as insufficient for the support of their own national development. In May Slovaks, Serbs and Romanians all had mass assemblies that articulated wide-ranging demands for national autonomy. Beyond wanting their languages to be used in schooling and administration, they envisioned fundamental changes in the structure of the Hungarian kingdom for their own national benefit. Slovak leaders called for federalization on a national basis, Serb leaders demanded their own autonomous crownland of Vojvodina in southern Hungary, and Romanian leaders rejected the union of Transylvania and Hungary that was soon to come into effect.[17]

Slovene preferences for a strong Austria led Germans in Styria to found a German Nationalist Association to protect 'German interests'. An Association of Germans from Bohemia, Moravia and Silesia was similarly created to protect the 'badly threatened interests of Germans'.[18] For the German liberals preparing their first national parliament in Frankfurt, Bohemia presented their greatest nationalist challenge. They took it as a given that Bohemia would be a part of the new German nation-state. Ignaz Kuranda even suggested they invite the distinguished historian František Palacký to join the pre-parliament.[19]

Palacký was well-known in Germany and had travelled across the country in the 1840s meeting with prominent professors and writers. They were aware that he represented some vague group of people known as the Czechs, but they had little awareness of who exactly these Czechs were and even less so why they should not want to be part of Germany.[20] In a widely publicized letter, Palacký wrote that while he respected the efforts and sentiments motivating the creation of a German nation-state, he could not participate in it for a simple reason: 'I am not a German ... I am a Bohemian of Slavonic blood'. While his nation had indeed long been ruled by a German house, this tie was purely dynastic, and he emphasized that the 'Bohemian nation' had never been under German rule. Besides this issue of sentiment, he placed himself categorically against the undermining of Austria in any way, whose existence he described as 'a great and important matter not only for my own nation but also for the whole of Europe, indeed, for humanity and civilization itself'. If Austria had not existed, 'it would have been in the interests of Europe and indeed of humanity to endeavour to create it as soon as possible'.[21]

The shocked liberals in Frankfurt sent a delegation to Prague in an attempt to smooth over differences and ensure elections would happen in Bohemia. At its head was the Prague-native Kuranda—one of four Jewish deputies that would ultimately sit in the Frankfurt National Assembly—

who relayed worrying conclusions to the committee on his return. They found the city 'completely changed' by what appeared to be a new *Völkerwanderung*, presided over by a decidedly anti-German clique of traitorous Slavs that hoped 'to build a great Slavic empire, with the Czech tribe serving as its leader'. Germans meanwhile were afraid to show their patriotism for fear of Czech 'terrorism'. In a city 'that was German just a few weeks ago, the Germans do not even find the freedom to speak openly about their interests and wishes in the most modest way'.[22]

The delegation held a meeting with the Bohemian National Committee, which only deepened the gulf between the two sides. It was broken off after the rabid German nationalist Ernst Schilling exclaimed that Prague 'was a completely German city, both in its spirit and learning' and that 'Czech literature was incapable of advancing the cause of liberty, for this concept was alien to the Slavs'.[23] Elections to the Frankfurt National Assembly ultimately took place across Germany, including in German areas of Austria, but not in dozens of Slavic-majority regions of Bohemia and Moravia. The Frankfurt National Assembly claimed authority over them, but they had no representation there. In some Slovene-majority parts of Carinthia and Carniola, too, electors expressed strong reservations about the idea of superseding Austria with a German nation-state, some declining to elect a representative in protest.[24]

Instead, Slavs in the Habsburg Monarchy were preparing for an altogether different kind of assembly, one that had come to Kuranda's attention at the rancorous meeting in Prague: a great Slav Congress. In early April, various Slavic delegations—including prominent figures like Ľudovít Štúr and Ljudevit Gaj—drawn to Vienna with their own petitions met informally to find common ground for cooperation. A clear divide quickly emerged between Galician Poles and other Austrian Slavs. Poles, many themselves nobles, expected a great war with Russia that would require German and Hungarian assistance, while Czechs, Slovaks, Slovenes, and Croats were trying to keep Austria together to protect against German and Hungarian aspirations. To make matters worse, the fledgling Ruthenian national movement was calling for a partition of Galicia into Polish and Ruthenian halves.[25] Poles had a developed political program that had existed for decades. They had several failed uprisings under their belts, and concrete traditions of political independence to look back to. To them, the Pan-Slavic mysticism that prevailed in Central Europe was a mystery. The co-leader of the Galician Poles Florian Ziemiałkowski confided in his diary that 'our situation with respect to the Slavs is dreadful. Broadly speaking, it is very hard to sympathize with them'.[26]

Štúr was undeterred by Galician resistance. After arriving in Prague on 20 April he immediately began organizing a gathering of leading Slavs to discuss issues of common interest. He garnered the support of a diverse array of figures including Karel Havlíček, the Sorb Jan Pětr Jordan, Palacký, Pavel Josef Šafárik, and patriotic Czech nobles. The organizers of the resulting Slav Congress took great pains to ensure the approval of the authorities in Vienna. It was decided early on to exclude non-Austrian Slavs except as guests, and a statement was prepared that acclaimed their 'loyalty to the dynasty and our unalterable determination to remain in the Austrian Empire against public accusations in the Germanic press of Pan-Slavism, separatism, and Russianism'.[27] While the deference shown to the Habsburg authorities succeeded in winning the congress official approval, the same could not be said for German or Hungarian public opinion.

The radical Viennese daily *Die Constitution* warned that the only alternative to Austria's annexation to Germany would be 'Slavicization'. The correspondent of the *Oesterreichisch deutsche Zeitung* asked readers to ponder the fate of 'Germanic Prague' and whether it was a taste of what was to come for Vienna.[28] Worries were not limited to Austria. The *Breslauer Zeitung* warned that the Slav Congress would launch the creation of a 'vast Pan-Slav republic'. Kuranda's *Grenzboten* meanwhile gave a Pan-Germanist riposte to Palacký's musings on the purpose of Austria. 'Austria had sense and meaning only as a German power', its destiny being 'to elevate the Slavic primitives to the level of German civilization, and to bring them as a dowry to [Germany]; from the moment when the Austrian government ... is no longer able to fulfil this calling, Austria collapses and deserves to disintegrate'.[29]

* * *

For the first time in over half a century, Frankfurt was once again at the centre of Germany. On 18 May 1848, 330 delegates from across the German Confederation gathered in the Emperor's Hall of the Römer (Frankfurt's city hall). Portraits of Leopold, Francis, and countless other Habsburg emperors looked down on them from the walls as they began their ceremonial procession to the Paulskirche. This was the city's main Lutheran church, completed only fifteen years before, a symbolic contrast to the Catholic cathedral in which Roman emperors had once been crowned. Black-red-gold banners adorned the church-turned-parliament. In time, a five-meter-tall painting would be hung above the podium showing a symbolic representation of *Germania* holding a sword in one hand and the German tricolour in the other, with broken shackles on the floor and rays of sunlight shining out in the distance.[30]

The well-heeled men were overwhelmingly from the educated middle class: professors, teachers, civil servants, legal professionals, freelance intellectuals. Nonetheless, they provided a striking and unique portrait of Germany. As Wilhelm Zimmermann recalled, one saw deputies from the farthest east of Prussia 'where the Cossack stands guard' alongside Italian-speakers from the southern tip of Alpine south Tyrol; wealthy aristocrats in 'princely garb' rubbed shoulders with farmers who tilled the soil with their own hands; benches were shared by Jesuits, Protestants, Jews, and secular philosophers; those who suffered years of exile in France spoke after men who cut their teeth in pre-March assemblies and conservative nobles who might have opposed both.[31]

Over the weeks and months, this medley of delegates came to be organized into loosely defined political clubs that formed a relatively broad political spectrum. There was a clear 'centre-right' majority of moderate liberal constitutionalists who wanted to defend the March achievements and supported constitutional monarchy. Their main opponents on the 'centre-left' and 'left' generally favoured a stronger parliament and 'sovereignty of the peoples'. Some were even outright republicans, but in general this more democratic tendency had been shut out of Frankfurt.[32]

The latter instead fell back on extra-parliamentary agitation, their efforts largely focused on the most liberal southwest German states and the Rhineland. In the latter, Karl Marx had set up shop and began publishing the *Neue Rheinische Zeitung* on 1 June, a daily newspaper dedicated to spreading the views and ideals of the Communist League. It was one of hundreds of new political periodicals that sprung up across Germany thanks to the abolition of censorship. Through these papers and countless new associations, Germans discussed and debated politics with hitherto unseen levels of freedom, helping the divisions between various political movements and tendencies become clearer than ever. Radicals hoped to push the revolutions forward by harnessing the power of students, workers and the lower-middle class. Constitutionalist liberals hoped to protect the March achievements against the twin threats of reaction and social revolution. Conservatives and reactionaries plotted in the background while Catholics and national minorities mobilized to defend their interests against potential encroachments.

THE LOST PARTITION

As the Frankfurt National Assembly convened, there were far more questions than answers around what exactly the institution would become. Early on, deputies overwhelmingly voted to make their decisions binding on all German states as they set up a cabinet meant to serve as Germany's central government, but they had little power of enforcement without the agreement of German princes. The vast majority agreed that Germany would be a constitutional monarchy. But who would be its monarch?

Habsburgs and Hohenzollerns were natural candidates, but neither appeared willing to unconditionally accept such a role. Even though the Habsburg Archduke John—a Florentine-born son of Leopold II—was elected regent in late June, the relationship of the Habsburg emperor's non-German lands to this new Germany was ambiguous. John's assumption of the role was highly controversial within the family and he in any case had no authority to decide on Austria's relationship to the future Germany.[33] Just a week after the parliament's opening one Viennese deputy hoped to resolve the conundrum by demanding the 'annexation [by the new Germany] of Austrian lands not belonging to the German Confederation'. Above all 'this includes Hungary, as the main country of the German Danube', the overarching goal being the creation of a 'huge, united, free Central Europe [Mitteleuropa] that holds the balance of East and West, between republic and autocracy, with a strong fist'.[34]

Echoing Schuselka's 1843 pamphlet *Is Austria German?*, the Bohemian Count Friedrich Deym similarly insisted deputies recognize that from Bukovina to Dalmatia 'every educated person speaks German; it is only the German element that everywhere brings civilization to the Slavic and Magyar lands'.[35] He saw Germany's mission as being to become a vast Central European power of seventy to a 100 million people that would stand against 'East and West, against the Slavic and Latin peoples, the sea power of the English, and become the largest, strongest people in the world'.[36] In a more conciliatory fashion Julius Fröbel argued for a 'Central European Confederation' with its centre in Vienna in which non-German peoples would be allowed their own statehood.[37] These and other proposals for a 'Central European-German Confederation', 'Central European League of Nations', or a 'United Central European States' found no great resonance.[38]

It was not just linguistic and national concerns that worried deputies, but religious ones as well. As much as deputies spoke of one 'Germany', it would be radically different depending on how it was put together. A Germany without the German lands of the Habsburg Monarchy would

113

have a Protestant majority, but with their inclusion it would be predominantly Catholic. If the Habsburgs included their crownlands outside of the German Confederation, too, this hypothetical Germany would be not only overwhelmingly Catholic, but also one-third Slavic, in addition to the millions of Hungarians, Jews, Romanians, Italians and others suddenly drawn into this bewilderingly diverse 'Germany'. It would have been a mockery of the very idea of a nation-state.

Debates about the potential extent of the future Germany were inevitably couched in the language of great power politics and historical missions. The idea that Germany would one day have to fight a major war—especially with Russia—was taken as a given. Germany was treated both as a potential bulwark of a generalized Occident but also as a unique power in its own right. The right-wing deputy Wilhelm Wichmann saw its 'world historical mission' as 'self-assertion against a despotic East and a republican West'.[39] The left-wing deputy Carl Vogt, meanwhile, spoke of a 'holy war' which would one day be fought 'between the culture of the West and the barbarism of the East'. He emphasized that this would not be a 'cabinet war' fought by princes like in the past, but a 'war of peoples'.[40]

Commonplace too were predictions that Europe would in the future be divided into families of peoples, as Jacob Grimm suggested in his *History of the German Language* published in June 1848. In a few generations, Grimm said, only Romance-language-speakers, Germans, and Slavs would share power in Europe, and so he hoped that Germanic peoples would be able to set aside their differences.[41] Ernst Moritz Arndt echoed these sentiments in parliament later in the year, also with reference to the Danes, who he hoped would act as a 'brother people with us so that no eastern barbarism and savagery now threatening us from all Slavic and Gaulish peoples can force its way in'. Even England, he went on to say, 'is a people of the same blood and [will] not abandon us in a great struggle of nations'.[42] Others followed similar arguments to, for example, call for an alliance with Hungary to help Germany 'one day conquer the German Danube' and create a 'strong Central Europe' which would in the future unite with other Germanic nations to face down the Romance and Slavic peoples.[43]

Optimistic nationalists like Schuselka pointed out that 'millions of Slavs' both inside and outside of German areas had been Germanised 'not with force, but rather through the spiritual power of German *Bildung*'. Who was to say 'that this will not subsequently happen with other millions!'[44] But the majority of deputies had little desire to bring tens of

THE LOST PARTITION

millions of non-Germans into a nascent state already struggling to deal with a paltry few million. The Prussian Georg Beseler even opined that unlike 'entirely German' Prussia, 'Austria is not a German power, it only has German components'.[45]

* * *

At 9am on 2 June 1848, dozens of leading Slavs from across the Habsburg Monarchy convened at the National Museum in Prague. They made their way into the heart of Prague's old town for a religious service before moving on to the Žofín Palace situated on a small island in the Vltava River. A huge banner in Habsburg black and gold conspicuously decorated the hall in which they convened.[46] The moderate doyen of Pan-Slavism Pavel Josef Šafárik gave an uncharacteristically rousing speech to close out the day. 'Brothers!' he exclaimed, 'either we in fact purify ourselves and demonstrate that we are capable of liberation or we will be transformed in a flash into Germans, Magyars, and Italians … The path from oppression to liberation is not without struggle: either victory and unshackled nationhood, or an honourable death and after death, glory!'[47]

The Slav Congress' participants were tasked with the vague brief of discussing how Slavs could best cooperate with each other and other European nations to further their common national wellbeing. Discussions were divided into three sections, one for Czechs, Slovaks, and Moravians, one for south Slavs, and one for Poles and Ruthenians. The litany of disagreements showed precisely why there would be no Slavic revolution. Slovenes questioned why south Slavic discussions were so dominated by 'Illyrians'. Poles and Ruthenians clashed over Galicia. In both the Polish-Ruthenian and Czecho-Slovak sections the question of whether Austria's preservation should really be their primary goal loomed, as did questions around the primacy of Pan-Slavism over individual Slavic identities.

Germans and Hungarians may have still had their internal political differences in 1848, but they had at least developed strong senses of cultural unity rooted in their respective unitary literary standards. Slavs had never achieved such unity except in the theories of the Pan-Slavist movement. Unlike the Germans and Hungarians, they also lacked a common state on which to build a political identity. In a sense, the purpose of the Slav Congress was to find such a political centre in the Habsburg Monarchy. The abandonment of Hungarian state identity by the Croats and the young Slovak nationalist movement led by Štúr took them a step in this direction but left the Poles unconvinced. Even Štúr found himself disheartened by the linking of 'state' and 'national' right—implying traditions of statehood were necessary for a nation's existence—by the Czechs and Poles, which in his eyes was no different from the argument used in Hungary to justify Magyarization.[48] Failing to come to a common view on the political meaning of Pan-Slavism, the only thing that emerged from the congress was a manifesto addressed to the nations of Europe, which rehashed a familiar set of Slavic grievances and demands alongside some general liberal principles.[49] The congress was cut short when an unrelated uprising broke out in Prague as more radical revolutionaries attempted to take control of the city. It was brutally crushed by the military commander of the city, Prince Alfred Windischgrätz—whose wife was killed by a stray bullet on the first day of unrest—and the whole of Bohemia was soon put under martial law.[50]

The Slav Congress and its violent aftermath fanned the flames of anti-Slavic sentiment in Germany. Alfred Meissner, a deputy from Moravia, related his experience passing through Prague on the way to Frankfurt to the *Kölnische Zeitung*. This well-known German city was transformed into a 'gaudy, big caravansary, boasting of strange foreign guests from the East ... Wherever one looked—un-European uniforms, rattling swords, fluttering feathers of the Slav tricolour ... How did these lovely barbarians get to civilized German Prague?' Even Prague residents also took part, to 'provide proof that they could look no less un-European and barbaric than their South Slavic brethren if they wanted to'.[51] It is little wonder then that Kuranda's otherwise staunchly liberal *Grenzboten* celebrated Windischgrätz's reconquest of the city.[52] Windischgrätz for his part legitimized and mythologized his local coup by 'uncovering' a Pan-Slavist conspiracy aimed at turning Austrian Slavs against the Germans and Hungarians. They had supposedly even been planning a massacre of rich Germans and Jews in Prague only stopped by his intervention.[53]

In the German press Slavs were mocked for supposedly needing to use German because they could not understand each other. The radical Viennese journalist Sigmund Engländer showed how intertwined such mockery was with outright hostility when he wrote that their need to use German was 'the most telling proof that they are firmly rooted in Germandom and that to dislodge them from this natural ground would simply mean their destruction'.[54] First reports from the opening caused a fiery debate in the Frankfurt National Assembly, with speakers demanding immediate military action. The assembly tasked a special Austro-Slav committee with investigating the Slav Congress, presenting its conclusions to the parliament on 1 July. It denounced supposed Pan-Slavist designs aimed at turning Austria into a 'great Slav empire' and demanded Austria take immediate steps to ensure elections took place there.[55]

Germany's troublesome Central European entanglements inevitably influenced the proceedings in Frankfurt. While it was generally agreed that individuals of whatever background would have equal rights in the new state, German linguistic, and therefore national predominance was taken for granted. German nationalists—like their Hungarian counterparts—hoped minorities would be content with all the new rights conferred by citizenship and assimilate to the dominant national culture. Liberal Jews indeed embraced this idea, seeing the revolution as a way to finally bring full emancipation. The liberal Viennese Rabbi Adolf Jellinek even warned of the fanaticism of 'Czechomania' and 'Pan-Slavism' while celebrating the inherent cosmopolitanism of German nationalism.[56] The Frankfurt National Assembly saw it as superfluous to differentiate between citizens and Germans, eventually specifying: 'the German people consists of the citizens of the states that form the German Reich'.[57]

In both Hungary and Germany, politicians frequently deferred to their western counterparts on such questions, emphasizing that a modern nation-state could only have one language of politics and public life.[58] Amidst debates on Bohemia's status, Arndt asked the assembly rhetorically: 'What would the French say if the Bretons, Basque, and old Ligurian ethnic groups [*Volksteile*] ... declared that [they] wanted to be Bretons, Provençals, and no longer French?'[59] The Frankfurt-based *Deutsche Reichstags-Zeitung* declared in even more belligerent language in the wake of the Slav Congress that Slavs would either be integral parts of the German nation like the Bretons and Alsatians in France, Gaels and Irish in Britain, or 'they are and should be their serfs'.[60] Kossuth envisioned the Slavs, Romanians, and Germans in Hungary in similar terms as comparable to the Bretons in France or the Welsh and Irish in Britain.[61]

Over the summer of 1848, the Frankfurt deputies had a chance to debate these questions openly with direct reference to Bohemia and the province of Posen, which the Prussian authorities had divided in two since their crushing of the nascent Polish uprising in May. In one of the most famous speeches of the parliament, the liberal deputy Wilhelm Jordan dismissed German desires to revive the Polish state as an exercise in 'idiotic sentimentality' and instead called for Germans to embrace a 'healthy national egoism'. He deployed familiar cultural, historical, and naturalistic arguments for German superiority over the Slavs, concluding that 'it is none other than the right of the stronger, the right of conquest'.[62] On 28 July the parliament voted on a motion to declare the partition of Poland a 'shameful injustice' and the 'sacred duty of the German people' to help reconstruct an independent Poland. Barely 100 voted in the affirmative while 458 voted against.[63]

Much of the parliament was also souring on Austria by then, questioning both its commitment to the March achievements and its suitability for integration. A further uprising in Vienna in May had caused the court to flee to Innsbruck and left the Habsburg capital in the hands of revolutionaries. Windischgrätz's occupation of Bohemia and Field Marshal Joseph Radetzky's reconquest of northern Italy in July and August showed the emperor was not averse to making use of the military forces still under his control. On 22 July an Austrian parliament convened in Vienna after elections held across the non-Hungarian parts of the Habsburg Monarchy. Tasked with producing a constitution for the whole Habsburg Monarchy, its work and ambitions seemed to directly contradict those of the German National Assembly. It was decidedly multinational and nearly a quarter of the deputies were farmers or small landowners. This brought Austria's German character into question while providing a negative example of what a multinational parliament would look like. The Württemberg envoy in Vienna reported incredulously that the man appointed chairman by seniority was a peasant from Bukovina who spoke only 'the Romanian dialect'. Germans were firmly in the minority, and the 'mythical times of the Tower of Babel seemed to be returning'.[64]

* * *

Hungary's revolutionary parliament opened on 5 July in the old capital of Buda. The euphoria of the March days had long since faded. Emperor-King Ferdinand I had acquiesced to the Hungarian government's demands that the rebellious Croatian Ban Jelačić be dismissed, but he simply ignored the command, instead being given dictatorial powers by the assembly in Zagreb and remaining steadfast in his demands that Croatia be separated from Hungary entirely. To make matters worse, the Serbs in southern Hungary had joined his revolt.[65]

Relations between Vienna, Zagreb and Budapest were tense throughout the summer. Despite Ferdinand's early support for the liberal April Laws, many in his court saw the Hungarian Revolution as the primary threat to the integrity of the Habsburg Monarchy. Conversely, many in the Hungarian government were hoping for non-Hungarian parts of the monarchy to be absorbed into German, Italian and Polish nation-states, thus leaving it independent by default.[66]

It was therefore not entirely clear where the Hungarian government's loyalties lie: with 'the Revolution' as a pan-European phenomenon, or with the Habsburgs. Széchenyi, who had always believed in working with the court rather than against it, viewed the looming confrontation with despair as the ruin of his life work. 'Magyaria is buried, and history will remember the Hungarians as a rotten, despicable people' he wrote in his diary. On 31 August, the Austrian court officially informed Hungary that it considered all the revolution's achievements to be in violation of the pragmatic sanction. A delirious Széchenyi attempted suicide.[67] On 11 September, without explicit commands but with vague assurances from the court, Jelačić invaded Hungary. As he told his soldiers, in order to preserve the monarchy 'I must act on behalf of His Majesty, if necessary against His Very Highest Will'.[68]

The following day Batthyány resigned and Lajos Kossuth took a leading role in preparing the country's defence, touring the countryside to raise volunteers. The nationalist fervour being unleashed as Hungarians defended their homeland from invasion was clearly not appreciated by the court. When Franz Philipp von Lamberg, freshly appointed by Ferdinand as commander of all Austrian military forces in Hungary and Croatia, arrived in Buda on 28 September, he was quickly seized by a mob and lynched on the bridge between Buda and Pest. This incident tipped the scales at court in favour of a full-scale reaction, and on 3 October 1848 Ferdinand announced he was dissolving the Hungarian parliament and declaring martial law in the country, appointing Jelačić supreme commander of Hungary. Kossuth now officially became prime minister, dedicated to defending the revolution and all its achievements.[69]

In Germany the tide was turning too. Viennese revolutionaries led by radical students and democrats revolted against the court's confrontation with Hungary, murdering the minister of war and taking control of Vienna as the parliament and court (which had returned to the city in August) fled to Moravia. This final stage of the revolution was crushed by Windischgrätz and Jelačić at the end of the month at the cost of thousands of casualties. Martial law was instituted and a shocked German liberal public watched as the radical deputy Robert Blum—who as a member of the Frankfurt National Assembly they expected to have immunity—was tried and executed by a military court. Soon after, the Prussian King Frederick William IV forced the Prussian National Assembly in Berlin into the provincial surroundings of Brandenburg an der Havel—a prelude to its dissolution a month later.

Despite its Moravian exile, the Austrian parliament pressed ahead with its most important task: drafting a constitution for the Habsburg Monarchy. But what exactly was 'Austria'? Was it a single state, a collection of crownlands, a union of nations, or of states? No simple answer was forthcoming when the constitutional subcommittee debated the matter in January 1849. Palacký put forward the most radical proposal, arguing that 'nations' should become the basic units of the empire, but this was eventually rejected by the majority who continued to see historic crownlands as the basic building blocks of the monarchy.

Yet here too there was no agreement on the exact numbers, on whether they were true 'states' as the Bohemians argued, or on their relationship to nations. The subcommittee contained three Slavic Bohemians and three German Moravians. One of the latter complained on the second day that there should be a German Bohemian represented there too, to which Palacký's future son-in-law František Rieger riposted that the 'Bohemian' (Czech) element in Moravia and Carinthia would have to be represented. 'Moravia knows no Bohemian element, only a Moravian one!' the German Moravian countered. 'I will not get into the distinction between Czechs and Moravians, but I believe I know the "Moravian" language better than my Moravian colleague [here]' Rieger shot back. In late January 1849 a constitutional subcommittee discussed a draft that defined Austria as 'an indivisible constitutional hereditary monarchy formed out of' thirteen 'independent crownlands'. Ultimately, they recognized that on the local level nationalities should have their own representation. This Kremsier constitution was in the end ignored by the court, which proclaimed its own 'irrevocable' constitution in March 1849 (which was revoked on 31 December 1851).[70]

Amidst the revolutionary tumult, Ferdinand had finally been convinced to step aside in December 1848. He was replaced by his eighteen-year-old nephew Franz Joseph. Like his great-grandfather Leopold before him, Franz Joseph had inherited a realm on the brink of collapse. In January 1849, Kossuth's government withdrew to Debrecen as it faced war on several fronts, but in April his armies mounted a successful reconquest of Pest. He declared independence and the deposition of the Habsburgs, turning the Hungarian Revolution into a true war for independence. It took Russian intervention on behalf of the Habsburgs to defeat the Hungarians. Their country was placed under martial law and Kossuth and other revolutionary leaders escaped into exile, many condemned to death as traitors in absentia and hung in effigy. Those who failed to escape, including thirteen generals and former Prime Minister Batthyány, were executed by the Austrian army, becoming martyrs for the cause of Hungarian freedom.

As German courts regained their confidence, they crushed the revolutionary centres one by one. In October 1848 the Frankfurt National Assembly had voted to include Habsburg lands as part of the German Confederation in the new Germany on the condition that they could only be unified with non-German lands in a purely personal union. This was rejected out of hand by the Austrian Minister-President Felix zu Schwarzenberg, who emphasized that the Habsburg Monarchy was indivisible, rejecting the pretentions of both Hungarian and German nationalists. In March 1849 he went even further, demanding that the *entirety* of the Habsburg Monarchy enter the new Germany, little more than a negotiating tactic on the way to his envisioned restoration of the German Confederation. The Frankfurt National Assembly had no intention of building a multinational 'Reich of seventy million' as Schwarzenberg proposed, narrowly voting instead to elect the Prussian King Frederick William IV as German emperor.[71]

It fell to Eduard von Simson as president of the national assembly to undertake the great mission to bring the crown of Germany to its elected head. Simson and his delegation were received warmly in Berlin and formally met with the king on 3 April 1849. While the trust the German people had placed in him 'touched him deeply', he pointed out that he could not accept the crown without 'the free consent of the crowned heads, the princes and free cities of Germany'.[72] The stunned deputies suffered through a formal state dinner with the blasé king, who acted as if their offer meant nothing and belittled their authority.[73] In private, he was even more disparaging of what he called an 'iron collar of servitude' and a crown 'of dirt and clay'.[74] Little did they know that the Romanticist king spent the early months of 1848 dreaming not of constitutions, but of a fantastical historicist scheme that would have seen an elected 'King of the Germans' serve as head of government to a Habsburg 'Roman Emperor'. The highest crown in Europe, he thought, belonged to Vienna, not Berlin.[75]

Though Frederick William rejected the crown of a constitutional German Reich drawn up by the liberal-dominated Frankfurt assembly, he had not abandoned the notion of German unity entirely. He instead began to negotiate directly with other princes to see if a new constitutional arrangement could be agreed upon which would bind Germany's princely states together while warding off future revolutionary challenges. In late May 1849 the kings of Prussia, Saxony, and Hanover presented a constitution which was meant to be a compromise between proposals including and excluding Austria. It would create a more unified Prussian-led Germany with Austria loosely attached through a confederal arrangement. Frederick William continued to insist over the summer that he wanted 'to make Austria mightier and greater than ever before'.[76] Austria's young Emperor Franz Joseph and his minister-president were unconvinced.

This led to a brief and strange period in which there were two competing German projects, both being pursued by princes rather than 'the people'. The Prussian-led Erfurt Union held elections in January 1850 and its parliament assembled in March, consisting of deputies from a dozen German states that had stuck with the scheme until then. Meanwhile Austria acted as if the old confederation had only been suspended, supported by the other German kingdoms and a spattering of smaller states. The two sides came to the brink of war in late 1850, but Prussia and Austria came to an agreement in the end, pushing the question of the German Confederation to a conference in Dresden the following spring, at which it was duly revived with only a few modifications.

In the first half of the nineteenth century writers, princes, nobles, scholars, and politicians had developed radically different visions of what Central Europe was and what it should become. Conservative establishments clung to a system of territorial states under continued nominal Habsburg leadership. While many Germans wanted to see a strong and united German nation-state, many more were content with a loose confederal tie binding together a collection of states that had no shortage of local identities and interests they were unwilling to abandon in the name of some abstract German nation. 'Austro-Slavists' hoped the entire Habsburg Monarchy could become a Slavic state, institutionalizing the German-Slavic duality of Central Europe. Provincial nobles hoped to reconcile the two, to assert national rights within the wider framework of a conservative order where nation and state remained congruous. Hungarian reformers espoused a different model, effectively wanting to do in Hungary what they pleased while leaving Germany to its own devices. They envisaged a German-Hungarian or possibly German-Hungarian-Polish-Italian Central Europe in which the aspirations of

THE LOST PARTITION

smaller Slavic nations were ignored entirely. In 1848 all these visions collided, with regional, local, national, and imperial dynamics all inherently intertwined. But despite the wealth of visions, and the millions of pages of pamphlets, books, letters, newspapers, and magazines, the political solutions would ultimately be decided by the same people as always: aristocrats, princes, Habsburgs, and their loyal servants.

7

INTO THE FURNACE OF MODERNITY

At approximately 10:30 a.m. on 28 July 1857, a train rolled into Trieste. It had passed across marshes and rivers, through dramatic mountains, and along the glistening Adriatic before arriving at the brand-new Trieste Central Station. Six hours earlier, Emperor Franz Joseph had boarded it in Laibach for its inaugural journey. Construction had commenced nearly a decade before, with engineers forced to battle rivers, dry karst mountains, and powerful Adriatic winds to bring it to fruition. For the first time ever, the great imperial capital of Vienna was connected by rail to Austria's principal Adriatic port. It was an achievement worthy of the emperor's presence.

He was accompanied by four Archdukes, two ministers, the chief of police, and countless other dignitaries including Prussia's trade minister, Saxony's finance minister, and representatives of dozens of shipping and rail companies from other German states. As he laid down the keystone on the viaduct, the emperor announced 'with great satisfaction' the completion of a work which 'after overcoming the greatest difficulties, is now complete and which, I hope, with God's help, is destined to increase the prosperity of the provinces of My Empire and especially that of my most faithful city Trieste'. The opening of the line was accompanied by two days of festivities.[1]

While the grandest of transformations hoped for in 1848 had failed to take root, the political, social, and economic forces that had been unleashed ensured that Central Europe would never be the same. The princes and their coteries continued to rule, but they were forced to reckon with the fact that stability could not be guaranteed by returning to pre-1848 methods of governance. Instead, they would use the tools of the modern state to regulate their societies and economies, bringing modernization, economic growth, and even a degree of political liberalization with the broad aim of ensuring stability through prosperity. The French Revolution had turned enlightened Central European regimes towards conservatism, but the home-grown revolutions of 1848 had turned conservatives into radical reformers willing to accept the social and economic transformations that marked their industrializing and urbanizing societies as long as power ultimately remained in their hands.

Even though governments were appointed from above, they were largely 'pragmatic, centrist coalitions', more likely to be led by former revolutionaries than reactionary nobles.[2] One of the most important pragmatic centrists, Otto von Manteuffel (Prussia's interior minister in 1849 and minister-president from 1850 to 1858), told the Prussian parliament in 1849 that returning to the 'decaying conditions of the past' was like 'scooping water with a sieve'.[3] Austria's Minister-President Felix von Schwarzenberg similarly remarked in a letter to Metternich in 1850 that whoever sought a return to the pre-revolutionary era was seeking 'the impossible'.[4]

The phantom 'Austrian Empire' that had been declared in 1804 as a theoretical title to make up for the loss of the Roman imperial one was suddenly declared a single unitary state by Emperor Franz Joseph in 1851. Language, education, law, and much more were to be made uniform irrespective of the history, identity, or political traditions of each province. No central parliament was left standing, with ministers appointed by and responsible only to the emperor. Provincial diets were transformed from bodies based on estate privileges to ones based on property, income, and education.[5] But real power lay with the governors imposed from above and the bureaucrats tasked with implementing their policies.

Prussia became a constitutional state in 1848–50, retaining the elected assemblies that had been established in the revolutions—including a central parliament—but with a highly restrictive franchise that was expected to return a reliably conservative majority. The lower house was elected on an indirect three-class franchise based on the amount of tax one paid.[6] So the richest were disproportionately represented, but the well-off bourgeoisie nonetheless retained a forum for political participation. Ministries were appointed by and responsible to the king, however, not the central parliament.

The transformations experienced by German states in the 1850s are perhaps better termed accelerations, with social and economic developments that were present before 1848 merely being given new stimulation. Unlike before the revolutions, when the growth of industrial capitalism was limited by feudal economic restrictions, in the 1850s and 1860s it was unleashed thanks to the loosening or outright banishment of restrictions on the freedom of labour, enterprise, and capital. The Prussian state statistician Karl Friedrich Wilhelm Dieterici commented in 1855 that at 'the present time industry is penetrating human affairs with such power and significance that a comparison with earlier conditions is scarcely possible'.[7] However, there were considerable variations in its impact across Central Europe—not so much between 'Germany' and 'Austria' as between various interconnected economic regions 'created by concentrations of natural resources, market relations, and local social structures', all linked to an international economy in different ways.[8]

The increasing awareness of Central Europe's place in a globalizing world economy led by Western European states was part of what inspired Austria's minister of trade Karl Ludwig von Bruck to propose the unification of Austria with the rest of Germany into a single economic union. By 'means of this commercial unification of Central Europe Austria' would, 'thanks to her central position between East and West, North and South … necessarily become the centre of the great international trade movement'. The state would be strengthened internally and its connection to Germany solidified like never before.[9] Originally from the Rhineland and only ennobled in 1844, Bruck was an enthusiastic economic liberal who had made a name for himself in Trieste. He spearheaded the foundation of the Habsburg Monarchy's first business paper, the *Österreichischer Lloyd*, in 1833, with the company behind it becoming the first to introduce regular steamships into the Adriatic.[10] In his short tenure as trade minister from 1848–51 he laid the groundwork for Austria's far tighter economic linkage with the rest of Germany, even if his dream of a Central European economic union would never come to fruition.

He oversaw the formation of a German-Austrian Telegraph Organization in 1850 alongside an Austrian-German Postal Union. German states—Austria included—also loosened passport requirements in 1850 (though the Habsburgs would only abolish internal passport requirements in 1857).[11] A litany of other treaties saw restrictions on trade and movement loosened and in 1857 Austria even entered into a currency union with *Zollverein* (German Customs Union) states, though this did not last.[12] Having humiliated Prussia by forcing it to abandon its nascent Erfurt Union, Austria's position in Germany looked unassailable at the head of a union of conservative princes and their modernizing governments.

Countless German emigres settled into Austrian state administration, showing that Vienna remained attractive as a place to make one's career. Franz Joseph married his Bavarian cousin Elisabeth (familiarly known as 'Sisi') in 1854. Chairs in branches of German jurisprudence and literature were established at Austrian universities, and the German language itself was imposed uniformly on the whole country as the language of administration and higher education.[13] The government hoped to de-politicize linguistic questions by making German the common imperial language—as Joseph II had done before—while allowing the free development of vernaculars in the private and cultural sphere.

A modern system of gymnasiums (secondary schools) was set up by the first minister of education Leo von Thun. In 1860 reforms of elementary schools followed, and within a decade teaching was professionalized. Attempts were made to turn teachers from suspect revolutionaries into those who 'plant in [pupils'] young minds ... true fear of God, loyalty to the King, love for the Fatherland'.[14] Nonetheless, school reforms were interpreted by many liberals as something to celebrate. The idea of universal, uniform, compulsory education was a crucial stepping stone to the building of a responsible, educated citizenry. In Saxony's new school law this aim was made explicit, the child of every Saxon guaranteed in state schools 'general human and civic education', garnering the praise of the liberal-minded Maximilan Robert Preßler.[15] Austria, by contrast, seemed to liberals to be taking a huge backwards step when it turned to the Catholic Church. It signed a concordat with the Holy See in 1855 that ceded to the church wide-ranging powers over education. But the concordat also represented a step forward insofar as it prevented the state from meddling in the internal affairs of the church, thereby affecting a broader separation between church and state.[16]

The procession of German visitors to Prague in 1848 that had lamented the Slavic flood into a once-German city had little to worry about in the 1850s. Reinforced by Thun's educational reforms and its imposition as an empire-wide administrative language, German remained dominant in cities across the Habsburg Monarchy. Recalling his childhood in 1840s and 1850s Prague, the Czech journalist Servác Heller remarked that it was a 'German city' where 'all who adhered to fashion Germanized, for German was in vogue'.[17] Even Agram—despite the fact that Croatia was not and had never been a part of 'Germany'—gave Antun Nemčić and countless others the impression that it was 'more a German than Croatian city'.[18]

Streets and shopfronts bore German names. German print media predominated. Booksellers in Agram and other northwest Croatian cities were generally themselves from German-speaking lands and many even refused to stock Slavic titles. Musical societies, theatres, and clubs were almost all German, the default language of educated social discourse. As had been the case before the revolutions, Croatian nobles and educated commoners alike were not just fluent in German but often produced literature in it.[19] That included 'national awakeners' like Ljudevit Gaj, Ivan Kukuljević-Sakcinski, and Antun Mihanović. Indeed, German had long been taught in Croatian schools not as a foreign language, but as if it were a native one.[20]

Ofen-Pest too, briefly united as Budapest by the revolutionary government in 1848, became a stage onto which the Austrian regime projected its own vision of Hungary. The Hungarian National Museum was painted Habsburg yellow and all public buildings had to paint their entrances in the dynastic black and gold. Hungarian red-white-green lettering and national costume were banned. Those who insisted on putting up Magyar signs had to provide German translations below.[21] These were only the cosmetic changes. Countless clubs and associations were also shut down and the government strictly supervised publishing, education, and social life to ensure Germanophone and loyalist tendencies in society were favoured. Institutions controlled by local notables often proved willing collaborators.

The quasi-official *Pester Zeitung* celebrated Pest's transformation into a modern German city 'almost at the level of Vienna, inhabited by the same human stock, of the same nation according to blood and language'. Magyars could not claim the city as their own, another article claimed, because 'all of the splendid buildings, the splendid shop windows, the splendid vaults! This is *German* culture! *German* efforts have been made, and *German* spirit has flowed, just as the city's inhabitants are German'.[22] It was a view that would no doubt have been encouraged by the sizable community of those who came from the Austrian half of the monarchy, amounting to eleven per cent of the two towns together in 1857.[23] According to the 1850 military census, about half of the population was German and only a third Magyar, the rest made up of Jews, Slovaks, Serbs and others. Even in Pest Germans still outnumbered Magyars by a narrow margin, while in Ofen there were nearly four times as many Germans as Magyars.[24]

The spirit of economic liberalism was so strong that some even thought nationalism had had its moment. The German-Bohemian Theodor Pisling argued that in stark contrast 'to the less or not at all cultivated' European East and Southeast, to say nothing of 'the Orient', in the 'highly civilized parts of West and Central Europe' national peculiarities were being eroded to such a degree that it was fruitless to speak of ethnographic nations by 1861. The 'separatist action' of the 'harsh ethnographic idea of nationality' stood in stark contrast to 'the progress of culture and civilization'.[25] Such a dismissal of Slavic national projects was hardly new amongst Austro-German liberals, but notable in the 1850s was that many erstwhile Slavic nationalists agreed. Count Leo von Thun—once an enthusiastic proponent of the Czech language and participant in the Slav Congress—expressed doubts about the abilities of even the most developed Slavs, the Czechs, 'to further spread *Bildung* in their native language'.[26] The Czech historian Adolf Maria Pinkas advised his son to give up on the Czech national idea in the mid-1850s, arguing that 'particularist tendencies' had become 'mere utopias', while another Czech historian admitted to his friend 'that [he] considered the Bohemian national cause to be lost'.[27]

Carl Freiherr von Czoernig, the semi-official ideologue of what would come to be known as Austrian 'neo-absolutism', noted in his famed assessment of the period, *Austria's Redesign 1848–1858*, that he 'who wishes to judge the current conditions in the whole of Austria according to the circumstances of 1847 would come upon an enormous anachronism; he would be standing with his judgements closer to the year 1758 than to the year 1858'.[28] It was an exaggeration, but not an extreme one. With meticulous statistical detail, he described the endless list of areas where the centralized government had left its mark. Hungary's backwards dirt roads were transformed into modern paved ones. The postal system was modernized and expanded so that by 1856 it could handle nearly triple the volume of mail than in 1848. The electric telegraph system grew ten-fold, connecting the whole monarchy like never before, and so on.[29]

Nothing was more important to and emblematic of the industrialization of society than the railroad. The opening of the Vienna-Trieste railway came just twenty years after Austria had received its first line. By the beginning of the neo-absolutist regime, the network had expanded to 1,300 kilometres. A decade on that figure would be 3,000 kilometres, with Hungary's network alone exploding from just 200 to 1,700.[30] The growth of the railways in other German states was no less impressive. Prussia's network grew from 3,285 kilometres in 1848 to 7,504 in 1860. This made up a majority of non-Austrian Germany's nearly 15,000.[31]

While these networks had facilitated 614 million kilometres of individual passenger travel in 1848—which included the journeys of many revolutionaries—this had more than doubled by 1860. Just 168 million freight transport kilometres had meanwhile become 1,675 million.[32]

Such increases were observable in just about every facet of industrial life. In Prussia, output in mining and metal production doubled between 1850 and 1860. The boom in coal production—which fed the expansion of railways and factories—was particularly impressive. The Ruhr produced 1.7 million tonnes of coal in 1850, but 11.6 million by 1870. Silesia meanwhile went from producing 975,000 tonnes to 5.8 million.[33] In the Kingdom of Saxony, between 1856–61 the amount of horsepower provided by steam engines increased by the same amount it had between the arrival of the first steam engine in 1822 and 1856.[34] By 1856 three-quarters of steam engines in use in the kingdom were produced there, and by 1861 a large proportion of factories exclusively used steam power.[35] Between and within German states there was a great deal of variation in both urbanization and industrialization. Saxony rapidly became the most industrialized German state while Hanover remained largely rural and sparsely populated. Much of Prussia remained the same even as the Rhineland and Silesia became world centres of industry. In the Habsburg lands Bohemia led the way, but even there industrialization spread in stages.[36] Hungary lagged behind, while peripheral provinces like Galicia and Dalmatia remained largely untouched by the great transformations of the era.

Industrialization brought increasing financialization of the economy, with the rise of private investment banks and other financial institutions facilitating large-scale investments.[37] Increased revenues brought into the coffers of German states by this burgeoning industrial and financial economy were not always enough to make up for growing, debt-financed expenditure. One way or another, more and more money was needed to expand the size and reach of state education, administration, and especially the military. Austria doubled its expenditure on domestic administration between 1847 and 1856, much of it going towards an expanding system of district offices that required courts and offices to be built across the monarchy.[38] It was symbolic of a desire for efficient uniformity in governance that was hardly unique to the Habsburgs. Before 1848 Prussia had 144 different provincial systems of property tax, four totally different criminal law systems, and several different systems of municipal administration.[39] By 1866 not just Prussia, but every German state had a uniform criminal code, usually accompanied by a wide range of other judicial reforms.[40] The path to full equality of all citizens of a given state proceeded slower and unevenly, with Jews in particular still facing a litany of restrictions after 1848, but the direction of travel was clear enough.

Franz Joseph's so-called Silvesterpatent of 1851 rolled back many revolutionary achievements, but serfdom remained abolished, restrictions on Jews were loosened, and citizens were more equal before the law and market than ever before. This contributed in no small part to the rapid urbanization that would become a feature of late-nineteenth- and early-twentieth-century Central European life. While major cities like Vienna, Berlin, Hamburg, and Ofen-Pest had been steadily expanding in the years leading up to 1848, in the decades after they were transformed into true modern metropolises. Sleepy provincial towns became bustling regional hubs linking peripheral regions to the rest of Europe thanks to the growing rail networks.[41] Vienna and Berlin had populations of around 200,000 around 1800. A century later they were both nearing two million. Hamburg began the nineteenth century with 132,000 inhabitants but finished it with 768,000. For the towns of Ofen, Pest, and Alt-Ofen that would later be amalgamated into Budapest, the figures were 50,000 and 800,000.[42]

These were new cities both in scale and kind. Their growth from small, medieval corporate entities into industrial metropolises required local transformations no less dramatic than those that were occurring on the state or imperial level. To take the example of Central Europe's second-largest city: in the 1850s Berlin's powerful police chief Carl Ludwig von Hinckeldey established a regular fire brigade, public baths for the poor, a street-cleaning system, new waterworks, planted trees throughout the city, and introduced its famous public notice columns. And this was all tangential to his main achievement of a reorganized police force with regular street patrols.[43] While not every Central European city experienced such modernization as early as the 1850s, by the end of the century even somewhere like the provincial Bohemian town of Budweis would have seen the installation of gas streetlamps, a modern sewage system, and all the other trappings of a modern city.[44] The provincial Hungarian city of Temesvar even received an electric tramway in 1898, two years after the Hungarian capital had opened the first metro line in continental Europe.[45]

Perhaps nothing symbolized the transformations of urban space more than the tearing down of old city walls and the amalgamation of multiple old entities into single administrative units. Modern Zagreb was created only in 1850 with the unification of the towns of Gradec, Kaptol, and other surrounding settlements. The unification of Budapest followed in 1873. Berlin tore down its old city walls in 1860. The dismantling of Vienna's city walls was ordered by Franz Joseph three years prior. In their place Vienna laid down an elegant ring road—the *Ringstrasse*—which transformed the urban landscape. This tied into the other great symbol of new Central European urbanism, which was the sprouting of impressive civic buildings like schools, courts, theatres, museums, and city halls on or along pleasant squares, parks, and boulevards, from the great imperial capital Vienna all the way down to the smallest German, Hungarian, Croatian, or Galician town.

With the tearing down of city walls, the medieval city gate was replaced symbolically by the railway station. These structures had originally been modest and functional, confined to the outskirts of cities. But from the middle of the century, with the proliferation of railroads and their increasing centrality to life, railway stations became increasingly elaborate and—aided by the outwards expansion of cities—central.[46] They were surrounded by cafes, shops, and hotels catering to all manner of clientele. Inns serving beer became a common sight across the Habsburg Monarchy, generally with German or Czech names to prove their authenticity.[47] While beer had been brewed in the region for centuries before the nineteenth century, it took on an entirely new scale and significance thanks to the social and industrial innovations of the nineteenth century.

At the century's beginning, brewing was a highly localized industry strictly controlled by guilds and traditional regulations. Only gradually did Enlightenment scientific advances find their application. As in every guild-dominated industry, most brewers were extremely resistant to changes that could only threaten their privileges. They perhaps also believed that beer brewing was an art acquired through practical experience rather than a science that could be perfected and commodified. By 1899 a writer in *Agramer Lloyd* could lament with romantic nostalgia that brewing 'had lost its coarse poetry', by then a careful business run by technicians and industrialists rather than the master brewers themselves.[48] One of the earliest proponents of applying enlightened methods to beer brewing, the Bohemian Franz Andreas Paupie, wrote dramatically of the 'envy, hatred and persecution' suffered as a result of his controversial views. His 1794 two-volume treatise *The Art of Beer-Brewing* nonetheless became a seminal text in the development of modern Central European beer-brewing.[49]

In England it was already becoming an industrially-produced good, encouraging Anton Dreher and Gabriel Seldmayr to visit in 1833. They were friends and owners of two of the largest Central European breweries in Vienna and Munich, respectively. Industrialized brewing pioneered in England would find fertile soil in Bavaria, where it was already one of the most important industries and where light 'lager' beers fermented in vast underground cellars would become a regional—later global—standard. Thanks to advances in artificial refrigeration, brewers across Central Europe began to mimic the subalpine Bavarian conditions to produce similar lager beers, powered as the century went on by coal-fired steam engines, transported on railroads, and financed by new financial instruments.

In the early 1840s a Bavarian brewer was brought to Bohemian Pilsen to develop what would become the world-famous Pilsner beer. A few years later the burghers of Budweis decided they needed a modern brewery and produced a similar light Budweiser lager of no less renown.[50] By the 1890s the Budweis brewery owned refrigerated warehouses as far as Hamburg, Berlin, and Zagreb to aid distribution.[51] Industrial lager breweries based largely on Bavarian and Bohemian technologies would spread across Central Europe by the end of the century, making the industrial brewery and its tall chimney a common sight in countless small towns and cities.[52]

Buildings across Central Europe spoke a strikingly familiar architectural language. There were local flourishes, but the cultural, economic, political, financial, and administrative relationships between urban centres were such that architecture produced more commonalities than distinctions. For most of the nineteenth century architects in the Habsburg Monarchy were trained exclusively in Vienna,[53] the largest city in the whole region, a cultural capital both for Habsburg subjects and Germans more broadly, as well as the site of the region's most ambitious architectural redesign. In other words, there were no autochthonous Hungarian or Polish models for a modern city.

The case of Friedrich Schmidt is illustrative. Schmidt, who designed Vienna's elaborate neo-Gothic City Hall, led one of the most prominent architectural studios in late-nineteenth-century Vienna. Himself originally from Württemberg, architects from all over Central Europe flocked to Vienna to work under him. From there, they fanned out across the region, replicating his ornate neo-Gothicism far and wide. For example,

Hermann Bollé, a Cologne-native, became the most important architect in Croatia, restoring or building countless iconic structures including Zagreb's Cathedral and Mirogoj Cemetery. Pest-natives Imre Steindl and Frigyes Schulek were similarly important to Hungary more broadly, the former designing its famously elaborate parliament building and the latter restoring Buda's beautifully ornate Matthias Church.[54]

Between 1870 and 1913 the Vienna firm Fellner & Helmer built forty-eight majestic theatre buildings between the Rhine and the Dnieper, most billed as 'national' or 'state' theatres.[55] Their work extended to palaces, hotels, department stores, and other buildings emblematic of the modern city. And the impact of Central European architecture went well beyond the limits of the historical Central Europe. Fellner & Helmer were called across the Carpathians into Iasi (modern Romania) and Odesa (modern Ukraine) to build similarly characteristic theatres that still stand to this day. This was symptomatic of a wider cultural aura emanating into the Balkans, where over the course of the nineteenth century a series of Christian nation-states were established after freeing themselves from Ottoman rule. Greece, Romania, and Bulgaria would all even find themselves ruled by German princes. Serbia was the exception for having avoided a German monarch, but it was also the country where Central European influences penetrated the deepest.

When it came to modernizing and 'de-Ottomanizing' Serbian state and society, Central Europe consistently provided the models. That went for military dress, ideas of monarchical statehood, legal codes, and even the rebuilding of Belgrade—situated right on the border with Hungary—in emulation of Vienna and its glorious Ringstrasse.[56] The Serbian writer Milan Đakov Milićević noted in 1876 that Belgrade was a city totally transformed from its earlier Ottoman form, where Greek and Turkish were heard more often than Serbian. Now: 'Houses, shops, crafts, clothes and customs—all that is modelled according to that which is seen in the West, to be exact, in our closest neighbourhood'. Indeed, so enamoured was the Serbian youth in Belgrade with the 'closest neighbourhood', he complained, that waiters and journeymen sooner offered their services in German than Serbian.[57]

As standardized textbooks and readers in the Reich and Habsburg Monarchy would tell their students in German, Czech, Croatian, and other vernaculars, that 'closest neighbourhood' was called 'Central Europe'. Some included the Low Countries and largely German-speaking Switzerland in the mix, but all agreed that it was a simple geographic fact that Germany and the Habsburg Monarchy were located in 'Central Europe'. The Reich was the 'main country of Central Europe' one Bavarian reader put it. Austria-Hungary was just 'a part of Central Europe' said an Austrian equivalent.[58]

* * *

Barely 'had we begun to look forward to a better future than it melted away before our eyes like a mist'.[59] The Bohemian Karel Havlíček's eulogy for the revolution, written in 1850, reflected a widespread sense of disappointment amongst erstwhile revolutionaries. After his nervous breakdown, the Hungarian politician István Széchenyi spent the rest of his life in a mental asylum before taking his own life in 1860. Joining Lajos Kossuth and thousands of Hungarian revolutionaries in exile were thousands of disappointed German liberals that uprooted themselves and their families to make a new life elsewhere in Europe or in the New World. But perhaps none were as disillusioned as the Austro-Slavists. Their ostentatious loyalty to the Habsburgs had brought them nothing and the experience of the Slav Congress left little hope for future cooperation. Ján Kollár—having stayed out of the revolutionary upheavals entirely—died in 1852. His lifelong Pan-Slavist collaborator Pavel Josef Šafárik had a mental breakdown and died in 1861. Even the young Havlíček, who was inspired after 1848 to call for a 'smaller ... southwestern or Central European' Pan-Slavism, would find himself forced into exile in Tyrol and died of tuberculosis at the age of thirty-four in 1856.[60]

While not everyone was as enamoured with the 1850s as the propagandists of neo-absolutism, neither were most as despondent as Štúr, Széchenyi, Šafárik, or the thousands of émigré '48ers. In the 1850s associational life survived through various ostensibly nonpolitical clubs and societies. The press too was much freer after 1848 than it had been after 1815, with governments turning to managing public opinion rather than pre-emptively censoring publications. And as was always the case in Germany, the multiplicity of states provided ample space for those whose politics may have been unwelcome in their own home state to remain politically active. Frankfurt's relative freedom turned it into a centre of liberal politics in the 1850s, hosting a variety of democratic and nationalist clubs and associations despite the fact that it was also home to the confederal diet.[61] The more favourable institutional atmosphere meant that by the latter half of the 1850s the tide began to turn against the conservative establishment, with liberals scoring huge victories in representative institutions left standing after the revolutions. By 1862 an exiled revolutionary like Friedrich Kapp could marvel upon his return at 'people's greater independence, their participation in political affairs, economic expansion, and self-confidence'.[62]

German and Hungarian liberals maintained similar views on their respective revolutions. Though they had failed, many liberals felt comfortable working for or with thoroughly reactionary regimes because they could continue to advance their liberal agenda. Many of their values and aims were indeed compatible with the princely state: responsible ministries, budgetary oversight, emancipation of the Jews, freedom of enterprise, secular schooling. But the question of full constitutionalism was much more difficult to square with Central Europe's post-revolutionary constellation. The regularization of political life brought by liberal political and social mores enshrined in a constitution was thought to be the key to the creation of a truly liberal society governed by and for free, responsible men. The movement for German unification on liberal nationalist principles was therefore intimately tied up with such visions of a constitutional polity and society.

For many German liberals it was impossible to imagine such a transformation in their own princely states, which they often saw as the province of small-mindedness and petty princes. The same was not quite true in the Habsburg Monarchy, where constitutional life within a princely state meant the building of a constitutional great power. Nor was it necessarily true in Prussia, a state which Protestant German liberals increasingly looked to as the potential basis for a future united Germany. After all, the princely state reigned supreme, and German history seemed to indicate that it was the only driver of change. This was a view accepted even by most liberals, in no small part because of the failure of the revolutions. The liberal nationalist historian Heinrich von Treitschke observed that for Germans the state was 'a cultural power from which we expect positive achievements in all areas of national life'.[63] Or, as the exiled liberal August Ludwig von Rochau put it in a more distilled form, the 'discussion of the question: who should rule ... belongs to the realm of philosophical speculation; practical politics only has to do with the simple fact that it is power alone that can rule'.[64]

For most archconservatives, the idea that non-nobles, no matter how much income, property, or education they possessed, should be able to dictate to a prince how his country was to be ruled remained anathema.

But even in Prussia, where an influential circle of archconservatives clustered around the *Neue Preußische Zeitung* newspaper (nicknamed the *Kreuzzeitung*) had a direct line to King Frederick William IV through his close friend Leopold von Gerlach, they were forced to contend with the transformed circumstances of the 1850s that left them just one faction amongst many around a weakened king. They could not, for example, stop the king from keeping Otto von Manteuffel on as Minister President from 1850–58. The son of a high-ranking Saxon official hailing from Lower Lusatia, Manteuffel saw his mission as breaking the last vestiges of feudal aristocratic privilege and imposing the uniformity of the state in its place.[65]

This necessarily entailed curtailing the special legal position of the Junker class that had long thought itself born to rule in Prussia while it was simultaneously being undercut by wider social and economic changes. In 1856, forty-three per cent of Prussian estates were already in the hands of non-noble families. By the 1880s they would hold more than two-thirds in East Prussia, that symbolic bastion of Junker privilege.[66] All the while aristocrats continued to dominate the upper reaches of the Prussian state, the officer corps, and the courts as if nothing had changed.[67] This tension between the advances made by bourgeois members of society in the economic sphere and their lack of power would be a continuous source of frustration for middle-class German liberals well into the twentieth century.

Ironically, in what Austria's interior minister Alexander von Bach sardonically referred to as 'the former kingdom of Hungary', it was the nobility that resented the power of the bureaucracy rather than the other way around. Before 1848, Hungarian politics and administration had remained a preserve of the nobility. State administration was understood within this framework of noble traditions and privileges, while bureaucratism was perceived as something entirely foreign. Something 'German'.[68] In the 1850s this foreign, German bureaucracy was suddenly imposed upon the whole of Hungary, reaching deep into the heartlands of the Hungarian nobility. Coming off the heels of a failed bid for independence, it was all but destined to be viewed as little more than punishment.

The struggles faced by Austria and Prussia in the 1850s were largely down to the disparate and conflicting territories and populations they ruled over. Smaller princely states seemingly found it easier to adapt to the new era, spending the 1850s by and large brimming with confidence. Saxony's post-revolutionary government, embodied by Friedrich Ferdinand von Beust, lasted uninterrupted until 1866. It implemented agrarian reforms, passed a belated freedom of enterprise law in 1861, reformed the justice system, expanded infrastructure, and in 1865 introduced the first German Civil Code.[69] Despite maintaining draconian restrictions on the freedom of the press, assembly, and association, the government implemented a litany of liberal policies and allowed liberals to return to parliament unhindered, cowed as they might have been.[70] Modernization had become the raison d'être of conservative governance, and in this regard the government could boast that Saxons had plenty to be proud of. The government-friendly *Budissiner Nachrichten* could proclaim by 1865 that Saxony had no need 'to yearn for Great Powerdom' because unlike Prussia or Austria it had 'a constitutional life ... prosperity, low taxes and good finances'. As a result 'concord reigns between King and people' and 'fantasies entertained by the large states cannot disturb our well-being, for there is room enough in the smallest hut for a satisfied heart'.[71]

Hanoverians could similarly read in their newspapers of all the fantastic achievements of their princely government, of the railways, the growth of industry, and the modernization of urban life. Unlike Saxony, Hanover somewhat strangely did have pretentions to Great Power status. King George V and his circle saw their state as a future maritime power thanks to its favourable geographic position. He referred to his country not as a 'middling state' but as a '*Mittelreich*'.[72] This had consequences for the neighbouring port-city-states of Hamburg, Bremen, and Lübeck. Hanover refused to allow a Paris-Hamburg railway line to be built because its path to Great Power status was allegedly to be paved by the prosperity of its own ports. Saxony played at railway politics too, lobbying Bavaria and Austria not to build direct rail links to Prussia so that it could act as a crossroads between the three most important German states.

As the above partially indicates, patriotism for the princely state was as strong as ever, bolstered by the achievements of the post-revolutionary era. At the 1851 Great Exhibition in London a common *Zollverein* display scandalized Saxon and Württemberg representatives when they found that only the Prussian coat of arms bore a royal crown. 'Württemberg is mistaken for a town' complained its exhibition commissioner. To make up for the slight he proudly raised a banner emblazoned with 'Wurtemburg [sic]'.[73] Princely patriotism was not directed against Germany, but against the pretentions of Austria or Prussia to dominate Germany (and partially against other rival princely states or free cities). It was about loyalty to the dynasty within the framework of a decentralized German nation, rather than asserting that the princely state itself should or could be a totally sovereign and independent nation-state.

The exception was Bavaria. Its King Maximilian II—who had come to power amidst the revolutions and would reign until 1864—was singularly and uniquely focused on the 'elevation of Bavarian national feeling'. He saw this as part of the same process of legitimization through conservative modernization that other states were pursuing.[74] If nationalism was the force of the future, then the survival of the princely state depended on harnessing it. In a circular distributed in 1851, his minister of religion and education decreed how history was to be taught in Bavarian schools. As was traditionally the case, the Wittelsbachs, the Bavarian dynasty, were to be put front and centre, but pride in Bavaria's ancient history, independence, and self-sufficiency were also to be emphasized. A centralized Germany '[contradicted] the German character', and therefore Bavaria through its separateness was in fact as German as could be.[75] The opening of a Bavarian National Museum in 1855 was thus highly symbolic. It represented Bavarian ambitions to be more than just a part of a unitary German nation. In the face of such confident princely patriotism, German liberals could see few avenues to national unity that did not go through the princes themselves. The great question was whether it would be a Hohenzollern or Habsburg prince that led the way, or if all the princes could come together to form a closer national bond by mutual consent.

8

CENTRAL EUROPE REMADE

For the last time in history, a Habsburg led his own troops into war. On 24 June 1859, nearly 300,000 soldiers massed near the Lombard town of Solferino. The battle that followed—pitting Austrian forces led by Franz Joseph himself against France and Sardinia—was the largest on the European continent since the Battle of Leipzig in 1813. Casualties were light, but the consequences enormous. Austria's defeat at Solferino marked the end of centuries of Austrian hegemony on the Italian peninsula, forcing it to cede Lombardy as well as the Habsburg-ruled duchies of Tuscany, Modena and Parma to what would soon become a unified Italian nation-state.[1]

The embarrassment for Franz Joseph was compounded by the fact that his neo-absolutist system was propping up an army it could not even afford. Already heavily indebted before the war, by its end the monarchy was teetering on the edge of bankruptcy. His ministers debated ways to bring the crisis under control over subsequent months, but state finances continued to worsen as it became clear that only fundamental reform could restore fiscal credibility. Ministers, bureaucrats, aristocrats, and even the emperor himself came to recognize that the neo-absolutist system would have to go.

It was little consolation that Prussia was mired its own political crisis. Both leading German powers would spend the 1860s embroiled in constitutional conflicts between conservative courts and liberal oppositions. But one emerged split in two, and the other stronger than ever at the head of a united German nation-state—a stunning achievement which nobody did more to bring about than Otto von Bismarck. Born east of Berlin into an old Pomeranian noble family, Bismarck was, in the designation of one biographer, an Ur-Prussian.[2] He was precisely the kind of provincial

Junker whose social influence was on the retreat in the face of a rising liberal bourgeoisie. This is also what drove him into politics as a young provincial landlord in 1847. A resolute conservative throughout the revolutions of 1848, he emerged on the other side as a confidant of the *Kreuzzeitung* circle. In 1851 he was sent to Frankfurt as Prussia's delegate to the confederal diet, a position he despised as irrelevant but that would make a lasting impression on his vision of Germany.

It was there that he came to believe that Prussian and Austrian interests in Germany were irrevocably at odds; the German Confederation nothing but a feeble barrier to Prussian ambitions. From Frankfurt he watched as the confederation stood inertly through two great political crises that threatened the balance of power in Europe. The first was the Crimean War, in which Austria's vacillating saw it remain neutral and alienate its erstwhile Russian ally, leaving it isolated on the international stage. This opened the door for the second crisis: the Austro-Sardinian war in 1859, which Franz Joseph was goaded into starting himself. Both crises were avidly discussed in a German press that grew more and more vocal as the 1850s went on. There were fears that France might march on Germany next. There were hopes that Sardinia's unification of Italy could be repeated north of the Alps.

Only in 1848 had most German liberals really come to grips with what it meant that Austria was a multinational state. The 1850s showed how its entanglements—in Italy, the Balkans, and Eastern Europe—could threaten the security of Germany itself. By 1859 a group of prominent German liberals decided they had seen enough. They issued a declaration from Eisenach calling for the replacement of the confederation with a centralized nation-state led by Prussia. It was 'the duty of every German man to support the Prussian government to the best of his ability, insofar as its efforts proceed from the assumption that the mission of the Prussian state essentially coincides with Germany's needs and mission and that it directs its activities towards the introduction of a strong and free constitution for Germany'.[3] Later that year they formed a German National Association in Frankfurt to lobby for this '*kleindeutsch*' (lesser German) unification. At its height in 1862–3 it was the largest mass movement in Central Europe.[4]

It was matched three years later by a more conservative, and less successful, German Reform Association that advocated a '*großdeutsch*' (greater German) solution that would have included Austria in any unified German state, generally understood as meaning a federal unification or even just the closer integration of the states of the German Confederation. As Karl Ludwig von Bruck—the former Austrian trade minister now serving as minister of finance—put it in 1859, a 'unitary state' on the model of France or Russia 'contradicts German nature and history to the utmost'.[5] This tradition of 'federal nationalism' was as old as German nationalism itself, endorsed by Goethe and many others throughout the years as the country's natural state, stressed particularly by Catholics, particularists, dynastic loyalists, and conservatives in general.[6] But for the liberal Austrian patriot Bruck the 'greater German' solution had an added benefit. Austria's firm binding to the rest of Germany would put the Habsburg state on a much firmer foundation to carry out its own internal task of spreading culture to the various peoples of the monarchy.[7]

That strengthening the German Confederation would be in Austria's interests was something that Bismarck wholeheartedly agreed with. 'The clinging to the Slavic-Romanian half-breed state on the Danube, the whoring with pope and emperor, is at least as treasonable against Prussia and the Protestant confession, indeed against Germany, as the most despicable Rhenish Confederation', he complained after the supposedly missed chance of 1859. 'To France we can, at most, temporarily lose a province, but we can lose all of Prussia to Austria, now and forever'.[8] Bismarck was no German nationalist. Far from it. He was a Prussian monarchical conservative through and through, one who saw the elevation of the Hohenzollern dynasty and its state as his life mission. But he was notoriously flexible, and his political career would be marked by a series of unexpected alliances. As he liked to put it, deploying his favourite metaphor: 'Man can neither create nor direct the stream of time. He can only travel upon it and steer with more or less skill and experience'.[9]

With neo-absolutism discredited, the main political cleavage at the highest levels of Austrian politics in the 1860s would be between federalists who wanted to see the empire reformed into a loose confederation of autonomous crownlands, centralists who wanted a liberal empire with a single central parliament, and Hungarians who simply demanded their special status be recognized.[10] Franz Joseph leaned heavily towards the federalist position in the October Diploma of 1860. It satisfied some landowners but did little to convince the bankers he needed to finance his state that true structural reforms had placed it on sounder financial footing. He was thus soon forced to lean more towards the centralists in the February Patent of 1861. This called into being a bicameral Reichsrat (Imperial Council) with an appointed upper chamber and elected lower one.

While the lower house was meant to have 343 members, only 203 participated, of whom 130 belonged to one of three liberal factions that would collectively come to be known as the 'Constitutional Party'.[11] These largely Germanophone liberals cast themselves as the sole political force committed to constitutional rule as set out by Franz Joseph in 1860–61. They enjoyed an overwhelming majority in the rump lower house, but also the emperor's own confidence from 1860–65 under the government dominated by Anton von Schmerling, which in their eyes gave them a mandate to build a centralized, liberal state in which German language and culture would predominate. Schmerling was a longtime civil servant who had briefly served as minister-president in the Frankfurt National Assembly in 1848. It was he who, more than anyone, decided the shape of Austria in the years after the fall of neo-absolutism, steering it on this decidedly liberal and centralist course.

The Reichsrat was left a rump largely because the Hungarians refused to participate. Led by Ferenc Deák, Hungarian nationalists insisted that the April laws of 1848 could be the only legal basis for Habsburg rule in Hungary, while Schmerling argued that the failed bid for independence invalidated all previous constitutional arrangements.[12] Deák and most other Hungarian politicians maintained that Hungary was a separate state entitled to a separate constitutional life from the remainder of the Habsburg Monarchy, with all the lands of the Crown of St. Stephen—including Croatia-Slavonia and Transylvania—under its rule. Anything less than this was considered unacceptable.

Such arguments based on 'state right' were taken up by Czech and Croat nationalists too. In 1859, František Palacký along with his son-in-law František Ladislav Rieger emerged as the leaders of the National Party that acted as the political voice of the Czech national movement. While initially working within the confines of the centralist constitutional regime, Palacký and the 'Old Czechs' as they came to be called found themselves increasingly alienated as they waged a fruitless struggle against the Austro-German liberal majority in the Bohemian Diet. In 1863, after proposals for electoral reform were soundly rejected by that Austro-German majority, Old Czech leaders met in Palacký's house and narrowly voted to boycott the central Reichsrat in Vienna. They were joined by a group of conservative Great Landowners with whom they had formed a loose alliance on the basis that both rejected the liberal vision of a centralized Austrian state and instead sought to win recognition of Bohemia's unique state right.

Leading Croatian nationalists of various stripes embraced the idea of state right with equal vigour. The traditional Pan-Slavic orientation of Croatian nationalism was given new impetus by the figure of Josip Juraj Strossmayer. A native of Essek, of distant Austro-German descent, Strossmayer had become a convinced Pan-Slavist in the pre-1848 era while training to become a priest and, by 1847, a bishop. His vision of the Habsburg Monarchy was fundamentally 'Austro-Slavist', hoping to see it reorganized on a federal basis in which a unified South Slav entity would be formed on the basis of Croatian state right. In 1861 he entered politics, acting as one of the founders and leaders of the renewed National Party. Like their Hungarian counterparts and, later, the Old Czechs, Croatian politicians refused to participate in the Reichsrat, asserting that their country had no common affairs with Vienna.[13]

* * *

As in Austria, it was military spending that plunged Prussia into crisis. Wilhelm I, who was serving as regent for his incapacitated brother, watched with horror when in 1858 liberals increased their representation in the Prussian Landtag from sixty to over 200 representatives while Conservative Party support collapsed.[14] He pressed ahead anyway with an expensive army reform bill. A particularly outraged faction of liberals formed the even more obstinate German Progress Party, which then became the largest party in parliament following new elections in 1861. After parliament was once again dissolved for rejecting the army reform bill, the German Progress Party won an even larger victory, facing down a hardline cabinet appointed by Wilhelm, now king. He was despondent and contemplated abdicating before he was convinced by his minister of war to appoint Otto von Bismarck as minister-president.

Coming after such a prolonged crisis, the liberal public largely saw Bismarck's appointment as the last gasp of a desperate regime—he was expected to last weeks, months at most.[15] Certainly not, as it turned out, twenty-eight years. This was especially true after Bismarck's first public appearance in front of the budgetary commission of the lower house. Though he brought an olive branch he had collected in Avignon to symbolize his commitment to bridge-building, his words told a very different story. 'Germany does not look at Prussia's liberalism, but its power', he told them. 'Bavaria, Württemberg, Baden may indulge liberalism, and that is why nobody will assign to them Prussia's role'. Instead, 'Prussia must gather its strength and hold it together for the favourable moment that has already been missed several times'. Then followed perhaps his most famous utterance: it was 'not through speeches and majority decisions that the great questions of the time will be decided—that was the great mistake of 1848 and 1849—but by iron and blood'.[16]

When 'I hear so shallow a Junker like this Bismarck brag about the "iron and blood" with which he intends to subjugate Germany', wrote Heinrich von Treitschke, 'the baseness is exceeded only by the absurdity'.[17] Bismarck's speech was an enormous and unintended faux pas. It made him seem out of step not only with the liberal nationalist public, but with the king who had just appointed him—a king who felt he was under siege by an intransigent liberal opposition, and who was certainly not dreaming of conquering Germany. Bismarck was nonetheless kept on, repaying the king's trust by breaking the constitutional deadlock. He simply governed without parliamentary approval of the budget, exploiting the so-called 'gap theory' that the Prussian constitution of 1850 left sufficient ambiguity for budgetary matters to revert to the monarch. By ensuring the military remained generously funded, Bismarck kept the greatest tool for defence against internal threats as well as the expansion of Prussia's power abroad. Austria's first constitutional government, meanwhile, was slashing its military budget, from 179 million gulden in 1861 to 96 million by 1865.[18]

Were it not for Bismarck, Franz Joseph would have had little immediate reason to fear his northern neighbour. Ludwig von Gerlach expressed established conservative sentiment in describing Austro-German cooperation as the 'vital foundation, the real basis for a German constitution'.[19] Relations between the two states were warm in the early 1860s, encouraging Franz Joseph's mission to reform the confederation into a somewhat livelier political body. For most German states it was more a question of how the princely union should be reformed than if it should be. In October 1861, the Saxon leader Friedrich Ferdinand von Beust officially proposed a reorganization of the German Confederation to the German public. This would have seen the 'third Germany' institutionalized in a triple executive alongside Prussia and Austria, and two assemblies representing governments and parliaments. In trying to satisfy everyone Beust satisfied no one: his proposal was rejected by the other major German states.[20]

Two months later Prussia's foreign minister put forward his own counterproposal of dual-track federalism, with Germany being dominated by

Prussia, and joined with Austria in a confederal arrangement. This was unacceptable both to Austria and the other German states that would have fallen under Prussian domination. Austria's own foreign minister in turn felt compelled to put forward an Austrian proposal. In February 1862 Austria, with the support of the kingdoms of Bavaria, Saxony, Hanover, and Württemberg, formally rejected the Prussian proposal and signed a secret agreement to oppose any Prussian plans for a Germany excluding Austria.[21] This came to a stalemate later in the year in Frankfurt. Once Bismarck came to power, he studiously upheld Prussian opposition, succeeding in defeating an Austrian reform plan at the confederal diet in early 1863 by a vote of nine to seven. This intransigent Bismarckian opposition brought Wilhelm I to tears later that year when Franz Joseph called a meeting of all the German princes in Frankfurt, and Bismarck through sheer force of personality convinced the Prussian king not to attend, thereby killing yet another Austrian reform attempt. As Wilhelm famously lamented: 'it is difficult to be king under Bismarck'.[22]

Austria's failures in Germany paled in comparison to its constitutional struggles at home. While Prussia forged ahead under Bismarck by ignoring its liberal-dominated parliament, Austria was unfocused, riven by conflicting parties and interest groups vying not just to influence decision making, but to redefine the entire decision-making apparatus of the state. Schmerling's attempts to build a liberal Austria were consistently undermined by the fact that Hungarian politicians refused to participate, eventually leading Franz Joseph to abandon the project of a centralized Habsburg Monarchy altogether. Going over the head of his own government, Franz Joseph opened negotiations with Hungarian politicians in 1865 to break the impasse, bringing down Schmerling's government in the process. The Bohemian Count Richard Belcredi took his place, tasked with achieving a settlement with Hungary. In July the Austrian Reichstag was dissolved and in September the February Patent was suspended, returning Austria to a state of suspended constitutional animation.

Against this backdrop, a crisis broke out that finally compelled the German Confederation to act over the troubled duchies of Schleswig and Holstein. In a famous though apocryphal quotation attributed to British Prime Minister Lord Palmerston, the Schleswig-Holstein question was said to be so complicated that only three people understood it: 'the Prince Consort, who is dead—a German professor, who has gone mad—and I, who have forgotten all about it'.[23] Fundamentally, it was a dispute over succession and the duchies' relationship to the German Confederation. It resulted in a military confrontation between Germany—led by Prussia and Austria—and Denmark. The former scored an easy victory before a joint occupation of the two duchies ensued while their ultimate fate was decided. Bismarck understood this as the opportunity Prussia had been waiting for. He convinced the king and those around him that the time had come to confront Austria. Manoeuvring to annex Schleswig-Holstein would act as the pretext.[24] In early 1866 the Austrian government's decision to allow the Schleswig-Holstein estates to call a united assembly was disputed by Prussia, and the two slid towards war.

The months-long build up made it unambiguously clear that Prussia had little support in Germany for a war against Austria.[25] The Habsburgs, for centuries the leading house in Germany, officially had the German Confederation on their side. That included all the kingdoms save Prussia, as well as most of the mid-sized states. It included even liberal public opinion, which saw in a potentially grinding and bloody civil war a steep price to pay for unclear prospects of national unification, even if this did not extend to genuinely pro-Austrian feelings. Prussia simply no longer recognized the confederation, staking not just its position in Germany but its entire existence on a war that many thought Austria would win. To Bismarck, it was as clear an opportunity to establish Prussian hegemony in northern Germany as he was ever going to get. Franz Joseph, for his part, had no less ambitious plans. He wished first and foremost to finally avenge the loss of Silesia, then to give Lusatia to Saxony and partition the Prussian Rhine between Hanover, Hesse, Bavaria, and Württemberg.[26] As Bismarck had remarked in 1859, it was to Austria alone that Prussia could lose everything.

There is perhaps no conflict in European history whose significance was so inversely proportionate to its length. Hostilities ceased barely a month after they had begun. In the first Austro-Prussian confrontation since the Silesian Wars, Prussia emerged victorious. The German Confederation was officially dissolved. Prussia annexed Schleswig-Holstein, Hanover, Hesse, Nassau, and Frankfurt. Saxony only narrowly avoided annexation, restored as a strange sister kingdom in a North German Confederation dominated by Prussia to which all of northern Germany now belonged.[27] Only Bavaria, Baden, and Württemberg remained wholly independent, under pressure to follow the rest of non-Austrian Germany into some kind of union. Central Europe had been remade.

* * *

With hindsight, the Austro-Prussian War was a turning point in Central European history. The Habsburgs, who had led or presided over Germany for centuries, were expelled from German affairs altogether, paving the way for unification on a Prussian basis. But it was not immediately clear that Austria had stumbled out of German history. Many in Austria thought the time had finally come to focus on their own affairs, that the severed link with Germany could serve as an opportunity to finally focus on building stable foundations for a sovereign Habsburg state. But others saw this new constellation as temporary, plotting their day of retribution. Austro-German liberals perhaps did not go that far but saw the war as reflective of the failings of Austria's political system rather than an estrangement from Germany.[28] While not clearly taking one side or the other, Franz Joseph proceeded with what was widely interpreted as an act of defiance.

A few months after his defeat, he appointed none other than Friedrich Ferdinand von Beust as his foreign minister, who later became the first Austrian statesman since Metternich to hold the title of chancellor. He had been dismissed from his post in Saxony because Bismarck refused to deal with him. The day before his appointment was announced, Beust had laid out his agenda to Franz Joseph's cabinet, placing the settlement of constitutional issues firmly at the top. Internal stability would help Austria maintain the independence of the south German states.[29] This first part of his plan was swiftly implemented, with much of the work done long before Beust's tenure. The Hungarian diet had been convened in December of 1865 to give the court a legal negotiating partner. A subcommittee led by Ferenc Deák and Gyula Andrássy had drafted the Hungarian demands, and an outline published the day before the outbreak of the Austro-Prussian War.

As defeat loomed, Palacký, Rieger, Strossmayer, Ivan Mažuranić, and several Polish politicians met in Vienna in an attempt to forge a common federalist program to stave off the threat of Austro-Hungarian dualism, which they feared would result in a Magyar-dominated Hungary on the one hand and a German-dominated 'Austria' on the other, leaving the Slavs divided and oppressed in both. Palacký had laid out his federalist vision with his pamphlet on *The Austrian State Idea* in which he expanded this notion of state right to the entire monarchy. At the meeting this plan was reiterated, with Palacký proposing a federalized state comprised of five entities: Bohemia, Austria, Hungary, Galicia, and a South Slav state. Dualism, he thought, would spell disaster for the monarchy: he warned

Germans and Magyars that it would mark 'the birth of Pan-Slavism in its least desirable form'. The court, however, thought differently.[30]

In January 1867, Vienna resumed its negotiations with the Hungarians, producing a draft agreement eventually agreed to by both sides. It transformed the Habsburg state into a dual monarchy in which Hungary would share ministries of war, foreign affairs and finance with the 'Austrian' half, but otherwise have its own parliament with legislative powers. It also allowed for the union of Transylvania with the rest of Hungary.[31] Lajos Kossuth penned a stirring letter from exile, warning the compromise would spell disaster for Hungary, but the Hungarian parliament was undaunted and approved it. On 8 June 1867, Franz Joseph was crowned king of Hungary, replaying in Budapest the great drama his great-grandfather Leopold II had experienced in Pressburg.

Just two weeks later, dozens of the monarchy's leading Slavs embarked on a journey that seemed to make good on Palacký's earlier warning. They were heading to St. Petersburg, then on to Moscow where an ethnographic exhibition was planned. It was theoretically apolitical, but the timing of the trip and general sense of outrage amongst the Slavic politicians from the Habsburg Monarchy led supporters and opponents alike to bill it as a much grander heir to the ill-fated Prague Slav Congress of 1848. One no longer suffused with ostentatious displays of loyalty to the Habsburgs.

Palacký was the spiritual head of the delegation that included Slavs from across Central Europe, Rieger and Ljudevit Gaj among them and even including two Sorbs. From the moment they reached 'ethnographic Russia', they were feted as honoured guests and wildly popular celebrities. The state railways gave them free passage while a luxurious hotel gave them free lodgings. Huge crowds gathered to meet them in St. Petersburg and Moscow. Nobles and notables threw banquets and dinners in their honour while museums, churches, and learned societies hosted them as distinguished guests. Even Tsar Alexander II welcomed them for an audience. 'I am happy to see you Slavic brethren on native Slavic soil' he warmly told them.[32]

The thrill of novelty could only go so far. The visit was clearly political, undertaken as the dawn of dualism in the Habsburg Monarchy threatened the political subjugation of its Slavs, and yet speakers had to carefully avoid discussing politics. Official Russian support did not translate into any desire to jeopardize the peace in Europe through wild claims on Habsburg territory. To make matters worse, Polish political leaders across Europe were disgusted by the whole affair and were nowhere to be seen. In 1863 Poles had risen yet again against their Russian rulers, their failed uprising resulting in the abolition of their autonomy and direct incorporation into Russia. The notion that national freedom could be achieved through this Russifying autocracy appeared patently absurd to the Poles.

Indeed, the course of the congress made clear to leading Central European Slavs that the Russian idea of Pan-Slavism was quite different to their own. Though the Russian Pan-Slavists were not able to lay out their vision overtly, they did so implicitly through the 1867 publication of the Slovak nationalist Ľudovít Štúr's *Slavdom and the World of the Future*. The hitherto unseen manuscript had been written in German at the height of postrevolutionary despair in the 1850s. It marked a radical break with previous Pan-Slavist thought in Central Europe, Štúr arguing Slavs should take up the Russian language and Orthodox faith and work towards a federation under Russian leadership.[33] It was precisely what leading Russian Pan-Slavists themselves envisioned, seeing the Slavs as a natural whole inherently incompatible with the Romano-Germanic world of the West.

Palacký, Rieger, and other Slav leaders had gone to Russia hoping for concrete political support but left with nothing but fond memories and suspicions of Russian Pan-Slavism. As Palacký wrote soon after: 'Czechs fought for their national individuality and preserved it at the cost of countless sacrifices. They will not desire to surrender it in exchange for any dubious promises. The same applies to all the other Slavs, particularly those of the South'. The 'Slavic nation' that had been posited for centuries was fracturing under the weight of its own contradictions. For the second time in as many decades, Slavs had come together to find that they shared many good intentions, but too few concrete interests. Some would soon make their peace with the dualist system, while others resigned themselves to the fact that no foreign intervention would save them from its fetters. Few still clung to the hope that out of the many 'tribes' of the 'Slavic nation' any unity could ever be found.[34]

* * *

Franz Joseph and Beust broke the Habsburg state in two, hoping that this would help prevent Germany become one—but Bismarck was hardly rushing to incorporate the 'south-German, Catholic, Bavarian element' into the nascent Prusso-German state.[35] His focus was squarely on consolidating the territories annexed by Prussia, solidifying Prussian control over the newly-founded North German Confederation. The outrage of Prussia's war was not forgiven overnight. Hanover's House of Guelph, with connections at courts in St. Petersburg and London and an exiled home in Vienna, agitated for the restoration of its throne.[36] It could even count on a largely symbolic volunteer *Welfenlegion* (Guelphic Legion) with over 1,000 members to help it.[37] Even if they lacked a political outlet for their frustrations, Frankfurters were no less outraged about the loss of their centuries-old freedom, particularly since they had not even been party to the war. Only a single person toasted to the Prussian king at an official ceremony marking the city's annexation.[38] It was not so straightforward to turn Hanoverians, Frankfurters, or Nassauers into Prussians overnight. The Prussian government therefore allowed some quasi-federal institutions to survive in these annexed territories. Hanover and Nassau kept their local districts, for example, and Frankfurt its currency.[39]

In a similar vein, Prussia trod carefully when it came to the North German Confederation. Saxony may have been spared outright annexation, but this was hardly seen as a gesture of goodwill. The pro-Prussian agitation of Saxon national liberals even helped bring about a conservative, particularist backlash that coloured the first elections to the North German Reichstag in early 1867. A majority supported parties that were at best lukewarm towards German unification, with national liberals failing to win a single seat. The influential Saxon national liberal Julius Hermann Moritz Busch lamented in the summer of 1867 that a trip to the countryside around Leipzig had proven the strength of particularism and anti-Prussian feeling. The masses, under the influence of bureaucrats and priests with a romantic attachment to the Wettins, believed Prussians to be little better than 'cannibals' or 'robbers'.[40] A whole spectrum of Saxon opinion from the democratic left to the conservative right were united in their hatred for 'Prussian Caesarism' and its living embodiment: Bismarck.[41]

Anti-Prussian forces were triumphant in southern Germany too. While they had reluctantly consented to the creation of a *Zollparlament* (customs parliament) to discuss issues of common interest to the *Zollverein*, it was far from certain that this would be a first step to German unity. Harnessing fears of a Prussian-dominated Germany and its consequences for Catholic Bavaria, a loose coalition of Bavarian conservatives and particularists managed to capture the majority of Bavarian seats in the first elections. In Württemberg the government-supported People's Party won all the apportioned seats, the pro-Prussian German Party winning none. Even in Baden, where prince, parliament, and ministers were most supportive of a united Germany, particularists managed to find a broad base of support.[42] Further particularist sentiment was aroused by the adoption of Prussian military regulations in the southern German states, the Austro-Prussian War having supposedly proven Prussian military superiority.[43] But many interpreted this as the scorned 'Prussianization' of society through the backdoor. In Württemberg the minister of war was forced to resign after commenting that the Prussian system was 'barbaric and un-German'.[44]

Bavaria's exceptionally strong identity was seemingly strengthened in these years by the stunning success of the newly formed Bavarian Patriots' Party, which harnessed Bavarian patriotism, Catholic clericalism, dynastic loyalty, and anti-Prussianism to become the strongest political force in Bavaria. Remarkably, the Patriots' Party managed a stunning victory even in Bavarian Landtag elections in 1869 despite a restrictive franchise and liberal gerrymandering. It won seventy-eight of 153 seats in May, rising to eighty-three in November. Armed with a powerful democratic mandate, the Patriots' Party forced the resignations of liberal education and interior ministers and, in their greatest triumph, the pro-unification foreign minister Count Chlodwig zu Hohelohe-Schillingsfürst.[45] Bismarck concluded in early 1869 that German unity was 'not at the moment a ripe fruit'.[46]

Once again, it was a succession crisis that would reshape the map of Central Europe. This time it was in distant Spain, where a military junta considered filling their country's vacant throne with a candidate from the Swabian Catholic branch of the Hohenzollerns. The mere suggestion that a German prince related to the Prussian royal house could sit on the Spanish throne provoked frenzied outrage in France. Even though the Hohenzollern candidate withdrew himself from consideration, the incident culminated in a French declaration of war, drawing in the whole North German Confederation. The prospect of a belligerent French invasion of southern Germany was enough to send Baden, Württemberg, and Hesse into Prussia's arms. Bavaria too, with some reluctance, entered the war. Its particularist-dominated Landtag was unsure of how to proceed, ultimately approving of war credits requested by the royally-appointed Bavarian government while refusing to sanction a declaration of war. Bavaria would nevertheless go to war without a declaration.[47]

The Franco-Prussian War completed Bismarck's transformation from provincial Prussian Junker into German national hero. Led by Prussia's impressive army, bolstered by contingents from the South German states, Germany fought and won as a nation. The patriotic fervour unleashed by the war convinced even the most recalcitrant of German princes that a united Germany had to come about. The precise terms would be haggled over for months, producing contradictory symbolism and expectations. The constitution of the North German Confederation was simply expanded southwards, accepted by Baden and Hesse without reservations. Württemberg and Bavaria proved tougher to win over, the latter negotiating for itself a number of concessions.[48]

But the most recalcitrant of all the princes proved to be the king of Prussia himself. The day before a new German Reich was proclaimed, Wilhelm wept that he would soon 'take leave of the old Prussia', before flying into a rage at his ministers.[49] He would remain king of Prussia in the new state, but would be forced to step into a new, uncertain role as hereditary leader of a centralized union of German princely states and free cities. The other princes refused to call this new leader the 'Emperor of Germany', instead compromising on 'German Emperor', which did not imply that he was emperor of *all* German lands given that Austria remained outside the new Reich. On 18 January 1871, most—but not all—German princes gathered in the palace of Versailles outside the besieged French capital. In Louis XIV's grand Hall of Mirrors, a new German Reich was proclaimed.

* * *

Central Europeans were, as ever, masterfully adept at rearranging polities into new configurations. Like a game of musical chairs, every reorganization reduced the number of states and consolidated the ones that remained. The Napoleonic Wars reduced thousands of imperial polities to thirty-nine German states plus the various Habsburg and Hohenzollern territories outside the German Confederation. The aftermath of the revolutions of 1848 then saw the Habsburg territories folded into a single Austria. The Austro-Prussian War once again reduced the number of German states, incorporating most of the remainder into a North German Confederation around the same time that the 1867 *Ausgleich* (Austro-Hungarian compromise) split Austria in two. Then, the Franco-Prussian War finally brought most of Germany's princes together into a single Germany.

In 1871 Central Europe arrived at the political configuration most familiar to posterity: the German Reich in the north and Austria-Hungary in the south. But the notion that these were simply two unitary states as we would think of them in the twenty-first century is misleading. The two halves of Austria-Hungary had their own armies under the 'common army'. The German Reich meanwhile had four distinct armies—the Royal Saxon Army, the Bavarian Army, the Württembergian Army, and the Royal Prussian Army—which each sported only their own cockades before Kaiser Wilhelm II decreed in 1897 that they should in addition wear the 'national' black-white-red.[50] One was not a citizen of 'Austria-Hungary' or the 'German Reich', but rather of Austria, Hungary, Prussia, Bavaria, Saxony, and so on.

The imperial titles of German Emperor and Austrian Emperor harkened back to the Holy Roman Empire, not to overseas or even continental empires. Neither even corresponded to territories, but to constitutional positions atop composite states. In Germany there were still kings of Bavaria, Saxony, and Württemberg, grand dukes of Baden, Hesse, Mecklenburg-Schwerin, Mecklenburg-Strelitz, Oldenburg, and Saxe-Weimar, dukes of Anhalt, Brunswick, Saxe-Altenberg, Saxe-Coburg and Gotha, and Saxe-Meiningen, seven princes, and three free cities. The Habsburg 'Empire'—or even more erroneously, 'Austro-Hungarian Empire'—was even less of the kind of 'empire' the word is associated with today.[51] The 'Austrian Empire' ceased to exist in 1867—although Franz Joseph remained 'Emperor of Austria' outside of Hungary—replaced by the Kingdom of Hungary and 'The Kingdoms and Lands Represented in the Imperial Council'. The latter was also commonly referred to as 'Cisleithania', the lands on 'this' side of the Leitha river from the perspective of Vienna, as opposed to Hungarian lands which were beyond the Leitha, referred to as Transleithania. Cisleithania consisted of the three kingdoms of Bohemia, Dalmatia, and Galicia, the archduchies of Upper and Lower Austria, the duchies of Bukovina, Carinthia, Carniola, Salzburg, Silesia, and Styria, the margraviates of Istria and Moravia, the princely counties of Gorizia and Gradisca, Tyrol, and Voralberg, and the Free City of Trieste. The Kingdom of Hungary was divided into Hungary proper and the Kingdom of Croatia-Slavonia, which itself claimed to also represent the Kingdom of Dalmatia.

Central Europe therefore remained a confusing patchwork of states and societies. The new German Reich consisted of twenty-five distinct administrative divisions, Cisleithania of nineteen, and Hungary of two. Each of these units had a unique history and identity, with its own particular social, cultural, and economic background and conditions. In the decades after 1871, the exact nature of these various constitutional arrangements came under constant questioning and critique. Franz Joseph was emperor in Austria but mere king in Hungary. Wilhelm I and his successors were 'German Emperors', but also kings of Prussia, *primus inter pares* (first among equals). The significance—and in some cases insignificance—of such distinctions only became clear with time.

9

THE AGE OF NATIONALISM

In the wake of the 1848 revolutions, the Hungarian writer and one-time revolutionary minister of education József Eötvös turned his attention to 'one of the most peculiar phenomena of our time'—nationality. This was an idea 'which in the past century almost seemed to be forgotten, [that is] now ... exerting a greater influence than perhaps ever before on all states in Europe'.[1] By 1871 this age of nationalism had produced German, Italian, and Hungarian nation-states the likes of which had been nothing but a dream in 1848. Calls for Croatian, Czech and Polish nation-states had only grown louder while Romanian and Serbian states to the southeast seemed to represent the first steps in the building of much more expansive ones. But what exactly was nationality? What was a nation? Did the terms refer to the same concept? Few denied that nations or nationalities existed. But there was little agreement about what exactly they were, how they could be measured, or what role they should have in public life.

The new expectations and ambitions of a growing middle class inspired by liberal arguments for the inclusion of much wider sections of the population in the business of government had made old corporate notions of nationhood obsolete by 1871. The nation was generally thought of as a great mass of people, who through education could be raised up to a higher level of political and cultural being. It was often suggested that a nation could only be enlightened in its own language, and this had inspired the cultivation of vernaculars and the construction of national-literary cultures. But by 1848 these projects could hardly claim to represent the totality of political, cultural and social life in Central Europe, and it remained unclear how nationhood related to the world as it was rather than how some hoped it would be.

In Frankfurt, Budapest, Zagreb, Prague, Vienna, Kremsier, and beyond national revolutionaries pointed to many markers as proof of one's belonging to the nation, the most prominent being language. Yet language often offered a confused picture. Jacob Grimm thought the Dutch and Scandinavians were also German by virtue of their language.[2] Pan-Slavists lumped all Slavs together, something many thought ridiculous. Language was a vessel for the building of a common political and cultural life, an element of mythologized heritage, and the social glue that held the national community together. But it was also malleable, difficult to define, could be picked up or abandoned, and was something that most educated people had more than one of. As Eötvös put it: 'language alone is not nationality, it is one of the means of preserving nationality by isolating one people from others', thereby making independent development possible.[3]

One of Germany's most chauvinistic liberal nationalists—the historian Heinrich von Treitschke—even boasted in 1871: 'We Germans have never understood the principle of nationality in the crude and exaggerated sense that all German-speaking Europeans must belong to our state'.[4] Indeed, Germany's liberals were overwhelmingly thrilled by the new Reich founded in 1871, even though millions of German speakers were left outside of it. Gone were past worries that Prussian authoritarianism would corrupt this grand achievement. The left-liberal Progress Party that had emerged in Prussia in the early 1860s in opposition to princely absolutism was eclipsed by the far more popular National Liberal Party founded in 1867—Treitschke was one of the founders and leaders—representing the alliance of princely state and nationalist middle class in the interests of building a liberal nation-state.

They would dominate German politics until 1879, less due to their prominence in parliament—though they won the most seats in every Reichstag election between 1871 and 1878—than to their strategic alliance with Bismarck, who deferred to them on countless matters of domestic policy. The liberal Eduard Lasker later recalled the 1866–80 period as among the 'the most magnificent phenomena in the history of reform in Prussia and Germany, if not the history of reform in all civilized nations'. He pointed to the constitutions of the North German Confederation and German Reich, which established a unified Reichstag with universal male suffrage; the new penal code and other judicial laws; reform of the monetary system and the founding of a national bank; the new imperial commercial code; and laws governing joint stock companies, the imperial court, the national press, and even new military laws.[5]

THE AGE OF NATIONALISM

What these liberal triumphs masked was that ministers like Bismarck were not actually responsible to the Reichstag, while the Prussian Landtag maintained a restrictive franchise that divided voters into three classes, giving greater weight to the wealthy elites. German liberals themselves were, like their Austrian and Hungarian counterparts, thoroughly elitist. The National Liberal Party was a party of local notables—bureaucrats, schoolteachers, lawyers, judges, editors, shopkeepers—led by a self-constituted group of national notables.[6] Even after they fell out of favour in 1879, national liberals exerted an outsized influence on German society and culture through their prominent roles in journalism, academia and associational life. Indeed, it was from their ranks that the German Reich would largely derive its sense of self.

They were central to the development of a pro-Prussian school of German historiography, which portrayed the Prussian state as having a special progressive mission in German history. The 'patriarch' was Johann Gustav Droysen, whose magnum opus was a fourteen volume *History of Prussian Politics* published over the years 1855–86. It drew a straight line of continuity from the Teutonic Knights bringing 'superior German culture' to the East in the Middle Ages through the generations of savvy Hohenzollern state-builders up to the founding of the German Reich. In his footsteps followed others like Treitschke, a prolific and popular publicist, lecturer, and historian who left an indelible mark on a whole generation of Germans with his partisan pro-Prussian views. Ironically, he was from Saxony and his father, a military general, publicly disavowed him due to his Prussian chauvinism. And, finally, there was Heinrich von Sybel, the editor of the hugely influential historical magazine the *Historische Zeitschrift*. As trusted director of the Prussian archives, Sybel was given official sanction to write an official history of *The Founding of the German Empire under William I*.[7]

Together, figures like Droysen, Treitschke and Sybel painted a picture of German history centred on the Prussian state and its mission to unify Germany. It was a partial one, which was perhaps unsurprising given the demographic makeup of the Reich's national liberals. Between 1867 and 1917 the National Liberal Party would send just fifty-one Catholic deputies to the Reichstag compared with 569 Protestants. Even in heavily Catholic Bavaria the equivalent figures for the Landtag were seventy-eight Protestants to thirty-three Catholics.[8] The party that acted as the political manifestation of middle-class German nationalism was in fact an overwhelmingly Protestant, Prussian-oriented party, albeit one whose representatives largely came from territories not part of Prussia in 1866.[9] Textbooks approved by state ministries of education in southern German states meanwhile deemphasized or ignored Prussia's leading role in German unification. One Bavarian schoolbook even claimed that in 1870 German princes had simply come together to restore 'old imperial unity'.[10]

In the first all-German elections in 1871, turnout was just fifty-one per cent. Half voted for parties that were either unenthusiastic or hostile to unification, though since ministers were not actually responsible to the Reichstag these deputies had little practical power.[11] In Saxony, Bavaria, Württemberg and many other states, a strong sense of particularism was maintained and often promoted by local governments, even if few rejected the Reich outright.[12] State governments retained control over education, policing, railways, and even kept their own ministries of foreign affairs, since they remained according to the 1871 constitution subjects of international law. Most soon scaled these down to a minimum, but Saxony and Bavaria maintained diplomatic missions in Vienna. Bavaria even maintained ones in Bern, St. Petersburg, and Paris. These positions were little more than sinecures but are revealing as to the peculiar nature of the German Reich.[13]

It was both a nation-state, symbolically represented by a parliament elected from all states by universal male suffrage, and a princely federation consisting of distinct states with their own long histories, identities, and governments. The latter, not the former, was paramount. The Kingdom of Prussia was the Reich's undisputed hegemon, representing around sixty per cent of its population and similar share of its land area. Berlin was at once the German imperial and Prussian royal capital, where the German Reichstag, Prussian Landtag, and all of the bureaucracies were situated, but until the First World War more were employed in the Prussian bureaucracy than the 'national' one.[14] Bismarck, meanwhile, served in an almost uninterrupted dual role as minister-president of Prussia and chancellor of Germany from the German Reich's formation until 1890, considering the Prussian post unquestionably the leading one. While the Reichstag may have been elected by Germans from across the country, in practice the imperial government was appointed by and responsible to nobody but the Prussian king (and German emperor) himself.

Its constituent states formed a single nation-state and yet they communicated with each other through their own ministries of foreign affairs, and in a way that still recognized Vienna as a not-quite-foreign city. Prussia's king ruled as German emperor, but his kingdom had its own diplomatic relations with other German states. Ironically, the Reich itself had no representative in the Vatican until 1882. There were Bavarian and Prussian ones, but they were treated as equals.[15] This points to what would become the main cleavage in German society in the first decade after unification. For most of the nineteenth century German rulers had focused on building bridges between Protestants and Catholics, in large part thanks to the changes in the map of Germany after 1815, but divisions persisted.[16] Generations of Catholic Germans had feared a Prussian-dominated Reich precisely because they knew it would leave them a minority in a Protestant state. Liberals and Protestants alike meanwhile saw the Catholic Church as a reactionary force that threatened to destroy the Reich from within. This was part of a much wider European conflict between dawning secular liberalism and a more muscular clerical Catholicism that sought to regain its once-leading position in society.

In 1864 Pope Pius IX issued the controversial Syllabus of Errors, in which he condemned a litany of aspects of modernity as heresies. A few years later the Vatican Council met for the first time in over three centuries with the aim of redefining the church's position in a modernizing world. A host of modern '-isms' were once again condemned. For both Bismarck and liberals, this turn represented one of the greatest threats facing Germany. As Bismarck put it, there was only one 'constitutional and political standpoint: that of the complete freedom of the church in ecclesiastical matters and the resolute repulsion of any attack on the realm of the state'. This supposed Catholic encroachment on the secular state required a legislative counterattack that would come to be known as the *Kulturkampf* (culture war). It was launched in earnest when the Reichstag passed the 'pulpit law' in December 1871, which punished with up to two years imprisonment any cleric who publicly discussed state affairs while exercising his duties. A spate of repressive laws followed in the Reichstag and Prussian Landtag with the aim of breaking the power of the Catholic Church in Germany.[17]

The countless bishops and priests who were imprisoned for failing to comply with the *Kulturkampf* laws became martyrs to a community that felt itself under siege by an overbearing Protestant state.[18] Catholics built up powerful associational networks, supported by their own press and what was effectively their very own party: the Centre Party. Founded in 1870, its vote share peaked at the height of the *Kulturkampf* in 1874, winning the highest percentage of any party with 27.7 per cent of the vote in a country about thirty-six per cent Catholic. They were the largest single group in a broad coalition that opposed the dominant liberal self-conception of Germany as it was being developed in the 1870s—joined by princely particularists, some conservatives, and representatives of national minorities, the largest of which was the Polish minority.[19]

The Reich's three million Poles only represented about five per cent of the population but ten per cent of Prussia's. Their concentration in West Prussia, East Prussia, Posen, and Silesia made them an outsized target of concern for Prussian and imperial governments. Most Polish-inhabited parts of Prussia had never been a part of either the Holy Roman Empire or the German Confederation. Thus when Prussian Poles were transformed into German citizens, they saw this as a direct attack on their national identity and an outrageous annexation of Polish lands to Germany.[20] One Polish deputy even told the Reichstag: 'We want, gentleman, to remain under Prussian rule until God decides otherwise for us, but we do not want to be incorporated into the German Reich'.[21] In effect, Polish leaders wanted to retain an a non-national Prussian monarchy apart from the German nation-state it was building. Yet Poles and Polish political leaders were by no means disloyal to their Hohenzollern rulers.

Since 1863, Polish nationalists had turned away from fruitless wars for independence towards conservative loyalism in the hope of winning concessions, tied up with the idea that self-determination could be achieved by building up the nation from below. The loyalist trend in Prussia was embodied by the Polish Party, an organization almost exclusively led by nobles who claimed to represent the whole Polish national movement even as they faced pressure from a growing Polish middle class (while most rural Poles remained detached from nationalist politics, many thinking of themselves not as Poles but rather Masurians, Kashubs, or Silesians).[22]

Since Poles were overwhelmingly Catholic, they were disproportionately affected by the *Kulturkampf*. Many of the measures undertaken in the 1870s targeted not just the church, but also the position of the Polish language and Polish political elites (though most historians see this as secondary to the *Kulturkampf*'s main purpose). Polish regions were denied self-government out of fear that they could become nationalist strongholds. The restrictive three-class franchise ensured that even in Polish-majority provinces like Posen and West Prussia Poles were outnumbered by Germans two-to-one in the provincial assemblies. In 1876 German was even proclaimed the official language of Posen province, leading to bilingual signs coming down and places being renamed. The Prussian interior minister justified the repressive measures through the imperative of assimilation: 'We must work to make the Poles Prussian and then German, but they must become Prussian *and* German'.[23]

Bismarck's list of 'enemies of the Reich' was long. It included particularists, Catholics, Poles, even many liberals. But there was one organization in particular that he saw as so dangerous that it needed to be banned outright. In 1875, the Socialist Workers' Party of Germany came into being through a merger of the General German Workers' Association (founded by Ferdinand Lassalle) and the Social Democratic Workers' Party (led by August Bebel and Wilhelm Liebknecht). Representing the burgeoning workers' movement, it called for universal suffrage, replacing standing armies with militias, total secularization of public life, and a raft of protections for workers. However, it also had much grander revolutionary visions of the 'liberation of the working class' through the radical reordering of 'prevailing social and political conditions'. Indeed, Bebel and Liebknecht truly were enemies of the Reich. The latter denounced the North German Confederation in its own Reichstag as a 'creation of violence' based on 'the division, subjugation, and enfeeblement of Germany'. Both had been arrested for allegedly plotting high treason in 1870.[24]

This first act of state persecution did little to deter them. Heavily industrialized Saxony—the birthplace of Bebel and Liebknecht's party—became the first German state in which socialist candidates won a plurality of the votes in the Landtag election of 1874. The now-united Socialist Workers' Party increased their share to nearly forty per cent in 1877, with Bebel elected to represent the Wettin king's very own constituency in Dresden-Old City.[25] By then their Social Democratic party had hundreds of local branches with tens of thousands of members, acting as a unified party that sought to advance the cause of workers' rights everywhere. Conservative and liberal elites alike were terrified by this upswell of working-class militancy but hesitated to ban the party outright as Bismarck demanded.

It was a stroke of luck then when two failed assassination attempts on the emperor-king gave Bismarck the chance to blame the Social Democrats and call a new election revolving around the threat they posed to the Reich. One semi-official paper warned that they would lead Germany down the road to 'national impoverishment, the ongoing degradation of the nation's morals, the weakening of our defensive power'. Bismarck got the majority he wanted and in late 1878 a Law Against the Publicly Dangerous Endeavours of Social Democracy was passed that banned the

Socialist Workers' Party and countless associated organizations, to be renewed every two years and enforced by each individual state.[26]

For Bismarck, the security of the Reich was more than just an internal matter. In 1873 he had used the threat of international socialism to help broker the 'Three Emperors' Alliance' with Russia and Austria-Hungary, the cornerstone of a foreign policy that sought to ensure Germany would never be surrounded by enemies. But in 1878 that alliance began to falter. After the Ottoman Empire suffered a crushing defeat to Russia and its Balkan allies, the great powers hastily organized a congress in Berlin to ensure its consequences would not upset the balance of power in Europe. Romania, Serbia, and Montenegro were all officially recognized as independent while Bosnia & Herzegovina fell under Austro-Hungarian occupation.

Bismarck had tried to play the mediator, but Russia was frustrated by what felt like minor gains. The Three Emperors' Alliance broke down and as relations between Berlin and St. Petersburg cooled, Bismarck took the chance to push for something he had advocated since 1875: a separate alliance with Austria-Hungary. He passionately made his case through the summer and autumn of 1879. He pointed to 'German tribal ties', historical memory, and language as things that would make the alliance not only more popular than one with Russia, but also more durable. Despite Wilhelm's opposition, Bismarck got his way. In October 1879 Germany and Austria-Hungary concluded a defensive alliance. If either was attacked by Russia, they would come to each other's aid. Just over a decade after Austria had been expelled from Germany, the Habsburg state was once again tied to it.[27]

* * *

The Austro-Hungarian compromise of 1867 was a turning point in Hungarian history. Generations of Hungarian politicians had demanded the right to legislate their own affairs. The price they ultimately paid was loyalty to the Habsburg dynasty and an effective renunciation of the rebellious legacy of 1848, even if the liberal April Laws of that year were restored. This gave the Hungarian elite a free hand to finally transform the Kingdom of Hungary into the Magyar nation-state they had long dreamt of, even if—lacking their own army and foreign policy—they would never be truly sovereign within the bounds of the compromise.

Gyula Andrássy—who led the first post-compromise government—had been a revolutionary sentenced to death in absentia and hung in effigy in 1849. His minister of education József Eötvös served in the same post in 1848. Nonetheless, these two men represented the moderate 'centre-right' faction in favour of the compromise, whose leader was the national patriarch Ferenc Deák. The opposition consisted of several factions that rejected the compromise and instead wanted to see Hungary effectively independent with its own parliament-controlled army and foreign policy, tied to the rest of the Habsburg Monarchy in a personal union at most. From 1871–73 Deák, Eötvös, Andrássy, and other leading politicians died, retired from political life, or—in Andrássy's case—went on to serve as the common Austro-Hungarian minister of foreign affairs. When economic crisis hit in 1873 and threw the state's finances into disarray, the two dominant parties began to inch towards an agreement with each other.[28]

In early 1875, the pro-compromise forces merged into a new Liberal Party with Kálmán Tisza at its head. It would rule until 1905 with a total stranglehold on Hungarian political life; Tisza served as prime minister from 1875 to 1890. Its ideological orientation was enigmatic. On the one hand it entrenched liberalism as state ideology and celebrated the liberal achievements that preceded Tisza's tenure. On the other, Tisza was more like Bismarck than a liberal ideologue; a proponent of Realpolitik, to whom ruling was an end in itself. One opposition paper commented critically in 1882: 'Liberalism is as far removed from current Hungarian government policy as truth is from lies'.[29]

The Liberal Party became so synonymous with the state that the lines between them were often blurred. In 1910 over half of the Liberal Party's MPs in northern Hungary had served as local officials, often having acted as little more than party functionaries.[30] The suffrage law passed in 1874 limited the electorate for the lower house to just five or six per cent of the population, only slightly larger than the *Natio Hungarica* (corporate Hungarian nation) of old. Indeed, by 'ancestral right' anyone whose family name appeared on a voting register pre-1848 was given the vote even if they did not meet the general requirements based on property, land, and tax paid.[31] The parliament was elected by open ballot in single-member, first-past-the-post constituencies gerrymandered in 1877 to suit the Liberal Party's needs. Oppositional districts were packed with as many voters as possible while those containing national minorities were made as large as possible. Electoral chicanery was ubiquitous, but the Liberal Party indeed had the support of most aristocrats, large and medium landowners, civil servants, and the burgeoning financial elite.[32]

In the new liberal Hungary, Budapest took over Vienna's traditional role as the agent of centralization. Legal equality of all citizens was established in 1868 and the last vestiges of feudal privileges abolished. Laws were passed regulating the rights of counties and municipalities, curtailing the traditional rights of the former while drastically reducing the number of the latter. Further reforms during Tisza's reign saw the traditional privileges of Zipsers, Cumans, and Transylvanian Saxons abolished, and their former territories integrated into neighbouring counties.[33] Jews were finally fully emancipated, free to make huge social and economic advances. The half that did not adhere to strict Orthodoxy were generally enthusiastic about Magyarization and would find themselves vastly over-represented in many areas of public life. Hungary's political elite admired and encouraged Jewish assimilationism knowing full well that the only path to a Magyar Hungary was the assimilation of its minorities. It aimed to turn its various 'nationalities' into a single political 'nation' based on the Magyar language and the Hungarian national movement that had been built through it since the late eighteenth century.

The clearest distillation of this outlook was the Nationalities Act of 1868. It distinguished one, indivisible Hungarian nation, consisting of all the country's equal inhabitants, from the many nationalities that inhabited the country. Though it nominally recognized the right of these nationalities to use their own languages in public life, later laws tended to reinforce the dominant position of Magyar. It paid lip service to liberal notions of equality of nationalities while clearly giving preference to the thoroughly Magyarized idea of the Hungarian nation.[34]

The central state and its many organs became a symbolic preserve of a Magyar-inflected Hungarian nation, with social mobility increasingly dependent on knowing the new language of public life. Schools, courts and public administration were Magyarized and increasingly so over the years as the provisions of the Nationalities Act were portrayed as impractical and even utopian. Assimilation did indeed occur, and knowledge of the new state language rose continually, but this was largely thanks to Magyar's prestigious role and the assimilatory power of increasingly Magyar-dominated cities rather than the transformation of the large non-Magyar swathes of rural Hungary. Schooling in a language most minority-nationality children did not understand did not turn them into Magyars, but simply hindered their education, much like the imposition of German had done during neo-absolutism.[35]

The Magyarizing state took a generally hostile stance towards minority expressions of national identity. Representatives of non-Magyar nationalities, who made up around half the country, would never have more than five per cent of the seats in the Hungarian parliament.[36] After 1867 they had practically no say in the direction of Hungarian politics.

There was thus little that could be done in 1874 when the government shut down the Slovak *Matica* (cultural institution) that had operated out of Martin since 1863, on the grounds that it was a covertly Pan-Slavist political organization. The only three Slovak gymnasiums (secondary schools) were closed around the same time.[37] The only Slovak party in Hungary—the Slovak National Party, which claimed to speak for all Slovaks—was weak and withdrawn. The same was true of the Romanian party in Transylvania, which protested the union with Hungary by taking a passive stance that did little to help the position of Romanians in Hungary. Despite being the largest single minority, the restrictive electoral franchise made Romanians practically invisible in Hungarian politics. That went even for the counties in which Romanians formed huge majorities. Changes in governance in the 1850s and 1860s had advanced the use of Romanian in county assemblies and administration, but the Magyar elites managed to walk these changes back and re-assert Magyar dominance.[38]

Hungary's millions of German-speakers had wildly different attitudes and approaches to the Magyarizing state. In general, they proved loyal Hungarians and many embraced Magyarization.[39] Some had Magyarized long before 1867, such as the Danube Swabian family of Sándor Wekerle, who in 1892 became Hungary's first non-noble prime minister.[40] Even those who did not necessarily embrace the language—like the largely monolingual German majority of Pressburg—displayed their loyalty to and identification with the Hungarian state through symbolic gestures.[41]

The Transylvanian Saxons were more divided. They accepted the dualist system but condemned the loss of their medieval autonomy and resented any attempts to deprive them of their language or culture. Four Saxon-dominated counties managed to make use of the constitutional structure to ensure strict Magyar-German-Romanian trilingualism in their administration, but their autonomy was severely limited within the newly centralized state. Some Saxons like Georg Daniel Teutsch, a prominent local historian, tried to alert their Reich brethren to their fate, but few took note. Treitschke may have embraced the cause of 'the subjugation of our loyal Saxon compatriots' by the 'arrogance of the Magyars', but the Reich cared only for the integrity of its Habsburg ally.[42]

* * *

Every 'nation has a holy city which it thinks about with piety and pride',[43] according to the Hungarian writer and revolutionary leader Mór Jókai. In the first half of the nineteenth century, Agram (Zagreb), Ofen-Pest (Buda-Pest), Prag (Prague), and Laibach (Ljubljana) hosted museums, clubs, newspapers, and other organizations dedicated to advancing the Croatian (or 'Illyrian'), Czech, Hungarian, and Slovene national causes, but they remained cities in which German language and culture dominated. The neo-absolutist regime intensified this presence, but also sowed the seeds of its eventual demise, particularly in the Lands of the Crown of Saint Stephen (the Hungarian lands). Centres of Germanization became centres of nationalization, an ambition that transcended many of the divisions that would emerge within national movements.

After the fall of the hated neo-absolutist system in 1860, the Croatian Sabor (diet) voted to scrap German from gymnasiums (secondary schools) in a symbolic assertion of national sovereignty. The minority that opposed the measure was booed throughout the debate by rowdy crowds from the galleries above. German was retained only because the emperor refused to sanction the measure.[44] The same patriotic crowds—numbering just a few dozen—caused a far bigger scene at what became the final German-language performance of the German theatre in Zagreb in 1860. They pelted the performers with eggs and rotten apples and onions, after which a young Croatian actor mounted the stage and proclaimed that from then on only Croatian would be heard there. The following day the theatre switched to performing German works in Croatian translation but eventually closed down.[45] Overnight in November, German inscriptions on shops and streets were covered in black, presumably by similar crowds of agitators.[46] In June 1860 Franz Joseph appointed a native Croat as *ban*, giving him permission to make the 'national language' official, at a time when Croatian tricolours, national dress, and the language itself were already becoming ubiquitous.[47]

Nationalist street agitation to complement the work of nationalist politicians had been pioneered in Ofen-Pest. In the 1830s the patriotic youth took to threatening German shopkeepers to change their signs to Magyar, resorting to theft or rock-throwing if they failed to comply. The German-dominated Ofen Town Council conceded in 1832 that street signs should be bilingual, but this was far from the kind of national transformation that Hungarian nationalists demanded. As the centre of the Hungarian national movement, Pest steadily took on a Magyar character. By the end of the 1850s there were thirty-one Hungarian periodicals published there compared with just eleven German ones.⁴⁸ The German theatres in Ofen and Pest, despite official support, struggled to regain their formerly dominant position in the cities' cultural lives.⁴⁹

Like in Zagreb, Hungarian nationalists were ready to spring into action after the fall of neo-absolutism. This they did at breakneck speed, with the Buda and Pest town councils announcing they would switch their operations entirely to Magyar already in the summer of 1860. This followed enormous public celebrations of the poet Ferenc Kazinczy's birth the previous year, after which Hungarian patriotism burst back into public life. The carnival season, St. Stephen's Day, and funeral services for István Széchenyi in 1860 proved to be even larger Hungarian patriotic celebrations, where Hungarian costumes, songs, colours, and dances were put proudly on display.⁵⁰ Courses on Austrian history and German literature made way for their Hungarian equivalents at the university in Pest. Professors who did not speak Magyar were simply let go. Over the course of the 1860s there would be hundreds of name changes across Buda-Pest, transforming it into a symbolically Hungarian city.⁵¹

In Prag and Laibach, the path to Czech and Slovene national conquest was much more arduous owing to the size and prominence of the German communities in the cities and the crownlands they were situated in. Most German Bohemians, Moravians and Silesians thought of their land as fundamentally German. The same was true for German Styrians, Carinthians and Carniolans, despite the fact that some—like those in Laibach—lived in urban German islands surrounded by seas of Slavs. Unlike in Hungary and Croatia, where German-speakers proved open to Hungarian and Croatian nationalism, the growing power of Slavic national movements did not provoke sympathy, but a lasting German counter-reaction.

After Prague's 1861 local elections, bilingualism was quickly introduced into the municipal bureaucracy and Czech became the main language of primary school instruction.⁵² Collections for the construction of a Czech National Theatre were large enough for a temporary structure to be erected in 1862, which provided a base for the flourishing of Czech theatrical and musical life.⁵³ While Czech nationalists controlled just a third of the Bohemian diet, in Prague they had the chance to build a nation-state on a municipal scale. That much was confirmed already in 1868, when on the occasion of the laying of the cornerstones of the Czech National Theatre building some 100,000 to 200,000 Czechs descended on the city, requiring over 100 special trains to accommodate the influx.⁵⁴

Czech nationalists would control Prague until the fall of the Habsburg Monarchy in 1918 as Germans were turned into an embattled minority in a vast Czech metropolis. Germans from Bohemia emigrated in large numbers to Vienna or other German-speaking Bohemian cities but largely avoided Prague. In the 1860s association after association would be divided along national-linguistic lines—including even non-political professional associations of physicians, jurists and businessmen—the city's bourgeoisie effectively splitting in two. The symbolic divide was cemented in 1882 when the university in Prague was split into Czech and German sections. The new mayor Tomáš Černý added insult to injury in the eyes of the besieged Germans when he praised 'our ... beloved, golden Slavic Prague', provoking the resignation of the five remaining German representatives on the city council two days later.[55] Prague was truly 'lost to Germandom'.

Laibach, the small provincial capital of Carniola, was until 1860 a city no less dominated by German language and culture than Agram, Prague, or Ofen-Pest. This despite the fact that while the other Slovene-inhabited duchies of Styria and Carinthia were mostly German, Carniola was overwhelmingly Slovene. It held its first municipal elections after the fall of neo-absolutism in early 1861, in which Mihael Ambrož's moderate camp emerged victorious. He had the support of both Germans and Slovenes in an election not marked strongly by national divisions. When the municipal council met, the Slovene nationalist contingent pushed for equal status between Slovene and German in the council, but this was rejected by the majority.[56] Slovene nationalists were not just in the minority but were vehemently attacked by the exclusively German press.[57]

An even more vitriolic and sustained attack on the whole Slovene national movement—and Slavic national movements in Austria more generally—came from the turncoat Karl Deschmann. A celebrated Carniolan natural scientist, he was elected to the Reichsrat in Vienna on the Slovene nationalist ticket in 1861. However, he turned on the movement soon after arriving. Over the course of the following year, he wrote a series of articles and pamphlets accusing the Slovene national movement of being beholden to backwards clericalism. This culminated in his pamphlet *Germandom in Carniola*, in which he argued Carniola was a fundamentally German land and that it was the duty of Germans there to elevate the Slovenes to a higher cultural level.[58]

After Ambrož's death, Slovene nationalists won control of the municipality and the mayorship in 1864, but just four years later the pendulum swung back to the Germans, who won an absolute majority. They organized themselves into a 'Constitutional Union' that envisioned Carniola as just one piece of a centralized, liberal Austrian state. They would keep Laibach in their hands for over a decade, until 1882. Worse still for Slovene nationalists, in 1873 the Austrian liberals convincingly won local elections to the Reichsrat in Vienna and in 1877 took control of the Carniolan Assembly itself. Only when Slovene nationalists finally retook the city hall in 1882 did Slovene have the chance to displace German in schools, administration, and theatre, a shift symbolically cemented by the erection of bilingual or Slovene street signs.[59]

This struggle to overturn German dominance in Ljubljana was in many ways the rule rather than the exception. Proudly Hungarian Budapest, Croatian Zagreb and Czech Prague concealed the fact that the 'German character' of most Habsburg cities was far more resilient. That included important Hungarian cities like Pressburg and Temeswar, which would retain their German majorities into the twentieth century.[60] Moravia's capital of Brünn, Silesia's Troppau, Bohemian Budweis, Styrian Marburg, Carniolan Cilli, and Croatian Essek all had resilient German characters.

In the Austrian half of the monarchy, German pre-eminence was reinforced from above thanks to the dominance of Germanophone liberals grouped together in the Constitutional Party. They did not so much represent a modern political party as a loose association of local bourgeois notables from across the Austrian duchies and Bohemian lands. Candidates for political posts were chosen in the backrooms of venerable social clubs like the German Casino in Prague, with nothing approximating a party structure to provide a semblance of party democracy.[61] Indeed, many of the most prominent Austrian liberals were those from crownlands with sizeable Slavic minorities or even majorities. Given the hegemonic status of German language and culture in Habsburg-ruled cities over the preceding century it was hardly a surprise that such local notables were overwhelmingly German-speaking, even though many were of Slavic or Jewish descent.

In their eyes the German language was associated not with the absolutism of the Habsburg court, but with the progressive fruits of German culture. Following on from a long liberal nationalist tradition, they saw Germanness as effectively synonymous with liberal bourgeois values. Their chief enemies were the clericalism of the church, the reactionary nobility and federalist schemes that would have emboldened them. Also following on from a long tradition, Slavs and their nationalist movement were cast as lackeys of these reactionary forces. In 1867, after passing the Austro-Hungarian Compromise, the liberal-dominated Austrian Reichsrat appointed a subcommittee of seven—later expanded to nine—parliamentarians tasked with redefining the nature of the state. Eight of the nine were Germanophone liberals. Over the course of 1867 they drafted a series of laws that amounted to a constitutional revolution in the Austrian half of the monarchy, which included the Austrian duchies, Bohemian lands, Galicia, Bukovina, Dalmatia, and Istria.

They provided for the independence of the judiciary, checked the power of the monarch, and laid out a series of fundamental rights for every citizen including freedom of speech, religious belief, assembly, and more. Jews were fully emancipated, henceforth completely equal to their fellow Austrians. They also established a bicameral central parliament, with an upper house consisting of hereditary peers and a lower house consisting of members elected by regional diets, themselves directly elected. Franz Joseph sanctioned the laws in December 1867. In addition to an elected central parliament, Austria's constitutional revolution created Landtags (provincial diets) as well as democratic and highly autonomous municipalities. With their restrictive franchises that favoured the traditionally Germanized middle and upper-classes, Landtags would largely be dominated by Austro-German liberals in the decades after 1860. The same was true of the Reichsrat itself, which was in liberal hands until 1879. With the Reichsrat, government, and most Landtags under their control, they set about pursuing their own revolution from above, passing liberal reforms targeting the church, bureaucracy, education, and army.[62]

Their envisioned Austrian state would be liberal, but also distinctly German, conflicting with the very spirit of the constitution they had drafted in 1867, which guaranteed national and linguistic rights. But the article that protected these rights was vague on a number of counts. One of the central points of contention was the precise definition of 'languages customarily used in a province' (*landesübliche Sprachen*). This provision and ones like it did, however, open a path for Czechs, Slovenes, and Poles to enjoy schooling in their native language, thereby challenging the presumed role of German as the only language of higher culture and education in the monarchy.

This was far less than national activists would have liked, but more than was offered to Sorbs living in Saxony and Prussia. Sorbs were not only divided between these two states, but also by religion and language. Prussia—where the vast majority of Sorbs lived—did nothing to aid Sorbian national development, let alone to help bridge the linguistic or confessional divides that existed between them. Earlier in the century Prussian officials had declared Sorbian a 'deeply decayed language' that could not 'possibly be suitable for the kind of instruction of the young which our times demands'. The state therefore discouraged its use in schools and churches. The Saxon government was more tolerant, allowing school instruction to be carried out in Sorbian, but with the important caveat that children also be taught to read and write German.[63] Strong assimilatory pressures meant that by the mid-to-late nineteenth century Sorbs were increasingly bilingual, with those living in urban areas showing a strong tendency to assimilate entirely. 'The fate of the Wendish language is sealed' wrote a contemporary German ethnographer: 'The small language island is nowadays only just an ethnographic curiosity'.[64] Sorbian speakers who had once numbered perhaps a quarter of a million were reduced to just 106,618 in 1900.[65]

* * *

In his 1882 *Die Lehre von Staatenverbindungen*, the prominent legal scholar Georg Jellinek pointed out that the 'unitary state' was foreign to the political development of Central European states. They were instead defined by their composite nature, a never-ending source of controversy only complicated by the dawn of constitutionalism. This was especially true in the case of Austria-Hungary. The compromise that created it had been predicated on the notion that the Kingdom of Hungary retained its fundamental statehood; but Bohemians, Croatians, and Austrian centralists all argued that their own 'historical-political individualities' of choice possessed fundamental statehood too. As democratized party politics dawned on the Habsburg Monarchy, high-level national struggles would largely take place at this constitutional level. Past romanticist notions of Pan-Slavic unity, or even Czechoslovak and Yugoslav unity, faded into the background as the monarchy's Slavs leaned on their claims to state right to advance their nationalist aspirations.[66]

In 1868 pro-Hungarian—'unionist'—Croatian politicians concluded a compromise with Budapest that gave the Kingdom of Croatia-Slavonia autonomy in education, administration, religious affairs, and justice.[67] Croatia-Slavonia would maintain its own political life centred on the Sabor while sending delegates to both houses of the central parliament in Budapest. A Croatian minister without portfolio would sit in the Hungarian cabinet while an appointed *ban* represented the royal government. As with the Austro-Hungarian compromise, both sides interpreted it in their own way. Croatian legal scholars and politicians claimed it confirmed Croatian statehood, while Hungarians contended there was no separate Croatian state at all.[68]

The party most aggressively opposed to the politics of the compromise was the small Party of Right that had been founded in 1861. It demanded near-total independence from both Vienna and Budapest on the grounds that Croatia was a sovereign kingdom by state right. Its leader, Ante Starčević, had been an Illyrianist in his youth, but in the 1850s came to reject just about every single one of its postulates. In large part this was thanks to a series of polemical exchanges with the Serbian philologist Vuk Karadžić, who claimed most Croats were simply Serbs, if they existed at all. Starčević thus came to insist on an aggressive assertion of the Croatian name—as opposed to more generalized 'Illyrian' or 'Yugoslav' concepts. His program was broadly liberal and democratic, but also thoroughly nationalistic, rejecting cooperation with other Slavs and espousing profound anti-Serbianism.[69]

Without his knowledge, his party co-founder Eugen Kvaternik launched a futile armed uprising in 1871 to win Croatian independence, easily crushed by the imperial army and leading to the party's marginalization for the remainder of the decade. The National Party, with its roots in the Illyrian movement, took a more sanguine approach, accepting the compromise and even welcoming pro-Hungarian unionists into its ranks in 1873 as the patriotic Ban Ivan Mažuranić took power. The Kingdom of Croatia-Slavonia's autonomy may have been limited, but Croatian was deployed in education and administration and the state lent its support to nationalist initiatives. Mažuranić passed a raft of reformist and liberal legislation, unifying the country administratively, emancipating Jews, and establishing a Croatian university in Zagreb in 1874. Despite its limitations, it was certainly a far cry from the oppressive days of neo-absolutism.

Thanks to an informal arrangement with Vienna, Galicia was able to achieve a similar degree of autonomy. The local Polish nobility was effectively given free rein to develop their province according to their wishes, asserting a conservative, loyalist, and Polish-Galician quasi-national identity.[70] Symbolic of Galicia's special place in the Austrian half of the monarchy was the maintenance of a minister without portfolio in the Viennese cabinet, sometimes even referred to as the Galician 'ambassador' or 'mission'.[71] Polish became the official language of administration, politics, and education, extending to the universities of Krakow

THE AGE OF NATIONALISM

and Lwów (Lemberg).[72] The 'mini-compromise' represented a symbolic end to Austria's largely fruitless attempts to integrate Galicia into German-speaking Central Europe.

While Galicia's new position was a triumph for the dominant Poles, it represented a defeat for the nascent Ruthenian (Ukrainian) national movement. Since first emerging in earnest in 1848, self-consciously recognizing an affinity between the millions of 'Ruthenians' living in the Russian Empire and calling for a division of Galicia in two, it had steadily found more adherents amongst the Greek Catholic clergy, students, intellectuals, and the small self-consciously Ruthenian middle class. They were strongly represented in the Galician diet throughout the 1860s, during which their conflict with the Poles only grew more intense.

Many in the Ruthenian movement thus increasingly looked eastwards for salvation, embracing a 'Russophile' orientation as a cudgel against Polish pretensions to dominance over them. At the time the dominant view in the Russian Empire was that Ruthenians or Ukrainians were simply 'Little Russians', one branch of a greater Russian whole that also included 'Great Russians' and 'White Russians'. The Galician Russophiles propagated this in their own Russian Council founded in 1870 (which they claimed served as a direct continuation of the Supreme Ruthenian Council of 1848) as well as in their own newspaper and literature. But this Russophile party in Galicia did little to arrest the decline of Ruthenian political fortunes over the course of the 1870s, nor did it represent a lasting reorientation of their national identity. It was a younger generation of 'Ukrainophiles' who proved to be more successful in the long run, celebrating the vernacular and embracing the Ukrainian name as part of an effort to assert the distinctiveness of the Ukrainian nation. They coalesced around the National Council in 1885, which they claimed was the true successor of the 1848 Supreme Ruthenian Council.[73]

In Bohemia, repeated attempts were made from 1867 to 1871 to find a compromise that would satisfy the nationalist Old Czechs and their noble allies. Cisleithania's first five minister-presidents would all find themselves brought down by this seemingly intractable problem. Franz Joseph prevaricated, unsure of how he could satisfy the centralist desires of Austro-German liberals, the privileged dualism of the Hungarians, and the federalist ambitions of the Czechs all at once. The closest they came was a series of draft laws in 1871 that would have recognized Bohemia's state right and committed Franz Joseph to being crowned king of Bohemia, but the emperor eventually decided against it amidst a wave of

Austro-German protest. Their national aspirations again frustrated, the Old Czechs continued their boycott of the Reichsrat.[74]

Their dissatisfaction only underlined the growing complacency of Austro-German liberals. Like all liberals, they saw themselves as agents of the forward march of history. The disgruntled clerics, aristocrats, and Slavic nationalists opposed to them they thought of as too disorganized and backwards to present a real challenge. But the crash of the Vienna stock market in 1873 profoundly shook the faith so many had placed in the power of economic progress since the 1850s. In 1879, after sixteen years of boycotts, the Old Czechs were convinced to enter the Reichsrat. Fresh elections to the Reichsrat provided the Constitutional Party with 175 seats. A new conservative-Slav coalition headed up by Franz Joseph's childhood friend Eduard von Taaffe had 178. A progressively expanding franchise combined with the fruits of the local triumphs of national movements would soon turn Austrian liberals into just one political force amongst many.

10

THE SPIRIT OF SECESSION

In September 1892, the Association of Berlin Artists extended a prestigious invitation. After his successful show in Kristiania, Berlin's leading association of visual artists decided to give the relatively unknown Norwegian painter Edvard Munch an exhibition in its newly built neo-Renaissance palazzo. It was to be the first ever one-man show in the association's fifty-year history. At the opening on 5 November 1892, Munch's triumph quickly turned to scandal. Not expecting the avant-garde nature of his work, conservative members of the association were horrified to see what they had sponsored. The *Frankfurter Zeitung* reported: 'An impressionist, and a mad one at that, has broken into our herd of fine, solidly bourgeois artists'. Amidst outraged demands for the show to be cancelled, a special members' assembly met a week after its opening. A heated meeting followed in which a narrow majority ordered the show to be cancelled 'out of reverence to art and artistic effort'.[1]

Chaotic scenes ensued. Shouting, screaming and fighting seemed to presage the 'total rupture' that one artist had predicted if the show was cancelled. A group of younger members banded together and stormed out of the hall while older ones tried to restrain them. Forty-eight of these rebels soon published an open declaration in a leading Berlin paper condemning the vote 'as a measure that contravenes common decency'. Berlin's cultural scene only narrowly—and temporarily—avoided a 'secession'.[2] Munch became a celebrity overnight. Shows across Germany followed, eventually bringing him to Munich.

Earlier that year, the Bavarian capital had experienced the first full-blown 'secession' when ninety-six artists had resigned from the city's equivalent of the Association of Berlin Artists to form their own breakaway group. Its goal was to be more open to new artistic currents than the staid conservative artistic establishment. The 'secessionist' movement would eventually spread to Vienna in 1897, Berlin in 1898, and just about every other major Central European city. As the contemporary art historian Hermann Uhde-Bernays put it, the 'core of the argument was about novelty: a new art, new theatre, new opera, new concerts in new concert halls; it was about a rejuvenation of old schools, about a new and fresh life'.[3]

The 'rejuvenation of old schools', the search for a 'new and fresh' life. These were the very same ideas that energized a new political generation that radically redrew the political map of every Central European society in the decades after 1880. The liberal parties and movements that had dominated until then were elitist and 'anti-popular', managed by notables who had a stranglehold on social, cultural and political life. Those who wanted change were left with little choice but secession. As a general rule, the more successful a national movement was, the fewer major secessions there were and the later they came. Hungary's hegemonic Liberal Party, for example, comfortably ruled without any serious challenge until 1905. But their counterparts in Austria experienced a crisis of purpose almost immediately after their fall from power in 1879.

At a major liberal conference in 1880 nationalists associated with the 'Young' faction tried to push Austrian liberalism in a more avowedly German nationalist direction. They concluded that Austrian liberalism had failed and Austro-Germans should embrace a more communitarian ethnic nationalism in its place. The brainchild of this school of thought was the Linz Program of 1882, whose leading proponents included Victor Adler, Georg von Schönerer and Heinrich Friedjung.[4] It called for Hungary, Galicia, and other overwhelmingly non-German parts of Austria to be given their independence to aid Austria's total Germanization, the country's only path to national rejuvenation.[5] The Franco-Prussian War over a decade before had provoked similar calls and programs from Austro-Germans that continued to grow in the 1870s as a rising generation demanded a more assertive progressive German nationalism to take the place of elitist liberalism.[6]

By the early 1880s the underlying political, social, and cultural state of the country had changed to such an extent that this program suddenly found a much broader appeal. Not only had Austrian liberals fallen from power after losing many seats in the Reichsrat in 1879, but the first census in 1880—which asked for 'language of daily use'—made clear just how weak the position of 'Germandom' was in many parts of Austria. German Laibach was outnumbered by Slovene Ljubljana more than three to one.

THE SPIRIT OF SECESSION

Over the following twenty years the Slovene-speaking population would grow by sixty-two per cent while German speakers declined by five per cent.[7] The situation in Prague and its surroundings was even more dire, with German-speakers outnumbered by Czech-speakers by more than five to one; by 1910 it would be twelve to one.[8] Little more than thirty years prior Austro-Germans read confident 'scientific' estimates that Bohemia had three Germans for every four Czechs, with Germans outnumbering Czechs in Prague nearly two to one—all based on the questionable assumption that those who used German in their day-to-day professional life must have been Germans.[9] From the ivory tower of their German Casinos, they had overestimated both their size and their strength and were now forced to contend with the consequences.[10]

'Until now I have only ever considered myself an Austrian' wrote the Austro-German liberal Julius Alexander Schindler in 1881. He had seen himself as a 'citizen of a great empire', that was willing to 'lovingly communicate its own customs, knowledge and skills to other more backward state-compatriots'—unlike the German Reich, which was content to 'merely manage and enjoy its acquired cultural heritage'. But with the recent 'handing over of state life' to backwards Slavs, who acted as 'lackeys of feudalism and ultramontanism [that is, promoting the supreme authority of the Pope]', he was forced to reconsider his allegiances. After 'a long, fruitless hope and wait for the final victory of the Austrian state idea, now I too remember that I am a German by birth and *Bildung*'.[11]

Other liberal organizations across Austria came to similar conclusions, often under the influence or even direction of the figures behind the Linz Program. The Liberal Association of Linz became the German Association. The Constitutional Society of Germans in Bohemia became the German Club. The Laibach Turnverein (gymnastic club) became the Laibach German Turnverein. By the mid-1880s nearly half of all liberal political associations in Moravia had German in their name. Newspapers underwent a similar conversion, like Styrian Cilli's *Cillier Zeitung*, which renamed itself *German Watch* in 1883 after spending the previous year publishing articles in support of the Linz Program and even full speeches of Schönerer.[12]

Perhaps the most important of all German nationalist organizations was the German School Association, founded in 1880 by the activists behind the Linz Program. Its aim was to help fund German schools and teachers in borderlands where otherwise German children might be 'lost' to the national enemy that had politically triumphed. By the latter part of the decade, it had over 100,000 members in nearly 1,000 local chapters, making it 'one of the largest bourgeois voluntary associations in the German-speaking world'.[13] Many of the ancestors of Austria's German-speakers had embraced German *Bildung* as emblematic of a certain set of universalist middle class values that promised to help raise all of Austria's peoples to a higher level of civilization. Now, their descendants were redefining this German *Bildung* as a precarious heritage under siege by rival nationalists.[14]

Austro-Germans began to put up statues of Emperor Joseph II in municipalities under their control in the early 1880s, celebrating him as an enlightened promoter of German culture. Usually erected in front of buildings that housed local German nationalist organizations, they often looked nearly identical because they came from the same ironworks in Moravia. Their unveilings were accompanied by speeches in which Joseph was praised for recognizing that only German culture could 'oust the remainders of semi-barbarism' and build a 'mighty barrier against the East'. In Budweis it provided the occasion to emphasize that it 'is and remains a German city'.[15] Czech and Slovene nationalists responded by building up their own private organizations to wage the national struggles.[16]

Large organizations that took interest in the plight of their supposed co-nationals everywhere—like the school associations—helped build a sense of solidarity and identity between nationalists no matter the states they lived in. The German School Association kept its members abreast of the latest developments on the German 'borderlands', or of the latest developments in German nationalism more broadly, without any real distinction between Reich and Austrian Germans. One 1885 publication warned against using foreign words and informed its readers that a General German Language Association was being formed to maintain the purity of the German tongue.[17] Many of its subscribers were no doubt members of other German nationalist associations, which flourished in the Reich no less than in Austria.

By the 1880s, the 'Polish problem' in the east had become a mainstream concern for Reich Germans in a seeming reflection of the 'dangers' of Slavicization faced by their Austrian compatriots. An 1883 article showed in meticulous statistical detail that the German population in Prussia's eastern provinces was declining—startling not only because it signalled the dreaded 'Polonization' of large swathes of Prussia, but also because it was a stark reversal of previous trends.[18] Like elsewhere in Central Europe, the tendency for most of the nineteenth century had been the progressive Germanization of urban centres. But from the 1870s this began to change, affecting country and town alike. Between 1871 and 1895 the number of towns in Posen with a German-Jewish majority halved. The interior minister Robert von Puttkamer warned the Reichstag in 1885 that in a variety of eastern provinces the Polish element was rapidly outgrowing the German.[19]

The spectre of national conquest and death loomed large in the rhetoric of nationalists of all stripes. In the early nineteenth century Ján Kollár had lamented that in eastern Germany, 'Every town, every village, every river and mountain that had a Slavic name seemed ... like a grave or a monument in this huge cemetery'.[20] Decades later the liberal Austrian deputy Armand von Dumreicher echoed the sentiment in noting that in many regions of Austria 'German creations remain, but the German people are gone. Yet even here the stones speak; they speak for those who were and are no more'.[21] By the final decades of the century this spectre was even reaching into the heart of the Reich.

For many German nationalists the natural solution was more proactive measures from the government aimed at 'inner colonization', a position that even Bismarck came to endorse. Against a wider backdrop of anxieties about Polish advances as well as political crisis in the Reichstag, Bismarck demanded from his cabinet in 1886 'a more rigorous resumption of resistance to Polonization, even the encouragement of Germanization'. Prussia undertook a frenzy of anti-Polish measures.[22] The most notorious of all was the Settlement Law of 1886, which established a Royal Prussian Settlement Commission in the Provinces of West Prussia and Posen. This was given an official mandate to buy up Polish-owned lands and then sell them on to German settlers, but despite settling about 22,000 German families the commission failed to change the ethnic balance in any province.[23] A similar scheme in Austria, initiated by the private nationalist association Südmark, to settle Germans in Slovene-majority southern Styria also had little impact.[24]

Nonetheless, the endeavour provided an opportunity to broadcast to the nationalist public the issues facing Germandom in the 'borderlands', catalysing the growth of an increasingly vitriolic ethnic nationalism. German-Slavic 'borderlands' became an ideological battleground for nationalists of all stripes to project their fears and fantasies.[25] Towards the turn of the century these nationalist conflicts and struggles became increasingly internationalized as the local linguistic struggles of earlier decades gave way to more organized and regularized mass politics. Census figures were touted as objective measures of national strength and 'property'. Activists lobbied parents to send their children to the 'correct' school. Nationalist publications wrote about their activities as grand messianic struggles against implacable national enemies, seeking to assert their 'national' ownership over land and urban centres.

Like elsewhere in Europe, Charles Darwin's theory of natural selection was hugely influential in Central Europe from the 1870s, fuelling interest in its putative consequences for human societies and the study of different 'races'.[26] Indeed, for the pioneering sociologist Ludwig Gumplowicz, 'race' was essential to understanding the political development of human societies. A Polish Jew from Krakow, Gumplowicz would act as one of the most eloquent proponents of Social Darwinist thinking as a professor at the University of Graz from 1875. Politics in his eyes was really about the struggle between different races for survival and supremacy. That went even for Austria-Hungary, a state he saw as defined by German and Hungarian racial domination over 'less developed' Slavs. A state was not merely a 'loose accumulation of individuals' but rather an 'organism' consisting 'of dissimilar elements, whether we call them classes, estates, tribes, peoples or nations'.[27]

Such ideas lent credence to the idea that Germans and Slavs were not simply two conflicting nations, but two different biological races locked in a struggle for existence. When the Südmark hosted a visitor from Berlin, he reported that German settlers 'must often rebuild their houses from the foundations up, since the German master race cannot live in a pigsty the way the Slav does'.[28] If Germans and Slavs were indeed such different 'races', then it was questionable whether they could ever truly share a common political home. This vision of society as fundamentally conflictual, with unequal human groups locked in constant struggle, would be most forcefully expressed in Houston Stewart Chamberlain's best-selling *The Foundations of the Nineteenth Century* published in 1899. Chamberlain was an Englishman, but the book was written and published in German. He lived in Vienna, married to the daughter of the great composer Richard Wagner, where he had imbibed the spirit of racialist German nationalism and developed it into an all-encompassing view of European history. It was the fate of two races in particular, he argued, that defined its contours. Not the German and the Slav, but the 'Aryan' and the Jewish.[29]

* * *

THE SPIRIT OF SECESSION

On 10 September 1882, around 300 men descended on a venue in central Dresden. In the ballroom where they met, proud busts of the Austrian and German emperors as well as the king of Saxony stood on the podium. On the wall was a framed letter from Otto von Bismarck thanking the innocuously named German Reform Association for its greetings. But pride of place in this authoritative display was given to something odd: a life-size portrait of a Hungarian peasant girl, standing on a path leading to a synagogue.[30]

Around five months earlier, the subject of the painting, Eszter Solymosi, had gone missing in the small eastern Hungarian village of Tiszaeszlár. She had been sent to buy extra paint needed for her family's spring cleaning but never made it home. Her distraught mother went about questioning the villagers, eventually encountering József Scharf, a local Jew. This had happened somewhere before, he assured her. A child was lost and people started blaming the Jews, but it turned out she'd 'been sleeping among the tussocks'. The seeds of suspicion planted by this encounter did not take long to sprout. Two days later Eszter's mother asked the local and district authorities to investigate the synagogue to no avail. Rumours and accusations festered, eventually leading to an official inquiry. The heavy-handed local investigators soon launched a blood libel against over a dozen village Jews.[31]

Eszter's alleged ritual murder became an antisemitic cause célèbre in Hungary and beyond. The portrait on display in Dresden was reproduced in countless smaller prints, pictures and books, and inspired a far more graphic painting of the murder itself, produced in Zagreb in October 1882, which authorities rushed to confiscate.[32] It provided a visceral emotional catalyst for a burgeoning new wave of political antisemitism that had culminated in the Congress for the Safeguarding of Non-Jewish Interests in Dresden. Presiding over it was the Protestant clergyman Adolf Stöcker, a court chaplain to Emperor Wilhelm I. Most attendees were German, including several radical antisemitic rabble-rousers who had risen to prominence over the previous decade. Three Hungarian members of parliament joined them, including Győző Istóczy, who later founded the country's first antisemitic party. And from Austria one of the central figures behind the Linz Program, Georg von Schönerer, joined too.[33]

In 1873 Europe had entered a period of prolonged economic crisis, producing widespread economic insecurity and anxiety. The liberal promise of a progressively better society in which the volatile and fluid market mechanism took over from the rigid and hierarchical world of yesteryear seemed to many a false promise. Conservative landowners, priests, artisans, and shopkeepers alike saw the entire project of a liberal society as the roots of their misery. Calls grew for the return of protectionism, the revival of guilds, and laws against 'usury' and 'peddling'. The eloquent leader of the Reich's Catholic Centre Party proclaimed in 1879 that his party would serve as the 'liquidator' of the 'bankruptcy' of the 'liberal economy'.[34] But what would this mean for one of the liberal era's greatest achievements, the emancipation of the Jews?

For the mainstream of every established party—including the Centre Party—there was no question of rolling this back. But after the stock market crash of 1873, anti-Jewish sentiment had begun to crop up in the German press. Conservative publicists began painting a picture of a corrupt alliance between greedy liberals and usurious Jews wrecking the economy with immoral speculation.[35] The antisemitic and formerly liberal journalist Otto Glagau would coin a simple phrase that encapsulated the thrust of this new kind of anti-Jewish sentiment: 'The social question is the Jewish question'.[36] Stöcker was the founder of the anti-liberal Christian Social Party, which was meant to give political expression to this whole conservative strain of anti-modernism, blending social conservatism with an extensive program of economic paternalism. A year after its founding in 1878, he embraced what Wilhelm Marr had recently deemed 'antisemitism'.

In 1880 three prominent German 'antisemites' organized a petition that demanded a ban on Jewish immigration and the exclusion of Jews from public positions. This was presented to Bismarck in 1882 with over 200,000 signatures, mostly from north and east Prussia.[37] At the Dresden conference in 1882, the eight antisemitic resolutions passed failed to satisfy two of the attendees, who criticized the supposedly 'soft' language and called for immediate, extreme action. Just six months later a far smaller congress met in Saxon Chemnitz, presided over by Otto Glagau with an even more racist tone.[38] Most of the original attendees stayed away, and the movement to build an 'antisemitic international' fizzled out.

Over the course of the 1880s, antisemitism nevertheless continued to find new adherents, provoking fresh political secessions. Victor Adler and Heinrich Friedjung—who had drafted the Linz Program alongside Schönerer—were both of Jewish descent. The rise of political antisemitism contributed to Adler's total break with German nationalism, and he would go on to become a founder of the Austrian Social Democratic

Party. Friedjung, meanwhile, doubled down on his Greater German nationalism, but found himself coming up against radical ethnic nationalists who denied he could be German at all. In 1885 the liberal deputies in the Reichsrat split into a moderate German Austrian Party and a more radical German Club. Friedjung took over the editorship of the German Club's house paper, and sixteen antisemitic members left the party in protest.[39]

This aggressive form of political antisemitism played on popular anti-liberal and anti-modernist anxieties, but it was often accompanied by a firm belief that Jews simply could not be authentic members of a given nation. Since their emancipation, Jews or people of Jewish descent had become more and more prominent in Central European life. They made up ten per cent of Vienna's population in 1880 and nearly twenty per cent of Budapest's.[40] In Vienna as in Hungary more broadly, Jews were vastly overrepresented in finance, law, industry, journalism, and education.[41] Even in Croatia-Slavonia, where they were less than one per cent of the population, they represented seventeen per cent of all lawyers and about a quarter of all doctors in 1910.[42]

The success of Jewish Central Europeans in integrating into mainstream Christian society and various bourgeois professions provoked antisemites to combine their anti-modernism, anti-liberalism and anti-capitalism with racism, social Darwinism and ideas of national purity. Jews were cast as parasitic capitalists exploiting the common folk and as racial inferiors who corrupted the wider nation.[43] Since the birth of modern German nationalism as a liberal, bourgeois phenomenon, Germanness had been open to effectively anyone ready to embrace standard High German in speech and writing and the culture associated with it. Even though legal emancipation had always lagged and prejudices remained, Jews learned German, took on German names, and ascended to the ranks of 'polite society'.

Similarly, in Hungary they had become a bulwark of Magyardom, and the political elite steadfastly defended Hungarian Jews against antisemitic attacks. Istóczy was interrupted and laughed at when making speeches in parliament, his party eventually folding in 1892.[44] In Croatia too, the axiom that a Jew could remain 'faithful to the religion of his fathers' and a be 'faithful son of his homeland' had undergirded the somewhat belated emancipation of Jews in 1873 and represented the stance of 'official' liberalism.[45] Despite being against Jewish emancipation early on in his reign, in subsequent decades Franz Jospeh went out of his way to engage with various Jewish synagogues, reciprocated in their overwhelming loyalty to the dynasty.[46]

Schönerer's struggle to win over the liberal nationalist mainstream to antisemitism was indicative of the broader tension between the politically oriented nationalism of established liberal institutions and the ethnically rooted nationalism espoused by secessionist radicals. His attempts to get the German School Association to take an antisemitic stance consistently floundered, with the organization steadfastly adhering to the established notion that Jews could be and were Germans if they embraced the German language.[47] The exclusivist institutions of Prague's embattled German community were similarly hostile to antisemitism, with Prague Jews overwhelmingly identifying as German.[48]

These were, however, the kind of notable-dominated institutions that the radical nationalists despised. The Association of German Students founded in Germany in 1880 would be open only to Christian students, a position taken by a similar Viennese organization two years later. Meanwhile the *Burschenschaften* (student fraternities) declared later that decade that 'Jewish subjects of the Reich' were not German and therefore could not be members of the fraternities.[49] Christian university students in Hungary similarly demanded a decrease in the number of Jewish students in 1881, though without success.[50] Many associations added an 'Aryan paragraph' to their statutes, stating that only people from the 'Aryan race' could be members. This was an anti-egalitarian attitude that sought to replace the aristocracy of noble blood with the aristocracy of the 'noble race' to which Jews supposedly did not belong.[51]

Antisemitism in the Reich was aided by the fact that one of its earliest and most prominent proponents was Heinrich von Treitschke. He seamlessly synthesized political antisemitism with older nationalist themes, linking early-nineteenth-century cosmopolitanism to the 'oriental ancestry' of its proponents, who also supposedly had an inner affinity with France.[52] That his position was condemned by many of his peers, such as Johann Gustav Droysen and Theodor Mommsen, contributed to a certain sense of complacency within the Reich's Jewish communities.[53] But in 1892 the German Conservative Party, one of the main pillars of the Prussian party system, adopted a platform that called for the Christian basis of the state to be reaffirmed, opposing the 'multifarious and obtrusive Jewish influence that disrupts our people's lives'.[54] Antisemitism had finally become impossible to ignore.

Jewish communities were hesitant to respond due to an uneasiness about overemphasizing their Jewishness at a time when they wanted to present themselves as just as German as their Christian counterparts. This was a particularly acute concern due to the growing prominence of 'Eastern Jews'. The vast majority of European Jews lived in miserable conditions in the Russian 'Pale of Settlement', denied not only political rights but even the most basic protection from the state. A wave of violent pogroms in 1881 was followed by yet more restrictions aimed at driving Jews out of the Russian countryside. An unprecedentedly large and constant stream of Jewish emigration began not just from Russia, but from Europe itself, with the United States of America the overwhelmingly popular destination. The emigrants tended to be poor, not well-educated, and Yiddish-speaking. To the highly assimilated Jews of Central Europe, their eastern coreligionists were unrecognizably foreign.[55]

As the German sociologist Franz Oppenheimer would later write, 'national' Jewishness was almost non-existent among Jews in Western and Central Europe. German Jews were '*national Germans*; the eastern Jews, on the other hand, are only rarely *national Russians*. They are *national Jews* as much as they are *cultural Jews*'.[56] Jews in the Russian Empire were generally far more religiously observant, barely integrated into Christian society, and subject to widespread, state-endorsed persecution. Jews in Germany, Austria and Hungary were less interested in the fate of these eastern Jews than in fighting off attempts by radical nationalists to deny them their place within the German, Austro-German or Hungarian nations.

When, in 1893, a centralized organization for German Jews was finally founded—one that would be the largest Jewish organization in Germany for decades—it bore the telling name of Central Association of German Citizens of the Jewish Faith. It grounded its defence against antisemitism in a liberal understanding of political nationhood. The first paragraph of its statutes demanded 'German-mindedness' from its members, placing Germanness even above 'Jewishness' in its values.[57] But for some Jews, the rise of modern political antisemitism combined with the plight of their eastern co-religionists prompted a more concerted attempt to grapple with their Jewish identity.

Theodor Herzl was the paradigmatic example. Born to a wealthy, assimilated, German-speaking Jewish family in Pest in 1860, he trained as a lawyer in Vienna before turning to playwriting and journalism. He spent the early 1890s as the *Neue Freie Presse*'s correspondent in Paris, bearing witness to the explosion of antisemitism associated with the Dreyfuss Affair and eventually becoming a convert to the Jewish national cause. He became convinced that the only defence against antisemitism in Europe was for Jews to found their own state as part of a general program of national renewal.

His plan was outlined in his seminal 1896 pamphlet *The Jewish State*, published in German in Leipzig and Vienna, which became a foundational text for the Zionist movement. It embraced the notion that there was a separate Jewish nation, seeking secession not only from European nationalisms, but from Europe itself. In 1897, in no small part thanks to Herzl's magnetic and energetic personality, the nascent movement was organized into an international Zionist Organization whose professed aim was to create a Jewish nation-state somewhere outside of Europe. While it won adherents—particularly amongst Jewish university students in the Habsburg Monarchy—in the first years after its founding it was, like many secessionist movements, a marginal attempt to grapple with the decline of liberalism in Central Europe. Upon Herzl's death in 1904 a Jewish nation-state was nowhere nearer to reality.[58]

* * *

Zagreb woke up to a shock on 7 August 1883. As strollers passed by government finance and customs buildings, they were suddenly confronted with plaques bearing a joint Croatian-Hungarian coat of arms surrounded by bilingual Croatian-Magyar inscriptions. Croatian nationalists saw the plaques not only as a symbolic affront, but also a blatant violation of the compromise which had defined Croatian as the country's sole official language. Anti-Hungarian demonstrations erupted across Croatia-Slavonia. In Zagreb agitated crowds emerged day after day, tearing down some of the plaques and smashing the windows of offending buildings.[59]

The incident brought about the fall of Ban Ladislav Pejačević, his duties handed over to an Austrian general who reasserted state authority throughout Croatia. Only after an embarrassed Hungarian government passed a law replacing the plaques with 'silent' ones (without any inscriptions) a few months later did Franz Joseph feel confident enough to restore civilian rule. At Hungarian Prime Minister Tisza's request, he appointed Károly Khuen-Héderváry as the new *ban* of Croatia-Slavonia on 1 December 1883. While Héderváry was the scion of a magnate family with considerable landholdings in Slavonia, he was a Tisza-loyalist and member of the ruling Liberal Party: his interests were firmly aligned with those of Budapest.

THE SPIRIT OF SECESSION

From the very beginning, the Croatian-Hungarian compromise had been controversial. Although Croatia-Slavonia achieved autonomy, it was left without Dalmatia, one of the historical lands of the 'Triune Kingdom'. To make matters worse, the port city of Fiume (Rijeka to Croats) was a 'separated body', considered a direct part of Hungary, while a huge expanse of Croatia-Slavonia was still ruled directly from Vienna as the Military Frontier. Ban Ivan Mažuranić's failure to have this frontier region reintegrated led to his resignation in 1880, and made clear how distant were ambitious national goals like the integration of Dalmatia, south Slav unity or full separation from Hungary.

In 1881 Franz Joseph decided to finally integrate the Military Frontier after all, with by-elections to the Sabor for the new districts taking place in early 1883. The highly restrictive franchise meant that most districts had only a few dozen voters, the overwhelming majority electing compromise-friendly representatives of the National Party. The most successful opposition party was Ante Starčević's Party of Right. Despite its inactivity in the early 1870s, this nationalist party had become incredibly popular amongst students and young intellectuals. Towards the end of the decade, it began to intensify its activities, reaching even into the lands of the frontier where it was able to appeal to local notables with their own grievances against the government.[60]

Still, Croatia's nationalists were pessimistic. The franchise limited the electorate to just about 45,000 men, half of whom were civil servants expected to reliably support the government.[61] The National Party, which had once been synonymous with Croatian national rebirth, was turned by Hédervary into a vessel for supporting the government's moderate liberal nationalism firmly within the bounds of the compromise with Hungary. In 1887 his electoral machinations paid huge dividends when the opposition parties suffered huge defeats. Hédervary would end up serving as *ban* until 1903, twenty years in which Croatian nationalists came to feel that the dualist system meant little more than Hungarian rule.

Social developments seemed to offer no consolation. Despite the symbolic triumph of Croatian language and culture, German retained a privileged position in urban life. When German Studies was introduced at the University of Zagreb in 1896 all the lectures were held in German, simply assuming native-level command of the language. Croatian authors continued to include large blocks of German text in their writings, expecting their educated audience would understand it. German visitors like the philologist Hermann Hirt could still comfortably note in 1896 that,

'Throughout Croatia one hardly remembers they have left the German-speaking area'.⁶²

Nevertheless, language or even religious background were not necessarily indicative of one's political ideology. The brothers Josip and Jacob Frank, for example, were born into a German-speaking Jewish family in Essek. Jacob was a prolific publicist of establishment-liberal orientation and was the first owner of the local German paper *Die Drau*. Though it supported the government, it was by no means 'anti-national', praising Croatian cultural advances and reporting widely on South Slavs more generally.⁶³ His brother Josip, meanwhile, was a convert both to Catholicism and the Croatian nationalist cause. While working as a lawyer in Zagreb, he became an enthusiastic and active supporter of the Party of Right, eventually becoming one of Starčević's closest collaborators. In 1895 the Party of Right split in two after a short-lived alliance with the Independent National Party. Starčević and Frank led the secessionist faction—which came to be known as the 'Frankists'—that hoped to reorient Croatian politics towards Vienna and thus achieve true Croatian statehood.⁶⁴

If the case of Bohemia was anything to go by, Vienna in fact had little to offer. In 1889 yet another attempt was launched at a compromise in Bohemia. Eduard von Taaffe's government arranged extensive negotiations between itself, the Old Czechs, some German liberals, and great landowners. They came to an agreement surprisingly quickly, agreeing in 1890 to effectively partition Bohemia in two halves, one German and one bilingual Czech-German, sitting together in the Landtag in their own national curias. What none of those involved seem to have properly accounted for was the sea change in Czech politics that meant the Old Czechs no longer represented the bulk of Czech nationalist opinion.⁶⁵

Frustrated with endless boycotts as well as an unpalatable alliance with conservative aristocrats, the 'Young Czechs' had seceded from the party of their elders in 1874 to form their own National Liberal Party. They rejected the heritage of Palacký and instead claimed to be the heirs of Karel Havlíček—an early rejecter of Pan-Slavism—espousing a more radical program that called for universal manhood suffrage and the strengthening of the Czech peasantry at the expense of the great landowners. Their popularity steadily rose in the 1880s, but it was the 1890 compromise attempt that catapulted them to the forefront of nationalist politics. They mercilessly criticized the Old Czechs for ostensibly selling out to the Germans, a message that helped them win the most Czech votes in the 1891 elections to the Reichsrat, as they embraced the issue of Bohemian state right that had once defined their elders. Even many Old Czechs turned on the compromise, but the damage had been done. In the 1895 Bohemian Landtag elections the Old Czechs were reduced to just three seats while the Young Czechs took ninety and became the largest party in the country.[66]

As in Croatia, the secession from and subsequent eclipse of the older generation reflected (alongside a wider gulf in values) frustration with the failure of their tactics to realize nationalist dreams. That Prague was a Czech metropolis seemed like little consolation when the state institutions were still dominated by Germans, and Moravia and its capital of Brünn, alongside Bohemian cities like Budweis, remained firmly under German control.

Even dualist Hungary, for all its Magyarizing policies, fell short of the expectations of many of its nationalists. When the pro-Austro-Hungarian-compromise 'Deák Party' and moderate anti-compromise 'Left Centre' merged in 1875 to form the Liberal Party, factions against the merger seceded from both. In 1884 those that seceded from the latter merged with the 'Far Left' to form the Independence Party. It rejected the compromise and celebrated Kossuth and his failed bid for independence, by the late 1890s becoming the largest opposition party in the country—aided by the return of Kossuth's son Ferenc to Hungary—despite being little more than a protest party. Since it rejected the compromise, it was almost impossible to imagine how it could ever take power. They themselves seemed to agree, not even bothering to run enough candidates to actually win a majority in elections, while rallying to Ferenc Kossuth more due to his name than his aptitude for politics.[67]

The Hungarian government trumpeted the steadily rising number of those that claimed Magyar as their mother tongue in the censuses of 1880, 1890, 1900, and 1910 as evidence of the success of their whole political project. Yet a quarter of Hungary was still bi- or multilingual in 1910 and German still seemed to pose an irresistible attraction for so many living in urban centres.[68] In Pozsony—historic Pressburg—a common joke went that the city was Slovak in the morning when the market was open, Magyar in the afternoon when workers filled offices and students schools, and German in the evening when the city flocked to cafes, restaurants, and pubs.[69]

The largely German-speaking elites did not object to measures like the erection of bilingual street signs in 1880, the symbolic use of Magyar in private associations, or even learning Magyar itself. But nor did they see it as any reason to abandon their culture of German literacy either. Despite decades of rural immigration, in 1910 Pozsony remained a diverse hodgepodge of languages with a noticeable German predominance. The numbers of native German and Magyar speakers were roughly equal at 32,790 and 31,705, with native Slovak speakers trailing behind at 11,673, but amongst these three largest linguistic groups in the city seventy-five per cent spoke German, seventy per cent Hungarian, and thirty-seven per cent Slovak.[70] Most jobs advertised required both German and Magyar, while jobseekers often touted their knowledge of the three local languages. To those, like the chairman of the local Magyarizing association, it was a disappointment that this 'pearl in the Hungarian crown' was still so conspicuously non-Magyar.[71]

Even the great national capital itself was certainly far from a purely Magyar metropolis. In 1880, sixty-two per cent of those that claimed Magyar as their mother tongue in Budapest also spoke German. In 1910, ninety-two per cent of the roughly half of Magyar speakers in the city that knew another language spoke German, a percentage basically unchanged since 1880 and one that could also be observed in Zagreb, Essek, Pressburg, and countless other urban areas. All in all, nearly half of Budapest knew German. Despite its diminished status, German retained its unique position as the 'first second language' of choice and indeed by 1910 had more speakers than ever in Hungary and Croatia-Slavonia.[72]

The triumph of national cultures therefore did not spell the end of German's role as the lingua franca of the educated, but only its partial relegation to the status of a prestigious auxiliary language. German was not just the language of 'the Germans'. It was the language of industry and commerce, of advanced science and sociology, of Einstein and Freud, Marx and Weber. Even though Magyars, Croats, Czechs, and Poles could study at universities in their native tongues, they flocked in ever-greater numbers to German-language universities in Cisleithania and the Reich.[73] Despite the protests of nationalists, 'child exchanges' were still common in linguistically mixed areas—so common that the central committee of the Czech Nationalist Union of Northern Bohemia complained that local notables that sat on the boards of nationalist organizations themselves continued to send their children on language exchanges.[74] Despite Central Europe's growing divisions, the social glue of German literacy showed few signs of abating.

11

THE NEW OLD REGIME

For six months in 1900, Paris hosted the largest and most extravagant world's fair ever seen. It was perhaps the first fitting successor to the 1851 Great Exhibition in the Crystal Palace in London, which had sparked a craze for 'international' or 'world' fairs. In an age of rapid industrialization and globalization, countries were keen to showcase their technological advancements, agricultural products, and artistic refinement, but usually it was much more of a national than the claimed international affair. At Paris's previous 'world's fair', held in 1889 on the centenary of the French Revolution and for which the Eiffel Tower was built, no major European power even attended. Monarchs had no desire to celebrate the most famous revolt against one of their own. The 1900 edition was different. With varying enthusiasm, every great power in Europe leaped at the opportunity to showcase its splendour. They prepared for years, the most important of them given prime real estate along the Seine to build their own special pavilions. Alongside the fair, Paris hosted the second edition of the revived Olympic games and over 100 international conferences on everything from dentistry and publishing to fencing and postal regulations. Millions of visitors streamed through the city's streets over the course of the year.[1]

The Central European states represented in Paris exuded confidence, not only in their achievements in art, industry and commerce, but in the success of the political ideas they represented. Austria-Hungary and the German Reich had been born 1867 and 1871 as products of war and compromise, engendering bitter disappointment as well as cautious optimism. Few believed the new political arrangements were ideal. Critics proliferated over the years. But the victors of these new settlements certainly felt that by 1900 they had plenty to celebrate.

The growth in the German Reich's power, prestige and wealth was comparable perhaps only with that of the United States of America around the turn of the century. From a newly unified country of forty-one million in 1871, it had grown to a stunning sixty-eight million by 1914. Its economy nearly doubled between 1896 and 1912, leaving its Habsburg ally looking like an industrial minnow by comparison.[2] It was young and vigorous, as the German catalogue for the fair pointed out, with sixty-one per cent of its population under the age of thirty.[3] In the final decades of the nineteenth century the Reich had become the workshop of the world. Its universities were cutting-edge, its cities modern, its technology advanced. Even its social policies were markedly progressive. From the early 1880s Bismarck had pioneered a system of 'state socialism', providing workers with pensions, insurance and basic protections against exploitation in an attempt to foster social harmony.

The Reich's economic success had a powerful integrative effect. It made Germans feel like the whole of their princely states was much greater than the sum of their parts. In 1888, the free cities of Hamburg and Bremen had finally decided to join the customs union which had integrated much of Germany even before the final unification in 1871. Gone were the days when, as at the Crystal Palace in 1851, Württembergian or Saxon patriots wanted to make themselves seen. There was now a single German pavilion that in theme and content betrayed little of the country's divisions. It was built in the style of a Hanseatic town hall, symbolic of the commercial image the Reich sought to project. The impressive technological achievements appeared to prove that Germany was ahead in every aspect of industry, from cranes to synthetic chemicals. That industrial might had already convinced many Germans that the country could become a true world power, and as such needed to pursue *Weltpolitik*—'world politics'. In the main German retrospective work on the fair, an industrial lobbyist wrote that the question of whether the Reich would adopt a consistent *Weltpolitik* would determine 'whether Germany will be a great world-empire at the end of the present century, or whether it will have sunk into complete political insignificance'.[4]

It was a sentiment that resonated at the very pinnacle of the German state. In 1888 a young Wilhelm II took the reigns of Prussia and Germany, dismissing Bismarck soon after and embracing an ambitious 'New Course' to turn the Reich into a true world power. Wilhelm was a lover of the modern, of trains, cars and zeppelins. He devoured newspapers, keeping abreast of all the latest developments in his realm and the world at large. In the late nineteenth century there were few things as modern as building a vast overseas empire. In 1897, Wilhelm's foreign minister Bernhard von Bülow famously called for Germany to find its 'place in the sun', an ambition which the monarch wholeheartedly shared. Overseas colonies that had been accumulated since 1884 in Africa, China and the Pacific were touted as the building blocks of the Reich's future *Weltpolitik*. To support it, Germany embarked on a hugely expensive naval program in 1897 with the ambition of eventually building a fleet capable of taking on the British in the North Sea. Colonies, the navy and the patriotic Kaiser himself were symbols of a new Germany that had finally transcended its many divisions and taken its place on the stage of world history as a unified nation-state.[5]

Just a short walk up the Seine, visitors could marvel at the equally proud Hungarian pavilion. Unlike its German counterpart, its focus was on culture and history. Utilizing a series of characteristic architectural and artistic styles, it presented a narrative of Hungarian history stretching back 1,000 years. A highlight was the 'Hussar room', showcasing Hungary's great martial export. In the eighteenth and nineteenth centuries this style of light cavalry had become a necessity for every European army, helping spread the fashion for moustaches that by 1900 had reached its zenith. Lest the exhibition be accused of dwelling too much on the past, it proudly displayed a new 'national' style that combined secessionist art nouveau with folk decorative themes. According to one visitor, the 'ensemble of the most contradictory' elements even managed to 'present a certain unity'.[6]

The whole thing was a scaled down version of the much grander Millenium Exhibition that had taken place in Budapest four years before to celebrate 1,000 years since the Magyar conquest of the Pannonian Plain. As part of the festivities, four monuments were erected in ethnically-mixed extremities of the country, a symbolic assertion of the unity of the state under Magyar auspices. The other nationalities were presented as ethnographic curiosities in the form of replica peasant villages, matched in equal number by Magyar counterparts. Continental Europe's first metro line opened for the occasion, inaugurated by Franz Joseph I, or King Ferenc József as the Hungarians knew him.

Even more significant was the grandiloquent neo-Gothic parliament building, which at least appeared complete even if it had missed its 1896 target date. The Danube skyline would henceforth be dominated not by the Habsburg castle on German Buda, but the almost absurdly ornate parliament building in Hungary's holy city Pest. The metro, the parliament and the exhibition in general marked Budapest's nineteenth-century transformation from a city of 'dust and mud' into one of the most vibrant, dynamic and modern cities in the world. It was a grand display of the ruling Hungarian liberal nationalist ideology, emphasizing the leading role of the Magyar element in the country's 1,000 years of statehood, as well as loyalty to the Habsburgs within the framework of the 1867 compromise. Rapid modernization was presented as the fruits of both.[7]

Austria could not claim the same nation-state mantle as Hungary or Germany. But what it lacked in national unity it made up for in characteristic Habsburg splendour. Two pavilions down stood a handsome Baroque palace that would not have been out of place in Vienna, Ljubljana, Prague, or Lwów. Upon entering, the visitor was confronted with an opulent atrium. Under a canopy of calming palm trees stood statues of Rudolf and Leopold I. Rudolf was the first Habsburg to be invested with what became the family's Austrian heartlands in the Middle Ages. In a foundational religious-political myth, he had given away his horse to a priest carrying the Eucharist to give a dying man his last rites. His humility was rewarded with a promise of world power. Because of this, Corpus Christi processions became one of the main public rituals, at which the legitimacy of the House of Habsburg, rooted in its piety and defence of Catholicism, was reinforced year after year.

The Corpus Christi procession in Vienna in 1898 had a special resonance, for it came in the year of Franz Joseph's golden jubilee, celebrating fifty years on the throne. Unlike the previous jubilee, accompanied only by 'a solemn day of contemplation', this one was to be celebrated with great pomp in order to reinforce the unifying symbols of faith and monarchy at a time when national conflicts were reaching a crescendo. The procession in June went off without a hitch, which seemed to portend a successful jubilee celebration later in the year. But unexpected tragedy struck in early September when the Empress-Queen Elisabeth was assassinated by an Italian anarchist in Switzerland.

The monarchy went into mourning. This tragedy derailed most of the planned jubilee celebrations, but also reinforced Franz Joseph's stoic, grandfatherly image. In 1867 his brother had been executed by revolutionaries in Mexico after an ill-fated monarchist attempt to install him as emperor there. Then in 1889 Franz Joseph's only son and heir had taken his own life in a scandalous suicide pact with his teenage mistress. Now he had lost his wife, herself a beloved icon in the monarchy. The popular press was flooded with effusive expressions of loyalty and reverence for a monarch who had faithfully carried out his duties for decades even through so much death and suffering. The Catholic hierarchy took this a step further. In a pastoral letter read to congregations across the overwhelmingly Catholic monarchy, Franz Joseph was elevated to a Christ-like figure in a grand display of fervent religious devotion.[8]

This dynastic patriotism stood front and centre of the Austrian pavilion in Paris. Surrounding the statues of Rudolf and Leopold was a cycle of bronze statuettes of musical icons including Mozart, Haydn, Beethoven, and Schubert embellishing the pillars in the gallery. On the ground floor, the right wing of this suitably supranational construction was occupied by the city of Vienna, which besides celebrating its majestic aesthetic qualities contained exhibits on the city's hygiene and social welfare policies. Other rooms held displays of the Austrian postal and telegraph services, of bathhouses and mineral water, an ethnographic exhibition of Dalmatia, and a joint Polish and Czech art exhibition. There was also a branch of the Austrian Länderbank, a restaurant run by the Viennese brewery founded by lager pioneer Anton Dreher, and an exhibit of the Austrian Press Association. Over 1,000 political dailies from across the monarchy were plastered across the walls in an impressively celebratory display of the rich print culture that had defined Austrian politics over the previous century.[9] All in all, the pavilion presented an image of Austria as an elegant, cultured, and modern liberal state rooted in Habsburg rule.

Though the three Central European exhibits in Paris differed considerably, they shared a noticeable common attachment to secessionist art.[10] This regional manifestation of art nouveau had been embraced with particular enthusiasm by artists across Central Europe, often as a means to creating a new truly national style of art, design, and architecture that went beyond the historicism of the late nineteenth century.[11] It was one example of how, for all the probing, criticizing and questioning of the fin-de-siècle, Central Europeans were being drawn closer together and to the rest of the world than ever before thanks to urbanization, industrialization, rising literacy rates, migration, and mass politics. For every social critic there were thousands of men and women going about their day-to-day lives in their democratized princely states, where portraits of moustachioed rulers hung in entrance halls, where they rubbed shoulders with officers in pristine uniforms in neoclassical theatres painted in Habsburg yellow, where liberals, nationalists and socialists ate the ubiquitous *Cremeschnitte* side by side in equally ubiquitous coffeehouses, where in schools children learned about the glory of the Habsburg, Hohenzollern,

Wettin, or Wittelsbach dynasties, and where men and women of countless backgrounds interacted every day.

Industrialization and urbanization in the decades after 1848, and especially after 1880, meant not only the mass migration of peasants into towns and cities, but also unprecedented levels of linguistic, religious and national intermingling. Saxony and Bohemia, as two of the most industrialized territories within their respective states, saw especially high levels of migration, but other industrializing areas were no less attractive for migrants. Hundreds of thousands of Czechs, Poles, Silesians, and Masurians made their way to industrial centres in the Ruhr and Saxony or major metropolises like Hamburg, Bremen and Berlin.[12]

Most German state governments and industry leaders saw little to worry about in such patterns of migration, especially considering that many of these Slavic migrants spoke German and blended seamlessly into their surroundings. This was especially true for the Protestant, Polish-speaking Masurians, a quarter of whom lived in the Rhineland and Westphalia by 1914. They studiously avoided association with Catholic Poles, emphasizing that they were Prussian Protestants. By 1910 ninety per cent of them cited German as their native language, indicating an even more rapid rate of assimilation than in Masuria itself.[13] For Slavic immigrants of all types that settled down in the Reich it was common for their children to assimilate to German culture, much to the chagrin of Slavic nationalist activists.[14] One Czech worker described an entirely typical process of assimilation with regards to his sister, who settled down with her husband in Dresden. Though they continued to speak Czech at home, the children adopted the German of their surroundings. They would speak to the children in Czech and receive replies in German.[15]

Despite nationalist—or indeed religious—attempts to place every individual into a neatly labelled box, personal identities often defied easy categorization, particularly for the 'elites'. Striking examples of this were the differing life paths of three nobles of Polish descent: August Urbanski, Oskar Halecki and Emilj Laszowski. All three were born to fathers of Polish descent serving the imperial army and Croatian mothers. They were all multilingual but spoke German at home. Urbanski was the only one to follow in his father's footsteps, clinging to a supranational Austrian patriotism even beyond the life of the state that produced it. His 'home was the entire old and great Austria'. Halecki, who was born and raised in Vienna, could have easily become an 'Austrian' too. But his father's testament commanded that his son study in Krakow and reconnect with

THE NEW OLD REGIME

the family's roots, which he duly did. Laszowski meanwhile was raised in Croatia in the German-speaking environment of his maternal noble Šufflays near Karlovac. He too could have ended up an Austrian, but after briefly studying medicine at Graz moved to Croatia to study law and eventual became a founding member of the patriotic Society of the Brethren of the Croatian Dragon, leading it for nearly thirty years.[16]

In other cases, national affiliations changed over the generations. In 1833, Samuel Hoitsy's pamphlet *Should we become Magyars?* sparked a whole debate around Magyarization, with Hoitsy himself answering firmly negatively on behalf of Hungary's Slavs. His son Pal Hoitsy, meanwhile, became one of the most notorious Magyar imperialists of the late nineteenth century, dreaming of Hungary annexing the whole Balkan peninsula and hearing Magyar spoken on the streets of Sofia.[17] To embrace nationalism was ultimately a choice. A personal, social and political choice—and by no means the only one available to Central Europeans of the fin-de-siecle.

* * *

The 1900 world's fair was billed as a celebration of the nineteenth century—a century in which, bumps in the road notwithstanding, liberalism had proceeded on a triumphant march through the economic, social and political institutions of Europe. Yet by the turn of the century, voters across Central Europe were turning to parties that rejected liberalism. In particular, two relatively new movements now attained hitherto unseen levels of mass support: social democracy and Christian socialism.

Though they did not reject the states they lived in, they hoped to radically transform them according to their own visions. They appealed to the losers from liberalism, who could point to the nineteenth century as an age of increasing uncertainty and anxiety, if not perpetual decline and immiseration. For all the wealth that had been created by industrialization, those that enjoyed it were a minority, and generally seemed uninterested in the plight of the losers of this great transformation. Social democrats opposed them as selfish capitalists. Christian socialists scorned them as usurious Jews and their enablers. The millions of workers that had migrated into new industrial centres hoping for a better life worked long hours in terrible conditions for low pay. They lived in abysmal conditions, often suffering from disease and malnutrition. To Social democrats, this was evidence of the impossibility of reconciling capitalism with the betterment of the working class. To Christian socialists, it was evidence of the moral rot at the heart of secular liberalism.

'Pauperization' or 'proletarianization' were fates that terrified skilled craftsmen and artisans alike. Bakers, brewers, tailors, shoemakers, bookbinders, watchmakers, toolmakers, and potters sat precariously between the toiling proletariat and the comfortable bourgeoisie. Liberalism provided opportunities but also exposed them to the danger of competition from large factories backed by huge sums of capital. Both the working and lower-middle classes could point to liberalism, to capitalism, to the haughty bourgeoisie as the roots of their suffering.

In Germany, Social Democrats had been driven underground by Bismarck in 1878, but in the 1880s built up strong networks of clandestine and disguised associations and publications and were still able to run for office as independent candidates. Just how much Bismarck's anti-socialist policies had failed was made patently clear in 1889 when the coal-mining region of the Ruhr was gripped by a huge wave of strikes, which were violently suppressed. Instead of acquiescing to Bismarck's demands for a harsher crackdown, Wilhelm II dismissed the 'iron chancellor' and allowed the anti-socialist law to lapse. In 1890 the Social Democratic Party (SPD) was officially founded as a legal organization. The party attempted to reconcile its revolutionary roots with decades of practical electoral experience. The result was an incongruous mix of prophesizing a future socialist revolution with a practical list of reforms to be pursued by parliamentary means before it: universal democratic suffrage, popular militias, women's equality, workers protections, and so on. Already in 1890, the SPD became the most popular party in Germany, but a franchise that favoured rural over urban districts meant its share of seats was disproportionately small.

Like middle-class urban Protestants who tended to vote liberal, Catholics who coalesced around the Centre Party, and rural Protestants who preferred the Conservative Party, socialist workers came to form their own 'social-moral milieu' of which party politics was only one manifestation. Social democracy was a mass movement that encompassed millions of ordinary working Germans, many of whom were members of socialist-affiliated trade unions that by 1913 had 2.5 million members. They formed their own associations and societies modelled on their bourgeois equivalents, they gathered in their own pubs and clubs, they had their own ritualized celebrations like May Day, and they had their own cultural canon that included classics like Goethe but also socialist theorizers like Marx and Engels. They gathered and socialized, played sports and games, and used their newfound solidarity to negotiate for fairer wages and workplace protections.[18]

In Cisleithania, Social Democrats won nearly a quarter of the vote in 1897, but this only made them the second-most-popular party. The top spot was taken by the recently formed Christian Social Party, whose firebrand leader Karl Lueger would soon after be sworn in as mayor of Vienna. His party promised a revolutionary brand of reformist Christian welfarism, deploying antisemitism to play on the anxieties of a Catholic lower-middle class that felt itself under the thumb of a wealthier and more successful Jewish bourgeoisie as well as a lower Catholic clergy that wanted to become more politically active after a century of cultural retreat.[19]

The rise of the Christian socialists was a shock to the Austrian establishment. Bishops looked askance at the political activity of their subordinates, especially since Christian socialist clerics often claimed to be revolting against the bishops. Liberals and all those that respected their achievements were aghast at the antisemitic rabble-rousing and attempts to reassert Christianity in public life. And the high bourgeoisie were scandalized by the notion that a party of antisemitic shopkeepers, bakers and priests should rule over them. The party was so controversial that Lueger's appointment as mayor of Vienna came after four successive refusals on the part of Franz Joseph to confirm him, largely because of the 'illness' of his antisemitism.[20]

Even within the restrictive confines of Hungary's liberal party-state, political Catholicism was beginning to make its mark. The impetus was a fiery and controversial 'culture war' that erupted in the mid-1890s. Hungary did not have true separation of church and state but rather supported several Christian churches while giving Judaism and Islam only 'recognition'. Everyone had to be a member of some church or another, registered from their birth through their mother or father, whose marriages themselves were entirely under the purview of the church. In 1894 the Hungarian government secularized the institution of marriage under Prime Minister Sándor Wekerle, following this up in 1895 by officially making Judaism a 'state church' on par with the main Christian denominations.

A storm of outrage swept over Catholic Hungary that forced Wekerle's resignation, crossing ethnic boundaries and energizing a generation of young radicals. They held mass rallies, distributed pamphlets, and in 1894 founded the Christian socialist Catholic People's Party to wage the struggle for a 'Christian Hungary'. The party attracted many Slovaks into its ranks, putting up some as candidates for parliament, such as the young priest Andrej Hlinka. According to one Slovak Catholic journalist, the struggle in Hungary was not one between nationalities, but one of 'Jewish liberalism' against the 'Christian people'.[21] Indeed, antisemitism was central to the party's messaging from the outset. One of its founders, the priest Ottokár Prohászka, had been amongst those arguing that a 'Jewish spirit' ruled over Hungary and that 'Christian culture' would 'fail' if it did not 'cast out the poison' of 'Jewish morality'.[22] Christian socialism found fertile ground across Catholic parts of the Habsburg Monarchy thanks to a deep sense of aggrievement. Many Catholics believed that they were the true oppressed and downtrodden of the liberal system, not the Jews who liberals so steadfastly defended. Even where they ostensibly condemned racial antisemitism, they asked why liberals demanded they tolerate Jews and yet—as in Germany during the *Kulturkampf*—persecuted Catholics.[23] 'Today, in the golden age of liberalism, the Jews are the lords of Hungary' wrote one author in the Catholic *Constitution* in 1904. 'They have the land, the money, the banks and loans, as well as the companies'. Doctors, lawyers, theatres, the arts, literature, the press, universities, and schools were all added to the list of things that proved just how 'infested' with Judaism Hungary had become.[24]

Christian socialism found adherents in Bohemia, Moravia, Galicia, and Croatia-Slavonia, many of whom praised Lueger's advances against the 'lying liberalism' that had hitherto defined the dualist system, but its greatest successes with Habsburg-ruled Slavs came amongst the Slovenes and Slovaks. Both were overwhelmingly peasant nations without native nobilities, ruled from urban centres where German or Hungarian predominated with a secular liberal spirit antithetical to the Catholic worldview of the pious rural masses. Lacking a strong enough nationally-minded middle class, the kind of liberal nationalist politics that triumphed amongst Germans, Hungarians and others remained the preserve of a small minority of Slovene and Slovak politicians.

By appealing precisely to those rural masses at a time when an expanding franchise was giving them more of a voice in the Reichsrat, the Slovene People's Party (founded in 1892 as the Slovene Catholic Party) rapidly became the most popular party amongst Slovenes in Carniola, Carinthia and Styria. Like Lueger's Christian Social Party, it billed itself as a party of Slovene workers and peasants, seeking to protect them from the moral and social ills of modern capitalism while battling against the pernicious influence of 'German' liberalism. Indeed, the Archbishop of Ljubljana

Anton Jeglič—an enthusiastic supporter of the party—effectively equated German and liberal influence, with his war on the latter bringing harsh criticism from both the imperial and Vatican authorities for supposedly also targeting the former.[25]

It was an indication of just how much nationalism still bedevilled attempts at transnational politics. The whole Slovak Catholic movement eventually split from the Hungarian Catholic People's Party due to its overly pro-Magyar stance, in 1906 forming their own Slovak People's Party, with the priest Andrej Hlinka serving as the spiritual leader. Though collaborating with the Slovak National Party, it proved to be far more successful and quickly displaced it as the main political representative of the Slovak national movement. By then Lueger's own German chauvinism had lost him most of his erstwhile Slavic supporters as he positioned his party as resolutely German as much as Catholic and Habsburg loyalist. The Social Democratic Party of Austria, founded in 1889, faced a similar struggle. Socialists thought about nationalism primarily in terms of class. Some international socialists like Rosa Luxemburg argued that class solidarity made national differences irrelevant, but the Austrian Marxists argued that the advance of capitalist modernity was making nations more relevant, not less, with the average worker and peasant finding themselves more differentiated than ever 'by the diversity of national education and civilization'.[26]

Indeed, the leading theorists of this school were themselves deeply indebted to German nationalism, believing that German culture still had a 'civilizing' role to play amongst the 'unhistoric' nations under Habsburg rule.[27] The Prague-born but Vienna-raised Victor Adler—one of the party's founders—had been one of the young nationalists behind the Linz Program before shifting leftwards. The editor of the party journal, Karl Renner, supported the exclusive use of German as the official language of the Austrian half of the monarchy on account of its superior level of cultivation. Party ideologue Otto Bauer meanwhile boasted that the 'greatness of a nation depends not only on its numbers, but also on the height of its morals and its culture ... Who will deny that German science, German philosophy, German poetry, and German art can stand their ground with any culture of any nation?'[28] Renner and Bauer became the main theorisers of the 'Austro-Marxist' idea that nations should be given non-territorial autonomy within the wider Habsburg state as a solution to the national question.[29]

Austrian Social Democrats did not, however, think that nationalism should be given ideological preference over socialism as such. As tensions between national movements grew—particularly in Bohemia—this opened space on the political spectrum for those who promoted the interests of workers but also wanted to pursue more assertive nationalist politics. In 1897 a Czech National Social Party was founded as a splinter of the Young Czechs' left wing, hoping to attract workers to a more nationalist alternative to social democracy. Six years later, German Bohemians responded with their own German Workers' Party—growing out of organizations affiliated with the Pan-German radical Georg von Schönerer—to mobilize against the supposed Czech onslaught. Much like in Saxony and other parts of the Reich, Czech workers were accused in the solidly German parts of Bohemia of undercutting wages, stealing German jobs, and otherwise poisoning the German character of the country. A group of politically active workers considered social democracy not just insufficiently nationalist, but the root cause of their malaise. The party program of 1913 put it bluntly that 'Marx's teachings on internationalism' were of 'immeasurable harm for the Germans of Central Europe'. The German working class and petty bourgeoisie needed aggressively national politics to secure their economic position. National socialism, not Marxist socialism.[30]

* * *

The rise of ethnic nationalism, social democracy and Christian socialism were signs of just how weak liberalism had become as a political force in Central Europe by the turn of the century. Yet aspects of liberalism continued to inspire a new generation of reformers, who sought in different ways to find a synthesis between liberalism, socialism and nationalism. They believed in the importance of nations but saw state right and national romanticism as distractions from improving the social, economic and moral conditions of the people that comprised those nations. They rejected Marxism but seriously grappled with this 'social question' and what its resolution might entail. And, ultimately, they saw liberal ideals such as democratic governance, social equality, personal autonomy and freedoms as prerequisites for national flourishing. Though figures like the German pastor Friedrich Naumann, the Hungarian sociologist Oszkár Jászi, and the Czech professor Tomáš Masaryk came from different backgrounds and had their own idiosyncratic views, they all represented an attempt to rejuvenate the liberal nationalist tradition.

Born into a pious Lutheran family in Saxony in 1860, Friedrich Naumann followed in his father's footsteps and became a pastor. He joined the 'inner mission' that sought to bring workers in godless cities back into the fold of the church, seeing first-hand the abysmal living conditions of the working classes in Hamburg, Chemnitz and Frankfurt. He soon came to believe that the social question was 'the task of our time'. Initially, Naumann saw the best avenue for its resolution within a Protestant Christian framework in Adolf Stöcker and his antisemitic Christian socialism.[31]

In large part thanks to a close friendship with the sociologist Max Weber, Naumann drifted away from Stöcker and by the 1890s had developed his own unique brand of liberal nationalism.[32] A passionate and charismatic orator with a voluptuous 'Bismarckian figure', Naumann won himself a devoted following through his progressive speeches at the Evangelical Social Congresses and beyond, drawing the ire of Stöcker and the conservative clergy. The culmination of his political work would be the National Social Association founded in 1896, really a political party that sought to convince all Germans—especially the working class—that the liberal imperialist nation-state could work for them. As its program put it, national and social policy were one and the same and could only be achieved by extending the power of the German Reich.[33]

Naumann was a left-liberal, believing in democratic suffrage, women's rights, social welfarism, and a civic understanding of nationhood that accepted Jews, Poles, Danes, and Catholics as equal members of the German nation. But his eclectic embrace of modern ideas also made him sympathetic to the erratic and personalistic Emperor Wilhelm II, whose imperialism and great power politics both he and his close friend Weber supported, even if they believed more democratic oversight was needed in its pursuit. What both ultimately sought was the eradication of all particularisms, of all divisions in the German nation that had persisted through the founding of the Reich, and the construction of a harmonious society without strong social divisions. It was a vision that appealed to educated, liberal Protestant intellectuals, but few workers. The National Social Association folded in 1903 after repeated failings at the ballot box, with Naumann and most of his supporters joining the liberal Radical Union.[34]

When the head of Hungary's National Civic Radical Party Oszkár Jászi first met Naumann in 1916, he found him a kindred spirit. Jászi was fifteen years Naumann's junior; of a different generation, nation, and political persuasion. But Jászi's career too had been spent in search of a synthesis of the main ideological trends shaping the modern world in the interests of transforming Hungary into a truly democratic nation-state. He was born in 1875 in a provincial capital in northeast Hungary. His family was Jewish but converted to Calvinism soon after his birth. He went on to study law and political science in Budapest before entering the civil service as a minor clerk. His intellectual horizons were, however, far broader than the narrow confines of state office.

Jászi was part of a whole circle of young left-wing intellectuals. He was not interested in Marxism, however, but rather the cosmopolitan, humanistic liberalism of the Hungarian Reform Era of the early nineteenth century. The 'sham jingoism of the Compromise era' stood in stark contrast to 'the true values of the Hungarian past' as he saw it. In 1900 Jászi and many of his radical friends founded the journal *Twentieth Century*, which he later described as a 'revolutionary initiative' which 'rejected the political, intellectual and indeed moral foundations' of Hungarian society and demanded radical reforms.

Jászi thought Hungary was dominated by a single feudal-agrarian class that had monopolized political power and suppressed the hopes and interests of all others. His solution was not the 'economic struggle' prescribed by the Marxists, but 'struggle across the whole front, economically, politically, and ideologically'. He wanted Hungarian politics to move far beyond the binary of '67er versus '48er, dismissing this as 'constitutional ideology'. True change would have to come with radical democratization and reform targeting just about every aspect of politics and society. But he rejected any notion that this was an 'unpatriotic' endeavour, the traditional charge against the socialist left. Not only were the civic radicals not socialists, but they were simply 'working honourably for a New Hungary'. The country's restrictive franchise precluded any kind of mass radical movement, but through the pages of *Twentieth Century* and the influential Sociological Society, Jászi's 'civic radicalism' continued to find new adherents.[35]

Tomáš Masaryk was the oldest of the three democrats considered here. Born in 1850 to a Slovak father and Moravian mother, he was educated in Brno and Vienna before going on to complete a PhD at Leipzig in the late 1870s. Fluent in German, he arrived in Prague in 1882 to take up a post at the newly opened Czech section of Charles University as a total outsider to the city and to Czech society at large. He found it stuffy and old-fashioned, full of professors obsessed with ideas no longer fit for the modern world. He instead encouraged his students and followers to look beyond Central Europe to the democracies of the West for political and social inspiration. Germany and Austria-Hungary were beholden to what he called 'theocracy', a hierarchical spirit that permeated every aspect of their societies, supported by the irrationality and unscientific doctrines of the church. Germans, Austrians and Hungarians voted in elections, but they remained subjects without an ounce of the democratic spirit that ruled in France, England and the USA. 'The real democrat will everywhere feel and act democratically', he wrote, 'not only in parliament, but also in the community, in the party, in the circle of his friends, in the family'. Democracy to him was not just about politics but 'a new world view and a new way of life'.[36]

Masaryk's radical democratic spirit manifested itself in unique ways. In an overwhelmingly Catholic country, he was a Protestant convert. In a thoroughly patriarchal society, he adopted his American wife's name—Garrigue—as his own. In a nation dominated by a patriotic romanticism, he argued for science rather than feeling to act as the basis of national life. As one biographer put it, Masaryk was 'an unrelenting critic of conventional wisdom, established institutions, customary practices and habits in Bohemia and in Austria-Hungary as a whole'. Even when it cost him dearly, he was never afraid to speak his mind. When he spoke against the authenticity of supposedly ancient Czech manuscripts, he was labelled a 'loathsome traitor'. When he defended a poor Jew against blood libel, he become 'the most isolated man among the Czech public'. Yet slowly he built a cult following more consequential than any enjoyed by either Naumann or Jászi.[37]

His acolytes were charmed by his warm and welcoming demeanour and impressed by his wit and readiness to swim against the current. At a time when Czech politics seemed to be going nowhere, when the Young Czechs seemed more interested in dogmatism than national enlightenment and nationalists of all stripes whipped themselves into an antisemitic frenzy, Masaryk seemed to offer a different path. As a follower of Ludwig Gumplowicz's sociological theory of state, he rejected the Czech fixation on state right. He interpreted it as a reflection of how beholden Czech politics was to the nobility and the clergy and how ignorant it was of society at large. The Realist Party he founded in 1900 was the only Czech party save the Social Democrats that rejected this central nationalist demand.[38]

Looking beyond the dualist Austro-Hungarian framework also allowed Masaryk to build new bridges. When he first arrived in Prague there was little cooperation between Czech and Slovak politicians. Earlier in the century, Slovak Pan-Slavists like Ján Kollár had been enthusiastic advocates of a single shared Czechoslovak literary standard, considering Czechs and Slovaks a single branch of the great Slavic national tree. But later Slovak nationalist generations rejected this, embracing their own Slovak standard that to Czechs seemed to signal a lack of interest in their Bohemian brethren. By the late nineteenth century Slovak politics were parochial and dominated by conservative clerics based in isolated Martin in the foothills of the Tatra mountains.

For many young Slovaks who studied in Vienna and Prague, the ideas they found there were thus a revelation—especially those espoused by the half-Slovak Masaryk. In 1898 many of them gathered together to form the journal *Hlas*. They did not reject dualist Hungary, but called for democratic, progressive reforms to transform it from a 'medieval feudal state' in which Slovaks lived 'almost in serfdom' into one in which Slovaks could 'be reborn morally'. 'Hlasists' criticized the leaders of the Slovak National Party as out of touch, calling for closer cooperation with Czechs across the border. Masaryk's Realist Party reciprocated the embrace. Its party programs endorsed the notion of a single Czechoslovak nation, even while not seeking to deny Slovaks their individuality.[39]

Masaryk helped bring about a similar sea change in attitudes amongst younger south Slavs. Amongst them too, the Pan-Slavist postulate of a single Yugoslav nation with a single literary standard had withered away in the second half of the nineteenth century as Slovene, Croat and Serb nationalists pursued their own individual development within the confines of the dualist system. Indeed, the Croatian Party of Right, which was popular amongst students and intellectuals, was openly anti-Serb while the dominant Serbian party in Croatia-Slavonia—the Serb Independent Party—subscribed to the philologist Vuk Karadžić's belief that Croats did not even exist.[40] Once again, it was the younger generation influenced by Masaryk that would challenge this status quo. In October 1895 a few dozen frustrated Croatian students burned a Hungarian flag on Zagreb's main square while Franz Joseph was visiting the city. The students were all expelled from the University of Zagreb. Encouraged by their ringleader Stjepan Radić, many went on to continue their studies in Prague.

Radić was the son of poor, illiterate peasants from a village near Zagreb. He was myopic, physically unimpressive, and hot-headed. But he was also energetic, intellectually curious and intelligent, following his older brother to Zagreb to attend gymnasium (secondary school) and eventually enrolling in the law faculty of the university. Deeply moved by the plight of the peasantry, Radić undertook periodic journeys by foot through Croatia, Slavonia, Dalmatia, Serbia, the Slovene lands and beyond. From an early age he had been a Slavophile, undertaking a 'pilgrimage' to the Russian Empire in 1889. While at university, he sought out all the leading figures of Croatian life to discuss and debate the great political issues of the day.

He was disappointed by Starčević, the founder of the Party of Right and idol of so many young Croatian nationalists, whose dismissive attitude towards the peasantry chafed. Radić was arrested in 1893 for an indignant comment against Ban Héderváry made at a public commemoration, ending up in prison for four months and expelled from the university. He used the time to learn Czech, already having made arrangements to continue his studies in Prague. The 'beautiful and great Slavic city' amazed him. His Slavophilia was transposed onto the most advanced of Slavic nations, with Radić embracing many of Masaryk's basic political critiques. The old parties and their national romanticism were to be discarded. French and Czech influence was to replace German and Magyar rule. And the common folk were to be placed on a pedestal as the true representatives of the nation.[41]

The 'Progressive Youth' that came under the influence of Masaryk's ideas discarded their narrow national chauvinism and embraced the idea of pan-Yugoslav cooperation. In the early years of the twentieth century this young generation would take a leading role in Croatian politics, forming a united Serb-Croat opposition that sought to finally bring down Héderváry's regime and replace it with a truly national one, embracing the Yugoslavist notion that Croats and Serbs were the same people. By that point, however, Radić had broken with the opposition and founded his own party alongside his older brother Antun: the Croatian People's Peasant Party. 'The peasant isn't a class, he is the nation in the full sense of the word', wrote Antun. It was their mission to bring this truth to the forefront of politics. 'The peasant knows much. Only he doesn't know that he is a person'.[42]

12

BETWEEN WESTERN CIVILIZATION AND EASTERN BARBARISM

Franz Jospeh's diamond jubilee fell on 2 December 1908, sixty years from the day he took the reins of a semi-feudal country in the midst of a revolutionary upheaval that threatened to partition it into four. By 1908 he was a constitutional monarch standing atop two vast, modern states over which he had little direct control. Besides the jealously guarded prerogatives of diplomacy and war, the direction of politics and society was driven largely by ministers, civil servants, businessmen, and an ever-growing pool of voters. The emperor struck an increasingly distant, almost semi-mythical figure. There was a sense, however, that the monarchy was teetering on the brink, with the image of the staid old emperor the only thing holding it together. Unlike the jubilee ten years prior, marked by deference to a mourning monarch, the diamond jubilee was marred by Italian, Magyar and Slav boycotts that effectively took away its entire purpose. Rather than a display of the bonds of imperial unity, it was a stark demonstration of just how frayed they had become.

In 1897, Austria-Hungary entered what seemed to be a permanent state of crisis. It began, as so many crises did, in Bohemia. The Galician Count Kasimir Felix Badeni—appointed minister-president of Austria in 1895—hoped to finally solve the Gordian Knot of Bohemian politics by passing an ordinance that required every civil servant in the country to be proficient in both German and Czech by 1901. The German reaction to the so-called Badeni Ordinances of 1897 shook the Habsburg state to its core and alienated—perhaps irrevocably—Czech nationalists from Germans, the Habsburg Monarchy, and even Central Europe itself.

In the debate that erupted in the Bohemian Landtag, one Christian Social deputy asserted frankly that Czech was nothing but the language of the kitchen. A German nationalist colleague went further, comparing Czechs to 'Eskimos and Zulus'.[1] Violent riots broke out across Bohemia, spreading even to Vienna and Graz. In the latter, rioters clashed with the army. After Bosnian troops shot a protestor dead, huge anti-army demonstrations followed.[2] The Radical League of Germans in Bohemia had just 7,000 members in 1895. By 1900 it had 60,000.[3] German organizations in Bohemia, Saxony and even Bavaria proclaimed their commitment to replacing Czech with German beer.[4] By the end of the year Georg von Schönerer had launched his Away from Rome movement, calling for Austro-Germans to abandon the anti-national Catholic Church and convert to Protestantism as part of a general Pan-Germanist program to unite them with their Reich brethren.

Amidst growing chaos and disorder, the Reichsrat reconvened on 23 September 1897. It too immediately devolved into chaos thanks to the obstructionism of Austro-German deputies. As the weeks passed it only got worse. After a few particularly heated days in late November in which knives were drawn and some deputies threatened to bring revolvers, Badeni decided to dismiss the parliament and resigned.[5] Now came the Czech counter-reaction. Demonstrations and brawls broke out in various Bohemian cities, culminating in an anti-German riot in Prague. They broke windows, looted stores, and harassed passers-by before martial law was declared in the city on 2 December.[6] The mayhem unleashed by the Badeni ordinances shocked Germans not only in the Habsburg Monarchy, but in the German Reich too.

At the height of the parliamentary chaos, the celebrated German scholar Theodor Mommsen made a shockingly incendiary intervention. On the front page of the leading Viennese liberal daily, he published a pseudo-anonymous letter addressed to the Germans of Austria. He warned in apocalyptic tones that 'the apostles of barbarization are at work, burying the German work of half a millennium in the abyss of their un-Kultur'. He beseeched them: 'Be tough! The Czech skull does not accept reason but is open to punches'.[7] Friedrich Naumann noted in 1900: 'Interest in Austria is growing stronger than ever before in Germany. No national party can avoid taking part in the struggle of Germans on the Moldau and Danube'. After all, 'the life of Germanness, of the Central European community of states' was at stake, he argued.[8] Four fifths of all German professors ended up signing a petition that drew attention to the great dangers 'which threaten the ancient site of German science and the entire German people in Bohemia and Moravia'.[9]

WESTERN CIVILIZATION AND EASTERN BARBARISM

The open intervention of so many Reich Germans in the internal affairs of Austria deeply alienated many Czechs. It was bad enough that they had to struggle against the weight of Germandom in Austria, but with this backed up by the weight of the Reich the Czech cause would have been entirely hopeless. When the Badeni ordinances were repealed in 1899, it only seemed to confirm that Czech national aspirations could never be achieved within a German-dominated Central Europe. Paul de Lagarde— one of the great prophets of anti-modernism—argued in his popular *Deutsche Schriften* that the 'German question' was a 'Central European one [that] can only be answered correctly as such'.[10] German national renewal meant pursuing the divine mission of unification with Austria, involving the 'population transfers' of Slovenes, Czechs and Magyars to far-off parts of Europe where they could die off in peace, if they proved unable to assimilate to the superior German nation.[11] Ernst Hasse, a member of the Reichstag and president of the Pan-German League, wrote in 1905 that *Weltpolitik* could only be pursued in conjugation with a 'continental policy in Central Europe'. 'Before we seek a great Germany in the far corners of the world, we must create a greater Germany in Central Europe'.[12]

Condescending notions of German superiority were by no means confined to the fringes of German politics. In 1903, as part of a series of geographical studies on various regions of the world guided by the 'father of geopolitics' Halford Mackinder, a volume on Central Europe appeared by the German geographer Joseph Partsch. The Silesian Partsch described Central Europe not only as a natural geographic whole, but an area in which Germans acted as the 'standard bearers of culture, knowledge and progress'.[13] Indeed, if Central Europeans wanted to 'reach greatness', they had to embrace unity on the basis of German language and culture since they already 'consciously or unconsciously, willingly or unwillingly, [belonged] to the sphere of German civilization'.[14]

Representatives of other Central European nations were well aware of how Pan-German radicals were increasingly entertaining visions of Central Europe as a space of natural German domination. A pre-political Tomáš Masaryk wrote to Lagarde in 1881 '[expressing] his gratitude' for Lagarde's work, while noting he wanted to later correct Lagarde's 'accusations' against Czechs.[15] The Young Czech leader Karel Kramář took a different approach. Many in his party had already become solidly Russophile thanks to the wider anti-German struggle, but Kramář developed a whole political program he called 'neo-Slavism' that sought to totally reorient Czech politics towards Russia.[16]

'The idea of a Slavic Austria is an unslavic idea' because it was an 'idea of antagonism with Russia', which would itself represent the 'suicide of the Slavs' wrote the journalist Josef Holoček. Russia was not a barbaric Oriental power as the Germans charged, but a European nation of good people with a wise ruler in Alexander III. All Slavs had come to recognize that one enemy threatened them: the German *Drang nach Osten* (drive to the East). Fighting back this drive was their common interest. 'That common need unites all Slavs'.[17] The revival of Pan-Slavism in certain Czech nationalist circles was a damning indictment of the failure of the Habsburg state to satisfy the national demands of the Czech national movement. And if they could not be satisfied, the monarchy's whole future was under question. As Kramař put it: 'The Bohemian question is, in fact, *the* real Austrian question'.[18]

In June 1905 a Prague German paper published an alarming report. The small Saxon town of Ostritz right across the border had recently experienced rapid Slavicization due to a flood of Czech workers. The story was reprinted throughout Saxon papers and caused a sensation in the Reich. The Prussian government felt compelled to officially ask the Saxon Foreign Ministry whether the story was true, with Saxon officials subsequently refuting its central claim that a third of the town was Czech. But by then such reports were a familiar sight in the German press. The *Trautenauer Wochenblatt* had claimed in 1895 that 'Czech nationalist leaders not only want the Czechization of Bohemia, Moravia, Austrian Silesia, and Austria' but to 'Czechify any part of Germany where Slavs once lived'. Bautzen was allegedly to be the first conquest for this 'Czech empire'.[19]

Rabidly nationalistic organizations like the Pan-German League were particularly active in Saxony, where they tried to portray the local struggle against Czech immigration as common to Germans on both sides of the border. Even though Mommsen dismissed it as a collection of 'national fools', it counted amongst its members half of the city council of Dresden by 1905. It hosted lectures with titles like 'Should the Reich Germans Stand Back Quietly and Watch the Extermination of Germandom in Austria?'[20]

The fall of the Badeni government at the end of 1897 spread the monarchy's crisis into Hungary. The decennial negotiations around the compromise had been concluded without fanfare, but the Reichsrat had been dissolved before it could ratify the new agreement. Hungary's liberal government saw little need for concern, extending the 1887 agreement for another year. But the anti-compromise opposition went into a frenzy.

The customs union between the two halves of the monarchy had simply expired, they argued, while denouncing the government's actions as the most outrageous crime against the Hungarian constitution.

The opposition—led by the Independence Party—now embraced the kind of parliamentary obstructionism that had become so common in Vienna. The turmoil came to a head in November 1904 as the parliament came to a vote on an expensive army bill. The government changed voting rules in parliament in an attempt to permanently overcome the gridlock through a waving of handkerchiefs, causing more outrage and a secession from the Liberal Party before the opposition formed a single 'Coalition'. On 13 December 1904 they came to the house of deputies early and physically destroyed its furniture and decorations. Parliament was soon dissolved and in late January 1905 Hungarians went to the polls to elect a new government.

The Coalition won 231 seats to the Liberal Party's 159. The Independence Party alone had 166. Hungary's parliamentary majority now rejected the very foundations of the common Austro-Hungarian state. In Vienna, panic set in, with intermittent negotiations between the Austrian court and the Hungarian Coalition failing to resolve the crisis. When Franz Joseph appointed a new caretaker Hungarian government, it was denounced as unconstitutional by the Coalition, who illegally sat in parliament and passed a resolution calling for the country to take up passive resistance. Local governments were ordered not to raise taxes or recruits and to treat the appointed government as illegitimate.[21] As chaos and confusion reigned in Hungary, news broke of a shocking political alliance. The Croat-Serb opposition—united across Croatia, Slavonia and Dalmatia—had signed a resolution allying itself with the Hungarian opposition. It had been working towards this position for years, seeing it as a welcome opportunity to finally break through the gridlock of the dualist system.

Franz Joseph turned to the nuclear option. He ordered his caretaker government to prepare the introduction of universal male suffrage in Hungary, knowing full well this would spell disaster for the Magyar elites. The opposition eventually agreed to renounce its most unpalatable demands as it inched towards power, agreeing to accept the dualist system, approve new recruits, and put electoral reform at the top of their agenda. What followed was a bizarre series of political reshufflings characteristic of Hungary's incestuous political system. Sándor Wekerle, who had withdrawn from public life a decade before after his first stint as prime minister, was chosen to lead the new government. He was a respected politician known for his deep knowledge of financial affairs. Though historically a member of the Liberal Party, by now he was de facto independent. The Liberal Party was in any case soon dissolved as new elections brought an overwhelming victory for the former opposition. The cabinet was split between members of the Independence Party and the new Constitution Party which Wekerle now joined.[22]

Having been forced to renounce the anti-Habsburg stance that had made it so distinct, the Independence Party turned towards internal national consolidation, quickly dashing Croat-Serb hopes for a more favourable settlement with Budapest. The conflict came to a head over the Lex Kossuth legislation, which mandated that state railway employees be fluent in Magyar, seen by the Croatians as yet another violation of their compromise with Hungary. More obstructionism and parliamentary chaos followed as the 'new course' of the Croat-Serb politicians fell to pieces.[23] The Hungarian government followed this up with the even more controversial Lex Apponyi, which required all schoolteachers to be fluent in Magyar, resulting in an enormous decline in the number of schools with non-Magyar instruction from an already paltry level.[24] Political leaders of minority nationalities that had largely come to accept the territorial integrity of the Hungarian state were left dejected and alienated. Slovaks increasingly looked to Prague, Romanians towards Bucharest, and Serbs towards Belgrade.

* * *

Friedrich Naumann was elated. In 1903 electoral disappointment had led to the dissolution of his short-lived National Social Association. Now, in 1907, voters in the small Württemberg town of Heilbronn had voted to send Naumann to be their deputy in the German Reichstag. The campaign had been taxing. Naumann made dozens of public appearances, his last one coming the evening before the vote as he made his case for his own candidature under the banner of the Radical Union.[25] Naumann's personal triumph came at a time of political crisis in the Reich.

In 1904 a colonial uprising broke out in German South West Africa. The German general sent to quell the revolt acted ruthlessly and genocidally. For many in the Reich the violence carried out in their nation's name was scandalous. When Chancellor Bernhard von Bülow sought Reichstag approval for a budget supplement to help suppress the rebellion, he was voted down by the Social Democrats, Poles, and Centre Party. He thus called an election for January 1907, using all the means at his disposal to whip the Reich into a nationalist frenzy. It worked. The Social Democratic Party lost about half its seats, and the 'Bülow Bloc' was formed including the Conservative Party, the National Liberal Party and Naumann's liberal Radical Union.

Bülow's majority proved short-lived, however, breaking up by 1909 and forcing his resignation. Wilhelm II appointed Theobald von Bethmann Hollweg in his place. What followed in 1912 was an even worse blow to the government. In an election marked by strong antisemitic agitation by parties of the right, the SPD achieved its best ever vote and seat share, winning nearly thirty-five per cent of the former and a little over a quarter of the latter. The SPD and Centre Party together had over half of the seats in the Reichstag while the newly-unified left-liberal Progressive People's Party—which Naumann had joined—came fourth. Never before had the Reich had a parliament so opposed to the government and the emperor and so committed to parliamentary rule.

Emperor Wilhelm II had never wanted to be a grandfatherly symbol atop a sprawling modern state like his Austrian counterpart, but an active embodiment of the Reich's monarchical executive. How he could fulfil this role alongside his appointed ministers was never clear. Indeed, he effectively wanted to take on the domineering role that Bismarck had once played himself. Wilhelm lacked his talent for politics, however, and his erratic personality made the kind of careful diplomatic balancing act pioneered by Bismarck all but impossible. Wilhelm's personal fixation was *Weltpolitik*—turning Germany into a true world power. Under the strong direction of Admiral Alfred von Tirpitz, he pursued a policy of vigorous naval expansion from 1898, provoking a futile and expensive arms race with Britain. He was convinced that the strategy would be successful in deterring Britain from joining any future wars against the Reich.[26] His blundering foreign policy not only alienated Britain but also pushed France and Russia closer together. By the second decade of the twentieth century Central Europe's two great powers faced the very real prospect of war against both East and West.

Franz Joseph and the tight circle around him, for their part, were focused squarely on Austria-Hungary's only real area of potential influence: the Balkans. In the century leading up to 1914, the Ottoman Empire's position in Europe had been in steady decline. Serbia, Greece, Romania, and Bulgaria had all achieved their independence, though their economic backwardness and political instability made the peninsula a constant source of worry in the capitals of Europe. A crisis in 1878 had resulted in the Habsburgs occupying the province of Bosnia and Herzegovina, drawing the monarchy further into the mountainous region at a time when nationalists in neighbouring Serbia were clamouring for their country to unify all South Slavs—including those under Habsburg rule—on the model of Italy or Germany.

The spectre of Pan-Slavist subversion was the excuse given when in 1908 Austria-Hungary decided to annex Bosnia outright. It was an international scandal, worsening the country's relations with Britain and Russia. To lend credence to the concerns justifying it, the authorities arrested fifty-three prominent Serb politicians who were part of the Serb Independent Party. After being held for ten months without charge, they were officially accused of being part of a nefarious conspiracy aimed at the destruction of Austria-Hungary and charged with high treason. The trial took place in Zagreb in 1909, during which the paucity of evidence was on display for all to see. Masaryk was outraged by the whole affair. He saw it as just the latest piece of evidence of how morally bankrupt the undemocratic Austro-Hungarian regime was. He tried to rouse the Reichsrat where he sat as a deputy to investigate the evidence but failed to get the two-thirds majority he needed. Over thirty prison sentences were eventually handed out.[27]

The treason trial was an embarrassment for Vienna, making its diplomats appear weak. Crisis soon came to the Balkans again when Italy decided to take advantage of perceived Ottoman weakness and attacked Libya in 1911. Italian victory encouraged the Christian Balkan states to put aside their differences and launch a multi-pronged assault on the remaining Ottoman territories in the Balkans, hoping to finally realize longstanding expansionist dreams. Vienna sat on the sidelines hoping a Turkish victory would result after a long and grinding war that would ideally weaken Serbia.[28] But instead the Habsburg high command was left watching nervously as the Balkan League scored victory after victory in late 1912 and early 1913, cheered on by Slavic nationalists in Central Europe and Russia alike. Austria-Hungary mobilized at great expense to prevent Serbia from gaining an outlet to the Adriatic, but in the grand scheme of things it was a largely irrelevant victory. The course of the Balkan Wars and Austria-Hungary's inability to shape it convinced Franz Joseph that next time they would have to either stay out entirely or be all in.[29]

This meant nothing less than an eventual war with Serbia. A poor and extremely rural state with less than a tenth of Austria-Hungary's population should hardly have posed a great challenge to Franz Joseph's enormous army. But war with Serbia also likely meant war with Russia. In such an event Vienna naturally hoped for Berlin's assistance. Germany was not prepared to assist in 1912 but nonetheless saw Austria-Hungary's power as essential to its own standing in the world. In October that same year Wilhelm II paid a visit to his close friend Franz Ferdinand, the Habsburg crown prince, at his Bohemian estate. He took the opportunity to swing by Vienna and speak with the Austro-Hungarian Foreign Minister Leopold Berchtold. 'A war between East and West cannot be permanently avoided' Wilhelm told him, casting any potential conflict as the result of the inevitable clash of Slavs and Germans. He noted that at Franz Ferdinand's estate, all the Bohemian and Hungarian aristocrats in attendance had agreed that the inexorable rise of Slavic nations was terrifying. He concluded with a characteristic comment: 'The Slavs were not born to rule, but to serve, and this must be taught to them'.[30]

'Austria stands at a turning point', he would write in December, 'and it has become an *existential question*, whether it will remain *German* and *German*-ruled—thereby *alliable*—or be overrun by Slavdom and therefore *unalliable*'. Germany was faced not only with a potential war against Russia, but a '*race war*' of the Germans 'against the overconfident Slavs. A *race war*, from which we will not be spared, because it concerns the future of the Habsburg Monarchy and the *existence* of our fatherland'.[31] The chief of the German general staff Helmuth von Moltke expressed a similar vision of the coming 'European war' in a message to his Austro-Hungarian counterpart in early 1913, in which he promised that Austria-Hungary could count on German support in the future 'struggle between Germandom and Slavdom'.[32] To the Reich's military leadership, Russia seemed like an existential threat, a barbaric eastern Slavic colossus that it was better to defeat sooner rather than later. By 1914 they too were prepared for war.

13

PLUNGE INTO THE ABYSS

On 28 June 1914, the heir to the Austro-Hungarian throne Franz Ferdinand was assassinated by a Serb nationalist in the capital of Habsburg Bosnia. Decision-makers in Vienna quickly realized the moment for decisive action had come. After receiving a famous 'blank cheque' from Berlin, Austria-Hungary presented Belgrade with an ultimatum designed to be rejected. Exactly a month after the Sarajevo assassination, Austria-Hungary declared war on Serbia. The complicated web of guarantees and alliances soon meant that the German Reich and Austria-Hungary were fighting a two-front war against a Triple Entente of France, Great Britain and Russia.

As the news of war spread, huge crowds gathered in the streets of Central European cities singing patriotic songs and professing their loyalty to monarch and nation. In Vienna and Berlin there was a sense that it was a purely defensive war, that the nefarious forces that sought to constrain the Reich's rise and see Austria-Hungary torn apart were finally making their move.[1] This contributed to the outpouring of enthusiasm that accompanied the war's outbreak, even if it was far from universal. Private reservations left less of a mark than public displays of solidarity and support. In the Reich in particular, it would come to be mythologized as the 'spirit of 1914', the coming together of the whole nation irrespective of party, class, religion, or confession.[2] Kaiser Wilhelm II epitomized it with his statement to the Reichstag on 4 August 1914: 'I no longer recognize any parties, I see only Germans'.[3] This was reciprocated by the main political parties in the Reichstag—before the war forming an anti-government majority—who passed war credits unanimously as they prepared to take a backseat in the coming war.

In Austria-Hungary, there was a renewed sense of duty and loyalty to the Habsburg dynasty. Politically conscious Croats, Slovenes, Poles, and

Czechs went to war hoping it would pave the way to the realization of their own national ambitions under the Habsburg sceptre. Even in oft-rebellious Hungary crowds greeted news of mobilization and war with nationalistic fervour and a sense of public unity. On 2 August Crown Prince Karl travelled to Budapest and paraded through the city in the uniform of a Honvéd Hussar, greeted by 200,000 people on the streets.[4] Germans in Austria, too, felt proud to be fighting side-by-side with their Reich compatriots, a feeling that extended well beyond the Pan-Germanist fringe.[5] This feeling was reciprocated across the border. One leading German daily hailed the coming war with cries of: 'Hurrah Germania! Two Germanic peoples against the Russians and French, two powerful, viable peoples against megalomaniac cultural barbarism and an already overripe civilization'.[6]

The distinction between a superficial Western 'Civilization' and a purer and more profound German 'Kultur' became hugely influential amongst German intellectuals during the war.[7] It seemed to perfectly sum up every negative judgement of the Western foe and every positive German contrast. The 'ideas of 1789' versus the 'ideas of 1914'; 'merchants versus heroes'; 'idealism versus utilitarianism'.[8] A sense of prewar estrangement rapidly became an unbridgeable gulf. In the Franco-British 'West', the war was quickly cast as a war of Western civilization against German barbarism. Academic cooperation between scholars in the Entente and Central Powers was replaced by polemical exchanges that did nothing but convince both sides that their cause was just.[9] The Reich's decision to invade neutral Belgium in an attempt to knock France out of the war proved doubly disastrous, drawing Britain into the war and also exposing the country to blistering international criticism for atrocities carried out against the neutral country.[10] Accusations of German barbarism only provoked German accusations of Entente barbarism, especially well-founded in German eyes thanks to the Western alliance with the great 'Slavic half-Asiatic power' in the East. Like many others, the philosophers Ernst Haeckel and Rudolf Eucken singled out Britain in particular for fighting 'on the side not only of barbarism, but also of moral wrong' and ascribed to it 'the immense guilt and world-historical responsibility' for the war.[11]

Though not published until after the war, the novelist Thomas Mann's *Reflections of a Nonpolitical Man* was emblematic of the wartime mindset. He interpreted the Great War as a struggle unlike any that had come before. It was much more than a cabinet war of old. More even than a mere great power conflict. It was a struggle for the very existence of Germany—for its *Kultur*, threatened as it was by obliteration 'like mist before the sun' by an arrogant West and its 'Civilization', which was not only 'psychologically anti-German [but] also necessarily politically anti-German'.[12] According to Mann there had been 'the most complete unanimity from the first moment of the intellectual roots' of the First World War: Germany's irreconcilable 'protest' against the West's pretentions to universal civilization. This was essentially 'a new outbreak, perhaps the grandest, the final one, as some believe, of Germany's ancient struggle against the spirit of the West, as well as the struggle of the Roman world against stubborn Germany'.[13]

* * *

For a war that would be marked by unprecedently brutal industrial warfare, the First World War began with an anachronistic display of chivalry. The head of Serbia's armed forces Radomir Putnik found himself in Budapest when the war broke out. A man with decades of military experience who had recently led the Serbian army through two victorious Balkan wars, the Austro-Hungarian general staff hoped to seize the opportunity to keep him out of action. But against their wishes, Franz Joseph had Putnik escorted safely back to Serbia.[14] There he presided over the defeat of the invading Habsburg army, which he had beaten back by December 1914. It was a phenomenal embarrassment, compounded by Russia's sweep into defenceless Galicia and Bukovina that sent a million refugees fleeing westwards and devastated Austro-Hungarian agriculture.[15] Any hope of a quick and easy conquest of Serbia was in tatters. A long war would evidently be devastating for huge swathes of the monarchy.

The German offensive in the west fared better, pushing the frontline deep into French territory, but was still inconclusive. Millions of soldiers on both sides became bogged down in brutal trench warfare. Disappointment in the west was at least somewhat compensated for by triumph in the east. After an unexpected Russian invasion of East Prussia threatened to throw the entire German war plan into disarray, the elderly Paul von Hindenburg was called out of retirement to lead the small eighth army against the numerically superior Russians. By the end of August 1914, Hindenburg had rallied and scored a huge victory at the Battle of Tannenberg. In November he was elevated to Supreme Commander of the East. Hindenburg—and to a lesser extent his chief of staff Erich

Ludendorff—would become heroic figures in Germany as they presided over an astonishingly successful eastern campaign, pushing deep into Russian territory over the course of 1915.

So universal was Hindenburg's popularity that the stalwart Junker general joked with some senior Social Democrats that he 'was quite popular with the comrades and would soon have to acquire a red beret'.[16] Hindenburg memorabilia spread like wildfire across the Reich, his face appearing on posters, cups, glasses, plates, matchboxes, and more.[17] A thirteen-meter-tall wooden statue of Hindenburg appeared in Berlin in September 1915, which people could hammer a nail into in exchange for a donation for war widows and orphans.[18] Hundreds of these 'nail figures' would appear across Germany and Austria-Hungary during the war, becoming the most ubiquitous visual symbol of the Central European war community.[19]

German successes in east and west quickly brought the question of war aims to the fore. Already in late August and early September of 1914, political groups in the Reich put forward ambitious plans for European reconstruction under German auspices once the war came to its expected victorious conclusion. A particularly expansive plan was drafted by the leader of the Pan-German League, Heinrich Claß. Its wide circulation put pressure on the government to define its own approach, outlined in Chancellor Bethmann Hollweg's secret and since-infamous 'September Program'.[20] It sought nothing less than securing 'the German Reich in West and East for all time' by drastically weakening France, pushing Russia far back into the East, and building up a new German-led Central European order.[21]

The Central Powers' occupation of Russian Poland raised the long dormant 'Polish question' with particular urgency. The charismatic socialist and unwavering Polish patriot Józef Piłsudski had been allowed to build up a Polish Legion in August which fought alongside the Central Powers with the aim of restoring Poland's unity. It was wildly popular in Galicia, where Piłsudski became something of a folk hero. The Austrian authorities allowed the formation of a Supreme National Committee that united a broad spectrum of Polish political leaders in a single organization dedicated to the realization of a united Polish state under Habsburg rule.[22] This so-called 'Austro-Polish solution' was advocated in Vienna too, though proved controversial with the Hungarians. The issue was further complicated by concurrent debates around the forming of a Reich-Austro-Hungarian customs union, itself a highly contentious issue in Berlin,

Vienna and Budapest. This would have signified an institutionalization of the bond created by the war, one that would inevitably outlive it and pave the way for the integration of the three states. Walther Rathenau—Germany's future foreign minister—saw 'the Central European customs union as the great civilizing mission that the war can grant our history'.[23]

Austro-Germans similarly understood the political potential of such a union as a means of cementing the bond between Reich and Austrian Germans. Some even went to Berlin to lobby privately.[24] The nationalist historian Heinrich Friedjung's 'Memorandum from German-Austria' proved particularly influential, read and discussed at the highest levels of the Reich government. It presented a close economic and military union between the two Central Powers as a panacea for all the ills of Germandom in Central Europe. It would preserve the monarchy, Germandom's predominance within it, and the alliance in one fell swoop.[25]

However, in the official negotiations that followed, the non-national government of the multinational Habsburg state found arguments emphasizing Pan-German brotherhood unconvincing if not borderline hazardous.[26] Any agreement between Vienna and Berlin would ultimately have to be as equals and respect the former's internal arrangements with Budapest. The fact that this constitutional bedrock of Austria-Hungary was subject to decennial negotiations due in 1917 effectively precluded any new treaties with the Reich.

In May 1915, Friedrich Naumann sat down to pen his own contribution to this debate. No single work would do so much to stimulate discussions of Central European unity as Naumann's wildly popular book *Mitteleuropa*. Published in 1915—and translated into English in 1916 as *Central Europe* and French in 1917 as *L'Europe centrale*—the book sold over 100,000 copies by the end of the war, making it the second most popular non-fiction book published in the German Reich, bested only by Bismarck's reminiscences.[27] Naumann, by then a liberal member of parliament, set out a hypothesized postwar Europe dominated by a powerful economic and political zone in Central Europe with Germany at its core. German would be the natural lingua franca, but all nations and languages would be free to develop.

His rather liberal vision was the work of a minor, non-governmental politician, but for many in the West, Mitteleuropa became a byword for expansive Pan-Germanist war aims.[28] Indeed, although it was met with an enthusiastic reception in German Bohemia, it divided Czechs, Poles and Hungarians. In 1916 Naumann travelled to Bohemia and Hungary and met with leading politicians to strengthen the Central European war bond. Many met him with suspicion and others depressed him with their lack of solidarity.[29] One man he did win over to his cause was Oszkár Jászi, who had been spending the war reporting from the front. 'A little long-winded and slipshod but his basic thinking is right' he noted down in his diary after attending a lecture by Naumann. Over the following three months the topic of Central Europe became a point of heated debate amongst Hungarian radicals, with Jászi coming out firmly in favour of Naumann's plan. He criticized his compatriots who could only see in the Reich 'Prussian militarism and the rule of the Junker class'. Germany still 'better represents human progress than does the Entente' he wrote.[30] But Tomáš Masaryk had by then come to the precise opposite conclusion, seeing Naumann's plan as little more than refined German imperialism. In December 1914 Masaryk had gone into exile, seeing his nation's future not in Central Europe, but in the West.

The anti-Slavic tone of much of the German war discourse alienated many Habsburg Slavs, particularly since it was accompanied by outbursts of violence and paranoia from the military establishment. In a small town near Graz, Slovenes that took part in a Sokol festival on the day of Franz Ferdinand's assassination were arrested for 'Serbophile machinations'.[31] Anti-Serb riots, meanwhile, broke out in the wake of the assassination across the Habsburg Monarchy. Even in Munich an allegedly Serb-owned café was attacked by pro-Austrian demonstrators.[32] What the military saw as the country's circle of enemies was far greater than just Serbs. It included anti-Habsburg Czechs, irredentist Italians, treacherous South Slavs, as well as pro-Russian Ruthenians. Hence the anti-Habsburg Czech politician Vaclav Klofáč was arrested for high treason soon after the outbreak of war, later to be joined by several other prominent Czech politicians.[33] Along the front with Serbia the army was even more jittery, viewing the civilian population with an exaggerated sense of suspicion that led to the execution of some 3,000 Serbian civilians.[34]

* * *

On 21 October 1916, a young man walked into the restaurant of the upscale hotel Meissl & Schadn in Vienna and murdered Minister-President Karl von Stürgkh with three shots from a pistol as he sat there eating his lunch. The assassin was the son of the great Austrian socialist Victor Adler. He later explained it was a protest for peace and against the wartime absolutist regime.³⁵ Exactly a month later, the seemingly eternal Emperor Franz Joseph passed away at the age of eighty-six. His grand-nephew, the new Emperor Karl I, struck a markedly less impressive figure. At his Hungarian coronation as King Karl IV later that year, he nearly wobbled off his horse while wearing the Holy Crown of Saint Stephen. The Countess Katalin Károlyi wondered if such 'emblems of power had been intended for the colossi of a bygone era'. They were, in any case, 'too heavy for Karl; his task too, no doubt; an empire in full disintegration'.³⁶

In 1916 the Central Powers had begun to feel the pinch of economic isolation occasioned by a total British blockade that Wilhelm II's expensive navy proved powerless to break. It culminated in the brutal 'turnip winter' of 1916–17, by which point the demands of the war were taking a severe toll on Central European civilians. Basic daily rations by the summer of 1917 offered less than half the number of calories contemporary nutritionists thought necessary to survive.³⁷ Hunger provoked feelings of resentment, envy and apathy. It also fuelled petty crime and corruption. Personal loss and deprivation inevitably drove many to wonder what it was all for in the first place. Antisemitism began to flourish as Jews were blamed for cowardice and war profiteering, exacerbated by the huge influx of Jewish refugees from Eastern Europe. In Vienna and Budapest, they numbered about 75,000 and 25,000 respectively, but inflated figures circulated that added to fears of a Jewish 'invasion'.³⁸

At the start of the war emergency legislation allowed constitutional structures to be swept aside, resulting in arbitrary arrests, the suspension of civil rights, and what felt to many like the establishment of an unrestricted military dictatorship.³⁹ In Germany this was epitomized by the elevation of Hindenburg and his deputy Ludendorff to leadership of the entire German war effort in August 1916. Much of their attention the previous year had been devoted to the administration of 'Ober Ost', a vast military fiefdom carved out of occupied Russian territory that the two tried to turn into a model autarkic military state.⁴⁰ They transplanted much of that ethos onto the Reich itself, instituting an expansive plan of economic control designed to direct as many resources as possible to the war effort.

The 'Hindenburg plan' only exacerbated the fraying of the bonds of unity that so many Germans had celebrated over the previous several years. By 1917 two vehemently opposed camps had crystallized that represented the deep polarization of German society. One called for a negotiated end to the war without annexations or indemnities, enjoying majority support in the Reichstag from the Centre Party, SPD, and the liberal Progressive People's Party. The other called for a continuation of the war to its victorious end, to be followed by massive annexations. Without a base in the Reichstag, this camp coalesced around the virulently nationalistic, extra-parliamentary Fatherland Party founded in 1917 by Alfred von Tirpitz and Wolfgang Kapp. They enjoyed the support of the huge swathes of German society that were still entirely committed to the war and could not imagine it resulting in anything other than an overwhelming German victory. They saw demands for a negotiated peace as little more than treason, a 'stab in the back' for a brave German army heading to victory. Socialists and Jews became the primary targets for nationalist scorn, sometimes joined by Catholics and Poles as enemies of the Reich supposedly sabotaging it from within.[41] The Fatherland Party represented the radicalization of a German right that had become obsessed with dreams of imperialist grandeur and national unity which only the war could fulfil.[42]

By this point the Habsburg Monarchy was also being threatened with outright dissolution if it failed to placate growing calls for federalization. Masaryk was just one of a number of Slavic politicians that had gone into exile over the course of the war, convinced that national goals would be better serviced by aligning themselves with the Entente than by sticking with the Central Powers. The triumvirate of Masaryk, Edvard Beneš and the Slovak Milan Rastislav Štefánik established a Czechoslovak government-in-waiting in early 1916, amalgamating the self-determination of Czechs and Slovaks into a single joint project.[43] In July 1917 the exiled Yugoslav Committee signed an agreement with the government of Serbia committing to a future unified South Slavic state that similarly tied together the fate of Slovenes, Croats, Bosnians, Serbs, and Montenegrins. A month later Roman Dmowski formed a Polish National Committee in Switzerland, soon recognized by France as the legitimate representative of the Polish people. In April of 1918 they would all meet in Rome at an Entente-backed Congress of Oppressed Nationalities of the Austro-Hungarian Empire, expressing if nothing else a common desire to see the collapse of Habsburg power in Central Europe.

The exiles were aided in their mission by sympathetic observers in the Entente powers, who helped propagandize their calls for independence at a time when few had heard of—much less cared for—strange peoples like Czechoslovaks or Yugoslavs. The French historian Ernest Denis, a Czechophile, anti-German, and anti-Austrian Protestant, founded and edited a bimonthly publication entitled *The Czech Nation*.[44] In Britain, the roaming scholar of Austria-Hungary Robert Seton-Watson, foreign editor of *The Times* Wickham Steed, and historian Arthur Evans acted as the crucial intermediaries, patrons and propagandists.[45] The exiles themselves were, not coincidentally, exceptionally pro-Western and pro-Entente. Masaryk was a committed Anglophile, Beneš and Štefánik Francophiles in equal measure. They found in the word 'Mitteleuropa' the perfect encapsulation of everything they were against, the first issue of the exile journal *The New Europe* expressing itself as an antidote to the 'Pangerman project of "Central Europe"'.[46]

On the ground, tensions were rising between the governments of the Central Powers and the representatives of various nationalities. The 'Austro-Polish solution' was definitively abandoned in November 1916 when an independent Poland was proclaimed instead, though it remained a mere puppet regime. Naumann optimistically wrote that this signalled 'the creation of a community of struggle between Poles and all Central Europeans. From now on we are brothers-in-arms!' Only through 'struggle, death, effort and victory' would the 'Central European spirit become something alive'.[47] The following summer, when Piłsudski and most of his legionnaires refused to swear an oath of allegiance to a 'king of Poland' (yet to actually be named), he was imprisoned by the Germans.[48] Unlike the German Reichstag, which sat throughout the war, the Austrian Reichsrat had been disbanded in 1914. It was recalled in 1917 in the hope that it would help stabilize the monarchy, but in its very first session on 30 May Slavic delegates demanded the monarchy's federalization.

In the name of 'representatives of the Bohemian people' from 'all three lands of the crown of Saint Wenceslaus', František Staněk called for 'the transformation of the Habsburg-Lothringian Monarchy into a federal state of free and equal national states'. Moreover, he expressed their more ambiguous striving 'to unite all the tribes of the Czechoslovak people into a democratic state', which would have meant joining Slovak areas of Hungary to this proposed federal unit. Staněk was followed by the Slovene Anton Korošec, speaking on behalf of the United South Slavic Club, who 'on the basis of the national principle and Croatian state right' called for 'the unification of all Slovene, Croat, and Serb inhabited areas of the monarchy into an independent' democratic 'state body under the sceptre of the Habsburg-Lothringian dynasty'.[49] The message was clear. They had suffered and died for the monarchy, and now they expected their reward.

The calls for national self-determination were growing more and more intense, soon catalysed by two great promises from East and West. The Russian Empire was struck by a revolution in March 1917, just weeks before the United States entered the war on the side of the Entente. Sensing an opportunity to knock the great eastern colossus out of the war for good, the German high command decided to send the far-left revolutionary Vladimir Lenin into the fray. In November his radical Bolshevik faction within the Russian Social Democratic Party staged a coup d'etat with the hope of leading a world revolution.

The day after taking power, Lenin issued a 'Decree on Peace' calling for an immediate end to the war, a 'just and democratic peace ... without annexations and reparations'. Lenin's slogan of 'land, bread, and peace' promised a concrete, material way forward for the hungry, impoverished, war-weary masses, and not just in the Russian Empire. The idealistic president of the United States Woodrow Wilson felt compelled to respond. On 8 January 1918 he outlined what would become his famous fourteen points. They envisioned a progressive world order based on international cooperation between independent nation-states. Whether under the auspices of progressive Wilsonianism or revolutionary Bolshevism, national self-determination was set to define the world of the future.

By 1918 this was not really even disputed within the Central Powers, but the primacy of military concerns and the inflexibility of existing political arrangements made the realization of any national demands all but impossible. Armies were the very embodiment of the princely states that ruled over the whole region. They were machines that turned the average man into a cog irrespective of his personal loyalties or desires. Whatever hopes people had for social or national aspirations to be realized by the war, they remained purely theoretical, to be decided at a later point. But Lenin and Wilson promised a world in which they would not have to wait, in which social or national revolutions could be welcomed and secured in the near future. Habsburgs and Hohenzollerns could not even feed their people, much less provide them with a bright new future. By 1918 German and Austro-Hungarian societies were coming apart at the seams.

In March 1918, a peace treaty was signed with Bolshevik Russia which the Central Powers desperately hoped would provide them with much needed resources, especially grain from Ukraine. But their military fortunes were entirely dependent on a spring offensive launched on the western front a few weeks later. Despite initial successes, it stalled. In

PLUNGE INTO THE ABYSS

August the Western Entente powers launched their own offensive, slowly pushing the German army back as the high command began to accept that the war was lost. In October political representatives of the various nationalities ruled by the Habsburgs began to go their own ways, forming national councils that claimed to speak for their entire nations.

Watching these concerning developments, the Reich's ambassador in Vienna convened an emergency meeting with the diplomatic corps there, including the envoys of other German states such as Bavaria and Saxony. He had been reliably informed that the Czechs were on the verge of declaring independence, jeopardizing the stability of Germany's closest ally. But with the war all but lost, the real worry was the fate of their co-nationals. The Reich would have to prepare to defend the imperilled Germans of Austria, they concluded. Emperor Wilhelm II concurred. The struggle between Slavdom and Germandom had brought the Germans of Central Europe closer together. They would now 'feel drawn to us, to the centre', he opined. It would be best for them, therefore, 'to join the German Reich, in some form or another, in order to preserve the existence and future of its race'.[50] But soon there would be no Hohenzollern realm into which to welcome the lost Germans of Habsburg Austria.

PART III

THE FALL
1918–1948

14

GEESE INTO THE FOG

'On February 23 I arrived at Buchs on the Swiss-Austrian frontier' wrote the English journalist Ellis Ashmead-Bartlett in 1919. 'Here one left civilization behind, and entered the devastated zone'. It was a land without 'food, wine, warmth or comfort' where hardly 'a normal man, woman or child was to be seen'. Restaurants were stripped bare, advertisements posted for goods that were impossible to find. The once-proud Austrian officials wore 'rags' rather than uniforms—a better sight still than the shivering half-starved children who begged alongside maimed soldiers on the streets.

Vienna, where it seemed the old elites were too deluded to recognize the diminution of their city's status, was a dirty, freezing, hungry city overrun by a 'cosmopolitan throng' from 'every tribe and race of Central and Eastern Europe'. In this scene of abject misery and poverty, 'the Jew stood out prominently and dominated every situation' he wrote. 'The little Jews swarmed over Vienna, and devoured its decaying remains like flies round a raw steak on a hot summer's day'. The Englishman's blasé antisemitism reflected what had become a common sentiment across the continent as a result of the war. Budapest he found in a better state than Vienna, but with a tense political atmosphere that 'seemed likely to burst forth at any moment into an upheaval, which might menace the existing social structure of all the neighbouring states'.[1]

Ashmead-Bartlett concluded his 1923 *The Tragedy of Central Europe* with uncertainty. 'The future of all the nations east of the Rhine is in the melting pot and the final form in which they will emerge may not be seen for many years to come. The war set the pot boiling and the peace has not yet cooled the seething metal to its final shape. What fresh ethnographical, economic, and political groupings will arise only time can show'.[2]

CENTRAL EUROPE

In the autumn of 1918, most Central Europeans had come to place their hopes for salvation on President Wilson's promise of a 'just peace'. This drove Emperor Karl's belated endorsement of national self-determination at a time when Wilson no longer even recognized the integrity of the Habsburg Monarchy.[3] Kaiser Wilhelm II appointed the liberal Prince Max von Baden—heir to the Grand Duchy of Baden—as chancellor in a vain attempt to do the same, but it was too little too late. A mutiny in the naval town of Kiel had been spreading across northern Germany since early November, with workers' and soldiers' councils (usually referred to in English by the Russian word 'soviet') establishing control over countless towns and cities. They raised the red flag of revolution, giving a symbolic unity to their uncoordinated movement.

One by one the German princes laid down their crowns. On 9 November tens of thousands of protestors streamed onto the streets of Berlin demanding Emperor Wilhelm II go. Without his knowledge or approval, his abdication was announced by Chancellor Max that same day, who then passed the chancellorship on to the socialist Friedrich Ebert.[4] Wilhelm II slipped into exile in the Netherlands, where he would remain until his death. There he belatedly renounced 'for all time the rights to the crown of Prussia and associated rights to the German imperial crown'.[5] The house paper of the Austrian Social Democratic Party put it succinctly: 'Habsburg and Hohenzollern, Austria and Prussia—they dominated, divided, split up the German peoples. Now their time is over'.[6]

The collapse of empires east of the Rhine would create victors and vanquished, but few new certainties. Ancient borders were replaced by amorphous fronts; hallowed imperial capitals by competing centres of authority. Old hierarchies crumbled and violence took their place. The princes and their houses, with their centuries of all but universally recognized legitimate rule over Central Europe, no longer mattered. It was the people and only the people with whom political legitimacy now resided. But 'the people' were brutalized, impoverished, disoriented, and polarized by four years of war. A staggering eighty-six per cent of German men and seventy-eight per cent of Austro-Hungarian men aged eighteen to fifty had passed through the armed forces in the First World War. Over three million had been killed.[7]

Millions more had been left wounded or traumatized by the fighting. Grief for the loss of loved ones cut across all social and national lines. Countless soldiers, officers and civilians were radicalized into far-right or far-left politics. Some believed they had been 'stabbed in the back' by treacherous pacifists, socialists and Jews. Others held the governing class, their state, and all it represented responsible for the catastrophe of a war that had led to nothing but suffering. Some had been radicalized while fighting communists in the expanses of Eastern Europe, or had been persuaded by those very same communists to join their crusade while in Russian prisoner-of-war camps. As the war officially came to an end, these radicals and the ideas they now espoused flooded back into their starving and disease-stricken homelands, bringing the violence of war home with them.

The provincial revolutionary wave had been slow to reach Berlin, but by the time Chancellor Ebert entered office some socialists felt sufficiently confident to proclaim a republic. Indeed, two such proclamations were issued on 9 November from the balcony of the Reichstag, by the moderate Philipp Scheidemann and the radical Karl Liebknecht, presaging a division within the socialist movement that would only grow over the following year. Two days before the revolution in Berlin, a republic had been declared in Bavaria by the socialist Kurt Eisner. It was accompanied by the capture of barracks, ministries, railway stations, post offices, and telegraph lines, leaving Munich in Eisner's hands by the morning of 8 November.[8] He was originally from Berlin but embraced and encouraged the wave of anti-Prussian and anti-Berlin sentiment that had gripped the Reich—Bavaria in particular—in the waning months of the war.[9] By 11 November he had already announced that until Bavaria's precise relationship to other German states was settled, Bavarian troops would refrain from wearing the German cockade. Bavarian conservatives, for their part, wanted to play no part in a red German republic. Bavarian members of the Centre Party gathered in Regensburg and proclaimed the foundation of a right-wing Bavarian People's Party that demanded 'Bavaria for the Bavarians!'[10]

For their own reasons, the Bavarian left and right alike opened the door to Bavarian separation from the Reich. A similar spectre had already been raised in western Germany, where longstanding dissatisfaction with 'Prussianism' combined with the disastrous outcome of the war and fear of revolution on the Bolshevik-Russian model led to demands for separation from Prussia, the Reich, or both. Most Westphalian citizens were 'different from the rabid masses of Berlin and also from the fanatics of the East that have principally plunged us into this misfortune', opined the Dortmund-based paper *Tremonia*. Another paper described Berlin as the 'metropole of the Slavic east'.[11] Anti-Bolshevism, anti-Prussianism and anti-Slavism were seamlessly combined in the phrase 'Away from Prussia!', now treated as a proxy for the barbaric world of Eastern Europe.[12] On 4 December a large gathering took place in Cologne which many separatists hoped would result in a declaration of a Rhenish Republic led by Cologne Mayor Konrad Adenauer. While Adenauer demurred, he nonetheless took over as chair of the Rhenish Committee for the Establishment of a West German Republic the following day and became a figurehead for the movement to separate the Catholic Rhineland from Prussia.[13]

Separatism—whether revolutionary or reactionary—was not so much indicative of a desire to abandon 'Germany' as it was the uncertainty of the revolutionary events. The moribund Reich government was under transitional rule by republicans who thought only a democratically elected assembly could decide the country's future, but conservatives watched with despair at the fading away of the hallowed princely states. On the nationalist right many believed they had not lost the war at all but had instead been 'stabbed in the back' by revolutionaries at home. After all, the Central Powers had achieved a stunning victory in the east and spent four years fighting in the west deep in French territory. What they found at home, meanwhile, was a world turned upside down by a dirty, faceless revolutionary mass. One right-wing nationalist compared the revolutionary 'mob' to 'rats ... with the filth of the gutters on them, grey, furtive, with little red-rimmed eyes'.[14]

This disgust fuelled his decision to join one of over 100 paramilitary Freikorps brigades that formed in the wake of the war. Though they had no definite ideology, their culture was often marked by brutal violence, antisemitism, anti-socialism, and a passionate desire for 'national renewal'. Hundreds of thousands passed through their ranks, brawling with their revolutionary counterparts on the streets of German cities, hoping to beat back the nebulous tide of 'Slavonic-Jewish Bolshevism'; fighting in the German-Polish borderlands—Silesia in particular—hoping to stave off the threat of annexation to Poland; or marauding the vast chaotic expanses of Eastern Europe, where they had been told to stay by the Western Entente powers to ward off the Bolshevik advance. One right-wing paramilitary activist characteristically described it as a 'godforsaken wasteland of slime' without 'a glimmer of Central European *Kultur*'. The last Freikorps units returned to Germany on 13 December 1919.[15]

Radical socialists at home, meanwhile, demanded immediate revolution, reconstituting themselves as the Communist Party of Germany in late 1918. Unhappy with Ebert's moderate direction, they tried to overthrow the government on 5 January 1919. When this failed, these so-called 'Spartacist' revolutionaries turned to armed struggle. Ebert fatefully turned to Freikorps militias, a pattern that would be repeated across Germany over the following year as moderate republicans deployed radical nationalists to stave off 'Bolshevik' revolution. Karl Liebknecht and Rosa Luxemburg, the leaders of the communist party, were captured, abused and murdered by Freikorps troops as the uprising was crushed.[16]

West- and south-German separatism, the tumultuous events in Berlin, and a desire to show the Entente powers that a new Germany was being born convinced Ebert that the upcoming Reichstag would have to meet (temporarily) outside of Berlin. Kassel, Erfurt, Eisenach, Würzburg, Mamberg, and Frankfurt all put themselves forward to host the new assembly, but the government ultimately decided on the small town of Weimar.[17] The town of Goethe, of enlightened cosmopolitanism, was seen as the total antithesis of Berlin and Potsdam, of Bismarck and Wilhelm, of cold Realpolitik and Prussian militarism. It was symbolism they hoped would not be lost on their Western counterparts who themselves had long observed a distinction between these 'two Germanies'.[18]

The triumph of the more cultured and democratic Germany seemed to be clear from the January 1919 elections undertaken with universal suffrage irrespective of sex, religion, property, or class. Germans returned a parliament overwhelmingly supportive of a democratic republic, with the Social Democratic Party, Centre Party, and liberal German Democratic Party together winning seventy-six per cent of the vote.[19] These three parties would come to be known as the Weimar Coalition, founders of a new democratic German nation-state born out of the ruins of the delegitimized Prussian-led Reich. To symbolize the country's rebirth, they adopted the revolutionary black-red-gold as the country's official flag in place of the old black-white-red, much to the chagrin of the nationalist right.[20] They sought not only to create a new democratic state, but also to overcome the narrow confines of Bismarck's 'little German' Reich. Already on the day of the Weimar parliament's opening, Ebert called for the representatives to authorize the government to immediately negotiate German-Austria's accession to Germany, to 'reknit the bond that the violence of 1866 once tore asunder'.[21]

Far from an expression of German imperialism or radical nationalism, the widespread hope that Austro-Germans would finally be united with their Reich brethren was seen as a progressive fulfilment of the ideals of 1848 in line with Wilson's principles of national self-determination. This was, not coincidentally, how the Austrian revolutionaries had been positioning their own political project since October. Watching the various nationalities of the monarchy go their own way, Austro-German representatives gathered on 21 October 1918 to form a Provisional National Assembly. The venue chosen was the building of the Lower Austrian Diet where the Austrian Revolution had begun in 1848.[22] Like in Weimar, it was an act of political harmony, bringing together Christian Socials, Social Democrats, and liberal German Nationals under the eventual leadership of Karl Renner. Meeting him over a decade before, the Russian revolutionary Leon Trotsky had derisively concluded that Renner was 'as far from revolutionary dialectics as the most conservative Egyptian pharaoh'.[23] There could have been no better man to spearhead a moderate national revolution of Germans in Austria.

The Moravian-born Renner—like most Austrian Social Democrats—was a great believer in the value and virtues of German *Kultur*.[24] During the war this evolved into enthusiastic support for the integration of Central Europe into a single state in which German language and culture would clearly have a special role.[25] By late 1918, however, it was clear that Central Europe's Wilsonian future entailed the emergence of a new system of independent nation-states. With the Habsburgs totally delegitimized, the monarchy collapsing, and any hope of its federal reorganization fading, the Provisional National Assembly was forced to imagine an independent existence for Austrian Germans.[26] An *Anschluss* (a joining with Germany) was thought the only alternative. When the news of Wilhelm II's abdication of a German republic reached Vienna, Social Democratic leaders encouraged Emperor Karl to do the same.[27] He fled Vienna instead, *sans abdication*.

On 12 November the Provisional National Assembly met and declared a republic, accompanied by the abolition of the emperor's authority, the feudal upper house, the provincial diets, and all the imperial ministries. All officers and civil servants were henceforth released from their oaths of authority to the imperial state.[28] The second article of the law adopted by the assembly declared 'German-Austria is an integral part of the German Republic'. As a note sent the following day to President Wilson put it: 'The German nation in Austria, having exercised its right to self-determination ... wishes to restore the close constitutional tie with Germany torn up by the sword 52 years ago'.[29]

The *Anschluss* was not merely a question of German-Austria's unification with Germany, but also its very borders. The young republic's claimed boundaries stretched deep into the Bohemian lands where German majorities could be found.[30] But German-Austria had no effective means to enforce this claim, nor was it clear exactly how ancient Bohemian lands could suddenly be integrated into a new German state. The Reich's ambassador in Vienna had already observed in October that the desire for annexation was not equal across German-speaking Bohemia: 'For us Prussians it is not exactly flattering that the desire for unification with [Prussian] Silesia is much weaker in eastern Bohemia than that for the unification with Saxony and Bavaria in the western regions'.[31] Indeed, anxieties about domination from Berlin—whether out of dislike for Prussianism, Protestantism or socialism—coloured how many Austrians viewed the *Anschluss* question, reflecting wider uncertainty around Germany's development. Preliminary negotiations in spring 1919 bore little fruit, dependent in any case on approval from the Entente powers in a peace conference neither Germany nor Austria were taking part in.[32]

Hungary's attempts to embrace democracy and Wilsonian self-determination to stave off the collapse of the country proved even more futile than those of Austria. On 26 October 1918 representatives of the country's leading opposition parties gathered in the Pest mansion of the liberal aristocrat Mihály Károlyi and formed a Hungarian National Council. Károlyi had been the Hungarian opposition's most vigorous peace advocate since 1916, a committed progressive democrat who supported universal suffrage, land redistribution, and the secularization of public life.[33] He had joined forces with Oszkár Jászi, who had laid out a vision of transforming Hungary into a multinational, democratic 'eastern Switzerland' over the previous year. Just a few days later, with the streets of Budapest in chaos, Károlyi was officially asked to form a government, which he did, appointing Jászi his minister of nationalities. 'This war was the responsibility of feudal Hungary', Jászi wrote. The democrats hoped they would not have to bear its burden.[34]

On the day of Károlyi's appointment, mutinying soldiers shot wartime prime minister István Tisza dead in his home. It was just one sign of just how much state's authority was withering away in the face of social revolution, leaving it powerless to defend against the national revolutions chipping away at its territory from all sides. Károlyi consented to harsh armistice terms imposed by the Entente powers, that saw Hungary voluntarily disarm and Entente troops occupying large swathes of the country ahead of their expected annexation to Romania, Czechoslovakia, and an expanded Serbo-Yugoslav state. Károlyi eventually declared Hungary an independent republic on 16 November, leading it first as prime minister and later as president.

His presence at the top of the new republic was living proof of its unquestionable democratic, pacifist and pro-Entente credentials. Károlyi hoped his firm commitment to Wilsonianism would secure the country a more favourable peace, supported by Jászi's concrete plans for a multinational federation.[35] But the republican coalition in Hungary was noticeably shakier than in Austria or Germany, entirely lacking the infrastructure and legitimacy provided by mass political parties. By December 1918 Jászi was worriedly writing to Károlyi about how there was 'no sign of the organization of popular forces, of the establishment of a new, democratic public life'.[36] Instead, the forces of counterrevolution seemed to be growing stronger alongside far-left radicals. In late November the small Party of Communists in Hungary was founded by Béla Kun and fellow former soldiers who had been radicalized as prisoners-of-war in Russia.

On 20 March 1919 the head of the Entente's military mission in Hungary Fernand Vix delivered a note to President Károlyi demanding he allow the Romanian army to advance significantly further into Hungary. Károlyi was shocked and refused to carry out the demand. Recognizing the note represented a total defeat of his pacifist politics, he and other government leaders concluded that a socialist government would have to be formed which would hopefully garner the support of Soviet Russia. Events rapidly overcame Károlyi and by 22 March his resignation had been forced and a socialist unity government had been formed that included Kun's radical party.[37] Jászi, who had resigned months before, noted in his diary: 'Plan for Russian alliance. *Levee en masse*. Toward dark and bloody chaos'.[38]

Hungary was transformed practically overnight into a 'Soviet' Republic.[39] It was born and would die amidst a war it had little chance of winning. The enemies surrounding it were backed militarily by France, while the remaining Entente powers remained firmly committed to the erstwhile kingdom's partition. What little popularity the socialist government had in the country was largely squandered by an aggressively radical program of nationalization, expropriation, and cultural revolution combined with a 'Red terror' that left hundreds dead.[40] The 'Soviet' republic could only really claim full authority over Budapest, being despised in the countryside and opposed by right-wing groups at home and in exile.

About 100,000 Hungarians—including Jászi and 10,000–15,000 officers—fled the communist regime to Austria in 1919, where the aristocrat

Karl von Schönborn-Buchheim provided the influential Anti-Bolshevik Committee with a headquarters at his Viennese palace.[41] It was one of many paramilitary organizations that drew in former officers committed to overthrowing the new regime, many of whom were noble or middle-class refugees from lands destined to fall under the control of Hungary's neighbours. In other words, they were the dispossessed elites of what had recently become the 'old regime'.[42] They shared with the Freikorps of Germany a desire for radical national renewal through violent revenge against socialists, pacifists, Jews, and anyone else deemed to be responsible for the nation's suffering.

The most consequential counterrevolutionary force was a full-on rival government formed in Szeged, a large agricultural city on the Great Hungarian Plain southeast of Budapest. A contingent of about 3,000 French troops occupied the city in December 1918, providing a safe haven for Hungarians fleeing both the successor states and the regime in Budapest. Doubly radicalized by the humiliations of the national and social revolutions that had destroyed all the certainties of Hungarian political life, the counterrevolutionary government formed there in May 1919 would from the start be committed to the overthrow of the order of 1918 and all it represented.[43] The militant nationalist, anti-communist, and irredentist culture nurtured in Szeged produced a novel—albeit vague—ideology that marked a definite break with the Hungarian liberalism of old.[44] This was especially true of its more radical wing, represented by Gyula Gömbös, who added to the explosive mix a strong dose of antisemitism, blaming 'international Jewry' for Hungary's misfortunes.[45] The former Austro-Hungarian Admiral Miklós Horthy became the figurehead of the Hungarian counterrevolution, tasked with organizing an army to topple the socialist-communist regime.[46]

There was a general sense of chaos and spreading revolution in Central Europe. The head of the Bavarian revolutionary government Kurt Eisner was shot dead on the street by the radical aristocratic nationalist Anton Arco-Valley on 22 February 1919. In response, one of Eisner's followers walked into the Bavarian parliament and fired two shots at the head of the Majority Social Democratic Leader Erhard Auer—one of Eisner's chief critics—leaving two people (but not Auer) dead.[47] The political situation in Bavaria began to spiral out of control, eventually catalysed by the revolution in Hungary, where Béla Kun called for Austrian and Bavarian socialists to follow in their footsteps. In early April the far-left proclaimed its own 'Soviet' republic in Munich, causing the Majority Socialist government to flee to the town of Bamberg in northern Bavaria.[48] The Austrian government, totally dependent on the Entente powers to feed its citizens and desperate to stave off an occupation, declined to join its two neighbours in this revolutionary episode, instead following Berlin in cracking down on communists with the help of right-wing paramilitaries.[49]

After just 133 days, the Hungarian 'Soviet' republic was toppled by a Romanian invasion in August 1919. The time had come for Horthy's counterrevolutionary crusade. Less a *Reconquista* than a violent sweep of the western Hungarian countryside to root out suspected communists, Horthy's men matched the 'red terror' of the socialist-communist regime with a 'white terror' of their own. While it officially only targeted those who participated in the communist regime, the zealousness of the radicalized right-wing paramilitaries often led them to target those who they thought represented everything wrong with the present crisis: the Jews. That thirty of forty-eight commissars in the 'Soviet' republic had been Jewish seemed to confirm the connection between Jewishness and godless Bolshevism—often rendered simply as 'Judeo-Bolshevism'.[50] This, coupled with the explosion of antisemitism in the waning years of the war, inspired violent antisemitic pogroms across Hungary that left thousands of Jews dead.[51] Horthy strode into Budapest on a white stallion with his national army on 16 November 1919 after the Romanians had vacated the city. He condemned the national capital as a 'guilty and sinful city', one that had 'dragged the Holy Crown and the national colours in the dust'.[52]

By then Bavaria's own communist republic had long since been crushed, deeply shocking the otherwise sleepy bourgeois city of Munich. Even during the reign of the 'Soviet' republic, a certain normality remained. As government troops surrounded the city in late April, however, everything descended into chaos. Trams stopped running, workers stayed at home, and panicked residents cowered in their apartments as the sound of artillery fire grew closer and closer. Members of the Bavarian 'Red Army' executed ten hostages in cold blood, a prelude to days of violent fighting in the streets that left over 600 people dead, including hundreds of civilians. More than 2,000 supporters of the communist regime were sentenced to death or long prison terms in the aftermath.[53]

* * *

On 8 November 1918, two German officers arrived at Magdeburg prison. In the garden they found the imprisoned former leader of the Polish

Legions Józef Piłsudski and his second-in-command Kazimierz Sosnowski on their daily walk. They informed the bewildered Poles that they were free to go, with the two hastily packed off to Berlin to catch a train to Warsaw.[54] The war was at an end, Magdeburg under revolutionary control, and the monarchy on the verge of collapse.

Piłsudski's arrival in Warsaw on 10 November created an electric atmosphere. Somehow the war had defeated all three partitioning powers, leaving Poland stumbling towards what generations of Polish patriots could only dream of. The following day Piłsudski met with the Regency Council of the German client kingdom, which gave him the title of commander in chief and tasked him with forming a national unity government before dissolving itself. While this government in Warsaw was by then just one of five rival centres of power—with other Polish governments declared in Lublin, Krakow, Poznan, and France—all eventually coalesced around the heroic, martial figure of Piłsudski.[55]

Four days after Piłsudski's arrival in Warsaw, Karel Kramář took the stage to address the parliament of the newly independent Czechoslovak Republic. 'For too long, we have felt the barbarism of cultural oppression' under the 'heavy bonds of Austrian and Hungarian violence'. To a rapturous standing ovation, he announced: 'All ties that bound us to the Habsburg-Lorraine dynasty are severed'.[56]

Romanian and Serbian troops meanwhile streamed into Hungary to take up their positions along the demarcation line agreed to by President Károlyi. A couple of weeks later representatives of the unrecognized State of Slovenes, Serbs, and Croats arrived in Belgrade to negotiate their unification with Serbia, officially proclaimed on 1 December as the Kingdom of Serbs, Croats, and Slovenes.[57] That same day a dramatic display of national self-determination took place in Transylvanian Alba Iulia: 100,000 Romanians gathered to witness the formation of a Great National Assembly consisting of 1,228 delegates from all over the Romanian-inhabited lands of the former Hungarian kingdom to proclaim their union with the motherland.[58]

The new Czechoslovak government also rapidly moved to secure its territorial claims. Using a combination of Czech units from the former Austro-Hungarian army as well as returned legionnaires, it occupied the German-inhabited territories of the Bohemian crownlands with little resistance in November. In neither the starving German-Austrian state nor in the chaotic Reich was there appetite for intervention.[59] The conquest of Slovakia was much more fraught. In many towns filled with

Hungarian loyalists the Czechoslovak troops were met with a frosty reception, their inhabitants thinking the occupation would be temporary. Even in Slovak areas Czech troops sometimes alienated the Catholic locals with blasphemous behaviour like stabling their horses in churches and celebrating the Czech proto-Protestant Jan Hus.[60]

In Pozsony—which would soon be rechristened Bratislava—German and Hungarian-speaking workers went on strike while shopkeepers kept their doors shut to voice their displeasure with the new regime. A confrontation between legionnaires and anti-Czechoslovak crowds left nine dead and dozens wounded. Further east, the pro-Hungarian Zipser Germans touted the idea of their own republic. As their local paper proclaimed in October: 'We were Germans and are Germans and want to remain Germans! And as Germans we were Hungarian and are Hungarian and want to remain Hungarian!' In mid-December they were peacefully occupied, accompanied by what was then the customary tearing down of symbols of Hungarian authority and the establishment of Slovak rule. Still further east the Czechoslovak troops were met with resistance, later even beaten back by the Hungarian Soviet Republic which then attempted to set up its own Slovak Soviet Republic in Sáros county. With French help, Czechoslovak forces regrouped and pushed to what had become the demarcation line in the summer of 1919.[61]

The minor show of force required for Czechoslovakia to secure its new borders paled in comparison to Poland's path to statehood. The collapse of the Central Powers had led the Soviets to repudiate the Treaty of Brest-Litovsk, promising to reconquer all the territories once held by the Russian Empire and link up with the revolutions in Central Europe. The Polish state was reborn straight into a war with a vast revolutionary power, forced to organize its defence with exhausted soldiers, suspicious civilians, and officers from four different armies.[62] Its very existence was at stake, but what exactly its 'existence' would look like was also an open question. As Piłsudski would put in in February 1919: 'At this moment Poland has practically no borders and everything we can get in the West depends on the Entente'. In the East it was a different matter: 'here there are doors that open and close depending on who opens them and how wide they open them with force'.[63]

Piłsudski did not want Poland to be just another European state, but a great Commonwealth like it once was. He believed it was 'doomed to greatness'.[64] He had been born and raised near Vilna, the old capital of the Grand Duchy of Lithuania. He nurtured an understanding of

Polishness characteristic of Lithuanian Poles in the Russian Empire, one that held on to a multinational, federative vision of Polish statehood, even if Polish language and culture were expected to play leading roles.[65] This necessitated competition and even war not only with the Bolsheviks and their satellite republics, but also nationalist republics that had been declared in Lithuania and Ukraine. Failing to win Lithuania over to his federalist schemes, Piłsudski first attempted to overthrow its government before eventually occupying Vilna in 1920, poisoning relations between the two states for decades. He managed to secure an alliance with Ukraine, but this lost all relevance with the westward Soviet advance in 1920.[66] By August they were at the gates of Warsaw, forcing a last-ditch defence of the city that came to be known as the 'miracle on the Vistula'.[67] The Soviets were eventually beaten back, and peace was concluded between the two exhausted countries in 1921. Tens of thousands of soldiers had been killed on both sides, as had countless civilians in brutal violence that weak central authorities could do little to stop.[68]

Poland's final borders were decided by a mix of negotiations, war and plebiscites.[69] It was left as neither the multinational commonwealth Piłsudski dreamed of nor the narrowly ethnographic Poland that his opponents advocated. When the country had been partitioned 123 years before, it was a noble republic in which 'Polishness' was largely synonymous with the noble political nation that ruled over an extremely heterogeneous population. In the intervening years understandings of nationhood had radically changed, with the most 'modern' nationalists advocating an ethnic or even racial understanding of nations as organic entities caught in a naturalistic struggle for existence and dominance. In a Polish context, the chief proponent of this conception was Roman Dmowski and his National Democracy movement. He and Piłsudski represented two poles of Polish opinion.[70]

Poland—like all the victorious successor states—was ultimately conceived of as a thoroughly national project that bore little resemblance to the old commonwealth. Its 1921 constitution's dramatic proclamation that 'We, the Polish nation, thank Providence for liberating us from a century and a half of slavery' exclusively reflected Polish nationalist myths and visions.[71] In a similar vein, Germans and Hungarians were barred from participating in the first postwar Yugoslav elections while Czechoslovakia's 1920 constitution was drafted without the input of the huge German and Hungarian minorities unwillingly annexed to the country.[72] After all, as the declaration of independence in 1918 had made clear, the 'Czechoslovak nation' was the country's 'state-forming' nation.[73]

Bohemian state right was asserted in the interests of territory, but 'Bohemia' as understood by the new republic was a historically Czech state formation. This view was infamously put forward by Masaryk in the waning stages of the war, when he noted that Germans 'originally came into the country as immigrants and colonists'.[74] His attempts to clarify his awkward comment did little to change the reality that those not belonging to the 'Czechoslovak nation' would be a minority in someone else's nation-state. This was the future that Transylvania's 'historic nations' were also forced to contend with as they found themselves being absorbed into the expanded Romanian state.[75] The newly annexed territories were integrated on the basis that they were 'reunifying' the Romanian nation. Regional peculiarities were seen as something to be overcome as quickly as possible.[76] Its new constitution adopted in 1923 emphasized that 'the Kingdom of Romania is a unitary and indivisible national state'.[77]

The question of whether south Slavs should have the same coloured the debates leading up to the adoption of a constitution in 1921 for the new Kingdom of Serbs, Croats, and Slovenes, though unification had already occurred as a fait accompli. As the Habsburg Monarchy collapsed, its former south Slav territories were in total chaos. In what was until recently the Kingdom of Croatia-Slavonia, looters and robbers were running amok, and some even feared Bolshevik agitators could push the country towards revolution.[78] Slovene and Dalmatian politicians meanwhile nervously waited for the Serbian army to occupy the Adriatic coast before the Italians could get there first. The arrest of a former Austro-Hungarian general supposedly planning to overthrow the new regime raised the spectre of counterrevolution.[79] The National Council of Slovenes, Croats, and Serbs in Zagreb decided almost unanimously to send a delegation to negotiate unification with Serbia. Only Stjepan Radić voted against.[80] He questioned the very legitimacy of the unelected council to decide the fate of millions, famously beseeching his colleagues: 'Don't rush like geese into the fog!'[81]

Yet Radić's voice was only one of many that questioned the new political order, in particular the signing away of Croatian statehood (even though the Kingdom of Croatia-Slavonia had in effect already abolished itself).[82] Despite the long Croatian tradition of Yugoslavism reaching back to the Illyrian movement, the prominence of Croatian exiles in the Yugoslav Committee, and the nearly unanimous decision of the National Council to unify with Serbia, Croatia rapidly became the centre of autonomist opposition to a unitary Yugoslav state. A few days after the new state had been proclaimed in Belgrade, over a dozen people were left dead in Zagreb after a clash between armed supporters and opponents of the new regime.[83]

Discontent grew in the countryside as the Serbian army brought in to restore order made the locals feel as if they were under foreign occupation.[84] In early 1919 Radić's Peasant Party openly began to agitate for an independent Croatian republic, after which he was thrown in jail. That did little to arrest the party's rise and in the first all-Yugoslav elections in 1920 it became the third largest party, the largest of the federalist and autonomist opposition. A unitarist constitution was passed with a slender majority on 28 June 1921, a Serbian Orthodox holiday, with the Peasant Party, Slovene People's Party, and communists all abstaining.

* * *

German, Austrian and Hungarian republican dreams of winning a favourable peace for their defeated countries crumbled as the Entente powers dictated the peace terms from mid-1919 to early 1920. In the treaties of Versailles, Saint-Germain and Trianon, the three new republics were treated as defeated powers, not fellow democracies that had overthrown the yoke of Habsburg-Hohenzollern feudalism. They suffered huge territorial losses, were saddled with large indemnities, and were forced to drastically reduce their armed forces. In all three the peace treaties produced shock and outrage. Particularly resented was the fact that they were nominally forced to accept responsibility for the war.

The political consequences of the peace would loom large over these three principal successors to the defeated Central Powers. The *Anschluss* of German-Austria to Germany was explicitly prohibited, with the transitory Republic of German-Austria becoming the internationally recognized Republic of Austria instead.[85] Austrian claims to any lands of the Bohemian crown were rejected.[86] The mixed Slovene-German duchies of Carinthia and Styria were meanwhile partitioned on vaguely ethnic lines, while Italian-speaking South Tyrol was ceded to Italy. Of ten million people who identified German as their primary language of daily use in the Austrian half of the old Habsburg Monarchy, only 6.1 million found themselves living in the new republic.[87] Shorn of their political homeland amongst Germans in Bohemia and Moravia, Austrian liberals rapidly became irrelevant in the new Austrian state, which was left with two opposing blocs of Christian Socialists and Social Democrats. Conservative fears of socialist domination by Berlin were replaced by fears of socialist domination by 'Red Vienna', the bloated erstwhile imperial capital suddenly trapped in a tiny and overwhelmingly rural, conservative and Catholic Austrian republic.

The efforts of Czechoslovak, 'Yugoslav', Romanian, and Polish politicians had been wildly successful in winning the Entente powers over to their extensive and often contradictory territorial claims. While the Bohemian lands included huge German minorities, they were claimed in their entirety thanks to the doctrine of Bohemian state right. Hungarian state right meanwhile was dispensed with in the name of Slovak self-determination, while even huge areas of the erstwhile Hungarian kingdom that contained Magyar majorities were also annexed on the grounds that they were needed for the Czechoslovak state to be viable. In a similar vein, the vast majority of southern Slav-inhabited territories of the former Austro-Hungarian monarchy became a part of the new Kingdom of Serbs, Croats, and Slovenes. But so too did the extremely diverse province of Vojvodina, including border areas that were majority Magyar. Altogether, it inherited about half-a-million Magyars, compared with 750,000 in Czechoslovakia. Nearly one-and-a half-million Magyars represented Romania's largest minority.

Thus, the Treaty of Trianon not only left the old Kingdom of Hungary truncated but also left over three million Magyars living outside of the country. For Hungarians used to thinking of their kingdom as an indivisible, eternal whole, the picture was even more grim. A startling 71.4 per cent of its territory had been lost to neighbouring countries along with 63.6 per cent of its population. More territory of the former kingdom was left with Romania than Hungary itself.[88] For Magyars it was universally understood as a national catastrophe. Hungarian politics over the following decades would be indelibly shaped by a desire to overturn the Treaty of Trianon, something difficult to imagine without the overturning of the entire postwar order. Hungary was at least guaranteed a kind of internal stability thanks to the conservative nature of the government, which directed nationalist frustrations outwards rather than inwards. The same was not true in Germany, where the Treaty of Versailles was considered no less of an outrageous humiliation. It signed away a seventh of the Reich's territory and a tenth of its population along with all its overseas colonies. It accepted the responsibility of Germany and its allies for the war, which was the grounds on which the country would be forced to pay huge reparations. Its army would be reduced to a paltry 100,000 men.

GEESE INTO THE FOG

There were widespread calls in Germany for an outright rejection. Protests came from just about every angle. The Social Democratic Minister-President Philipp Scheidemann asked rhetorically: 'What hand would not wither that places itself and us in this bondage?' Leading associations of entrepreneurs and trade unions called it a 'death sentence for the German economy'. The Social Democratic minister-president of Prussia coined the phrase 'better dead than a Slav' in response to his state's loss of vast territories to Poland, all without a plebiscite except in the case of Upper Silesia (which would later be partitioned).[89] Paul von Hindenburg opined that 'as a soldier he was duty bound to prefer annihilation with honour to a dishonourable peace'.[90] The Reichstag eventually approved the treaty under the threat of occupation by the Entente powers, but it became a symbol of everything wrong with Weimar Germany.[91]

Debates around the cause of the war provoked less reflection on what had led to its outbreak than what had led to Germany's defeat. The most infamous moment in the official investigation into the causes of the war came on 18 November 1919, when Hindenburg gave his closing testimony. Citing words attributed to 'an English general', he asserted that the 'German Army was stabbed in the back'. 'It is plain enough upon whom the blame lies', he went on. 'If any further proof were necessary to show it, it is to be found in the utter amazement of our enemies at their victory'.[92] An idea already being espoused on the nationalist right was suddenly given a stamp of legitimacy from the heroic figure of Hindenburg. The German military had been victorious, betrayed by the civilian cowards responsible for the republic. 'In Germany, every loyal German man naturally hangs his head in shame', wrote one aristocratic officer in October 1918, 'that our Jewish-Social Democratic government has destroyed everything that the sword has achieved'.[93]

For many radical nationalists, there was no reason to wait to strike against the hated republic. When the government tried to dissolve a prominent Freikorps brigade, Wolfgang Kapp and Walther von Lüttwitz took control of Berlin (where the government had returned to from Weimar) and declared the government toppled in March 1920. They had the support of Hindenburg's old right-hand man Erich Ludendorff, who had made himself a focal point of elite resistance to the republic since returning to Germany in February 1919. His wildly popular memoir published after the war was already in its seventh German edition by 1921. Though he remained in the shadows in the Kapp Putsch, he was undoubtably a key figure in its preparation and its prospects for success.[94]

The army stood idly by as the legitimate government fled, saved only by a nationwide general strike supported by socialist, liberal and Christian trade unions.[95] The one lasting success for the anti-republican right was the resignation of the Social Democratic government in Bavaria. It was replaced by one headed by the archconservative Gustav von Kahr, who was heavily involved in a burgeoning right-wing paramilitary scene in Bavaria that he steadfastly protected from the government in Berlin.[96] The right was given one more victory in June 1920, when the 'Weimar coalition' was reduced to a minority, a position from which it would never recover. The national-conservative German National People's Party (DNVP)—the successor of the Fatherland Party—came third. It was the same year in which the Hungarian republic was totally abandoned, with a rump Kingdom of Hungary restored with Horthy as regent. Austria's grand coalition also collapsed in mid-1920, inaugurating a period of extreme polarization. The revolutionary hopes of 1918 had given way to extreme disillusionment.

For the most prominent postwar critics of the new order from the defeated Central European powers, the prewar world was remembered not as a golden age, but as the original sin of all their later sufferings. Critics of the prewar era—of Wilhelmine Germany, liberal Hungary, and Habsburg Austria—became prophets of the postwar world. Such was the fate of Arthur Moeller van der Bruck. Born in the Prussian Rhineland in 1876, his life drew him inexorably eastwards. He lived in the Baltic, married into a Baltic German family, published Dostoyevsky's complete works in German from 1906 to 1914, and finally spent the war serving in the Press and Propaganda Department for the eastern countries. Already a harsh critic of contemporary German culture before the war, in 1922 he began working on his ultimate critique of Germany's malaise and how the country could recover from it. Published the following year, he thought to name the book 'the third party' or 'third point of view' but ultimately settled on *The Third Reich*.[97]

He was one of many conservative polemicists who deepened their wartime belief in a fundamental divide between materialist Western 'civilization' and more profound German *Kultur*. Materialism, rationalism, republicanism—anything associated with 'the West' fell into the basket of the former.[98] To national conservatives, Weimar represented the unnatural imposition onto Germany of these Western values, akin to a spiritual Western occupation. For Germany to free itself, to shift to a path of national renewal, it would require, as Bruck argued, a revolution from the right—a 'conservative revolution' as this prominent strain of right-wing thought would come to be known. The third Reich would overcome the imperfect first and second Reichs of Charlemagne and Bismarck, which failed to fulfil their true national purpose and finally unite the German-speakers in a single state that would thereafter assume its natural leading position in Central Europe. The civilization of the West that had already penetrated too deeply into Wilhelmine society and after 1918 occupied Germany itself, would be cast aside. The Russian East—excessively submerged in reflective *Kultur*—would act as Germany's ally in this anti-Western crusade, so Bruck hoped, with the great synthesis between West and East in Germany itself.

In salons and magazines, through bestselling books and the DNVP, these national conservative views became articles of faith. Germany's corrupt past and need for a purer future, the pernicious influence of the West and possibility of alliance with the East, and the need to recapture the 'German spirit' by creating a single Greater Germany that would domineer over Europe: such were the ideas of a huge and influential nationalist right that dominated many leading institutions in German public life—the army, the universities, the civil service.

In Hungary, the dominance of right-wing reactionaries was even more complete, and they came to understand their country's past, present and future in terms not dissimilar to their German counterparts. Central was the historian Gyula Szekfű, described by Tibor Frank as the 'semi-official ideological oracle of the Horthy regime'.[99] A devout Catholic, Szekfű first gained notoriety as a prewar critic of the then-dominant school of national romanticism that saw in Hungarian history a struggle of the heroic Magyar gentry against Habsburg centralism. Szekfű developed an alternative view of Hungarian history during the war and its tumultuous aftermath.[100] Its first manifestation was his 1917 *The Hungarian State*—published in German—in which he argued that Hungary's destiny was in a 'German-Christian world', which he took to be effectively synonymous with the term Central Europe. This was a historical rather than political concept, he argued: the pressures emanating from West and East had created in the territories ruled by the Habsburgs in the heart of Europe a single 'Germanic-Christian' community of fate and interests, of which Hungary had always formed an offshoot.

The collapse of the Austro-Hungarian war effort, of the Central Powers, and of Hungary itself did not shake his historical faith in a Christian-German Central Europe but only made it deeper. Amidst the revolutionary tumult of 1918–19, Szekfű began writing *Three Generations and What Came Afterward*, a biting critique of Hungarian liberalism since 1848 and how it was responsible for the present catastrophe. Published in 1920, this was perhaps the most important text in interwar Hungary. It argued that 'everyone must agree that the recent liberal past was an age of deviation, from which we can only raise ourselves with organized work, and through the building of true national traditions'. Hope was only to be found in reestablishing Hungary's link with the 'Christian-Germanic cultural community' that stood in contrast to the secular liberalism exemplified by France.[101] It was in the misguided and failed attempt to mimic this Western liberal model that the seeds of Hungary's collapse were sown, with the abandoning of true national traditions only paving the way for the ascent of the 'Jewish spirit'.[102]

15

THE CENTRAL EUROPEAN CRISIS

'Apart from the Far East'—on the verge of a brutally destructive war between China and Japan—'Central Europe has become the most dangerous centre of crisis in the world' warned Gerhard Schacher in his 1936 *Central Europe and the Western World*. Issues like the *Anschluss*, 'Hungarian irredentism, the Habsburg question, [and] National Socialist risings' were 'symptoms' of 'an internal disequilibrium' which had arisen as a result of the war, still uncured nearly two decades after its end. In the preface to the book's English edition, the venerable journalist Wickham Steed was in full agreement with Schacher's gloomy assessment. Unless 'the Great Powers of Western Europe, are resolved to check the operation of destructive forces, the process of recovery cannot begin in Central Europe, or elsewhere, and civilized mankind will be heading for immeasurable disaster'.[1]

Despite the shedding so much blood together between 1914 and 1918, after the dust from the war had settled, Central Europeans went their own ways. Economic protectionism became the order of the day, breaking down long-established trade relations. Millions were forced to make a choice between becoming a 'national minority' in their own home or picking up everything to become a 'national majority' elsewhere. Even tiny parcels of territory occasioned decades-long rifts. Countries focused on guarding and consolidating their hard-fought sovereignty regarded each other with suspicion. Princes and their claims to historical rights gave way to the democratic right of nations to self-determination. German as a cosmopolitan language of high culture gave way to integrated national societies.

The building of unitary, centralized states dominated by a national majority was not based on any Central European model. It was imported wholesale from the West as countries once defined by their place between East and West now redefined themselves as representatives of the West in the East. As Masaryk had written about extensively during the war, the New Europe was to be the antithesis of 'Mitteleuropa'. But no state could create a democratic, Western, national society overnight. Especially not when the legacy of Central European civilization loomed so large.

That it would take time and require peace was certainly recognized by the leaderships of the successor states, who were aware that the vanquished would take time to accept the new order. One of the few fixtures of the international scene in postwar Central Europe was the system of anti-revisionist alliances supported by France. At the Paris Peace Conference France had been the strongest backer of extensive territorial gains for the new states to Germany's east with the hope that they would form an impregnable bulwark against future German or Russian aggression.[2] In the postwar years it solidified this with an alliance with Poland and backed the 'Little Entente' between Romania, Czechoslovakia and the Kingdom of Serbs, Croats, and Slovenes. The young radicalisms created by the war remained on the margins in the early 1920s. The new 'establishments' were essentially parties and people of the prewar era that had swept the princes aside. It was, after all, German universities, Viennese cafes, imperial armies, and weak and cacophonous parliaments that had shaped men like Masaryk, Horthy, Renner, Ebert, and their associates. It was not the threat of the new they feared, but that of the old.

The House of Habsburg—along with others such as the Bavarian Wittelsbachs—had not renounced claims to its inheritance. Already in 1921, the deposed Karl tried twice to regain the vacant throne of the rump Kingdom of Hungary. In their last meeting in the waning days of the war, when Admiral Miklós Horthy was head of the Austro-Hungarian navy, the latter had pledged, unprompted, with tears in his eyes: 'I will never rest until I have restored your Majesty to his thrones in Vienna and Budapest'.[3] It is little mystery what Karl expected from the now-Regent Horthy. But Karl's sudden appearance in the royal palace in Budapest in March 1921 was unexpected and unwanted. In a heated confrontation, Horthy refused Karl's demands to hand over power to his old sovereign. He feared—not without reason—that a Habsburg restoration would only lead to an occupation of Hungary. His small, disarmed state of 7.6 million was surrounded by a hostile and well-armed alliance of forty-three million.[4] Karl returned to Switzerland with his tail between his legs. In October he stepped onto a plane for the first time in his life to make an even more daring attempt to regain his throne. A majestic flight in the morning autumnal sun over the Alps and into the Pannonian Plain was the highlight of a chaotic endeavour that ended in disaster. Karl was exiled to distant Madeira, where he would die less than a year later, leaving his nine-year-old son Otto the pretender to the lost Habsburg patrimony.[5]

There was no question of such escapades in the other successor states. In the very heartland of the old monarchy, the dispossession of the House of Habsburg was written into the constitution. Karl was banned from ever setting foot in the Republic of Austria again, and his descendants would only be permitted insofar as they renounced the family's claims. This was followed by a wider abolition of noble titles in Austria, turning aristocrats into mere citizens. The same had been done in Czechoslovakia the previous winter, accompanied by extensive land reform, physically breaking the power of the old aristocracy that in Czech national mythology represented a foreign, German imposition. Toppled too were statues of Joesph II and Catholic Marian columns—representative of Habsburg and German rule. Countless stations, squares and streets took the names of Masaryk and US President Wilson.[6] While there was no question of abolishing titles of nobility in the kingdoms of Romania and 'Yugoslavia', land reform bills passed in the wake of the war had a similar goal in mind. In the latter only Slavs could apply for redistributed land—in practice mostly Serbs—while in the former 'national' elements were prioritized. Czechoslovakia was less explicit, but Germans and Hungarians still found themselves vastly underrepresented amongst the beneficiaries of land reform.[7]

Germany had little need or will for land reform.[8] Most large estates in eastern Prussia had in any case passed out of Junker hands, but there was a general unwillingness on the part of the moderate, embattled democratic government to countenance a truly radical break with the Wilhelmine past. Reactionary judges, civil servants and officers were left in their posts despite a blindingly obvious lack of commitment to democracy. During the Kapp Putsch in 1920, not only did the army refuse to intervene, but only a single person involved in the attempted overthrow of the republic received any jail time. For the charge of high treason, Traugott von Jagow was sentenced to just five years imprisonment, his sentence mitigated by the fact that he only did it for love of country. Erich Ludendorff was not even arrested, instead moving to Bavaria where he was supported by wealthy aristocrats and provided with a free car and adjutant by the Munich police.[9] In Bavaria Ludendorff intensified his political activities aimed at overthrowing the republic and restoring the Hohenzollern monarchy, perhaps with a period of military dictatorship if necessary. There was no better model than Horthy in Hungary.[10]

In May 1920, a small delegation appeared in Budapest bearing a letter from Ludendorff. He admired Horthy's counterrevolutionary crusade, and from late 1919 had been looking to replicate it on a European scale. His proposals for the man he called 'the saviour of the nationalist idea' were far-reaching and fantastical. Bavarian paramilitaries would be trained in secret in Hungary, where they could then be used to overthrow the regimes in Austria and Bavaria. Then, the combined Austro-Bavarian-Hungarian forces would invade and partition Czechoslovakia before moving on to Berlin and establishing Ludendorff there as dictator. In the final phase, the counterrevolutionary regimes would link up with anti-Bolshevik forces in Russia to overthrow the Soviet regime there before confronting the Entente and reversing the shame of 1918.[11] Horthy agreed to the plan, but it ultimately fizzled out.[12]

Nevertheless, the plan was emblematic of the outlook solidifying on the nationalist right in the defeated Central European states. They believed violent, radical action was needed to overturn the postwar order, to save their nations from the humiliation of 1918, and to punish the Jews, socialists and liberals responsible for it. Bavaria—where the Kapp Putsch had been successful in overthrowing the socialist-led government—became the epicentre of this burgeoning right-wing scene in Germany. Besides Ludendorff, it hosted the head of the Wittelsbach dynasty, supported by countless monarchist organizations, secretive occultist racialist societies, violent far-right paramilitaries, and extreme nationalist parties openly calling for dictatorship.

On 26 August 1921, two members of the Munich-based extreme nationalist Organisation Consul assassinated the former Minister of Finance Matthias Erzberger. Bavarian officials helped the assassins escape to Hungary.[13] Bavarian Minister-President Gustav von Kahr refused to recognize the state of emergency subsequently declared by President Ebert, eventually resigning in protest instead.[14] Less than a year later, members of Operation Consul staged an even more daring assassination of Foreign Minister Walther Rathenau, who was Jewish and had been dogged by antisemitic attacks his whole career. The government in Berlin this time responded with what was meant to be a law providing for the steadfast defence of the republic, banning any organization seeking to 'undermine the constitutionally established republican form of government of the Reich or of a state'. The Bavarian government—still in the hands of Kahr's Bavarian People's Party—challenged the legitimacy of the law, eventually wrangling concessions from Berlin that effectively made it a dead letter in Bavaria.[15]

In 1923 Germany's postwar crisis came to a head. After repeated defaults on reparations payments, France sent troops to occupy the industrial Ruhr. German outrage was only compounded by the government's feeble response of passive resistance. Inflation began to spiral out of control, causing unimaginable hardship for millions. The machinations of pro-French Rhenish separatists and widespread expectations of another communist uprising made it feel like the country was on the brink of civil war. A feeble spark came on 23 October when communists staged an uncoordinated uprising in Hamburg, Saxony and Thuringia that ended with a whimper two days later.[16]

Ludendorff continued to liaise between far-right paramilitaries, reactionary nationalists and even the military over the course of the year. The anti-republican right was awash with plots, conspiracies, and schemes. Some envisioned a monarchical restoration, others a nationalist dictatorship, and some a fascist one on the model recently provided by Mussolini in Italy. In September Ludendorff lent his public support to the Kampfbund, an alliance of several Bavarian far-right paramilitaries with tens of thousands of members.[17]

The Kampfbund's political leader, Adolf Hitler, had become a fixture of the Bavarian far-right scene over the previous four years. He drew huge crowds into the city's beer halls with rabble-rousing antisemitic speeches that lambasted the 'November criminals' and called for radical national renewal. He presented himself as 'nothing more than a drummer and rallier' paving the way for a future dictatorship.[18] Even if Hitler did harbour grander ambitions, it was prudent for the unknown Austrian to play second fiddle to Ludendorff, the man already seen by much of the nationalist right as the future dictator.[19]

As an anonymous soldier in the Bavarian army, Hitler had first discovered his talent for speaking when his army superiors tasked him with lecturing his fellow soldiers for purposes of 're-education' following the collapse of the Bavarian Soviet republic.[20] He was eventually assigned to observe the small far-right German Workers' Party, which recruited the gifted orator. As his star rose, his influence in the party grew. In early 1920 it was renamed the National Socialist German Workers' Party in an attempt to emphasize its populist credentials. It had taken advantage of the crisis year of 1923 to rapidly expand its membership from 15,000 to 55,000.[21]

The unrelated small German Workers' Party in Austria (which had been founded in Bohemia in 1904) had similarly added 'national socialist' to its name two years earlier.[22] Hitler did not take inspiration from the Austrian German Workers' Party, but they shared a common origin in the world of fringe radical German nationalism in the Habsburg Monarchy. 'I lived my youth enmeshed in the border struggle for German language, culture, and thought', Hitler later recalled, 'of which the great majority of the German people had no idea during peacetime'. Not far from the Bohemian frontier, the great issue of the day in his quasi-hometown of Linz was the immigration of Czechs, part and parcel of the great 'defensive battle against advancing Slavdom', as a former classmate of his put it.[23] Hitler moved to Vienna at the age of eighteen with dreams of becoming a great artist. The great imperial metropolis both repelled and amazed him. Though it is difficult to ascertain precisely what his political beliefs were in these years, he might have been at least sympathetic to Pan-German nationalism.

Pan-Germanism was a racist, antisemitic, eugenicist, and profoundly anti-Habsburg subculture that saw the Habsburg state as an impediment to German national flourishing and wanted German areas of Austria to be annexed to the Reich. It contained much of the ideological and symbolic content that would later become known to the world through Hitler and the Nazi Party. The eccentric Guido von List advocated restoring the 'Aryan race' through selective breeding and made impassioned calls for a 'strong man from above' to lead society out of its current malaise. In List's works and countless other Pan-German publications that advocated the unification of Germans everywhere, the Swastika was used as an ostensibly ancient Aryan symbol.[24]

Though encountering and perhaps even sympathizing with all this earlier in his life, Hitler's true politicization was a result of the Reich German experience of the First World War and its aftermath. Having moved to Munich in 1913, he experienced the feeling of national unity and purpose in 1914 as well as the bitter sting of 'betrayal' and the shock of defeat as it set in after the Treaty of Versailles.[25] He had a strong sense of Germans as a 'race' threatened by their 'inferiors' but also an acute awareness of Reich German politics and sensitivities. In his speeches he promised to negate the humiliation of 1918, the failure of the Second Reich, but also the humiliation of the whole Habsburg history of Central Europe, the original sin of the First Reich.

THE CENTRAL EUROPEAN CRISIS

On 9 November 1923 these two strains were given their symbolic synthesis. An ill-fated putsch attempt ended with Hitler and Ludendorff marching side-by-side into central Munich, hoping to renew their troubled German nation through a combination of old-school aristocratic conservatism and decidedly modern racialist nationalism. 'What a combination', one fellow-traveller gushed: 'Ludendorff, the General, with all that name implied of caste and authority, and Hitler, the dynamic corporal, coming from the people!'[26] They met unexpected resistance from the army and after exchanges of fire eighteen people were left dead.[27] The 'Beer Hall Putsch' had ended ignominiously.

Bavarian conditions once again proved fortuitous for the radical right. While the subsequent trial of Hitler and Ludendorff for high treason should have been handed to a special court for the defence of the republic in Leipzig (pursuant to the law passed in the wake of Rathenau's assassination), the Bavarian government convinced Berlin to have the case tried in a Bavarian 'People's Court' instead. The trial began on 26 February, becoming little more than a forum for the defendants. The highly sympathetic lay judges wanted to acquit Hitler outright, but ultimately he was given the minimum sentence of five years. Though by law he should have been deported as a foreigner, they concluded that this could not possibly apply 'to a man that thinks and feels as German as Hitler'.[28] Ludendorff—far and away the more prominent of the two—had grabbed the headlines, but Hitler had stolen the show with his passionate oratory.

Ludendorff was exonerated, free to return to radical right politics while Hitler relaxed in comfortable confinement. The same month the trial ended Ludendorff led the far-right National Socialist Freedom Movement to a record 6.5 per cent of the vote in elections to the Reichstag. But in new elections held in December it had dropped to three per cent. Under Foreign Minister Gustav Stresemann, Germany's finances and relations with the Western powers were normalized, paving the way for the country's entrance into the League of Nations in 1926. Even the army reconciled itself to the new republic, hoping that stabilization rather than revolution would lead to the country's revival as a military power.[29] Although Hitler was released in 1925, after just eight months in prison, and allowed to re-found his party, he was banned from using his greatest skill—public speaking. That same year Ludendorff was convinced to run for president on behalf of the radical right, garnering a measly one per cent of the vote. His old boss, the even more esteemed general and national hero Paul von Hindenburg, won comfortably.

Republican consolidation and conservative nostalgia had triumphed over the extreme right.

* * *

For the young states to Germany's east, the rabble-rousing of a fringe demagogue in the beer halls of Munich was the least of their worries. Even before they had secured their sovereignty and their borders, they were beset by pressing questions of political, social and economic integration. Poland was a country conjured up from the ruins of three separate empires. Romania and the new Kingdom of Serbs, Croats, and Slovenes expanded from more homogeneous Balkan cores, but still had multiple legislative systems, currencies, rail systems, customs areas, and even calendars to harmonize. Even Czechoslovakia, which started out in the best position, inherited a dual legal system. The Bohemian lands inherited Austrian laws and Slovak and Ruthenian ones those of Hungary.[30]

Consolidating law, administration and economies proved far easier than making real the theoretical unity of nations that had in fact never—or not for centuries—shared a common political, social or economic life. Each was a majoritarian, unitary, centralized nation-state whose existence was officially recognized as the fruits of the labour of a single nation and its representatives over the centuries. And yet in reality they were patchworks of peoples and places with long histories and traditions that did not easily gel together.

This was a problem the Vienna-trained Serbian geographer Jovan Cvijić turned his attention to in a 1918 article sketching out 'The Zones of Civilization of the Balkan Peninsula'. Unlike the kind of ethnographic maps that had become *de riguer*, his map showed a rich quilt of overlapping cultural layers that had accumulated over the centuries. All along the Adriatic coast stretched the influence of 'Italo-Mediterranean' civilization. Pockets of Islam dotted across the peninsula marked out the remainders of 'Turco-Oriental' civilization. Crosses and stars scattered largely across the Slovene and Croat lands as well as core Serbia meanwhile betrayed the presence of 'Central European' civilization and 'national civilization based on the civilizations of Central and Western Europe'. The backdrop for all of this was the dark green sea of the rural 'patriarchal regime' that supposedly represented the ur-culture of South Slavic peasants.[31]

This final point was presented as the justification of the whole Yugoslav project, with this common peasant culture supposedly proving they were a single nation after all. Setting aside the accuracy of his map or the historical claims underpinning it, the approach he took is crucial to understanding the realities of national integration after the war. It was less a question of integrating solid blocs of nationally homogeneous territory, as ethnographic maps suggested, but rather bringing together urban areas shaped by wildly different cultural, political and social institutions as well as countrysides hardly touched by these urban nodes. In Bukovina and Transylvania, Romanians formed 44.5 and 51.9 per cent of the population, respectively. But in urban areas, they were a small minority, often invisible on the margins of polite society. Urban areas were centres of Magyar and German language and culture, often surrounded by seas of Romanian peasants, but also rural Jews, Magyars, Germans, Ukrainians, and others. In Transylvania in particular, these Magyar and German-dominated cities appeared bewilderingly foreign to Romanians—places where they went to shed their culture or to be scorned and rejected as poor peasants unfit for civil life.[32]

Poland's first census, meanwhile, revealed a country that was only 69.2 per cent Polish. Ruthenians made up 15.2 per cent, Jews (counted as a separate nationality) eight per cent, Belarusians four per cent, and Germans three per cent.[33] Yet reducing everyone to either a 'national majority' Pole or a 'national minority' captured little of the complex social reality. Prussian Poland, Galicia, Congress Poland, and the 'eastern borderlands' (once an integral part of the Russian Empire) left behind hugely different legacies for their inhabitants.

Prussian Junkers, urban Germans in Łódź, and Galician German farmers were likely to have very different perspectives on what it meant to suddenly live in a Polish nation-state. The same went for *déclassé* Polish nobles from old Lithuania, Catholic workers from Silesia, and German-speaking former Austrian officers. Of the country's three million Jews, most lived in desperate rural poverty. But Jews were also vastly over-represented in Poland's cities, where many were highly educated professionals who embraced German or Polish nationalisms, or Marxist and Zionist ideas entirely foreign to their rural coreligionists.[34] 40,000 people 'who could not define their nationality in any other way' meanwhile identified themselves as 'locals'. A decade later a slightly different question about mother tongue yielded over 700,000 national 'locals', all in the eastern province of Polesia where they represented sixty-two per cent of the population.[35]

Attitudes towards the millions of 'national minorities' in Poland bitterly divided public opinion. The face of tolerance—Piłsudski—decided to step back from public life after the Polish-Soviet War. Gabriel Narutowicz, a moderate close to Piłsudski, was subsequently elected president. Despised by the nationalist right for having supposedly been elected by Jews, just five days after taking office he was assassinated by a right-wing art critic.[36] Hyperinflation and endemic political instability plagued the young republic, with a national strike in late 1923 leading to violent confrontations between strikers and the army that left dozens dead. By 1926 Poland had seen fourteen different governments, with thirty different parties in the fractured Sejm (the lower house of parliament) and over three times as many active in the country.[37] Watching the imperilled country from the sidelines, Piłsudski eventually came to believe that radical action was needed to 'cleanse' the state from what he saw as the evils of parliamentarism. In May 1926 he overthrew the government in a bloody coup that left hundreds dead. It was an inauspicious beginning for the rescue of a democracy.

Poland at least had a clear national majority. The same could not be said about Czechoslovakia and the new south Slav monarchy. Wartime claims that Serbs, Croats, and Slovenes 'are one people with the same traditions, the same tongue, the same tendencies, but whom evil fate has divided' or that 'Slovaks are Bohemians [Czechs]' took on a farcical quality in the postwar years.[38] Czechs and Slovaks as well as Serbs, Croats, and Slovenes stubbornly retained their identification with their own individual nations, reflected in radically different voting patterns. And even when added together, Czechs and Slovaks represented just sixty-five per cent of Czechoslovakia's population in 1921. In what was later renamed Yugoslavia, Slavs made up well over eighty per cent of the population, but they were divided into more than half a dozen distinct national groups whose divergent expectations for the new state turned disagreements into paralyzing political conflicts.

While the new Kingdom of Serbs, Croats, and Slovenes professed to represent a single South Slav—or Yugoslav—nation with three 'tribal names', it was really the Serbian state tradition that played the leading role in the new country's formation. It was a unitary monarchy centred in Belgrade, ruled by a Serbian monarch supported by an overwhelmingly Serbian army. The dominant understanding of Yugoslavism in Serbia was really a kind of Greater Serbianism that saw the country as having liberated its fellow South Slavs from the Habsburg yoke. There were therefore thousands of educated, politically conscious Croats and Slovenes that found themselves marginalized in a new state with ideologically shaky foundations. Educated officers who had faithfully served one of Europe's great powers and fought in one of its largest and most advanced armies found themselves subordinated to less educated Serbian equivalents.[39] In Croatia, the old elite were doubly marginalized by the meteoric rise of Radić's Croatian Peasant Party, which consistently won the vast majority of Croatian votes across the whole former Triune Kingdom. It was a totally new force that fit comfortably neither into the Yugoslavist nor nationalist traditions that had dominated politics in Central European Croatia-Slavonia for the last century.

Radić saw the peasantry as the only true representatives of the Croatian nation—not the urban bourgeoisie that had fashioned itself into the political nation of Habsburg Croatia. 'Roman-European civilization' was a dirty word, something synonymous with feudal and capitalist oppression that could only be overcome with truly national, peasant-oriented politics.[40] In a Faustian bargain, the Croatian Peasant Party renounced its republicanism and entered government in 1925 in an effort to change the state from within. This was not as successful as some had hoped, and tensions between the various parliamentary groups reached a head in 1928. In a heated parliamentary session on 20 June, a Montenegrin deputy pulled a revolver and shot two Croatian Peasant Party deputies dead while fatally wounding Radić. The shocking murder of Croatia's most popular politician—in the parliament itself of all places—threatened to drive the country into chaos.

And yet in an article published in late January 1929, Czechoslovakia's foreign minister and President Masaryk's right-hand man Edvard Beneš struck a surprisingly optimistic tone when assessing the condition of Central Europe in its new form. While those mentally stuck in the prewar world would inevitably decry the achievements of the postwar years, anyone taking a 'democratic view of the history and development of the European nations and of world politics in general' would inevitably assess these years positively. He pointed out that all postwar European states had their struggles, and those of the new states of Central Europe should by no means invalidate their existence or achievements. Despite the tumultuous events in Belgrade, the 'fundamental ideas on which the Jugoslav state' rested supposedly remained unchanged. 'In general', he went on, 'it may be asserted that all the new States which owed their origin to the rebellion of oppressed peoples, have during the first decade of their existence shown a considerable measure of stability'. Indeed, the ten years since 1918 proved that 'democracy found fruitful soil and struck firm roots in Central Europe'.[41]

This was a classic piece of Masaryk-Benešian propaganda, the likes of which flooded Western Europe during the interwar years, reinforcing the message that Czechoslovakia was the most liberal and democratic—the most Western—of any state in the region. Beneš' article was published in the London-based *Slavonic and East European Review* just two weeks after King Alexander I abolished the Vidovdan constitution and took the country he would soon rename Yugoslavia down the path of a unitarist dictatorship. Piłsudski—whose coup was anything but democratic—moved from 1929 in a more decidedly dictatorial direction. In June 1930 a royal coup d'etat brought Carol II to the Romanian throne.

Beneš understandably wanted to defend the considerable achievements of the Czechoslovak republic, which—with exaggeration—he called 'the prototype of a completely democratic State'.[42] Czechoslovakia managed to avoid the temptations of dictatorship, but it did so with what might nowadays be termed a 'managed democracy', presided over by a revered quasi-monarchical figure in Masaryk. Representatives of the five main Czech political parties maintained a policy of unofficial cooperation behind the scenes. Beneš himself served as foreign minister from the state's inception until 1935, when he took over from the eighty-five-year-old Masaryk as president.

Many in Czechoslovakia praised Piłsudski's 'cleansing' coup for having saved democracy from the dangers of right-wing radicalism. Masaryk and Beneš contemplated a similar move in 1926 as the Czech National Fascist Community rose to 200,000 members and fears grew of a fascist coup.[43] Masaryk and his circle—euphemistically referred to as 'the Castle'—managed to stave off the threat of Czech chauvinism, but others loomed. These came not from the German minority—which had largely accepted the new state and enjoyed generous rights to German-language social, cultural and political life—but from the Slovaks, who were meant to be part of the 'state-forming' Czechoslovak nation. From 1925 the most popular party in Slovakia was the clerical-nationalist Slovak People's Party led by the priest Andrej Hlinka, which demanded autonomy for the country and rejected the notion of a Czechoslovak nation. Additionally, the communists regularly garnered about ten per cent of the vote across Czechoslovakia. The country's long-term democratic survival was not as secure as its political elites would have wanted. But the nail in the coffin for Beneš' rosy assessment was entirely out of his control.

* * *

THE CENTRAL EUROPEAN CRISIS

In October 1929 the global stock market crashed, catapulting the world into the Great Depression. Millions across Central Europe were plunged into poverty and uncertainty. Industrial production plummeted, severely affecting Germany, Austria, Czechoslovakia, and Hungary. Agriculture fared no better, with prices hovering at between a third and a half of their pre-Depression levels until 1939, meaning even largely rural countries like Poland, Yugoslavia and Romania were severely impacted. Between 1929 and 1933 unemployment doubled in Austria, and still stood at twenty-two per cent in 1937. German unemployment meanwhile peaked at about one third of the working-age population in February 1932. In a sign of just how bad things had become, per capita beer consumption in Germany fell by forty-three per cent between 1929 and 1933.[44]

No political party exploited the crisis so successfully as the German Nazi Party. After 1925 Hitler began to present himself not as the 'drummer' of a national revolution but its leader. But the leader's first electoral test was a fiasco. In 1928 a measly 810,127 voters opted for the Nazis—2.6 per cent. The Nazis failed to even to surpass the Bavarian People's Party, who won 945,644 votes despite their base being confined to a single state. The national-conservative German National People's Party (DNVP) still dominated the nationalist right with over four million votes. But returning to the polls two years later at the depths of their economic despair, Germans—rural Protestants in particular—voted in droves for Hitler's party. The Nazis came second with 18.3 per cent of the vote. Two years on, an even more dramatic swing catapulted the party into first place with 37.3 per cent. The rise of the Nazis looked meteoric and unstoppable.

Hitler presented a reassuring face to industrialists, the military and the middle classes in order to convince them that Nazism meant national renewal and not a new revolution, but this was a façade. Nazi paramilitaries brawled with communists in beer halls and on the streets while its leaders nurtured dreams of a Germany 'cleansed' of Jews, socialists and other 'degenerate' elements. Hitler's virulent antisemitism was as strong as ever, and in prison he had integrated a new radical idea into his worldview: the need to secure 'living space' in the East for the German people.

This was a change from the early postwar years, when he had entertained the notion of 'brotherhood towards the East'. Anti-Bolshevik emigres formed an important part of the radical right constituency of postwar Munich, with the Baltic German Alfred Rosenberg acting as one of the Nazi Party's formative ideologues. If only the Bolsheviks could be overthrown, they hoped, then Russia could become a antisemitic ally of the future national-socialist Germany.⁴⁵ Hitler's propaganda chief Joseph Goebbels opined that Nazis had 'more in common with "Eastern Bolshevism" than with "Western capitalism"', while Gregor Strasser called for 'German Central Europe—fighting the West, with temporary support from the East'.⁴⁶

As late as 1926 others in the party saw Russia as a potential ally. But by then Hitler was certain that the messianic visions of German renewal would play out in what he saw as the grand, wild, barbaric expanses of Eastern Europe: it was too tainted by 'sub-humans' and 'Judeo-Bolshevism' to be an ally.⁴⁷ Central Europe as a concept played no discernible role in Hitler's thinking. If anything, his ambition was to make it synonymous with a Greater Germany. But really his thinking followed in a long tradition of Austrian Pan-Germanists who wished to see Galicia, Hungary and South Slavic areas put out of sight and out of mind. In the West, Germany would find its revenge; in the East, its salvation.

The positive vision of the East entertained by many leading Nazis in the 1920s was similar to the outlook of the national conservatives who dominated the nationalist right before Hitler's rise. The Pan-German nationalism, anti-republicanism, anti-socialism, and antisemitism of national conservatives were to a large degree represented by the anti-republican DNVP, particularly when it veered to the right in 1928 after coming under the leadership of Alfred Hugenberg.⁴⁸ But its electoral fortunes faded as those of the Nazis rose. In April 1930, the country had already taken a step towards dictatorship. President Hindenburg had appointed a presidential cabinet—his constitutional right—through which Germany was being ruled by decree. Many on the right would have been happy to transform this into a proper dictatorship, but by 1932 it was difficult to see how this could be done without what was far and away the largest party in the country.

The more traditional forces of the nationalist right still could not countenance a Nazi government. After the government failed a vote of no confidence, new elections were slated for November 1932. The Nazis lost thirty-four seats, but the calculus had barely changed. Over the next two fateful months, Hindenburg was slowly convinced that there was no alternative to a Nazi government. On 30 January 1933 he appointed Adolf Hitler chancellor of Germany atop a Nazi-DNVP coalition. Less than a month later, a lone Dutch communist set fire to the Reichstag. Hitler wasted no time in claiming an imminent communist revolution, convincing the elderly Hindenburg to issue a decree suspending civil rights 'in

THE CENTRAL EUROPEAN CRISIS

defence against Communist state-endangering acts of violence'. Fresh elections marked by widespread Nazi violence and intimidation grew the party's parliamentary delegation by ninety-two. By the end of the month the notorious Enabling Act had been passed, allowing Hitler to bypass the Reichstag and President Hindenburg entirely.

Hitler and his party rapidly set about reshaping the country in their image, meeting shockingly little resistance. Organizations opposed to the Nazi party were banned. Effectively every organization was forced to either Nazify or abolish itself under the process 'coordination'. This also meant adopting a key tenet of the Nazi worldview: the absolute and irrevocable exclusion of Jews from all areas of national life. Over the course of 1933, a raft of legislation either excluded or severely restricted the participation of Jews in the civil service, legal profession, press, universities, schools, cultural life, even medicine and farming.[49] Individual state governments were rapidly taken over, to be abolished entirely in January 1934. The 'unity of party and state' left little room for alternative centres of authority.[50] On 1 August Hitler's cabinet decreed that the office of the president would be merged with that of the chancellor upon Hindenburg's death. The following day Hindenburg passed away. Hitler was transformed from mere chancellor into the *Führer* of the German Reich.

* * *

The mid-1930s were years of turmoil in all of the successor states. Austria—its very existence threatened by the rise of the Austrian Nazi Party—creeped down the path of authoritarianism before a short civil war in 1934 resulted in its transformation into a fully-fledged Catholic-conservative dictatorship. It was no longer a republic but a 'Federal State' whose new constitution was issued not in the name of the people, but in the name of God. It repudiated not only Austrian constitutional development since 1920, but the whole project of a liberal Austria going back to 1867. Austrian Nazis saw this as antithetical to their vision of Austria as just part of a greater German whole. They murdered the authoritarian Chancellor Engelbert Dolfuss in a failed coup attempt in July 1934, subsequently leading to the banning of the Nazi party.[51]

A similarly bloody changing of the guard occurred in Yugoslavia. On 9 October 1934 King Alexander arrived in Marseilles to strengthen ties with the French. Alexander and French Foreign Minister Louis Barthou drove through the streets in an open-top car when a man emerged and shot the king dead. In the ensuing chaos, the French foreign minister was also killed. The gunman was part of a radical Macedonian terrorist organization working in conjunction with the fascist Croatian Ustaša movement that agitated for a violent destruction of the Yugoslav state. Like many fascist parties, it revelled in violence. The knife, revolver, machine gun and time bomb were praised as 'idols ... the bells that will announce the dawning and resurrection of Croatia'.[52] Exiled in Italy, this small fascist movement with its roots in the old pro-Austrian Frankist party was marginal in Croatian political life, but its mere existence spoke to a profound radicalization of the extreme right across Europe.

In Romania, two distinct fascist movements emerged in the 1920s, their popularity skyrocketing after the Great Depression. The Iron Guard and the National-Christian Defence League both called for the exclusion of Jews from public life, the establishment of a corporatist dictatorship, and the final creation of a 'purified' national state. The leaders of the Iron Guard in particular were young and educated, many too young to have even fought in the war. Their violent energies were directed squarely at an urban bourgeoisie world that to them appeared entirely foreign, in the hands of Jews, Hungarians and Germans instead of Romanians.[53]

The Polish fascist National Radical Camp founded in 1934 espoused a similar worldview, presenting itself as a youthful national movement that would save the country from Jewish domination. A month after its foundation, the elderly and withdrawn Józef Piłsudski passed away, leaving behind an authoritarian regime uncertain of how to proceed without its charismatic leader. His successor as unofficial strongman was his old comrade Edward Rydz-Śmigły, a highly respected military leader that the regime tried to bill as the 'Second Marshal'. Poland drifted further in an authoritarian and nationalist direction under his rule.[54] It was a temptation resisted by Edvard Beneš when he succeeded Masaryk as president of Czechoslovakia in December 1935. He stood precariously atop the lone liberal democracy left in Central Europe.

By 1935 the threat of monarchical restorations had long faded from the scene. But the New Europe that promised so much in 1918 seemed to everyone to be crumbling before their very eyes. The Western powers appeared withdrawn. Democracies had fallen one after another. No Central European society lacked those that saw in ultranationalism, antisemitism, authoritarianism, and corporatism a bright vision of the future. Fascism, in a word, whose triumph and seeming success in the largest country in the region only emboldened fellow travellers. Nazi Germany offered a middle path between the godless 'Judeo-Bolshevism' of the East and the liberal capitalism of the West. Nazi Germany's international isolation had first been broken by Hungarian Prime Minister Gyula Gömbös. A convinced antisemite and veteran of the counterrevolutionary crusade, he praised Hitler and the 'national socialist movement' for providing 'a service of world-historical importance to all of humanity by putting an end to the communist threat in Germany'.[55]

While Mussolini's Italy had acted as the model fascist state since the early 1920s—inspiring its fair share of Central Europe fascists, Hitler included—the racial, antisemitic nationalism of the Nazis had a particularly strong resonance in Central European successor states. Indeed, it became a powerful force in its own right amongst German minorities in Romania and Yugoslavia increasingly under the sway of a Nazi-inspired 'renewal movement', while the much larger German minority in Czechoslovakia started to flock to the Nazi-friendly Sudeten German Party.[56] But the Bolshevik threat to which the Nazis presented themselves as the cure was one that Poles, Germans and Hungarians alike had faced in the aftermath of the First World War and that continued to have a powerful hold on the popular imagination.

The promise to crush the power of the Jews also resonated well beyond the fascist fringe, particularly on the Catholic right—strong in Austria, Poland, Slovakia, and elsewhere—where antisemitism was understood as part and parcel of a program of reestablishing the Christian foundations of state and society. Typical of the 'moderate' (not necessarily racial) antisemitism of the clerical right was the view expressed by the head of the Polish Catholic Church in early 1937. It was right to 'avoid' Jewish shops but wrong to 'plunder' them. It was necessary to 'find protection from the harmful moral influence of the Jews' but wrong to attack them.[57] Anti-Jewish laws were a common sight across the whole of the European continent in the 1930s, with laws limiting the immigration of Jews passed even in liberal democracies.[58]

In 1920, Hungary had become the first European country to limit the number of Jewish students at universities. Unofficially, Jews were also excluded from the bureaucracy and officer corps.[59] Poland had maintained similar barriers between institutions considered vital for the national state and the huge Jewish minority. Though it never passed outright antisemitic legislation, Jews had been reduced from about a quarter of Polish university students in 1921–22 to just eight per cent by 1938–9.[60] In 1938 more antisemitic legislation was passed in Hungary. In the interest of 'racial defence and national unity', the percentage of Jews in a whole array of professions was limited to twenty per cent. Another law the following year reduced the percentages further with the eventual aim of excluding Jews from state administration and justice entirely. Even Horthy, who had long served as a moderating influence on the more extreme elements of the nationalist right, came to believe in the necessity of antisemitic legislation in the interests of building a Hungarian middle class.[61]

The antisemitism of the Nazi German regime was still singular, firmly rooted in the modern political antisemitism that had emerged in the late nineteenth century, which blamed the Jews for all the ills of modern society. The sheer scale and extent of Nazi antisemitic laws, regulations and practices—numbering well over 1,000 by 1939—were intended to make life for Jews in Germany effectively unbearable.[62] The Nuremberg laws passed in September 1935 dispossessed Jews of German citizenship, a privilege reserved only for those with the correct 'blood'. Jews were no longer even second-class citizens, but 'subjects'.[63] At this time and long after, the Nazi leadership was in agreement that Jews should be encouraged to emigrate from Germany. Tens of thousands did so every year from 1933.

This was only part of Hitler's grand vision for Germany, however. He was firmly committed to overturning the humiliating terms of the Treaty of Versailles. While the country had been rearming in secret for years— made flagrantly public after 1933—no serious revisions could be made while the Rhineland was demilitarized, effectively leaving Germany's industrial heartland at the mercy of France. In March 1936 Hitler ordered German troops to re-enter the Rhineland. When the Western powers failed to offer resistance, the treaties signed in the aftermath of the First World War became a dead letter. There was little reason to believe that anyone would lift a finger for tiny, isolated Austria.

The very first page of Hitler's *Mein Kampf* was devoted to the importance of Austria's 'return to the great German motherland'.[64] The dream of an *Anschluss* of Austria to the wider German Reich was one that spanned the political spectrum. It was rooted in the simple reality that Austrians spoke German and largely considered themselves to be German. The corporatist Catholic dictatorship that had ruled Austria since 1934 was trying to forge an alternative Austrian identity, one rooted in Germandom but professing the uniqueness of Austrian state consciousness.[65] But it could offer little resistance when Hitler cowed it into submission in March 1938. German troops were met with rapturous cheers from crowds across the country as they moved in to secure it. Austria was rapidly 'coordinated' with the rest of the Reich. Almost forty per cent of the academic staff at the University of Vienna were dismissed, with Jewish students barred by the autumn. The large, wealthy, educated, and highly assimilated Jewish community of Vienna was shattered with remarkable speed and efficiency. The once-great imperial capital was reduced to a cultural backwater.[66]

Hitler's attention now turned to the three million formerly Austrian Germans that lived in Czechoslovakia. Over the course of the 1930s, Sudeten Germans had turned overwhelmingly to the Sudeten German Party led by Konrad Henlein. It had an often-contradictory relationship to the Nazi Party, aligned but not subordinate to it and encompassing a broad base of support that did not unanimously support the Sudetenland's annexation to the Reich. Ultimately, however, it would become a Nazi tool of subversion in Czechoslovakia by acting as the proof for the charge that Germans did not feel at home in the Czechoslovak state.[67] Hitler's ceaseless threats against Czechoslovakia irked the Western powers, who above all else wanted to avoid another European war. They convinced Hitler the issue could be settled by negotiations between the four powers—Italy, Germany, France, and Great Britain—who descended on Munich on 29 September 1938 to save the peace of Europe. The following day they had reached an agreement. The Sudetenland was handed over to Hitler's Germany without a fight.

British Prime Minister Neville Chamberlain famously declared that the Treaty of Munich meant 'peace in our time'. But others thought it only delayed the inevitable. Aurel Kolnai warned in his 1938 *The War Against the West* that national socialism's 'central impulse' was an 'absolute and conscious antagonism to Western Liberal civilization'. The line of continuity from ancient Greece through Rome and Christianity to the modern 'West' was one that Germany had failed to follow. Instead, Germany had always been at the margins of Western civilization, following a different, special path from Herder through Fichte, Treitschke, Nietzsche, and others to Hitler. 'The Germans live in the middle of Europe; they flood Europe; and yet nobody knows with certainty how far they really belong to Europe'. A new European war would not be one fought between states or peoples, but between two antithetical civilizations: between the Liberal West and Nazi Central Europe.[68]

16

THE DEATH OF A CIVILIZATION

In the early hours of 1 October 1938, German troops crossed into Czechoslovakia. Blaring through loudspeakers across Prague's Wenceslas Square, Prime Minister Jan Syrový tried to explain to his people why the government had opted to accept the 'Munich diktat'. 'I must tell you frankly ... the forces opposed to us at this moment compel us to recognize their superior strength and to act accordingly ... we were abandoned, and [we] were alone'.[1] Particularly painful was the French betrayal. As French policymakers recognized from the beginning, France was the great power that had the most to gain from the postwar order's maintenance.[2] For the French historian Joseph Aulneau, the failure to consolidate this new regional order would be disastrous. 'The condition of Central Europe dominates the condition of Europe itself', he warned in his sweeping 1926 *Histoire de l'Europe Centrale*. Imperfect as the postwar order may have been, it existed as 'a whole'. One 'breach in the wall and it collapses'.[3]

This was precisely how things went once Britain and France no longer sought to enforce the peace treaties. The new Czechoslovak-German border, set by an 'international commission' on 5 October, acquiesced to German demands that any territory at least fifty-one per cent German in the Austrian census of 1910 be handed over.[4] The rump Czechoslovak state was given three months to set a new border with Hungary, the Western powers now disappearing entirely as the German and Italian foreign ministers dictated a new border on 2 November.[5] About 1.2 million Czechs, Slovaks and Ruthenians abruptly found themselves assigned to a new state—over 700,000 Czechs in the Sudetenland alone. In the aftermath of the various territorial changes, about 100,000 Czechoslovak citizens fled the territory ceded to Hungary and over 200,000 Czechs, Jews and anti-fascists fled the Sudetenland.[6] Prague's Wilson Station became a scene of desperation, filled for weeks with men, women and children with nowhere to go.[7] Many had left at a moment's notice, their property, possessions and professions lost to the totalitarian dictatorship that had engulfed their homes.[8] Those Czechs that chose to remain faced the prospect of unremitting Germanization. Czech cultural life in the Sudetenland was simply abolished. Czech signs were painted over, monuments to Czech heroes toppled. Places named after Masaryk or Wilson were replaced by those bearing the names of Hitler and Göring.[9]

'Very well' opined the Prague daily *Lidové noviny* on 4 October, 'if we are not allowed to sing with the angels we will howl with the wolves'.[10] President Beneš resigned the next day, replaced by the non-partisan lawyer Emil Hácha. The 'Second Czechoslovak Republic'—officially renamed the Czecho-Slovak Republic—would be a repudiation of everything Masaryk and Beneš' pro-Western First Republic had stood for. If 'singing with the angels' meant becoming a Western liberal democracy, 'howling with the wolves' meant building a corporatist, authoritarian, nationalist state as a sign of respect if not reverence for Hitler's Germany. Slovakia's leading party—the Slovak People's Party now led by Catholic priest Jozef Tiso—was given free rein to pursue this with vigour. When Slovaks went to the polls in December 1938, the ballot paper asked a simple, leading question: 'Do you want a new, free Slovakia?' Jews—and in some cases Czechs—had to cast their vote in separate boxes. The 'United List' won ninety-eight per cent of the vote in this bizarre referendum-election. The following January the new government formed a commission tasked with solving the 'Jewish Question' in Slovakia.[11]

The fate of the Sudeten Jews—or those who the Nazis claimed were Jews—was already sealed. On the night of 9 November 1938, antisemitic pogroms raged like wildfire across the Reich. Historic synagogues—in Vienna, Dresden, Breslau, Frankfurt, Munich, and elsewhere—were burnt to the ground. Thousands of Jewish shops and properties were attacked, vandalized or ransacked. At least ninety-one Jews were murdered in cold blood, countless others humiliated and terrorized in what came to be known as *Kristallnacht*, or the night of broken glass.[12] It was the most shocking and violent episode of a years-long program of state-backed antisemitic persecution that by 1 September 1939 had forced 330,000 German and Austrian Jews into emigration, leaving just 175,000 behind.[13]

After Munich, one clerical Czech paper wrote optimistically that the reduction of the Czechoslovak state into a 'purely national state of Czechs and Slovaks' opened the path towards neutrality and safety from any future conflicts 'between the two European fronts'.[14] But Hitler never had any intention of allowing a Czechoslovak state to survive. It was a question of if, not when, it would finally be 'annihilated'.[15] Less than six months after Munich, Hitler made his move. After encouraging Slovakia's clerical fascists to declare their country's independence, he occupied the rest of the country without resistance. The freeing of Slovaks from the 'Czech yoke' was accompanied by the expulsion of 50,000 Czechs, joining the 10,000 already resettled over the previous five months.[16] Hungary took another chunk while a 'Protectorate of Bohemia and Moravia' was established in the non-Slovak lands occupied by Germany.

Czechs were allowed to retain their culture there, but Bohemian German papers declared with glee that 'Prague was again a German city'.[17] Decades of cultural retreat had finally been reversed; Germans were again in what they saw as their rightful place as the rulers of Bohemia. 'The Bohemian-Moravian countries belonged for a millennium to the living space of the German people' explained Hitler's decree establishing the protectorate. It was an act of self-preservation that Germany took 'decisive action for the reestablishment of the foundations of a Central European order'.[18]

By 1939, it was little mystery what kind of regional order the Nazis hoped to forge out of the ruins of old Central Europe. A 'racially pure' greater Germany would act as regional—if not continental—hegemon, with other nations permitted a degree of autonomy according to the whims of those in Berlin, and only insofar as their politics were more or less 'coordinated' with Nazi Germany's. Czechs were brought into Hitler's 'New Order' by force, but Slovakia joined willingly. As did Hungary, which in 1939 abandoned the League of Nations and signed up to Hitler's Anti-Comintern Pact instead, seeing in Germany the best hope for the recovery of territories lost in the Treaty of Trianon.

Poland proved much more difficult to win over. The largest of Germany's eastern neighbours had a strange place in Hitler's worldview. It had never featured prominently in his grand visions of the East, which were directed at the territory of the Soviet Union, especially Ukraine and Crimea. Despite the long history of anti-Polish sentiment in Germany, Hitler saw the country as a primarily geopolitical threat rather than a racial one.[19] In 1930 Hitler even spoke of an 'agreement with Poland [as] the first step towards the unification of Central Europe'.[20] Perhaps this reflected Polish Foreign Minister Józef Beck's view that Hitler was 'more of an Austrian, and in any case not a Prussian'.[21]

Prussian or not, Warsaw decided to stake its future on the Western powers rather than Germany. Just two weeks after the occupation of Czechoslovakia Hitler instructed his generals to begin planning an invasion of Poland. A few months later, on 22 August 1939, he impressed upon them what the coming war would mean in the starkest possible terms. Though no official transcript was taken, there is little doubt that he intended to wage the invasion of Poland with hitherto unseen levels of brutality. This was to be a new kind of war, aimed not at the establishment of boundaries but at the destruction of a people and their state, ultimately to be 'depopulated and settled by Germans'.[22] This did not just mean defeating the Polish army but subjecting the land-that-was-once-Poland to a brutally exploitative occupation from which it could never reemerge.

It would be a testing ground for many of the tools that would be deployed with far greater ferocity in the future eastern struggle. The Einsatzgruppen—special units of the SS tasked with following behind the army and murdering anyone deemed to be an enemy of the Reich—were to be of particular importance. It was symbolic that they had been formed in German-Slavic borderlands of past and present: Silesian Oppeln and Breslau, Prussian Allenstein, Pomeranian Krössinsee, and Vienna.[23] They stood waiting for the eventual order as the Nazi propaganda machine churned out story after story about alleged atrocities against Germans in Poland. On the morning of 1 September 1939, bombs began to rain down on Warsaw as battles broke out along the frontier. Two days later Great Britain and France declared war on Germany. The Second World War had begun.

Poland's allies could do little to help it. Even less so since the Soviet Union had secretly agreed to partition the country with Germany. In just three months Nazi forces killed 54,000 Polish civilians, targeting social, intellectual and political elites in an effort to 'decapitate' the Polish nation.[24] Jews were liable to be murdered at random irrespective of their social status.[25] About half of the Polish territory occupied by Germany was annexed outright. Hitler gave the *Gauleiters* (regional leaders) of these new territories the somewhat vague command that 'he only demanded a report from [them] after ten years that their area was German, that is purely German'.[26] This would be no simple task considering these territories contained only 600,000 Germans, but 8.9 million Poles and 603,000 Jews.[27]

Decrees reduced Poles to second-class citizens, banning them from using certain public amenities, providing them with lower rations, forbidding them from maintaining autonomous cultural life, and making them liable to be deported at will.[28] Cities became the focus of such efforts, with hundreds of thousands of Poles removed to make way for Germans. Their places were in part meant to be taken by Germans being resettled as part of the Nazi regime's 'back home to the Reich' policy. Whole German communities—consisting of several hundred thousand people—that had lived for centuries in Galicia, Bessarabia, the Baltic, and elsewhere were forcibly uprooted and utilized by the Nazi regime in its grand schemes of racial engineering. Being 'brought home' in fact meant being sent to colonize occupied Poland.[29] The 'General Government'—the half of the German occupation zone not annexed directly—served as a dumping ground for Poles, Jews and other 'undesirables', and was eventually so overwhelmed by the influx that deportations had to be halted.[30]

The barbarity with which Germany waged war on Poland and subsequently administered it was all the more striking considering the light touch shown in Western Europe and Scandinavia. In the spring and summer of 1940, Denmark, Norway, France, Belgium, and the Netherlands were all conquered with breathtaking speed. None of these countries was formally integrated into Germany.[31] As the leading Austrian Nazi and governor of the Nazi-occupied Netherlands, Arthur Seyss-Inquart, put it: 'In the east we have a National Socialist mission; over there in the west we have a function. Therein lies something of a difference'.[32] While acting as a brutal imperial conqueror in the East, Germany presented itself as a dispassionate—though certainly not benign—occupier in the West.

In those parts of Central Europe in which it had little direct interest, it acted as hegemon. In August 1940 the Axis powers negotiated a second 'Vienna Award' that returned a huge swathe of Romanian-ruled Transylvania to Hungary. Both countries—and Slovakia—would be pressured into joining the Tripartite Pact with Germany, Italy and Japan later that year. Romania was by then under the dictatorship of the rabidly racist, nationalistic and antisemitic Marshal Ion Antonescu, who would rule the country until 1944. Under intense pressure, Yugoslavia was compelled to join the Tripartite Pact on 25 March 1941, provoking a anti-Axis coup two days later. Within a month the country had been invaded and occupied by the Axis powers. The Slovene lands were partitioned between Germany, Italy and Hungary, the last of these also receiving a chunk of Vojvodina. Serbia-proper was occupied and most of Croatia, Bosnia and Dalmatia put under the control of a newly established Croatian puppet regime headed by the virulently anti-Serb and antisemitic

Ustaša movement. Huge population movements followed each of these transfers of territory. 'The political fact of "Mitteleuropa" has today been created' opined one scholar in what was once Germany's leading history journal. It did not exist, in his eyes, beyond the Third Reich. It was rather a product of it, an afterthought of German hegemony. 'The enemies of the Reich are therefore also the enemies of Central Europe'.[33]

* * *

By 1941, generations of German nationalist dreams had been fulfilled. Antisemites, greater German nationalists, monarchists, national conservatives, and Nazis could all share in the wonder of Hitler's achievements. Jews had been excluded from German life, the German lands once ruled by the Habsburgs welcomed into the Reich, the shame of 1918 vindicated, the folly of 1789 undone. A powerful, confident, fanatically racist Germany now had Europe in its hands. Hungarians, Slovaks and Croats who had felt cheated by the result of the First World War shared in the spoils.

And yet, for the man that stood atop it all, this was nothing but a prelude. Hitler's obsessions lay eastwards, in the final overthrow of 'Jewish Bolshevism' and the conquest of vast tracts of 'living space' for the German people. In spite of the non-aggression pact signed in 1939, Hitler decided in late 1940 that the time for war with the Soviet Union was ripe. Britain's hopes for an eventual victory with Soviet help would be extinguished and the isolated island empire forced to sue for peace, or so the reasoning went. Operation Barbarossa was launched on 22 June 1941. Three million German soldiers poured across the Soviet border, joined by hundreds of thousands of Romanians further south. They caught their enemies unprepared. By December the Germans were closing in on Moscow and Leningrad. With victory appearing only a matter of time, the Nazi regime wasted little time in setting in motion its wildly genocidal goals.

Already in May 1941, the tone had been set by the infamous 'Commissar Order'. It declared that Soviet 'political representatives and leaders ... had clearly proved through their previous subversive and seditious work that they reject all European culture, civilization, constitution, and order' and were 'therefore to be eliminated'.[34] This set the tone for a war that was cast in almost apocalyptic terms. 'It is the old struggle of the Germanic people against Slavdom, the defence of European culture

THE DEATH OF A CIVILIZATION

against Muscovite-Asiatic inundation, the repulse of Jewish Bolshevism', one general told his troops. It was nothing less than 'a fundamental sector of the struggle for existence of the German people'.[35]

The line between Jews and Bolsheviks already blurred by decades of antisemitic propaganda, they were in practice treated as one and the same enemy. From the beginning, the Einsatzgruppen targeted Jews on Soviet territory, but their wild murders grew in scale and intensity as the invasion progressed. In late September, when explosions caused by bombs planted by the Soviet secret police had struck German-occupied Kyiv, over 30,000 Jews were shot in just two days in retribution. A month later a similarly horrific massacre took place near Odesa in a joint Romanian-German operation after thousands of Jews had already been murdered by Romanian forces. It was part and parcel of the war against 'Judeo-Bolshevism'.[36]

From 1 September Jews over the age of six in Germany and the Protectorate of Bohemia and Moravia were forced to wear a Star of David in public, already a practice in the General Government as well as Croatia.[37] Soon after, deportations of German Jews eastwards began, though the process was confused by the cacophony of jurisdictions and authorities. In November, packed trains arrived in Kaunas from Berlin, Frankfurt, Munich, Vienna, and Breslau. The passengers from these cultured, historic cities were simply unloaded and shot.[38] The head of the SS, Heinrich Himmler, quickly ordered a halt to killings of Reich Jews in such a manner. The time was apparently not yet right for the murder of German Jews. Yet in the Warthegau the murder of Reich Jews was proceeding apace, while in the General Government (which had recently expanded into Galicia) Jews were similarly being slaughtered.[39] In the 'Independent State of Croatia', organized killings of Jews, communists and Serbs had already begun, claiming the lives of thousands over the summer.[40]

On 30 January 1939, Hitler had prophesized that if 'international Jewish financiers within Europe and abroad should succeed once more in plunging the nations into a world war, then the consequence will be not the Bolshevization of the world and therewith a victory of Jewry, but on the contrary, the annihilation of the Jewish race in Europe'. He returned to this 'prophecy' on 12 December 1941 in a speech given to leading Nazis, just after the United States entered the war. 'The world war is here, the destruction of the Jews must be the necessary consequence', noted Joseph Goebbels in his diary.[41] The 'final solution' was a question of how and precisely when, not if. The annihilation of European Jewry was part and parcel of a wider Nazi campaign against all those they deemed to be unfit to live amongst the 'Aryan race'. Roma were deported and murdered in their thousands alongside Jews in 1941. Tens of thousands of disabled Germans had been murdered by their own state over the previous two years. Homosexuals, communists, black people, even Jehovah's Witnesses were amongst those targeted by the Nazi regime. But perhaps the most confusing and contradictory aspect of the entire genocidal machinery of the Nazi state was its attitude towards the Slavs.

Two days after Barbarossa was launched, Himmler commissioned a report on the future German plans for the East. The result was the fantastically genocidal 'Generalplan Ost'. It envisioned the killing of over 100 million Poles, Ukrainians, Russians, Belarusians and others in order to clear the way for German settlement. How it was done—whether through starvation, murder in war, death through brutal forced labour— did not matter. What mattered was the ideological imperative of clearing the land of 'sub-humans' so that Germans could enjoy their 'living space'. Reinhard Heydrich, acting as Reich Protector of Bohemia and Moravia, presented a similar vision to German officials there in a speech he gave in Prague on 2 October 1941. 'Gentlemen, the final solution [for the Protectorate] must be the following: that this space must once and for all be settled by Germans'. Half could be 'Germanized'. The other half sterilized or removed.[42]

The organization of all these plans was no easy task, especially during wartime. Unlike Jews, who were slated for complete extermination, Slavs were not considered a 'race' but rather divided up into subgroups of varying 'racial value'. They were vaguely assumed to be inferior, with few qualms shown about treating them as such. But at the same time Nazi Germany was allied with Slavic Croats, Slovaks and Bulgarians, while centuries of mixing had rendered any serious 'racial' divide between Germans and Slavs effectively non-existent.[43] Despite these vagaries, Poland's leadership was targeted for extermination and millions of Poles deployed as slave labour, any political and cultural life deemed unnecessary. In territories directly annexed to Germany Poles were either to become German or face deportation.

The war in the East claimed the lives of millions of Soviet citizens, the callous disregard for their lives part and parcel of the Nazi dream of a land made free for German colonization. But to Europe and the world they presented the war as a grand 'crusade' against 'Judeo-Bolshevism', to which Italy, Croatia, Slovakia, Hungary, Finland, and especially Romania

THE DEATH OF A CIVILIZATION

would also contribute. Their war would culminate with the enormous battle of Stalingrad, the largest battle in human history. Between July 1942 and February 1943, it claimed the lives of a million Axis troops. A similar if not far greater number of Soviets also fell in the battle. It ended in defeat for Germany and its allies, a turning point in a war whose catastrophic destructiveness continued to grow.

* * *

In late July 1943, Hamburg was turned into a blazing inferno. Allied bombers mercilessly pummelled the city with incendiary bombs over ten days and nights. Up to 40,000 perished, mostly civilians engulfed by the infernal flames that burned as hot as 800 degrees Celsius.[44] Tenements and once-luxurious townhouses alike were turned into burnt-out shells. Nearly every major German city—and many mere towns—would soon become familiar with the terror that rained down from the skies. By the end of the war at least 350,000 had died in the Allied bombings of German cities.[45]

The eastern front slowly receded over the course of 1943, with losses of men and material taking a severe toll. The Allied landing in Sicily had brought Mussolini's downfall and forced a German occupation to keep Italy in the war. In the Balkans, meanwhile, the Axis failed multiple times to crush a communist partisan movement led by the charismatic Yugoslav leader Josip Broz Tito, whose ranks had swelled into the hundreds of thousands by the end of the year. In the summer of 1944, a million men were lost on the eastern front alone as the Soviets pressed up to the German border.[46] Meanwhile Allied forces poured into France and by September found themselves on the German border in the west.

Germany's impending defeat did nothing to blunt the ideological extremism of the Nazi regime and its fascist allies. When, in March 1944, Hungary was occupied by Germany to prevent it from seeking a separate peace, it was immediately taken as an opportunity to destroy the largest remaining Jewish community in Europe. Over the course of the year hundreds of thousands of Hungarian Jews were deported to German death camps, the vast majority killed on arrival. By the time Horthy was overthrown in October 1944 and replaced by the fascist Arrow Cross Party led by the fanatical antisemite Ferenc Szálasi, most Hungarian Jews had been deported.[47] Millions of Jews from across Europe had been murdered by the Nazi regime by the time that Heinrich Himmler ordered the gas chambers at Auschwitz-Birkenau to be dismantled in November 1944.

The Nazis were by then preparing for their last stand. A failed assassination attempt on Hitler in July only radicalized the regime further while strengthening his desire to fight until the bitter end. 'Every bunker, every block of houses in a German town, every German village must become a fortification in which the enemy bleeds to death or the occupiers are entombed in man-to-man fighting' Hitler demanded. Hundreds of thousands of German and foreign workers were enlisted in the backbreaking and fruitless labour of turning cities across Germany's east into fortresses that were to be defended until their total annihilation.[48] All the while, Allied bombs rained down from the sky, turning city after city into rubble. By February 1945 Dresden and Breslau were the only two cities with over half a million residents that remained intact.[49]

Dresden, the magnificent old seat of the House of Wettin, was eviscerated over four days in the middle of the month. Breslau was meanwhile surrounded by Soviet troops, the fanatical *Gauleiter* of Silesia Karl Hanke committed to fighting to the death. In preparation for the battle, much of the historic city centre had been razed to build an airstrip to keep the Germans supplied. Street-by-street fighting devastated much of the rest. The only time the airstrip was used was when Hanke fled Breslau before its surrender.[50] Tens of thousands of soldiers and civilians were killed and an entire historic city razed to the ground for nothing. The fall of Budapest and the fascist Arrow Cross regime came after a similarly costly siege that claimed the lives of over 100,000 Hungarians and tens of thousands more German soldiers. Over a quarter of the homes in the city were damaged and iconic structures like the Széchenyi Chain Bridge and the Royal Palace completely destroyed.[51]

The shrinking borders of the Reich contained an ever-growing population of miserable and traumatized refugees fleeing the horrors of Soviet occupation. East Prussia alone saw an exodus of about two million people in January 1945 in unbelievably harsh winter conditions. The roughly 500,000 that stayed behind suffered the wrath of the invading Soviet forces keen to exact revenge upon a German nation that had subjected their own people to such unimaginable cruelty.[52] Around four million Germans fled westwards that winter, the vast majority never to return.[53] 'There will be no mixture of populations to cause endless trouble', Winston Churchill told parliament in December 1944: 'A clean sweep will be made'.[54] By the time of Hitler's suicide on 30 April 1945 (while Berlin was being reduced to rubble) and the subsequent unconditional German surrender on 8 May, a new Europe was already taking shape.

THE DEATH OF A CIVILIZATION

As Allies from the start, Poland and Yugoslavia were confident that they would share in the spoils of victory. Czechoslovakia had been transformed into a Western ally under Edvard Beneš's government-in-exile. Romania switched sides at the last minute while Hungary fought on with the Axis to the end, to be treated as a defeated country alongside Germany, slated for an indefinite occupation. The functions of the German state were taken over by the four occupying powers—France, Britain, the United States, and the Soviet Union—with the former three each administering their own zone in the west of Germany and the Soviets one in the east. Berlin was divided between the four. For years in exile Czechoslovakia's president Edvard Beneš had advocated for the complete expulsion of Germans from his country following its eventual liberation. It took until 1942 for the Allies to be won over to the proposal, which became official policy in 1945.[55] The same would occur in Poland, whose borders were to be moved westwards along with millions of Poles. It was all to happen in a manner that was 'orderly and humane'.

In 1943 the Allies had expected between 3.5 and four million Germans from Poland and one million from Czechoslovakia to be expelled. In the former case it ended up being double, in the latter triple. In June and July 1945 occupied Germany was receiving 100,000 refugees per week.[56] Tens of thousands would die in the Sudeten expulsions, hundreds of thousands in those from Poland. The cumulative total of population transfers from 1944 to 1948 was staggering. A total of twelve million Germans were expelled from across Central and Eastern Europe while 2.1 million Poles were transferred from the Soviet Union to Poland and 650,000 Ukrainians went in the other direction. In Hungary, Romania and Yugoslavia the transfers were less dramatic, but still numbered in the hundreds of thousands in various directions.[57]

On 1 November 1943, Austria had been recognized by a joint Allied declaration as 'the first free country to fall victim to Hitlerite aggression'.[58] In time, the promotion of this polite fiction became the founding act of the second Austrian republic. As British, American and Soviet troops flooded in to take their posts in occupied Austria, the moderate, Moravian-born Karl Renner emerged from his internal exile to take charge of yet another Austrian revolution. In his first public proclamation, he decried the 'annexation' of a 'powerless and coerced people' in 1938.[59] This was a stark contrast to his reaction at the time, when he had endorsed the absorption of 'German-Austrians' into the greater German whole and celebrated that the 'sad interlude of the half-century of 1866 to 1918 is now vanished in our thousand-year common history'.[60]

CENTRAL EUROPE

Austria was not the only Central European state being liberated from its own history. In 1945 Czechoslovak President Edvard Beneš made clear that the expulsion of three million Germans was only part of the task at hand: 'we must de-Germanize the republic, everywhere and in its entirety'. The 'names, the landscape, the customs—everything that can be de-Germanized'. Streets, squares, buildings, villages, towns were renamed. German schools, associations and publications were shut down. In the de-Germanizing frenzy Czechs with German names were told to change them to Czech-sounding ones and German music was taken off the radio, two measures without much of a lasting impact. Anyone who declared themselves to be German or Hungarian in 1929 was simply stripped of their citizenship.[61] Poland's leaders took a similarly aggressive approach. Already in August 1944 the Polish government had stripped all 'Polish citizens of German nationality' of their citizenship and determined that they would all have to leave the territory of the future state. Using German at home or in day-to-day life or '[adhering] to German habits' was supposedly enough to make one a German.[62] The precise definition was less important than the fact that, as one communist leader put it: 'We will not have any ethnic minorities. We have proceeded to the concept of a nation-state … Thus we will remove the German from our country'.[63]

On 25 February 1947, the representatives of the Allied Powers in Berlin announced the 'state of Prussia … hereby dissolved'. They had freed Europe from the state that 'since time immemorial' had acted as the 'bearer of militarism and reaction in Germany'.[64] Most of its eastern territories would be taken by Poland, with a hefty chunk carved out for the Soviet Union around the town of Königsburg, rechristened Kaliningrad. Prussia served as a convenient scapegoat for all that was wrong with Germany and its history. The Nazis themselves, it was felt, had selectively claimed the heritage of Prussia to bolster their own legitimacy.[65] This seemed a natural enough continuity for those in the West already familiar with the terror of Prussian militarism from the First World War. Though Hitler was an Austrian who had served in the Bavarian Army, Britain's Foreign Minister Anthony Eden called him 'a symptom' of 'the Prussian spirit of military domination'.[66]

The mass ethnic cleansing of Germans from Poland, Czechoslovakia (there also Hungarians), and Yugoslavia (there also Italians) was based on notions of collective guilt justified with nationalist narratives that posited them as 'ancient Slavic lands' in which Germans (or Hungarians and Italians) were little more than 'invaders'. Their land was not being settled but 're-settled'. Not annexed, but 'recovered'.[67] In an attempt to draw settlers, often suspicious and reluctant, into these 'recovered territories', one Polish government announcement gave a typical portrayal: 'The conqueror has fled in panic across the Oder, leaving behind villages and cities, estates and factories, stocked ponds, and cultivated gardens. These empty lands lie waiting for us—their legitimate proprietors ... To the west!'[68]

Where Germans—or Hungarians—were not expelled with any comparable thoroughness, it was largely because they were too rural and small in number to threaten the new national states they lived in. And these were, above all else, national states that emerged from the rubble of the Third Reich. Poland, Czechoslovakia, Hungary, Romania, and self-liberated Yugoslavia mourned their national dead, but showed little special regard for the Jews that had been slaughtered by the Nazi regime, to say nothing of the Germans, Hungarians and Italians expelled to pay for Nazi crimes. Pogroms continued even after the war, contributing to the desire of many survivors of the Holocaust to leave Europe for good.[69] Hundreds of thousands of Jews emigrated to British-ruled Palestine, where within a few years the Zionist dream of an independent Jewish state would be fulfilled. Under the watchful gaze of the Red Army, communist coups swept across the new nation-states. As Europe slid into a Cold War, their borders became impenetrable walls between two different worlds. Eastern Europe had marched westwards; Western Europe had marched eastwards. Central Europe was nowhere to be found.

PART IV

THE LIFE
1948–

17

LIBERATED FROM HISTORY

Max Frisch stood with his hands in his pockets. He trudged through the rubble, gazing in all directions, astonished. He was standing in Frankfurt. Or so they said. The old streets through which processions of princes, electors, bishops, and emperors had once passed were buried under ruins that 'sunk into their own rubble'. The house where Goethe was born two centuries ago was remembered only by a plaque. Those where countless thousands had been born, lived and died were remembered not at all. Frankfurt reminded Frisch not of a city, but of the mountains of his Swiss homeland, where 'narrow goat paths lead over hills of debris, and all that still stands are the bizarre towers of a weathered ridge'.

What those towers—those ruins—might once have been Frisch did not mention. He might have passed by the Paulskirche, where the first German parliament had met nearly a century ago, now a hollow shell. Or perhaps the Römer, whose painted emperors had been whisked away for safekeeping, spared watching the destruction of the city where they had been crowned with such pomp and circumstance in centuries past. But Frisch wrote in his diary that looking at the grass growing out of ruined houses, at the dandelions sprouting in toppled churches, 'one could suddenly see how it grows on, how a jungle spreads over our cities, slowly, inexorably, a humanless flourishing, a silence of thistles and moss, a history-less Earth, then the chirping of birds, Spring, Summer and Autumn, the breath of years that no one anymore counts'.[1]

Frisch visited Frankfurt in May 1946, a year after the end of the Second World War, when the process of rebuilding had not yet begun in earnest. In his poetic estimation, it was easier to imagine nature reclaiming the ruins of this old centre of Central European civilization than it was to imagine how it could ever be again what it once was. On the ruins of what had fallen in the years from 1938 to 1948, everything would have to be built anew. What exactly was rebuilt, when, and how would reflect ideological projects as much as material necessity. After the First World War, legal systems, bureaucracies, armies, cities, and indeed societies remained largely intact, scarred and shaken as they may have been. They were inherited by new governments, not uprooted and replaced. But after 1945 Germans, Austrians, Poles, Czechs, Slovaks, Hungarians, Slovenes, Croats, Serbs, Jews, and others were forced to rebuild the foundations of civilized life from scratch. To restore legal order fit for a new world. To construct new, uncompromised bureaucracies, armies, and institutions. To rebuild countless cities, brick by brick. To provide people with the opportunity to live a new life, free from the burdens of the past. To begin anew, from what was later dubbed 'Year Zero'.

Not every city was a pile of rubble. And not every country that emerged—or failed to emerge—was treated equally by the victorious powers. 'Year Zero' was a zeitgeist, not a single year or a single starting point shared by all. It was the nearly universal feeling that the Second World War had marked an absolute break with the past. The abolition of Prussia, the removal of Austria from Germany, the flight or expulsion of over twelve million Germans from across Europe's east—all served a common purpose of correcting the stream of Central European history that had veered so wrongly off course. The history of a strange collection of lands once presided over by the House of Habsburg, and their equally strange path through the transformations of modernity, had definitively come to an end. The building of a new world was at hand.

* * *

Exactly four years on from the end of the war in Europe—on 8 May 1949—sixty-five delegates from the western zones of occupation officially endorsed the 'Basic Law for the Federal Republic of Germany', setting in motion the establishment of a West German state. In Soviet-occupied Berlin, meanwhile, a vast memorial complex was being inaugurated to commemorate the Soviet soldiers that had fallen in the Battle of Berlin. The centrepiece of this expression of a dawning communist East German state was a massive twelve-meter-tall statue of a Soviet soldier. Germany's partition in two was not planned from the beginning but became a by-product of worsening relations between the Western powers and the Soviet Union in the years after the war. As allies became adversaries, their visions of the future became irreconcilable.

LIBERATED FROM HISTORY

This changing state of Europe was immortalized in Winston Churchill's March 1946 speech in which he warned: 'From Stettin in the Baltic to Trieste in the Adriatic, an iron curtain has descended across the Continent. Behind that line lie all the capitals of the ancient states of Central and Eastern Europe. Warsaw, Berlin, Prague, Vienna, Budapest, Belgrade, Bucharest and Sofia'.[2] Over the following years this iron curtain would come to divide two entirely different worlds—in effect two entirely different civilizations, which, like Central Europe before them, were absolute novelties in European history. In Western Europe, a group of closely integrated liberal democracies emerged under the wider umbrella of a Euro-Atlantic world claiming the mantle of 'Western civilization'. In Eastern Europe, an even more tightly-knit collection of communist-ruled 'people's republics' emerged, taking inspiration and direction from Moscow.

Three months after the adoption of the Basic Law, Germans in the western zones of occupation went to the polls. Konrad Adenauer's Christian Democratic Union (CDU) narrowly emerged victorious, and he was elected the first chancellor of the Federal Republic of Germany, a position he remained in for fourteen years. While his chief internal rival, Jakob Kaiser, head of the CDU in the Soviet zone of occupation, wanted Germany to act as a bridge between East and West, and his chief political opponent, Kurt Schumacher, the head of the Social Democratic Party, wanted a neutral Germany within a neutral Central Europe, Adenauer had an entirely different idea of Germany.[3]

He was born in Cologne on 5 January 1876, just five years after the proclamation of the German Reich. He was a devout Catholic and had been a lifelong member of the Centre Party. From 1917 to 1933 he served as mayor of his hometown, spending the following twelve years fearing for his life in internal exile. Much like his Austrian counterpart Karl Renner, who was six years his senior, by the end of the war the sixty-nine-year-old Adenauer was something of a political dinosaur. As in Renner's case, it was precisely his seniority that made him well-placed to take charge at a time when so many people had been compromised by Nazi rule.

Adenauer concurred with Allied views that the roots of German militarism, imperialism and anti-Westernism lay in a Prussian state tradition that he was happy to see consigned to the history books.[4] Under very different circumstances three decades prior, he had publicly called for a 'West German republic', which if it remained a part of a federalized

Germany could have served as a pro-Western and democratic bulwark to counteract the eastern, militaristic tendencies of Prussia.[5] By 1949, with Prussia abolished and its heartlands occupied by the Soviets, the path was open for an even more expansive version of Adenauer's West German republic—one that would not just keep the balance but tip the scales entirely. As the Cold War dawned, the old Rhinelander had no doubts that Germans would find their natural home in a 'Western Europe' which was the only force that could 'halt the further intellectual and forceful advance of Asia'.[6]

'The West, the Christian West, is no geographical concept: it is a spiritual and a historical concept that also encompasses America', he told those at the first CDU rally in the British zone of occupation in 1947. 'It is this Christian West that we want to try and save'.[7] For Adenauer, 'the West' was much more than a transient arrangement of countries, or an alliance of convenience to face down the threat of Soviet communism. It was an ancient civilization rooted in Europe's Christian heritage that stretched across the Atlantic to the United States of America. Indeed, his preferred term was *Abendland*—the 'Occident', a slightly old-fashioned term that evoked a time when Europe was synonymous with a Christendom threatened by a barbaric 'Orient'. In his eyes, Germany belonged firmly to this Western, 'occidental' community of nations.

Luckily for Adenauer, this kind of Christian-Western civilizational rhetoric was on the rise on both sides of the Atlantic in the early twentieth century. In the nineteenth century Europe had been viewed with considerable suspicion in the United States. It was reluctantly dragged into both world wars by idealistic presidents who wanted to see the United Sates take a far more active role in global—and European—politics. But the notion that Europe and the United States shared common interests was far from obvious, particularly in the wake of the First World War. Whatever Europeans chose to do was seen by many in the United States as none of their business. In the decades after 1919, however, perspectives began to change, in part thanks to the German historian Oswald Spengler's bestselling *The Decline of the West*, which argued to readers on both sides of the Atlantic that European and American history were part of a single whole that seemed to be imperilled by the forces of modernity.[8]

In a speech that could well have come out of Adenauer's own mouth, US Senator James C. Eastland spoke in late 1945 of 'savage, barbarian Mongolian hordes [in Czechoslovakia] stalking the streets of Western civilization as its conquerors, and threatening not to stop at Vienna and Berlin but to push on to engulf the very civilization from which we ourselves have stemmed'.[9] Churchill too, in his 'iron curtain' speech, pointed to the danger communism posed to a common 'Christian civilization', a worry shared by Labour Foreign Minister Ernst Bevin, who mused to the American Secretary of State George C. Marshall that: 'It is not enough to reinforce the physical barriers which still guard our Western civilisation. We must also organize and consolidate the ethical and spiritual forces inherent in this Western civilisation of which we are the chief protagonists'.[10]

This belief in a common Western interest rooted in a common civilizational heritage—both imperilled by the existential threat of Soviet communism—was the prerequisite for the construction of the institutions that have come to define Euro-Atlantic integration. Unlike in 1919, victors and vanquished would be drawn together in a single community of fate. In 1949 the French former and future Prime Minister Georges Bidault told a group of his fellow pro-European politicians that: 'Three kinds of Europe are possible: an English Europe, which means no Europe at all. A Russian Europe, which means Asia. As for Europe for everyone, the basis for this is a Franco-German rapprochement'.[11] And so, in the interests of Europe and Western Civilization, the former foe rapidly became a close ally. West Germany would be a founding member of the European Coal and Steel Community that in 1952 set six Western European countries down the path to integration. Three years later, aided by British and American worries about the fate of Western civilization, the country officially joined the recently founded North Atlantic Treaty Alliance (NATO).[12] Politically, institutionally, 'civilizationally', Germany in its Adenauerian iteration had become an indisputably Western European country for the first time in its history.[13]

While the creation of a Western Europe as part of an institutionalized trans-Atlantic Western world was a novelty in European history, it could truthfully point to an old, shared history that had been inconveniently derailed by the secular ideologies of the nineteenth and twentieth centuries. The eastern powers that had led Germany astray over the previous 200 years—Prussia, Austria, even Saxony—had been removed from the picture. Charlemagne's medieval empire provided a clear antecedent of this institutionalized occidental civilization, conveniently including the same France, western Germany, northern Italy, and the Low Countries that after the Second World War embarked on a process of European integration spearheaded by Christian democratic parties. Those same parties inherited a Catholic tradition that conceived of Europe as a Christian civilization that stood above and beyond the transient claims of princes, nations or ideologies.[14]

For the countries of Europe's east, the way forward was nowhere near as clear. The Western orientation of many of the successor states, along with the Western-inspired political systems they had adopted, had been thoroughly discredited by decades of political instability, economic crisis, and—in Czechoslovakia's case—Western betrayal.[15] But the East was an unknown quantity. In the interwar years, the Soviet Union was effectively closed off to the rest of the world. Communist parties were banned in most Central European countries. Poland had been forced to fight a bloody war against the nascent Soviet state to attain its independence in the first place, while for Hungarians and many Germans 'Bolshevism' still evoked memories of the bloody revolutions in 1919, reinforced through the brutal crusade against 'Judeo-Bolshevism' during the Second World War.

Since 1919 the Communist International (Comintern) had been headquartered in Moscow, which communist parties across the world looked to for inspiration and direction. Thousands of foreign communists made the city their home, many falling victim to brutal and paranoid purges that swept the country in the 1930s. This organization, whose stated goal was global communist revolution, became an awkward liability for the Soviet leadership by the early 1940s, allied as the latter was with the 'imperialist' and 'bourgeois' powers of the West. In 1943 it was wound up altogether in an attempt both to assuage Soviet allies and to destigmatize European communist parties from their association with Moscow.

Already in August 1941—just two months after the Axis invasion—Stalin suggested to the head of the Comintern that it would be better if Poland's communist party was abolished and replaced with a 'workers' party of Poland' to make it more palatable to the Polish people. 'At the present stage, the struggle is one of national liberation' he wrote in his diary.[16] This point of view mirrored how the Soviets presented the war effort to their own people. Russian nationalism was rehabilitated during what would be dubbed the 'Great Patriotic War', following Stalin's wider belief that nationalism and communism were perfectly compatible.[17] Soviet radio stations targeting Europe's east bore names like 'For National Liberation', 'For Slovak Freedom', 'Free Yugoslavia', or 'Radio Kossuth'.[18] The partisan war of the Yugoslav communists led by Josip Broz Tito—a survivor of Stalin's Moscow purges—was labelled a 'National Liberation War' undertaken by a 'National Liberation Army'.

LIBERATED FROM HISTORY

Against the charge of godless Judeo-Bolshevism, communist parties positioned themselves as the only true fighters for national freedom.

A curious if sometimes forgotten aspect of this national turn was the Soviet embrace of Pan-Slavism. The theme of Slavic solidarity was doubly useful for Stalin in that it bound together the various Slavs of the Soviet Union—Ukrainians, Belarusians and Russians—as well as the Soviet Union and the three Slavic Allied countries in Eastern Europe. In his speech commemorating the anniversary of the October Revolution in 1941, Stalin spoke of freeing the 'subjugated Slavic peoples' as one of his war goals and warned that Hitler was ready to 'exterminate' them.[19] It was a message supported by a recently founded All-Slavic Committee tasked with spreading Pan-Slavic propaganda. Stalin would proclaim triumphantly on 9 May 1945 not the victory of communism but that, 'The centuries-long struggle of the Slavic peoples for their existence and independence has ended with victory over the German occupiers and German tyranny'.[20]

This rejuvenated Pan-Slavism found its way into the foundational texts of the postwar Polish and Czechoslovak states. The 'Manifesto of the Polish Committee for National Liberation', published by the pro-Soviet Lublin government established in 1944, announced that Polish and Soviet troops were fighting side-by-side to liberate the country. And not just liberate it, but also to conquer Silesia, Prussia, and other western territories that had traditionally been the demands of right-wing National Democrats.[21] 'History and the experience of the current war show that only the building of a great Slavic dam based on a Polish-Soviet-Czechoslovak understanding can protect against the onslaught of German imperialism'.[22]

The Košice Program of the postwar Czechoslovak government went even further in establishing the direction of Pan-Slavic politics. 'As an expression of never-ending gratitude' towards the 'victorious Slavic great power in the East', the government would make an alliance with the Soviet Union an 'indispensable guideline of its foreign policy'. Relations with Poland, Yugoslavia and Bulgaria would also be re-founded 'on the basis of Slavic brotherhood'. This 'Slavic orientation' extended even to cultural policies 'in accordance with the new importance of Slavism' in international and domestic politics. 'There will be a revision of our relation to German and Hungarian culture carried out through the unveiling of their reactionary elements in all areas'. The relationship to the Soviet Union, meanwhile, would be 'completely rebuilt from a cultural point of view'. All anti-Soviet content in school materials would be removed and the Russian language would be given pride of place in the new curriculum.[23] It was a remarkably frank expression of what it meant to become an 'Eastern European' state.

With hindsight, it is easy to view such proclamations as little more than the early stages of a predetermined Soviet takeover, but this is overly simplistic. The Košice Program was that of a cross-party coalition government that Edvard Beneš would preside over as president until 1948. Disillusionment with the West due to the Munich betrayal in 1938 and a sense of hope for the democratic national state promised by the East were widespread in the Czech lands, if less so in Slovakia.[24] The Czech philosopher Josef Ludvík Fischer summed this attitude up in a way that would be unthinkable in later decades: 'Central Europe is today only a continuation of Eastern Europe, with the Slavic bloc as its central core. Here, and not elsewhere, is our place … We got and will get nothing from the West'.[25]

Soviet Pan-Slavism allowed Czechs, Slovaks, Poles, and other Slavs to interpret the war as a great common struggle for Slavic liberation, which produced a final victory of Slavdom over Germandom, underscored by the expulsion of millions of Germans. The goal of what the old Westernizing Francophile Beneš embraced as the 'new Slavic politics'—as opposed to the 'old' Pan-Slavism associated with reactionary Russian imperialism—was nothing less than 'the gaining of a new place for all Slavic nations in Europe and in the world'.[26]

Communist parties, bolstered by their association with this eastern Slavic power that promised to elevate the role of the Czechs and Slovaks in world history, grew rapidly in the wake of the war. There was plenty of opportunism—and even coercion—but also genuine enthusiasm for what was, in effect, a utopian ideology. Even in Poland, where the Pan-Slavic propaganda was less successful and communism markedly less rooted, the Polish Workers' Party swelled to 550,000 members by 1946. In Hungary just 3,000 members in December 1944 grew to 600,000 by January 1946. Head and shoulders above the rest was the Communist Party of Czechoslovakia, which grew from 28,000 at the end of the war to over a million by March 1946, the largest party in Czech history.[27] It won thirty-eight per cent of the vote in the first postwar Czechoslovak election in 1946; forty-three per cent in Bohemia itself.

Czechoslovak communists presented the East as the inheritor of all the progressive traditions of the West. Turning eastwards was therefore not a step backwards, but a great leap forward. 'The Slavs are building on the great fundamental values of the Western revolutions and in many respects are ahead of the West' opined one communist journalist.[28] The postwar era was indeed one in which the left seemed to be on the march in both East and West, lending credence to the notion that communism represented the future. The era of the liberal bourgeoisie was over, and the 'working and agricultural masses' and their leaders were on the ascendant, noted President Beneš.[29]

In Britain, the Labour Party won the first postwar election in 1945 and reshaped the postwar British state with a raft of left-wing economic and social policies. In France the communists won the first postwar elections, while in Italy they cemented themselves as the leading party of the left, winning almost a third of the vote in 1948. Even in Poland, Czechoslovakia, Romania, and Hungary the main challengers to the far-left communists were not parties of the right—which were often banned and persecuted—but social democrats and left-agrarian populists. Whatever shape the postwar regimes took they clearly marked a strong leftward turn. As the Polish philosopher Krzysztof Michalski later recalled, communism was greeted as something inevitable. 'In people's eyes, the Red Army was a natural phenomenon, like volcanic lava'. And for the most enthusiastic proponents of communism, it 'represented history itself, the future and progress'.[30]

National liberation and class struggle converged in the single project of the 'people's republic'. Once again, Czechoslovakia was exemplary. While in exile during the war, President Beneš had remarked to the communist leader Klement Gottwald that the expulsion and expropriation of Germans would be 'a national revolution combined with a social revolution. By means of measures taken against German wealth as well as German national characteristics, the way will be opened to radical economic intervention and social change in the Bohemian lands'.[31] The 'people's republic' would therefore be a nation-state ruled by a spirit of collectivism in which the 'oppressors' of the past—'fascists', 'speculators', the 'bourgeois', 'imperialists'—would have no role. The large estates that provided the material basis for the existence of a landowning class that stood above the rest of society were confiscated and redistributed amongst the peasant masses. Never again would a Prussian Junker, Hungarian magnate, Bohemian aristocrat, or Polish nobleman hold the fate of any nation in their hands.

Industry, financial assets and property came under state ownership for the benefit of the whole nation. There were few qualms about uprooting millions of Germans, Italians, Hungarians, or even Poles from their ancestral homes and putting their assets and personal belongings in the ownership of the 'correct' national majority. The shadowy and oppressive forces of capitalism scorned by fin-de-siècle nationalists as the preserve of 'foreign' German, Hungarian, or Jewish interests were eradicated in favour of national collectivism.

Postwar Pan-Slavism reached a crescendo in the year or two after the war, epitomized by the All-Slavic Congress in Belgrade in 1946, where a General Slavic Committee was established as an organ of the 'new Slavic movement'. But as relations between the Soviet Union and its erstwhile Western Allies soured, subsequent Slavic congresses were awash with increasingly shrill anti-American, anti-Western, and anti-capitalist rhetoric in which 'Slavism' appeared to mean little more than loyalty to the Soviet Union and its foreign policy.[32] As the Cold War dawned, Pan-Slavism faded away as a transient curiosity in a much wider story of Soviet expansionism. Under communist rule, Czechoslovakia, Poland, Hungary, and Romania aligned themselves politically, diplomatically, culturally, socially, and economically with the implacably anti-western Soviet Union, cemented in the Warsaw Pact of 1955 and countless ancillary agreements. The exception was Yugoslavia, where communists had established the very first 'people's republic' immediately after the war thanks to their self-liberation on the back of a mass partisan movement. Tito and the Yugoslav communist leadership were enthusiastic Stalinists, for whom the 'new Slavic politics' was crucial both domestically and internationally. In an attempt to overcome the national divisions that had plagued the country before the war, the new Yugoslavia was a proudly federal state. Tito even hoped to make it the core of a much wider communist federation stretching across the Balkans, the first step being the absorption of Bulgaria. Stalin saw this push for a Balkan Federation as needlessly provocative, contributing to his growing suspicion of Tito. In 1948 this led to a total break between the Soviet Union and one of its most loyal allies. Yugoslavia would in subsequent years forge its own path between Eastern and Western Europe, leaving it uniquely placed in Cold War Europe as a non-aligned but communist-ruled country—a foil to Austria, which would be a non-aligned but democratic country.

Almost as an afterthought, Stalin allowed a German Democratic Republic to come into being in the Soviet zone of occupation on 7 October 1949. It presented the usual façade of liberal democracy but was a state built by and for communists that wanted to see their country reborn along Stalinist lines. The vast memorial complex built in Berlin served, as the Soviet city commander recounted, as a reminder of 'when, by whom, and for what price victory had been gained'. It was 'a symbol of the fight of the peoples of the world for socialism and democracy against the fire raisers of a new war'.[33]

The Soviet narrative of liberation—epitomized by the various war memorials erected in prominent locations across Eastern Europe—allowed local communists to present their nation as having been cleansed of the sins of the past. Communists everywhere cast themselves as the primary victims of fascist oppression as well as the sole force that could be counted on to fight fascism both past and present. 'Anti-fascism', directed against internal enemies and at the West, took over from war-time Pan-Slavism as the glue binding together the emerging communist world of Eastern Europe. It provided a myth of origin and a political mission that could give logic to the construction of a common civilization upon the community of fate known as Eastern Europe.

* * *

Central Europe's destruction and subsequent transformation into a disparate collection of nationally homogenized states divided in two by an iron curtain is most poignantly observed in its great urban centres. Some—like Berlin, Dresden, Wrocław, and Budapest—had been physically devastated, while others—like Vienna, Prague, Krakow, and Zagreb—had been left largely intact, but no city was untouched by the massive displacements that accompanied the war and its aftermath. No city was spared from being transformed into a site of Western or Eastern European civilization.

The Holocaust more than anything caused irreparable damage to the urban fabric of every single Central European city. In the eyes of many later writers, Jews had been the very bearers of Central European civilization—its 'intellectual glue' as Milan Kundera called them. There is some truth to this, insofar as Jews and Jewish converts formed a huge portion of the educated bourgeoisie concentrated especially in cities like Prague, Budapest and Vienna. But what made Jews so central to the urban culture of Central Europe was not really their Jewishness, but their cosmopolitanism. This was hardly unique to Jews, even if they had natural reasons to hold steadfast to their cosmopolitanism even as many around them turned to increasingly virulent ethnic or racial nationalism. The entire urban bourgeois culture of Central Europe was assaulted from multiple directions by multiple different political movements from the years 1918 to 1948.

Jews were the hardest and most universally hit, expelled from or murdered in every corner of Central Europe. Germans were naturally targeted in territories taken over by non-German states, but not in occupied Germany itself. Other 'national bourgeoisies' had highly diverse experiences in the war. Polish elites more than any others were targeted by both the Nazi and Soviet regimes. The Slovak fascist regime expelled Czechs, but did not murder them. Croatian fascists both murdered and displaced Serbs. For political reasons, many Croatian, Slovak, Hungarian, Romanian, Ukrainian, and Slovene elites were murdered or fled as Soviet or partisan armies advanced.

The Polish Bureau of War Losses estimated in 1947 that a stunning seventy-nine per cent of the six million Polish citizens who lost their lives between 1939 and 1945 had been urban residents—this in a country that was overwhelmingly rural. In Warsaw alone it was estimated that 800,000 out of 1.2 million prewar inhabitants lost their lives.[34] Lviv—once the Habsburg administrative capital of Galicia and after 1945 part of Soviet Ukraine—by 1946 only had perhaps ten per cent of its prewar population. In 1939 it was a city of 345,000, with about 160,000 Poles and 100,000 Jews, the two largest groups in the city. By 1971 it was a city of 566,000 in which Poles and Jews had all but disappeared. Ukrainians were 68.2 per cent of the population and Russians 22.3 per cent.[35]

In 1918, just one per cent of Silesian Breslau's population were Polish-speakers, and even by 1945 Germans outnumbered Poles by ten to one. Rechristened Wrocław by its new Polish rulers, the city was effectively cleansed of its prewar German inhabitants.[36] The prewar Jewish and German populations of Prague and Bratislava (once Pressburg/Pozsony) were almost entirely gone.[37] Across Carinthia, Carniola, Styria, Croatia, Slavonia, Bohemia, and Moravia, towns that had once had German-speaking majorities, pluralities, or substantial minorities—often indeed bolstered by Jewish inhabitants—were left by the 1960s cities overwhelmingly Slovene, Croatian and Czech.

To call the last remaining minorities in Eastern Europe after 1948 'minorities' does not quite do their situation justice. They were remnants of devastated communities; reminders of a past that the 'national majorities' around them condemned as a time of darkness and oppression. They were made invisible. Some—like the remaining Germans and Austrians in Yugoslavia—were not even recognized as minorities.[38] Even for those who had the chance to remain, the choice was a difficult one that many regretted or were made to regret. In Poland, most so-called 'autochthons'—German-speakers 'verified' as Poles in a lengthy process, and effectively banned from identifying as German in any manner—eventually emigrated to West Germany.[39] The 61,995 Germans and Austrians counted in the 1953 Yugoslav census were reduced to just 21,096 by 1961 through emigration and assimilation.[40] Communities that did survive in large numbers, such as the hundreds of thousands of Hungarians in Slovakia, often did so despite strong pressure from above. The Czechoslovak state claimed 350,000 Hungarians were actually Slovaks who had strayed from their roots and now had to 'return' to Slovak language and culture in order to be accepted in their homeland.[41]

Jews that remained in the wake of the Holocaust also struggled to find a place in the new peoples' republics, facing more hostility than sympathy from people that often decried their 'victim mentality'. Lingering antisemitism took a perverse turn in the early 1950s when the Soviet Union and its satellite states embarked on a series of antisemitic campaigns under the broad umbrella of 'anti-Zionism' and 'anti-cosmopolitanism'. Jewish communist leaders were cast as duplicitous traitors in stark contrast to their purely 'national' communist brethren. Some were even executed after highly publicized show trials, as was the fate of Czechoslovak communist Rudolf Slánský. And in 1951 the Hungarian Communist Party decreed that members of the 'former ruling class'—which in practice expanded to include people displaying 'bourgeois tendencies'—in Budapest and other cities should be forcibly relocated to the countryside to perform 'useful' labour. Between fifteen and thirty per cent of those deported were Jewish.[42]

In Romania too, 'anti-Zionist' show trials set the stage for a wider purge of ethnic minorities from the communist party in what remained one of the most ethnically diverse Eastern European satellites. This presaged an even more aggressive nationalist turn under Nicolae Ceauşescu, who mixed communist megalomania with prewar nationalist mysticism to create a uniquely isolationist form of national communism in the 1970s and 1980s.[43] Communist antisemitism in Eastern Europe would resurface with a vengeance in 1967 during the Six-Day War between Israel and surrounding Arab states, most notably in Poland. The relentless 'anti-Zionist' campaign there eventually resulted in a broad purge of Jews from the communist party and the emigration of 25,000 remaining Polish Jews, leaving just 10,000 by 1970.[44]

If the fate of much of the old Central European bourgeoisie was one of death, expulsion, emigration, and assimilation, the greater part was forced to contend with what it meant to live in a 'people's republic'. The comfortable existence that had marked their prewar world and all its cultural achievements would now be scorned, derided, and in many cases made impossible to reemerge. An eastern Ukrainian planner dispatched to Lviv by the Soviet authorities succinctly summed up this attitude in its extreme form when he described the city as one where 'the proud veil of European culture masks the offensive face of a capitalist barbarian'.[45]

The urban fabric of Central Europe's old metropolises under communist rule was rewoven to emphasize that they were cities that belonged to nations whose true representatives were not the decadent bourgeoisie—and certainly not the old nobilities—but the common peasants and proletariat. Mass rural migration to cities was a phenomenon that stretched back to the nineteenth century, but the historical cores of cities like Vienna, Buda, Zagreb, and Prague had been highly resilient to the changes happening around them. Even when Prague had swelled into a vast Czech metropolis, for example, the wealthiest districts in the city centre remained a stronghold of German-speakers both Christian and Jewish.[46] The grand apartments in ornate buildings surrounded by equally grand cafes, shops, theatres, and elitist clubs that regulated the social calendar of the Central European bourgeoisie acted as a kind of social fortress.

As such, communists now targeted these spacious bourgeois apartments with equal vigour as the vast estates of the former nobility, if not quite with equal thoroughness.[47] In cities emptied of their prewar Jewish and German inhabitants, apartment buildings that once housed doctors, lawyers and academics became curious sites of rural-urban cultural fusion—and confusion—as their new inhabitants kept livestock in their gardens and basements.[48] In the capitals of Poland, Romania and Yugoslavia, the transplantation of 'national majorities' from the countryside into the cities shocked their remaining bourgeoisie inhabitants.

One native Varsovian described her city as dominated by a 'suburban rabble' that behaved like 'Gypsies' and kept 'potatoes in bathtubs and laundry in the washbowl and toilet'. A Bucharest publicist lamented that a 'European francophone city of the highest cultural rank' had been reduced to a provincial backwater where people not only could not speak foreign languages but could not even speak their own language properly.[49] In time, the rubble would be cleared away, the animals banished to the countryside, and the country bumpkins re-educated into the ways of the city. But the haughty old urban world of Central Europe was carried forward by a vanishing minority.

Not even death could save some from oblivion for their failure to conform to the needs and tastes of the 'people's republic'. In 1948 the newly established communist authorities in Prague banned the work of what had become the city's most famous author, Franz Kafka. Though he died in anonymity in 1924, his work achieved stunning posthumous acclaim, in large part thanks to German-speakers like Hannah Arendt and Klaus Mann who had emigrated to the West and helped turn Kafka into the literary icon of mid-century American culture.[50] Kafka was, as the literary scholar who first established his fundamental link to Prague put it, a stranger to Czech society in three senses: as a Jew, as a German, and as a member of the bourgeoisie.[51] Even had he survived, his existence as a German-speaking Prague Jew hardly could have.

18

THE BIRTH OF AN IDEA

It was impossible to erase the past entirely after 1945, but it is difficult to imagine how the rupture could have been greater. The new cities, states and societies built out of the ruins of Central Europe were those of liberal, capitalist democracies or communist party-states—of Western or Eastern European civilization. They no longer looked inward for inspiration, but to the lands of capitalist opportunity in the West or the socialist paradise in the East. There was no longer any Central European alternative, no longer any notion that the people brought together in the nineteenth century by accidents of history should be forced to build upon a common fate together.

Realities often did not match the lofty ambitions of those who claimed to be establishing a new world totally free from the burdens of the past. Former Nazis were just about everywhere in postwar East and West Germany alike as well as Austria. West Germany did not even accept the new eastern border with Poland, with enormous and influential organizations of expellees pressuring the government to make no concessions on the matter. Social democrats, meanwhile, continued to criticize Adenauer for prioritizing Westernization over reunification and turning the country into the frontline of the Cold War.

References to 'Central Europe' did not entirely disappear either, an early indication of how many people refused to come to terms with their country's new Western or Eastern European identity. This was especially true in the East, where after 1948 it rapidly dawned that their new model was simply a transplantation of Soviet Stalinism: totalitarian one-party dictatorship buoyed by a personality cult centred on a party leader, and the pursuit of radical social transformation through a command economy prioritizing heavy industry. Free expression and association disappeared and any public questioning of the party's leading role in society and the country's unbreakable bond with the Soviet Union became unthinkable.

The new regimes condemned not only the long centuries of Habsburg rule as a time of barbaric feudal oppression, but even the old 'bourgeois' regimes as little more than tools of capitalist oppression. Even Tomáš Masaryk—Czechoslovakia's great pro-Western 'philosopher king'—disappeared from the pantheon of great Czechs and Slovaks, his name erased from public places, his bespectacled visage removed from countless streets and squares, his life's work recast as a misguided prelude to the true national and social revolution of 1945–8.[1]

For those who rejected the Soviet alignment of their country, the alternatives were Western alignment on the West German model, or the kind of neutrality demanded by West German Social Democrats. But calls for countries to act as bridges or syntheses between East and West were fantasies in Cold War Europe. The iron curtain's descent was the final act in a long, bloody process that did not just remove Central Europe from the map but made impossible its return—so long, at least, as the Soviet Union was committed to upholding communist rule across Eastern Europe.

When workers in East Germany revolted against worsening living conditions in 1953, the Soviet army helped the local communists keep their own people in check. In 1956 an anti-Soviet uprising brought the downfall of the Stalinist leader Mátyás Rákosi in Hungary. His replacement Imre Nagy attempted to make good on the general anti-Soviet mood by removing his country from the Warsaw Pact and pledging to hold free elections. The Soviets responded by brutally crushing the revolution, leaving thousands dead and causing 200,000 Hungarians to flee into exile.

The only non-Soviet alternative remained Yugoslavia, which looked like a beacon of liberty compared with neighbouring Warsaw Pact regimes. Initially shocked by their expulsion from the communist world, Yugoslav communists developed their own kind of socialism that entailed considerably more economic and social freedom, extending to Yugoslavs being able to travel freely to the West. Without the baggage of Soviet Eastern Europe, many leading Yugoslav communists saw their country as simply a progressive European state.

Miroslav Krleža forcefully argued that there was no other way to understand the country. Widely considered the greatest Croatian writer of the twentieth century, Krleža had strong left-wing convictions that translated into support for Tito and communism in Yugoslavia. In a series of interviews conducted by the Bosnian historian Predrag Matvejević in

THE BIRTH OF AN IDEA

the late 1960s and early 1970s, Krleža was asked point blank what he thought about the notion of a literary 'Central European complex' that critics often emphasized. There were few better people to ask. Krleža was born in Zagreb in 1893. One of his early literary inspirations was the great Hungarian national poet Sándor Petőfi, who he studied in his Magyar classes. He spoke German fluently, alongside an almost bookish Croatian. In the preface to a 1992 edition of his childhood memoir *Childhood in Agram*, Miroslav Burić wrote that: 'By his themes, style, education and erudition Krleža is a true Central European writer who naturally belongs to the western cultural circle'.[2]

Krleža's 'broad forehead [began] to wrinkle and his facial expression soured' when Central Europe was mentioned, Matvejević wrote. While Krleža conceded that one could argue that 'within the framework of the decomposition of the Austro-Hungarian colonial empire' some vaguely similar literary sensibilities could be detected, the notion of a 'Central European complex' was a 'phantom'. 'Nowadays this is the summoning of long-dead ghosts in a spiritualist séance simply called writing feuilletons about unfamiliar things ... "Central Europe" today is just a formula of quiet nostalgia for bygone days when the Spanish dynasty still ruled: *"Die schönen Tage von Aranjuez sind vorbei"'* ('The beautiful days of Aranjuez are over'). All the authors people liked to include in the rather short list of characteristically Central European writers were, in his words, 'apologists of the Austrian mistake'. He invoked French, Italian, Scandinavian, German, and Croatian literature in an enthusiastic attempt to confirm there was not and had never been a cultural unity called Central Europe.[3]

* * *

In the world of the Cold War, Eastern Europe was a fact. Indeed, the more time Western and Eastern Europeans spent siloed off in their own separate worlds, the more their societies diverged as they were shaped by the vastly different political circumstances prevailing in each half of the continent. Eastern Europe became so entrenched in the minds of Europeans that it took the birth of an entirely new idea to make possible the claim that some Eastern European nations were in fact rightfully a part of the West. A new idea of Central Europe.

By the late 1940s, the rising tide of optimism that had accompanied great promises of 'national and democratic revolution' under communist rule had receded. The inflexible totalitarian reality of Stalinism was exposed for all to see. In the mid-1950s the worst excesses of Stalinism were walked back and condemned, but the one-party state and its stranglehold on social, cultural and economic life remained. The situation in Czechoslovakia was particularly disappointing for those that had once welcomed communism. Not only had a 'Czechoslovak road to socialism' failed to materialize, but the kind of internal liberalization taking place in Poland, Hungary and even the Soviet Union itself during the post-Stalin 'thaw' years evaded them under the orthodox communist Antonín Novotný.

It was especially unfortunate because, unlike the largely rural societies that blanketed most of Eastern Europe, Bohemia and Moravia were already highly industrialized in 1945 and therefore had the least to gain from the aggressive program of rapid industrialization demanded by Stalinist planners. By the mid-1950s Czechoslovak industry was plagued by shortages, breakdowns and obsolete equipment. Yet Novotný's Czechoslovakia had been the first Eastern European state—following the Soviet Union in 1936—to proclaim the 'victory of socialism'. In 1960 a new constitution transformed it into the Czechoslovak Socialist Republic, a self-congratulatory gesture that confirmed the country was proceeding along the path to communism. The constitution's adoption had even been preceded by nationwide 'discussions' to give it a veneer of democratic legitimacy, supposedly involving over four million people across nearly 50,000 public meetings.[4] To be facing stagnation while celebrating reaching a higher state of social being was bad enough, but in 1963 national income even fell in the wake of a prematurely abandoned five-year plan. The party leadership was forced to recognize that reform was necessary.[5]

Slowly, bureaucratically, a great reform plan was devised—the New Economic Model. It envisioned subtle democratization in the economy by giving workers on the ground more input into how resources were distributed. As the party's tight grip loosened, however slightly, the door to free discussion outside of the sphere of the party-state began to open. A noticeable liberalization of intellectual life began to take hold within the narrow boundaries set by the party. Film and literature became forums for relatively free expression, even if criticism of the party remained strictly taboo.[6] By 1964 the three leading weekly cultural periodicals together had a circulation of over 250,000, with a collective readership of about a million in a country of just fourteen million. Leading the way was the Czech-language journal of the Czechoslovak Writers' Union, *Literární noviny*.[7]

THE BIRTH OF AN IDEA

The past several decades of Czech and Slovak history had brought epochal changes to both nations and all those surrounding them. And yet in official channels recent history could only be addressed or discussed with ideological platitudes. In the pages of *Literární noviny* and its Slovak counterparts, however, writers continually pushed the envelope in an attempt to sate a deep societal hunger to discuss and interpret their recent past. President Novotný resented the atmosphere of liberalization, eventually cracking down with a new censorship law that came into effect in early 1967. The number of 'suggestions'—euphemism for censorship—faced by the editors of *Literární noviny* skyrocketed. The outbreak of the Six-Day War only added fuel to the fire. In what was perceived as a shameless act of mimicry, Czechoslovak propaganda followed the Soviet Union's harsh anti-Israel stance, which was impossible to publicly challenge. Writers began to feel that they were under siege, at risk of being deprived of the only critical Czech-language forum in the country.[8]

Against this backdrop of mounting pressure, the communist leadership allowed the Writers' Union to go ahead with their fourth congress in late June 1967, expecting to use it as an opportunity to assert its authority. The day before it opened, the union followed the Stalinist protocol that party members—who were in any case the vast majority—meet in advance to agree on a common position so that no real debate could occur at the wider event. The keynote speaker was the Politburo member and close Novotný ally Jiří Hendrych. He criticized *Literární noviny*'s 'open attacks on the party' and praised the work of the censors. He was followed by the outgoing head of the union Jiří Šotola, who calmly presented a report on the brash censorship that its journal had been suffering. Unity even within the party ranks could not be taken for granted.

The following hot June day, the congress opened in a grand late-nineteenth-century building not far from Prague's main railway station. Fittingly for a socialist republic, since 1955 it had served as the Central Cultural House of Railwaymen. After an official speech of welcome, Milan Kundera stepped up to the podium. He announced that the Union's central committee had decided to dispense with 'the usual introductory speeches, which were always exceedingly long, authoritative, and boring'. Instead, he set an irreverent tone that would come to define the congress. Speaking directly to his country's leading writers, he reminded them of the central role that language and literature had played in the Czech national revival of the nineteenth century. 'It is the Czech writers who were responsible for the very existence of the nation and remain so today', but after some two decades of communism they seemed to be losing their way. It was, as he presented it, an existential threat to the Czech nation.

Kundera had been born in Moravia in 1929 and come of age under the shadow of Nazi occupation. He had embraced communism in his youth with the kind of naïve enthusiasm common to many of his generation, initially deploying his literary talents to produce socialist realist poetry in the 1950s. A well-known communist poet, he became a lecturer at the famed film academy which produced many of the leading lights of the Czechoslovak New Wave such as Miloš Forman. Even as his disillusionment with the regime grew in the 1960s, as a party member and renowned author of communist poetry he stood firmly within 'the system'.[9] It was his role as a party intellectual that enabled the publication of his first novel in 1967—*The Joke*—a biting and quasi-autobiographical satire of the excesses of Stalinism and its zealous young proponents.[10]

Kundera's speech at the 1967 Writers' Congress went well beyond criticism of past party failings. He went on to accuse the communist regime of vandalizing Czech history and identity, of creating a regime full of people 'who live purely in their own immediate present tense, without culture or awareness of historical continuity'. People were unmoored from the 'world of Graeco-Roman antiquity and the world of Christianity, those two mainsprings of the European spirit which give it its strength and tension'. The communist regime had created people who are 'quite capable of turning their country into a wasteland with no history, no memory, no echo or beauty'.[11]

Jiří Hendrych followed this dramatic expression of cultural desperation with an ill-placed intervention, berating the audience with familiar ideological platitudes about the dangers of subversion and ideological pluralism. Pavel Kohout—another internal critic—spoke immediately after him, drawing a comparison between the fate of Israel and that of the Czechs to criticize the censorship regime, which he credited with breeding apathy that in turn led to ignorance.[12] Then came Alexander Kliment, who defended free speech and expressed his solidarity with the Russian dissident writer Aleksandr Solzhenitsyn, who had made his own attack on Soviet censorship in an open letter to the Fourth Congress of Soviet Writers that took place earlier in the year. Kohout abruptly announced that he had a Czech translation with him and asked if the congress wanted to hear it. The crowd responded with applause and the chairman took a vote to confirm. Just one was against, while two abstained.[13] A furious

THE BIRTH OF AN IDEA

Hendrych donned his hat, picked up his briefcase, and stormed out of the hall. As he passed the row where Kundera and other leading writers were sitting, he cried: 'You have lost everything, absolutely everything!'[14]

Hendrych returned for the second day, but only to confirm his worst fears. First the film critic Antonín J. Liehm warned that faith in socialism had waned to such an extent that society was gripped by an 'idealisation of the cultural life of the West'. The comments of the non-party playwright Václav Havel were expectedly critical but paled in comparison to those of Ludvík Vaculík. Excoriating the communist regime for reducing citizens to serfs, Vaculík dismissed not just the leadership of the party, but their whole socialist project as a miserable failure. 'All we have done so far is to follow dumbly in the wake of dehumanised, American-style civilization, reproducing the mistakes of East and West alike'. This was the conclusive piece of evidence party officials had been waiting for. One attendee recalled a frantic Ideological Department official indignantly telling him: 'What did I tell you? Do you still say there's no plot?'[15]

Hendrych decided to act. On the third day he convened the communist faction before the congress could open, informing it that the whole event had been hijacked by a group of radicals. He demanded the party members elect a new Writers' Union committee, but his reading of the list of 'recommended' candidates was interrupted by angry interjections that devolved into a shouting match. In the end only Vaculík, Kohout, Ivan Klima, and the non-party Havel were thrown off the committee. The congress reconvened with a two-hour delay and ended without incident.

In the wake of the congress Vaculík, Liehm and Klíma were expelled from the party and the central committee brought *Literární noviny* under the control of the Ministry of Culture.[16] There was no meaningful reflection on what had led to such an open rebellion. Not in Prague, at least. The congress and its aftermath were a largely Czech affair. Though Novotný's 1960 constitution was highly centralized, there was a separate Communist Party of Slovakia in which the reformist Alexander Dubček had served as first secretary since 1963. While Novotný cracked down, Dubček welcomed liberalization. While Czech writers and communists clashed, their Slovak counterparts maintained cordial relations. Novotný and Dubček seemed to represent two diametrically opposed visions of Czechoslovakia's future. When the Central Committee of the Czechoslovak Communist Party met in late October, Dubček and other Slovaks openly criticized Novotný's authoritarian methods, provoking heated debates between reformers and orthodox communists. As the central committee adjourned, a threatened Novotný sought external support. Soviet General Secretary Leonid Brezhnev visited Prague in December, but to Novotný's chagrin announced that he would not involve himself in Czechoslovak party quarrels. Heated debates followed when the central committee met again at the end of the month. The reformists eventually won out. On 5 January 1968 Novotný stepped down as first secretary and Dubček took his place. The 'Prague Spring' had begun.

Over the following months Dubček pursued a program of wholesale reform that sought to live up to the lofty promises espoused by communist parties across Eastern Europe. His vision was by no means shared by his sister parties across the Eastern Bloc, however. Dubček pursued a wholesale liberalization of society, with the aim of—eventually—enabling the return of multi-party democracy as well as the federalization of Czechoslovakia. It was the promise of a unique 'Czechoslovak manner of constructing and developing socialism'—which came to be known as 'socialism with a human face'—that had been greeted with such enthusiasm in the late 1940s.[17]

One of the most significant steps was the abolition of censorship in March 1968, which created a veritable eruption of public debate and discussion. The Writers' Union's journal alone, re-founded as *Literární listy*, reached a circulation of 300,000.[18] The other communist regimes across the Eastern Bloc watched with trepidation. Few questioned Dubček's commitment to communism, but they worried that the reforms could take on a life of their own and open the door to anti-communist subversion. Such fears were even being stoked by the Soviet KGB, which sent to its allies in Poland and East Germany a worrying report, 'On the Activities of the Counter-revolutionary Underground in Czechoslovakia'. It warned that 'counterrevolutionary and revisionist forces' supported by international imperialism had long been seeking to restore capitalism and separate Czechoslovakia from the international socialist community. 'Already [at the congress] the reactionary core of the Writers' Union (Kohout, Liehm, Vaculi, Havel, Kundera) succeeded in forcing the decision in which a political platform opposing the [communist party] was formulated', it pointed out ominously. When the leaders of the Eastern Bloc states met in Dresden on 23 March 1968, Brezhnev warned of the danger posed by this 'counterrevolutionary conspiracy' of writers.[19]

Bit by bit, the worst fears of orthodox communists began to materialize. In the 4 April 1968 edition of *Literární listy*, an article appeared, 'On the Theme of an Opposition', by Václav Havel. Unlike Kundera and most other authors who spoke at the Writers' Congress, Havel was not and had never been a communist. He was from a well-off Prague family and as punishment for this bourgeois background had been prevented from going to university, instead turning to the theatre and becoming an internationally renowned playwright. As one of the few non-communists with a prominent public profile, his article came as a shock to the whole system. He argued that despite all the flowery liberal rhetoric, nothing in the country would change until 'noncommunist points of view are accorded a certain basic political and moral recognition'—until, in effect, a true political opposition was allowed that could compete with the Communist Party on equal footing.[20]

An awkward political dance continued throughout the spring and early summer as reformist Czechoslovak communists did their best to affirm their commitment to the Soviet-led Eastern European order. Ultimately, they failed to convince their allies and hardliners at home. On 20 August 1968, hundreds of thousands of Warsaw Pact troops flooded into Czechoslovakia. This would swell to almost half-a-million foreign troops bolstered by 6,000 tanks. Soviet paratroopers stormed the headquarters of the central committee of the Czechoslovak Communist Party. Dubček and his colleagues were arrested by the KGB and sent to Moscow where, after days of intense negotiations, they were forced to sign an agreement effectively agreeing to roll back all the major reforms introduced during the Prague Spring.[21] Dubček was eventually removed as first secretary in April 1969. The country was then set on the path of what was euphemistically called 'normalization' under the watchful guard of Soviet troops.

To Kundera, the Prague Spring had still been a moral triumph. In his essay 'The Czech Fate', published in *Literární listy* in December 1968, he argued that there was 'no nation in the world that, in a comparable ordeal, had stood its ground like ours and showed such determination, reason and unity'. The essay provoked an acerbic response from Havel, published in January 1969: 'All of us, that is the entire Czech nation, must undoubtedly be delighted to find out that, for our performance in August, we have gained the approbation of Milan Kundera, that somewhat sceptical intellectual cosmopolitan, who tends to see but our negative side'. Havel accused Kundera of the same 'pseudo-critical illusionism' which he claimed to be critiquing. All it did was 'quietly lead us away from our responsibility for the current events and our duty to authentically enter them'. Kundera responded with his own increasingly personal attack on

Havel, whose worldview he presented as forcing him into errors and lies that blinded him to the reality of the 'Czech fate'.[22]

The public barbs and insults traded between Kundera and Havel were their final cries before official oblivion. Their polemic was the last time either writer was published in their homeland while it remained under communist rule. They became 'dissidents', a term that only gained currency in the late 1970s and 1980s as their plight became a topic of global concern, but one that consigned them to two very different fates.[23] While Havel remained in his country, Kundera packed his bags and moved to Paris in 1975. But his obsession with the 'Czech fate' would never escape him. As he put it in his response to Havel: 'Fate is assigned to us. Man is determined to death and Bohemia lies in Central Europe'.[24]

* * *

Milan Kundera was a latecomer to the life of an Eastern European exile. He had lived through the war as a teenager, greeted communism with joyful expectation, and enjoyed a position as one of his country's leading writers right through the Prague Spring. Until then, there was no reason for him to flee. The same was not true for the waves of Jews, Poles, Hungarians, Czechs, Slovaks, Croats, and others that had been washing up on Western shores for decades fleeing Nazism, war and communism.

Exiles and émigrés were forced to confront their homelands' Eastern European fate. The Polish government-in-exile in London and the thousands of officers, civil servants, lawyers, and other elites of the old Poland associated with its community maintained an air of indignant withdrawal. They were, by and large, virulently anti-communist, many from the eastern provinces annexed to the Soviet Union. They gathered in smoky clubs where they reminisced about a Poland that was rapidly fading into memory. They sent their children to Polish Saturday schools in vain attempts to forestall their eventual Anglicization. Themselves overwhelmingly male, many married into British society anyway.[25] Right-wing émigrés across Western Europe, North America and Australia similarly clung on to the dream of a lost homeland they imagined uncorrupted by communist influences. They refused to engage with the changing countries they left behind and instead agitated mercilessly against the regimes that ruled them.

In Paris, Vienna, Munich, and other major continental metropolises, literary exiles discussed, debated, and plotted how they could continue to engage with their captive homelands from abroad. In 1947, the first issue of what was perhaps the most influential of all émigré periodicals appeared in Rome: *Kultura*. At a time when others were expectantly waiting for a war that would catapult them back to Warsaw—one that of course never came—the men and women behind *Kultura* decided that a living cultural link needed to be created that could sustain Polish culture in exile but in communion with the homeland. They did not want to live in the 'imprisonment of the London ghetto' as editor-in-chief Jerzy Giedroyć put it.[26] *Kultura* served as the model for the Czech journal *Svědectví*, published by the Catholic exile Pavel Tigrid, who took a similar approach in aiming to foster dialogue between exiles and their homeland. Tigrid had been one of the few voices who protested the 'idealization of the East' after the war and argued in an Adenauerian vein that Czechs belonged 'morally, politically, culturally, and religiously to Western European civilization'.[27]

Many émigrés settled still further afield, finding new homes in Western—especially American—universities, from which they spoke directly to the educated public of the West. This was Oskar Halecki's fate. As a devoutly Catholic Polish patriot, he saw no future in a communist Poland, instead building a life for himself in the world of American academia. It was a strange twist of fate for a Viennese-born son of a noble Croatian mother and an imperial officer father of Polish descent (who knew no Polish). Halecki was a cosmopolitan European the likes of which became increasingly rare over the course of the century. He possessed an arsenal of languages beyond his native German—Polish, French, English, Italian, Croatian, and Russian.[28]

His area of historical specialism was the old Polish-Lithuanian Commonwealth, a topic he had arrived at through researching his own family lineage.[29] In his first published work he praised the commonwealth's multinationalism as a model for Austria-Hungary to follow as it crumbled around him during the First World War. In the interwar years he emerged as one of the young Polish republic's most prominent historians, putting his linguistic abilities to work in the service of international historical cooperation. In 1923, at the first International Congress of Historians in Brussels, he presented a paper on the problems of chronology and geographical divisions in 'Eastern Europe'. He defined this term in a strictly geographical sense, without 'civilizational' connotations, but emphasized the role of Poland as a historical civilizing force. Polish historians in the interwar years largely embraced this view of Eastern Europe as a simple geographical term while placing their country firmly within a wider Western world.[30]

This was not without controversy. The Czech historian Jaroslav Bidlo challenged Halecki's conception, putting forward the alternative view that Eastern Europe was in fact a world defined by Slavism and Greco-Orthodoxy, something that made it opposed to the Romano-German West.[31] In Germany, meanwhile, a whole school of '*Ostforschung*' (research on the East) had developed that sought to bolster German claims to 'living space' in the East by proving its inherently backwards character and the singularity of the German civilizing mission there.[32] Even in Halecki's thoughts, the notion of a geographically distinct but integrally Western 'Eastern Europe' underwent a curious metamorphosis during the Second World War.

For the first time, he began to deploy the term 'East-Central Europe' instead, developing it after the war into a fully-fledged paradigm for understanding European history. In his 1950 *The Limits and Divisions of European History* he explicitly rejected the notion of a unified Central Europe while asserting the fundamental Europeanness of an Eastern Europe that ended at 'Eurasian' Russia's borders.[33] In his 1952 *Borderlands of Western Civilization*, he presented his narrative of 'East-Central European' history as that of—as the title suggests—the eastern borderland of Western Civilization. It ended with an appeal to the United States to help liberate the 'at least' 100 million Europeans who were supposedly 'united with the Americans by the most intimate bonds of religion, race, and culture [and who] could be a stronghold of peace at the very frontier of Western civilization'.[34]

Both his books received a warm reception in Adenauer's West Germany when they were published in translation in 1957. Halecki was, like the leaders of the CDU, a Catholic conservative who believed in the unity of Western Civilization—especially in its trans-Atlantic form—and saw Soviet communism as an existential threat to its survival. Halecki's wider goal, one he shared with many postwar Catholic intellectuals, was to challenge the Marxist materialist view of history, but from a pluralist perspective rather than retreating to a kind of Catholic religious ghetto.[35]

19

THE LIFE OF AN IDEA

By the time of Halecki's death in 1973, he had left his mark on a whole generation of Western students and scholars focused on the smaller nations of Soviet-ruled Eastern Europe. But the implications of his works, his passionate insistence on the notion that Poland, Hungary, Czechia, and other nations trapped behind the iron curtain, fundamentally 'belonged' to the West, left no discernible mark on the fate of those nations. In fact, never had the division of Europe into two looked so set in stone. In 1969 the United States and Soviet Union entered a period of *détente*—a relaxing of tensions—leaving little prospect of American intervention in Soviet-ruled Europe. In West Germany the first Social Democratic chancellor took office that same year, radically transforming the country's foreign policy. 'Central Europe' was on the agenda in Washington, Moscow and Berlin, but only as part of the 'normalization' of the postwar status quo.[1] The West, it seemed, was abandoning 'East-Central Europe' to its Eastern European fate.

Even worse, it seemed to be convincing itself that this was a natural state of affairs. This was precisely what troubled Kundera. In 1973 he had met the American novelist Philip Roth in Prague. The two eventually became close, in no small part thanks to the interpreting and translation of Kundera's wife Věra, whose English was considerably better than his. In 1974 Roth successfully pitched Penguin Books to publish a series of translated novels under the title 'Writers from the Other Europe'. The editor's note to each edition noted that it wanted 'to bring together outstanding and influential works of fiction by Eastern European writers'. Kundera hated it. The 'regional contexte is very bad ... more over wrong, irreal [sic]', he wrote to Roth in an agitated letter, not waiting as he usually did for Věra to make it more legible. In another, he railed against the notion of an 'Other Europe' as 'a batard born from Yalta, by the father Stalin and the mother Roosevelt [sic]'.[2]

Kundera's third novel, *The Book of Laughter and Forgetting*, published in French translation in 1979, begins with a fictionalized account of the communist seizure of power in Czechoslovakia in 1948, described as 'a fateful moment of the kind that occurs once or twice in a millennium'.[3] In an interview with Philip Roth published the following year and later added as an afterword to the book, Kundera expanded on his view of recent Czech history, of the 'Czech fate'. 'As a concept of cultural history, Eastern Europe is Russia, with its quite specific history anchored in the Byzantine world', he claimed. 'Bohemia, Poland, Hungary, just like Austria, have never been part of Eastern Europe. From the very beginning they have taken part in the great adventure of Western Civilization'. Developing an argument he would return to with even more force a few years later, he argued that the 'postwar annexation of Central Europe (or at least its major part) by Russian civilization caused Western culture to lose its vital center of gravity'.[4]

The direction of Kundera's thoughts coincided with a much wider movement to reappraise the position of 'Eastern European' nations within the wider cultural and historical map of Europe in the late 1970s and early 1980s. Though banned from publishing or working in the theatre, Václav Havel continued to write plays that were distributed through *samizdat*— self-published and distributed informally. The same was true of countless writers, playwrights, poets, and other intellectuals who had been shut out of official life. They took 'normal' jobs as stokers, brewers, or security guards but continued their writing in secret, sharing it with their fellow 'dissidents' and anyone else who cared to read it. In late 1976, spurred on by the arrest of the members of underground psychedelic rock band The Plastic People of the Universe, Czechoslovakia's leading dissidents penned a charter condemning the regime's limitations on free expression and announcing the creation of a forum, Charter 77, for the promotion of human rights. Havel was one of its three spokesmen and, in time, the leading one. In 1978 he wrote his most famous essay, 'The Power of the Powerless', which circulated widely in *samizdat* amongst Poles, Hungarians and Slovaks as well as Czechs. It became perhaps the defining expression of anti-communist dissident writing.[5]

It was by then a product of an increasingly rich trade of publications between East and West. In the early years of the Cold War, émigré publications like *Kultura* and *Svědectví* had only small readerships back home.

But over the decades, as dissatisfaction in communist Eastern Europe grew but intellectual life remained stultified, the number of people behind the iron curtain reading and writing for these open forums in the West steadily grew.[6] *Samizdat* writings found their way into these publications, which in turn made their way back into the hands of their contributors, enriched with writings of those living in the West. In this way, an alternative public sphere developed that straddled the iron curtain, uniting Czechs, Slovaks, Hungarians, and Poles in what Jessie Labov dubbed a 'transatlantic Central Europe'.[7]

The term 'Central Europe' was a commonplace on the pages of *Svědectví* from its very first issue in 1956, which announced in its opening line: 'This journal comes out at a time of revolution in Central Europe'.[8] While the Hungarian Revolution was crushed and the Polish internal revolution came to nothing, the notion that the Soviet satellite states of Eastern Europe should instead be referred to as Central Europe remained. Dozens of writers used it over the years in both historical and contemporary contexts. One Munich-based letter-writer in 1980 lamented the 'increasingly widespread habit' of speaking of the whole Eastern Bloc as one 'Eastern Europe', something 'clearly at odds with reality'.[9]

Proponents of this Central European idea faced an obvious problem. To most of the world Eastern Europe appeared perfectly in line with reality. It referred to a half of the European continent ruled by communist parties espousing similar visions of state and society. Historians and economists gave depth to this view, reading back into 'Eastern European history' a whole narrative of perennial backwardness. If Central Europe could not be found in political or social reality, then where could it be found? The answer proffered in the pages of dissident journals was that it could be found in literature.

The Czech philosopher Václav Bělohradský, for example, pointed to Jaroslav Hašek's classic *The Good Soldier Švejk*, a satirical novel about an affable Czech soldier in Austro-Hungarian service who blunders his way through the First World War and exposes the moral bankruptcy of the Habsburg state in the process. In an essay published in 1980, Bělohradsky criticized the communist regime's appropriation of Švejk. 'The unity of Central European civilization is obscured by the disintegration of its political unity. This does not change the fact that Švejk does not belong to "Slavic literature", but to the same city as Kafka, to the same space as Musil'. It was precisely because Milan Kundera was conscious of this, argued Bělohradsky, that he became the only Czech writer of the communist epoch to be widely read in the West.[10]

Kundera had by then taken up the literary motif as well. In June 1978, on the pages of the Rome-based *Listy* (founded in 1971 by exiled reformist communists who billed it as 'the magazine of the Czechoslovak socialist opposition'), Kundera's first systematic treatment of Central Europe had appeared in Czech, translated from a French essay published in *Les Nouvelles littéraires* earlier that year. He too focused on literature, on Švejk and Kafka, on the power of the written word and those who transcribe it to convey a reality that reaches deeper than politics.[11]

The notion of a literary Central Europe clearly resonated beyond Czechoslovakia. In 1981, the Polish author Czesław Miłosz, who had recently won the Nobel Prize in Literature, presented his own attempt to understand the literary culture of Central Europe, at the University of Michigan's 'East European Festival'. After a long period of *détente*, the fate of Eastern Europe had returned to the international agenda. The election of the Polish cardinal Karol Józef Wojtyła as Pope John Paul II in 1978 provided what was often the sole non-communist institution under communist regimes with a powerful figurehead. Then in 1980 Ronald Reagan was elected US president on a platform of ending *détente* and adopting a more confrontational attitude towards the Soviet Union. The Polish communist regime was meanwhile facing the first real challenge to its rule in decades as the first independent trade union, 'Solidarity', ballooned to some ten million members.

Explaining the fate of captive nations in Europe's east suddenly seemed more pressing than ever. Ladislav Matějka, a Czech professor at the University of Michigan, was so impressed with the contributions at the festival that he decided to collate them into a new annual journal that would be born the following year as *Cross Currents: A Yearbook of Central European Culture*. Miłosz's address, 'On the Poetry of Central Europe', opened the first issue. He concluded with a call to intellectual arms, addressed to the poets from 'East-Central Europe', to break out of their 'closed national compartments hostile or indifferent to each other' and bring 'to light what unites those countries in their present struggle for cultural identity'.[12]

On 21 September 1983, US Vice President George H. W. Bush gave a speech in the opulent Hall of Ceremonics in Vienna's Hofburg Palace on the topic of 'U.S. Policy Toward Central and Eastern Europe'. In the same room that once hosted the throne from which old Central Europe was ruled, Bush reflected on the meaning of Europe's division into two after five days spent travelling through Eastern Europe. While the sight

THE LIFE OF AN IDEA

of the iron curtain—of barbed wire, soldiers standing with machine guns, and attack dogs on chains—gave the impression that one stood at a 'lonely outpost on the edge of Western civilization', the reality was quite different. It represented instead a 'fictitious division down the very center of Europe', one that cut 'Central Europe' out of the 'European mainstream' in which it had historically stood. Miłosz and Kundera were quoted, as was another 'great Mitteleuropean, His Holiness Pope John Paul II'. While the countries of 'Eastern Europe' were criticized for their record on human rights, the 'nations' and 'people' of 'Central Europe' were praised for their spirit of freedom and democracy.[13]

It was a fitting synthesis of the various intellectual springs that had contributed to the development of the idea of Central Europe during the Cold War, expressed through the prisms of individual and national experiences by Halecki, Kundera, Miłosz, and countless others, but always coming back to the same concept of a 'part of the West in the East'. Unlike German Social Democrats, who decades before deployed Central Europe as a prospective neutral zone between Cold War East and West, or historians who wrote about Central Europe in centuries past, these dissident writers spoke of Central Europe as a real, living, breathing place—a culturally united part of the West that was submerged under the Soviet tide. But whenever it receded—in Hungary in 1956 or in Czechoslovakia in 1968—it revealed a region more European than Europe, precisely because they had to fight for their place in Europe to be recognized.

This was, ultimately, Kundera's argument in the most famous expression of the idea of Central Europe, his 1983/4 essay. Originally written in French under the title 'A Kidnapped West or the Tragedy of Central Europe', its first appearance was in fact in Swedish translation in 1983. The French original appeared later that same year, while in 1984 it was published in German and in English in the British magazine *Granta* and (in its most famous iteration) in the *New York Review of Books*. Each version bore a different title and was marked by slight alterations that Kundera tailored to its audience.[14] But the fundamental message remained the same.

For a Hungarian, Czech or Pole, 'the word *Europe* does not represent a phenomenon of geography but a spiritual notion synonymous with the word *West*. The moment Hungary is no longer European—that is, no longer Western—it is driven from its own destiny, beyond its own history: it loses the essence of its identity'. The real tragedy was not merely its subjugation by the Soviet Union, not only the physical and spiritual blows of the early twentieth century, but that 'Europe'—the West—'sees in Central Europe only Eastern Europe'. The 'disappearance of the cultural home of Central Europe', which was 'one of the greatest events of the century for all of Western civilization', went 'unnoticed and unnamed' because 'Europe no longer perceives its unity as a cultural unity'. Culture in Europe had already 'bowed out'.

Given its outsized influence, it is easy to forget just how much criticism Kundera's essay received when it was originally published—and not just from Russians like Joseph Brodsky, with whom Kundera would enter a polemical exchange later in the decade due to his rejection of Russia's Europeanness, but even from many of his fellow Czechs. Many of these critiques were published in *Svědectví*'s first issue of 1985, alongside the polemical exchange between Kundera and Havel at the end of the Prague Spring on the topic of the 'Czech fate'. Milan Hauner, a Czech-German historian at the University of Wisconsin-Madison, accused Kundera of an unforgivable display of historical amnesia. 'The Germans with a certain number of Hungarian allies also fought against "Russian barbarism" and "died for Europe"', he pointed out. The absence of a treatment of Nazism and its implications for Central Europe was incomprehensible, especially considering 'Hitler himself, who in Kundera's long article never appears, was a product of Central European culture *par excellence*; Stalin was not'.[15]

Nevertheless, the deceptively simple idea undergirding the whole essay—that 'captive nations' in Eastern Europe were rightfully part of 'the West'—proved alluring and enduring. In the 1980s Communist regimes were mired in deep crises of political legitimacy only exacerbated by the reformist turn of the Soviet Union under Mikhail Gorbachev. With the utopia appearing ever more distant, communists leaned increasingly on a kind of 'bureaucratic nationalism' in an effort to stave off the threat of democratization and bolster their own authority.[16] Their struggling economies were by then so behind those of the West that it was 'the West', not communism, that their people imagined as a utopia on earth.

* * *

In June 1989, Debrecen welcomed the European Parliament's foreign policy spokesman. At Lajos Kossuth University, he gave a speech on 'Hungary's Chances of Catching Up'. He later invited members of the Hungarian Democratic Forum (MDF) to an upscale dinner at the Grand

Hotel Aranybika in the centre of town. The MDF was one of many non-Communist Party organizations that had sprung up across the Eastern Bloc since Mikhail Gorbachev had welcomed a new reformist age. The most successful of all—Poland's Solidarity movement—had just won a crushing victory in the country's first free and fair elections after years of martial law provoked by its original rise earlier in the decade. The end of communism in Poland was nigh.

As wine flowed, the diners spoke about the fantastical prospect of a borderless, united Europe under the shadow of Debrecen's huge Soviet military base. On a whim, MDF member Ferenc Mészáros suggested they have a picnic across the iron curtain. The idea brewed in his mind over the following days before he suggested it at a meeting of the Debrecen MDF. His fellow activist Mária Filep volunteered to organize it. Soon they had a name, the Pan-European Picnic; a logo, a dove carrying barbed wire in its beak; and a date in mid-August. They got in touch with the European parliamentarian whose dinner had inspired the whole thing, and he pledged his support. His name was Otto von Habsburg.[17]

As a young boy, Otto had been forced to flee Hungary as revolutions swept his father from the family's centuries-old thrones. At the age of nine, the last Habsburg crown prince became the pretender to the various titles once held by his father. Otto was banned from ever returning to his family's Austrian homeland unless he renounced this heritage. Already a man reaching middle-age, who had lived his whole life as a roving exile, in the late 1950s he began manoeuvring for a return to Austria. He was finally able to legally re-enter it on 31 October 1966.

In 1973, Otto became the president of the Paneuropean Union, founded in 1923 by the Bohemian aristocrat Richard von Coudenhove-Kalergi as one of the first organizations advocating the unification of the continent. He remained on the margins of politics until the head of the Bavarian Christian Social Union Franz Joseph Strauss offered to make him a candidate for the first ever elections to the European Parliament in 1979. He accepted. While on the campaign trail, Otto found himself in a remote Bavarian village. After some German tunes, the local brass band played the Radetzky March, Otto rushing to 'conduct' to great applause. He was elected as the MEP for Upper Bavaria, remaining in his post until 1999. For the first time in over a century, a Habsburg had entered German politics.[18]

His most important role was as the spokesman of the Political Affairs Committee from 1981, which effectively made him a lobbyist for

European foreign policy. True to his Paneuropeanist convictions, his focus was enlargement. In previous decades most had come to accept the continent's division into two, including the majority on the committee. Otto, however, demanded that whenever 'general European topics were being debated, there should be an empty chair' for 'those nations missing from our community'. After two years of debate, his proposal finally carried the day. Symbolically at least, the European Parliament was repudiating the continent's division.[19]

For Otto von Habsburg, the fate of the countries once ruled by his father and ancestors which were trapped behind the iron curtain was more than just political. It was personal. When he spoke to activists from the MDF, he spoke of 'we' and 'our' Hungary in fluent Magyar.[20] Though he did not make it to the Pan-European Picnic himself, he sent his daughter, and the event proved to be a stunning success. It was where, as the German Chancellor Helmut Kohl later said, the 'first stone was removed from the Berlin Wall'.[21]

Just three months later, masses overwhelmed the guards at the Berlin Wall and breached it in several places. It was the most symbolic episode in a revolutionary wave that was sweeping over Eastern Europe in 1989, soon to reshape the map of Europe for good. As similar demonstrations erupted elsewhere, communist regimes and their parties crumbled. They promised elections, lost them, then disappeared into history. The bewildering speed of the changes and the enthusiasm with which Poles, Hungarians, Czechs, Slovaks, and others demanded liberalism, democracy and their 'return to Europe' seemed to prove what some writers had been claiming for decades: that Central Europe had been there all along, a submerged and forgotten part of the West, whose people had been itching to rejoin the European mainstream if only they could be given the chance. With the overthrow of communism, that is precisely what they got.

20

THE RETURN OF CENTRAL EUROPE?

In death, Central Europe came back to life. In July 2011, the old Habsburg anthem once again rang out in St. Stephen's Cathedral in the heart of Vienna. Hundreds of mourners stood solemnly before a coffin draped in Habsburg black-gold. When the funeral service came to an end, the coffin made its way out of the church, past the Hofburg, and bent around the Ringstrasse. Following was a procession of figures conjured up from a bygone epoch. Bourbons, Hohenzollerns, Wittelsbachs. Hussars in red trousers and gold-embroidered coats. Soldiers in the light blue uniform of the Austro-Hungarian army. Austrians, Magyars and Slavs in colourful folk dress carrying flags with emblems of crownlands that have long since passed into the history books. Hundreds of thousands of Austrians watched the live broadcast from their homes as the coffin arrived at the Capuchin Church. There, Otto von Habsburg's body was laid to rest in the Imperial Crypt alongside generations of Habsburg rulers. The next day—also following family tradition—Otto's heart was buried at an abbey in Hungary, the urn adorned with a wreath in Hungarian national colours. A final goodbye to the boy that was once fated to be emperor.[1]

In the years since the revolutions of 1989, old Central European legacies once condemned to oblivion have sprouted again with a bewildering regularity. On 16 October 1990—decades after his removal by the communists—Ban Josip Jelačić returned to Zagreb's main square accompanied by feverish national celebration. Like a phoenix rising from the basement of the Yugoslav Academy of Arts and Sciences, his emergence wiped 'Republic Square' off the map and heralded the dawn of an independent Croatia.[2] A decade later, Hungarians triumphantly reincarnated their own Central European ghost. On 1 January 2000, a heavily armed motorcade rolled along the streets of Budapest, driving from the

Hungarian National Museum to the parliament building on the Danube. A glass cabinet emerged out of one of the armoured cars, carried up into parliament by an honour guard. It contained the crown of St. Stephen. It was received in parliament by a special Corporation of the Holy Crown, created just weeks before and consisting of the highest officeholders of the republic. The law which established it announced in the preamble that the 'Holy Crown' embodied 'the continuity and independence of the Hungarian state' stretching back a millennium.[3]

Otto von Habsburg was celebrated not as a man seeking to recapture his family's lost crown, but as a great European and a 'peacemaker' who promoted 'the coexistence of peoples and cultures, languages and religions'.[4] The Holy Crown of St. Stephen was invoked not to claim the territories that once belonged to the Kingdom of Hungary, but because it 'created the possibility for Hungary's entry into Europe'.[5] The same Croatian president who presided over Jelačić's return told his country in 1991 that Croatia fought its war for independence from Yugoslavia (1991–95) not only for 'its territorial integrity, its freedom and democracy' but also for the 'normal conditions when Croatia can join Europe, where she historically belongs'.[6]

This was the promise of the revolutions of 1989; the promise of Central Europe. By correcting the aberration of communism, the formerly 'captive nations' of Eastern Europe could rejoin the Western mainstream where they rightfully belonged. In practice, this meant the establishment and consolidation of liberal democracy and free market capitalism on the Western model, paving the way for their accession to the European Union and, for many, NATO.

The speed of this transition was staggering. By the end of 1989 Poland, Hungary, Czechoslovakia, and Romania had all overthrown their communist regimes and were hurtling towards radical economic and political reforms. Recently a dissident persecuted by the state, Václav Havel had become the first democratic president of Czechoslovakia in decades, while the following year the head of the Solidarity movement Lech Wałęsa became president of Poland. East Germany meanwhile disappeared off the face of the Earth less than a year after the fall of the Berlin Wall as its former territories were simply absorbed into the Western Federal Republic of Germany.

As the new rulers found—whether liberal ex-dissidents, Catholic conservatives or communists-turned-social democrats—there was a prescriptive bundle of policies that accompanied becoming a 'normal' Western

THE RETURN OF CENTRAL EUROPE?

country. These included deregulation, privatization and liberalization, all powered by the idea that a free society could only be built up through the weakening of the state's role in the economy. The speed of this capitalist transformation (often dubbed 'shock therapy') differed from country to country but generally brought enormous upheavals. Inflation skyrocketed, unemployment rose, and output collapsed.[7]

The historian Tony Judt would later jokingly call this the 'revenge of the Austrians'. It was Austro-Hungarian-born economists like Friedrich von Hayek and Ludwig von Mises who had carried forward the free-market principles of the 'Austrian school' of economics into the twentieth century and proselytized them in Western exile.[8] Their ideas offered the ideological foundations of the Thatcherite and Reaganite revolutions that took the United Kingdom and United States by storm in the 1980s before spreading to Europe and the world through the so-called Washington Consensus. Thus, in a roundabout way, ideas born in Austria-Hungary had made their way back to its former lands.

The initial hardships of the transition to free-market capitalism were eventually overcome, with steady growth and democratic consolidation in the late 1990s and early 2000s paving the way for the accession of Poland, Hungary, Czechia, Slovakia, Slovenia, and the Baltic States to the European Union in 2004. This was the crowning triumph of a transition that seemed to prove what Kundera, Halecki and other proponents of the idea of Central Europe had always argued: that Central Europe was a real place that belonged in the West; belonged to the West. Their nations had differentiated themselves from each other, escaping the rigid, homogenized world of Eastern Europe, and willingly joined the West as free and equal democracies.

At the precise moment of their triumph, the Central Europe 'debate' faded into the background. With their integration into Europe, it was no longer a pressing matter to argue for the fundamental Europeanness of Poland, Hungary, Czechia, or other formerly Eastern European countries. It was now taken as a given. Who needed to delve into the murky depths of nineteenth-century literature to rediscover some lost world of Central Europe when a Europe including its Western and Central parts was an established fact? But this also begs the question: had the Central Europe posited by its Cold War proponents ever really existed outside of their own utopian visions? Had a 'Central Europe' really 'returned'?

Insofar as Central Europe exists in the 2020s, it is as a collection of nation-states once part of communist Eastern Europe, who are now accepted as part of 'the West'. But it is difficult to pinpoint what precisely makes them 'Central European'. Even though the Visegrád Four (Poland, Hungary, Czechia, Slovakia) banded together to harmonize their joint accession to European institutions, their geopolitical visions have since diverged considerably, as have their visions of 'Central Europe'.

For Poles, it is not Czechs, Slovaks or Hungarians that play a central role in their historical or geopolitical thinking, but the territories of the former Polish-Lithuanian Commonwealth, what Halecki dubbed 'Jagiellonian' Europe: Poland, Lithuania, Ukraine, and Belarus.[9] These countries share little to no history with Hungary beyond the communist period. The Central Europe of post-communist Hungarians is not Jagiellonian, but Danubian. After the Russian invasion of Ukraine in 2022, Poland embraced Ukraine's plight as synonymous with its own historical struggle against Russian domination, while Hungary treated it as a far-off conflict Hungarians had nothing to do with.

Václav Havel's great political rival and eventual successor as Czech president—the liberal-conservative Václav Klaus—meanwhile dismissed Central Europe altogether, asserting that Czechia was simply part of the West.[10] This came off the back of Czechoslovakia's dissolution in 1992—the so-called Velvet Divorce—after which Slovakia was dominated by the populist strongman Vladimír Mečiar, whose style of rule was so disliked by Western leaders that Slovakia's very 'return to Europe' came under question. No matter, Mečiar commented: 'if they don't want us in the West, we shall turn East [to Russia]'.[11]

The situations of Slovenia and Croatia differ still further. As Yugoslavia disintegrated in the early 1990s, both were forced to fight wars of independence. In the former case it lasted just ten days, with Slovenia making a rapid 'return to Europe' akin to the Visegrád countries. In 2000 its parliament thus proudly declared that Slovenia 'is a Central European country' whose foreign policy was focused on rebuilding cultural, economic and political ties with its fellow countries in the region. In practice the most important of these was not a post-communist country at all, but Austria.[12]

Croatia had no such celebration of Central European status. In 2013 it became the latest (as of 2025) post-communist country to enter the European Union. Its 'return to Europe' was the most arduous of all, forced to fight a four-year-long war that devastated much of the country in order to win its independence from what its nationalist President Franjo Tuđman called 'the Balkan darkness of the so-called Yugoslavia'. Indeed, Croatia seemed to care less about entering Central Europe than it did about escaping the Balkans. Tuđman said in his state of the union address in 1997 that 'by its civilization and culture, Croatia belongs to the Central European and Mediterranean circles of Europe', the 'political links with the Balkans between 1918 and 1990' representing nothing but a 'short episode in Croatian history'.[13]

What emerged from the ruins of communist Eastern Europe was not a suppressed cosmopolitan Central Europe, but a series of nation-states forged in the upheavals of the early twentieth century that had destroyed that very same Central European world. It is only natural that since 1989 each of these nation-states has interpreted that legacy in their own way, trying to come to terms with their own histories and places in a new world not as 'Central Europeans', but as Poles, Hungarians, Czechs, Slovaks, Slovenes, Croats.

Decades on from the fall of the Berlin Wall, they do once again share a common civilization. But it is one defined by the Cold War political inheritance of the United States, by the rise of a culture of English literacy, and by integration into a generalized 'West' and its institutional structures. It is certainly not, as it once was, defined by the disparate feudal inheritance of the House of Habsburg, a culture of German literacy, and a conscious position between an Anglo-French West and a Russo-Slavic East.

Few if any of those who dreamt of their country's rightful place in Central Europe during the Cold War wanted a return to that Habsburg-German world of old. Indeed, there could be no return to it because it had been so thoroughly obliterated over the course of the first half of the twentieth century. The revolutions of 1989 were akin to those of 1918: a shuffling of power groups rather than a sudden wholesale break with the immediate past. By all accounts, post-communist European countries have inherited far more of their present-day social, political, cultural, and economic heritage from their Eastern European past than their distant Central European past. The peoples' republics created through the levelling of past social and national divisions are still with us, democratized and integrated into the 'West' as they may be.

For some of the most ardent anti-communists, 1989 thus felt like a false revolution. 'If the old communists lived long enough to see the world of today', wrote the conservative idealogue Ryszard Legutko in *The Demon in Democracy*, 'they would be devastated by the contrast between how little they themselves had managed to achieve in their antireligious war and how successful the liberal democrats have been'. For Legutko, liberalism and communism were both products of modernity, which needed to be cast away for the true national revolution to succeed. Legutko is one of the leading ideologists of the right-wing Polish Law and Justice party, which polarized Poland when it ruled from 2015 to 2023 with its uncompromising conservative policies.[14] This anti-liberal revolt against the 'incomplete' revolutions of 1989 went further in Poland than anywhere except Hungary, where Viktor Orbán transformed the dissident Fidesz party into a hegemonic national conservative party that upholds a system of 'illiberal democracy'.

Both parties promise a rejection of the post-1989 neo-liberal spirit of 'no alternatives'. To the idea of 'end of history', they reply that history is as important as ever. Against the primacy of the individual, they promote the national collective. And against the internationalist institutions that define the 'global West' they assert the rights of the sovereign state. Many commentators once saw this right-wing movement as a peculiar Central European condition: a revival of 1920s national conservatism that had been frozen by the long years of communist rule. But the seemingly inexorable rise of right-wing and far-right parties across Europe in the early 2020s made Hungary and Poland less the exceptions to the rule than the precursors to wider European developments. Orbán's Hungary, Law and Justice's Poland—they are not movements rooted in a distant Central European past, but ones that emerged in the context of Eastern European post-communist transition and blossomed as their countries became fully integrated into 'Western civilization' in its modern form. 'Twenty-seven years ago, here in Central Europe we believed that Europe was our future', announced Orbán in a 2017 speech, but 'today we feel that we are the future of Europe'.[15]

* * *

With the benefit of hindsight, it is easy to forget the Central Europe debates of the 1980s, and to dismiss the idea of Central Europe as the literary obsession of a few men and women trampled by the march of history. But that would perhaps be to ignore the profundity of what the 'return to Europe' meant for the countries that successfully completed it, and to ignore why the idea of Central Europe was embraced with such enthusiasm in the first place.

The course of the Lisbon Conference was a case in point. In 1988, writers from both sides of the iron curtain came together in an unprecedented literary gathering. On 7 May all twenty-eight gathered around a table for the first of two days of discussions on the 'literature of Central and Eastern Europe'. They had all prepared their own papers to read but the moderator—Michael Scammell—announced that these would be jettisoned in favour of a more natural dialogue. He underestimated how difficult communication could be between writers from two entirely different worlds.

After exchanges between Polish, Hungarian, Serbian, and Slovene writers opened the proceedings, the Russian writer Tatiana Tolstaya—a distant descendent of Leo Tolstoy, on her first trip outside of the Soviet Union—commented with incredulity at the 'stubbornness with which everybody talks about Central Europe', as if it were some 'special place which somehow unifies you' and as if 'it is bad to be an Eastern European, that it is somehow worse than being a Western European'.

Tolstaya, Joseph Brodsky and other Russian writers set forth their reasoning for why Central Europe did not exist, laying bare their own incredulity at the thought that it even could exist. The Russians had no trouble in referring to Poles, Hungarians, Czechs, Yugoslavs, and so on as Eastern Europeans, but performed all manner of mental gymnastics to avoid putting them together into a single basket as Central Europeans. Their confused and often bizarrely abstract comments on a concept that everyone else present understood perfectly well reeked to an indignant Danilo Kiš of a 'pedagogical tone' that made him 'feel like a small child being taught elementary lessons'. Accusations of 'imperialist' and 'colonial' thinking were targeted at the Russian authors, further aggravating the situation. 'I am afraid that there is a certain taboo in Russian literature' Czesław Miłosz concluded, 'and this taboo is empire'.[16]

Four years later, Rutgers University in New Jersey hosted a sequel to the Lisbon Conference. Many of the original attendees were there, including Brodsky, Tolstaya and Miłosz. But gone was the sense of utopian optimism that had once been synonymous with Central Europe, overshadowed by a black cloud of national conflict in the former Yugoslavia and the difficult realities of post-communist transition. Brodsky was cold towards the only Ukrainian writer there, who he had met before, telling her: 'I don't remember you. Ukraine—where is this?' Unbeknownst to her, he had written a chauvinistic anti-Ukrainian poem after the country declared its independence in August 1991, expressing a not-uncommon Russian view of Ukrainians as provincial schismatics from a greater Russian cultural empire. Of the other former

Soviet satellites, which he refused to call Central European, Brodsky told Miłosz at Rutgers that 'the choices they have made' will turn them into 'client states of Germany'.[17]

Tolstaya would be even more dismissive of both Ukraine and the 'Eastern Europeans' two decades later in an interview on Russian TV. In her frank reminiscences of what she called the 'dispute of the Slavs among themselves', she ridiculed Central European writers as nothing more than metaphorical 'toddlers' being put into a 'special, intermediate kindergarten group' by the West. Their performance was embarrassing, in stark contrast to Brodsky, who made 'an amazing appearance, because the whole great Russian culture stood behind him, and he carried it like a big flag'.[18] The decades since 1989 seem to have confirmed what the Central European writers at Lisbon suspected: Russians were struggling to face their imperial past. Brodsky and Tolstaya's refusal to countenance the rejection of Eastern Europe as a sphere of Russian influence reflected deep uncertainty within Russia of its national identity and place in the world. Ukraine's quest for sovereignty only exacerbated this.

Ukrainians were on the margin of the margin of historical Central Europe in Habsburg-ruled Galicia, Bukovina, and Transcarpathia. Indeed, those 'Ruthenians' who lived there were on the margins of their own national story. Most of Ukraine in its 1991 borders was historically a part of the Russian Empire and the Polish-Lithuanian Commonwealth before it, not Central Europe. What shaped modern Ukrainian history from the eighteenth to twentieth centuries was by and large not German-speaking cities, Habsburg rule, and a position between East and West. It was rather the struggle between Polish and Russian elites for hegemony over Ukraine, the dominance of their languages in its urban centres, and its firm envelopment in the vast Eurasian empire ruled from Moscow.

In 2021 Russian President Vladimir Putin penned an essay arguing that Ukraine was rightfully part of a single greater Russian whole and its separation could only be evidence of a nefarious 'anti-Russia' ideological project invented by Austrians and Poles to destroy Russia. His minister of defence made it obligatory reading for Russian officers.[19] This came seven years after Putin had taken advantage of a crisis of legitimacy in Ukraine to annex the Crimean Peninsula and provoke separatist uprisings in Russian-speaking parts of the country, bolstered by direct Russian intervention. In February 2022 he took this a step further. Russian troops, missiles and tanks poured over the border as Putin launched the largest war in Europe since the Second World War.

THE RETURN OF CENTRAL EUROPE?

For those who remembered the Soviet interventions in Czechoslovakia and Hungary and the debates about Central Europe that they eventually led to, the parallels were uncanny. When Milan Kundera passed away in 2023—after authorizing the publication of his 'The Tragedy of Central Europe' in book-length format—a flood of obituaries in French, German and English praised the prescience of his words, deploying phrases like Ukraine's 'Kunderian problem' and its 'Kunderian war'. Kundera had rejected the notion that there was some 'Slavic soul' that made Eastern Europe a natural whole, a civilization apart from the West. Ukrainians were doing the very same as they attempted their own 'return to Europe'. Henry Kissinger opined in 2022 that 'Ukraine has become a major state in Central Europe for the first time in modern history'.[20] The Central Europe once defined by Habsburgs, by the dominance of German high culture, and by a position *between* West and East, has long passed into history. But the idea of Central Europe lives on.

NOTES

INTRODUCTION

1. 'The Lisbon Conference on Literature'; Kirschbaum, 'The Verbatim Drama'.
2. 'Dmytro Kuleba: Ukraine is back in Central Europe', *Ministry of Foreign Affairs of Ukraine* (20 September 2021), https://mfa.gov.ua/en/news/dmytro-kuleba-ukraine-back-central-europe (last accessed 23/03/25); Sinnhuber, 'Central Europe'.
3. Rob Cameron, 'Central or Eastern? Schwarzenberg, Lavrov tussle over map of Europe', Radio Prague International, 12 February 2009, https://english.radio.cz/central-or-eastern-schwarzenberg-lavrov-tussle-over-map-europe-8587521 (last accessed 23/03/25).
4. Kundra, *Putinovi agenti*, 34–5.
5. Kundera, 'The Tragedy of Central Europe'.
6. Miller, 'Тема Центральной Европы', 23–5.
7. Miłosz, 'Central European Attitudes', in Schöpflin and Wood eds., *In Search of Central Europe*, 122.
8. Schöpflin and Wood eds., *In Search of Central Europe*; Graubard ed., *Eastern Europe … Central Europe … Europe*; Burmeister et al. ed., *Mitteleuropa. Traum oder Trauma?*; Papcke and Weidenfeld eds., *Traumland Mitteleuropa?*; Trávníček ed., *V kleštích dějin*; Vodopivec ed., *Srednja Evropa*.
9. All translations are my own unless otherwise stated. Hanák, 'Schöpferisch Kraft', in Burmeister et al. eds., *Mitteleuropa*, 20.
10. Fukuyama, 'The End of History?', 4.
11. Wolff, *Inventing Eastern Europe*, 15.
12. Kundera, *A Kidnapped West*.
13. A full transcript of the speech can be found at the website of the French Embassy in the US: https://franceintheus.org/spip.php?article11311 (last accessed 23/03/25).
14. For a critique: Ther, 'Beyond the Nation'.
15. Suny, 'History and the Making of Nations', 569–88.
16. See for example Connelly, *From Peoples into Nations*, 241–65.
17. An issue raised in Sheehan, 'What is German History?' and tackled head on in Sheehan, *German History 1770–1866*.
18. See for example contributions by Frank, Suppanz, Hackmann, Stobiecki, Ludanyi, and Okey in Frank and Hadler eds., *Disputed Territories and Shared Pasts* and Heiss, Klimó, Kolář, and Kováč in Berger and Lorenz eds., *The Contested Nation*.
19. Le Rider, *La Mitteleuropa*, 3–5; Burmeister et al. ed., *Mitteleuropa. Traum oder Trauma?*, 7–10.

1. BEFORE CENTRAL EUROPE

1. Schulin, *Vollständiges Diarium*, 277; Hommel, *Briefe*, 113–116.
2. Goethe, *Dichtung und Wahrheit*, 30–31.
3. Metternich, *Aus Metternich's nachgelassenen Papieren*, Vol. 1, 11.
4. Glatthorn, 'The Imperial Coronation of Leopold II and Mozart', 90; Wolff, *Mozart at the Gateway*, 47–50.
5. Schulin, *Vollständiges Diarium*, 280.
6. Hommel, *Briefe*, 123.
7. Schulin, *Vollständiges Diarium*, 285; Hommel, *Briefe*, 123.
8. Hommel, *Briefe*, 125; 106.
9. Ibid., 3.
10. Ibid., 17–19; 26–39.
11. Ibid., 89–98; 64–86.
12. Rudolph, 'Meaningless Spectacles?' in Gelder ed. *More Than Mere*, 75.
13. Hommel, *Briefe*, 165.
14. Glatthorn, 'The Theatre of Politics and the Politics of Theatre', 192–206.
15. Metternich, *Aus Metternich's nachgelassenen Papieren*, Vol. 1, 11.
16. Siemann, *Metternich*, 68–9.
17. Mikolletzky, 'Leopold II', in Schindling and Ziegler eds., *Die Kaiser*, 277.
18. Ibid., 281–2; Wandruszka, *Leopold II*, Vol. II, 206–11.
19. Wandruszka, *Leopold II*, Vol. II, 249–52.
20. Ibid., 252–4.
21. Godsey, 'Pageantry', in Gelder ed., *More than Mere*, 253–4.
22. Ibid., 254–6.
23. O'Reilly, 'Lost Chances of the House of Habsburg'; Stollberg-Rilinger, *Maria Theresa*, 24–5; Rady, *The Habsburgs*, 175.
24. Anderson, *The War of the Austrian Succession*, 83–4.
25. Blanning, *Frederick*, 119.
26. Ibid., 185.
27. Stollberg-Rilinger, *Maria Theresa*, 552–62.
28. Friedrich, *The Other Prussia*, 164–8; Plokhy, *The Gates of Europe*, 143–5.
29. Szakaly, 'Pragmatism triumphant', in Szijártó, Blockmans, and Kontler eds., *Parliamentarism*, 291.
30. Schulin, *Vollständiges Diarium*, 334.
31. Renna, 'The Holy Roman Empire'.
32. Kaldellis, *Romanland*, 3–37.
33. Moser, *Von Deutschland*, 550.
34. Wilson, *The Holy Roman Empire*, 174.
35. Hardy, 'Were there', in Damen and Overlaet eds., *Constructing*, 39–40.
36. Sheehan, *German History*, 25.
37. Godsey Jr., *Nobles and Nation*, 80–91; Stollberg-Rilinger, *The Holy Roman Empire*, 25–6.
38. Heiss, *The History of the Empire*; Vayrac, *L'etat present de l'Empire*.
39. Stollberg-Rilinger, *Maria Theresa*, 40–1.
40. Schulin, *Vollständiges Diarium*, 280.

41. Lukowski, *The European Nobility*, 13.
42. Vermes, *Hungarian Culture and Politics*, 55–72.
43. Szelényi, *The Failure of the Central European Bourgeoisie*, 86.
44. Varga, *A Hungarian Quo Vadis*, 38.
45. Almási and Šubarić, 'Introduction', in Almási and Šubarić eds., *Latin at the Crossroads*, 1.
46. Miskolczy, '*Hungarus* Consciousness', in ibid., 82.
47. Balázs, *Hungary and the Habsburgs*, 127; Szelényi, *The Failure*, 74–86.
48. Schauff, *Die Feyerlichkeiten*, 108–120.
49. Ibid., 43–55; Löschenkohl, *Beschreibung*, ch. 1 and 2.
50. Schauff, *Die Feyerlichkeiten*, 60–4.
51. Löschenkohl, *Beschreibung*, ch. 3.
52. Schauff, *Die Feyerlichkeiten*, 72–91.
53. Agnew, 'Ambiguities', 8–9.
54. Krueger, *Czech, German, and Noble*, 76–9; Hroch, *Na prahu*, 18–22.
55. Debrois, *Urkunde*, 44–66; *Krönungsbegebenheiten Kaisers Leopold II.*, 42–3; 61–2.

2. THE ENLIGHTENMENT CHALLENGE

1. Debrois, *Urkunde*, 165–6.
2. Palacký, *Joseph Dobrowsky's*, 6–8; Brandl, *Život*, 259.
3. Kleinschnitzová, 'Josefa Dobrovského'.
4. Török, *Exploring*, 54.
5. Whaley, 'The Protestant Enlightenment in Germany', in Porter and Teich eds., *The Enlightenment*, 107.
6. Ibid.
7. Gossman, *Medievalism*, viii.
8. Burke, *Languages and Communities*, 18.
9. Dülmen, *The Society of the Enlightenment*, 14–17.
10. Blanning, *The Culture of Power*, 49–50.
11. Burke, *Languages and Communities*, 19.
12. Blackall, *The Emergence of German as a Literary Language*, 3.
13. Ibid., 32–3.
14. Ibid., 33–48.
15. Blanning, *Reform and Revolution*, 11–12.
16. Blanning, *The Culture of Power*, 200; Zande, 'Prussia and the Enlightenment', in Dwyer ed., *The Rise of Prussia*, 97; Cerman, 'The Enlightenment in Bohemia', in Cerman et al. eds., *The Enlightenment in Bohemia*, 24.
17. Blackall, *The Emergence*, 47.
18. Blitz, *Aus Liebe zum Vaterland*, 42–6; Kohn, *The Idea of Nationalism*, 144–6; Sheehan, *German History*, 4; Wilson, *The Holy*, 255–92.
19. Szelenyi, 'From minority to Übermensch', 216–32; Geiger, 'Njemci u Hrvatskoj', 320–1.
20. Polenz, *Deutsche Sprachgeschichte*. Vol. III, 454; Elmentaler, 'Hochdeutsch und Platt', in Elmentaler ed., *Deutsch und seine Nachbarn*, 31–9.
21. Blanning, *Frederick*, 118–19.

22. Ibid., 299–301.
23. Greenfeld, *Nationalism*, 310; Zande, 'Prussia and the Enlightenment', in Dwyer ed., *The Rise of Prussia*, 92–6; Carsten, *Geschichte der preußischen Junker*, 40–51.
24. Stollberg-Rilinger, *Maria Theresa*, 123–4; 191–250.
25. Scott, 'Reform in the Habsburg Monarchy', in Scott ed., *Enlightened Absolutism*, 152–4; 182.
26. Khavanova, 'Maria Theresa's Monarchy', in. Szijártó et al. eds., *Parliamentarism*, 184.
27. Khavanova, 'Multilingualism versus proficiency', in Rjéoutski and Frijhoff eds., *Language Choice*, 98–9.
28. Blitz, *Aus Liebe zum Vaterland*.
29. Whaley, *Germany and the Holy Roman Empire*, 411.
30. Piirimäe, 'Thomas Abbt's Vom Tode Fur Das Vaterland'; Redekop, 'Thomas Abbt', 90.
31. Stollberg-Rilinger, *Maria Theresa*, 156–61.
32. Wiesinger, 'Die sprachlichen Verhältnisse', in Gardt et al. eds., *Sprachgeschichte*, 323–6.
33. Brnardić, *Svijet Baltazara Adama Krčelića*, 31.
34. Scott, 'Reform', in Scott ed., *Enlightened Absolutism*, 173; Szabo, *Kaunitz*, 22–31.
35. Scott, 'Reform', in Scott ed., *Enlightened Absolutism*, 164–6; Cerman, 'The Enlightenment universities', in Cerman et al. eds., *The Enlightenment in Bohemia*, 59–60.
36. Kann, *A Study in Austrian*, 146–9.
37. Balázs, *Hungary and the Habsburgs*, 64; Brnardić, 'The Enlightenment Choice of Latin', in Almási and Šubarić eds., *Latin at the Crossroads*, 134; Khavanova, 'Multilingualism versus proficiency', in Rjéoutski and Frijhoff eds., *Language Choice*, 92.
38. Khavanova, 'Joseph von Sonnenfels's Courses', 55–69; Khavanova, 'Multilingualism versus proficiency', in Rjéoutski and Frijhoff eds., *Language Choice*, 97; Trencsényi et al. eds., *History of Modern Political Thought in East Central Europe, Volume I*, 58.
39. Schulze, *The Course*, 46.
40. Šimeček, *Geschichte des Buchhandels*, 35.
41. Wiesinger, 'Johann Siegmund Valentin Popowitsch', 65; Obad, *Roda Roda*, 17–18; Nübler, 'Tschechische und deutsche Gelehrte', in Koschmal et al. eds., *Deutsche*, 70–1.
42. Barany, 'Hoping Against Hope', 336; Tibensky, 'Matthias Bel 1684–1749', in Winter and Jarosch eds., *Wegbereiter*, 47; Winter, *Halle als Ausgangpunkt*, 1–29; 47–9.
43. Ujvári, 'Abriss der deutschsprachigen', 66; Meier, 'Deutschsprachige Literatur', 236; Lengyel and Tüskés eds., *Learned Societies*, 30.
44. Seidler, 'The Long Road of Hungarian', in Almási and Šubarić eds., *Latin at the Crossroads*.
45. While there was a literary journal published before it in 1784, only one edition was produced: Ujvári, 'Abriss der deutschsprachigen', 70.
46. Živković, 'Publicistika', 62–5.
47. Freifeld, 'The De-Germanization', in Bullivant et al. eds., *Germany and Eastern Europe*, 148–155.
48. Rapant, *K počiatkom*, Vol. 1, 6–13.
49. Šubarić, 'From the Aftermath of 1784', in Almási and Šubarić eds., *Latin at the Crossroads*, 194.

50. Khavanova, *Нация, отечество, патриотизм*, 118–19.
51. Miskolczy, 'Hungarus Consciousness', in Almási and Šubarić eds., *Latin at the Crossroads*, 72–3.
52. Quoted in Almási and Šubarić, 'The new discourses of nation (Part 1)', 903.
53. Khavanova, *Нация, отечество, патриотизм*, 115.
54. Seidler, 'The Long Road', in Almási and Šubarić eds., *Latin at the Crossroads*, 158; Vermes, *Hungarian Culture and Politics*, 142.
55. See Seidler and Seidler eds., *Das Zeitschriftwesen im Donauraum*.
56. Almási and Šubarić, 'Introduction', in Almási and Šubarić eds., *Latin at the Crossroads*, 4–6.
57. Fried, 'Mehrsprachigkeit', in Dóbék et al. eds., *Media and Literature*, 26.
58. Khavanova, 'Multilingualism versus proficiency', in Rjéoutski and Frijhoff eds., *Language Choice*, 105.
59. Evans, 'The politics of language', in Scott and Simms eds., *Cultures of Power*, 213–14.
60. Sundhaußen, *Der Einfluß der Herderischen Ideen*, 77–8; Kamusella, *The Politics of Language*, 435–6.
61. Evans, *Austria, Hungary, and the Habsburgs*, 179–82; Péter, *Hungary's Long Nineteenth Century*, 5.
62. Rapant, *K počiatkom*, Vol. II, 53–74.
63. Krueger, *Czech, German, and Noble*, 214.
64. Quoted in Agnew, *Origins of the Czech National Renaissance*, 51.
65. Šołta, 'The Sorbs', in Kasper ed., *Language and Culture*, 31.
66. Tolstoy, *Путешествие*, 133; 115.
67. Wollman, 'Kdo', 348–61.
68. Kopitar, *Grammatik*, III–IV.
69. Šesták, 'Der tschechische Austroslavismus', in Moritsch ed., *Der Austroslavismus*, 25; Trencsényi et al., *Negotiating Modernity*, 58; Greenfeld, *Nationalism*, 296–300.
70. Hösler, *Von Krain*, 98.
71. Strsoglavec, 'Anton Tomaž Linhart', 325.
72. Ibid., 330; Merchiers, *Cultural Nationalism*, 25–38.
73. Hassel, *Statistischer Umriss*, 23; Stone, *Slav Outposts*, 223.
74. Lencek, 'Note', 93–7.
75. Pohrt, 'Karl Gottlob von Anton', 716–17.
76. Ibid., 721.
77. Blanning, *The Culture of Power*, 249.
78. Blackall, *The Emergence of German*, 495.
79. Iggers, *The German Conception of History*, 37.
80. Blackall, *The Emergence of German*, 495; Piirimäe, *Herder*, 27.
81. Blanning, *The Culture of Power*, 253.

3. FINIS ROMAE

1. Wandruszka, *Leopold II*, Vol. II, 382.
2. Palacký ed., *Leben*, 35.
3. Wandruszka, *Leopold II*, Vol. II, 289.
4. Vierhaus, *Deutschland im 18. Jahrhundert*, 202–215.

5. Gooch, *Germany*, 74–5.
6. Hommel, *Briefe*, 32–3.
7. Ziegler, 'Franz', in Schindling and Ziegler eds., *Die Kaiser*, 289–93.
8. Kusber, 'Wahrnehmungen, in Roll and Schnettger eds., *Epochenjahr 1806?*, 133.
9. Wilson, 'Bolstering', 723–4.
10. Quaasdorf, *Kursachsen*, 366.
11. Leo, *Aus meiner Jugendzeit*, 22–3
12. Wilson, 'Bolstering, 731–5.
13. Braun, 'Das Reich', in Roll ed., *Epochenjahr 1806?*, 7–8.
14. Whaley, *Germany*, 644.
15. Burgdorf, 'Once', in Evans and Wilson eds., *The Holy Roman Empire*, 55–61.
16. Quaasdorf, *Kursachsen*, 369.
17. Burgdorf, 'Das Vahlkampfsche Schweigen', in North and Riemer eds., *Das Ende des Alten Reiches*, 172–205; Burgdorf, *Ein Weltbild*, 172–225; Coy, 'Introduction', in Coy, Marschke, and Sabean eds., *The Holy Roman Empire*, 1–7; Wilson, *The Holy Roman Empire*, 288; Burgdorf, 'Once', in Evans and Wilson eds., *The Holy Roman Empire*, 56.
18. Burgdorf, 'Once', in Evans and Wilson eds., *The Holy Roman Empire*, 52.
19. Hassel, *Statistischer Umriss*, III–IV.
20. Scattered mentions of '*Mitteleuropa*' are observable in German texts prior to Hassel, but they are rare, isolated, and unexamined. See Johann Georg Hager, *Geographischer Büchersaal*, Vol. 3, Chemnitz (1778), 220; *Göttingische Anzeigen von gelehrten Sachen*, Vol. 1, Göttingen (1793), 73–80; Julius August Remer, *Versuch einer Geschichte der französischen Constitution*, Helmstedt (1795), 88.
21. Melton, *The Rise of the Public*, 105–106.
22. 'Hassel: Johann Georg Heinrich H.', in *Allgemeine Deutsche Biographie*, Vol. 10, 760.
23. Hassel, *Statistischer Umriss*, IV.
24. Ibid., V.
25. *Oberdeutsche Allgemeine Literaturzeitung im Jahre 1806*, 1133–6.
26. Török, *The Science of State Power*, 34–8; 128–9.
27. Curiously, 'Mitteleuropa' disappeared from the second edition three years later. Zeune, *Gea. Versuch einer wissenschaftlichen Erdbeschreibung*, 32.
28. Butter, *Die unerlaßlichen Bedingungen*, 100; *Vaterländische Blätter*, 107.
29. *The British Press*, 26 November 1805, 2; *Globe*, 26 November 1805, 2; *The Literary Panorama*, Vol. I (1807), 309–311; *The Oxford Review; Or Literary Censor*, Vol. I (1807), 114–15.
30. As late as the First World War Woodrow Wilson's *Inquiry* used the terms 'Central Europe', '*Mittel-Europa*', and 'Mid-Europe' interchangeably, Dhand, *The Idea of Central Europe*, 104.
31. Ibid., 92–3.
32. Niedzzwiedzz, 'How did Virgil…?', in Siedina ed., *Latinitas*, 34–7.
33. Blanning, *The Pursuit of Glory*, 116.
34. Vermeulen, *Before Boas*, 274.
35. Milton, *A Brief History of Moscovia*, 32.
36. Delanty, *Inventing Europe: Idea, Identity, Reality*, 28.

37. Ibid., 27.
38. Roller, *Ancient Geography*.
39. Fisch, 'Zivilisation, Kultur', 679–724.
40. The classic account of this transformation is given in Wolff, *Inventing Eastern Europe*. For a critique see Schmale, 'Das östliche Europa', in Augustynowicz and Pufelska eds., *Konstruirte (Fremd-?)Bilder*.
41. Sheehan, *German History*, 259–61.
42. Ibid., 261–74.
43. Clark, *Iron Kingdom*, 320–44.
44. Vierhaus, 'Bildung'; Kohn, 'The Paradox of Fichte's Nationalism', 326.
45. Iggers, *The German Conception*, 47–60; Sorkin, 'Wilhelm von Humboldt'.
46. Levinger, *Enlightened Nationalism*, 106.
47. Hagemann, 'Francophobia and Patriotism', 412–20.
48. Rowe, *From Reich to State*, 234–45.
49. Bahr, 'Geothe's Concept of Volk', in Vaszonyi ed., *Searching for Common Ground*, 136–7.
50. Siemann, *Metternich*, 251.
51. Carl, 'Der Mythos des Befreiungskrieges', in Langewiesche ed., *Föderative Nation*, 81.
52. Siemann, *Metternich*, 438–40.
53. Kraehe, *Metternich's German Policy*, Vol II, 5.
54. Ziegler, 'Franz', in Schindling and Ziegler eds., *Die Kaiser*, 318–19.
55. Wilson, *The Holy Roman Empire*, 665; Kraus, *Das Ende des alten Deutschland*, 88–90.
56. Vushko, *The Politics*, 139.

4. THE AGE OF COSMOPOLITANISM

1. Murko, *Deutsche Einflüsse*, 305; 334–5.
2. Siemann, *Metternich*.
3. Ibid., 129–31.
4. *Taschenausgabe der österreichischen Gesetze*, 10–11.
5. Clark, *Iron Kingdom*, 458–9.
6. Ibid., 427.
7. Green, *Fatherlands*, 22.
8. Osterkamp, *Vielfalt ordnen*, 218–19; Barclay, *Frederick William*, 50.
9. Ringer, 'Bildung'.
10. Sorkin, *The Transformation*, 15–36; Hertz, *How Jews Became Germans*.
11. Meinecke, *Cosmopolitanism and the National State*, 29.
12. Siemann, *Metternich*, 64–6; Baár, *Historians and Nationalism*, 58.
13. Levinger, *Enlightened Nationalism*, 112.
14. Düding, 'The Nineteenth-Century German Nationalist Movement', in Schulze ed., *Nation-Building*, 32.
15. Press, 'False Fire'.
16. Williamson, 'What Killed'.
17. Fillafer, *Aufklärung habsburgisch*, 54.
18. Echternkamp, *Der Aufstieg des deutschen Nationalismus*, 389–95; Green, *Fatherlands*, 100–103.

19. Baár, *Historians and Nationalism*, 48–50; Vick, *Defining Germany*, 48–57.
20. Bismarck, *Gedanken und Errinerungen*, 1.
21. Kohlrausch, *Die Teutsche Geschichte*, 1–3.
22. Echternkamp, *Der Aufstieg des deutschen Nationalismus*, 595.
23. Godsey Jr., *Nobles and Nation in Central Europe*, 61.
24. Ibid., 48–71.
25. Green, *Fatherlands*, pp. 103–109; Heinzen, *Making Prussians*, 122–37.
26. Sked, 'The Nationality Problem in the Habsburg Monarchy', in Moggach and Jones eds., *The 1848 Revolutions*, 324–31.
27. Zacek, *Palacký*, 19.
28. Ibid., 56.
29. Meyer, 'Das konstitutionelle Deutschland und der Westen', in Reinalter ed., *Die Anfänge des Liberalismus*, 193–9; Schröder, 'Between East and West?' in Bavaj and Steber eds., *Germany and 'the West'*, 147.
30. Kamusella, *The Politics of Language and Nationalism*, 383.
31. Wolff, *The Idea of Galicia*, 81–9; Vushko, *The Politics*, 101–103.
32. Kamusella, *The Politics of Language and Nationalism*, 381.
33. Liulevicius, *The German Myth of the East*, 73.
34. Echternkamp, *Der Aufstieg des deutschen Nationalismus*, 414–15.
35. Düding, 'The Nineteenth-Century German Nationalist Movement', in Schulze ed., *Nation-Building*, 34–5.
36. Kałążny, 'Hambach', in Hahn and Traba eds., *Deutsch-Polnische*, Vol. 2, 111–121.
37. Liulevicius, *The German Myth of the East*, 74.
38. Pásztorová, *Metternich*, 33–8.
39. Deak, *Forging*, 38–60.
40. Murko, *Deutsche Einflüsse*, 303–304; 316–17.
41. Ibid., 301.
42. Ibid., 355.
43. Orton, 'Did the Slavs Speak German', 515.
44. He in fact caveats with the same two words twice in the same lecture: Schlegel, *Geschichte der alten und neuen Literatur*, 259; 270.
45. Ibid., 271.
46. Hösler, *Von Krain zu Slowenien*, 86.
47. Maxwell, 'Latin as the Panslavonic Language, 1790–1848', in Almási and Šubarić eds., *Latin at the Crossroads*, 245–6.
48. Ibid., 246.
49. Zajc, *Gdje slovensko prestaje*, 28–34.
50. Murko, *Deutsche Einflüsse*, 128–47.
51. Though in the Czech he calls this 'Serbian'. Kollar, *Ueber die literarische Wechselseitigkeit*, 11.
52. Ibid., 9.
53. Ibid.
54. Ibid., 6–11.
55. Sundhaußen, *Der Einfluß Herderschen Ideen*, 127–8.

56. Kropej, 'The Cooperation of Grimm Brothers', 224.
57. Banac, *Nacionalno pitanje*, 86.
58. Zajc, *Gdje slovensko prestaje*, 49.
59. Ibid., 50.
60. Novak, *Višejezičnost i kolektivni identiteti iliraca*, 313–15; 337–40.
61. Banac, *Nacionalno pitanje*, 76–83.
62. Zajc, *Gdje slovensko prestaje*, 72.
63. Scherber, 'Von der Zweisprachigkeit', in Bernik and Lauer eds., *Die Grundlagen*, 163–4.

5. REFORM AND REVOLT

1. Paget, *Hungary*, Vol. II, vii.
2. Ibid., 231–2.
3. Barany, *Stephen*, 11–57.
4. Ibid., 57–101.
5. Ibid., 114–134.
6. Freifeld, 'The De-Germanization', in Bullivant et al. eds., *Germany and Eastern Europe*, 148; Vermes, *Hungarian Culture and Politics*, 210–212.
7. Maxwell, 'Budapest and Thessaloniki'.
8. Sundhaußen, *Der Einfluß Herderschen Ideen*, 87.
9. Barany, *Stephen*, 169.
10. Ibid., 203–43.
11. Ibid., 295–6.
12. Vermes, *Hungarian Culture and Politics*, 259.
13. Péter, *Hungary's Long Nineteenth Century*, 188–202.
14. Vermes, *Hungarian Culture and Politics*, 261–72; Barany, *Stephen*, 305–12.
15. Pajkossy, 'Gefangenschaft', in Fazekas et al. eds., *Széchenyi*, 99–106.
16. Ibid., 103.
17. Barany, *Stephen*, 375–81.
18. 'Politische Rückblicke', *Die Grenzboten*, Vol. 3, No. 1 (1844), 3–5.
19. Šedivý, 'The Austrian Empire, German Nationalism', 25.
20. Barlcay, *Frederick William*, 189.
21. Šedivý, 'The Austrian Empire, German Nationalism', 31–5.
22. Clark, *Revolutionary Spring*, 150.
23. Clark, *Iron Kingdom*, 440–41.
24. Barclay, *Frederick William*, 24–50.
25. Clark, *Iron Kingdom*, 441–3.
26. Jones, *Karl Marx*, 55–121.
27. Loewenheim, 'German Liberalism', in Brock and Skilling eds., *The Czech*.
28. Clark, *Iron Kingdom*, 450–8; Barclay, *Frederick William*, 103–105.
29. Hodenberg, 'Weaving Survival'.
30. Siclova, '1848', in Moggach and Jones eds., *The 1848*, 257–62; Moggach 'German Republicans', in ibid.
31. Gogol, *Toward a Dialectic*, 47.

32. Andrian-Werburg, *Oesterreich und dessen Zukunft*, 7; 2.
33. Ibid., 8.
34. Petre, 'Kopitar und Herder', in Krauss et al. ed., *Slawisch-deutsche Wechselbeziehungen*, 569; Kollar, *Ueber die literarische Wechselseitigkeit*, 8–9.
35. Miskolczy, '*Hungarus* Consciousness'.
36. Maxwell, *Everyday Nationalism*, 21–9; Thun, *Die Stellung der Slowaken in Ungarn*, 7; 27–8.
37. Boia, *History and Myth*, 37.
38. Adler, 'Nation and Nationalism'.
39. Sikirić-Assouline, *U obranu hrvastkih municipalnih prava*, 28.
40. Roksandić, 'Controversies on German Cultural Orientation', in Ingrao and Szabo eds., *The Germans and the East*, 145.
41. Ibid.
42. Varga, *A Hungarian Quo Vadis*, 118; 123; 126.
43. Wolff, *Inventing Eastern Europe*, 314–15.
44. Schuselka, *Ist Oesterreich deutsch*, 18; 38–50.
45. Pfizer, *Das Vaterland*, 293–9.
46. Ibid., 56–7.
47. Kořalka, *Tschechen*, 39–40; Loewenheim, 'German Liberalism', in Brock and Skilling eds., *The Czech*, 155–7.
48. Zacek, *Palacký*, 68.
49. Trencsényi et al. eds., *Negotiating Modernity*, 186.
50. Sked, 'The Nationality Problem in the Habsburg Monarchy', in Moggach and Jones eds., *The 1848*, 337.
51. Kořalka, *Tschechen*, 87–9.
52. Trencsényi et al. eds., *Negotiating Modernity*, 174.
53. Almasy, 'An Unintended Consequence', 8.
54. Maxwell, *Choosing Slovakia*, 118.
55. Ibid., 127.
56. Mann, 'Karel Havlíček: a Slav Pragmatist', 413–17; Kořalka, *Tschechen*, 47–8.
57. Wierzbicki, *Wschód-Zacchód*, 108–142.
58. Vushko, *The Politics*, 206–220.
59. Boaglio, 'Language and power', in Schjerve ed., *Diglossia*.
60. Kořalka, 'Prag-Frankfurt', in Lutz and Rumpler eds., *Österreich*, 127; Nimni, 'Marx, Engels'.
61. Lukowski, *Disorderly Liberty*, 205.
62. Vital, *A People Apart*, 113–14; Wistrich, *The Jews*, 24–5.
63. Vital, *A People Apart*, 234–6.
64. Wistrich, *The Jews*, 29–31.
65. Tilly and Kopsidis, *From Old Regime*, 104–114.
66. Barclay, *Frederick William*, 127–9.
67. Siemann, *The German Revolution*, 91–4.
68. Rath, *The Viennese*, 13–15.
69. Spira, 'Lajos Batthyány', 81.

NOTES pp. [105–114]

6. THE LOST PARTITION

1. Rath, *The Viennese*, 34.
2. Siemann, *The German*, 57–8.
3. Clark, *Revolutionary Spring*, 295–7; Rath, *The Viennese*, 40–2.
4. Spira, *A Hungarian Count*, 15–30.
5. Hahn, *The 1848*, 89–105.
6. Siemann, *The German*, 77–9.
7. Deak, *The Lawful Revolution*, 100.
8. Ibid., 74–5; Clark, *Revolutionary Spring*, 309.
9. Clark, *Revolutionary Spring*, 309.
10. Füster, *Memoiren*, 58–9.
11. Schulze, *The Course of German Nationalism*, 30.
12. Clark, *Revolutionary Spring*, 539.
13. Hofman, *Die Prager Zeitschrift*, 88.
14. Deak, *The Lawful Revolution*, 147–52.
15. Massan, 'Der Austroslavismus', in Moritsch ed., *Der Austroslavismus*, 55–60.
16. Švoger, 'Ban Josip Jelačić', 248–67.
17. Deak, *The Lawful Revolution*, 122–8.
18. Judson, *Exclusive Revolutionaries*, 41–2.
19. Loewenheim, 'German liberalism', in Brock and Skilling eds., *The Czech*, 159.
20. Kořalka, *Tschechen im Habsburgerreich*, 180–4.
21. Trencsényi and Kopeček eds., *Discourses of Collective Identity*, Vol. II, 322–9.
22. Jucho, *Verhandlungen des Deutschen Parlaments*, Vol. I, 291–6.
23. Orton, *The Prague Slav Congress*, 28.
24. Melik, 'Frankfurstke volitve 1848', 103–106.
25. Wagner ed., *Die revolutionsjahre 1848/49 im Königreich Galizien-Lodomerien*, 11–73.
26. Ziemiałkowski, *Pamiętniki*, 69–70.
27. Žáček, *Slovanský sjezd*, 65–6.
28. Orton, *The Prague Slav Congress*, 41.
29. Žáček, *Slovanský sjezd*, 188–190; 'Prag und der neue Panslavismus', 385.
30. Valentin, *Geschichte*, Vol. II, 11.
31. Zimmermann, *Die deutsche Revolution*, 742–6.
32. Siemann, *The German Revolution*, 124–6.
33. Hamann, 'Die Habsburger', in Lutz and Rumpler eds., *Österreich*, 215.
34. Wollstein, *Das "Großdeutschland" der Paulskirche*, 268–9.
35. Vick, *Defining Germany*, 165.
36. Petersen, 'Deutsche Antworten', in Fahlbusch et al. eds., *Völkische Wissenschaften*, 68–9.
37. Fröbel, *Wien, Deustchland und Europa*.
38. Wollstein, *Das "Großdeutschland" der Paulskirche*, 273–5.
39. Ibid., 284–5.
40. Wigard, *Stenographischer Bericht*, Vol. 8, 5823.
41. Grimm, *Geschichte der Deutschen Sprache*, foreword.
42. Wigard, *Stenographischer Bericht*, Vol. 3, 2050.
43. Carl von Moering's speech, in ibid., 1113–14.

44. Schuselka, *Deutsche Fahrten*, Vol. 2, 108.
45. Vick, *Defining Germany*, 167.
46. Orton, *The Prague Slav Congress*, 64–5.
47. Ibid., 66.
48. Maxwell, *Choosing Slovakia*, 135.
49. Palacký, 'Manifesto of the First Slavonic Congress to the Nations of Europe', 309–13.
50. Siemann, *The German Revolution*, 154–5.
51. 'Bilder Aus Frankfurt—Aus der Fahrt zum Parlamente', *Kölnische Zeitung* (16 July 1848), 1.
52. Loewenheim, 'German liberalism', in Brock and Skilling eds., *The Czech*, 164.
53. Orton, *The Prague Slav Congress*, 107–115.
54. Orton, 'Did the Slavs Speak German', 517–20.
55. Orton, *The Prague Slav Congress*, 109.
56. Wistrich, *The Jews*, 29–31.
57. Vick, *Defining Germany*, 113–19.
58. Kořalka, *Tschechen*, 40–2.
59. Wigard, *Stenographischer Bericht*, Vol. I, 214.
60. Koralka, 'Welche Nationvorstellungen', in Jaworski and Luft eds., *1848/49*, 37.
61. Deak, *The Lawful Revolution*, 45.
62. Wigard, *Stenographischer Bericht*, Vol. II, 1143–51.
63. Baron, 'The Impact of the Revolution', 236.
64. Siemann, *The German Revolution*, 139–40.
65. Spira, *A Hungarian Count*, 208–218.
66. Deak, *The Lawful Revolution*, 147–52.
67. Spira, *A Hungarian Count*, 276–301.
68. Deak, *The Lawful Revolution*, 137–59.
69. Ibid., 159–77.
70. Wheatley, *The Life and Death*, 33–47.
71. Vick, *Defining Germany*, 165–8; Sondhaus, 'Schwarzenberg'.
72. Simson, *Erinnerungen*, 183–4.
73. Dow, *A Prussian Liberal*, 84–5.
74. Barclay, *Frederick William IV*, 194; 192.
75. Ibid., 190.
76. Ibid., 200.

7. INTO THE FURNACE OF MODERNITY

1. Kupka, *Die Eisenbahnen Österreich-Ungarns*, 127–9.
2. Clark, 'After 1848', 173–4.
3. Ross, *Beyond the Barricades*, 31.
4. Vocelka, *Franz Joseph*, 94.
5. Osterkamp, *Vielfalt ordnen*, 185.
6. Clark, *Iron Kingdom*, 501.
7. Sheehan, *German Liberalism*, 79.
8. Sheehan, *German History*, 746.

9. Hagen, *Österreichs Mitteleuropa*, 32–42.
10. Reill, *Nationalists Who Feared the Nation*, 84–5.
11. Murdock, *Changing Places*, 34.
12. Hagen, *Österreichs Mitteleuropa*, 79–184.
13. Evans, *Austria, Hungary, and the Habsburgs*, 277–9.
14. Green, *Fatherlands*, 190–8.
15. Preßler, *Deutschlands Schulreform*, 5–10.
16. Boyer, *Austria*, 57.
17. Cohen, *The Politics of Ethnic Survival*, 29.
18. Novak, *Višejezičnost*, 65.
19. Deželić, *Iz njemačkoga Zagreba*, 10–62.
20. Novak, *Višejezičnost*, 56.
21. Nemes, *The Once and Future Budapest*, 150.
22. Maxwell, 'Hungaro-German Dual Nationality', 30.
23. Hanak, *Ungarn in der Donaumonarchie*, 297.
24. Nemes, *The Once and Future Budapest*, 152.
25. Pisling, *Germanisirung oder Czechisirung*, 9–10.
26. Aichner and Mazohl eds., *Die Korrespondenz*, 72.
27. Stölzl, *Das Ära Bach*, 67.
28. Czoernig, *Oesterreich's Neugestaltung 1848–1858*, iv.
29. Ibid., 317–20; 447–62.
30. Good, *The Economic Rise*, 82.
31. Fremdling, *Eisenbahnen und deutsches Wirtschaftswachstum*, 48.
32. Ibid., 17.
33. Sheehan, *German History*, 739; 742.
34. Bazillion, *Modernizing Germany*, 266.
35. Ibid., 267.
36. Kořalka, *Die Tschechen*, 83–5.
37. Brophy, 'The Political Calculus of Capital'; Sheehan, *German History*, 735–6; Good, *The Economic Rise*, 84.
38. Deak, *Forging a Multinational State*, 118–19.
39. Ross, *Beyond the Barricades*, 59; 113; 76–7; 134–5.
40. Ibid., 74.
41. Sheehan, *German History*, 763.
42. Nemes, *The Once and Future Budapest*, 8–9.
43. Barclay, *Friedrich Wilhelm IV*, 240–44.
44. King, *Budweisers into Czechs*, 49.
45. Horel, *Multicultural Cities*, 330.
46. Schivelbusch, *The Railway Journey*, 171–7.
47. Horel, *Multicultural Cities*, 347.
48. Kolar-Dimitrijević, 'Presjek', 153.
49. Paupie, *Die Kunst des Bierbrauens*; Meußdoerffer and Zarnkow, *Das Bier*, 107–111.
50. Šimková, 'The Birth of the Scientific Brewer', 221–8.
51. King, *Budweisers*, 107.

52. Tufegdžić and Blagojević, 'Golden Era of Lager Breweries'.
53. Horel, *Multicultural Cities*, 137.
54. Wiebenson and Sisa eds., *The Architecture*, 187–90.
55. Ther, *In der Mitte der Gesellschaft*, 343.
56. Hoare, *Serbia*, 111; 113–15; 154–70.
57. Milićević, *Кнежевина Србија*, 23–4.
58. No thorough examination of 'Central Europe' in nineteenth-century educational materials has been done, but a wealth of individual examples testify to how unremarkable it was. Franjo Klaić, *Čitanka za gradske produžne učione u kraljevini Dalmaciji, Hervatskoj i Slavoniji*, Vienna (1868), 114; Michael Öchsner, *Lehr- und Lesebuch für die männlichen deutschen Feiertags-oder Fortbildungs-Schulen*, Munich (1891), 151; *Viertes Lesebuch für die Volksschulen*, Prague (1868), 166–70; *Lesebuch für die Oberklassen der katholischen Volksschulen Bayerns*, Munich (1896), 179; *Věstník Vládní pro školy obecné v markrabství Moravském*, Brno (1885), 88; 100.
59. Mann, 'Karel Havlíček: a Slav Pragmatist', 421.
60. Štasný ed., *Slovanství v národním životě*, 209.
61. Palmowski, *Urban Liberalism*, 44.
62. Kapp, *Vom radikalen Frühsozialisten*, 77, translation taken from Sheehan, *German History*, 869.
63. Smith, *German Nationalism and Religious Conflict*, 37.
64. Rochau, *Grundsätze*, 2.
65. Ross, *Beyond the Barricades*, 55.
66. Rosenberg, *Machteliten*, 88; Blackbourn and Eley, *The Peculiarities*, 182.
67. Barclay, *Friedrich Wilhelm IV*, 219.
68. Evans, *Austria, Hungary, and the Habsburgs*, 177.
69. Neemann, 'Models of Political Participation', in Retallack ed., *Saxony*, 120–21.
70. Ibid., 124; Zeise, 'Die bürgerliche Umwälzung', in Czok ed., *Geschichte Sachsens*, 366–7.
71. Green, *Fatherlands*, 267; Retallack, 'Why Can't a Saxon', 28.
72. Green, *Fatherlands*, 76.
73. Green, 'Representing Germany?', 847–8.
74. Hanisch, *Für Fürst und Vaterland*, 398–9.
75. Ibid., 326–8.

8. CENTRAL EUROPE REMADE

1. Evans, *The Pursuit*, 242.
2. Engelberg, *Bismarck. Urpreuße und Reichsgründer*.
3. Huber, *Dokumente zur deutschen Verfassungsgeschichte*, Vol. 2, 104–105.
4. Erdődy, 'Unity or Liberty', in Dénes ed., *Liberty and the Search*, 96–8; Green, *Fatherlands*, 51.
5. Bruck, 'Die Aufgaben Österreichs', in Charmatz ed., *Minister Freiherr von Bruck*, 243.
6. Langewiesche, *Nation, Nationalismus, Nationalstaat*, 55–81.
7. Bruck, 'Die Aufgaben Österreichs', in Charmatz ed., *Minister Freiherr von Bruck*, 243–1.

8. Gall, *Bismarck*, 136–7.
9. Pflanze, *Bismarck and the Development of Germany*, 17.
10. Osterkamp, *Vielfalt ordenen*, 191.
11. Boyer, *Austria*, 64–5.
12. Ibid., 67–8; Kwan, *Liberalism and the Habsburg Monarchy*, 38–40.
13. Heka, 'Hrvatsko-Ugarska Nagodba u zrcalu tiska', 939.
14. Sheehan, *German History*, 863.
15. Gall, *Bismarck*, 253–5.
16. Kohl ed., *Die politischen Reden*, 29–30.
17. Cornicelius ed., *Heinrich von Treitschkes Briefe*, Vol. 2, 238.
18. Deak, *Beyond Nationalism*, 50–51.
19. Sheehan, *German History*, 900.
20. Kötzschke and Kretzschmar, *Sächsische Geschichte*, 351.
21. Sheehan, *German History*, 874–5.
22. Steinberg, *Bismarck*, 196–7.
23. Heywood, 'Palmerston's Joke', 112–114.
24. Sheehan, *German History*, 891–900.
25. Ibid., 906–908.
26. Boyer, *Austria*, 78–9.
27. Retallack, *Germany's Second Reich*, 110–124.
28. Judson, *Exclusive Revolutionaries*, 107–108.
29. Schmitt, 'Count Beust and Germany', 22–6.
30. Tomljanovich, *Biskup*, 170–73; Kořalka, *František Palacký*, 454–7.
31. Boyer, *Austria*, 73–85.
32. Petrovich, *The Emergence*, 219–22.
33. Maxwell, *Choosing Slovakia*, 135–7.
34. Petrovich, *The Emergence*, chs. 1–8; Kořalka, *František Palacký*, 462–71.
35. Pflanze, *Bismarck and the Development*, 369.
36. Heinzen, 'The Guelph "Conspiracy"', 261–7.
37. Heinzen, *Making Prussians, Raising Germans*, 50–51.
38. Palmowski, *Urban Liberalism*, 49–63.
39. Heinzen, *Making Prussians, Raising Germans*, 46.
40. Busch, *Tagebuchblätter*, Vol. 3, 552–6.
41. Retallack, *Red Saxony*, 38–9.
42. Pflanze, *Bismarck and the Development*, 396–9.
43. Deak, *Beyond Nationalism*, 84–5.
44. Pflanze, *Bismarck and the Development*, 409.
45. Fink, 'For Country', in Speirs and Breuilly eds., *Germany's Two Unifications*, 158–60.
46. Pflanze, *Bismarck and the Development*, 433–4.
47. Fink, 'For Country', in Speirs and Breuilly eds., *Germany's Two Unifications*, 161–3; Chrastil, *Bismarck's War*, 10–11.
48. Pflanze, *Bismarck and the Development*, 484–9.
49. Ibid., 497.
50. Schieder, *Das Deutsche Kaiserreich*, 74–5.

51. Judson, 'L'Autriche-Hongrie était-elle un empiré?'; Connelly, 'Was the Habsburg Empire an Empire?'

9. THE AGE OF NATIONALISM

1. Eötvös, *Ueber die Gleichberechtigung*, 3.
2. Benes, *In Babel's Shadow*, 123–51.
3. Eötvös, *Ueber die Gleichberechtigung*, 7.
4. Treitschke, 'Oesterreich und das deutsche Reich', 668.
5. Langwiesche, *Liberalismus in Deutschland*, 165.
6. Nipperdey, *Die Organisation der deutschen Parteien*, 42–175; Eley, 'Notable Politics', in Jarausch ed., *In Search of a Liberal Germany*; Kühne, 'From Electoral Campaigning', in Blackbourn and Retallack eds., *Localism*, 107–108.
7. Retallack, *Red Saxony*, 33–6; Berger, 'Prussia', in Dwyer and Berger eds., *The Rise of Prussia*, 37–40.
8. Smith, *German Nationalism and Religious Conflict*, 34.
9. Schieder, *Das Deutsche Kaiserreich*, 11–12.
10. Kennedy, 'Regionalism and Nationalism', 14.
11. Green, *Fatherlands*, 298–9.
12. Bennette, *Fighting for the Soul of Germany*, 28–9.
13. Hetzer, 'Außenpolitik als deutscher Bundesstaat', in Berwinkel and Kröger eds., *Die Außenpolitik*, 28–41.
14. Clark, *Kaiser Wilhelm II*, 40.
15. Hetzer, 'Außenpolitik als deutscher Bundesstaat', in Berwinkel and Kröger eds., *Die Außenpolitik*, 28–41.
16. Bennette, *Fighting for the Soul of Germany*, 15–21.
17. Engelberg, *Bismarck. Das Reich*, 104–152.
18. Smith, *German Nationalism*, 42–8.
19. Schieder, *Das Deutsche Kaiserreich*, 13–21.
20. Blanke, *Prussian Poland*, 12–13; 83–4.
21. Schieder, *Das Deutsche Kaiserreich*, 19–20.
22. Karch, *Nation and Loyalty*, 53–61.
23. Blanke, *Prussian Poland*, 17–47.
24. Chickering, *The German Empire*, 179–83; Retallack, *Red Saxony*, 94–102.
25. Retallack, *Red Saxony*, 111–127.
26. Ibid., 132–70; Chickering, *The German Empire*, 184.
27. Engelberg, *Bismarck. Das Reich*, 275–95; Kořalka, 'Deutschland und die Habsburgermonarchie', in Wandruszka and Urbanitsch eds., *Die Habsburgermonarchie*, Vol. VI/2, 59–78.
28. Katus, *Hungary in the Dual Monarchy*, 115–20.
29. Gottas, *Ungarn*, 43.
30. Lorman, *The Making of the Slovak People's Party*, 24–6.
31. Janos, 'The Decline of Oligarchy', in Janos and Slottman eds., *Revolutions in Perspective*, 9–10.
32. Gottas, *Ungarn*, 45–52.

33. Katus, *Hungary*, 136–9.
34. Berecz, 'The Hungarian Nationalities Act'.
35. Berecz, *The Politics of Early Language Teaching*, 196–219.
36. Gottas, *Ungarn*, 49.
37. Babejová, *Fin-de-Siecle Pressburg*, 49–50.
38. Berecz, 'Hungarian, Romanian and German'.
39. Babejová, *Fin-de-Siecle Pressburg*, 51–2.
40. Geyr, *Sándor Wekerle*, 36–7.
41. Horel, *Multicultural Cities*, 74; Babejová, *Fin-de-Siecle Pressburg*, 59–63.
42. Kwan, 'Transylvanian Saxon Politics'.
43. Nemes, *The Once and Future Budapest*, 3.
44. Novak, *Višejezičnost*, 59; Gross, *Počeci moderne Hrvatske*, 462.
45. Žepić, 'Zur Geschichte', 219; Batušić, *Geschichte*, 103–110.
46. Deželić, *Iz njemačkoga Zagreba*, 65.
47. Gross, *Počeci*, 443–6.
48. Nemes, *The Once and Future Budapest*, 156.
49. Freifeld, 'The De-Germanization', in Bullivant et al. eds., *Germany and Eastern Europe*, 158–64.
50. Nemes, *The Once and Future Budapest*, 160.
51. Ibid., 166.
52. Cohen, *The Politics of Ethnic Survival*, 37–9.
53. Ther, *In der Mitte*, 262–6.
54. Ibid., 267.
55. Srb, *Politické dějiny*, Vol. 1, 608; Kořalka, *Tschechen in Habsburgerreich*, 138.
56. Matić, *Nemci v Ljubljani*, 11–21.
57. Ibid., 13–15.
58. Ibid., 28–30.
59. Štergar, 'The Evolution of Linguistic Policies', in Prokopovych et al. eds., *Language Diversity*, 57–8.
60. Horel, *Multicultural Cities*, 500–502.
61. Kwan, *Liberalism and the Habsburg Monarchy*, 16.
62. Boyer, *Austria*, 129–44.
63. Stone, *Slav Outposts*, 225–7; Andree, *Wendische Wanderstudien*, 162–4.
64. Andree, *Wendische Wanderstudien*, 191.
65. Glaser, *Minority Languages*, 98–105; 103; Walde, 'Katholisches versus evangelisches', 15–28.
66. Wheatley, *The Life and Death*, 4–7; 104–25.
67. Heka, 'Hrvatsko-Ugarska Nagodba u zrcalu tiska', 949–61.
68. Heka, 'Analiza Austro-Ugarske I Hrvatsko-Ugarske Nagodbe', 871–3.
69. Gross, *Počeci*, 381–91; Gross, *Izvorno pravaštvo*, 53–60; Veselinović, 'Pregled razvoja'; Bartulin, 'From Independence', in Fitzpatrick ed., *Liberal*.
70. Wolff, *The Idea of Galicia*, 222–3.
71. Szymczak, *Galicyjska „ambasada" w Wiedniu*, 7.
72. Boyer, *Austria*, 125.

73. Massan, 'Der Austroslavismus', in Moritsch ed., *Der Austroslavismus*, 61–4.
74. Kwan, 'Austro-German Liberalism'.

10. THE SPIRIT OF SECESSION

1. Prideaux, *Edvard Munch*, 135.
2. Paret, *The Berlin Secession*, 50–54; Ibid., 136.
3. Quoted in Charles and Carl, *The Viennese Secession*, 35; Hanák, *The Garden and the Workshop*, 32–8.
4. Judson, *Exclusive Revolutionaries*, 202.
5. Berchtold ed., *Österreichische Parteiprogramme*, 198–203.
6. Cvirn, *Trdnjavski trikotnik*, 66–76.
7. Matić, 'Die Deutschen und Slowenen'.
8. Cohen, *The Politics of Ethnic Survival*, 65.
9. Schnabel, *Tafeln zur Statistik von Böhmen*, table 8.
10. Judson, *Exclusive Revolutionaries*, 203–204.
11. Schindler, *Exkursionen*, V–VII.
12. Judson, *Exclusive Revolutionaries*, 205–206; Matić, *Nemci v Ljubljani*, 399; 361; Cvirn, *Trdnjavski trikotnik*, 105–106.
13. Judson, *Exclusive Revolutionaries*, 207–20; Kořalka, 'Deutschland und die Habsburgermonarchie', in Wandruszka and Urbanitsch eds., *Die Habsburgermonarchie*, Vol. VI/2, 81–3.
14. Judson, *Guardians of the Nation*, 26.
15. Wingfield, *Flag Wars and Stone Saints*, 17–45.
16. Judson, *Guardians of the Nation*, 16.
17. Judson, *Exclusive Revolutionaries*, 210–11.
18. Blanke, *Prussian Poland*, 41–2.
19. Ibid., 106; 41.
20. Murko, *Deutsche Einflüsse*, 355.
21. Judson, 'Inventing Germans', 54.
22. Blanke, *Prussian Poland*, 56–82.
23. Eddie, 'The Prussian Settlement Commission', in Nelson ed., *Germans, Poland*.
24. Judson, *Guardians of the Nation*, 100–139.
25. Cornwall, 'The Struggle'.
26. Weikart, 'The Origins of Social Darwinism in Germany'.
27. Gumplowicz, *Raçe und Staat*, 19; 3; Turda, *The Idea of National Superiority*, 38–48.
28. Judson, *Guardians of the Nation*, 120–21.
29. Turda, *The Idea of National Superiority*, 51–60; Friedländer, *Nazi Germany & the Jews*, 87–90.
30. Véri, 'The Tiszaeszlár Blood Libel', in König and Schulz eds., *Antisemitismus*, 265–6.
31. Handler, *Blood Libel*, 40–74.
32. Véri, 'The Tiszaeszlár Blood Libel', in König and Schulz eds., *Antisemitismus*, 269–72; Véri, 'Imagining ritual murder', in Hauser and Janáčová eds., *Visual Antisemitism*, 38–42.
33. Aronsfeld, 'The first anti-Semitic international', 65–7.
34. Rosenberg, 'Political and Social Consequences'.
35. See for example Meyer, *Politische Gründer*.

36. Volkov, 'Kontinuität und Diskontinuität', 231; Volkov, *The Rise of Popular Antimodernism*, 172–3.
37. Pulzer, *The Rise of Political Anti-Semitism*, 88–96.
38. Aronsfeld, 'The first anti-Semitic international', 68–71.
39. Judson, *Exclusive Revolutionaries*, 244.
40. Boyer, *Political Radicalism*, 79; Viragh, 'Becoming Hungarian', 1.
41. Hanak, *Ungarn in der Donaumonarchie*, 302; Wistrich, *The Jews*, 165–73.
42. Goldstein, *Židovi u Zagrebu*, 15.
43. Pulzer, *The Rise of Political Anti-Semitism*, 33–55.
44. Ranki, *The Politics of Inclusion and Exclusion*, 55–68.
45. *Saborski dnevnik Kraljevinah Hrvatske*, 641; Vulesica, *Die Formierung*.
46. Unowsky, 'Reasserting Empire', in Wingfield and Bucur eds., *Staging the Past*.
47. Pulzer, *The Rise of Political Anti-Semitism*, 159.
48. Cohen, *The Politics of Ethnic Survival*, 154–66.
49. Reinharz, *Fatherland or Promised Land*, 29.
50. Ranki, *The Politics of Inclusion*, 54.
51. Biddiss, 'Gobineau and the Origins of European Racism'.
52. Pulzer, *Jews and the German State*, 17–20.
53. Reinharz, *Fatherland or Promised Land*, 23.
54. Ibid., 38–9.
55. Vital, *A People Apart*, 282–370.
56. Reinharz, *Fatherland or Promised Land*, 129–31.
57. Ibid., 39–70.
58. Vital, *A People Apart*, 438–75; Wistrich, *The Jews*, 347–80.
59. Pavličević, *Narodni pokret*, 120–31.
60. Turkalj, 'Stranka prava'.
61. Biondich, *Stjepan*, 20.
62. Žepić, 'Zur Geschichte', 215–21.
63. Obad, *Roda Roda*, 39–59.
64. Veselinović, 'Pregled'.
65. Kořalka, *Tschechen*, 153–7.
66. Vojtěch, *Mladočeši*.
67. Konrad, 'Jews and politics', 174.
68. Hanak, *Ungarn in der Donaumonarchie*, 308.
69. Babejova, *Fin-de-Siecle*, 85–91.
70. Horel, *Multicultural Cities*, 74.
71. Babejova, *Fin-de-Siecle*, 22–156; Ibid.
72. According to census data collected from 1880 to 1910.
73. Szögi, 'Ungarländische' and Luetić, 'The Migration', in Iveljić ed., *The Entangled*; Molik, 'Polnische Studenten'.
74. Zahra, *Kidnapped Souls*, 2–3.

11. THE NEW OLD REGIME

1. Mandell, *Paris 1900*, 3–70.

2. Koenen, *Der Russland-Komplex*, 37; Whiteside, *Austrian National Socialism*, 21–6.
3. *Weltausstellung in Paris 1900*, 3.
4. Vosberg-Rekow, 'Die wirtschaftspolitische Bedeutung', in Malkowsky ed., *Die Pariser Weltausstellung*.
5. Chickering, *The German Empire*, 391–402; Berger, 'Building', in Berger and Miller eds., *Nationalizing*, 257–65.
6. Mora, 'Ungarn auf der Weltausstellung', in Malkowsky ed., *Die Pariser Weltausstellung*, 261–4.
7. Székely, 'The Resetting of the Main Historical Group', in Székely ed., *Ephemeral Architecture*; Barenscott, 'Articulating Identity'.
8. Schedel, 'Emperor, Church, and People'; Unowsky, *The Pomp and Politics*, 79–104.
9. Mora, 'Oesterreich auf der Weltausstellung', in Malkowsky ed., *Die Pariser Weltausstellung*, 241–3; Pendl, *Österreich auf der Weltausstellung*, 24–7.
10. Visible even in their catalogues: see Pendl, *Österreich auf der Weltausstellung*; *Magyarország a Párisi nemzetközi kiállitáson*.
11. A mission they would continue well into the twentieth century: see Clegg, *Art, Design & Architecture in Central Europe*, 49–144.
12. Ehmer et al., 'Migration Patterns', 25; Hauschildt, 'Polish Migrant Culture,' 157; Klessmann, 'Comparitive Immigrant History', 337; Karch, *Nation and Loyalty*, 71.
13. Blanke, *Polish-Speaking Germans?*, 85–6.
14. Hauschildt, 'Polish Migrant Culture,' 167; Murdock, *Changing Places*, 51–2.
15. Beneš, *Workers and Nationalism*, 60–61.
16. Romsics, *Myth and Remembrance*, 16–17; Agičić, *Srednjoeuropske teme*, 105–113; Agičić, 'W poszukiwaniu chorwackich korzeni', in Dąbrowska ed., *Oskar Halecki*, Vol. 3; Augustynowicz, 'Wiedeńska geneologija Oskara Haleckiego', in Dąbrowska ed., *Oskar Halecki*, Vol. 2; Rhode, 'Drei polnische Historiker', 529–30; Stipančević, 'Neznani svijet Email Laszowskog'.
17. Janos, 'The Decline of Oligarchy', in Janos and Slottman eds., *Revolutions in Perspective*, 26; Holec, *Trianon*, 23–6; Miskolczy, '*Hungarus* Consciousness', in Almási and Šubarić eds., *Latin at the Crossroads*, 89.
18. Chickering, *The German Empire*, 210–212.
19. Boyer, *Political Radicalism in Late Imperial Vienna*, 41–166.
20. Wistrich, *The Jews of Vienna*, 179.
21. Lorman, *The Making*, 58–60.
22. Hanebrink, *In Defense*, 27.
23. Vulesica, *Die Formierung*, 106–118; Blaschke, *Katholizismus und Antisemitismus*, 70–106.
24. Bede, 'Fathers of Budapest', 629–32.
25. Gottsmann, 'Parteipolitik', 321–5.
26. Bauer, 'The Concept of the "Nation"', in Bottomore and Goode eds., *Austro-Marxism*, 107; Smith, *The Bolsheviks and the National Question*, 7–14.
27. Connelly, *From Peoples into Nations*, 270–4.
28. Blum, *The Austro-Marxists*, 55–6; 95.
29. Smith, *The Bolsheviks and the National Question*, 10.
30. Whiteside, *Austrian National Socialism*, 72–6; 82; 100; Beneš, *Workers*, 92–5.

31. Bacher, *Friedrich Naumann*, 22–5.
32. Mommsen, *Max Weber*, 1–20; 36–163.
33. Ibid., 69–70; Bacher, *Friedrich Naumann*, 41–4.
34. Shanahan, 'Friedrich Naumann'; Zimmermann, 'A Road not Taken'; Hübinger, 'Maschine und Persönlichkeitt' in Bruch ed., *Friedrich*.
35. Litván, *A Twentieth Century*, 1–69.
36. Skilling, *T. G. Masaryk*, 23.
37. Ibid., xii; 5; 85.
38. Prendergast, 'The Sociological Idea'.
39. Skilling, *T. G. Masaryk*, 64–75.
40. Biondich, *Stjepan Radić*, 14–18.
41. Ibid., 10–52.
42. Aralica, *Kmet*, 74–5; 82.

12. BETWEEN WESTERN CIVILIZATION AND EASTERN BARBARISM

1. Connelly, *From Peoples into Nations*, 250.
2. Deak, *Beyond Nationalism*, 68.
3. Judson, *Exclusive Revolutionaries*, 256–9.
4. Wingfield, *Flag Wars and Stone Saints*, 53–9.
5. Ibid., 63–7.
6. Ibid., 71–3.
7. *Neue Freie Presse*, No. 11923, 31 October 1897, 1.
8. Jaworski, 'Friedrich Naumann', in Mommsen et al. eds., *První*, 196; Naumann, *Deutschland und Oesterreich*, 3.
9. Mommsen, 'Österreich-Ungarns aus der Sicht', in Rumpler ed., *Innere Staatsbildung*, 214.
10. Lagarde, *Deutsche Schriften*, 77.
11. Stern, *The Politics of Cultural Despair*, 1–92; 56–69; Lougee, *Paul de Lagarde*, 184–93.
12. Brechtefeld, *Mitteleuropa*, 34–5.
13. Dhand, *The Idea of Central Europe*, 5.
14. Partsch, *Central Europe*, 142.
15. Stern, *The Politics of Cultural Despair*, 85.
16. Jirásek, *Češi, Slováci a Rusko*, 189–215.
17. Holoček, *Ruskočeské Kapitoly*, 122–36.
18. Kramař, 'Europe and the Bohemian Question', 184.
19. Murdock, *Changing Places*, 63–4.
20. Chickering, *We Men Who Feel Most German*, 3; Ibid., 69–75.
21. Geyr, *Sándor Wekerle*, 209–216.
22. Ibid., 217–23.
23. Gross, *Vladavina*, 178–202.
24. Sugar, 'An Underrated Event', 299–301.
25. Bacher, *Friedrich Naumann*, 84–6.
26. Röhl, *Wilhelm II*, 1047–52.
27. Suppan, 'Masaryk', in Winters and Pynsent eds., *T. G. Masaryk*.

28. Höbelt, 'Why fight a Third Balkan War?', in Cornwall ed., *Sarajevo*, 154.
29. Ibid., 152–4.
30. Kazbunda, *Otázka česko-německá*, 311–314.
31. Röhl, *Wilhelm II*, 962–3.
32. Ibid., 977–8.

13. PLUNGE INTO THE ABYSS

1. Watson, *Ring of Steel*, 61–73.
2. Verhey, *The Spirit of 1914*, 186–202; Bruendel, *Volksgemeinschaft oder Volksstaat*, 67–71.
3. Röhl, *Wilhelm II*, 1178.
4. Freifeld, *Nationalism and the Crowd*, 304–306.
5. Vermeiren, *The First World War*, 77–87.
6. Ibid., 64.
7. Bruendel, *Volksgemeinschaft oder Volksstaat*, 73.
8. Koenen, *Der Russland-Komplex*, 57–9.
9. Bruendel, *Volksgemeinschaft oder Volksstaat*, 38–47.
10. See Horne and Kramer, *German Atrocities*.
11. Hoeres, *Krieg der Philosophen*, 122.
12. Mann, *Reflections of a Nonpolitical Man*, 30; 24.
13. Ibid., 38.
14. Rothenberg, *Army of Francis Joseph*, 182–5.
15. Watson, *Ring of Steel*, 186–204.
16. Goltz, *Hindenburg*, 22–3.
17. Ibid., 25–6.
18. Ibid., 27–33.
19. Watson, *Ring of Steel*, 221–2.
20. Kapp, 'Bethmann-Hollweg, Austria-Hungary and Mitteleuropa', 220–1.
21. Fischer, *Griff nach der Weltmacht*, 113–20.
22. Drozdowski, 'Powstanie Legionów Polskich'.
23. Kapp, 'Bethmann-Hollweg, Austria-Hungary and Mitteleuropa', 218.
24. Kapp, 'Divided Loyalties', 129–31.
25. Kapp, 'Bethmann-Hollweg, Austria-Hungary and Mitteleuropa', 232–4.
26. Dhand, *The Idea of Central Europe*, 82.
27. Elvert, 'Irrweg Mitteleuropa', 124; Bacher, *Friedrich*, 119.
28. Dhand, *The Idea of Central Europe*, 46–7; Greiner, 'Articulating Europe', 137–43.
29. Kárník, 'Idea' and Jaworski, 'Friedrich Naumann', in Mommsen et al. eds., *První*.
30. Litván, *A Twentieth Century*, 101–111.
31. Deak and Gumz, 'How to Break a State', 1119–21.
32. Agičić, 'Civil Croatia', 305–307; Vermeiren, *The First World War*, 61.
33. Cornwall, 'Traitors and the Meaning of Treason', 122–32.
34. Gumz, *The Resurrection and Collapse*, 34–45.
35. Callahan, 'Putting World War I on trial', 241–2.
36. Uslu, 'Nous sommes les amis de l'Entente', 271.
37. Watson, *Ring of Steel*, 352.

38. Hanebrink, *A Specter Haunting Europe*, 53–5.
39. Deak and Gumz, 'How to Break a State'; Scheer, 'One Empire or Two States?'
40. Liulevicius, *War Land*, 14–126.
41. Bruendel, *Volksgemeinschaft oder Volksstaat*, 191–202.
42. Ibid., 175–284.
43. Hadler, 'Utváření česko-slovenské spolupracé', in Mommsen et al. eds., *První*.
44. Michel, 'Le rôle d'Ernest Denis'.
45. Seton-Watson and Seton-Watson, *The Making of a New Europe*, 125–42; 154–64; 171–6.
46. Kopyś, 'Die Haltung'; Ibid., 179.
47. Naumann, 'Polen in Mitteleuropa'.
48. Watson, *Ring of Steel*, 497–501.
49. *Stenographische Protokolle über die Sitzungen des Hauses der Abgeordneten des österreichischen Reichsrates im Jahre 1917*, Vol. XXII, 34.
50. Vermeiren, *The First World War*, 319–21.

14. GEESE INTO THE FOG

1. Ashmead-Bartlett, *The Tragedy of Central Europe*, 14–15; 32–46.
2. Ibid., 304.
3. Strong, *Austria*, 91–102.
4. Gerwarth, *November 1918*, 112–114.
5. Röhl, *Wilhelm II*, 1247.
6. Vermeiren, *The First World War*, 335.
7. Watson, *Ring of Steel*, 2; Steiner, *The Lights That Failed*, 4.
8. Gerwarth, *November 1918*, 92–6.
9. Mitchell, *Revolution in Bavaria*, 24–6.
10. Holste, *Warum Weimar*, 61–6.
11. Ibid., 55–6.
12. Gerwarth, 'The Central European Counter-Revolution', 182.
13. Holste, *Warum Weimar*, 57–8; Erdmann, *Adenauer in der Rheinlandpolitik*, 28–48.
14. Salomon, *The Outlaws*, 14.
15. Gerwarth, 'The Central European Counter-Revolution', 182; Liulevicius, *War Land*, 227–43; Gerwarth, 'Fighting the Red Beast', in Gerwarth and Horne eds., *War in Peace*.
16. Broué, *The German Revolution*, 238–58; Gerwarth, *November 1918*, 173.
17. Holste, *Warum Weimar*, 79–154.
18. Hanna, *The Mobilization of Intellect*, 9–10; 106–141.
19. Gerwarth, *November 1918*, 160–2.
20. Hochman, *Imagining a Greater Germany*, 52–67.
21. Gerwarth, *November 1918*, 165.
22. Strong, *Austria*, 105–106; Haas, 'Konflikt při uplatňování nároků na právo sebeurčení', in Mommsen et al. eds., *První*, 116–20.
23. Trotsky, *My Life*, 208.
24. Whiteside, *Austrian National Socialism*, 66–8.
25. Blum, *The Austro-Marxists*, 34–49; 55–6; 172–76.

26. Boyer, *Austria*, 588–608.
27. Strong, *Austria*, 113; Ibid., 612.
28. Strong, *Austria*, 118.
29. 'Schreiben des Staatsamts', in Michaelis and Schraepler eds., *Ursachen und Folgen*, Vol. III, 287.
30. Boyer, *Austria*, 612–20.
31. Alexander, 'Die erste Phase', in Seibt ed., *Die böhmischen Länder*, 229.
32. Boyer, *Austria*, 627–33.
33. Uslu, 'Nous sommes les amis de l'Entente', 267–77; Hanebrink, *In Defense of Christian Hungary*, 48–9; 62–3.
34. Litván, *A Twentieth Century*, 137–50.
35. Uslu, 'Aux origines de la «note Vix»', 366–74.
36. Litván, *A Twentieth Century*, 162–3.
37. Pastor, *Hungary Between Wilson and Lenin*, 137–47.
38. Litván, *A Twentieth Century*, 180.
39. Kenez, 'Coalition politics', in Janos and Slottman eds., *Revolutions in Perspective*.
40. Hanebrink, *In Defense of Christian Hungary*, 71–5.
41. Gerwarth, 'The Central European Counter-Revolution', 183.
42. Mócsy, *The Uprooted*, 91–103.
43. Ibid., 112–31.
44. Hanebrink, *In Defense of Christian Hungary*, 47–76.
45. Sakmyster, 'From Habsburg Admiral to Hungarian Regent', 134–6.
46. Berend, *Decades of Crisis*, 139; Gerwarth, 'The Central European Counter-Revolution', 185–6.
47. Gerwarth, *November 1918*, 175–6.
48. Ibid., 176–180.
49. Maderthaner, 'Utopian Perspectives', in Bischof et al. eds., *From Empire to Republic*, 60; Berend, *Decades of Crisis*, 136–7.
50. McCagg, 'Jews in Revolutions', 78; Friedländer, *Nazi Germany & the Jews*, 90–5; Hanebrink, *In Defense of Christian Hungary*, 84–9.
51. Bodó, 'Interwar Hungary', in Ramet ed., *Interwar East Central Europe*, 122–3.
52. Gerwarth, 'The Central European Counter-Revolution', 187–8; Sakmyster, 'From Habsburg Admiral to Hungarian Regent', 138.
53. Gerwarth, *The Vanquished*, 130–31; Mitchell, *Revolution in Bavaria*, 330–1; Weber, *Becoming Hitler*, 47–55.
54. Pilsudska, *Pilsudski*, 269–70.
55. Zimmermann, *Jozef Pilsudski*, 279–93.
56. Národní shromáždění československé 1918–1920. Stenoprotokoly, 1. schůze (14 November 1918), https://www.psp.cz/eknih/1918ns/ps/stenprot/001schuz/s001001.htm#_h (last accessed 30/03/25).
57. Krizman, *Raspad Austro-Ugarske*, 222–9.
58. Egry, 'An Object of Desire', in Dobre et al. eds., *Myth-Making*, 100–105.
59. Haas, 'Konflikt při uplatňování nároků na právo sebeurčení', in Mommsen et al. eds., *První světová válka*, 159–64.

60. Holec, *Trianon*, 71–92.
61. Ibid., 93–8; Bobrík, 'Nemci na Slovensku a slovenská otázka', in Mommsen et al. eds., *První světová válka*, 109–11.
62. Chwalba, *Przegrane zwycięstwo*, 15–25; Böhler, *Civil War in Central Europe*, 51–58.
63. Pajewski, *Budowa drugiej Rzeczpospolitej*, 97.
64. Ibid., 34.
65. Snyder, *The Reconstruction of Nations*, 57–9.
66. Zimmermann, *Jozef Pilsudski*, 350–60.
67. Ibid., 361–9.
68. Böhler, *Civil War in Central Europe*, 146–86.
69. Pajewski, *Budowa drugiej Rzeczpospolitej*, 97–118.
70. Davies, *Heart of Europe*, 113–129.
71. Handelsman ed., *Konstytucje polskie*, 111.
72. Geiger, 'Njemci u Hrvatskoj', 325–6; Kárník, *České země*, Vol. 1, 94–7; 37–44; Orzoff, *Battle for the Castle*, 62.
73. Ramet and Leff, 'Interwar Czechoslovakia', in Ramet ed., *Interwar East Central Europe*, 78.
74. Hahn, 'Masaryk and the Germans', in Winters and Hanak ed., *T.G. Masaryk*, Vol. 3, 106–108.
75. Dăncilă, 'The Dynamic of Post-War Political Structures,' in Olschowsky et al. eds., *Central and Eastern Europe*.
76. Calcan, 'The administrative unification', 17–27; Fazakas et al., 'Transylvania as Part of Romania', in Veress ed., *Constitutional History of Translyvania*, 301–303.
77. Cojocaru, 'The Constitution of United Romania', 25–35.
78. Banac, '"Emperor Karl has become a Comitadji"'.
79. Krizman, *Hrvatska u Prvom svjetskom ratu*, 341–7.
80. Matijević, 'Narodno vijeće Slovenaca, Hrvata i Srba', 64.
81. Radić, *Politički spisi*, 323–35.
82. Djokić, *Elusive Compromise*, 25–6.
83. Gabelica, 'Žrtve sukoba na Jelačićevom trgu', 468–76.
84. Banac, *Nacionalno pitanje*, 144–6; Newman, 'Post-imperial and Post-war violence', 256–9.
85. Low, *The Anschluss Movement*, 436–7.
86. Suppan, 'Saint-Germain and Trianon', 43–5.
87. Ibid., 66.
88. Vardy, 'The Impact of Trianon', 21.
89. Winkler, *Weimar*, 89–92.
90. Mommsen, *The Rise and Fall of Weimar*, 74.
91. Steiner, *The Lights That Failed*, 62–7.
92. Goltz, *Hindenburg*, 67–8.
93. Conze, 'Only a dictator', in Urbach ed., *European Aristocracies*, 132–3.
94. Lockenour, *Dragonslayer*, 76–92.
95. Mommsen, *The Rise and Fall of Weimar*, 81–4.
96. Koepp, 'Gustav von Kahr'.
97. Stern, *The Politics of Cultural Despair*, 183–253.

98. Elvert, *Mitteleuropa!*, 45–56.
99. Frank, 'Conflicting Sovereignties', in Tibor and Hadler eds., *Disputed Territories*, 42.
100. Vardy, *Modern Hungarian Historiography*, 43–68.
101. Hanebrink, *In Defense of Christian Hungary*, 79–80.
102. Pok, 'Germans, Hungarians', in Braham and Miller eds., *The Nazis' Last Victims*, 47–8.

15. THE CENTRAL EUROPEAN CRISIS

1. Schacher, *Central Europe*, 7–8; iv.
2. Steiner, *The Lights That Failed*, 20–6; Wandycz, *France and Her Eastern Allies*, 3–131.
3. Brook-Shepherd, *The Last Habsburg*, 211.
4. Steiner, *The Lights That Failed*, 84.
5. Sakmyster, 'From Habsburg Admiral to Hungarian Regent', 143–4; Brook-Shepherd, *The Last Habsburg*, 281–300.
6. Glassheim 'National Mythologies', 468–9.
7. Berkes, 'The League of Nations', in Becker and Wheatley eds., *Remaking Central Europe*, 288–92.
8. Gerschenkron, *Bread and Democracy*, 91–112.
9. Lockenour, *Dragonslayer*, 93; 95.
10. Lohalm, *Völkischer Radikalismus*, 193.
11. Kántás, 'Secret Negotiations'; Gerwarth, 'The Central European Counter-Revolution', 177.
12. Lockenour, *Dragonslayer*, 94–5.
13. Bookbinder, *Weimar Germany*, 106.
14. Landauer, 'The Bavarian Problem: Part I', 113–14; Koepp, 'Gustav von Kahr'.
15. Mommsen, *The Rise and Fall*, 126–7.
16. Ibid., 147–50.
17. Ibid., 153–71.
18. Pechel, *Deutscher Widerstand*, 280.
19. Kershaw, *Hiler 1889–1936*, 169–219; Weber, *Becoming Hitler*, 279–90.
20. Kershaw, *Hitler 1889–1936*, 109–28.
21. Mommsen, *The Rise and Fall*, 153–8.
22. Whiteside, *Austrian National Socialism*, 105–106; 121.
23. Hamann, *Hitler's Vienna*, 17.
24. Ibid., 205–48.
25. Weber, *Becoming Hitler*.
26. Ludecke, *I Knew Hitler*, 65.
27. Evans, *The Coming*, 194.
28. Steger, 'Der Hitlerprozess'; Landauer, 'The Bavarian Problem: Part II', 222.
29. Mommsen, *The Rise and Fall*, 202–203.
30. Landau, 'The Economic Integration', in Latawski ed, *The Reconstruction of Poland*, 145–7; Bakić, *Britain and Interwar Danubian Europe*, 7; Radu, 'Romania and the Great War', 157; 160; 162; Kuklík, *Czech Law*, 86–90.
31. Cvijic, 'The Zones of Civilization'.
32. Livezeanu, *Cultural Politics in Greater Romania*, 1; 9–10; 53; 135–6; 144–53.

33. Gawrecki, 'The Determination of Nationality', 45–6.
34. Steiner, *The Lights That Failed*, 260; Stachura, 'National Identity and the Ethnic Minorities', in Stachura ed., *Poland Between the Wars*, 62.
35. *Pierwszy powszechny spis*, 56; Labbé, 'National indifference', in Ginderachter and Fox eds., *National Indifference*, 167.
36. Biskupski, 'The Polish Second Republic', Ramet ed., *Interwar East Central Europe*, 44.
37. Ibid., 45–6.
38. Seton-Watson and Seton-Watson, *The Making of a New Europe*, 157; 124.
39. Banac, *Nacionalno pitanje*, 147–9; Deak, *Beyond Nationalism*, 209.
40. Aralica, *Kmet, Fiškal, Hajduk*, 18–83.
41. Beneš, 'Central Europe after Ten Years', 245–51.
42. Ibid., 251.
43. Orzoff, *Battle for the Castle*, 99–105.
44. Berend, *Decades of Crisis*, 253–7; Boyer, *Austria*, 803; Stachura, 'Introduction' in Stachura ed., *Unemployment and the Great Depression*, 14; Evans, *The Coming of the Third Reich*, 243.
45. Weber, *Becoming Hitler*, 207–230.
46. Borejsza, *A ridiculous hundred million Slavs*, 58.
47. Kershaw, *Hitler*, 91; 169–72; ibid., 65–71.
48. Mommsen, *The Rise and Fall*, 253–60.
49. Friedländer, *Nazi Germany & The Jews*, 27–39; 49–60.
50. Evans, *The Third Reich in Power*, 47–9; Majer, *"Non-Germans" under the Third Reich*, 24–35.
51. Boyer, *Austria*, 759–96.
52. Goldstein and Goldstein, *The Holocaust in Croatia*, 92.
53. Connelly, *From Peoples into Nations*, 396–8; Livezeanu, *Cultural Politics*.
54. Biskupski, 'The Polish Second Republic', in Ramet ed., *Interwar East Central Europe*, 50–51.
55. Gerlach and Aly, *Das letzte Kapitel*, 40.
56. Biber, *Nemci v Jugoslaviji*.
57. Friedländer, *Nazi Germany & The Jews*, 216.
58. Gerlach, *The Extermination of the European Jews*, 311–32.
59. Berend, *Decades of Crisis*, 105–107.
60. Hagen, 'Before the "Final Solution"', 372.
61. Gerlach and Aly, *Das letzte Kapitel*, 41–8.
62. Walk ed., *Das Sonderrecht für die Juden im NS-Staat*.
63. Friedländer, *Nazi Germany & The Jews*, 141–4.
64. Hitler, *Mein Kampf*, Vol. 1, 1.
65. Boyer, *Austria*, 797–802.
66. Ibid., 810–34.
67. Boyer et al., 'Die Sudetendeutsche Heimatfront'.
68. Kolnai, *The War*, 6–11; 17–27; 539.

16. THE DEATH OF A CIVILIZATION

1. Henderson, *Eyewitness*, 230–1.
2. Wandycz, *France and Her Eastern Allies*, 21–3.

3. Aulneau, *Histoire de l'Europe Centrale*, 3; 623.
4. Caquet, *The Bell of Treason*, 205–207.
5. Ther, *The Dark Side*, 88; Ibid., 210–11.
6. Ther, *The Dark Side*, 104; 88–9.
7. Caquet, *The Bell of Treason*, 198.
8. Zelený ed., *Vynání*.
9. Wingfield, *Flag Wars and Stone Saints*, 253–7.
10. Tomášek, *Deník druhé republiky*, 29.
11. Procházka, *The Second Republic*, 62–4; Lorman, *The Making of the Slovak People's Party*, 216–17.
12. Gilbert, *Kristallnacht*, 23–41.
13. Ibid., 226–7.
14. Henderson, *Eyewitness*, 231.
15. Kershaw, *Hitler 1936–1945*, 87–93; 157–73.
16. Ther, *The Dark Side*, 104–105.
17. Wingfield, *Flag Wars and Stone Saints*, 254.
18. Lemkin ed., *Key Laws*, 1200.
19. Borejsza, *A ridiculous hundred million Slavs*, 82–109.
20. Wagener, *Hitler*, 122.
21. Borejsza, *A ridiculous hundred million Slavs*, 80.
22. Baumgart, 'Zur Ansprache Hitlers'; Domeier, 'World Domination and Genocide'; Rossino, *Hitler Strikes Poland*, 9–10.
23. Rossino, *Hitler Strikes Poland*, 29–57.
24. Borodziej, *Geschichte Polens*, 193.
25. Rossino, *Hitler Strikes Poland*, 88–120.
26. Kershaw, *Hitler 1936–1945*, 251.
27. Mazower, *Hitler's Empire*, 72.
28. Ibid., 92–4; Borodziej, *Geschichte Polens*, 191–8.
29. Ther, *The Dark Side*, 90–95.
30. Mazower, *Hitler's Empire*, 78–89; Borodziej, *Geschichte Polens*, 198–201.
31. Mazower, *Hitler's Empire*, 102–113.
32. Liulevicius, *The German Myth of the East*, 171.
33. Rumpf, 'Mitteleuropa', 510; 525.
34. Kershaw, *Hitler 1936–1945*, 357.
35. Ibid., 359.
36. Hanebrink, *A Specter Haunting Europe*, 131–2; 137–8.
37. Goldstein and Goldstein, *The Holocaust in Croatia*, 121–6.
38. Longerich, *Holocaust*, 297–300.
39. Ibid., 277–304.
40. Goldstein and Goldstein, *The Holocaust in Croatia*, 245–65.
41. Longerich, *Holocaust*, 124; 306.
42. Bryant, 'Either German or Czech', 691–6.
43. Borejsza, *A ridiculous hundred million Slavs*; Connelly, 'Nazis and Slavs'; Elvert, *Mitteleuropa!*, 311–26.

44. Overy, *The Bombing War*, 327–38; 435–6; Trentmann, *Out of the Darkness*, 26–7.
45. Overy, *The Bombing War*, 476–7.
46. Kershaw, *The End*, 92.
47. Karsai, 'The Last Phase', in Braham and Miller eds., *The Nazis' Last Victims*, 105.
48. Kershaw, *The End*, 69–70; 101–103.
49. Thum, *Uprooted*, xxxi.
50. Ibid., xxi-xxxi.
51. Ungváry, *Battle for Budapest*, 330–32.
52. Kershaw, *The End*, 177–81.
53. Ther, *The Dark Side*, 151.
54. James ed., *Winston S. Churchill*, Vol. 7, 7069.
55. Glassheim, 'National Mythologies', 471–2; Ther, *The Dark Side*, 143–5.
56. Ther, *The Dark Side*, 145–6.
57. Ibid., 197–8.
58. Michaelis and Schraepler eds., *Ursachen und Folgen*, Vol. XXIII, 106.
59. Boyer, *Austria*, 863–4.
60. Botz, *Nationalsozialismus in Wien*, 204–211.
61. Wiedemann, „Komm mit uns das Grenzland aufbauen!", 347–50; Douglas, *Orderly*, 101–103.
62. 'Rozporządzenie Krajowej Rady Ministrów z dnia 1 sierpnia 1944 r. o utracie obywatelstwa przez Niemców', *Dziennik Ustaw Rzeczpospolitej Polski*, Vol. III, No. 2, 17–18.
63. Thum, *Uprooted*, 58.
64. Michaelis and Schraepler eds., *Ursachen und Folgen*, Vol. XXIII, 372.
65. Simms, 'Prussia, Prussianism, and National Socialism', in Dwyer ed., *Modern Prussian History*, 254–61; Kolnai, *The War Against the West*, 528–39.
66. Kettenacker, 'Preußen in der alliierten Kriegszielplanung', 319.
67. Grzechnik, "'Recovering' territories", 674–88; Niebuhr, 'Enlarging Yugoslavia'; Trencsényi et al., *A History of Modern Political Thought in East Central Europe, Volume II*, 294–5; 302; 311–13; Krzoska, 'Historische Mission', 87–8; Mevius, *Agents of Moscow*, 114–17.
68. Thum, *Uprooted*, 66–7.
69. Douglas, *Orderly and Humane*, 182–6.

17. LIBERATED FROM HISTORY

1. Frisch, *Tagebuch*, 36–7.
2. James ed., *Winston S. Churchill*, Vol. 7, 7290.
3. Schwarz, *Vom Reich zur Bundesrepublik*, 299–344; 423–564. On social democrats more generally, Ash, 'Mitteleuropa?', in Graubard ed., *Eastern Europe*, 3–10.
4. Doering-Manteuffel, *Die Bundesrepublik Deutschland*, 30–35.
5. Craig, *The End of Prussia*, 74–8.
6. Foschepoth, 'Westintegration statt Wiedervereinigung', in Foschepoth ed., *Adenauer und die Deutsche Frage*, 31–4; Mensing ed., *Adenauer. Briefe 1945–1947*, 191.
7. Jackson, *Civilizing the Enemy*, 186.
8. Ibid., 104–11.

9. Ibid., 134.
10. James ed., *Winston S. Churchill*, Vol. 7, 7291; ibid., 217.
11. Kaiser, *Christian Democracy*, 232.
12. Jackson, 'Defending the West'.
13. Foschepoth, 'Westintegration statt Wiedervereinigung', in Foschepoth ed., *Adenauer und die Deutsche Frage*; Doering-Manteuffel, 'Wie westlich sind die Deutschen?'.
14. Kaiser, *Christian Democracy*, 164–302.
15. Abrams, *The Struggle for the Soul of the Nation*, 104–117.
16. Banac ed., *The Diary of Georgi Dimitrov*, 191–2.
17. Mevius, *Agents of Moscow*, 20.
18. Dostaly, 'Новое славянское движение', 176; Mevius, *Agents of Moscow*, 31.
19. Behrends, 'Die „sowjetische Rus" und ihre Brüder', 104; Hauner, 'Von der Verteidigung', in Behring et al. eds., *Geschichtliche Mythen*, 304.
20. Behrends, 'Die „sowjetische Rus" und ihre Brüder', 109.
21. Krzoska, 'Histoirsche Mission', 87–8.
22. 'Manifest Polskiego Komitetu', 9.
23. 'Das Kaschauer Programm', in Schieder ed., *Dokumentation der Vertreibung*, Vol. IV/1, 182–203.
24. Trencsényi et al., *A History of Modern Political Thought in East Central Europe, Volume II*, 295–303; Behrends, 'Die „sowjetische Rus" und ihre Brüder', 106–107.
25. Fischer, 'Západ, či východ?', in Hlaváček ed., *Západ nebo Východ?*, 725.
26. Abrams, *The Struggle for the Soul of the Nation*, 165; Hauner, 'Von der Verteidigung', in Behring et al. eds., *Geschichtliche Mythen*, 298–302.
27. Abrams, *The Struggle for the Soul of the Nation*, 12.
28. Ibid., 161.
29. Beneš, *Úvahy o slovanství*, 9.
30. 'The Lisbon Conference on Literature', 86–7.
31. Douglas, *Orderly and Humane*, 30.
32. Ražnjević, 'O Slavenskom komitetu Hrvatske', 113–14.
33. Hanebrink, *A Specter Haunting Europe*, 191–2.
34. Thum, *Uprooted*, 92; Connelly, *From Peoples into Nations*, 511.
35. Tscherkes, 'Stalinist Visions', 205–206.
36. Thum, *Uprooted*, xvii; 77–8.
37. Musil, 'Prague, Present Meets Past', 255; Luther, 'Ethnicity and Nationalism'.
38. Geiger, *Nestanak folksdojčera*, 34.
39. Thum, *Uprooted*, 65; Blanke, *Polish-speaking Germans?*, 288–305.
40. Geiger, 'Njemci u Hrvatskoj', 329–30.
41. Mevius, *Agents of Moscow*, 157.
42. Hanebrink, *A Specter Haunting Europe*, 231–2.
43. Tismaneanu and Iacob, 'The Romanian Ideology', in Rainer ed., *Underground Streams*.
44. Hanebrink, *A Specter Haunting Europe*, 161–98.
45. Tscherkes, 'Stalinist Visions', 208.
46. Cohen, *The Politics of Ethnic Survival*, 65–104.
47. Rainer, 'Conservative', in Rainer ed., *Underground*, 152.

48. Thum, *Uprooted*, 98–100.
49. Brzostekm 'The Ruralization of Bucharest and Warsaw' in Borodziej et al. eds., *Mastery and Lost Illusions*, 99–101.
50. Goodman, *The Nonconformists*, 30–51.
51. Eisner, *Franz Kafka*.

18. THE BIRTH OF AN IDEA

1. Skilling, *Against the Current*, viii–ix.
2. Krelža, *Djetinjstvo u Agramu*, preface.
3. Matvejević, *Razgovori s Krležom*, 63–73.
4. Skilling, 'The Czechoslovak Constitution'.
5. Kusin, *The Intellectual Origins of the Prague Spring*, 83–9.
6. Ibid., 53–62.
7. French, *Czech Writers and Politics*, 220–32.
8. Ibid., 250; Hamšík, *Writers Against Rulers*, 17–24.
9. Hrubý, 'Přerod komunistické víry'.
10. French, *Czech Writers and Politics*, 239–40.
11. Hamšík, *Writers Against Rulers*, 173–4.
12. *IV. sjezd Svazu československých spisovatelů*, 39–44.
13. Ibid., 46.
14. Hamšík, *Writers Against Rulers*, 46.
15. Ibid., 60.
16. French, *Czech Writers and Politics*, 259–72.
17. Zwick, *National Communism*, 108.
18. Sabatos, 'Criticism and Destiny', in Cashman ed., *1948 and 1968*, 186.
19. Dokument 121', in Karner et al. eds., *Prager Frühling*, 1004–1007; Williams, *The Prague Spring*, 71–2.
20. Havel, 'On the Theme of an Opposition' in Havel, *Open Letters*, 25–35.
21. Williams, *The Prague Spring*, 112–92.
22. Baer ed., *Preparing Liberty in Central Europe*, 143–64.
23. Bugge, 'A Western Invention?'.
24. Baer ed., *Preparing Liberty in Central Europe*, 156.
25. Patterson, 'The Polish Exile Community in Britain'.
26. Giedroyć, 'Rozmowa', in Klępka ed., *Zostało tylko słowo*, 69–73.
27. Stewart, '"We did not want an émigré journal"', in Neubauer and Török eds., *The Exile and Return*, 252–5; Abrams, *The Struggle*, 166–71.
28. Rhode, 'Drei polnische Historiker', 529–30.
29. Kłoczowski, 'Koncepcja Europy Środkowo-Wschodniej', in Dąbrowska ed., *Oskar Halecki*, Vol. II, 200–202.
30. Kłoczowski, 'East Central Europe'; Bömelburg, 'Oskar Halecki', in Dąbrowska ed., *Oskar Halecki*, Vol. I, 213–15.
31. Kłoczowski, 'Koncepcja Europy Środkowo-Wschodniej', in Dąbrowska ed., *Oskar Halecki*, Vol. II, 202.
32. Zahra, 'Looking East'; Mühle, 'Putting the East in Order', in Nelson ed., *Germans, Poland, and Colonial Expansion*.

33. Halecki, *The Limits and Divisions*, 129–31; Filipowicz, 'Oskar Halecki a Rosja', in Dąbrowska ed., *Oskar Halecki*, Vol. I.
34. Halecki, *Borderlands of Western Civilization*, 515.
35. Bömelburg, 'Oskar Halecki', and Stobecki, 'Oskar Halecki', in Dąbrowska ed., *Oskar Halecki*, Vol. I, 216–20; 228–36.

19. THE LIFE OF AN IDEA

1. Geyer, *Foreign Relations of the United States*, 212; 246; 271; 313; 367–8.
2. Goodman, *The Nonconformists*, 187–9; 195–204.
3. Kundera, *The Book of Laughter and Forgetting*, 3.
4. Ibid., 229–30.
5. Bolton, *Worlds of Dissent*, 115–200; Falk, *The Dilemmas of Dissidence*, 215.
6. Labov, *Transatlantic Central Europe*, 147–51; Bolecki, '*Kultura*', and Stewart, '"We did not want an émigré journal"', in Neubauer and Török eds., *The Exile and Return*, 168–77; 264–73.
7. Labov, *Transatlantic Central Europe*.
8. *Svědectví*, No. 1 (1956), 1.
9. *Svědectví*, No. 60 (1980), 629.
10. Bělohradský, 'Útěk k uniformě', 33–4.
11. Kundera, 'Z kulturního testamentu Střední Evropy'. It was also later published in the *NYRB* as 'The Czech Wager', 22 January 1981.
12. Milosz, 'Looking for a Center'.
13. Taylor ed., *Foreign Relations of the United States*, 56–64. The article by Kundera quoted by Bush was published in the 24 October 1982 edition of the *New York Times* under the title 'The Making of a Writer; "All I Cared About Was Women and Art"'.
14. Sabatos, 'Shifting contexts'.
15. Hauner, 'Dopis redacki'.
16. Banac, 'Political Change and National Diversity', in Graubard ed., *Eastern Europe*, 151–61.
17. Longo, *The Picnic*, 4–8.
18. Brook-Shepherd, *The Last Habsburg*, 183–90.
19. Ibid., 189.
20. Longo, *The Picnic*, 5–6.
21. Ibid., xi–xii.

20. THE RETURN OF CENTRAL EUROPE?

1. Höyng, 'Die Begräbnisfeier'; '413.000 nahmen "Abschied von Otto Habsburg"', *Der Standard*, 17 July 2011; 'Habsburg funeral sparks nostalgia and admiration', BBC News, 18 July 2011.
2. Walton, 'The Ban's mana'.
3. Péter, *Hungary's Long*, 17–18.
4. 'Begräbniszeremonie von Otto von Habsburg', *Der Standard*, 16 July 2011.
5. Péter, *Hungary's Long*, 18.
6. Lindstrom, 'Between Europe', 317–19.

7. Ther, *Europe Since 1989*, 11–18; 79–89.
8. Rupnik, 'After 1989', in Ignatieff and Roch eds., *Rethinking*, 265.
9. Kłoczowski, 'Koncepcja', in Dąbrowska ed., *Oskar*, Vol. II, 206–7.
10. Trencsényi, 'Central Europe', in Mishkova and Trencsényi eds., *European*, 179–80.
11. Duleba, 'Slovakia's', in Kucharczyk and Mesežnikov eds., *Diverging*, 164.
12. Lindstrom, 'Between Europe', 324.
13. Ibid., 325.
14. Legutko, *The Demon*, 167–8.
15. Rupnik, 'After 1989', in Ignatieff and Roch eds., *Rethinking*.
16. 'The Lisbon Conference on Literature'; Kirschbaum, 'The Verbatim Drama'.
17. Chernetsky, 'Silences'; Desnitsky, 'De-imperializing Joseph Brodsky'.
18. Kirschbaum, 'The Verbatim Drama'.
19. Maxwell, 'Popular and Scholarly'.
20. Jacques Rupnik, 'Jacques Rupnik: « Milan Kundera a esquissé une certaine idée de l'Europe »', *Le Monde*, 16 July 2023; Paul Berman, 'Paul Berman: "The largest European war since World War II turns out to be a Kunderian war"', *Le Monde*, 19 July 2023; Adam Soboczynski, 'Der Mann, der die Russen kannte', *Die Zeit*, 19 July 2023; Jacques Rupnik, 'War, identity, irony: how Russian aggression put central Europe back on the map', *The Guardian*, 25 August 2023; Henry Kissinger, 'How to avoid another world war', *The Spectator* (17 December 2022).

BIBLIOGRAPHY

Primary Sources

IV. sjezd Svazu československých spisovatelů (Protokol): Praha 29.-29. června 1967, Prague: Československý spisovatel (1968).

Aichner, Christof and Mazohl, Brigitte eds., *Die Korrespondenz des Ministers für Cultus und Unterricht Leo Thun-Hohenstein (1849–1860). Auswahledition zu den Reformen von Unterricht und Bildung in der Habsburgermonarchie*, Vienna: Böhlau (2022).

Andrian-Werburg, Victor Franz von, *Oesterreich und dessen Zukunft*, Hamburg: Hoffmann und Campe (1843).

Ashmead-Bartlett, Ellis, *The Tragedy of Central Europe*, London: Thornton Butterworth (1923).

Baer, Josette ed., *Preparing Liberty in Central Europe: Political Texts from the Spring of Nations 1848 to the Spring of Prague 1968*, Stuttgart: ibidem-Verlag (2006).

Banac, Ivo ed., *The Diary of Georgi Dimitrov 1933–1949*, New Haven: Yale University Press (2003).

Bělohradský, Václav, 'Útěk k uniformě a pád pořádku', *Proměny*, Vol. 18, No. 2 (1981), 33–46.

Beneš, Edvard, 'Central Europe after Ten Years', *The Slavonic and East European Review*, Vol. 7, No. 20 (1929), 245–60.

———, *Úvahy o slovanství. Hlavní problémy slovanské politiky*, Prague (1947).

Berchtold, Klaus ed., *Österreichische Parteiprogramme 1868–1966*, Munich: R. Oldenbourg (1967).

Bismarck, Otto Fürst von, *Gedanken und Erinnerungen*, New York: J. G. Cotta'sche Buchhandlung Nachfolger (1898).

Bottomore, Tom and Patrick Goode eds., *Austro-Marxism*, Oxford: Clarendon Press (1978).

Busch, Moritz, *Tagebuchblätter*, 3 Vols., Leipzig (1899).

Butter, Wilhelm, *Die unerlaßlichen Bedingungen des Friedens mit Frankfreich. Eine freimüthige und prüfende Darstellung der öffentlichen Meinung*, Wiesbaden (1815).

Charmatz, Richard, *Minister Freiherr von Bruck. Der Vorkämpfer Mitteleuropas*, Leipzig: Verlag von G. Hirzel (1916).

Cornicelius, Max ed., *Heinrich von Treitschkes Briefe*, 2 Vols., Leipzig: Verlage von G. Hirzel (1913).

Czoernig, Carl Freiherr von, *Oesterreich's Neugestaltung 1848–1858*, Stuttgart: J. G. Cotta'scher Verlag (1858).

Debrois, Johann, *Urkunde über die vollzogene Krönung seiner Majestät des Königs von Böhmen Leopold des Zweiten*, Prague (1818).

BIBLIOGRAPHY

Desnitsky, Andrei, 'De-imperializing Joseph Brodsky: "On the independence of Ukraine" and other poems', *Studies in East European Thought*, Vol. 76 (2023), 609–622.

Deželić, Velimir, *Iz njemačkoga Zagreba*, Zagreb: Tisak Antuna Scholza (1901).

Eötvös, Josef von, *Ueber die Gleichberechtigung der Nationalitäten in Oesterreich*, Pest: C. A. Hartleben's Verlag (1850).

Frisch, Max, *Tagebuch 1946–1949*, Frankfurt: Suhrkamp Verlag (1950).

Fröbel, Julius, *Wien, Deutschland und Europa*, Vienna: Verlag von Joseph Keck and Sohn (1848).

Füster, Anton, *Memoiren vom März 1848 bis Juli 1849. Beitrag zur Geschichte der Wiener Revolution*, Frankfurt: Literarische Anstalt (1850).

Geyer, David C., *Foreign Relations of the United States, 1969–1976, Volume XL: Germany and Berlin, 1969–1972*, Washington: United States Government Printing Office (2007).

Goethe, Johann Wolfgang von, *Aus meinem Leben. Dichtung und Wahrheit. Erster Theil*, Tübingen (1811).

Grimm, Jacob, *Geschichte der Deutschen Sprache*, Leipzig: Verlag von S. Hirzel (1868).

Gumplowicz, Ludwig, *Raçe und Staat. Eine Untersuchung über das Gesetz der Staatenbildung*, Vienna: Verlag der G. J. Manz'schen Buchhandlung (1875).

Hamšík, Dušan, *Writers Against Rulers*, London: Hutchinson & Co. (1971).

Handelsman, Marceli ed., *Konstytucje polskie 1791–1921*, Warsaw (1922).

Hassel, Georg, *Statistischer Umriss der sämtlichen Europäischen Staaten in Hinsicht ihrer Grösse, Bevölkerung, Kulturverhältnisse, Handlung, Finanz- und Militärverfassung und ihrer aussereuropäischen Besitzungen*, Braunschweig: Friedrich Vieweg (1805).

Hauner, Milan, 'Dopis redakci The New York Review of Books', *Svědectví*, No. 74 (1985), 356–9.

Havel, Václav, *Open Letters: Selected Writings 1965–1990*, New York: Alfred A. Knopf (1991).

Heffter, Moritz Wilhelm, *Der Weltkampf der Deutschen und Slaven seit dem Ende des fünften Jahrhunderts nach christlicher Zeitrechnung*, Hamburg: Friedrich und Andreas Perthes (1847).

Heiss, Johann von, *The History of the Empire*, London: R. Francklin (1730).

Hitler, Adolf, *Mein Kampf*, 2 Vols., Munich (1939).

Hlaváček, Petr ed., *Západ nebo Východ? České reflexe Evropy 1918–1948*, Prague: Academia (2016).

Henderson, Alexander, *Eyewitness in Czecho-Slovakia*, London (1939).

Holoček, Josef, *Ruskočeski Kapitoly*, Prague (1891).

Hommel, Rudolf, *Briefe über die Kaiserwahl während derselben aus Frankfurt geschrieben*, Leipzig: Georg Joachim Göschen (1791).

Huber, Ernst Rudolf ed., *Dokumente zur deutschen Verfassungsgeschichte*, 5 Vols., Stuttgart: Verlag W. Kohlhammer (1978–97).

James, Robert Rhodes ed., *Winston S. Churchill: His Complete Speeches 1897–1963*, 7 Vols., London: Chelsea House Publishers (1970–74).

Jucho, Friedrich Siegmund ed., *Verhandlungen des Deutschen Parlaments. Zweite Lieferung*, Frankfurt am Main: J. D. Sauerländer's Verlag (1848).

Karner, Stefan et al. eds., *Prager Frühling. Das internationale Krisenjahr 1968. Dokumente*, Cologne: Böhlau (2008).

Klępka, Krzysztof ed., *Zostało tylko słowo. Wybór tekstów o "Kulturze" paryskiej I jej twórcach*, Lublin: Wydawnictwo FIS (1990).

BIBLIOGRAPHY

Kohl, Horst ed., *Die politischen Reden des Fürsten Bismarck*, Vol. 2, Stuttgart (1892).

Kohlrausch, Friedrich, *Die Teutsche Geschichte. Erste Abtheilung*, Elberfeld (1818).

Kollar, Jan, *Ueber die literarische Wechselseitigkeit zwischen den verschiedenen Stämmen und Mundarten der slawischen Nation*, Pest (1837).

Kopitar, Jernej, *Grammatik der Slavischen Sprache in Krain, Kärnten und Steyermark*, Ljubljana: Wilhelm Heinrich Korn (1808).

Kramař [Kramarz], Karel, 'Europe and the Bohemian Question', *The National Review*, Vol. 40, No. 236 (October 1902), 183–205.

Krleža, Miroslav, *Djetinjstvo u Agramu godine 1902–03*, Samobor: Anindol (1992).

Krönungsbegebenheiten Kaisers Leopold II. als Königs von Böhmen, wie auch der Kaiserinn Mar. Ludovica, Prague: Joh. Jos. Diesbach (1791).

Kundera, Milan, *The Book of Laughter and Forgetting*, London: Penguin Books (1983).

———, 'The Tragedy of Central Europe', *The New York Review of Books* (26 April 1984).

———, 'Z kulturního testamentu Střední Evropy', *Listy: Časopis československé opozice*, Vol. VIII, No. 5 (1978), 37–9.

———, *A Kidnapped West: The Tragedy of Central Europe*, London: Faber & Faber (2023).

Lagarde, Paul de, *Deutsche Schriften*, Göttingen: Dieterichsche Verlagsbuchhandlung (1892).

Lemkin, Raphael ed., *Key Laws, Decrees and Regulations Issued by the Axis in Occupied Europe*, Washington: Board of Economic Warfare (1942).

Leo, Heinrich, *Aus meiner Jugendzeit*, Gotha: Friedrich Andreas Perthes (1880).

'The Lisbon Conference on Literature: A Round Table of Central European and Russian Writers', *Cross Currents*, No. 9 (1990), 75–124.

Löschenkohl, Hieronymus, *Beschreibung der königl. Hungarischen Krönung als Seine Apostolische Majestät Leopold der Zweyte*, Vienna (1790).

Ludecke, Kurt, *I Knew Hitler: The Story of a Nazi Who Escaped the Blood Purge*, London: Jarrolds (1938).

Magyarország a Párisi nemzetközi kiállitáson. Képzőművészeti iparművészeti, történelmi, és oktatásügyi csoportok, Budapest: Hornyansky Viktor (1900).

Malkowsky, Georg ed., *Die Pariser Weltausstellung in Wort und Bild*, Berlin: Kirchhoff & Co. (1900).

'Manifest Polskiego Komitetu Wyzwolenia Narodowego', *Rocznik Lubelski*, No. 2 (1959), 7–14.

Mann, Thomas, *Reflections of a Nonpolitical Man*, New York: New York Review of Books (2021).

Matvejević, Predrag, *Razgovori s Krležom. VII. dopunjeno i prošireno izdanje*, Zagreb: Prometej (2001).

Mensing, Hans Peter von ed., *Adenauer. Briefe 1945–1947*, Siedler Verlag (1983).

Metternich, Klemens Wenzel von, *Aus Metternich's nachgelassenen Papieren. Erster Theil*, Vol. 1, Vienna: Wilhelm Branmüller (1880).

Meyer, Rudolf, *Politische Gründer und die Corruption in Deutschland*, Leipzig: Verlag von E. Bidder (1877).

Michaelis, Herbert and Ernst Schraepler eds., *Ursachen und Folgen. Vom deutschen Zusammenbruch 1918 und 1945 bis zur staatlichen Neuordnung Deutschlands in der Gegenwart*, XXVI vols.

BIBLIOGRAPHY

Milićević, Milan đakov, *Кнежевина Србија*, Belgrade: Državna štamparija (1876).

Miłosz, Czesław, 'Looking for a Center: On the Poetry of Central Europe', *Cross Currents: A Yearbook of Central European Culture*, No. 1 (1982).

Milton, John, *A Brief History of Moscovia: And of Other Less-Known Countries Lying Eastward of Russia as far as Cathay*, London: Blackamore Press (1929).

Moritsch, Andreas ed., *Der Austroslavismus. Ein verfrühtes Konzept zur politischen Neugestaltung Mitteleuropas*, Vienna: Böhlau Verlag (1996).

Moser, Friedrich Karl, *Vom dem Deustchen National-Geist* (1765).

Moser, Johann Jacob, *Von Deutschland und dessen Staats-Verfassung*, Stuttgart: Johann Benedict Mezler (1766).

Naumann, Friedrich, *Deutschland und Oesterreich*, Berlin: Verlag der "Hilfe" (1900).

———, 'Polen in Mitteleuropa', *Polnische Blätter*, Vol. 42, No. 5 (20 November 1916), 182–7.

Oberdeutsche Allgemeine Literaturzeitung im Jahre 1806, Vol. 19, No. 1, Munich (1806).

Paget, John, *Hungary and Transylvania*, London: John Murray (1839).

Palacký, Franz, *Joseph Dobrowsky's Leben und gelehrtes Wirken*, Prague: Gottlieb Haase Söhne (1833).

———, 'Manifesto of the First Slavonic Congress to the Nations of Europe', *The Slavonic and East European Review*, Vol. 26, No. 67 (1948), 309–313.

——— ed., *Leben des Grafen Kaspar Sternberg, von ihm selbst beschrieben*, Prague (1868).

Partsch, Joseph, *Central Europe*, New York: D. Appleton and Company (1903).

———, *Mitteleuropa*, Gotha: Justus Perthes (1904).

Paupie, Franz Andreas, *Die Kunst des Bierbrauens*, 2 Vols., Prague (1794).

Pendl, Erwin, *Österreich auf der Weltausstellung Paris 1900*, Vienna: A. Hartleben's Verlag (1900).

Pfizer, Paul Achatius, *Briefwechsel zweier Deutschen*, Stuttgart: J. G. Cotta'schen Buchhandlung (1831).

———, *Das Vaterland*, Stuttgart: Hallberger'sche Verlagshandlung (1845).

Pierwszy powszechny spis Rzeczpospolitej Polskiej z dnia 30 września 1921 roku, Warsaw (1927).

Pisling, Theodor, *Germanisirung oder Czechisirung. Ein Beitraf zur Nationalitätenfrage in Böhmen*, Leipzig (1861).

'Prag und der neue Panslavismus', *Die Grenzboten*, 7. Jahrgang, 1. Semester, II. Band (1848), 383–8.

Preßler, Maximilian Robert, *Deutschlands Schulreform vom Kindergarten bis zur Hochschule mit besonderer Beziehung auf Sachsen*, Leipzig: Verlag von Georg Wigand (1850).

Radić, Stjepan, *Politički spisi*, Zagreb: Znanje (1971).

Rochau, August Ludwig von, *Grundsätze der Realpolitik angewendet auf de Zustände Deutschlands*, Stuttgart: Verlag von Karl Göpel (1853).

Saborski dnevnik Kraljevinah Hrvatske, Slavonije i Dalmacije. Godina 1872–1875, 2 Vols., Zagreb (1875).

Salomon, Ernst von, *The Outlaws*, New York: Kraus Reprint (1983).

Schauff, Johann Nepomuk, *Die Feyerlichkeiten bey der Krönung Seiner kaiserlich-königlich-apostolischen Majestät Leopold des Zweyten als König von Ungarn zu Preßburg den 15ten November 1790*, Preßburg (1790).

BIBLIOGRAPHY

Schieder, Theodor ed., *Dokumentation der Vertreibung der Deutschen aus Ost-Mitteleuropa*, 5 Vols., Bonn: Bundesministerium für Vertriebene, Flüchtlinge und Kriegsgeschädigte (1954–62).

Schindler, Julius Alexander, *Exkursionen eines Österreichers 1840–1879*, 2 Vols., Leipzig: Verlag von Duncker & Humboldt (1881).

Schlegel, Friedrich von, *Geschichte der alten und neuen Literatur. Vorlesungen gehalten zu Wien im Jahre 1812*, Berlin: M. Simion (1841).

Schnabel, G. N., *Tafeln zur Statistik von Böhmen*, Prague (1848).

Schacher, Gerhard, *Central Europe and the Western World*, New York: Henry Holt and Company (1936).

Schulin, Johann Philipp, *Vollständiges Diarium der römisch-königlichen Wahl und Kaiserlichen Krönung Ihro nunmehr allerglorwürdigst regierenden Kaiserlichen Majestät Leopold des Zweiten*, Frankfurt am Main: Verlag der Jägerischen Buchhandlung (1791).

Schuselka, Franz, *Ist Oesterreich deutsch? Eine statistische und glossierte Beantwortung dieser Frage*, Leipzig: Weidmann'sche Buchhandlung (1843).

———, *Deutsche Fahrten*, 2 volumes, Vienna: Jasper, Hügel & Manz (1849).

Simson, Eduard von, *Eduard von Simson. Erinnerungen aus seinem Leben*, Leipzig: Verlag von G. Hirzel (1900).

Stenographische Protokolle über die Sitzungen des Hauses der Abgeordneten des österreichischen Reichsrates im Jahre 1917, XXII Vols., Vienna: K. k. Hof und Staatsdruckerei (1861–1918).

Taschenausgabe der österreichischen Gesetze. Neunzehnter Band: Die Staatsgrundgesetze. Die Reichsverfassung. Die Landesverfassungen, Vienna: Manz'sche k. k. Hofverlags- und Universitäts-Buchhandlung (1882).

Thun, Leo von, *Die Stellung der Slowaken in Ungarn*, Prague: Calve'sche Buchhandlung (1843).

Tolstoy, Pyotr Andreeyevich, *Путешествие стольника П. А. Толстого по Европе (1697–1699)*, Moscow: Nauka (1992).

Treitschke, Heinrich von, 'Oesterreich und das deutsche Reich', *Preußische Jahrbücher*, Vol. 28 (1871), 667–82.

Trotsky, Leon, *My Life: An Attempt at an Autobiography*, New York: Pathfinder Press (1970).

Vaterländische Blätter für den österreichischen Kaiserstaat, Vol. 1, Vienna: Strauß (1817).

Vayrac, Jean de, *L'etat present de l'Empire*, Paris: Andre Cailleau (1711).

Wagener, Otto, *Hitler aus nächster Nähe. Aufzeichnungen eines Vertrauten 1929–1932*, Frankfurt: Verlag Ullstein (1978).

Wagner, Rudolf ed., *Die Revolutionsjahre 1848–49 im Königreich Galizien-Lodomerien (einschließlich Bukowina). Dokumente aus österreichischer Zeit*, Munich: Verlag "Der Südostdeustche" (1983).

Walk, Joseph ed., *Das Sonderrecht für die Juden im NS-Staat. Eine Sammlung der gesetzlichen Maßnahmen und Richtlinien—Inhalt und Bedeutung*, Heidelberg: C. F. Müller Juristischer Verlag (1981).

Weltausstellung in Paris 1900. Amtlicher Katalog der Ausstellung des Deutschen Reichs, Berlin (1900).

Wigard, Franz ed., *Stenographischer Bericht über die Verhandlungen der deutschen konstituierenden Nationalversammlung zu Frankfurt am Main*, 9 volumes, Frankfurt (1848–49).

BIBLIOGRAPHY

Žáček, Václav ed., *Slovanský sjezd v Praze roku 1848. Sbirka dokumentů*, Prague: Nakladatelství Československé akademie věd (1958).

Zelený, Karel ed., *Vynání Čehů z pohraničí 1938*, Prague: Ústav mezinárodních vztahů Praha (1996).

Ziemiałkowski, Floryan, *Pamiętniki Floryana Ziemiałkowskiego. Część druga. Rok 1848*, Krakow: Drukarna A. Koziańskiego (1904).

Zimmermann, Wilhelm, *Die deutsche Revolution*, Karlsruhe: Kunstverlag (1851).

Secondary Sources

Abrams, Bradley F., *The Struggle for the Soul of the Nation: Czech Culture and the Rise of Communism*, Lanham: Rowman & Litterfield (2004).

Adler, Philip, 'Nation and Nationalism Among the Serbs of Hungary 1790–1870', *East European Quarterly*, Vol. 13, No. 3 (1979), 271–85.

Agičić, Damir, 'Civil Croatia on the Eve of the First World War (The Echo of the Assasination and Ultimatum)', *Povijesni prilozi*, Vol. 14, No. 14 (1995), 301–317.

———, *Srednjoeuropske teme*, Zagreb: Srednja Europa (2020).

Agnew, Hugh LeCaine, *Origins of the Czech National Renaissance*, Pittsburgh: University of Pittsburgh Press (1993).

———, 'Ambiguities of Ritual: Dynastic Loyalty, Territorial Patriotism and Nationalism in the Last Three Royal Coronations in Bohemia, 1791–1836', *Bohemia*, Vol. 41 (2000), 3–22.

Almási, Gábor and Lav Šubarić eds., *Latin at the Crossroads of Identity: The Evolution of Linguistic Nationalism in the Kingdom of Hungary*, Leiden: Brill (2015).

———, 'The new discourses of the nation: The origins of nationalism in late eighteenth-century Hungary (Part 1)', *Nations and Nationalism*, Vol. 28, No. 3 (2022), 894–908.

Almasy, Karin, 'An Unintended Consequence: How the Modern Austrian School System Helped Set Up the Slovene Nation', *Austrian History Yearbook*, FirstView (2023), 1–19.

Ammon, Ulrich, Die *deutsche Sprache in Deutschland, Österreich und der Schweiz. Das Problem der nationalen Varietäten*, Berlin: Walter de Gruyter (1995).

Anderson, M.S., *The War of the Austrian Succession, 1740–1748*, London: Longman (1995).

Andree, Richard, *Wendische Wanderstudien. Zur Kunde der Lausitz und der Sorbenwenden*, Stuttgart: Verlag von Julius Maier (1874).

Aralica, Višeslav, *Kmet, Fiškal, Hajduk. Konstrukcija identiteta Hrvata 1935–1945*, Zagreb: Ljevak (2016).

Aronsfeld, C. C., 'The first anti-Semitic international 1882–83', *Immigrants & Minorities*, Vol. 4, No. 1 (1985), 64–75.

Augustynowicz, Christoph and Agnieszka Pufelska eds., *Konstruirte (Fremd-?)Bilder. Das östliche Europa im Diskurs des 18. Jahrhunderts*, Berlin: De Gruyter (2017).

Aulneau, Joseph, *Histoire de L'Europe Centrale*, Paris: Payot (1926).

Austensen, Roy A., 'Austria and the "Struggle for Supremacy in Germany"', *The Journal of Modern History*, Vol. 52, No. 2 (1980), 195–225.

Baár, Monika, *Historians and Nationalism: East-Central Europe in the Nineteenth Century*, Oxford: OUP (2010).

Babejová, Eleonóra, *Fin-de-Siecle Pressburg: Conflict & Cultural Coexistence in Bratislava 1897–1914*, New York: Columbia University Press (2003).

BIBLIOGRAPHY

Bacher, Frederick, *Friedrich Naumann und sein Kreis*, Stuttgart: Franz Steiner (2017).

Bakić, Dragan, *Britain and Interwar Danubian Europe: Foreign Policy and Security Challenges, 1919–36*, London: Bloomsbury Academic (2017).

Balázs, Eva H., *Hungary and the Habsburgs 1765–1800: An Experiment in Enlightened Absolutism*, Budapest: Central European University Press (1997).

Banac, Ivo, *Nacionalno pitanje u Jugoslaviji. Porijeklo, povijest, politika*, Zagreb: Globus (1984).

———, '"Emperor Karl Has Become a Comitadji": The Croatian Disturbances of Autumn 1918', *The Slavonic and East European Review*, Vol. 70, No. 2 (1992), 284–305.

Barany, George, *Stephen Szechényi and the Awakening of Hungarian Nationalism, 1791–1841*, Princeton: Princeton University Press (1968).

———, 'Hoping Against Hope: The Enlightened Age in Hungary', *The America Historical Review*, Vol. 76, No. 2 (1971), 319–57.

Barclay, David E., *Frederick William IV and the Prussian Monarchy 1840–1861*, Oxford: Clarendon Press (1995).

Barenscott, Dorothy, 'Articulating Identity through the Technological Rearticulation of Space: The Hungarian Millennial Exhibition as World's Fair and the Disordering of Fin-de-Siecle Budapest', *Slavic Review*, Vol. 69, No. 3 (2010), 571–90.

Baron, Salo W., 'The Impact of the Revolution of 1848 on Jewish Emancipation', *Jewish Social Studies*, Vol. 11, No. 3 (1949), 195–248.

Baumgart, Winfried, 'Zur Ansprache Hitlers vor den Führern der Wehrmacht am 22. August 1939', *Vierteljahrshefte für Zeitgeschichte*, Vol. 19, No. 2 (1971), 294–304.

Bavaj, Ricardo and Steber, Martina ed., *Germany and 'the West': The History of a Modern Concept*, New York: Berghahn (2015).

Bazillion, Richard J., *Modernizing Germany: Karl Biedermann's Career in the Kingdom of Saxony, 1835–1901*, New York: Peter Lang (1990).

Becker, Peter and Wheatley, Natasha eds., *Remaking Central Europe: The League of Nations and the Former Habsburg Lands*, Oxford: OUP (2020).

Bede, Ábel, 'Fathers of Budapest, Daughters of the Countryside: Recontextualizing Cultural Change in Fin-de-Siecle Hungary', *Hungarian Historical Review*, Vol. 13, No. 4 (2024), 623–54.

Behrends, Jan C., 'Die „sowjetische Rus" und ihre Brüder. Die slawische Idee in Russlands langem 20. Jahrhundert', *Osteuropa*, Vol. 59, No. 12 (2009), 95–114.

Behring, Eva, Ludwig Richter, and Wolfgang F. Schwarz eds., *Geschichtliche Mythen in den Literaturen und Kulturen Ostmittel- und Südosteuropas*, Stuttgart: Franz Steiner Verlag (1999).

Beneš, Jakub S., *Workers & Nationalism: Czech and German Social Democracy in Habsburg Austria, 1890–1918*, Oxford: OUP (2017).

Benes, Tuska, *In Babel's Shadow: Language, Philology, and the Nation in Nineteenth-Century Germany*, Detroit: Wayne State University Press (2008).

Bennette, Rebecca Ayako, *Fighting for the Soul of Germany: The Catholic Struggle for Inclusion After Unification*, Cambridge: Harvard University Press (2012).

Berecz, Ágoston, *The Politics of Early Language Teaching: Hungarian in the primary schools of the late Dual Monarchy*, Budapest: Pasts, Inc., Cenral European University (2013).

———, 'Hungarian, Romanian and German in the Counties of Dualist Hungary', *Südost-Forschungen*, 80 (2021), 141–73.

BIBLIOGRAPHY

———, 'The Hungarian Nationalities Act of 1868 in Operation (1868–1914)', *Slavic Review*, Vol. 81, No. 4 (2022), 994–1015.

Berend, Ivan T., *Decades of Crisis: Central and Eastern Europe Before World War II*, Berkeley: University of California Press (1998).

Berger, Stefan and Chris Lorenz eds., *The Contested Nation: Ethnicity, Class, Religion and Gender in National Histories*, Palgrave Macmillan (2008).

Berger, Stefan and Alexei Miller eds., *Nationalizing Empires*, CEU Press (2015).

Bernik, France and Reinhard Lauer eds., *Die Grundlagen der slowenischen Kultur*, Berlin: De Gruyter (2010).

Berwinkel, Holger and Martin Kröger eds., *Die Außenpolitik der deutschen Länder im Kaiserreich. Geschichte, Akteure und archivische Überlieferung (1871–1918)*, Munich: Oldenbourg Verlag (2012).

Biber, Dušan, *Nacizem in Nemci v Jugoslaviji, 1933–1941*, Ljubljana: Cankarjeva Založba (1966).

Biddiss, Michael D., 'Gobineau and the Origins of European Racism', *Race and Class*, Vol. 7, No. 3 (1966), 255–70.

Biondich, Mark, *Stjepan Radić, the Croat Peasant Party, and the Politics of Mass Mobilization, 1904–1928*, Toronto: University of Toronto Press (2000).

Bischof, Günter, Plasser, Fritz, and Berger, Peter eds., *From Empire to Republic: Post-World War I Austria*, New Orleans: University of New Orleans Press (2010).

Blackall, Eric A., *The Emergence of German as a Literary Language*, Ithaca: Cornell University Press (1959).

Blackbourn, David and Geoff Eley, *The Peculiarities of German History: Bourgeois Society and Politics in Nineteenth-Century Germany*, Oxford: OUP (1984).

Blackbourn, David and James Retallack eds., *Localism, Landscape, and the Ambiguities of Place: German-Speaking Central Europe, 1860–1930*, Toronto: University of Toronto Press (2007).

Blanke, Richard, *Prussian Poland in the German Empire (1871–1900)*, New York: Columbia University Press (1981).

———, *Polish-speaking Germans? Language and National Identity among the Masurians since 1871*, Cologne: Böhlau Verlag (2001).

Blanning, T.C.W., *Reform and Revolution in Mainz, 1743–1803*, Cambridge: Cambridge University Press (1974).

———, *The Culture of Power and the Power of Culture: Old Regime Europe 1660–1789*, Oxford: OUP (2002).

———, *The Pursuit of Glory: Europe 1648–1815*, London: Allen Lane (2007).

———, *Frederick the Great: King of Prussia*, London: Allen Lane (2015).

Blaschke, Olaf, *Katholizismus und Antisemitismus im Deutschen Kaiserreich*, Göttingen: V&R (1997).

Blitz, Hans-Martin, *Aus Liebe zum Vaterland. Die deutsche Nation im 18. Jahrhundert*, Hamburg: Hamburger Edition (2000).

Blum, Mark E., *The Austro-Marxists, 1890–1918: A Psychobiographical Study*, Lexington: The University of Kentucky Press (1985).

Böhler, Joachim, *Civil War in Central Europe, 1918–1931: The Reconstruction of Poland*, Oxford: OUP (2022).

BIBLIOGRAPHY

Boia, Lucian, *History and Myth in Romanian Consciousness*, Budapest: CEU Press (1997).

Bolton, Jonathan, *Worlds of Dissent: Charter 77, The Plastic People of the Universe, and Czech Culture under Communism*, Cambridge: Harvard University Press (2012).

Bookbinder, Paul, *Weimar Germany: The Republic of the Reasonable*, Manchester: Manchester University Press (1996).

Borejsza, Jerzy W., *A ridiculous hundred million Slavs: Concerning Adolf Hitler's world-view*, Warsaw: IH PAN (2017).

Borodziej, Włodzimierz, *Geschichte Polens im 20. Jahrhundert*, Munich: C.H. Beck (2010).

Borodziej, Włodzimierz, Stanislav Holubec, and Joachim von Puttkamer eds., *Mastery and Lost Illusions: Space and Time in the Modernization of Eastern and Central Europe*, Munich: Oldenbourg Wissenschaftsverlag (2014).

Bösch, Frank, *Die Adenauer-CDU. Gründung, Aufstieg und Krise einer Erfolgspartei 1945–1969*, Stuttgart: Deutsche Verlags-Anstalt (2001).

Botz, Gerhard, *Nationalsozialismus in Wien. Machtübernahme, Herrschaftssicherung, Radikalisierung, Kriegsvorbereitung*, Vienna: Mandelbaum (2018).

Boyer, John W., *Political Radicalism in Late Imperial Vienna: Origins of the Christian Social Movement, 1848–1891*, Chicago: The University of Chicago Press (1981).

———, 'Die Sudetendeutsche Heimatfront (Partei) 1933–1938: Zur Bestimmung ihres politisch-ideologischen Standortes', *Bohemia*, Vol. 38, No. 2 (1997), 357–85.

———, *Austria, 1867–1955*, Oxford: OUP (2022).

Braham, Randolph L. and Scott Miller eds., *The Nazis' Last Victims: The Holocaust in Hungary*, Detroit: Wayne State University Press (1998).

Brandl, Vincenc, *Život Josefa Dobrovského*, Brno: Matica moravská (1883).

Brechtefeld, Jörg, *Mitteleuropa and German Politics: 1848 to the Present*, Palgrave Macmillan (1996).

Brnardić, Teodora Shek, *Svijet Baltazara Adama Krčelića: Obrazovanje na razmeđu tridentskoga katolicizma i katoličkoga prosvjetiteljstva*, Zagreb: Biblioteka Hrvatska Povjesnica (2009).

Brock, Peter and H. Gordon Skilling eds., *The Czech Renascence of the Nineteenth Century*, Toronto: Toronto University Press (1970).

Brook-Shepherd, Gordon, *The Last Habsburg*, New York: Weybright and Talley (1968).

Brophy, James M., 'The Political Calculus of Capital: Banking and the Business Class in Prussia, 1848–1856', *Central European History*, Vol. 25, No. 2 (1992), 149–76.

Broué, Pierre, *The German Revolution 1917–1923*, Leiden: Brill (2005).

Bruch, Rüdiger vom ed., *Friedrich Naumann in seiner Zeit*, Berlin: De Gruyter (2000).

Bruendel, Steffen, *Volksgemeinschaft oder Volksstaat. Die „Ideen von 1914" und die Neuordnung Deutschlands im Ersten Weltkrieg*, Berlin: Akademie Verlag (2003).

Bryant, Chad, 'Either German or Czech: Fixing Nationality in Bohemia and Moravia, 1939–1946', *Slavic Review*, Vol. 61, No. 4 (2002), 683–706.

Bucur, Maria and Nancy M. Wingfield eds., *Staging the Past: The Politics of Commemoration in Habsburg Central Europe, 1848 to the Present*, West Lafayette: Purdue University Press (2001).

Bugge, Peter, 'A Western Invention? The Discovery of Czech Dissidence in the 1970s', *Bohemia*, Vol. 59, No. 2 (2019), 273–91.

Bullivant, Keith, Geoffrey Giles, and Walter Pape eds., *Germany and Eastern Europe: Cultural Identities and Cultural Differences*, Amsterdam: Rodopi (1999).

BIBLIOGRAPHY

Burg, Peter, *Die deutsche Trias in Idee und Wirklichkeit. Vom alten Reich zum deutschen Zollverein*, Stuttgart: Franz Steiner Verlag (1989).

Burgdorf, Wolfgang, *Ein Weltbild verliert seine Welt. Der Untergang des Alten Reiches und die Generation 1806*, Munich: R. Oldenbourg Verlag (2006).

Burke, Peter, *Languages and Communities in Early Modern Europe*, Cambridge University Press (2009).

Burmeister, H.-P., F. Boldt, Gy. Meszaros eds., *Mitteleuropa. Traum oder Trauma? Überlegungen zum Selbstbild einer Region*, Bremen: Edition Temmen (1988).

Calcan, Ghoerghe, 'The Administrative Unification of the Completed Romania. The Stages of the Administrative Integration of Transylvania, 1918–1925', *Transylvanian Review of Administrative Sciences*, No. 30 (2010), 16–29.

Callahan, Kevin J., 'Putting World War I on trial: The moral peace activism of Austrian socialist Friedrich Adler through political assassination', *Peace & Change*, Vol. 46, No. 3 (2021), 241–68.

Carsten, Francis L., *Geschichte der preußischen Junker*, Frankfurt: Suhrkamp (1988).

Cashman, Laura ed., *1948 and 1968—Dramatic Milestones in Czech and Slovak History*, Abingdon: Routledge (2010).

Caquet, P. E., *The Bell of Treason: The 1938 Munich Agreement in Czechoslovakia*, London: Profile Books (2018).

Cerman, Ivo, Rita Krueger, and Susan Reynolds eds., *The Enlightenment in Bohemia: religion, morality, and multiculturalism*, Oxford: Voltaire Foundation (2011).

Charles, Victoria and Klaus H. Carl, *The Viennese Secession*, New York: Parkstone International (2011).

Chernetsky, Vitaly, 'Silences and Displacements: Revisiting the Debate on Central European Literature from a Ukrainian Perspective', *Zeitschrift für Slavische Philologie*, Vol. 72, No. 1 (2016), 69–84.

Chickering, Roger, *We Men Who Feel Most German: A Cultural Study of the Pan-German League, 1886–1914*, Boston: George Allen & Unwin (1984).

———, *The German Empire: 1871–1918*, Cambridge University Press (2025).

Chrastil, Rachel, *Bismarck's War: The Franco-Prussian War and the Making of Modern Europe*, London: Allen Lane (2023).

Chwalba, Andrzej, *Przegrane zwycięstwo. Wojna polsko-bolszewicka 1918–1920*, Wołowiec: Wydawnictwo zarne (2020).

Clark, Christopher, *Kaiser Wilhelm II: A Life in Power*, London: Allen Lane (2000).

———, *Iron Kingdom: The Rise and Downfall of Prussia, 1600–1947*, London: Allen Lane (2006).

———, 'After 1848: The European Revolution in Government', *Transactions of the Royal Historical Society*, Vol. 22 (2012), 171–97.

———, *Time and Power: Visions of History in German Politics, from the Thirty Years' War to the Third Reich*, Princeton: Princeton University Press (2019).

———, *Revolutionary Spring: Fighting for a New World, 1848–1849*, London: Allen Lane (2023).

Clegg, Elizabeth, *Art, Design & Architecture in Central Europe 1890–1920*, New Haven: Yale University Press (2006).

BIBLIOGRAPHY

Cohen, Gary B., *The Politics of Ethnic Survival: Germans in Prague, 1861–1914*, West Lafayette: Purdue University Press (2006).

Connelly, John, 'Nazis and Slavs: From Racial Theory to Racist Practice', *Central European History*, Vol. 32, No. 1 (1999), 1–33.

———, *From Peoples into Nations*, Princeton: Princeton University Press (2020).

———, 'Was the Habsburg Empire an Empire?', *Austrian History Yearbook*, No. 54 (2023), 1–14.

Cornwall, Mark, 'The Struggle on the Czech-German Language Border, 1880–1940', *The English Historical Review*, Vol. 109, No. 433 (1994), 914–51.

———, 'Traitors and the Meaning of Treason in Austria-Hungary's Great War', *Transactions of the RHS*, Vol. 25 (2015), 113–34.

Cornwall, Mark ed., *Sarajevo 1914: Sparking the First World War*, London: Bloomsbury Academic (2020).

Coy, Jason Philip, Benjamin Marschke, and David Warren Sabean eds., *The Holy Roman Empire, Reconsidered*, New York: Berhahn Books (2010).

Craig, Gordon A., *The End of Prussia*, Madison: The University of Wisconsin Press (1984).

Cvijić, Jovan, 'The Zones of Civilization of the Balkan Peninsula', *Geographical Review*, Vol. 5, No. 6 (1918), 470–82.

Cvrin, Janez, *Trdnjavski trikotnik. Politična orientacija Nemcev na Spodnjem Štajerskem (1861–1914)*, Maribor: Obzorja (1997).

Czok, Karl ed., *Geschichte Sachsens*, Weimar: Hermann Böhlaus Nachfolger (1989).

Dąbrowska, Małgorzata ed., *Oskar Halecki i jego wizja Europy*, 3 Vols., Warsaw: Instytut Pamięci Narodowej (2012–14).

Damen, Mario and Kim Overlaet eds., *Constructing and Representing Territory in Late Medieval and Early Modern Europe*, Amsterdam: Amsterdam University Press (2022).

Davies, Norman, *Heart of Europe: The Past in Poland's Present*, Oxford: OUP (2001).

Deak, Istvan, *The Lawful Revolution: Louis Kossuth and the Hungarians, 1848–1849*, New York: Columbia University Press (1979).

———, *Beyond Nationalism: A Social and Political History of the Habsburg Officer Corps, 1848–1918*, New York: OUP (1990).

Deak, John, *Forging a Multinational State: State Making in Imperial Austria from the Enlightenment to the First World War*, Stanford: Stanford University Press (2015).

Deak, John and Jonathan E. Gumz, 'How to Break a State: The Habsburg Monarchy's Internal War, 1914–1918', *The American Historical Review*, Vol. 122, No. 4 (2017), 1105–1136.

Delanty, Gerard, *Inventing Europe: Idea, Identity, Reality*, London: Palgrave Macmillan (1995).

Dénes, Iván Zoltán ed., *Liberty and the Search for Identity: Liberal Nationalisms and the Legacy of Empires*, Budapest: Central European University Press (2005).

Dhand, Otilia, *The Idea of Central Europe: Geopolitics, Culture and Regional Identity*, London: I. B. Tauris (2018).

Djokić, Dejan, *Elusive Compromise: A History of Interwar Yugoslavia*, London: Hurst (2006).

Dóbék, Ágnes, Gábor Mészáros, and Gábor Vaderna eds., *Media and Literature in Multilingual Hungary 1770–1820*, Budapest: Reciti (2019).

Dobre, Claudia-Florentina, Ionuţ Epurescu-Pascovici, and Cristian Emilian Ghiţă eds., *Myth-Making and Myth-Breaking in History and the Humanities*, Bucharest (2011).

BIBLIOGRAPHY

Doering-Manteuffel, Anselm, *Die Bundesrepublik Deutschland in der Ära Adenauer*, Darmstadt: Wissenschaftliche Buchgesellschaft (1983).

———, 'Wie westlich sind die Deutschen?', *Historisch-Politische Mitteilungen*, Vol. 3, No. 1 (1996), 1–38.

Domeier, Norman, 'World Domination and Genocide: The "Lochner Version" of Hitler's Speech from 22 August 1939, a Key Document of National Socialist Ideology', *The Journal of Holocaust Research*, Vol. 38, No. 1 (2024), 35–54.

Dostaly, Marina Yu., '"Новое славянское движение" в СССР и Всеславянский комитет в Москве в годы войны', *Славянский альманах* (1999), 175–88.

Douglas, R. M., *Orderly and Humane: The Expulsion of the Germans after the Second World War*, New Haven: Yale University Press (2012).

Dow, James Elstone, *A Prussian Liberal: The Life of Eduard von Simson*, Washington: University Press of America (1981).

Drozdowski, Mateusz, 'Powstanie Legionów Polskich oraz Naczelnego Komitetu Narodowego w sierpniu 1914 roku. Zapomniany sukces politycznej elity Galicji', *Sowiniec*, No. 45 (2014), 21–49.

Dülmen, Richard van, *The Society of the Enlightenment: The Rise of the Middle Class and Enlightenment in Germany*, Cambridge: Polity Press (1992).

Dwyer, Philip G. ed., *The Rise of Prussia 1700–1830*, New York: Taylor and Francis (2000).

Echternkamp, Jörg, *Der Aufstieg des deutschen Nationalismus (1770–1840)*, Frankfurt: Campus Verlag (1998).

Ehmer, Josef, Steidl, Annemarie, and Zeitlhofer, Hermann, 'Migration Patterns in Late Imperial Austria', *Kommission für Migrations- und Integrationsforschung*, Working Paper Nr. 3.

Eisner, Pavel, *Franz Kafka and Prague*, New York: Golden Griffin Books (1950).

Elias, Norbert, *The Civilizing Process: Sociogenetic and Psychogenetic Investigations*, London: Blackwell Publishing (1994).

Elmentaler, Michael ed., *Deutsch und seine Nachbarn*, Frankfurt: Peter Lang (2009).

Elvert, Jürgen, *Mitteleuropa! Deutsche Pläne zur europäischen Neuordnung (1918–1945)*, Stuttgart: Franz Steiner Verlag (1999).

———, '"Irrweg Mitteleuropa". Deutsche Konzepte zur Neugestaltung Europas aus der Zwischenkriegszeit', in Duchhardt, Heinz and Morawiec Małgorzata eds., *Vision Europa. Deutsche und polnische Föderationspläne des 19. Und frühen 20. Jahrhunderts*, Mainz: Verlag Philipp von Zabern (2003), 117–37.

Engelberg, Ernst, *Bismarck. Urpreuße und Riechsgründer*, Berlin: Siedler (1985).

———, *Bismarck. Das Reich in der Mitte Europas*, Berlin: Siedler (1990).

Erdmann, Karl Dietrich, *Adenauer in der Rheinlandpolitik nach dem Ersten Weltkrieg*, Stuttgart: Ernst Klett Verlag (1966).

Evans, Richard J., *The Coming of the Third Reich*, London: Penguin (2004).

———, *The Third Reich in Power*, London: Penguin (2006).

———, *The Pursuit of Power: Europe 1815–1914*, London: Penguin (2017).

Evans, R.J.W., *Austria, Hungary, and the Habsburgs: Central Europe c. 1683–1867*, Oxford: OUP (2006).

Evans, R.J.W. and Peter H. Wilson eds., *The Holy Roman Empire, 1495–1806: A European Perspective*, Brill: Leiden (2012).

BIBLIOGRAPHY

Fahlbusch, Michael, Ingo Haar, Anja Lobenstein-Reichmann, and Julien Reitzenstein eds., *Völkische Wissenschaften: Ursprünge, Ideologien und Nachwirkungen*, Berlin: De Gruyter (2020).

Falk, Barbara J., *The Dilemmas of Dissidence in East-Central Europe: Citizen Intellectuals and Philosopher Kings*, Budapest: Central European University Press (2003).

Fazekas, István, Stefan Malfér, and Péter Tusor eds., *Széchenyi, Kossuth, Batthyány, Deák. Studien zu den ungarischen Reformpolitikern des 19. Jahrhunderts und ihren Beziehungen zu Österreich*, Vienna: Publikationen der ungarischen Geschichtsforschung in Wien (2011).

Fillafer, Franz Leander, *Aufklärung habsburgisch. Staatsbildung, Wissenskultur und Geschichtspolitik in Zentraleuropa, 1750–1850*, Göttingen: Wallstein Verlag (2020).

Fisch, Jörg, 'Zivilisation, Kultur', in Otto Brunner, Werner Conze, and Reinhart Kosselleck eds., *Geschichtliche Grundbegriffe*, Vol. 7, 679–774.

Fischer, Fritz, *Griff nach der Weltmacht. Die Kriegszielpolitik des kaiserlichen Deutschland 1914/18*, Düsseldorf: Droste Verlag (1971).

Fitzpatrick, Matthew P. ed., *Liberal Imperialism in Europe*, New York: Palgrave Macmillan (2012).

Foschepoth, Josef ed., *Adenauer und die Deutsche Frage*, Göttingen: Vandenhoeck & Ruprecht (1988).

Frank, Tibor and Frank Hadler eds., *Disputed Territories and Shared Pasts: Overlapping National Histories in Modern Europe*, London: Palgrave Macmillan (2010).

Freifeld, Alice, *Nationalism and the Crowd in Liberal Hungary, 1848–1914*, Washington DC: The Woodrow Wilson Center Press (2000).

Fremdling, Rainer, *Eisenbahnen und deutsches Wirtschaftswachstum 1840–1879*, Dortmund: Gesellschaft für Westfälische Wirtschaftsgeschichte E. V. (1975).

French, Alfred, *Czech Writers and Politics 1945–1969*, Canberra: Australian National University Press (1982).

Friedländer, Saul, *Nazi Germany & The Jews: The Years of Persecution 1933–39*, London: Pheonix Giant (1997).

Friedrich, Karin, *The Other Prussia: Royal Prussia, Poland and Liberty, 1569–1772*, Cambridge: Cambridge University Press (2000).

Fukuyama, Francis, 'The End of History?' *The National Interest*, No. 16 (1989), 3–18.

Gabelica, Mislav, 'Žrtve sukoba na Jelačićevom trgu 5. prosinca 1918', *ČSP*, Vol. 37, No. 2 (2005), 467–77.

Gagliardo, John G., *Reich and Nation: The Holy Roman Empire as Idea and Reality, 1763–1806*, Bloomington: Indiana University Press (1980).

Gall, Lothar, *Bismarck. Der weiße Revolutionär*, Frankfurt: Propyläen Verlag (1980).

Gardt, Andreas, Klaus J. Mattheier, and Oskar Reichmann eds., *Sprachgeschichte des Neuhochdeutschen*, Tübingen: Max Niemeyer (1995).

Gawrecki, Dan, 'The Determination of Nationality in Selected European Countries up to 1938', *Prager wirtschafts- und sozialhistorische Mitteilungen*, Vol. 22, No. 2 (2015), 27–54.

Geiger, Vladimir, 'Njemci u Hrvatskoj', *Migracijske teme*, Vo. 7 (1991), 319–34.

———, *Nestanak folksdojčera*, Zagreb: Nova Stvarnost (1997).

Gelder, Klaas Van ed., *More Than Mere Spectacle: Coronations and Inaugurations in the Habsburg Monarchy during the Eighteenth and Nineteenth Centuries*, New York: Berghahn (2021).

BIBLIOGRAPHY

Gerlach, Christian, *The Extermination of the European Jews*, Cambridge: Cambridge University Press (2016).

Gerlach, Christian and Götz Aly, *Das letzte Kapitel. Realpolitik, Ideologie und der Mord an den ungarischen Juden 1944/1945*, Stuttgart: Deutsche Verlags-Anstalt (2002).

Gerschenkron, Alexander, *Bread and Democracy in Germany*, Ithaca: Cornell University Press (1989).

Gerwarth, Robert, 'The Central European Counter-Revolution: Paramilitary Violence in Germany, Austria and Hungary after the Great War', *Past & Present*, Vol. 200, No. 1 (2008), 175–209.

———, *The Vanquished: Why the First World War Failed to End, 1917–1923*, London: Allen Lane (2016).

———, *November 1918: The German Revolution*, Oxford: OUP (2020).

Gerwarth, Robert and John Horne eds., *War in Peace: Paramilitary Violence in Europe after the Great War*, Oxford: OUP (2012).

Geyr, Géza Andreas von, *Sándor Wekerle 1848–1921. Die politische Biographie eines ungarischen Staatsmannes der Donaumonarchie*, Munich: Oldenbourg (1993).

Gilbert, Martin, *Kristallnacht: Prelude to Destruction*, London: Harper Press (2006).

Ginderachter, Maarten van and Jon Fox eds., *National Indifference and the History of Nationalism in Modern Europe*, London: Routledge (2019).

Glaser, Konstanze, *Minority Languages and Cultural Diversity in Europe: Gaelic and Sorbian Perspectives*, Clevedon: Multilingual Matters (2007).

Glassheim, Eagle, 'National Mythologies and Ethnic Cleansing: The Expulsion of Czechoslovak Germans in 1945', *Central European History*, Vol. 33, No. 4 (2000), 463–86.

Glatthorn, Austin, 'The Theatre of Politics and the Politics of Theatre: Music as Representational Culture in the Twilight of the Holy Roman Empire', Doctoral Dissertation (University of Southampton, 2015).

———, 'The Imperial Coronation of Leopold II and Mozart, Frankfurt am Main, 1790', *Eighteenth-Century Music*, Vol 14., No 1. (2017), 89–110.

Godsey Jr., William D., *Nobles and Nation in Central Europe: Free Imperial Knights in the Age of Revolution, 1750–1850*, Cambridge: Cambridge University Press (2004).

Gogol, Eugene, *Toward a Dialectic of Philosophy and Organization*, Leiden: Brill (2012).

Goldstein, Ivo, *Židovi u Zagrebu 1918–1941*, Zagreb: Novi Libe (2004).

Goldstein, Ivo and Slavko Goldstein, *The Holocaust in Croatia*, Pittsburgh: University of Pittsburgh Press (2016).

Goltz, Anna von der, *Hindenburg: Power, Myth, and the Rise of the Nazis*, Oxford: OUP (2009).

Gooch, George Peabody, *Germany and the French Revolution*, Longmans (1920).

Good, David F., *The Economic Rise of the Habsburg Empire, 1750–1914*, Berkeley: University of California Press (1984).

Goodman, Brian K., *The Nonconformists: American and Czech Writers Across the Iron Curtain*, Cambridge, MA: Harvard University Press (2023).

Gossman, Lionel, *Medievalism and the Ideologies of the Enlightenment: The World and Work of La Cure de Sainte-Palaye*, Baltimore: Johns Hopkins University Press (1968).

Gottas, Friedrich, *Ungarn im Zeitalter des Hochliberalismus*, Vienna: Verlag der Österreichischen Akademie der Wissenschaften (1976).

BIBLIOGRAPHY

Gottsmann, Andreas, 'Parteipolitik und katholische Kirche in der Donaumonarchie', *Römische Historische Mitteilungen*, Vol. 51 (2009), 317–36.

Graubard, Stephen R. ed., *Eastern Europe ... Central Europe ... Europe*, London: Routledge (1991).

Green, Abigail, *Fatherlands: State-Building and Nationhood in Nineteenth-Century Germany*, Cambridge: Cambridge University Press (2001).

———, 'Representing Germany? The Zollverein at the World Exhibitions, 1851–1862', *The Journal of Modern History*, Vol. 75, No. 4 (2003), 836–63.

Greenfeld, Liah, *Nationalism: Five Roads to Modernity*, Cambridge: Harvard University Press (1992).

Greiner, Florian, 'Articulating Europe During the Great War: Friedrich Naumann's Idea of *Mitteleuropa* and Its Public Reception in Germany, England and the USA', *Linue Culture Mediazioni / Languages Cultures Mediation*, Vol. 2, No. 2 (2015), 131–48.

Gross, Mirjana, *Vladavina Hrvatsko-srpske koalicije 1906–1907*, Belgrade (1960).

———, *Počeci moderne Hrvatske. Neoapsolutizam u civilnoj Hrvatskoj i Slavoniji 1850–1860*, Zagreb: Globus (1985).

———, *Izvorno pravaštvo. Ideologija, agitacija, pokret*, Zagreb: Golden marketing (2000).

Grzechnik, Marta, '"Recovering' Territories: The Use of History in the Integration of the New Polish Western Borderland after World War II', *Europe-Asia Studies*, Vol. 69, No. 4 (2017), 668–92.

Gumz, Jonathan E., *The Resurrection and Collapse of Empire in Habsburg Serbia, 1914–1918*, Cambridge: Cambridge University Press (2009).

Gyáni, Gábor ed., *The Creation of the Austro-Hungarian Monarchy: A Hungarian Perspective*, New York: Routledge (2022).

Hagemann, Karen, 'Francophobia and Patriotism: Anti-French Images and Sentiments in Prussia and Northern Germany During the Anti-Napoleonic Wars', *French History*, Vol. 18, No. 4 (2004), 404–425.

Hagen, Thomas J., *Österreichs Mitteleuropa 1850–1866. Die Wirtschafts-, Währungs- und Verkehrsunion des Karl Ludwig Freiherrn von Bruck*, Husum: Matthiesen Verlag (2015).

Hagen, William W., 'Before the "Final Solution": Toward a Comparative Analysis of Political Anti-Semitism in Interwar Germany and Poland', *The Journal of Modern History*, Vol. 68, No. 2 (1996), 351–81.

Hahn, Hans Joachim, *The 1848 Revolutions in German-Speaking Europe*, London: Routledge (2001).

Hahn, Hans Henning and Robert Traba eds., *Deutsch-Polnische Erinnerungsorte*, 4 Vols., Paderborn: Ferdinand Schöningh (2014).

Halecki, Oskar, *The Limits and Divisions of European History*, Sheed & Ward (1950).

———, *Borderlands of Western Civilization: A History of East-Central Europe*, New York: The Ronald Press Company (1952).

Hamann, Brigitte, *Hitler's Vienna: A Portrait of the Tyrant as a Young Man*, London: I.B. Tauris (2014).

Hanák, Péter, *Ungarn in der Donaumonarchie. Probleme der bürgerlichen Umgestaltung eines Vielvölkerstaates*, Vienna: Verlag für Geschichte und Politik (1984).

———, *The Garden and the Workshop: Essays in the Cultural History of Vienna and Budapest*, Princeton: Princeton University Press (1998).

BIBLIOGRAPHY

Handler, Andrew, *Blood Libel at Tiszaeszlar*, New York: Columbia University Press (1980).

Hanebrink, Paul, *In Defense of Christian Hungary: Religion, Nationalism, and Antisemitism, 1890–1944*, Ithaca: Cornell University Press (2006).

———, *A Specter Haunting Europe: The Myth of Judeo-Bolshevism*, Cambridge: The Belknap Press (2018).

Hanisch, Manfred, *Für Fürst und Vaterland. Legitimitätsstiftung in Bayern zwischen Revolution 1848 und deutscher Einheit*, Munich: R. Oldenbourg Verlag (1991).

Hanna, Martha, *The Mobilization of Intellect: French Scholars and Writers during the Great War*, Cambridge, MA: Harvard University Press (1996).

Hauschildt, Elke, 'Polish Migrant Culture in Imperial Germany', *New German Critique*, No. 46 (1989), 155–71.

Hauser, Jakub and Eva Janáčová eds., *Visual Antisemitism in Central Europe: Imagery of Hatred*, Berlin: Walter de Gruyter (2021).

Heinzen, Jasper, 'The Guelph "Conspiracy": Hanover as Would-Be Intermediary in the European System, 1866–1870', *The International History Review*, Vol. 29, No. 2 (2007), 258–81.

———, *Making Prussians, Raising Germans: A Cultural History of Prussian State-Building After Civil War, 1866–1935*, Cambridge: Cambridge University Press (2017).

Heka, László/Ladislav, 'Hrvatsko-Ugarska Nagodba u zrcalu tiska', *Zbornik Pravnog fakulteta Sveučilišta u Rijeci*, Vol. 28, No. 2 (2007), 931–71.

———, 'Analiza Austro-Ugarske i Hrvatsko-Ugarske Nagodbe (U povodu 150. objetnice Austro-Ugarske Nagodbe)', *Zbornik Pravnog fakulteta Sveučilišta u Rijeci*, Vol. 38, No. 2 (2017), 855–80.

Hertz, Deborah, *How Jews Became Germans: The History of Conversion and Assimilation in Berlin*, New Haven: Yale University Press (2007).

Heywood, James R., 'Palmerston's Joke About the Schleswig-Holstein Question', *Notes and Queries*, Vol. 67, No. 1 (2020), 112–14.

Hoare, Marko Attila, *Serbia: A Modern History*, London: Hurst Publishers (2024).

Höbelt, Lothar, 'The Austrians in the German National Assembly in 1848', *Parliaments, Estates and Representation*, Vol. 18, No. 1 (1998), 91–101.

Hochman, Erin R., *Imagining a Greater Germany: Republican Nationalism and the Idea of Anschluss*, Ithaca: Cornell University Press (2016).

Hodenberg, Christina von, 'Weaving Survival in the Tapestry of Village Life. Strategies and Status in the Silesian Weaver Revolt of 1844', in Jan Kok ed., *Rebellious Families*, Berhahn (2002), 39–58.

Hoeres, Peter, *Krieg der Philosophen. Die deutsche und die britische Philosophie im Ersten Weltkrieg*, Paderborn: Ferdinand Schöningh (2004).

Hofman, Alois, *Die Prager Zeitschrift "Ost und West". Ein Beitrag zur Geschichte der deutsch-slawischen Verständigung im Vormärz*, Berlin: Akademie Verlag (1957).

Holec, Roman, *Trianon. Triumf alebo katastrofa?*, Bratislava: Marenčin (2022).

Holste, Heiko, *Warum Weimar? Wie Deutschlands erste Republik zu ihrem Geburtsort kam*, Vienna: Böhlau (2018).

Höyng, Peter, 'Die Begräbnisfeier für Otto Habsburg aus der "Fenstersicht" von Thomas Bernhards "Auslöschung. Ein Zerfall" (1986)', *Journal of Austrian Studies*, Vol. 47, No. 2 (2014), 83–103.

BIBLIOGRAPHY

Horel, Catherine, *Multicultural Cities of the Habsburg Empire 1880–1914: Imagined Communities and Conflictual Encounters*, Budapest: Central European University Press (2023).

Horne, John and Kramer, Alan, *German Atrocities, 1914: A History of Denial*, New Haven: Yale University Press (2001).

Hösler, Joachim, *Von Krain zu Slowenien. Die Anfänge der nationalen Differenzierungsprozesse in Krain und der Untersteiermark von der Aufklärung bis zur Revolution. 1768 bis 1848*, Munich: R. Oldenbourg Verlag (2006).

Hroch, Miroslav, *Na prahu národní existence*, Mláda fronta (1999).

Hrubý, Karel, 'Přerod komunistické víry mladých intelektuálů Mlynář, Kosík, Kalivoda, Klíma, Kundera, Kohout, Vaculík', *Dějiny-Teorie-Kritika*, Vol. 2 (2017), 268–309.

Iggers, Georg G., *The German Conception of History: The National Tradition of Historical Thought from Herder to the Present*, Middletown: Wesleyan University Press (1968).

Ignatieff, Michael and Stefan Roch eds., *Rethinking Open Society*, Amsterdam University Press (2018).

Ingrao, Charles and Franz Szabo eds., *The Germans and the East*, West Lafayette: Purdue University Press (2008).

Iveljić, Iskra ed., *The Entangled Histories of Vienna, Zagreb and Budapest (18th–20th Century)*, Zagreb: Faculty of Humanities and Social Sciences, University of Zagreb (2015).

Jackson, Patrick Thaddeus, 'Defending the West: Occidentalism and the Formation of NATO', *The Journal of Political Philosophy*, Vol. 11, No. 3 (2003), 223–52.

———, *Civilizing the Enemy: German Reconstruction and the Invention of the West*, Ann Arbor: The University of Michigan Press (2006).

Janos, Andrew C. and William B. Slottman eds., *Revolutions in Perspective: Essays on the Hungarian Soviet Republic*, Berkeley: University of California Press (1971).

Jarausch, Konrad H. and Larry Eugene Jones eds., *In Search of a Liberal Germany: Studies in the History of German Liberalism from 1789 to the Present*, New York: Berg (1990).

Jaworski, Rudolf and Robert Luft eds., *1848/49: Revolutionen in Ostmitteleuropa. Vorträge der Tagung des Collegium Carolinum in Bad Wiessee vom 30. November bis 1. Dezember 1990*, Munich: R. Oldenbourg Verlag (1996).

Jirásek, Josef, *Češi, Slováci a Rusko. Studie vzájemných vztahů československo-ruských od roku 1867 do počátku světové války*, Prague: Vesmír (1933).

Jones, Gareth Stedman, *Karl Marx: Greatness and Illusion*, London: Penguin (2017).

Jovanović, Neven, 'Nikola Škrlec Lomnički o senatu i kontroli izvršne vlasti: Čedne želje i zaključci Hrvatskog sabora 1790', *Zbornik Pravnog Fakulteta u Zagrebu*, 50 (6) (2000), 1027–51.

Judson, Pieter M., 'Inventing Germans: Class, Nationality and Colonial Fantasy at the Margins of the Hapsburg Monarchy', *Social Analysis: The International Journal of Anthropology*, No. 33 (1993), 47–67.

———, *Exclusive Revolutionaries: Liberal Politics, Social Experience, and National Identity in the Austrian Empire, 1848–1914*, Ann Arbor: The University of Michigan Press (1996).

———, *Guardians of the Nation: Activists on the Language Frontiers of Imperial Austria*, Cambridge, Massachusetts: Harvard University Press (2006).

———, 'L'Autriche-Hongrie était-elle un empiré?', *Annales. Histoire, Sciences Sociales*, No. 3 (2008), 563–96.

BIBLIOGRAPHY

Kaiser, Wolfram, *Christian Democracy and the Origins of the European Union*, Cambridge: Cambridge University Press (2007).

Kaldellis, Anthony, *Romanland: Ethnicity and Empire in Byzantium*, Cambridge: Belknap Press (2019).

Kamusella, Tomasz, *The Politics of Language and Nationalism in Modern Central Europe*, London: Palgrave Macmillan (2009).

Kann, Robert A., *A Study in Austrian Intellectual History: From Late Baroque to Romanticism*, London: Thames and Hudson (1960).

Kántás, Balázs, 'Secret Negotiations between Hungarian, German (Bavarian) and Austrian Radical Right-Wing Politicians and Paramilitary Organisations after the Great War, 1919–1921', *International Journal of Arts, Humanities and Social Sciences Studies*, Vol. 6, No. 7 (2021), 37–44.

Kapp, Friedrich, *Vom radikalen Frühsozialisten des Vormärz zum liberalen Parteipolitiker des Bismarckreichs. Briefe 1843–1884*, Berlin: Insel Verlag (1969).

Kapp, Richard W., 'Bethmann-Hollweg, Austria-Hungary and Mitteleuropa, 1914–1915', *Austrian History Yearbook*, Vol. 19, No. 1 (1983), 215–36.

———, 'Divided Loyalties: The German Reich and Austria-Hungary in Austro-German Discussions of War Aims, 1914–1916', *Central European History*, Vol. 17, No. 2/3 (1984), 120–39.

Karch, Brendan, *Nation and Loyalty in a German-Polish Borderland: Upper Silesia, 1848–1960*, Cambridge: Cambridge University Press (2018).

Kárník, Zdeněk, *České země v éře První republiky*, 2 Vols., Prague: Nakladatelstvi Libri (2003).

Kasper, Martin ed., *Language and Culture of the Lusatian Sorbs throughout their History*, Berlin: Akademie Verlag (1987).

Katus, László, *Hungary in the Dual Monarchy 1867–1914*, New York: Columbia University Press (2008).

Kazbunda, Karel, *Otázka česko-německá v předvečer velké války*, Prague: Vydavatelství Karolinium (1995).

Kennedy, Katharine D., 'Regionalism and Nationalism in South German History Lessons, 1871–1914', *German Studies Review*, Vol. 12, No. 1 (1989), 11–33.

Kershaw, Ian, *Hitler 1889–1936: Hubris*, London: Penguin (2001).

———, *Hitler 1936–1945: Nemesis*, London: Penguin (2001).

———, *Hitler*, London: Penguin (2009).

———, *The End: Germany 1944–45*, London: Penguin (2012).

Kettenacker, Lothar, 'Preußen in der alliierten Kriegszielplanung, 1939–1947', in Lothar Kettenacker, Manfred Schlenke, and Hellmut Seier eds., *Studien zur Geschichte Englands und der deutsch-britischen Beziehungen. Festschrift für Paul Kluke*, Munich: Wihlelm Fink Verlag (1981), 312–40.

Khavanova, Olga, *Нация, отечество, патриотизм в венгерской политической культуре: движение 1790 года*, Moscow: Институт славяноведения (2000).

———, 'Joseph von Sonnenfels's Courses and the Making of the Habsburg Bureaucracy', *Austrian History Yearbook*, Vol. 48 (2017), 54–73.

King, Jeremy, *Budweisers into Czechs and Germans: A Local History of Bohemian Politics, 1848–1948*, Princeton: Princeton University Press (2002).

BIBLIOGRAPHY

Kirschbaum, Heinrich, 'The Verbatim Drama of Lisbon: Stenography of (Anti-)Imperiality', *Zeitschrift für Slavische Philologie*, Vol. 72, No. 1 (2016), 9–21.

Kleinschnitzová, Flora, 'Josefa Dobrovského řeč »Über die Ergebenheit und Anhänglichkeit der Slawishen Völker an das Erzhaus Östreich« z r. 1791', *Listy filologické*, Vol. 45, No. 2 (1918), 96–104.

Klessmann, Christoph, 'Comparative Immigrant History: Polish Workers in the Ruhr Area and the North of France', *Journal of Social History*, Vol. 20, No. 2 (1986), 335–53.

Koenen, Gerd, *Der Russland-Komplex. Die Deutschen und der Osten*, Munich: C.H. Beck (2023).

Koepp, Roy G., 'Gustav von Kahr and the Emergence of the Radical Right in Bavaria', *The Historian*, Vol. 77, No. 4 (2015), 740–63.

Kohl, Katrin, 'Hero or Villian? The Response of German Authors to Frederick the Great', *Publications of the English Goethe Society*, Vol. 81, No. 1 (2013), 51–72.

Kohn, Hans, *The Idea of Nationalism: A Study in Its Origins and Background*, New York: The Macmillan Company (1944).

———, 'The Paradox of Fichte's Nationalism', *Journal of the History of Ideas*, Vol. 10, No. 3 (1949), 319–43.

Kolar-Dimitrijević, Mira, 'Presjek kroz rad Zagrebačke pivovare d.d. do 1945. godine', *ČSP*, Vol. 24, No. 2 (1992), 149–68.

Kolnai, Aurel, *The War Against the West*, London: Victor Gollancz (1938).

König, Mareike and Oliver Schulz eds., *Antisemitismus im 19. Jahrhundert aus internationaler Perspektive*, Göttingen: V & R unipress (2019).

Konrád, Miklós, 'Jews and politics in Hungary in the Dualist era, 1867–1914', *East European Jewish Affairs*, Vol. 39, No. 2 (2009), 167–86.

Kopyś, Tadeusz, 'Die Haltung der tschechischen und polnischen politischen Eliten zur Mitteleuropa-Konzeption Friedrich Naumanns', *Bohemia*, Vol. 41, No. 2 (2000), 326–42.

Kořalka, Jiří, *Tschechen im Habsburgerreich und in Europa, 1815–1914*, Vienna: Verlag für Geschichte und Politik (1991).

———, *František Palacký (1798–1876)*, Prague: Argo (1998).

Koschmal, Walter, et al. eds., *Deutsche und Tschechen. Geschichte, Kultur, Politik*, Munich: C.H. Beck (2003).

Kötzschke, Rudolf and Hellmut Kretzschmar, *Sächsische Geschichte*, Frankfurt: Verlag Wolfgang Weidlich (1977).

Kraehe, Enno E., *Metternich's German Policy. Volume II: The Congress of Vienna, 1814–1815*, Princeton: Princeton University Press (1983).

Kraus, Hans-Christof, *Das Ende des alten Deutschland. Krise und Auflösung des Heiligen Römischen Reiches Deutscher Nation 1806*, Berlin: Duncker & Humboldt (2017).

Krauss, W., Stieber, Z., Bělič, J., and Borkovskij, V. I. eds., *Slawisch-deutsche Wechselbeziehungen in Sprache, Literatur, und Kultur*, Berlin: Akademie Verlag (1969).

Krizman, Bogdan, *Raspad Austro-Ugarske i stvaranje jugoslavenske države*, Zagreb: Školska knjiga (1977).

———, *Hrvatska u Prvom svjetskom ratu. Hrvatsko-srpski politički odnosi*, Zagreb: Globus (1989).

Kropej, Monika, 'The Cooperation of Grimm Brothers, Jernej Kopitar and Vuk Karadžić', *Studia Mythologica Slavica XVI* (2013), 215–31.

BIBLIOGRAPHY

Krueger, Rita, *Czech, German, and Noble: Status and National Identity in Habsburg Bohemia*, New York: OUP (2009).

Krzoska, Markus, 'Historische Mission und Pragmatismus. Die slawische Idee in Polen im 19. und 20. Jahrhundert', *Osteuropa*, Vol. 59, No. 12 (2009), 77–94.

Kucharczyk, Jacek and Grigorij Mesežnikov eds., *Diverging Voice, Converging Policies: The Visegrad States' Reactions to the Russia-Ukraine Conflict*, Warsaw: Heinrich-Böll Stiftung (2015).

Kuklík, Jan, *Czech Law in Historical Contexts*, Prague: Karolinum Press (2015).

Kundra, Ondřej, *Putinovi agenti. Jak ruští špioni kradou naše tajemství*, Brno: BizBooks (2016).

Kunze, Peter, 'The Sorbian National Renaissance and Slavic Reciprocity in the First Half of the Nineteenth Century, *Canadian Slavonic Papers*, Vol. 41, No. 2 (1999), 189–206.

Kupka, P. F., *Die Eisenbahnen Österreich-Ungarns 1822–1867*, Leipzig: Verlag von Duncker & Humblot (1888).

Kusin, Vladimir V., *The Intellectual Origins of the Prague Spring: The Development of Reformist Ideas in Czechoslovakia 1956–1967*, Cambridge: Cambridge University Press (1971).

Kwan, Jonathan, *Liberalism and the Habsburg Monarchy, 1861–1895*, Basingstoke: Palgrave Macmillan (2013).

———, 'Austro-German Liberalism and Bohemian State Rights, 1861–1879', *Střed*, Vol. 1 (2016), 109–50.

———, 'Transylvanian Saxon Politics and Imperial Germany, 1871–1876', *The Historical Journal*, Vol. 61, No. 4 (2018), 991–1015.

Labov, Jessie, *Transatlantic Central Europe: Contesting Geography and Redefining Culture beyond the Nation*, Budapest: CEU Press (2019).

Landauer, Carl, 'The Bavarian Problem in the Weimar Republic, 1918–1923: Part I', *The Journal of Modern History*, Vol. 16, No. 2 (1944), 93–115.

———, 'The Bavarian Problem in the Weimar Republic: Part II', *The Journal of Modern History*, Vol. 16, No. 3 (1944), 205–223.

Langewiesche, Dieter, *Liberalismus in Deutschland*, Frankfurt: Suhrkamp (1988).

———, *Nation, Nationalismus, Nationalstaat im Deutschland und Europa*, Munich: C.H. Beck (2000).

Langewiesche, Dieter and Georg Schmidt eds., *Föderative Nation. Deutschlandkonzepte von der Reformation bis zum Ersten Weltkrieg*, Munich: R. Oldenbourg Verlag (2000).

Latawski, Paul ed., *The Reconstruction of Poland, 1914–23*, New York: Palgrave Macmillan (1992).

Legutko, Ryszard, *The Demon in Democracy: Totalitarian Temptations in Free Societies*, New York: Encounter Books (2016).

Lencek, Rado L., 'Note: The Terms *Wende—Winde, Wendish—Windish*, in the Historiographic Tradition of the Slovene Lands', *Slovene Studies*, Vol 12., No. 1 (1990), 93–7.

Lengyel, Reka and Gábor Tüskés eds., *Learned Societies, Freemasonry, Sciences and Literature in 18th-Century Hungary: A Collection of Documents and Sources*, Budapest: MTA BTK (2017).

Le Rider, Jacques, *La Mitteleuropa*, Vendôme: Presses universitaires de France (1996).

Levinger, Matthew, *Enlightened Nationalism: The Transformation of Prussian Political Culture 1806–1848*, Oxford: OUP (2000).

Lindstrom, Nicole, 'Between Europe and the Balkans: Mapping Slovenia and Croatia's "Return to Europe" in the 1990s', *Dialectical Anthropology*, Vol. 27 (2003), 313–29.

BIBLIOGRAPHY

Litván, György, *A Twentieth-Century Prophet: Oscar Jászi 1875–1957*, Budapest: CEU Press (2006).

Liulevicius, Vejas Gabriel, *War Land on the Eastern Front: Culture, National Identity and German Occupation in World War I*, Cambridge: Cambridge University Press (2004).

———, *The German Myth of the East: 1800 to the Present*, Oxford: OUP (2009).

Livezeanu, Irina, *Cultural Politics in Greater Romania: Regionalism, Nation Building, and Ethnic Struggle, 1918–1930*, Cornell University Press (1995).

Lockenour, Jay, *Dragonslayer: The Legend of Erich Ludendorff in the Weimar Republic and Third Reich*, Ithaca: Cornell University Press (2021).

Lohalm, Uwe, *Völkischer Radikalismus. Die Geschichte des Deutschvölkischen Schutu- und Trutz-Bundes 1919–1923*, Hamburg: Leibniz-Verlag (1970).

Longerich, Peter, *Holocaust: The Nazi Persecution and Murder of the Jews*, Oxford: OUP (2010).

Longo, Matthew, *The Picnic: An Escape to Freedom and the Collapse of the Iron Curtain*, London: Bodley Head (2024).

Lorman, Thomas, *The Making of the Slovak People's Party: Religion, Nationalism and the Culture War in Early 20th-Century Europe*, London: Bloomsbury (2019).

Lougee, Robert W., *Paul de Lagarde 1827–1891: A Study of Radical Conservatism in Germany*, Cambridge, MA: Harvard University Press (1962).

Low, Alfred D., *The Anschluss Movement 1918–1919 and the Paris Peace Conference*, Philadelphia: The American Philosophical Society (1974).

Lukowski, Jerzy, *The European Nobility in the Eighteenth Century*, Basingstoke: Palgrave Macmillan (2003).

———, *Disorderly Liberty: The political culture of the Polish-Lithuanian Commonwealth in the eighteenth century*, London: Continuum (2010).

Luther, Daniel, 'Ethnicity and Nationalism in a Central European City (Bratislava in the first half of the 20th century)', *Human Affairs*, Vol. 6, No. 2 (1996), 179–92.

Lutz, Heinrich and Helmut Rumpler eds., *Österreich und die deutsche Frage im 19. und 20. Jahrhundert*, Vienna: Verlag für Geschichte und Politik (1982).

Majer, Diemut, *"Non-Germans" under the Third Reich: The Nazi Judicial and Administrative System in Germany and Occupied Eastern Europe, with Special Regard to Occupied Poland, 1939–1945*, Baltimore: The Johns Hopkins University Press (2003).

Mandell, Richard D., *Paris 1900: The Great World's Fair*, Toronto: University of Toronto Press (1967).

Mann, S. E., 'Karel Havlíček: a Slav Pragmatist', *The Slavonic and East European Review*, Vol. 39, No. 93 (1961), 413–22.

Matić, Dragan, *Nemci v Ljubljani 1861–1918*, Ljubljana: Narodna in univerzitetna knjižnica (2002).

———, 'Die Deutschen und Slowenen in Krain in der Zeit der Verfassungsära der Habsburgermonarchie', *Archivalische Zeitschrift*, Vol. 88, No. 2 (2006), 597–614.

Matijević, Zlatko, 'Narodno vijeće Slovenaca, Hrvata i Srba u Zagrebu', *Fontes: izvori za hrvatsku povijest*, Vol. 14, No. 1 (2008), 35–66.

Maxwell, Alexander, 'Budapest and Thessaloniki as Slavic Cities (1800–1914): Urban Infrastructures, National Organizations and Ethnic Territories', *Ethnologia Balkanica*, Vol. 9, 43–64.

BIBLIOGRAPHY

———, *Choosing Slovakia: Slavic Hungary, the Czechoslovak Language and Accidental Nationalism*, London: Tauris Academic Studies (2009).

———, 'Hungaro-German Dual Nationality: Germans, Slavs, and Magyars during the 1848 Revolution', *German Studies Review*, Vol. 39, No. 1 (2016), 17–39.

———, *Everyday Nationalism in Hungary 1789–1867*, Berlin: De Gruyter (2019).

———, 'Popular and Scholarly Primordialism: The Politics of Ukrainian History during Russia's 2022 Invasion of Ukraine', *Journal of Nationalism, Memory & Language Politics*, Issue 2, December (2022).

Mazower, Mark, *Hitler's Empire: How the Nazis Ruled Europe*, London: Penguin (2009).

McCagg Jr., William O., 'Jews in Revolutions: The Hungarian Experience', *Journal of Social History*, Vol. 6, No. 1 (1972), 78–105.

Meier, Jörg—'Deutschsprachige Literatur des 19. und 20. Jahrhunderts aus Preßburg/Pozsony/Bratislava', *Brücken: Zeitschrift für Sprach-, Literatur- und Kulturwissenschaft*, No. 1 & 2 (2007), 231–48.

Meinecke, Friedrich, *Cosmopolitanism and the National State*, Princeton: Princeton University Press (1970).

Melik, Vasilij, 'Frankfurtske volitve 1848 na Slovenskem', *Zgodovinski časopis*, Vol. II–III (1948–49), 69–134.

Melton, James van Horn, *The Rise of the Public in Enlightenment Europe*, Cambridge: Cambridge University Press (2004).

Merchiers, Ingrid, *Cultural Nationalism in the South Slav Habsburg Lands in the Early Nineteenth Century: The Scholarly Network of Jernej Kopitar (1780–1844)*, Munich: Verlag Otto Sagner (2007).

Mevius, Martin, *Agents of Moscow: The Hungarian Communist Party and the Origins of Socialist Patriotism, 1941–1953*, Oxford: OUP (2005).

Michel, Bernard, 'Le rôle d'Ernest Denis et du journal «La Nation tchéque» dans la naissance de la Tchéchoslovaquie', *Guerres mondiales et conflits contemporains*, No. 169 (1993), 17–25.

Miller, Alexei, 'Тема Центральной Европы, современные дискурсы и место в них России', *Новое литературное обозрение*, No. 6 (2001), 18–33.

Mishkova, Diana and Balázs Trencsényi eds., *European Regions and Boundaries: A Conceptual History*, New York: Berghahn (2017).

Mitchell, Allan, *Revolution in Bavaria, 1918–1919: The Eisner Regime and the Soviet Republic*, Princeton: Princeton University Press (1965).

Mócsy, István I., *The Uprooted: Hungarian Refugees and Their Impact on Hungary's Domestic Politics, 1918–1921*, New York: Columbia Univeristy Press (1983).

Moggach, Douglas and Jones, Gareth Stedman eds., *The 1848 Revolutions and European Political Thought*, Cambridge: Cambridge University Press (2018).

Mommsen, Hans, *The Rise and Fall of Weimar Democracy*, Chapel Hill: The University of North Carolina Press (1996).

Mommsen, Hans, Dušan Kováč, Jiří Malíř, and Michaela Marková eds., *První světová válka a vztahy mezi Čechy, Slováky a Němci*, Brno: Matice moravská (2000).

Mommsen, Wolfgang J., *Max Weber and German Politics 1890–1920*, Chicago: University of Chicago Press (1984).

Mueßdoerffer, Franz and Martin Zarnkow, *Das Bier. Eine Geschichte von Hopfen und Malz*, Munich: C.H. Beck (2014).

BIBLIOGRAPHY

Murdock, Caitlin E., *Changing Places: Society, Culture, and Territory in the Saxon-Bohemian Borderlands, 1870–1946*, Ann Arbor: The University of Michigan Press (2010).

Murko, Matthias, *Deutsche Einflüsse auf die Anfänge der böhmischen Romantik. Mit einem Anhang: Kollar in Jena und beim Wartburgfest*, Graz: Verlags-Buchhandlung 'Styria' (1897).

Musil, Jiří, 'Prague, Present Meets Past', *International Review of Sociology*, Vol. 16, No. 2 (2006), 243–72.

Nelson, Robert L. ed., *Germans, Poland, and Colonial Expansion to the East: 1850 Through the Present*, New York: Palgrave Macmillan (2009).

Nemes, Robert, *The Once and Future Budapest*, DeKalb: Northern Illinois University Press (2005).

Neubauer, John and Borbála Zsuzsanna Török eds., *The Exile and Return of Writers from East-Central Europe: A Compendium*, Berlin: Walter de Gruyter (2009).

Newman, John Paul, 'Post-imperial and Post-war Violence in the South Slav Lands, 1917–1923', *Contemporary European History*, Vol. 19, No. 3 (2010), 249–65.

Niebuhr, Robert, 'Enlarging Yugoslavia: Tito's Quest for Expansion, 1945–1948', *European History Quarterly*, Vol. 47, No. 2 (2017), 284–310.

Nimni, Ephraim, 'Marx, Engels and the National Question', *Science & Society*, Vol. 53, No. 3 (1989), 297–326.

Nipperdey, Thomas, *Die Organisation der deutschen Parteien vor 1918*, Dusseldorf: Droste Verlag (1961).

North, Michael and Robert Riemer eds., *Das Ende des Alten Reiche sim Ostseeraum. Wahrnehmungen und Transformationen*, Cologne: Böhlau Verlag (2008).

Novak, Kristian, *Višejezičnost i kolektivni identiteti iliraca: Jezične biografje Dragolje Jarnević, Ljudevita Gaja i Ivana Kukuljevića Sakcinskoga*, Zagreb: Srednja Europa (2012).

Obad, Vlado, *Roda Roda und die deutschsprachige Literatur aus Slawonien*, Vienna: Böhlau (1996).

Olschowsky, Burkhard, Piotr Juszkiewicz and Jan Rydel eds., *Central and Eastern Europe after the First World War*, Oldenbourg: De Gruyter (2021).

O'Reilly, William, 'Lost Chances of the House of Habsburg', *Austrian History Yearbook*, Vol. 40 (2009), 53–70.

Orton, Lawrence D., 'Did the Slavs Speak German at Their First Congress?' *Slavic Review*, Vol. 33, No. 3 (1974), 515–21.

———, *The Prague Slav Congress of 1848*, New York: Columbia University Press (1978).

Orzoff, Andrea, *Battle for the Castle: The Myth of Czechoslovakia in Europe 1914–1948*, Oxford: OUP (2009).

Osterkamp, Jana, *Vielfalt ordnen. Das föderale Europa der Habsburgermonarchie (Vormärz bis 1918)*, Göttingen: Vandenhoeck & Ruprecht (2020).

Overy, Richard, *The Bombing War: Europe 1939–1945*, London: Allen Lane (2013).

Pajewski, Janusz, *Budowa drugiej Rzeczpospolitej 1918–1926*, Krakow: Polska Akademia Umiejętności (1995).

Palmowski, Jan, *Urban Liberalism in Imperial Germany: Frankfurt am Main, 1866–1914*, Oxford: OUP (1999).

Papcke, Sven and Weidenfeld eds., *Traumland Mitteleuropa?: Beiträge zu einer aktuellen Kontroverse*, Wissenschaftliche Buchgesellschaft (1988).

BIBLIOGRAPHY

Paret, Peter, *The Berlin Secession: Modernism and Its Enemies in Imperial Germany*, Cambridge, Massachusetts: Belknap Press (1980).

Pastor, Peter, *Hungary Between Wilson and Lenin: The Hungarian Revolution of 1918–1919 and the Big Three*, New York: Columbia University Press (1976).

Pásztorová, Barbora, *Metternich, the German Question and the Pursuit of Peace*, Berlin: De Gruyter (2022).

Patterson, Sheila, 'The Polish Exile Community in Britain', *The Polish Review*, Vol. 6, No. 3 (1961), 69–97.

Pavličević, Dragutin, *Narodni pokret 1883. u Hrvatskoj*, Zagreb: Liber (1980).

Pažout, Jaroslav, '„Chceme světlo! Chceme studovat!". Demonstrace studentů z vysokoškolských kolejí v Praze na Strahově 31. října 1967', *Paměť a dějiny*, No. 1 (2008), 4–13.

Pech, Stanley Z., 'Passive Resistance of the Czechs, 1863–1879', *The Slavonic and East European Review*, Vol. 36, No. 87 (1958), 434–52.

Pechel, Rudolf, *Deutscher Widerstand*, Erlenbach: Eugen Rentsch Verlag (1947).

Péter, László, *Hungary's Long Nineteenth Century: Constitutional and Democratic Traditions in a European Perspective*, Leiden: Brill (2012).

Petrovich, Michael Boro, *The Emergence of Russian Panslavism 1856–1870*, New York: Columbia University Press (1956).

Pflanze, Otto, *Bismarck and the Development of Germany: The Period of Unification, 1815–1871*, Princeton: Princeton University Press (1963).

Piirimäe, Eva, 'Thomas Abbt's *Vom Tode für das Vaterland* (1761) and the French Debates on Monarchical Patriotism', *Trames*, Vol. 9, No. 4 (2005), 326–47.

———, *Herder and Enlightenment Politics*, Cambridge: Cambridge University Press (2023).

Pilsudska, Alexandra, *Pilsudski: A Biography by His Wife Alexandra Pilsudska*, New York: Dodd, Mead & Company (1941).

Plokhy, Serhii, *The Gates of Europe: A History of Ukraine*, New York: Basic Books (2015).

Pohrt, H., 'Karl Gottlob von Anton und die Slawen', *Zeitschrift für Slawistik*, Vol. 13, No. 1 (1968), 712–21.

Polenz, Peter von, *Deutsche Sprachgeschichte vom Spätmittelalter bis zur Gegenwart*, 3 Vols., Berlin: Walter de Gruyter (1999).

Porter, Roy and Miklaus Teich eds., *The Enlightenment in National Context*, Cambridge: Cambridge University Press (1981).

Prendergast, Thomas R., 'The Sociological Idea of the State: Legal Education, Austrian Multinationalism, and the Future of Continental Empire, 1880–1914', *Comparative Studies in Society and History*, Vol. 62, No. 2 (2020), 327–58.

Press, Steven Michael, 'False Fire: The Wartburg Book-Burning of 1817', *Central European History*, Vol. 42 (2009), 631–46.

Prideaux, Sue, *Edvard Munch: Behind the Scream*, New Haven: Yale University Press (2005).

Procházka, Theodore, *The Second Republic: The Disintegration of Post-Munich Czechoslovakia (October 1938—March 1939)*, New York: Columbia University Press (1981).

Prokopovych, Markian, Carl Bethke, and Tamara Scheer eds., *Language Diversity in the Late Habsburg Empire*, Leiden: Brill (2019).

Pulzer, Peter, *The Rise of Political Anti-Semitism in Germany and Austria*, New York: John Wiley & Sons (1964).

BIBLIOGRAPHY

———, *Jews and the German State: The Political History of a Minority, 1848–1933*, Oxford: Blackwell (1992).

Quaasdorf, Friedrich, *Kursachsen und das Ende des Alten Reiches. Die Politik Dresdens auf dem Immerwährenden Reichstag zu Regensburg 1802 bis 1806*, Leipzig: Leipziger Universitätsverlag (2020).

Radu, Sorin, 'Romania and the Great War: Political, Territorial, Economic and Social Consequences', *Pamięć i Sprawiedliwość*, Vol. 1 (2018), 138–67.

Rady, Martyn, *The Habsburgs: The Rise and Fall of a World Power*, London: Allen Lane (2020).

Rainer, János M. ed., *Underground Streams: National-Conservatives After World War II in Communist Hungary and Eastern Europe*, Budapest: Central European University Press (2023).

Ramet, Sabrina P. ed., *Religion and Politics in Post-Socialist Central and Southeastern Europe: Challenges since 1989*, Basingstoke: Macmillan (2014).

———, *Interwar East Central Europe, 1918–1941: The Failure of Democracy-building, the Fate of Minorities*, Abingdon: Routledge (2020).

Ranki, Vera, *The Politics of Inclusion and Exclusion: Jews and nationalism in Hungary*, New York: Holmes & Meier (1999).

Rapant, Daniel, *K počiatkom maďarizácie*, 2 Vols., Bratislava: Slovenská kníhtlačiareň (1927–31).

Rath, John R., *The Viennese Revolution of 1848*, Austin: University of Texas Press (1957).

Ravlić, Jakša, 'Ilirska čitaonica u Zagrebu', *Historijski zbornik*, Vol. 16, No. 1–4, 159–215.

Ražnjević, Tomislav, 'O Slavenskom komitetu Hrvatske kao instrumentu prosovjetske propagande 1946.—1948.', *ČSP*, Vol. 54, No. 1 (2022), 109–137.

Redekop, Benjamin W., 'Thomas Abbt and the Formation of an Enlightened German "Public"', *Journal of the History of Ideas*, Vol. 58, No. 1 (1997), 81–103.

Reill, Dominique Kirchner, *Nationalists Who Feared the Nation: Adriatic Multi-Nationalism in Habsburg Dalmatia, Trieste, and Venice*, Stanford: Stanford University Press (2012).

Reinalter, Helmut ed., *Die Anfänge des Liberalismus und der Demokratie in Deutschland und Österreich 1830–1848/9*, Frankfurt am Main: Europäischen Verlag der Wissenschaften (2002).

Reinharz, Jehuda, *Fatherland or Promised Land: The Dilemma of the German Jew, 1893–1914*, Ann Arbor: The University of Michigan Press (1975).

Renna, Thomas, 'The Holy Roman Empire was Neither Holy, Nor Roman, Nor an Empire', *Michigan Academician*, Vol. XLII (2015), 60–75.

Retallack, James, '"Why Can't a Saxon Be More Like a Prussian?" Regional Identities and the Birth of Modern Political Culture in Germany, 1866–67', *Canadian Journal of History*, XXXII (1997), 26–55.

———, *Germany's Second Reich: Portraits and Pathways*, Toronto: University of Toronto Press (2015).

———, *Red Saxony: Election Battles and the Spectre of Democracy in Germany, 1860–1918*, Oxford: OUP (2017).

———, ed., *Saxony in German History: Culture, Society, and Politics, 1830–1933*, Ann Arbor: University of Michigan Press (2000).

Rhode, Gotthold, 'Drei polnische Historiker—drei Persönlichkeiten der Zeitgeschichte: Zum Tode von Marian Kukiel (15. August 1973), Oskar Halecki (17. September 1973)

BIBLIOGRAPHY

und Stanislaw Kot (26. Dezember 1975)', *Jahrbücher für Geschichte Osteuropas*, Vol. 24, No. 4 (1976), 526–46.

Ringer, Fritz, 'Bildung: The social and ideological context of the German historical tradition', *History of European Ideas*, Vol. 10, No. 2 (1989), 193–202.

Rjéoutski, Vladislav and Willem Frijhoff eds., *Language Choice in Enlightenment Europe: Education, Sociability, and Governance*, Amsterdam: Amsterdam University Press (2018).

Röhl, John C. G., *Wilhelm II. Der Weg in den Abgrund 1900–1941*, Munich: C.H. Beck (2018).

Roll, Christine and Matthias Schnettger eds., *Epochenjahr 1806? Das Ende des Alten Reichs in zeitgenössischen Perspektiven und Deutungen*, Mainz: Verlage Philipp von Zabern (2008).

Roller, Duane W., *Ancient Geography: The Discovery of the World in Classical Greece and Rome*, London: I.B. Tauris (2015).

Romsics, Gergely, *Myth and Remembrance: The Dissolution of the Habsburg Empire in the Memoir Literature of the Austro-Hungarian Political Elite*, New York: Columbia University Press (2006).

Rosenberg, Hans, 'Political and Social Consequences of the Great Depression of 1873–1896 in Central Europe', *The Economic History Review*, Vol. 13, No. 1/2 (1943), 58–73.

———, *Machteliten und Wirtschaftskonjukturen. Studien zur neueren deutschen Sozial- und Wirtschaftsgeschichte*, Göttingen: Vandenhoeck & Ruprecht (1978).

Ross, Anna, *Beyond the Barricades: Government and State-Building in Post-Revolutionary Prussia, 1848–1858*, Oxford: OUP (2019).

Rossino, Alexander B., *Hitler Strikes Poland: Blitzkrieg, Ideology, and Atrocity*, Lawerence: University of Kansas Press (2003).

Rothenberg, Gunther E., *The Army of Francis Joseph*, Wes Lafayette: Purdue University Press (1976).

Rowe, Michael, *From Reich to State: The Rhineland in the Revolutionary Age, 1780–1830*, Cambridge: Cambridge University Press (2003).

Rumpf, Helmut, 'Mitteleuropa: Zur Geschichte und Deutung eines politischen Begriffs', *Historische Zeitschrift*, Vol. 165, No. 1 (1942), 510–27.

———, ed., *Innere Staatsbildung und gesellschaftliche Modernisierung in Österreich und Deutschland 1867/71 bis 1914*, Vienna: Verlag für Geschichte und Politik (1991).

Sabatos, Charles, 'Shifting contexts: The boundaries of Milan Kundera's Central Europe', in Brian James Baer ed., *Contexts, Subtexts and Pretexts: Literary translation in Eastern Europe and Russia*, Amsterdam: John Benjamins Publishing Company (2011), 19–32.

Sakmyster, Thomas, 'From Habsburg Admiral to Hungarian Regent: The Political Metamorphosis of Miklos Horthy, 1918–1921', *East European Quarterly*, Vol. XVII, No. 2 (1983), 129–48.

Schedel, James, 'Emperor, Church, and People: Religion and Dynastic Loyalty during the Golden Jubilee of Franz Joseph', *The Catholic Historical Review*, Vol. 76, No. 1 (1990), 71–92.

Scheer, Tamara, 'One Empire or Two States? Dualism and States of Emergency in Austria-Hungary Before and During the First World War', *First World War Studies*, Vol. 14, No. 1 (2023), 115–35.

Schieder, Theodor, *Das Deutsche Kaiserreich von 1871 als Nationalstaat*, Wiesbaden: Springer Fachmedien (1960).

BIBLIOGRAPHY

Schindling, Anton and Walter Ziegler eds., *Die Kaiser der Neuzeit. Heiliges Römisches Reich, Österreich, Deutschland*, Munich: C. H. Beck (1990).

Schivelbusch, Wolfgang, *The Railway Journey: The Industrialization of Space in the 19th Century*, Lemington Spa: Berg (1986).

Schjerve, Rosita Rindler ed., *Diglossia and Power: Language Policies and Practice in the 19th Century Habsburg Empire*, Berlin: Mouton de Gruyter (2003).

Schmitt, Hans A., 'Count Beust and Germany, 1866–1870: Reconquest, Realignment, or Resignation?', *Central European History*, Vol. 1, No. 1 (1968), 20–34.

Schöpflin, George and Nancy Wood eds., *In Search of Central Europe*, Barnes and Noble Books (1989).

Schulze, Hagen, *The Course of German nationalism: From Frederick the Great to Bismarck, 1763–1867*, Cambridge: Cambridge University Press (1985).

———, ed., *Nation-Building in Central Europe*, Leamington Spa: Berg Publishers (1987).

Schwarz, Hans-Peter, *Vom Reich zur Bundesrepublik. Deutschland im Widerstreit der außenpolitischen Konzeptionen in den Jahren der Besatzungsherrschaft 1945–1949*, Berlin: Klett-Cotta (1980).

Scott, H.M. ed., *Enlightened Absolutism: Reform and Reformers in Later Eighteenth-Century Europe*, London: Macmillan (1990).

Scott, H.M., and Brendan Simms eds., *Cultures of Power in Europe during the Long Eighteenth Century*, Cambridge: Cambridge University Press (2007).

Šedivý, Miroslav, 'The Austrian Empire, German Nationalism, and the Rhine Crisis of 1840', *Austrian History Yearbook* 47 (2016), 15–36.

Seibt, Ferdinand ed., *Die böhmischen Länder zwischen Ost und West. Festschrift für Karl Bosl zum 75. Geburtstag*, Munich: R. Oldenbourg Verlag (1983).

Seidler, Andrea and Wolfram Seidler eds., *Das Zeitschriftwesen im Donauraum zwischen 1740 und 1809. Kommentierte Bibliographie der deutsch- und ungarischsprachigen Zeitschriften in Wien, Preßburg und Pest-Buda*, Vienna: Böhlau (1988).

Seton-Watson, Hugh and Christopher Seton-Watson, *The Making of a New Europe: R.W. Seton-Watson and the last years of Austria-Hungary*, Seattle: University of Washington Press (1981).

Shanahan, William O., 'Friedrich Naumann: A Mirror of Wilhelmian Germany', *The Review of Politics*, Vol. 13, No. 3 (1951), 267–301.

Sheehan, James J., *German Liberalism in the Nineteenth Century*, Chicago: University of Chicago Press (1978).

———, 'What is German History? Reflections on the Role of the Nation in German History and Historiography', *The Journal of Modern History*, Vol. 53, No. 1 (1981), 1–23.

———, *German History 1770–1866*, Oxford: Clarendon Press (1989).

Siedina, Giovanna ed., *Latinitas in the Polish Crown and the Grand Duchy of Lithuania: Its Impact on the Development of Identities*, Florence: Firenze University Press (2014).

Siemann, Wolfram, *The German Revolution of 1848–49*, Macmillan Press (1998).

———, *Metternich: Strategist and Visionary*, Cambridge: Belknap Press (2019).

Sikirić-Assouline, Zvjezdana, *U obranu hrvatskih municipalnih prava i latinskoga jezika*, Zagreb: Srednja Europa (2006).

Šimeček, Zdenek, *Geschichte des Buchhandels in Tschechien und in der Slowakei*, Wiesbaden: Harrassowitz Verlag (2002).

BIBLIOGRAPHY

Šimková, Pavla, 'The Birth of the Scientific Brewer: International Networks and Knowledge Transfer in Central European Beer Brewing, 1794–1895', *Jahrbuch für Wirtschaftsgeschichte*, Vol. 65, No. 1 (2024), 209–235.

Sinnhuber, Karl A., 'Central Europe: Mitteleuropa: Europe Centrale: An Analysis of a Geographical Term', *Transactions and Papers (Institute of British Geographers)*, No. 20 (1954), 15–39.

Sked, Alan, 'Re-Imagining Empire: The Persistence of the Austrian Idea in the Historical Work of Heinrich Ritter von Srbik', *Radovi—Zavod za hrvatsku povijest*, Vol. 50, No. 1 (2018), 37–57.

Skilling, H. Gordon, 'The Czechoslovak Constitution of 1960 and the Transition to Communism', *The Journal of Politics*, Vol. 24, No. 1 (1962), 142–66.

———, *T. G. Masaryk: Against the Current, 1882–1914*, Basingstoke: Macmillan (1994).

Smith, Helmut Walser, *German Nationalism and Religious Conflict: Culture, Ideology, Politics, 1870–1914*, Princeton: Princeton University Press (1995).

Smith, Jeremy, *The Bolsheviks and the National Question, 1917–23*, Basingstoke: Macmillan Press (1999).

Snyder, Timothy, *The Reconstruction of Nations: Poland, Ukraine, Lithuania, Belarus, 1569–1999*, London: Yale University Press (2003).

Sondhaus, Lawrence, 'Schwarzenberg, Austria, and the German Question, 1848–1851', *The International History Review*, Vol. 13, No. 1 (1991), 1–20.

Sorkin, David, 'Wilhelm von Humboldt: The Theory and Practice of Self-Formation (Bildung), 1791–1810', *Journal of the History of Ideas*, Vol. 44, No. 1 (1983), 55–73.

———, *The Transformation of German Jewry, 1780–1840*, Oxford: OUP (1987).

Speirs, Ronald and John Breuilly eds., *Germany's Two Unifications: Anticipations, Experiences, Responses*, Basingstoke: Palgrave Macmillan (2005).

Spira, György, *A Hungarian Count in the Revolutions of 1848*, Budapest (1974).

———, 'Lajos Batthyány. Ein Vorkämpfer der bürgerlichen Umgestaltung Ungarns im 19. Jahrhundert', *Mitteilungen des Instituts für Österreichische Geschichtsforschung*, 95 (1987), 69–120.

Srb, Adolf, *Politické dějiny národa Českého od roku 1861 až do nastoupení ministerstva Badeonva R. 1895*, Prague: Knihtiskárna F. Šimáček (1899).

Stachura, Peter D. ed., *Unemployment and the Great Depression in Weimar Germany*, Basingstoke: Palgrave Macmillan (1986).

Štasný, Vladislav et al. ed., *Slovanství v národním životě čechů a slováků*, Prague: Melantrich (1968).

Steger, Bernd, 'Der Hitlerprozess und Bayerns Verhältnis zum Reich 1923/4', *Vierteljahrshefte für Zeitgeschichte*, Vol. 25 (1977), 441–66.

Steinberg, Jonathan, *Bismarck: A Life*, Oxford: OUP (2011).

Steiner, Zara, *The Lights That Failed: European International History 1919–1933*, Oxford: OUP (2005).

Stern, Fritz, *The Politics of Cultural Despair: A Study in the Rise of the Germanic Ideology*, Berkeley: University of California Press (1961).

Stipančević, Mario, 'Neznani svijet Email Laszowskog', *Arhivski vjesnik*, Vol. 53, No. 1 (2010), 279–310.

BIBLIOGRAPHY

Stollberg-Rilinger, Barbara, *Das Heilige Römische Reich Deutscher Nation. Vom Ende des Mittelalters bis 1806*, Munich: C.H. Beck (2013).

———, *Maria Thersa: The Habsburg Empress in Her Time*, Princeton: Princeton University Press (2021).

Stölzl, Christoph, *Die Ära Bach in Böhmen. Sozialgeschichtliche Studien zum Neoabsolutismus 1849–1859*, Munich: R. Oldenbourg (1971).

Stone, Gerald, *Slav Outposts in Central European History: The Wends, Sorbs and Kashubs*, London: Bloomsbury (2016).

Strong, David F., *Austria (October 1918–March 1919): Transition from Empire to Republic*, New York: Octagon Books (1974).

Strsoglavec, Đurđa, 'Anton Tomaž Linhart Between the German and Slovenian Language', *Poznańskie Studia Slawistyczne*, No. 5 (2013), 321–32.

Sugar, Peter F., 'An Underrated Event: The Hungarian Constitutional Crisis of 1905–6', *East European Quarterly*, Vol. XV, No. 3 (1981), 281–306.

Sundhaußen, Holm, *Der Einfluß der Herderschen Ideen auf die Nationsbildung bei den Völkern der Habsburger Monarchie*, Munich: R. Oldenbourg Verlag (1973).

Suny, Ronald Grigor, 'History and the Making of Nations', *Harvard Ukrainian Studies*, Vol. 22 (1998), 569–88.

Suppan, Arnold, 'Saint-Germain and Trianon, 1919–1920. The Imperialist Peace Order in Central Europe', *West Bohemian Historical Review*, Vol. X, No. 1 (2020), 39–67.

Švoger, Vlasta, 'Ban Josip Jelačić u očima svojih suvremenika', *Hrvatski akademije znanosti i umjetnosti*, Vol. 31 (2013), 247–71.

Sweet, Paul R., 'The Historical Writing of Heinrich von Srbik', *History and Theory*, Vol. 9, No. 1 (1970), 37–58.

Szabad, György, *Hungarian Political Trends Between the Revolution and the Compromise (1849–1867)*, Budapest: Akadémiai Kiadó (1977).

Szabo, Franz A. J., *Kaunitz and enlightened absolutism 1753–1780*, Cambridge: Cambridge University Press (1994).

Székely, Miklós ed., *Ephemeral Architecture in Central-Eastern Europe in the 19th and 20th Centuries*, Paris: L'Harmattan (2015).

Szelényi, Balázs A., 'Enlightenment from Below: German-Hungarian Patriots in Eighteenth-Century Hungary', *Austrian History Yearbook*, Vol. 34 (2003), 111–143.

———, *The Failure of the Central European Bourgeoisie: New Perspectives on Hungarian History*, New York: Palgrave Macmillan (2006).

———, 'From Minority to Übermensch: The Social Roots of Ethnic Conflict in the German Diaspora of Hungary, Romania and Slovakia', *Past & Present*, No. 196 (2007), 215–51.

Szijártó, István M., Wim Blockmans, and László Kontler eds., *Parliamentarism in Northern and East-Central Europe in the Long Eighteenth Century, Volume I: Representative Institutions and Political Motivation*, Oxon: Routledge (2023).

Szymczak, Damian, *Galicyjska „ambasada" w Wiedniu. Dzieje ministerstwa dla Galicji 1871–1918*, Poznan: Wydawnictwo Poznanskie (2013).

Ther, Philipp, 'Beyond the Nation: The Relational Basis of a comparative History of Germany and Europe', *Central European History*, Vol. 36, No. 1 (2003), 45–73.

———, *In der Mitte der Gesellschaft. Operntheater in Zentraleuropa 1815–1914*, Vienna: Oldenbourg Verlag (2006).

BIBLIOGRAPHY

———, *The Dark Side of Nation-States: Ethnic Cleansing in Modern Europe*, New York: Berhahn (2014).

———, *Europe since 1989: A History*, Princeton University Press (2016).

Thum, Gregor, *Uprooted: How Breslau Became Wrocław during the Century of Expulsions*, Princeton: Princeton University Press (2011).

Tilly, Richard H. and Michael Kopsidis, *From Old Regime to Industrial State*, Chicago: University of Chicago Press (2020).

Tokić, Mate Nikola, *Croatian Radical Separatism and Diaspora Terrorism During the Cold War*, West Lafayette: Purdue University Press (2020).

Tomášek, Dušan, *Deník druhé republiky*, Prague: Naše vojsko (1988).

Tomljanovich, William Brooks, *Biskup Josip Juraj Strossmayer. Nacionalizam i moderni katolicizam u Hrvatskoj*, Zagreb: Dom i svijet (2001).

Török, Borbála Zsuzsanna, *Exploring Transylvania: Geographies of Knowledge and Entangled Histories in a Multiethnic Province, 1790–1918*, Leiden: Brill (2016).

———, *The Science of State Power in the Habsburg Monarchy, 1790–1880*, New York: Berghahn (2024).

Trávníček, Jiří ed., *V kleštích dějin: Střední Evropa jako pojem a problem*, Brno: Host (2009).

Trencsényi, Balázs and Michal Kopeček eds., *Discourses of Collective Identity in Central and Southeast Europe (1770–1945). Texts and Commentaries. Volume II: National Romanticism*, Budapest: CEU Press (2007).

Trencsényi, Balázs, Maciej Janowski, Mónika Baár, Maria Falina, and Michal Kopoček, *A History of Modern Political Thought in East Central Europe, Volume I: Negotiating Modernity in the Long Nineteenth Century*, Oxford: OUP (2016).

Tscherkes, Bohdan, 'Stalinist Visions for the Urban Transformation of Lviv, 1939–1955', *Harvard Ukrainian Studies*, Vol. 24 (2000), 205–222.

Tufegdžić, Anica and Blagojević, Mirjana Roter, 'Golden Era of Lager Breweries in the Southern Austro-Hungarian Empire', *Industrial Archaeology Review*, Vol. 37, No. 1 (2015), 33–47.

Turda, Marius, *The Idea of National Superiority in Central Europe, 1880–1918*, Lewiston: The Edwin Mellen Press (2004).

Turkalj, Jasna, 'Stranka prava i izbori za Hrvatski sabor na području bivše Vojne krajine 1883. godine', *ČSP*, Vol. 36, No. 3 (2004), 1013–37.

Uffelmann, Dirk, 'The Imprint of Kundera's Strategic Anticolonialism on the Central European Roundtable in Lisbon (1988) and the Russian Discussants' Tactical Nominalism', *Zeitschrift für Slavische Philologie*, Vol. 72, No. 1 (2016), 39–53.

Ujvári, Hedvig, 'Abriss der deutschsprachigen Presselandschaft in Ungarn im 18. und zu Beginn des 19. Jahrhunderts', *Germanistische Studien VII* (2009), 63–76.

Umbach, Maiken ed., *German Federalism: Past, Present, Future*, Palgrave (2002).

Ungváry, Krisztián, *Battle for Budapest: 100 Days in World War II*, London: I.B. Tauris (2003).

Unowsky, Daniel L., *The Pomp and Politics of Patriotism: Imperial Celebrations in Habsburg Austria, 1848–1916*, West Lafayette: Purdue University Press (2005).

Urbach, Karina ed., *European Aristocracies and the Radical Right 1918–1939*, Oxford: OUP (2007).

Uslu, Ateş, '«Nous sommes les amis de l'Entente». Le comte Mihály Károlyi dans les années de la Grande Guerre', *ÖT KONTINENS*, No. 1 (2007), 263–87.

BIBLIOGRAPHY

———, 'Aux origines de la «note Vix»: contribution à l'histoire politique et diplomatique de la République Hongroise sous la présidence de Mihály Károlyi (janvier-mars 1919)', *ÖT KONTINENS*, No. 1 (2008), 353–74.

Valentin, Veit, *Geschichte der deutschen Revolution 1848–1849*, 2 vols., Berlin: Kiepenheuer & Witsch (1970).

Vardy, Steven B., *Modern Hungarian Historiography*, Boulder: East European Quarterly (1976).

———, 'The Impact of Trianon upon Hungary and the Hungarian Mind: The Nature of Interwar Hungarian Irredentism', *Hungarian Studies Review*, Vol. X, No. 1 (1983), 21–42.

Varga, Janos, *A Hungarian Quo Vadis: Political Trends and Theories of the Early 1840s*, Budapest: Akademiai Kiado (1993).

Vaszonyi, Nicholas ed., *Searching for Common Ground: Diskurse zur deutschen Identität 1750–1871*, Cologne: Böhlau Verlag (2000).

Veress, Emőd ed., *Constitutional History of Transylvania*, Springer (2023).

Verhey, Jeffrey, *The Spirit of 1914: Militarism, Myth, and Mobilization in Germany*, Cambridge: Cambridge University Press (2003).

Vermeiren, Jan, *The First World War and German National Identity: The Dual Alliance at War*, Cambridge: Cambridge University Press (2016).

Vermes, Gábor, *Hungarian Culture and Politics in the Habsburg Monarchy, 1711–1848*, New York: Central European University Press (2014).

Vermeulen, Han F., *Before Boas: The Genesis of Ethnography and Ethnology in the German Enlightenment*, Lincoln: University of Nebraska Press (2015).

Veselinović, Velimir, 'Pregled razvoja pravaške ideologije i politike', *ČSP*, Vol. 3 (2018), 583–621.

Vick, Brian E., *Defining Germany: The 1848 Frankfurt Parliamentarians and National Identity*, Cambridge: Harvard University Press (2002).

Vierhaus, Rudolf, 'Bildung', in Brunner et al. eds., *Geschichtliche Grundbegriffe*, Vol. I, Stuttgart: Ernst Klett Verlag (1974), 508–551.

———, *Deutschland im 18. Jahrhundert. Politische Verfassung. Soziales Gefüge. Geistige Bewegungen*, Göttingen: Vandenhoeck and Ruprecht (1987).

Viragh, Daniel, 'Becoming Hungarian: Jewish Culture in Budapest, 1867–1914', Unpublished Doctoral Thesis: University of California, Berkeley (2014).

Vital, David, *A People Apart: A Political History of the Jews in Europe 1789–1939*, Oxford: OUP (2001).

Vocelka, Michaela and Karl, *Franz Joseph I. Kaiser von Österreich und König von Ungarn 1830–1916. Eine Biographie*, Munich: C. H. Beck (2015).

Vodopivec, Peter ed., *Srednja Evropa*, Ljubljana: Mladinska knjiga (1991).

Vojtěch, Tomáš, *Mladočeši a boj o politickou moc v Čechách*, Prague: Academia (1980).

Volkov, Shulamit, *The Rise of Popular Antimodernism in Germany: The Urban Master Artisans, 1873–1896*, Princeton: Princeton University Press (1978).

———, 'Kontinuität und Diskontinuität im deutschen Antisemitismus 1878–1945', *Vierteljahrshefte für Zeitgeschichte*, Vol. 33, No. 2 (1985), 221–43.

Vulesica, Marija, *Die Formierung des politischen Antisemitismus in den Kronländern Kroatien und Slawonien 1879–1906*, Berlin: Metropol (2012).

BIBLIOGRAPHY

Vushko, Iryna, *The Politics of Cultural Retreat: Imperial Bureaucracy in Austrian Galicia, 1772–1867*, New Haven: Yale University Press (2015).

Walde, Martin, 'Katholisches versus evangelisches Milieu bei den Sorben', *Lětopis*, Vol. 53, No. 2 (2006), 15–28.

Walton, Jeremy F., 'The Ban's mana: post-imperial affect and public memory in Zagreb', *Cultural Studies*, Vol. 34, No. 5 (2020), 688–706.

Wandruszka, Adam, *Leopold II*, 2 Vols., Vienna: Verlag Herold (1963/65).

Wandruszka, Adam and Peter Urbanitsch eds., *Die Habsburgermonarchie 1848–1918*, 18 Vols, Vienna: Verlag der österreichischen Akademie der Wissenschaften (1973–2021).

Wandycz, Piotr S., *France and Her Eastern Allies*, Minneapolis: The University of Minnesota Press (1962).

Watson, Alexander, *Ring of Steel: Germany and Austria-Hungary at War, 1914–1918*, London: Penguin (2015).

Weber, Thomas, *Becoming Hitler: The Making of a Nazi*, Oxford: OUP (2017).

Weikart, Richard, 'The Origins of Social Darwinism in Germany, 1859–1895', *Journal of the History of Ideas*, Vol. 54, No. 3 (1993), 469–88.

Whaley, Joachim, *Germany and the Holy Roman Empire. Volume II: The Peace of Westphalia to the Dissolution of the Reich, 1648–1806*, Oxford: OUP (2012).

Wheatley, Natasha, *The Life and Death of States: Central Europe and the Transformation of Sovereignty*, Princeton: Princeton University Press (2023).

Whiteside, Andrew Gladding, *Austrian National Socialism Before 1918*, The Hague: Martinus Nijhoff (1962).

Wiebenson, Dora and Jozsef Sisa eds., *The Architecture of Historic Hungary*, London: MIT Press (1998).

Wiedemann, Andreas, *„Komm mit uns das Grenzland aufbauen!" Ansiedlung und neue Strukturen in den ehemaligen Sudetengebieten 1945–1952*, Wetzlar: Klartext (2007).

Wierzbicki, Andrzej, *Wschód-Zachód w koncepcjach dziejów Polski*, Warsaw: Państwowry Instytut Wydawniczy (1984).

Wiesinger, Peter, 'Johann Siegmund Valentin Popowitsch als Professor für Deutsche Sprache und Wohlredenheit an der Universität Wien 1754–1766', *Jahrbuch für Internationale Germanistik*, Jahrgang XLVII, Heft 2 (2015), 45–76.

Williams, Kieran, *The Prague Spring and its Aftermath: Czechoslovak Politics, 1968–1970*, Cambridge: Cambridge University Press (1997).

Williamson, George S., 'What Killed August von Kotzebue? The Temptations of Virtue and the Political Theology of German Nationalism, 1789–1819', *The Journal of Modern History*, Vol. 72, No. 4 (2000), 890–943.

Wilpert, Gero von, *Sachwörterbuch der Literatur*, Stuttgart: Kröner (2001).

Wilson, Peter H., 'Bolstering the Prestige of the Habsburgs: The End of the Holy Roman Empire in 1806', *The International History Review*, Vol. 28, No. 4 (2006), 709–736.

———, *The Holy Roman Empire: A Thousand Year of Europe's History*, London: Allen Lane (2016).

Wingfield, Nancy M., *Flag Wars and Stone Saints: How the Bohemian Lands Became Czech*, Cambridge: Harvard University Press (2007).

Winkler, Heinrich August, *Weimar 1918–1933. Die Geschichte der ersten deutschen Demokratie*, Munich: C.H. Beck (2005).

BIBLIOGRAPHY

Winter, Eduard, *Halle als Ausgangspunkt der deutschen Russlandkunde im 18. Jahrhundert*, Berlin: Akademie Verlag (1953).

———, *Die tschechische und slowakische Emigration in Deutschland im 17. und 18. Jahrhundert*, Berlin: Akademie Verlag (1955).

Winter, Eduard and Günter Jarosch eds., *Wegbereiter der deutsch-slawischen Wechselseitigkeit*, Berlin: Akademie-Verlag (1983).

Winters, Stanley B., Robert B. Pynsent, and Harry Hanak eds., *T. G. Masaryk (1850–1937)*, 3 Vols., Basingstoke: Macmillan (1990).

Wistrich, Robert S., *The Jews of Vienna in the Age of Franz Joseph*, Oxford: OUP (1990).

Wolff, Christoph, *Mozart at the Gateway to His Fortune: Serving the Emperor, 1788–1791*, New York: W. W. Norton & Company (2012).

Wolff, Larry, *Inventing Eastern Europe: The Map of Civilization on the Mind of the Enlightenment*, Stanford: Stanford University Press (1994).

———, *The Idea of Galicia*, Stanford: Stanford Universit Press (2010).

Wollman, Frank, 'Kdo "nasugeroval Evropě mythus o jednotě Slovanstva"?', *Sborník prací Filozofické fakulty brněnské univerzity*, Vol. 10, No. 8 (1961), 348–61.

———, *Slavismy a antislavismy za jara národů*, Prague: Academia Praha (1968).

Wollstein, Günter, *Das „Großdeutschland" der Paulskirche. Nationale Ziele in der bürgerlichen Revolution 1848/49*, Düsseldorf: Droste Verlag (1977).

Zacek, Joseph Frederick, *Palacký: The Historian as Scholar and Nationalist*, The Hague: Mouton (1970).

Zahra, Tara, 'Looking East: East Central European "Borderlands" in German History and Historiography", *History Compass*, Vol. 3, No. 1 (2005).

———, *Kidnapped Souls: National Indifference and the Battle for Children in the Bohemian Lands, 1900–1948*, Ithaca: Cornell University Press (2008).

Zajc, Marko, *Gdje slovensko prestaje, a hrvatsko počinje*, Zagreb: Srednja Europa (2008).

Žepić, Stanko, 'Zur Geschichte der deutschen Sprache in Kroatien', *Zagreber Germanistische Beiträge*, Vol. 11 (2002), 209–227.

Zeune, Johann August, *Gea. Versuch einer wissenschaftlichen Erdbeschreibung*, Berlin (1808).

Zimmerman, Joshua D., *Jozef Pilsudski: Founding Father of Modern Poland*, Cambridge, MA: Harvard University Press (2022).

Zimmermann, Moshe, 'A Road not Taken—Friedrich Naumann's Attempt at a Modern German Nationalism', *Journal of Contemporary History*, Vol. 17, No. 4 (1982), 689–708.

Živković, Daniela, 'Publicistika na njemačkom jeziku u Zagrebu u drugoj polovici 18. stoljeća', *Radovi—Zavod za hrvatsku povijest*, Vol. 22 (1989), 49–70.

Zwick, Peter, *National Communism*, Boulder: Westview Press (1983).

INDEX

Aachen, 17
Abbt, Thomas, 42
Abendland, 294
Académie Française, 37
Addresses to the German Nation (Fichte), 63
Adenauer, Konrad, 238, 293–4, 307, 317, 318
Adler, Victor, 178, 184, 203, 226
Age of Enlightenment (c. 1685–1815), 33–54, 63, 70, 71, 96, 133
Agram, Croatia, 45, 94, 128, 168, 171, 174, 188, 189, 192, 301, 304, 309
Agram Trial (1909), 218
Agramer Lloyd, 133
Alexander I, Emperor of Russia, 56, 75
Alexander I, King of Yugoslavia, 266, 269
Alexander II, Emperor of Russia, 150
Alexander III, Emperor of Russia, 214
All-Slavic Committee, 297
All-Slavic Congress (1946), 300
Allenstein, Prussia, 278
Allgemeine Zeitung, 96, 101
Allied-occupied Germany (1945–9), 285, 291–2, 294
Ambrož, Mihael, 170
Andrássy, Gyula, 149, 164–5
von Andrian-Werburg, Victor Franz, 91, 102

Anhalt, Duchy of (1863–1918), 155
Anschluss, 146–7, 213, 240, 241, 249, 255, 272–3
Anti-Bolshevik Committee, 243
Anti-Comintern Pact (1936), 277
antisemitism, 132, 137, 166, 172, 182–8, 201–2, 207, 217, 254, 258
   Bolshevism and, 244, 267–8, 271, 280, 281, 296
   communism and, 303
   Nazism and, 267, 270–72, 273, 276, 278, 280–83, 287, 301
   Tiszaeszlár affair (1882–3), 183
   World War I (1914–18), 227, 235, 237, 238, 258
von Anton, Karl Gottlob, 52, 53
Antonescu, Ion, 279
April Laws (1848), 107, 118, 164
archconservatives, 138
architecture, 134–5
Arco-Valley, Anton, 243
Arndt, Ernst Moritz, 65, 72, 77, 87–8, 114, 117
Arrow Cross Party, 283, 284
Art of Beer-Brewing, The (Paupie), 133–4
art, 177–8
'Aryan race', 182, 186, 260, 282
Ashmead-Bartlett, Ellis, 235
Association of Berlin Artists, 177
Association of German Students, 186
Auer, Erhard, 243

INDEX

Augustus II, Elector of Saxony, 40
Aulneau, Joseph, 275
Auschwitz-Birkenau, 283
Austria, 8, 9, 10, 19, 52, 62, 95
    Allied-occupied Austria (1945–55), 285, 292, 295, 302, 307
    Anschluss (1938), 272–3, 285
    Archduchy (1453–1804), 19, 20, 23, 34
    Austria-Hungary (1867–1918), *see* Austria-Hungary
    Empire (1804–67), *see* Austrian Empire
    Federal State (1934–8), 269, 271, 272
    Nazi State (1938–45), 272–3, 278
    Republic, First (1919–34), 7, 249–50, 257, 267, 268
    Republic of German-Austria (1918–19), 240–41, 249
    Napoleonic Wars (1803–15), 62, 65
Austria and Its Future (Andrian-Werburg), 91
Austria-Hungary (1867–1918), 6, 10, 149–50, 155–76, 193
    antisemitism in, 182–8, 201–2, 207
    armies, 155
    Ausgleich (1867), 149–50, 154, 155, 164, 172
    Badeni Ordinances (1897), 211–12, 214
    Balkan Wars (1912–13), 218–19
    Bosnia occupation (1878), 164, 218
    Christian socialism in, 201–2
    civil service, 211
    constitution (1867), 172
    Corpus Christi processions, 196
    decennial negotiations, 214, 225
    Dual Alliance (1879), 164
    economic crisis (1873–7), 183–4
    Franz Ferdinand assassination (1914), 221, 226
    Hungarian constitutional crisis (1905–6), 215–16
    Jews in, 166, 172, 174, 182–8, 201–2, 207, 227
    language in, 168–72
    liberalism in, 165, 172, 175–6, 178–80
    Linz Program (1882), 178–9, 184, 203
    Paris Exposition (1900), 195–7
    socialism in, 184–5, 201–4
    Tiszaeszlár affair (1882–3), 183
    Three Emperors Alliance (1873–87), 164
    World War I (1914–18), 221–31, 235
    Zagreb Trial (1909), 218
Austrian Empire (1804–67), 56, 62, 65, 66, 68–9, 76, 80, 91, 95, 126, 154
    bicameral Reichsrat, 143–4
    centralist movement, 143–5, 147
    Concordat (1855), 128
    Crimean War (1853–6), 142
    dual-track federalism proposal (1862), 147
    education in, 128
    federalist movement, 143, 145, 149
    industrialization in, 130–31
    modernization in, 127–38
    neo-absolutism (1848–61), 130, 136, 141, 143, 166, 168, 169, 174
    Prussian War (1866), 148–9, 153, 154
    revolutions (1848–9), 105–11, 113, 115–21, 130, 136, 142
    Sardinian War (1859), 141, 142
    Schleswig War (1864), 147–8
    Silvesterpatent (1851), 132
    unitary state declared (1851), 126
    urbanization in, 132

INDEX

Zollverein accession (1857), 127
Austrian Netherlands (1714–97), 20, 40, 42, 56
Austrian Press Association, 197
Austrian State Idea, The (Palacký), 149
Austrian-German Postal Union, 127
Austro-Slavists, 122, 136, 145
'Away From Prussia!', 238
Away from Rome movement, 212

von Bach, Alexander, 138
Baden, Grand Duchy of (1806–1918), 62, 105, 145, 148, 153, 154, 155, 236
von Baden, Max, 236
Badeni Ordinances (1897), 211–12, 214
Badeni, Kasimir Felix, 211, 212, 214
Balkan League, 218
Balkan Wars (1912–13), 218–19, 223
Baltic Germans, 38, 267
Baltic languages, 38, 54, 69
Bamberg, Bavaria, 244
Barthou, Louis, 269
Batthyány, Lajos, 92, 102, 106, 119–20
Battle of Berlin (1945), 292
Battle of Jena–Auerstedt (1806), 63
Battle of Solferino (1859), 141
Battle of Stalingrad (1942–3), 283
Battle of Tannenberg (1914), 223
Bauer, Otto, 203
Bavaria
    Electorate of Bavaria (1623–1806), 16, 22, 39, 40, 42
    Kingdom of Bavaria (1806–1918), *see* Kingdom of Bavaria
    Soviet Republic (1919), 243–4
    Weimar Germany (1919–33), 257–62, 267
Bavarian Army, 155
Bavarian People's Party, 237

Bavarian Soviet Republic (1919), 243–4
Bebel, August, 163
Beck, Józef, 277
Beer Hall Putsch (1923), 261
beer, 133–4, 212
van Beethoven, Ludwig, 197
Bel, Matthias, 46
Belarus, 8, 98, 282, 297
Belcredi, Richard, 147
Belgium, 19, 20, 23–4, 40, 42, 56, 222, 279
Belgrade, Serbia, 135, 300
Bělohradský, Václav, 321
Beneš, Edvard, 228, 229, 265–6, 270, 276, 285, 286, 298
Berchtold, Leopold, 219
Berlin, 64, 69, 77, 100, 107, 132, 133, 198, 237, 281, 284, 301
Berlin Wall, fall of (1989), 326, 331
Beseler, Georg, 115
Bessarabia, 279
Bessenyei, György, 47
von Bethmann Hollweg, Theobald, 217, 224
von Beust, Friedrich Ferdinand, 138–9, 146, 149
Bevin, Ernst, 295
Bidault, Georges, 295
Bidlo, Jaroslav, 318
Bildung, 63, 70, 95, 114, 130, 179, 180
Bildungsbürgertum, 64, 70
Bischofsteinitz, Bohemia, 33
von Bismarck, Otto, 10, 72, 141–8, 151, 158, 163–4, 194, 200, 217, 225, 239
Blanning, Tim, 54
Blum, Robert, 119–20
Bohemia
    Czechoslovakia (1918–92), *see* Czechoslovakia

407

INDEX

Kingdom of Bohemia (1198–1918), *see* Kingdom of Bohemia
Protectorate of Bohemia and Moravia (1939–45), 277, 281, 282
Republic of German-Austria (1918–19), 241
Bohemian Museum, 74
Bohemian Society of Sciences, 33–4, 54
Bollé, Hermann, 135
Bolshevism, 230, 238, 244, 268, 271, 280, 281, 296
Book of Laughter and Forgetting, The (Kundera), 320
Bosnia & Herzegovina, 19, 164, 218
Brandenburg
　Electorate of Brandenburg (1157–1806), 16, 22, 27
　Province of Brandenburg (1815–1947), 69
Bratislava, Slovakia, 6, 28, 45, 246
Bremen, 139, 198
Breslau, Silesia, 278, 281, 284, 302
Breslauer Zeitung, 111
Bretons, 117
Brezhnev, Leonid, 314
Brodsky, Joseph, 2, 324, 333–4
von Bruck, Karl Ludwig, 127, 143
Brünn, Moravia, 171, 191
Brunswick, Duchy of (1815–1918), 155
Buchs, Switzerland, 235
Buda, Hungary, 29, 49, 85, 118–19, 195, 304
Budapest, Hungary, 45, 132, 166, 168, 171, 185, 195–6, 227, 284, 301
Budissiner Nachrichten, 139
Budweis, Bohemia, 134, 180, 171, 191
Bukovina, Duchy of (1849–1918), 155, 172, 223
Bulgaria, 135, 217, 282, 297

Bülow Bloc (1907–9), 217
von Bülow, Bernhard, 195, 216, 217
Buric, Miroslav, 309
Burschenschaften, 67, 72, 186
Busch, Julius Hermann Moritz, 152
Bush, George Herbert Walker, 322
Byzantine Empire (330–1453), 25

Čakavian, 81
Calvinism, 39, 69, 91
capitalism, 4, 5, 61, 127, 185, 199–204, 268, 328–9
Carinthia, Duchy of (976–1918), 10, 34, 52, 73, 110, 120, 155, 169, 202, 249
Carl August, Grand Duke of Saxe-Weimar, 71
Carlsbad Decrees (1819), 72, 75, 76, 87
Carniola, Duchy of (1364–1918), 10, 34, 52, 83, 110, 155, 169, 170–71, 202
Carol II, King of Romania, 266
Catholic People's Party (Hungary), 201
Catholicism
　in Austria-Hungary, 201–3, 206, 212
　in Austrian Empire, 128
　in Austrian Federal State, 271, 272
　in Bavaria, 152, 159
　Christian democracy and, 295–6
　in Czechoslovakia, 246, 257, 271, 276
　Greek Catholic Church, 93, 97, 175
　Frankfurt National Assembly and, 113, 114
　in German Empire, 159, 161–2, 184, 198, 200, 201, 205, 238
　in Holy Roman Empire, 9, 18, 25–7, 38–9, 41, 42, 44–7, 54
　in Hungary, 91, 201–3
　in Poland, 175, 271

INDEX

in Prussia, 69, 70, 89
Ceaușescu, Nicolae, 303
Central Association of German Citizens, 187
Central Cultural House of Railwaymen, 311
Central Europe, 1–12, 59–62, 66, 135–6, 226, 287, 298, 301–2, 309, 321–6
  definitions of, 3, 8, 59
  denial of existence, 1, 2, 4
  Lisbon Conference (1988), 1–2, 4, 6
  origins of concept, 6, 59–62
  return of, 327–35
Central Europe and the Western World (Schacher), 255
Centre Party (Germany), 161, 184, 200, 216, 217, 228, 237, 239
Černý, Tomáš, 170
Chamberlain, Houston Stewart, 182
Chamberlain, Neville, 273
Charlemagne, Holy Roman Emperor, 17, 24, 25, 26, 88, 295
Charles University, 206
Charles VI, Holy Roman Emperor, 21–2
Charles X, King of France, 75
Chemnitz, Saxony, 184, 205
Childhood in Agram (Krleža), 309
China, 255
Christendom, 60–61
Christian democracy, 293–4, 295–6
Christian Democratic Union (CDU), 293–4, 318
Christian Social Party (Austria), 201
Christian socialism, 199, 200, 201–4, 205, 211, 240, 249
Churchill, Winston, 284, 293, 295
Cicero, 37
Cilli, Styria, 171, 179
Cillier Zeitung, 179

Cisleithania, 155, 192, 201
civilization, 11, 60, 61, 222–3, 294–5, 318, 323, 324
Claß, Heinrich, 224
coffeehouses, 105, 197, 256
Cold War (1947–91), 1, 6, 8, 294, 300, 307, 309, 322, 329
Cologne, 16, 25, 89, 238
Comenius, Jan Amos, 28
Commissar Order (1941), 280
communism, 4–5, 7, 91, 102, 112, 238–44, 292–305, 309–18, 319–26, 332
Communist International, 296
Communist League, 102, 112
Communist Manifesto, The (Marx and Engels), 102
Communist Party of Czechoslovakia, 313
Communist Party of Germany, 238–9, 259
Communist Party of Hungary, 242, 303
Communist Party of Slovakia, 313
Concerning the German National Spirit (Moser), 42
Confederation of the Rhine (1806–13), 56–7
Congress of Oppressed Nationalities (1918), 228
Congress of Vienna (1814), 65–6, 68, 74
Congress Poland (1815–1915), 75, 98, 151, 224
conservatism, 74, 76, 85, 86, 91, 112, 122, 137–8, 144, 184, 328–32
  modernization and, 126–7, 139
Conservative Party (Germany), 145, 186, 200, 217
Constitution Party (Hungary), 216
Constitution, Die, 111, 202
Constitutional Party, 144

409

INDEX

Constitutional Society of Germans, 179
constitutionalism, 57, 62, 101–2, 137, 173
    Austria-Hungary (1867–1918), 172
    Austrian Empire (1804–67), 143–4
    German Confederation (1815–66), 67–8, 75
    German Empire (1871–1918), 158
    Holy Roman Empire (800–1806), 19, 22, 24
    revolutions (1848), 105–23, 136–7
Corpus Christi processions, 196
cosmopolitanism, 4, 5, 9, 35, 50, 54, 70–71, 80, 85, 91, 95, 98, 186, 239, 255
Cossacks, 112
von Coudenhove-Kalergi, Richard, 325
Credit (Széchenyi), 85
Cremeschnitte, 197
Crimea, 277, 334
Crimean War (1853–6), 142
criminal codes, 131–2
Croatia, 2, 5, 8, 9, 10, 19, 93–4, 108, 115, 144, 157, 168, 173–4
    Independent State (1941–5), 279–80, 281, 282, 302
    Kingdom of Croatia (1527–1868), *see* Kingdom of Croatia
    Kingdom of Croatia-Slavonia (1868–1918), *see* Kingdom of Croatia-Slavonia
    Kingdom of Yugoslavia (1918–41), 248–9, 265, 270
    People's Republic of Yugoslavia (1945–63), 304, 307
    Republic (1991–), 327, 328, 330–31
Croatian language, 2, 81, 135, 168, 174, 188, 189
Croatian People's Peasant Party, 209, 249, 265
Croatian tricolour, 168

Croatian-Hungarian Party, 94
Cross Currents, 322
crown of St. Stephen, 328
Cumans, 166
Cvijic, Jovan, 262
Cyrillic, 93
Czech language, 33–4, 36, 50–52, 74, 77, 79, 96, 130, 179, 198, 207, 209
    Badeni Ordinances (1897), 211–12, 214
Czech Nation, The, 229
Czech National Social Party, 204
Czech Republic (1992–), 3, 5, 329
Czechia, 2, 3, 8, 10, 19, 33–4, 100, 115
    Czech Republic (1992–), 3, 5, 329, 330
    Czechoslovakia (1918–92), *see* Czechoslovakia
    Kingdom of Bohemia (1198–1918), *see* Kingdom of Bohemia
    Margravate of Moravia (1182–1918), 30
    Protectorate of Bohemia and Moravia (1939–45), 277, 281, 282
Czechoslovak Writers' Union, 310–15
Czechoslovakia (1918–92), 1, 2, 4, 228, 231, 245–6, 247–8
    Federative Republic (1990–92), 5, 328
    Nazi invasion (1938), 275–6
    Republic, First (1918–38), 7, 245–8, 250, 256–8, 262, 264–7, 270, 273, 296
    Republic, Second (1938–9), 276–7
    Republic, Third (1945–8), 285, 286, 287, 297–9
    Republic, Fourth (1948–60), 300, 303, 305, 308, 310
    Socialist Republic (1960–90), 1, 4, 310–16, 317, 319–24

INDEX

Czechs, migration of, 198, 204, 214, 260
von Czoernig, Carl Freiherr, 130

Dalmatia, 30, 34, 51, 66, 79, 81, 99, 131, 155, 172, 189, 215
Danica Ilirska, 81
Darwin, Charles, 182
Daughter of Slava, The (Šafařík), 79
Deák, Ferenc, 144, 149, 191
Debrecen, Hungary, 120, 324–5
Decline of the West, The (Spengler), 294
democracy, 204–9, 229, 239, 241–2, 255–7, 265–6, 270
Demon in Democracy, The (Legutko), 331
Denis, Ernest, 228–9
Denmark, 60, 147–8, 279
Deschmann, Karl, 170
Deutsche Reichstags-Zeitung, 117
Deutsche Schriften, 212
Deym, Friedrich, 113
Dietal Reports (Kossuth), 86
Dieterici, Karl Friedrich Wilhelm, 127
Dmowski, Roman, 228, 247
Dobrovský, Joseph, 31, 33–4, 50, 51–2, 53, 74, 77, 79
Dolfuss, Engelbert, 269
Drang nach Osten, 214
Drašković, Janko, 94
Drau, Die, 190
Dreher, Anton, 134, 197
Dresden, Saxony, 77, 163, 183, 284, 301
Dresden Conference (1851), 122
Dreyfus Affair (1894–1906), 187
Droysen, Johann Gustav, 159, 186
Dubček, Alexander, 313–14
Duchy of Anhalt (1863–1918), 155
Duchy of Brunswick (1815–1918), 155
Duchy of Bukovina (1849–1918), 155, 172, 223
Duchy of Carinthia (976–1918), 10, 34, 52, 73, 110, 120, 155, 169, 202, 249
Duchy of Carniola (1364–1918), 10, 34, 52, 83, 110, 155, 169, 170–71, 202
Duchy of Modena (1452–1859), 99
Duchy of Parma (1545–1859), 99, 141
Duchy of Salzburg (1810–1918), 73, 155
Duchy of Saxe-Altenburg (1602–1918)
Duchy of Saxe-Coburg and Gotha (1826–1918), 155
Duchy of Saxe-Meiningen (1680–1918), 155
Duchy of Silesia (1742–1918), 69, 90–91, 109, 155, 162, 171, 238
  Austrian, 30, 40, 155, 171
  Prussian, 40, 41, 42, 69, 90–91, 109, 148, 162
Duchy of Styria (1180–1918), 10, 34, 52, 73, 109, 155, 169, 171, 179, 202, 249
Duchy of Warsaw (1807–15), 75
von Dumreicher, Armand, 181
Düsseldorf, 74
Dutch language, 39, 158

East Germany (1949–90), 300, 308, 328
Eastern Europe, 3, 4, 6, 287, 293, 297–305, 317–18, 319, 321–6, 328
Eastland, James, 294–5
Ebert, Friedrich, 236, 238, 256
economic liberalism, 89, 127, 129
economic protectionism, 255
von Edelsheim, Wilhelm, 55
Eden, Anthony, 286
Edict of Toleration (1782), 100
education, 72–3, 135, 140, 160, 166
Egypt, 87
Eiffel Tower, Paris, 193

INDEX

Einsatzgruppen, 278, 281
Einstein, Albert, 192
Eisenach, 67, 91, 142
Eisner, Kurt, 237, 243
Electorate of Bavaria (1623–1806), 16, 22, 39, 40, 42
Electorate of Brandenburg (1157–1806), 16, 22, 27
Electorate of Hanover (1692–1814), 16, 27, 42
Electorate of Saxony (1356–1806), 16, 17, 22, 40, 42, 43, 52–3
Elisabeth, Empress of Austria, 128, 196
Enabling Act (1933), 269
Engels, Friedrich, 102, 201
England, 27, 38, 83, 89, 134
Engländer, Sigmund, 116
Enlightenment (c, 1685–1815), see Age of Enlightenment
Eötvös, József, 157, 158, 165
Erfurt Union (1850), 122
Erzberger, Matthias, 258
Escorial Palace, Madrid, 21
Essek, Croatia, 171, 190, 192
Estonia, 38
Eucken, Rudolf, 222
eugenics, 260
European Coal and Steel Community, 295
European Union, 5, 328, 329
Evangelical Social Congresses, 205
Evans, Arthur, 229

fascism, 259, 267–9
Fatherland, The (Pfizer), 95
Fatherland Party, 228, 252
Fellner & Helmer, 135
Ferdinand I, Emperor of Austria, 76, 106, 118–20
Fichte, Johann Gottlieb, 63, 273
Fidesz, 332
Filep, Mária, 325

financialization, 131
Finland, 282
First World War (1914–18), *see* World War I
Fiume, 94, 189
Forman, Miloš, 312
Foundations of the Nineteenth Century, The (Chamberlain), 182
Fourteen Points (1918), 230, 236, 240, 241, 242
France, 9, 11, 60, 73, 83
  Allied-occupied Germany (1945–9), 285
  Enlightenment (c. 1685–1789), 36–7, 38, 63
  Kingdom of France (843–1792), 22, 25, 27, 36–7, 38
  Empire, First (1804–15), 62–5
  Empire, Second (1852–70), 153–4
  July Monarchy (1830–1848), 87, 105
  Napoleonic Wars (1803–15), 56, 62–5, 73, 83, 100, 154
  Paris Peace Conference (1919), 256
  Prussian War (1870–71), 153–4
  Republic, First (1792–1804), 56
  Republic, Second (1848–52), 105
  Republic, Third (1870–1940), 187, 193, 242–3, 246, 256, 259, 269–70, 273, 275, 278
  Republic, Fourth (1946–1958), 285, 295, 299
  Revolution (1789–99), 19, 20, 55–6, 58, 126, 193
  Revolution (1830), 75
  Revolution (1848), 105
  Revolutionary Wars (1792–1802), 56
  World War I (1914–18), 221–2, 223, 224
  World War II (1939–45), 278, 279, 283

412

INDEX

Francis I, Holy Roman Emperor, 18, 22
Francis II, Holy Roman Emperor, 55–7, 65–6, 68, 69, 76, 111
Franconians, 39
Frank, Josip and Jacob, 190
Frank, Tibor, 253
Frankfurt, 15, 24, 25, 27, 42, 66, 100, 136, 148, 152, 205, 281, 291–2
Frankfurt National Assembly (1848–9), 108–18, 119–20, 121–2
Frankfurter Zeitung, 177
Frankish Kingdom (c. 509–843), 25
Franz Ferdinand, Archduke of Austria-Este, 219, 221, 226
Franz Joseph I, Emperor of Austria
   accession (1848), 120
   Ausgleich (1867), 149–50, 151, 154, 155, 156, 164, 172
   Balkan Wars (1912–13), 218–19
   Bohemian draft laws (1871), 175–6
   Croat *ban* appointments, 168, 188
   Croat protest (1895), 208
   death (1916), 227
   diamond jubilee (1908), 211
   golden jubilee (1898), 196–7
   Jewish community, relations with, 185–6
   Elisabeth, assassination of (1898), 196
   Elisabeth, wedding to (1854), 128
   Hungarian constitutional crisis (1905–6), 215–16
   Lueger, relations with, 201
   Millenium Exhibition (1896), 195
   October Diploma (1860), 143
   Prussian War (1866), 148–9
   Sardinian War (1859), 141
   Silvesterpatent (1851), 132
   Trieste railway opening (1857), 125
   unification proposals (1861–2), 146–7
   World War I outbreak (1914), 223
Frederick I, King of Prussia, 22
Frederick II, King of Prussia, 22, 40, 41, 42, 64, 69
Frederick William I, King of Prussia, 22, 40
Frederick William II, King of Prussia, 23–4, 27
Frederick William III, King of Prussia, 63, 65, 69
Frederick William IV, King of Prussia, 87–9, 101–2, 106–7, 120, 121–2, 138
Free City of Trieste (1849–1922), 125, 130, 155
Freikorps, 64, 67, 238–9, 243
Frencel, Michał, 51
French language, 9, 27, 35–7, 44, 46
French Revolution (1789), 19, 20, 55–6, 58, 126
French Revolutionary Wars (1792–1802), 56
Freud, Sigmund, 192
Friedjung, Heinrich, 178, 184, 185, 225
Frisch, Max, 291
Frisian language, 39
Fröbel, Julius, 113
Fukuyama, Francis, 5
Füster, Anton, 107

Gaj, Ljudevit, 81, 94, 110, 129, 150
Galicia, 10, 19
   Kingdom of Galicia (1772–1918), *see* Kingdom of Galicia
   Nazi occupation (1939–45), 279
gap theory, 146
General German Language Association, 180
General German Workers' Association, 163
George II, King of Great Britain, 38

INDEX

George III, King of the United Kingdom, 27
George V, King of Hanover, 139
von Gerlach, Leopold, 138
von Gerlach, Ludwig, 146
German Austrian Party, 185
German Club, 185
German Confederation (1815–66), 11, 66, 67–76, 87, 154
    Crimean War (1853–6), 142
    dual-track federalism proposal (1862), 147
    industrialization in, 130–31
    Kleindeutschland movement (1862–3), 142
    modernization in, 130–31, 132, 133, 138–40
    provincial systems, 131–2
    Revolution (1848–9), 106–18, 119–20, 121–2, 136
    Schleswig War (1864), 147–8
    urbanization in, 131, 132, 133
    Wartburg Festival (1817), 67, 71–2, 76
German Democratic Party, 239
German Democratic Republic (1949–90), 300, 308
German Empire (1871–1918), 6, 7, 154–7, 158–64, 193–5, 260
    antisemitism in, 182, 184, 186, 217
    Bülow Bloc (1907–9), 217
    constitution, 158
    Dual Alliance (1879), 164
    elections (1871), 160
    elections (1903), 205, 216
    elections (1907), 217
    establishment of (1871), 154–7, 158
    industrialization in, 198
    Jews in, 182, 184, 186–8, 217, 228
    Kiel mutiny (1918), 236
    Kulturkampf (c. 1871–87), 161–2, 202
    liberalism in, 158–9, 161–2, 163, 204–5
    migration in, 198, 204
    New Course (1890), 194–5
    overseas empire, 194–5, 216
    Paris Exposition (1900), 193–5
    Poles in, 162, 198
    population, 194
    religion in, 159, 161–2
    Revolution (1918), 236
    socialism in, 163–4, 200–201, 228
    state socialism, 194
    Three Emperors Alliance (1873–87), 164
    Weltpolitik, 194–5, 213, 217
    World War I (1914–18), 221–31, 236
German language, 6, 10, 28, 128, 189, 191–2, 211–12, 255
    Enlightenment and, 34, 36–9, 43–54
    nationalism and, 113, 162, 168–73, 178–82, 185, 203, 211–12
German National People's Party, 252, 253, 267, 268
German nationalism, 38, 54, 60, 63–5, 67–76, 80, 87–8, 95, 157, 178–82
    in Austria-Hungary (1867–1918), 178–82, 203, 211–14
    Pan-Germanism, 7, 111, 146–7, 204, 212–14, 224–5, 239, 240, 241, 249, 255, 260
    Revolution (1848–9), 107–18, 119–20, 121–2
    Unification of Germany (1866–71), 142–3, 146–8, 151–4
    Weimar Republic (1918–33), 252–3
    World War I (1914–18), 222–3, 225, 228, 231, 239–41
German Progress Party, 145
German Reform Association, 142, 183

INDEX

German School Association, 179–80
German Society, 43, 45
German South West Africa (1884–1915), 216
German tricolour, 107, 112
German Watch, 179
German Workers' Party (Austrian Republic), 260
German Workers' Party (Bohemia), 204
German Workers' Party (Weimer Republic), 259–60
German-Austrian Telegraph Organization 127
Germania (personification), 112
Germania (Tacitus), 38, 60
Germanomania, 65
Germans
   in Bohemia, 33, 110–11, 128, 168–71, 180, 179, 186, 191, 211–12
   in Croatia, 128–9, 168, 171, 189–90
   in Hungary, 38–9, 95, 129, 166, 167, 168, 191–2
   in Poland, 285, 286–7, 299, 302–3
   post-WWII expulsions, 285, 286–7, 299
Germany, 6–7, 8–11, 19, 60, 63–6
   Allied-occupied Germany (1945–9), 285, 291–2, 294
   Confederation (1815–66), *see* German Confederation
   Confederation of the Rhine (1806–13), 56–7
   Democratic Republic (1949–90), 300, 308, 328
   Enlightenment and, 36–9, 41–2, 43–54, 63, 70
   Erfurt Union (1850), 122
   Federal Republic (1949–), 9, 292–4, 303, 307, 308, 318, 325, 328
   Frankfurt National Assembly (1848–9), 108–18, 119–20, 121–2
   nationalism, *see* German nationalism
   North German Confederation (1866–71), 148, 152–4
   Reich, First (800–1806), *see* Holy Roman Empire
   Reich, Second (1871–1918), *see* German Empire
   Reich, Third (1933–45), 7, 269, 270–73, 275–84
   Revolution (1848–9), 106–18, 119–20, 121–2
   Revolution (1918–19), 236–9
   Unification (1866–71), 142–3, 146–8, 151–4
   Weimar Republic (1918–33), 7, 236–9, 250–53, 257–62, 267–9
Glagau, Otto, 184
globalization, 127, 193
Goebbels, Joseph, 268, 281
von Goethe, Johann Wolfgang, 15, 53, 58, 71, 77, 80, 143, 200, 239
Gömbös, Gyula, 243, 271
Good Soldier Švejk, The (Hašek), 321
Gorbachev, Mikhail, 1, 324
Göring, Hermann, 276
Gorizia, Princely County of (1754–1919), 155
Görlitz, Saxony, 52–3
Görres, Joseph, 65
Gossman, Lionel, 36
Gottsched, Johann Christoph, 38, 43–4
Gottsched, Luise, 43–4
Gottwald, Klement, 299
Gradec, Croatia, 132
Gradisca, Princely County of (1754–1919), 155
Grand Duchy of Baden (1806–1918), 62, 105, 145, 148, 153, 154, 155, 236

INDEX

Grand Duchy of Hesse (1806–1918), 148, 153, 154, 155
Grand Duchy of Lower Austria (1804–1918), 105–6, 155
Grand Duchy of Mecklenburg-Schwerin (1815–1918), 155
Grand Duchy of Mecklenburg-Strelitz (1815–1918), 155
Grand Duchy of Oldenburg (1815–1918), 155
Grand Duchy of Posen (1815–48), 69, 75, 98, 117
Grand Duchy of Saxe-Weimar (1809–1903), 155
Grand Duchy of Tuscany (1569–1860), 18, 20, 99, 141
Grand Duchy of Upper Austria (1804–1918), 73, 155
Granta, 323
Great Britain, Kingdom of (1707–1800), 35, 41
Great Depression (1929–39), 267, 270
Great Exhibition (1851), 139, 193, 194
Greece, 60, 135, 217
Greece, ancient, 37, 60, 273
Greek Catholic Church, 93, 97, 175
Greek Orthodox Church, 93, 318
Grenzboten, Die, 87, 89, 96, 111, 116
Grimm, Jacob, 80, 114, 158
Guelphic Legion, 152
Gumplowicz, Ludwig, 182, 207
Gustav III, King of Sweden, 27
gymnastics movement, 64, 71, 72, 88

von Habsburg, Otto, 257, 325–6, 327
Habsburgs, *see* House of Habsburg
Hácha, Emil, 276
Haeckel, Ernst, 222
Halecki, Oskar, 198, 317–18, 319, 323, 329
Halle, Prussia, 47

von Haller, Carl Ludwig, 73
Hambach festival (1832), 75
Hamburg, 25, 90, 132, 139, 198, 205, 283
Hanák, Péter, 4
Hanke, Karl, 284
Hanover
    Electorate of Hanover (1692–1814), 16, 27, 42
    Kingdom of Hanover (1814–66), 66, 73, 75, 131, 139, 147, 148, 152
    Kingdom of Westphalia (1807–13), 62
    Province of Hanover (1866–1946), 152
Hašek, Jaroslav, 321
Hasse, Ernst, 213
Hassel, Georg, 58, 62, 66
Hauner, Milan, 324
Havel, Václav, 5, 313–16, 320, 324, 328, 330
Havlíček, Karel, 97–8, 111, 136, 190
Haydn, Joseph, 197
von Hayek, Friedrich, 329
Hegel, Georg Wilhelm Friedrich, 95
Heller, Servác, 128
Hendrych, Jiří, 311, 312–13
Herder, Johann Gottfried, 49, 53, 63, 71, 84, 273
Herkel, Ján, 78
Herzl, Theodor, 187–8
Hesse, Grand Duchy of (1806–1918), 148, 153, 154, 155
Heydrich, Reinhard, 282
Himmler, Heinrich, 281, 282, 283
von Hinckeldey, Carl Ludwig, 132
von Hindenburg, Paul, 223–4, 227, 251, 261, 268–9
Hirt, Hermann, 189–90
historiography, 72–3, 121, 137, 140, 159–60

INDEX

Historische Zeitschrift, 159
Hitler, Adolf, 259–62, 267–9, 272, 276, 277–84, 286, 324
Hlas, 208
Hlinka, Andrej, 202, 203, 266
Hohelohe-Schillingsfürst, Chlodwig, 153
Hohenzollerns, *see* House of Hohenzollern
Hoitsy, Samuel, 199
Holeček, Josef, 214
Holocaust (1941–5), 280–83, 287, 301, 302
Holy Roman Empire (800–1806), 9–10, 11, 15–31, 57–8, 73, 260
    constitutionalism in, 19, 22, 57
    dissolution (1806), 57–8, 61
    eastern regions, 39–40
    Enlightenment in, 33–54
    French Revolution and, 56–7
    Jewish population, 100–101
    language in, 36–54
    prayers to emperors, 49, 40
    Silesian Wars (1740–63), 40, 41, 42, 69, 148
    western regions, 39
Hommel, Rudolph, 17
homosexuality, 282
Horthy, Miklós, 243, 244, 252, 256, 258
House of Guelph, 152
House of Habsburg, 6, 7, 9, 10, 11, 15–31, 68–9, 76, 135–6, 197, 255, 256, 331
    Ausgleich (1867), 149–50, 154, 155
    Austro-Prussian War (1866), 148–9
    Enlightenment and, 33–54
    French Revolution and, 56–7
    German nationalism and, 95
    Holy Roman Empire dissolution (1806), 57, 61
    Karl's restoration attempt (1921), 256–7
    Italian nationalism and, 99
    prayers to emperors, 49, 40
    provincial identities and, 73–4, 84
    revolutions (1848), 105–23
    unified state, ambitions for, 19, 20, 45, 69
    universalism, 26–7, 35, 53–4, 61–2
    World War I (1914–18), 221, 224, 228, 230, 231
House of Hohenzollern, 22–3, 34, 36, 37, 69, 113, 153, 197, 230, 231, 257
House of Wettin, 152, 163, 198, 284
House of Wittelsbach, 140, 198, 256, 258
Hugenberg, Alfred, 268
Huguenots, 81
von Humboldt, Alexander, 64
Hungarian Democratic Forum, 324
Hungarian State, The (Szekfű), 254
Hungary, 2, 3, 4, 8, 10, 19, 27–30
    Austria-Hungary (1867–1918), *see* Austria Hungary
    Kingdom, First (1000–1918), *see* Kingdom of Hungary, First
    Kingdom, Second (1920–46), 7, 252–4, 256, 258, 267, 271–2, 275, 277, 279
    People's Republic (1949–89), 1, 2, 4, 300, 303, 308, 310, 323
    Republic, First (1918–19), 241–3, 244, 250
    Republic, Second (1946–9), 296, 298, 299
    Republic, Third (1989–), 5, 324–5, 327–8, 329, 332
    Soviet Republic (1919), 242–3, 244, 246
Hus, Jan, 246

INDEX

Hussars, 195

Iasi, Romania, 135
Illyrian movement (1835–63), 81–2, 94, 115, 129, 168, 174, 248
Illyrians, 79, 174
Impressionism, 177
Independence Party (Hungary), 191, 215, 216
Independent National Party, 190
Independent State of Croatia (1941–5), 279–80, 281, 282, 302
industrialization, 90, 130–34, 193, 197, 198
International Congress of Historians, 317
Ireland, 117
Iron Guard, 270
Is Austria German? (Schuselka), 95, 107–8, 113
Islam, 201, 262
Israel, 303
Istóczy, Győző, 183, 185
Istria, Margravate of (1797–1918), 155, 172
Italian language, 27, 36, 37, 44
Italy, 9, 19, 27, 40, 60, 62, 99, 141, 157, 218, 226, 259, 299
    Fascist Italy (1922–43), 271, 273, 282, 283

Jagiellonian Europe, 330
Jahn, Friedrich Ludwig, 64, 71
Japan, 255
Jászi, Oszkár, 204, 205–6, 226, 241–2
Jeglič, Anton, 202–3
Jehovah's Witnesses, 282
Jelačić, Josip, 108, 118, 327
Jellinek, Adolf, 117
Jellinek, Georg, 173
Jesuits, 44, 112
Jewish State, The (Herzl), 188

Jews, 7, 114, 182–8
    in Austria-Hungary, 100, 166, 172, 174, 182–8, 201–2, 207, 227
    in Austrian Empire, 116, 117, 132, 137
    in Austrian Federal State, 271, 273
    in Croatia, 174, 185, 281
    in Czechoslovakia, 275, 281
    in Frankfurt National Assembly, 109, 112
    in German Confederation, 70, 109, 112, 114, 137
    in German Empire, 182, 184, 186–8, 217, 228, 237
    Holocaust (1941–5), 280–83, 287, 301, 302
    in Holy Roman Empire, 63, 69, 100–101
    in Hungary, 137, 166, 185, 187, 201–2, 244, 254, 271–2
    in Nazi Germany, 7, 270–72, 276, 280–83, 287
    in Poland, 23, 100, 263, 271, 278
    in Russian Empire, 187
    in Weimar Republic, 237, 258
    World War I and, 227, 235, 237
    World War II and, 280–83, 287
    Zionism, 188, 263, 287
John of Austria, Archduke, 113
John Paul II, Pope, 322
John the Baptist, 17
Johnson, Samuel, 60
Joke, The (Kundera), 312
Jordan, Jan Pětr, 111
Jordan, Wilhelm, 117
Joseph II, Holy Roman Emperor, 19, 20, 23, 42, 45, 48, 49–50, 56, 68, 69, 100, 180, 257
Judaism, 100, 201
'Judeo-Bolshevism', 244, 268, 271, 280, 281, 296
Junkers, 34, 69, 138, 146, 153, 224, 257, 263, 299

INDEX

Kafka, Franz, 305, 321, 322
von Kahr, Gustav, 258–9
Kaiser, Jakob, 293
Kajkavian, 81
Kaliningrad, 286
Kampfbund, 259
Kant, Immanuel, 35, 95
Kapp, Friedrich, 137
Kapp, Wolfgang, 228, 251
Kapp Putsch (1920), 251, 257
Kaptol, Croatia, 132
Karadžić, Vuk, 80, 82, 97, 174, 208
Karl I, Emperor of Austria, 222, 227, 236, 240, 256
Karlovac, Croatia, 94
Károlyi, Katalin, 227
Károlyi, Mihály, 241–2, 245
Kaunas, Lithuania, 281
von Kaunitz, Wenzel Anton, 44
Khuen-Héderváry, Károly, 188, 189, 209
Kiel mutiny (1918), 236
Kingdom of Bavaria (1806–1918), 88, 140, 148, 155
  army, 155, 259
  Catholicism in, 152, 159
  constitution (1808), 62
  diplomatic missions, 160
  Franco-Prussian War (1870–71), 153–4
  nationalism in, 88, 140
  Tyrolean Rebellion (1809), 65
  Unification of Germany, 147, 154, 155, 160
  World War I (1914–18), 231, 237
Kingdom of Bohemia (1198–1918), 9, 10, 16, 17, 19, 20, 21, 30–31, 33–5, 68, 155
  Badeni Ordinances (1897), 211–12
  Bohemian Museum founding (1818), 73–4
  centralist movement (1860s) and, 144
  Christian socialism in, 202
  constitutional laws (1867), 172
  draft laws (1871), 175–6
  Germans in, 33, 110–11, 128, 168–71, 180, 179, 191, 211–12
  industrialization in, 198
  Jews in, 116, 186
  language in, 50–52, 179
  nationalism in, *see* Czech nationalism
  Old Czechs, 144–5, 175–6, 190–91
  Revolution (1848–9), 109–11, 115–18, 130, 136, 150
  Slav Congress (1848), 110–11, 115–18, 130, 136, 150
  World War I (1914–18), 225–6
  Young Czechs, 190–91, 204, 207
Kingdom of Croatia (1527–1868), 28, 34, 36, 40, 45, 62, 79, 93, 100, 108
  architecture, 135
  centralist movement (1860s) and, 144
  Germans in, 128–9
  nationalism in, 96–7, 109–10, 115, 118, 144–5
  Revolution (1848), 115, 118
  Sabor, 93
Kingdom of Croatia-Slavonia (1868–1918), 168, 173–4, 188–90, 248
  anti-Hungarian protests (1883), 188
  Christian socialism in, 202
  constitutional crisis (1905–6), 215–16
  Germans in, 168, 171, 189–90
  Jews in, 174, 185
  nationalism in, 157, 168, 173–4, 188–90, 208–9
  Rakovica revolt (1871), 174
  Sabor, 168, 173, 189
Kingdom of Dalmatia (1797–1918), 66, 79, 81, 99, 131, 155, 172, 189, 215

419

INDEX

Kingdom of England (886–1707), 27, 38
Kingdom of France (843–1792), 22, 25, 27, 40
    Enlightenment (c. 1685–1789), 36–7, 38, 63
    Revolution (1789), 19, 20, 55–6, 58, 126
    War of the Austrian Succession (1740–48), 22
Kingdom of Galicia (1772–1918), 9, 23, 34, 36, 38, 41, 50, 68, 73, 97–9, 110–11, 155, 174–5
    Christian socialism in, 202
    constitutional laws (1867), 172
    industrialization in, 131
    revolutions (1848), 108, 110–11
    Russophiles, 175
    Tarnów uprising (1846), 98–9, 107
    Ukrainophiles, 175
    World War I (1914–18), 223, 224
Kingdom of Great Britain (1707–1800), 35, 41
Kingdom of Hanover (1814–66), 66, 73, 75, 131, 139, 147, 148, 152
Kingdom of Hungary, First (1000–1918), 9, 19, 20, 21, 23–4, 27–30, 40, 47–50, 62, 68, 73
    April Laws (1848), 107, 118, 164
    architecture, 135
    Ausgleich (1867), 149–50, 154, 155, 164
    Catholicism in, 91, 201–2
    centralist movement (1860s) and, 144, 147
    Christian socialism in, 201–2
    civil service in, 41, 45, 76, 138
    constitutional crisis (1905–6), 215–16
    diets, 49–50, 85–6, 91–2, 93, 94
    elections (1905), 215
    Germans in, 38–9, 95, 129, 166, 167, 168, 191–2
    Hussars, 195
    industrialization in, 131
    Jews in, 100, 166, 185, 187, 201–2, 227
    languages in, 28, 45, 47–50, 77, 84, 85, 91–2, 191–2
    liberalism in, 76, 85–6, 91, 165–7, 205–6
    Magyarization, 50, 77, 84–5, 91–2, 94, 116, 164, 166–9, 185, 191–2, 199, 216
    Millenium Exhibition (1896), 195
    modernization in, 131, 132
    nationalism in, 83–6, 92–5, 107, 108, 110, 144, 157, 168, 169, 191–2, 216
    Nationalities Act (1868), 166
    nobility in, 34, 41, 47–8, 49, 138
    Pan-Slavism in, 84, 92, 94
    Paris Exposition (1900), 195–6
    railways, 130, 216
    Revolution (1848–9), 105–6, 107, 108, 118–21, 122, 136, 206
    Romanians in, 167
    Slovaks in, 49, 167, 191, 192
    suffrage law (1874), 165
    Tiszaeszlár affair (1882–3), 183
    urbanization in, 132
    World War I (1914–18), 225–6
Kingdom of Hungary, Second (1920–46), 7, 252–4, 258, 267, 271–2, 287
    Karl's restoration attempt (1921), 256–7
    Munich Agreement (1938), 275, 277
    Vienna Award (1940), 279
    World War II (1939–45), 279, 282, 283, 284, 285, 302
Kingdom of Lombardy-Venetia (1815–66), 99
Kingdom of Poland (1815–1915), 75, 98, 151, 224

INDEX

Kingdom of Prussia (1701–1918), 9, 10, 20, 22–3, 34, 36, 38, 40–43, 62, 66, 69–70, 87–9, 239
army, 155
Austrian War (1866), 148–9, 153, 154
Congress of Vienna (1814), 66
constitution (1850), 146
censorship loosening (1840), 88
Crimean War (1853–6), 142
dual-track federalism proposal (1862), 147
French War (1870–71), 153–4
German Empire, position in, 159–60
German nationalism in, 63–5, 88
industrialization in, 131
Jews in, 100, 182, 186
Kleindeutschland movement (1862–3), 142
Kreuzzeitung, 138, 142
Landtag, 101–2, 145, 159, 160
languages in, 69
liberalism in, 87–9
mining industry, 131
modernization in, 131, 132
Napoleonic Wars (1803–15), 62, 63–5
nobility in, 138
Poles in, 162, 180, 198
provincial systems, 69, 131
railways, 130, 139
Revolution (1848–9), 106–7, 120, 121–2, 126
Schleswig War (1864), 147–8
Silesian Wars (1740–63), 40, 41, 42, 69, 148
Slavs in, 80
Sorbs in, 172–3
Stein-Hardenberg reforms (1806–19), 63, 69
Unification of Germany (1866–71), 142–3, 146–8, 151–4, 156
urbanization in, 132
Kingdom of Romania (1881–1947), 7, 217, 244, 248, 250, 257, 262, 267, 287
coup d'état (1930), 266
fascist movements, 270, 271, 279, 282
Little Entente (1920–21), 256
World War II (1939–45), 279, 282, 285, 302
Kingdom of Sardinia (1720–1861), 141, 142
Kingdom of Saxony (1806–1918), 66, 74, 75, 80, 152, 155, 160, 194
army, 155
Czechs in, 214
diplomatic missions, 160
industrialization in, 131, 198
post-revolutionary government (1849–66), 138–9
socialism in, 163
Sorbs in, 172
Unification of Germany (1866–71), 147, 148, 152
World War I (1914–18), 231
Kingdom of Serbia (1882–1918), 218–19, 221, 223
Kingdom of Serbs, Croats, and Slovenes (1918–29), 248, 250, 256, 262–3, 264, 267
Kingdom of Slavonia (1699–1868), 34, 38, 79, 81, 215
Kingdom of the Two Sicilies (1816–61), 105
Kingdom of Westphalia (1807–13), 62
Kingdom of Württemberg (1806–1918), 62, 139, 148, 152–3, 154, 155, 194
Kingdom of Yugoslavia (1918–41), 7, 247, 248–9, 250, 256, 257, 262–7, 269–70, 271
Kinsky, Franz Joseph, 52

421

INDEX

Kiš, Danilo, 333
Kissinger, Henry, 335
Klaus, Václav, 330
Klima, Ivan, 313
Kliment, Alexander, 312
Klofáč, Václav, 226
Knoll, Josef Leonhard, 96
Kohl, Helmut, 326
Kohout, Pavel, 312, 313, 314
Kollár, Adam František, 23, 49
Kollár, Ján, 76–9, 81, 84, 97, 136, 207–8
Kolnai, Aurel, 273
Kölnische Zeitung, 89, 116
Kolowrat, Franz Anton, 76
Königsberg, Prussia, 22, 35, 89, 286
Konrád, György, 2
Kopitar, Bartholomeus, 79, 80, 81
Korošec, Anton, 229
Košice Program (1945), 297–8
Kossuth, Ferenc, 191
Kossuth, Lajos, 86, 92, 105–6, 119, 120, 136, 150, 191
von Kotzebue, August, 71–2
Krakow, Poland, 74, 108, 301
Kramář, Karel, 213, 245
Krčelić, Baltazar Adam, 44
Kreuzzeitung, 138, 142
Kristallnacht (1938), 276
Krleža, Miroslav, 308–9
Krössinsee, Pomerania, 278
Kukuljević-Sakcinski, Ivan, 129
Kuleba, Dmytro, 2, 3
Kultur, 222–3, 238, 240, 252–3
Kultura, 317, 320
Kulturkampf (c. 1871–87), 161–2, 202
Kun, Béla, 242, 243
Kundera, Milan, 3–4, 5, 6, 301, 311–16, 319–24, 329, 335, 329, 335
Kundera, Věra, 319
Kuranda, Ignaz, 89–90, 96, 109, 111, 116

Kvaternik, Eugen, 174
Kyivan Rus' (c. 880–1240), 23

Labov, Jessie, 321
de Lagarde, Paul, 213
Laibach Turnverein, 179
Laibach, Slovenia, 45, 52, 168, 169, 170–71, 178
Lajos Kossuth University, 324
von Lamberg, Franz Philipp, 119
Länderbank, 197
Landeshoheit, 25
Lasker, Eduard, 158
Lassalle, Ferdinand, 163
Laszowski, Emilj, 198–9
Latin, 26, 27, 28–9, 36, 37, 44, 46, 47–8, 49, 50, 60, 77, 85, 91
Latvia, 8, 38, 54
Lavrov, Sergey, 2–3
Law and Justice, 332
League of Nations, 261
League of the Three Emperors (1873–87), 164
Legutko, Ryszard, 331–2
Leibniz, Gottfried Wilhelm, 37
Leipzig, Saxony, 43, 44, 77, 89–90, 152
Lemberg, 174
Lenin, Vladimir, 229
Leo III, Pope, 24
Leo, Heinrich, 57
Leopold I, Holy Roman Emperor, 196
Leopold II, Holy Roman Emperor, 15–21, 24, 27–31, 33–4, 54, 55, 111
Lessing, Gotthold Ephraim, 58
Liberal Association of Linz, 179
Liberal Party (Hungary), 165, 178, 188, 191, 215, 216
liberalism, 78, 136–7, 157, 178, 184, 188, 199–206, 332
  in Austria-Hungary, 165, 172, 175–6, 178–80, 185, 186

422

INDEX

in Austrian Empire, 87, 143–4, 147
in Austrian Republic, 249
in German Confederation, 67–76, 136–7, 142, 145–6
in German Empire, 158–9, 161–2, 163
Jews and, 174, 185, 186, 188
in Kingdom of Croatia-Slavonia, 174, 185
in Kingdom of Hungary, 76, 79, 85–6, 91, 137, 165, 254
in Kingdom of Prussia, 87–9, 145–6
revolutions (1848), 105–23, 136–7, 142, 157
Liebknecht, Karl, 239
Liebknecht, Wilhelm, 163
Liechtenstein, 8
von Liechtenstern, Joseph Marx, 59
Liehm, Antonín, 313, 314
Linhart, Anton Tomaž, 52, 53
Linz Program (1882), 178–9, 184, 203
Linz, Austria, 179, 260
Lisbon Conference (1988), 1–2, 4, 6, 332–3
von List, Guido, 260
Listy, 322
Literární listy, 314–15
Literární noviny, 310–11
literary reciprocity, 79, 98
Lithuania, 5, 7, 8, 60, 98, 246–7
 Nazi occupation (1941–5), 281
 Polish-Lithuanian Commonwealth (1569–1795), 23, 24, 41, 60, 246
 Republic, First (1918–40), 247
Little Entente (1920–21), 256
Ljubljana, Slovenia, 45, 52, 168, 169, 170–71, 178
Lloyd Palace, Pest, 83
Łódzz, Poland, 263
Louis Philippe I, King of the French, 75, 105
Louis XVI, King of France, 27, 56

Lower Austria, 20–21, 105–6, 155
Lübeck, 139
Ludendorff, Erich, 223–4, 227, 251, 257–8, 259, 261
Ludwig I, King of Bavaria, 88
Lueger, Karl, 201, 202, 203
Lusatia, 148
Lusatian Slavs, 52–3
Luther, Martin, 43–4, 67
Lutheran Lyceum, Pressburg, 74, 97
Lutheranism, 38, 39, 46–7, 69
von Lüttwitz, Walther, 251
Luxembourg, 8, 19
Luxemburg, Rosa, 203, 239
Lviv, 97, 302, 304
Lwów, 174

Macedonia, 269
Mackinder, Halford, 213
Macron, Emmanuel, 6
Madeira, 257
Madrid, Spain, 21
Magdeburg prison, 244–5
Magyars; Magyar language, 28, 36, 48–50, 166–9, 250, 263
 Magyarization, 50, 77, 84–5, 91–2, 94, 116, 164, 166–9, 185, 191–2, 199, 216
Magyar Hírmondó, 48
Magyar Kurír, 48
Mainz, 16, 25
Mann, Thomas, 222
Mannheimer, Isaac Noah, 107
von Manteuffel, Otto, 126, 138
Marburg, Styria, 171
Margravate of Istria (1797–1918), 155, 172
Margravate of Moravia (1182–1918), 19, 30, 46, 109, 120, 155, 171, 191, 202
Maria Theresa, Holy Roman Empress, 18, 20, 22, 23, 24, 40–45, 68, 99

INDEX

Marian columns, 257
Marie Antoinette, Queen consort of France, 27, 56
Marshall, George, 295
Martin, Slovakia, 167, 208
Marx, Karl, 89, 91, 100, 102, 112, 192, 201
Marxism, 203, 204, 206, 263, 318
Masaryk, Tomáš, 204, 206–9, 213, 218, 226–9, 248, 256–7, 265–6, 270, 276, 308
Masurians, 198
Matějka, Ladislav, 322
Maticas, 73, 167
Matvejevic, Predrag, 309
Maximilian II, King of Bavaria, 140
May Day, 200
Mažuranić, Ivan, 149, 174, 189
Mečiar, Vladimír, 330
Mecklenburg-Schwerin, Grand Duchy of (1815–1918), 155
Mecklenburg-Strelitz, Grand Duchy of, (1815–1918), 155
Mein Kampf (Hitler), 272
Meissner, Alfred, 116
'Memorandum from German-Austria' (Friedjung), 225
Merkur von Ungarn, 47, 49
Mészáros, Ferenc, 325
von Metternich, Klemens, 15, 18, 25, 37, 65–6, 68, 71, 72, 75, 85, 86, 106
Mexico, 196
Michalski, Krzysztof, 299
Mickiewicz, Adam, 98
Mihanović, Antun, 129
Military Frontier, 189
Military Order of Maria Theresa, 41
Millenium Exhibition (1896), 195
Miłosz, Czesław, 1, 2, 322, 333, 334
Milton, John, 60
von Mises, Ludwig, 329

Mitteleuropa (Naumann), 225
Mitteleuropa, 59, 256, 280
Modena, Duchy of (1452–1859), 99, 141
modernization, 125–40
Moeller van der Bruck, Arthur, 252
von Moltke, Helmuth, 219
Mommsen, Theodor, 186, 212
Montenegro, 164
Moravia, Margravate of (1182–1918), 19, 30, 46, 109, 120, 155, 171, 191, 202
Moscow, Russia, 150
Moser, Friedrich Karl, 42
Moser, Johann Jakob, 25
moustaches, 195
Mozart, Wolfgang Amadeus, 15, 31, 197
von Müller, Johannes, 57
Munch, Edvard, 177
Munich Agreement (1938), 273, 275, 296, 298
Munich, Bavaria, 134, 281
Mussolini, Benito, 259, 271, 283

Nagy, Imre, 308
Napoleon I, Emperor of the French, 56, 62–5
Napoleonic Wars (1803–15), 56, 62–5, 73, 83, 100, 154
Narutowicz, Gabriel, 264
Nassau, 148, 152
National Casino, 83, 85
National Democracy (Poland), 247
National Liberal Party (Bohemia), 190
National Liberal Party (Prussia) 158, 159, 217
National Party (Croatian), 144, 145, 174, 189
National Party (Slovak), 167
National Radical Camp, 270
National Social Association, 205, 216

424

INDEX

National Socialist Freedom Movement, 261
National Socialist German Workers' Party, 259, 267–9
National-Christian Defence League, 270
nationalism, 9, 11, 129–30, 140, 157–8, 203
   Croatian nationalism, 93–4, 108, 115, 144, 157, 168, 173–4, 188–90
   Czech nationalism, *see* Czech nationalism
   German nationalism, *see* German nationalism
   Hungarian nationalism, 83–6, 92–5, 107, 108, 110, 144, 157, 168, 169, 191, 216
   Italian nationalism, 99, 108, 157
   Polish nationalism, 98–9, 107–8, 157, 162
   Slovak nationalism, 167, 202, 203, 207–8
   Slovene nationalism, 168, 169, 170, 180, 202–3
natural selection, 182
Naumann, Friedrich, 204–5, 212, 216, 217, 225–6, 229
Nazism; Nazi Germany (1933–45), 7, 259, 267–9, 270–73, 275–84
   Anschluss (1938), 272–3, 285
   Czechoslovakia, invasion of (1938), 275–6
   Enabling Act (1933), 269
   Kristallnacht (1938), 276
   Molotov–Ribbentrop Pact (1939), 278, 280
   Munich Agreement (1938), 273, 275, 296, 298
   Nuremberg laws (1935), 272
   Poland, invasion of (1939), 278–9
   Rhineland remilitarization (1936), 272
   Soviet Union, invasion of (1941), 280
   Tripartite Pact (1940), 279
Nemčić, Antun, 128
neo-absolutism (1848–61), 130, 136, 141, 143, 166, 168, 169, 174
neo-Gothic architecture, 134–5, 195
neo-Slavism, 213
Netherlands, 9, 19, 27, 60, 80, 135, 158, 279
Neue Freie Presse, 187
Neue Preußische Zeitung, 138
Neue Rheinische Zeitung, 112
Neusatz, Hungary, 79
Neusohl, Slovakia, 46
New Europe, The, 229
New York Review of Books, 323
Nietzsche, Friedrich, 273
North Atlantic Treaty Organization (NATO), 5, 295, 328
North German Confederation (1866–71), 148, 152–4, 158
Norway, 80, 279
von Nostitz, Anton, 31, 33, 51, 52
Nouvelles littéraires, Les, 322
Novi Sad, Serbia, 79
Novotný, Antonín, 310–14
Nuremberg, Bavaria, 17
Nuremberg laws (1935), 272

October Diploma (1860), 143
Odesa, Ukraine, 135
Oesterreichisch deutsche Zeitung, 111
Ofen, Hungary, 45, 47, 49, 84, 129, 132, 168
Oken, Lorenz, 67
Old Church Slavonic, 93
Old Czechs, 144–5, 175–6, 190–91
Oldenburg, Grand Duchy of (1815–1918), 155
Olmütz, Moravia, 46
Olympic Games, 193

425

INDEX

Operation Barbarossa (1941), 280
Oppeln, Silesia, 278
Oppenheimer, Franz, 187
Orbán, Viktor, 332
Order of Saint Stephen, 41
Organisation Consul, 258
Österreichischer Lloyd, 127
Ostforschung, 318
Ostritz, Saxony, 214
Otto, Crown Prince of Austria, 257, 325–6, 327
Ottoman Empire (1299–1922), 20, 29, 49, 62, 79, 80, 81, 135, 164, 217–18, 262

Paget, John, 83
Palacký, František, 74, 79, 96, 109, 111, 120, 144, 149, 150, 151
Palestine, 287
Palm, Johann Philipp, 57–8
Pan-European Picnic, 325–6
Pan-German League, 213, 214, 224
Pan-Germanism, 7, 111, 146–7, 204, 212–14, 224–5, 239, 240, 241, 249, 255
    Anschluss, 146–7, 213, 240, 241, 249, 255, 272
    Nazism and, 260, 268, 272
Pan-Slavism, 77–82, 92, 94, 97–8, 145, 150–51, 167, 173, 208, 213–14, 218
    Russia and, 92, 97, 150–51, 213–14, 297
    Slav Congress (1848), 110–11, 115–18, 130, 136, 150
    Soviet Union and, 297–8, 300–301
    World War I and, 228, 229
Paneuropean Union, 325–6
Pannonian Plain, 27–8, 39, 195, 257
Papal States (756–1870), 99
Paris Exposition (1900), 193–9
Paris Peace Conference (1919), 256

Parma, Duchy of (1545–1859), 99, 141
Partitions of Poland (1772–95), 23, 40–41, 66
Partsch, Joseph, 213
Party of Right, 174, 189, 208, 209
pauperization, 90, 102, 200
Paupie, Franz Andreas, 133–4
Peace of Westphalia (1648), 27, 57
Pejačević, Ladislav, 188
Pelzl, Franz Martin, 50
Penguin Books, 319
Pest, Hungary, 47, 73, 83, 84, 85, 129, 132, 168, 195
Pester Zeitung, 129
Pesti Hírlap, 92
Peter I, Emperor of Russia, 51
Petőfi, Sándor, 309
von Petrasch, Joseph, 46
Pfizer, Paul, 95
Pietism, 46–7
Pilsen, 134
Piłsudski, Józef, 224, 229, 244–5, 246–7, 263–4, 266
Pinkas, Adolf Maria, 130
Pisling, Theodor, 129–30
Pius IX, Pope, 161
Plastic People of the Universe, The, 320
Poland, 2, 3, 8, 19, 60, 98
    Committee of National Liberation (1944), 297
    Congress of Vienna (1814), 74–5
    Kingdom of Galicia (1772–1918), *see* Kingdom of Galicia
    Kingdom of Poland (1815–1915), 75, 98, 151, 224
    nationalism, 98–9, 107, 108, 157, 162
    Nazi occupation (1939–45), 278–9, 281, 282, 302
    Partitions (1772–95), 23, 40–41, 66, 74, 98, 100

INDEX

People's Republic (1952–89), 2, 4, 300, 302, 304, 307, 310, 316–17
Polish-Lithuanian Commonwealth (1569–1795), 23, 24, 41, 60, 62, 66, 74, 98, 100, 246, 317, 330
Posen, Grand Duchy of (1815–48), 69, 75, 98, 107, 108, 117
Posen, Province of (1848–1920), 162, 181
Provisional Government (1945–7), 285, 286, 287, 299
Republic, First (1569–1795), 23, 24, 41, 60, 62, 66, 74, 98, 100, 246
Republic, Second (1918–39), 7, 245, 246–7, 262, 263, 266, 267, 270, 271, 277–8
Republic, Third (1989–), 2–3, 5, 328, 329, 332
revolutions (1848), 107–8, 110–11, 116
Soviet War (1919–21), 247, 264, 296
World War I (1914–18), 224, 228, 229, 238
World War II (1939–45), 278–9, 281, 282, 286–7, 297
Poles, 162–3, 172, 180, 192, 198–9
Polish Committee of National Liberation, 297
Polish language, 75, 162, 172, 192
Polish Legion, 224
Polish National Committee, 228
Polish Party (Prussia), 162, 216
Polish-Lithuanian Commonwealth (1569–1795), 23, 24, 41, 60, 62, 66, 74, 98, 100, 246, 317, 330
Polish-Soviet War (1919–21), 247, 264, 296
Pomerania, 69, 278
Popowitsch, Johann, 78

population transfers, 213, 285–7, 299–300
Portugal, 1–2, 5, 6, 19
Posen
  Grand Duchy (1815–48), 69, 75, 98, 117
  Province (1848–1920), 162, 181
Potsdam, 69
Pozsony, 191–2, 246
Prague, 30–31, 33, 44, 45, 128, 168, 301, 304, 305
  Germans in, 110–11, 128, 169–70, 171, 179, 186, 191
  Nazi occupation (1938–45), 275–6, 277
  Jews in, 116, 186
  Slav Congress (1848), 110–11, 115–18, 130, 136, 150
Prague Spring (1968), 1, 314–15, 324
Prešeren, France, 82
Pressburg, 28, 29–30, 45, 46, 47, 49, 74, 84, 97, 167, 191, 192
Pressburger Zeitung, 47, 48
Pressburgischen Gesselschaft, 47, 49
Preßler, Maximilan Robert, 128
Princely County of Gorizia (1754–1919), 155
Princely County of Gradisca (1754–1919), 155
Princely County of Tyrol (1140–1919), 65, 73, 106, 112, 136, 155, 249
Princely County of Voralberg (1140–1919), 155
princely states, 25, 37, 56, 70, 73, 90, 102, 122, 158
  modernization, 137–40
Principality of Transylvania (1570–1867), 19–20, 28, 34, 36, 39, 40, 45, 76, 86, 93, 109
Progress Party, 158
Progressive People's Party, 217, 228

427

INDEX

Progressive Youth, 209
Protectorate of Bohemia and Moravia (1939–45), 277, 281, 282
Protestantism
  in Czechoslovakia, 246
  in German Confederation, 89, 114
  in German Empire, 159, 161, 198, 200
  in Holy Roman Empire, 9, 36, 39, 40, 43–4, 46–7
  in Kingdom of Hungary, 46–7, 97
  in Kingdom of Prussia, 69, 89, 137, 159, 161
Prussia
  abolition (1947), 286, 292, 294, 295
  Free State (1918–47), 241, 251, 257, 297
  Kingdom of Prussia (1701–1918), *see* Kingdom of Prussia
Pulszky, Ferenc, 93
Putin, Vladimir, 334
Putnik, Radomir, 223
von Puttkamer, Robert, 181

race; racism, 182, 185, 260, 271–2, 277
Radić, Antun, 209
Radić, Stjepan, 208, 209, 248, 249, 265
Radical League of Germans, 212
Radical Union, 205, 217
Ragusa, Republic of (1358–1808), 51, 66
railways, 125, 130–31, 132, 139, 216
Rákosi, Mátyás, 308
Rathenau, Walther, 225, 258, 261
Reagan, Ronald, 322, 329
Realist Party, 207, 208
Reflections of a Nonpolitical Man (Mann), 222
Reform Judaism, 100

Regensburg, Bavaria, 57, 237
Reichenbach, Silesia, 24
Reichsrat, 143–5, 170, 171, 178, 185, 191, 212, 229
Reichstag
  Austrian Empire, 147
  German Empire, 158–9, 216, 228
  North German Confederation, 152, 158
  Weimar Germany, 261, 268
Renner, Karl, 203, 240, 256, 285, 293
Republic of Austria (1919–34), 7, 249–50, 257, 267
Republic of Croatia (1991–), 327, 328, 330–31
Republic of Czechia (1992–), 3, 5, 329, 330
Republic of Czechoslovakia
  First (1918–38), 7, 245–8, 250, 256–8, 262, 264–7, 270, 273
  Second (1938–9), 276–7
  Third (1945–8), 285, 286, 287, 297–8
  Fourth (1948–60), 300, 303, 305, 308, 310
Republic of France
  First (1792–1804), 56
  Second (1848–52), 105
  Third (1870–1940), 187, 193, 242–3, 246, 256, 259, 269–70, 273, 275, 278
  Fourth (1946–1958), 285, 295
Republic of German-Austria (1918–19), 240–41, 249
Republic of Germany (1918–33), 7, 236–9, 250–53, 257–62, 267–9
Republic of Hungary
  First (1918–19), 241–3, 244, 250
  Second (1946–9), 296, 298, 299
  Third (1989–), 5, 324–5, 327–8, 329
Republic of Lithuania, First (1918–40), 247

428

INDEX

Republic of Poland
  First (1569–1795), 23, 24, 41, 60, 62, 66, 74, 98, 100, 246
  Second (1918–39), 7, 245, 246–7, 262, 263, 270, 271, 277–8
  Third (1989–), 2–3, 5, 328, 329, 332
Republic of Ragusa (1358–1808), 51, 66
Republic of Romania (1989–), 5, 328
Republic of Slovakia
  First (1939–45), 277, 279, 282, 302
  Second (1992–), 5, 329, 330
revolutions (1848), 105–23, 136–7, 142, 206
Rheinischer Merkur, 65
Rhenische Zeitung, 89
Rhenish Committee, 238
Rhineland, 15, 25, 39, 66, 69–70, 87, 89, 131, 198, 259, 272
Rieger, František, 120, 144, 149, 150, 151
Riga, Latvia, 54
Rijeka, 94, 189
Robespierre, Maximilien, 63
von Rochau, August Ludwig, 137
Romania, 8, 9, 19, 93, 100, 135, 157, 164
  Republic (1989–), 5, 328
  Kingdom of Romania (1881–1947), *see* Kingdom of Romania
  People's Republic (1947–65), 299, 300, 303, 304
Romanians, 10, 28, 49, 91, 92, 93, 100, 109, 114, 117, 143, 167
Romanticism, 54, 72, 78, 79, 87–8, 98, 101
Rome, ancient (753 BCE–CE 476), 24, 26, 35, 37, 38, 273
Römer, Frankfurt, 16–18, 55, 111, 291
Roosevelt, Franklin, 320
Rosenberg, Alfred, 267

Roth, Philip, 319, 320
Rothschild, Mayer Amschel, 100
Rottenhan, Heinrich, 31
Royal Bohemian Society of Sciences, 33–4, 54
Royal Prussian Army, 155
Royal Saxon Army, 155
Rudolf, Crown Prince of Austria, 196
Rudolph II, Holy Roman Emperor, 30, 196
Ruhr, 131, 198, 259
Rushdie, Salman, 2
Russian Civil War (1917–23), 238
Russian Empire (1721–1917), 23, 51, 56, 59, 60, 62, 64, 66, 80, 110, 114, 209
  Balkan Wars (1912–13), 219
  Crimean War (1853–6), 142
  Ethnographic Exhibition (1867), 150
  Jews in, 187
  Kingdom of Poland (1815–1915), 75, 98, 151
  Ottoman War (1877–8), 164
  Pan-Slavism and, 92, 97, 150–51, 213–14
  Revolution (1917), 230, 297
  Three Emperors Alliance (1873–87), 164
  Ukraine and, 175
  World War I (1914–17), 221, 222, 223, 224, 230
Russian Federation (1991–), 2–3, 5–6, 334–5
Russian language, 79
Russian Revolution (1917), 230, 297
Rutgers University, 333–4
Ruthenians, 45, 97, 100, 108, 110, 115, 175, 226, 263
Rydz-Śmigły, Edward, 270

Šafařík, Pavel Josef, 79, 81, 97, 111, 115, 136

INDEX

Salieri, Antonio, 18
Salzburg, Duchy of (1810–1918), 73, 155
Salzmann, Christian Gotthilf, 35
samizdat, 320, 321
Sand, Carl, 71–2
Sardinia, Kingdom of (1720–1861), 141, 142
Sarmatians, 60
Sáros county, Hungary, 246
Saxe-Altenburg, Duchy of (1602–1918)
Saxe-Coburg and Gotha, Duchy of (1826–1918), 155
Saxe-Meiningen, Duchy of (1680–1918), 155
Saxe-Weimar, Grand Duchy of (1809–1903), 155
Saxons, 28, 39, 65, 93, 166, 167
Saxony, 77, 295
    Electorate of Saxony (1356–1806), 16, 17, 22, 40, 42, 43, 52–3
    Kingdom of Saxony (1806–1918), *see* Kingdom of Saxony
    Prussian Saxony (1816–1944), 69
Scammell, Michael, 333
Schacher, Gerhard, 255
Scharf, József, 183
Scheidemann, Philipp, 251
Schiller, Friedrich, 53, 80
Schilling, Ernst, 110
Schindler, Julius Alexander, 179
Schlegel, Friedrich, 78
Schleswig War (1864), 147–8
Schlözer, August Ludwig, 49, 51, 53
von Schmerling, Anton, 144, 147
Schmidt, Friedrich, 134–5
von Schön, Theodor, 89
von Schönborn-Buchheim, Karl, 243
Schönbrunn Palace, Vienna, 18, 43
von Schönerer, Georg, 178, 184, 186, 204, 212

Schubert, Franz, 197
Schulek, Frigyes, 135
Schulze, Hagen, 46
Schumacher, Kurt, 293
Schuselka, Franz, 95, 96, 107–8, 113, 114
von Schwarzenberg, Felix, 121, 126
Schwarzenberg, Karel, 3
Scotland, 27
secessionist movement (1892–1914), 177–8
Second World War (1939–45), *see* World War II
Seldmayr, Gabriel, 134
September Programme (1914), 224
Serb Independent Party, 218
Serbia, 2, 5, 8, 10, 19, 45, 135, 164, 217, 218
    Kingdom (1882–1918), 218–19, 221, 223
    Nazi occupation (1941–5), 279
    Principality (1815–82), 135, 157, 164, 217
    Yugoslavia (1918–92), 248–9, 264–5
Serbian language, 2, 80
Serbian Orthodox Church, 45, 93
Serbs, 10, 45, 73, 79–82, 93, 100, 109, 174, 215, 226, 281, 302
Seton-Watson, Robert, 229
Seven Years' War (1756–63), 22, 42
Seyss-Inquart, Arthur, 279
Should we become Magyars? (Hoitsy), 199
Sicily, 105, 283
Silesia
    Austrian Silesia (1742–1918), 30, 40, 155, 171
    Holy Roman Empire (1335–1742), 19, 22, 23–4
    Prussian Silesia (1742–1918), 40, 41, 42, 69, 90–91, 109, 148, 162
    World War I (1914–18), 238, 241, 251

430

INDEX

World War II (1939–45), 278, 281, 284, 297
Silesian Wars (1740–63), 40, 41, 42, 69, 148
Silesian weavers' uprising (1844), 90–91
Six-Day War (1967), 303, 311
Slánský, Rudolf, 303
Slav Congress (1848), 110–11, 115–18, 130, 136, 150
Slav tricolour, 116
Slavdom and the World of the Future (Štúr), 151
Slavonia, 34, 38, 79, 81, 94, 215
Slavonic and East European Review, 266
Slavs; Slavic languages, 6, 9, 10, 23, 28, 31, 33–4, 36, 38, 50–54, 69, 73, 74, 77–82
    four standards, 79–81, 97–8, 208
    migration, 198, 204, 214
    Pan-Slavism, *see* Pan-Slavism
    racial theories and, 182, 219, 231
Slovak language, 49, 77, 79, 191, 192
Slovak National Party, 167, 208
Slovak People's Party, 266, 276
Slovakia, 2, 3, 8, 19
    Czechoslovakia (1918–92), *see* Czechoslovakia
    Federative Republic (1990–92), 5
    Soviet Republic (1919), 246
    Republic, First (1939–45), 277, 279, 282, 302
    Republic, Second (1992–), 5, 329, 330
Slovaks, 3, 10, 34, 77, 97, 100, 109, 115, 167, 202, 203, 207–8
Slovene Catholic Party, 202
Slovene language, 52, 81, 82
Slovene People's Party, 202, 249
Slovenes, 10, 34, 97, 100, 109, 110, 168, 170–71, 178–9, 202, 226, 302
Slovenia, 5, 8, 10, 19, 329, 330

Social Darwinism, 182, 185
Social Democratic Party (Austria), 184–5, 201, 203–4, 236, 240
Social Democratic Party (Czechoslavonic), 207
Social Democratic Party (Germany), 200–201, 216, 217, 224, 228, 239, 251, 252, 293
Social Democratic Workers' Party, 163
social democrats, 199–201, 203–4
socialism, 91, 163–4, 194, 199–204, 228, 237, 249–50, 258
Socialist Workers' Party, 163–4
Societas eruditorum incognitorum, 46–7
Society of the Croatian Dragon, 199
Sociological Society, 206
Sokol movement, 226
Solidarity, 322, 328
Solymosi, Eszter, 183
Solzhenitsyn, Aleksandr, 312
von Sonnenfels, Joseph, 45, 46
Sontag, Susan, 2
Sorbs, 52–3, 150
Sosnowski, Kazimierz, 245
Šotola, Jiří, 311
Soviet Russia/Union (1917–91), 1, 7, 230, 238, 258, 267–8, 296, 300–301
    Allied-occupied Germany (1945–9), 285
    Battle of Stalingrad (1942–3), 283
    Cold War (1947–91), 1, 6, 8, 294, 300, 307, 309, 322
    Decree on Peace (1917), 230
    Czechoslovakia invasion (1968), 1, 315, 323
    Fourth Congress of Soviet Writers (1967), 312
    Hungary invasion (1956), 1, 2, 323
    Lisbon Conference (1988), 1–2, 4

INDEX

Molotov–Ribbentrop Pact (1939), 278
Nazi invasion (1941), 280, 282
Perestroika (1985–91), 324
Polish War (1919–21), 247, 264, 296
Warsaw Pact (1955), 300, 308
Spain, 9, 19, 21, 27, 60, 62, 65
Spanish language, 21, 44
Spartacist uprising (1919), 239
Spengler, Oswald, 294
SS (*Schutzstaffel*), 278
St. Petersburg, Russia, 150
St. Stephen's Cathedral, Vienna, 327
St. Stephen's Day, 169
Stalin, Joseph, 296–7, 300, 307, 309–10, 312, 320, 324
Staněk, František, 229
Starčević, Ante, 174, 189, 190, 209
State of Serbs, Croats, and Slovenes (1918), 245
state socialism, 194
steam engines, 131
Steed, Wickham, 229, 255
Štefánik, Milan Rastislav, 228, 229
Steindl, Imre, 135
Stephen I, King of Hungary, 29
Stephen of Austria, Archduke, 106
von Sternberg, Kaspar, 55, 74
Stöcker, Adolf, 183, 184, 205
Štokavian, 81
Strasser, Gregor, 268
Strauss, Franz Joseph, 325
Stresemann, Gustav, 261
Strossmayer, Josip Juraj, 145, 149
von Struve, Gustav, 105
Štúr, Ľudovít, 97, 110, 111, 115, 136, 151
von Stürgkh, Karl, 226–7
Styria, Duchy of (1180–1918), 10, 34, 52, 73, 109, 155, 169, 171, 179, 202, 249

Sudetenland, 33, 273, 275, 285
Šufflays, Croatia, 199
Svědectví, 317, 320, 324
Swabians, 38, 39
Swastika, 260
Sweden, 27, 57, 60, 80
Switzerland, 8, 19, 135, 228, 256
von Sybel, Heinrich, 159
Syllabus of Errors (1864), 161
Syrový, Jan, 275
Szálasi, Ferenc, 283
Széchenyi Chain Bridge, Budapest, 85, 284
Széchenyi, István, 83–6, 89, 94, 106, 119, 136, 169
Szeged, Hungary, 243
Szekfű, Gyula, 253–4
Szeklers, 93

von Taaffe, Eduard, 190
Tacitus, 38, 60
Tállyay, Dániel, 49
Tarnów uprising (1846), 98–9
Temesvar, Hungary, 132
Teutonic Knights, 159
Teutsch, Georg Daniel, 167
Thatcher, Margaret, 329
Theresianum, 41
Thirty Years' War (1618–48), 27, 30, 37
Thomasius, Christian, 37, 44
Three Emperors Alliance (1873–87), 164
Three Generations (Szekfű), 254
von Thun, Leo, 93, 128, 130
Thuringia, 77
Tigrid, Pavel, 317
von Tirpitz, Alfred, 217, 228
Tiso, Jozef, 276
Tisza, Kálmán, 165, 166, 188
Tiszaeszlár affair (1882–3), 183
Tito, Josip Broz, 283, 296, 300

INDEX

Tolstaya, Tatiana, 333–4
Tolstoy, Pyotr, 51
Tony Judt, 329
Tragedy of Central Europe, The (Ashmead-Bartlett), 235
'Tragedy of Central Europe, The' (Kundera), 3–4, 5, 6, 335
Transleithania, 155
Transylvania
    Austria-Hungary (1867–1918), 150, 166, 167
    Principality (1570–1867), 19–20, 28, 34, 36, 39, 40, 45, 76, 86, 93, 109
    Romanian Kingdom (1918–47), 7, 217, 244, 248, 263
    Vienna Award (1940), 279
Trautenauer Wochenblatt, 214
Treaty of Brest-Litovsk (1918), 246
Treaty of Munich (1938), 273, 275, 296, 298
Treaty of Reichenbach (1790), 24
Treaty of Saint-Germain (1919), 249
Treaty of Trianon (1920), 249, 250, 277
Treaty of Versailles (1919), 249, 250, 260, 272
Treaty of Westphalia (1648), 27, 57
von Treitschke, Heinrich, 137, 146, 158, 159, 186, 273
Tremonia, 237
Trier, Germany, 16, 25
Trieste, Free City of (1849–1922), 125, 130, 155
Triune Kingdom, 189
Troppau, Silesia, 171
Trotsky, Leon, 240
Tuscany, Grand Duchy of (1569–1860), 18, 20, 99, 141
Twentieth Century, 206
Tyrol, Princely County of (1140–1919), 65, 73, 106, 112, 136, 155, 249

Ukraine, 2, 3, 5–6, 8, 9, 10, 19, 98, 333–5
    Nazi occupation (1941–4), 281, 282, 302
    People's Republic (1917–21), 247
    Soviet Socialist Republic (1919–91), 277, 297, 304
    World War I (1914–18), 230
    see also Ruthenians
ultramontanism, 179
United Kingdom (1800–), 59, 83, 89, 117
    Allied-occupied Germany (1945–9), 285, 294
    general election (1945), 299
    Great Exhibition (1851), 139, 193, 194
    Munich Agreement (1938), 273, 296
    Thatcherism, 329
    World War I (1914–18), 221, 222
    World War II (1939–45), 278
United Nations, 2
United South Slavic Club, 229
United States
    Allied-occupied Germany (1945–9), 285
    Cold War (1947–91), 1, 6, 8, 294, 300, 307, 309, 322
    Fourteen Points (1918), 230, 236, 240, 241, 242
    Jewish migration to, 187
    Poland missile plan dispute (2009), 2–3
    Reaganomics, 329
    World War II entry (1941), 281
universalism, 26–7, 35, 53–4, 61–2
University of Berlin, 64
University of Bonn, 88
University of Göttingen, 38
University of Graz, 182
University of Jena, 76–7, 79

INDEX

University of Leipzig, 43, 44
University of Michigan, 322
University of Vienna, 78, 273
University of Wisconsin-Madison, 324
University of Zagreb, 189, 208
Upper Austria, 73, 155
Upper Silesia, 101, 251
urbanization, 61, 131–5, 197
Urbanski, August, 198
Ustaša, 270, 279–80

Vaculík, Ludvík, 313, 314
Varaždin, Croatia, 94
Vatican, 128, 161, 179, 203
Velvet Divorce (1992), 330
Venetian Republic (697–1797), 66
Versailles
    German Empire proclaimed (1871), 154
    Peace Conference (1919), 249, 250, 256, 260, 272
Vienna, Austria, 18, 20–21, 41, 43, 44, 49, 100, 132, 301, 304
    architects in, 134–5
    breweries in, 134
    city walls, dismantling of (1857), 133
    Corpus Christi processions, 196
    Jews in, 185, 186, 187, 227, 235, 273, 281
    Ringstrasse, 133, 135
    SS in, 278
    Trieste railway, 128, 130
    World War I (1914–18), 227, 235
Vienna Award (1940), 279
Vilna University, 75
Vilna, Lithuania, 246
Visegrád Group, 5, 330
Vix, Fernand, 242
Vojvodina, 109, 279
Völkerwanderung, 77, 95, 110
Voltaire, 24

Voralberg, Princely County of (1140–1919), 155
Vraz, Stanko, 82

Wagner, Richard, 182
Wales, 117
Wałęsa, Lech, 328
Wall Street Crash (1929), 267
War Against the West, The (Kolnai), 273
War of the Austrian Succession (1740–48), 22
War of the First Coalition (1792–7), 56
Warsaw, Poland, 245
Warsaw, Duchy of (1807–15), 75
Warsaw Pact (1955), 300, 308, 315
Wartburg Festival (1817), 67, 71–2, 76
Warthegau (1939–45), 281, 282, 302
Weber, Maximilian, 192
Weimar Coalition, 239
Weimar Republic (1918–33), 7, 236–9, 250–53, 257–62, 267–9
Weimar, 239
Wekerle, Sándor, 201, 215
Welfenlegion, 152
Weltpolitik, 194–5, 213, 217
Wends, 51, 52–3, 173
Wesselényi, Miklós, 86
West Germany (1949–90), 292–4, 303, 307, 308, 318, 325
Western Europe, 4, 6, 287, 293–5
Western Roman Empire (364–476), 77
Westphalia, 62, 198
Where from and Where To? (von Schön), 89
Whigs, 68
Wichmann, Wilhelm, 114
Wieland, Christoph Martin, 80
Wiener Neustadt, Austria, 41
Wiener Zeitung, 107

INDEX

Wilhelm I, German Emperor, 145, 147, 154, 156
Wilhelm II, German Emperor, 155, 194–5, 200, 217, 219, 221, 231, 240
Wilhelmsbad, Germany, 17
Wilson, Woodrow, 230, 236, 240, 257, 276
Windisch, Karl Gottlieb, 47
Windischgrätz, Alfred, 116, 118, 119
Wolfenbüttel, Saxony, 58
Wolff, Christian, 37, 38, 40, 44
Wolff, Larry, 5
World War I (1914–18), 6, 7, 221–31, 235
World War II (1939–45), 1, 4, 6, 7, 278–87
Wrocław, Poland, 301, 302
Württemberg, 42, 62, 139, 148, 152–3, 154, 155, 194
Württembergian Army, 155

Yalta Conference (1945), 320
Year Zero, 292
Yiddish, 187
Young Czechs, 190–91, 204, 207

Yugoslav Committee, 228, 248
Yugoslavia (1918–92)
    Federal People's Republic (1945–63), 285, 286, 300, 304, 308
    Kingdom (1918–41), 7, 247, 248–9, 250, 256, 257, 262–7, 269–70, 271
    Nazi occupation (1941–5), 279, 283, 296
    Socialist Federal Republic (1963–92), 5, 304, 328, 330
Yugoslavs, 81, 173, 174, 208, 209, 228, 229

Zagreb, Croatia, 45, 48, 94, 128, 133, 168, 171, 174, 188, 189, 192, 301, 304, 309
Zagreb Trial (1909), 218
Ziemiałkowski, Florian, 110–11
Zimmermann, Wilhelm, 112
Zionism, 188, 263, 287, 303
Zipsers, 38, 166, 246
Zois von Edelstein, Sigmund, 52
Zöllner, Johann Friedrich, 35
Zollverein, 76, 127, 139, 152